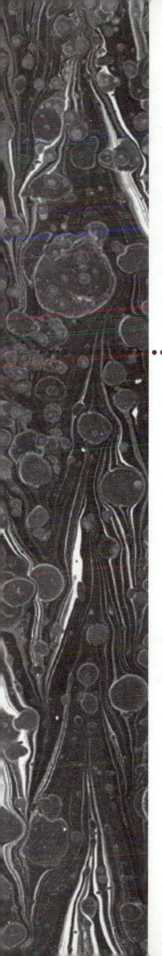

COGNITIVE PSYCHOLOGY

....

FOURTH EDITION

John B. Best
Eastern Illinois University

WEST PUBLISHING COMPANY
MINNEAPOLIS/ST. PAUL   NEW YORK   LOS ANGELES   SAN FRANCISCO

WEST'S COMMITMENT TO THE ENVIRONMENT

In 1906, West Publishing Company began recycling materials left over from the production of books. This began a tradition of efficient and responsible use of resources. Today, up to 95 percent of our legal books and 70 percent of our college and school texts are printed on recycled, acid-free stock. West also recycles nearly 22 million pounds of scrap paper annually— the equivalent of 181,717 trees. Since the 1960s, West has devised ways to capture and recycle waste inks, solvents, oils, and vapors created in the printing process. We also recycle plastics of all kinds, wood, glass, corrugated cardboard, and batteries, and have eliminated the use of Styrofoam book packaging. We at West are proud of the longevity and the scope of our commitment to the environment.

Production, Prepress, Printing and Binding by West Publishing Company.

 TEXT IS PRINTED ON 10% POST CONSUMER RECYCLED PAPER

British Library Cataloguing-in-Publication Data. A catalogue record for this book is available from the British Library.

Interior Text Design: Roslyn Stendahl
Copyediting: Deborah Drolin Jones
Text Composition: Carlisle Communications
Art: Carlisle Communications
Indexing: Catalyst Communication Arts
Permissions: Lynn Reichel
Interior Design Texture: Courtesy of Lauren Clark, *Marbelized Paper Patterns in Full Color*. Dover Publications, 1992.
Cover Image: Enkephalin is a naturally occuring pentapeptide isolated from the brain and probably functions as a neurotransmitter. © Dennis Kunkel/Phototake.

Library of Congress Cataloging-in-Publication Data

Best, John B.
    Cognitive psychology / John B. Best.—4th ed.
        p.   cm.
    Includes bibliographical references (p.   ) and indexes.
    ISBN 0-314-04445-0 (hard)
    1. Cognitive psychology. I. Title.
BF311.B485 1995
153—dc20

94-31727
CIP

DEDICATION

In memory of my daughter Adrienne

 # PREFACE

Yesterday, our older son (age 17) took our younger son (age 5) to the nearby creek to catch crayfish for the first time. They brought back some of their trophies, and I enjoyed showing the kindergartner how to pick up a "crawdad" without getting pinched. As I watched him examine the crayfish, I became aware of how quickly children develop. When I relived his development in my mind's eye, I could imagine him reacting to the crayfish in various ways: with incomprehensibility as a baby, with abject terror as a toddler, to intense curiosity now. Objectively, he wasn't very old, but how he had changed in just a few years!

Cognitive psychology is like that too. Although not a very old discipline in comparison to other scientific fields, it nevertheless continues to develop at an astonishing pace. To an author, this explosion of knowledge presents both opportunities and problems. It's certainly an exciting time to be a cognitive psychologist, and communicating the theories and findings of cognitive psychology to students such as yourself, who are hearing them for the first time, is an exciting opportunity for an author. However, one of the problems resulting from the explosion of knowledge and interest in cognition is that any book such as this one must be simply an "introduction" to the field. If I were to include coverage of every topic of interest to cognitive psychologists, the result would be an unmanageable volume from which no professor, no matter how skillful, could teach, or which no student, no matter how dedicated, could assimilate.

As it stands, there will be plenty in this book to keep you busy. I've been mindful of that, and I've tried to incorporate into the book some features that will enable you to learn the material in what I hope will be a painless manner. Each chapter begins with an overview. In the overviews, I've tried to use an anecdote as a springboard into the questions and issues of the chapter. Each chapter contains summary sections at various points. These should offer breathing spaces and logical starting and stopping places within the chapter. Each chapter also contains a focus section. In the focus section, I've tried to go into some specific research question or phenomenon in more detail than I do in the main narrative. One of the issues that students frequently bring up is the validity of the cognitive enterprise: Given that cognitive processes are so "interior" (the argument goes), how can we use scientific practices to study them? The focus sections are designed in part to show you how cognitive scientists go about making these interior processes more overt. From these sections, I also hope you'll get a clue about how cognitive scientists think. Each chapter closes with some concluding comments. The comments are intended as a summary, but I didn't want them to be simply a rehash of the material in the chapter. So, although the concluding comments summarize the chapter, I also intended them to point out some implications of the material in the chapter, to examine how certain "themes" or ideas in cognitive psychology are reworked in different areas, and so on. Following the concluding comments is a list of "key terms" that were used in the chapter. Most of the key terms also appear in the glossary. I recommend that you learn the definitions of all the key terms. Finally, many of the chapters include a section called "Using Your Knowledge of Cognition." Sometimes students complain that the material in cognitive psychology is rather abstract and, by implication, alien. The point of the "Using Your Knowledge" sections is to show you that cognitive psychology can be applied, sometimes without much difficulty, to many issues that may arise during a typical day.

Finally, I'd like to say, enjoy your course in cognition! It will be hard, but it needn't be dreaded. Moreover, I think you'll find that it's a course that you will look back on and come to regard as a solid foundation for your later studies in psychology or in related fields.

Thus far I've been addressing the student readership, but now some comments for the professional readership are in order. My intention is that the book be used by upper-division students who are taking their first course in cognition. The book can be covered comfortably in a semester-long course. Some knowledge of experimental psychology and statistics is presupposed, although most of the experiments in the book are described in enough detail that student readers who have not had those courses will be able to read the book and maintain good comprehension. Although almost every chapter contains some references to previous and future chapters, the chapters nevertheless can stand on their own, and so the sequence implied by the table of contents is just a suggestion.

As implied by comments to the student readership, users of previous editions will find that quite a bit has been changed. The material on computational vision that was previously found in Chapter 2 has been taken out in the interests of space and detail level. Whereas the previous edition contained one four-chapter sequence on memory, developments in that area have made that organization unwieldy. The current edition has a two-chapter sequence on memory. The first of these chapters (Chapter 4) focuses on the traditional information-processing view of memory, and the second chapter (Chapter 5) deals with a variety of memory processes. What was covered as "semantic memory" in previous editions is now covered as a two-chapter sequence on human knowledge, and these chapter have been largely rewritten for this edition. One chapter (Chapter 6) covers symbolic or local models of knowledge, and the second chapter (Chapter 7) covers connectionist or distributed models. Other less extensive changes have been incorported into Chapters 1, 3, 4, 5, and 11.

I created a manuscript by myself, but that's just the beginning. I'm very thankful to many people, without whose remarkable talents and prodigious efforts this book would never have come to be. At West Publishing, my editors Clark Baxter, Johanna Land and Peter Krall should author a case study about how to manage, nurture, and otherwise deal with Calamity-Jane-type authors like me. They've got it exactly right. Also Roslyn Stendahl who designed this terrific-looking book. Deborah Drolen Jones was the copy editor whose work is largely invisible to you, but whose clearheaded efforts smoothed out many a tangled sentence.

The previous edition of this book was reviewed by several specialists whose comments and criticisms have proved invaluable in shaping the current edition. They are:

Thomas R. Alley, *Clemson University*

Ian Begg, *McMaster University*

Jill Booker, *University of Indianapolis*

Patrick Brown, *University of Western Ontario*

Brian E. Butler, *Queen's University*

Raymond S. Corteen, *University of British Columbia*

Judith P. Goggin, *University of Texas at El Paso*

Jacqueline Johnson, *University of Virginia*

Mustaq Khan, *University of Western Ontario*

Stuart Klapp, *California State University, Hayward*

Harvey Marmurek, *University of Guelph*

David G. Payne, *State University of New York-Binghamton*

William Prinzmetal, *University of California, Berkeley*

L. G. Standing, *Bishop's University*

James J. Staszewski, *Carnegie Mellon University*

Edward Vela, *California State University, Chico*

Jerry L. Vost, *St. Norbert College*

At EIU, I must thank my graduate assistants, Christy Buehnerkemper, Damian Jones, Kathy Niebrugge, Beth Richfort, and Clint Waldhelm, and my undergraduate assistants, Michelle Berry and Amber Keith, for being so able to handle so many tasks. Whether it was tracking down a reference, helping with the permissions log, or keeping the lab running smoothly, these folks did everything that could be expected of them and more.

An author asks his or her family to make a sacrifice for the sake of the book and my family deserves my thanks for their support. Lorraine, Frank, and Matthew, thanks for your tolerance of my absences and your sympathy in my presence. Thanks for keeping the perspective that I sometimes failed to keep. As Matthew said recently in reponse to my having to go to the office on a day when everyone else was off: "Dad, playing with your son is more important than cognitive psychology." Indeed it is, and that's what I'm going to do right now. I hope your travels with this book are fruitful; enjoy your course.

John B. Best
Charleston, Illinois
May 30, 1994
Memorial Day

CONTENTS

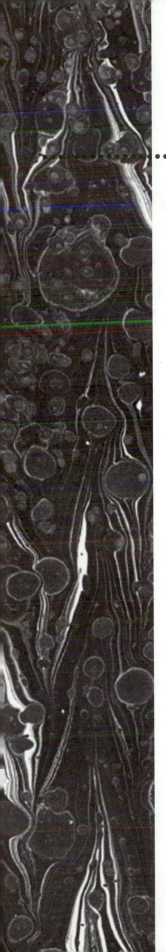

PART 1

INTRODUCTION

Preceding each section of this book is a part opener that describes some of the issues that are dealt with in the section. These part openers also provide a preliminary orientation to the material by describing some key phrases or concepts that are designed to help students organize the material as they read.

Students might get more out of this introduction if they understand at the outset that much of this chapter is concerned with "approaches" to cognition, and that these approaches have metaphors as their bases. There are two commonly used approaches in cognitive psychology. The information-processing approach has as its metaphorical base the idea that "the mind works like a computer," and the connectionist approach has as its metaphorical base the idea that "the mind works like a brain." Let's briefly consider what each of these metaphorical statements might mean.

It is intuitively obvious to many students that minds and computers have certain similarities. Both humans and computers have memories that are organized in particular ways, and both are capable of following directions on a line-by-line basis. Computers and people are similar in some other, less obvious ways, too. Both humans and computers *represent* information internally. In other words, they take in information from the world in one form (keystrokes or mouse-clicks in the case of computers, senses in the case of humans) and store it in some other form. Once stored, this information can be altered by the computer's program, or in the humans, by cognitive processes. Cognitive processes become the equiva-lent of mental programs according to the information-processing approach. These processes operate on the information we have stored, modifying it to suit our current purposes.

As obvious as the computer-mind similarity is, the brain-mind metaphor underlying the connectionist approach is even more obvious to many students—so obvious in fact that many students think this metaphor is simply a trivial cliché. But we should resist the temptation to dismiss the connectionist approach. Theorists and researchers have pointed out that digital computers do one thing at a time; the advantage of such machines is their incredible speed. But my cognitive system and yours are not at all like this. Relative to computing machines, our cognitive systems are much, much slower. But they possess an awesome advantage neverthe-less. Our cognitive systems can do more than one thing at a time; in fact, they are usually doing more than one thing at a time. This fact suggests that our cognitive systems, like our brains, work as *parallel* (many things at once) ma-chines, rather than as *serial* (one thing at a time) machines as computers do.

If you keep this distinction in mind as you wind your way through this chapter, I think you'll get a good grasp on why cog-nitive psychologists approach specific problems the way they do. One other thing: I hope you don't feel a need to decide which of these perspectives is "right" and which is "wrong." Both the information-processing and the connec-tionist approach have their uses, as we'll see directly.

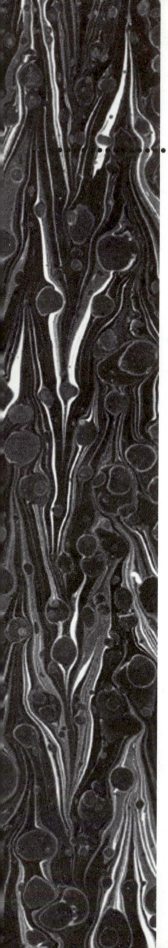

CHAPTER **1**

COGNITIVE PSYCHOLOGY: DEFINITIONS, ROOTS, AND METAPHORS

CHAPTER OUTLINE

OVERVIEW

Last week I did something that I thought was very strange. After supper, I told my wife that I was going to the grocery store to buy milk, and she asked me, as long as I was going out, to return a book to the library. Some minutes intervened while I did some other chores, and then I finally got going, almost forgetting the book, then remembering to put it on the passenger seat beside me in the car. The weather had turned quite a bit colder in the past week, and so I thought I could go to the grocery store first, leaving the milk in the car while I returned the book, without the milk being spoiled by warm temperatures. Having made this plan, I sort of put my mind on automatic pilot while I drove. I bought the milk, put it on the front seat next to the book, drove to the library, got out, went around to the passenger side, grabbed an object, walked into the library, walked all the way to the circulation desk, and met the somewhat quizzical eyes of the librarian before I realized that I had the milk, not the book. I sheepishly retreated and brought back the correct object a few minutes later.

On the drive home, I tried to figure out why I had made this mistake. At first, I couldn't come up with an answer. Milk gallons and books don't look alike; they don't have similar functions; and the objects weren't the same temperature, or the same weight. So how could I get them confused? To answer this question, we first must realize that my cognitive system created internal representations of both the milk and the book and, second, that these internal representations have properties all their own. Some of the properties are based on what I know about the object in question, and hence, these properties are stable and more or less unchanging over time. For example, I know that milk is food and that a book is not food, and these characteristics are part of my permanent internal representation of these objects. But some of the properties of the internal representation refer to characteristics that the object may possess temporarily, but not permanently. That is, our cognitive system seems to have a batch of "temporary files" into which an object can be placed for the time being, probably for the sake of some convenience. In these files the object may be represented on the basis of characteristics that it probably does not have permanently. Essentially, this is how I explained my mistake to myself: In my daydreaming, automatic-pilot state, both the objects on the front seat were represented simply as "things on the front seat" and were not "tagged" with their complete and permanent specification. Given that there were two things on the seat, I think that I had about a 50 percent chance of carrying the wrong object into the library.

From this example emerge several questions and themes that will be dealt with in this chapter, and that will come into play again and again throughout this book. What is the relationship of cognition to conscious awareness? How can human knowledge be described and explained? Are cognitive processes really as separate or as "modular" from one another as they seem to be in this case? We'll begin our exploration of these issues in this chapter.

This chapter also considers some of the many origins of cognitive psychology. Its roots are to be found in (among other places) linguistics, computer science, neurology, and human factors research. You may be somewhat surprised to find out that cognitive psychology has a relatively short history. Although the problems it investigates are ancient, virtually all of its founding figures are still alive.

In addition, this chapter will examine two approaches to the problems of cognitive psychology: the information-processing approach; and the connectionist approach. As we'll see, these approaches differ fundamentally in the assumptions they make about human cognition, although they don't necessarily differ in the predictions they make about human cognition. The chapter concludes with a description of some of the research methods and techniques that cognitive psychologists use.

 ## INTRODUCTION TO COGNITIVE PSYCHOLOGY

By the time you reach the period at the end of this sentence, you will have engaged in several distinct cognitive processes. Without any particularly strenuous effort on your part, you're grasping the meaning of this sentence right now, even as (perhaps) your attention has already begun to wander to an upcoming rendezvous, a test tomorrow, hunger pangs, or whatever. However, the ease with which we engage in cognitive processes shouldn't blind us to their complexity. The remaining 125,000 words of this text are spent in an effort to foster your appreciation of just how great that complexity is.

Neisser's Definition of Cognition

In 1967, Ulric Neisser published the now-classic text *Cognitive Psychology*, which offers the following definition: "Cognitive psychology refers to all processes by which the sensory input is transformed, reduced, elaborated, stored, recovered, and used." The definition is worth elaborating. As Neisser states, cognition begins with sensory input. Our cognitive processes are perhaps most useful in responding to information that is present in the world and that is capable of being picked up by our sensory apparatus. Next, the sensory input is transformed—that is, altered. Our sensory apparatus is finely attuned to certain kinds of energy present in the world. This sensory apparatus converts physical energy into neural energy, or as a cognitive psychologist might say, physical stimulation is encoded into neural events.

The notion of a code is an important idea in cognitive psychology and so deserves at least a brief description. To what does the process of encoding refer? Literally, a code is a system of signals used to represent letters or numbers in transmitting messages. For example, children make up secret alphabets and use them to send messages to their closest friends in school. These messages are coded; the symbols used are the result of some (presumably) systematic transformation of the alphabet, and the squiggles that children make up bear the same relationship to one another that characters in the alphabet do. If *e* is the most commonly occurring letter in English text, then the character representing *e* in the code also would be the most frequently occurring symbol.

Our nervous systems also are capable of coding events. That is, stimuli that are presented to us are first converted and then represented by patterns of neural activity. It's important to note that these patterns of neural activity preserve the information that was present in the stimulus. At the level that we want to talk about it, there's really nothing mysterious about this. If you could look inside yourself at any given point in time, you would see that your brain is constantly, vibrantly active at the neural level, and the specific activity that is going on is surely based on the specific stimuli that have impinged on you. We can talk about this pattern of activation at the neural level, in which case we're talking about a **neural code**. Or, we can describe the pattern of activation at an abstract level, in which case we're talking about a **cognitive code**. And I hope this comparison makes another point clear too: When I talk about the neural code "and" the cognitive code, I'm not really suggesting that they are two completely different things. It's appropriate to think of the cognitive code and the neural code as the same entity viewed from two different levels of analysis.

Now let's introduce one final level of analysis: the **mental level**. This should be the most familiar of the terms we've introduced so far, because the mental level corresponds to our consciousness, or our awareness of the stimuli around us, and our thoughts. What's the relationship of the mental level to both the cognitive and neural levels? Clearly, the neural code is not experienced directly, and so the neural code is not a part of our mental lives. But not all aspects of the cognitive code enter our awareness either.

To see this, think about the process of reading. If you set out to read a word, the meaning of this word almost certainly enters your awareness. The experience of "meaning entering your awareness" is hard to describe, but you know the experience you're having was produced by reading that particular word. However, other transformations of the physical energy were certainly involved, and probably none of these entered your awareness. For example, the light reflected from the page had to be converted into a code that preserved the lines of the letters; these lines had to be assembled in some meaningful way; the resulting pattern of lines had to be recognized as letters; and, presumably, at least some of the letters had to be identified. In each case, a cognitive code was created, although the results of such processing almost certainly did not enter your awareness.

Neisser describes the fate of the cognitive code in the next part of the definition. Once created, the cognitive code can be reduced or elaborated. The reduction of a cognitive code refers to the fact that neither the neural code nor the cognitive code preserves and retains *all* the characteristics of the original physical stimulation. This reduction isn't bad, because most of the physical energy in the environment isn't very informative and therefore isn't worth keeping. Even now, if you try to remember the exact words that began this chapter, you'll find it difficult to recall them, and you probably won't remember them accurately. Even when you read the words the first time, you probably recognized that the exact phrasing was not particularly important. What was important was the meaning of the introduction. Consequently, details like the exact phrasing, the style of the typeface, and so on, which may have been in the cognitive code for a short period of time, have now been reduced; they're no longer retrievable.

Elaboration of a cognitive code refers to the relating of specific mental events to one another. If, when you looked out the window, you noticed a tree and began to consider what characteristics of this particular tree resembled other trees in the area, you were elaborating a cognitive code.

In many cases, cognitive codes can be stored and recovered, and in addition, highly reduced cognitive codes can be fleshed out, or reconstructed. Reconstructions of cognitive codes occur quite commonly, and this ability seems to be based on our general knowledge of the world. Consider an example. Suppose you tell an acquaintance about the key volleyball game your intramural team won two weeks ago. Your account is almost certain to involve some reconstruction. Although some aspects of the game are sure to stand out vividly, some details have been reduced. To give a complete rendition of the game, however, these details must be filled in. How is this filling in accomplished? Knowledge of athletic contests in general, volleyball in particular, and chronological knowledge are probably all used. If you remember an incredible play you made to boost the score to 12–8 in favor of your team, and then you remember that your opponents came surging back to knot the score at 12 all, you may start to infer, and report, that they got the serve back on the next point and proceeded to reel off four straight points. To support this inference, you may try to recall where you were standing on the court when the opponents tied the score. If you believe you were still standing in the same place that you were in when you made the incredible play, then your belief about the order of the scoring is probably accurate: No rotation of players had apparently occurred in the meantime. But if you realize that you were standing in two different places when you made the play and later when the score became tied, then you know that the serve must have seesawed with no scoring, at least once, resulting in your rotating to a different spot on the floor. As this example hints, the processes involved in storing, recovering, and reconstructing cognitive codes are an aspect of our mental lives that we usually refer to as memory.

Perhaps the most important word of Neisser's definition of cognitive psychology is its last word: Cognitive processes create codes that are *used* by people. That is, the cognitive codes developed by individuals are the basis of their knowledge of the world. Such codes enable people to work, make decisions, study, play tennis, and so on.

Kinds of Knowledge and Types of Processing

Although the term *knowledge* encompasses a vast amount of territory, we can get some idea of the lay of the land by considering a few examples of knowledge in use. Consider the knowledge that Tamara has of her car's carburetor. She knows that this device measures out a tiny amount of gasoline, mixes it with air, and sprays the mixture into the engine's cylinders at just the right time. This knowledge can be quite useful to her sometimes, because she can use it to diagnose particular difficulties that her car is having. Like many people, however, Tamara doesn't know how to fix the carburetor; that requires a specialist. In contrast with her knowledge of carburetion, consider Tamara's knowledge of bicycle riding. She knows how to ride her own ten-speed bike, and she thinks she could ride just about any other ten-speed also. Tamara is certain that she would retain this knowledge even if several years elapsed without her riding a bicycle. Although she has knowledge of how to ride a bicycle, she can't explain what she does to keep her balance, how she makes a turn without falling over, and so on. In the case of the carburetor, Tamara has a certain amount of knowledge that she can describe verbally, but she has little practical knowledge. In the case of the bicycle, the situation is reversed. Tamara rides the bicycle well, but she can't describe what she does very completely.

Cognitive psychologists use two terms to describe these two seemingly different kinds of knowledge: **declarative knowledge** and **procedural knowledge.** Declarative knowledge refers to factual information that is somewhat static (i.e., unchanging) in nature, whose organization is often apparent to us, and which is usually describable. Let's take these items one at a time. Declarative knowledge often takes the form of a series of related facts. For example, the description of Tamara's carburetor knowledge mentioned a series of facts that are agreed upon by others who are familiar with carburetors. Even when our declarative knowledge is wrong, it's still expressible in this factual format, as would be true for someone who said, for example, that *Apollo 11* was the first Apollo spacecraft to land on the moon. In this definition, static means stationary or unchanging. I know that Abraham Lincoln was the sixteenth president of the United States. There's an excellent chance that I'll retain this knowledge to the end of my life, and I can't think of anything that would improve my grasp of this fact. We can control the organization of declarative knowledge in a very real sense. To see this, suppose I were to ask you to develop a system that we might use to categorize sports. How would you go about it?

You might start by dividing all sporting activities into two categories: those that involve a ball and those that don't. Then, you might proceed to further divide each of those categories into team versus individual sports.

In contrast with declarative knowledge, procedural knowledge refers to the knowledge underlying skillful actions, and its nature tends to be dynamic (i.e., changing). The organization of procedural knowledge is not very clear to us, nor is procedural knowledge usually very describable. It is more easily *shown* to someone than it is *told*. Using the bicycle example again, biking is an action that is best understood as a skill. When Tamara was six, she acquired this skill by falling off her bike numerous times. The acquisition of a skill often seems to involve making and detecting errors. Unlike my knowledge of Lincoln's presidency, Tamara's skill at bicycle riding continues to improve, as does her typing ability and her tennis serve. If Tamara were to stop doing any of these things for an extended period, her knowledge of how to do them would apparently decline. The knowledge probably wouldn't disappear altogether, but, nevertheless, procedural knowledge is dynamic in the sense that, with additional experience, we continue to improve; without it, the knowledge begins to decline.

The distinction between these two kinds of knowledge might best be summed up in the phrases "knowing how" and "knowing that." "Knowing how" refers to nonverbal knowledge of particular procedures that a person engages in to accomplish some objective. Whenever we hit a backhand, ride our bicycles, or make pancakes, we're using procedural knowledge to achieve some objective. "Knowing that" refers to knowledge that can be described more or less completely in a series of declarative sentences. When we describe how to program a computer or explain the workings of a camera, we're expressing declarative knowledge.

Cognitive psychologists have wondered about the relationship between declarative and procedural knowledge. Many—perhaps most—of our daily activities involve both kinds of knowledge. Nevertheless, a question that a cognitive psychologist might entertain concerns the cognitive codes in which procedural and declarative knowledge are represented: Are these codes fundamentally different from one another? If they are, then how does the brain know (in advance) what sorts of knowledge it will represent as a procedural knowledge code and what sorts as a declarative knowledge code? We'll try to answer that question later in the book.

The procedural-declarative distinction isn't the only one we can apply to our knowledge. Let's consider the generality of our knowledge. Even though you and I have actually shared only the sentences that you've read in this book, nevertheless there are many bits of knowledge that both you and I have in common and that we can retrieve effortlessly. For example, we both know the alphabet; we know that "thirty days has September"; and we both know that a home run scores at least one run in baseball. But there are many things that you know that I don't, and many things that I know and can retrieve easily that you couldn't possibly know (such as how many miles I have on my car, or how many pairs of maroon socks I own). Cognitive psychologists refer to the general knowledge about the properties of words and concepts that is shared by many as **semantic** knowledge or semantic memory (Tulving, 1972). Knowledge that each individual has that is based on his or her own experience, and thus is linked to a specific time or place, is referred to as **episodic** knowledge, or episodic memory.

Like the procedural-declarative distinction we looked at earlier, this division of knowledge also raises some interesting questions. For example, one issue concerns the possibility of a conversion of episodic to semantic memory. How many specific experiences are required to convert some portion of our episodic knowledge to semantic knowledge? Do you know what a hard-boiled egg tastes like? If the answer is yes, then how many did you have to eat before you could describe their taste? As an alternative possibility, it could be the case that semantic knowledge is actually something of an illusion: Maybe we really don't have knowledge "in general" about words or concepts. This would be the case if, when I asked you the question about hard-boiled eggs, what you actually retrieved was simply the taste of the last hard-boiled egg that you ate.

We've talked about some of the terms that cognitive psychologists might use to describe human knowledge, but cognitive psychologists also use a variety of terms to talk about the varieties of cognitive processing that people can bring to bear on a task. A good way to begin this discussion is to talk about the phenomenon of attention.

A complete discussion of attention is reserved for later, but right now, attention can briefly be defined as the concentration and focusing of mental activity (Matlin, 1983). In the dim light of morning, I must pay attention to the pair of socks that I get out of the drawer, lest I select a pair that doesn't go with the rest of my clothes. Paying attention seems to accentuate, or enhance, the sensory input that has been focused on. Thus, when I pay attention to eating my Black Forest torte, the flavor seems much more intense than it does when I pay attention instead to what my dinner companion is saying.

Attention is such a hallmark of our mental lives that it would be tempting to conclude that allocating attention is necessary to initiate any other cognitive processing. Such a conclusion would be erroneous, however. Evidence from our daily lives, which has been supported by experimental findings, suggests that cognitive processes can sometimes be initiated and sustained with little or no selective attention paid to them. Have you ever driven on an interstate highway while daydreaming about the events in your life, only to realize an hour later that you're not sure if you've already passed your exit? During the hour that you spent daydreaming, your cognitive processes continued to work because you made an untold number of decisions about passing other cars, maintaining speed, and so on. Yet these decisions did not seem to require any conscious effort.

Effortful cognitive processes that seem to require attention to initiate and sustain them are referred to as **controlled processes.** Processes that seem to be initiated and run without any conscious allocation of attention are referred to as **automatic.** Like the procedural-declarative knowledge distinction we have already examined, the automatic-controlled distinction allows cognitive psychologists to describe the type of cognitive processing that is taking place.

One form of the automatic-controlled distinction applies to the phenomenon of retrieval. **Explicit memory** refers to those situations in which a person is aware of using cognitive processes in an effort to retrieve something, or is otherwise conscious of being reminded. Such use of memory can be thought of as a controlled memory process. But there are numerous other situations that show that our cognitive and neural system sometimes retrieves things even though we have not become aware of using our memory (Roediger, 1990). This phenomenon is referred to as **implicit memory**, and such memories seem very much like automatic memory processing.

For example, subjects who are given a list of common words such as "table" may be asked to recall them after a certain time interval. At retrieval time, the subjects "try" to remember the words, and this is a straightforward example of explicit memory. As you might expect, subjects in such situations usually recall some but not all of the words that were presented. Here's what happens next. The subjects leave the laboratory, but instead of going home, they go into another laboratory where they are given a "word guessing game" that asks them to fill in the letters of a partially blanked-out word (such as _a b_e). Some of the words in the game are from the first list of words that the subjects were asked to recall; some are new words. Surprisingly, we find that the subjects are more likely to succeed on the partially blanked-out items from the first list than they are on new items. Also, the subjects in such situations frequently fill in the blanks successfully on items that they could not explicitly recall a short time earlier. Notice that the second task is not treated by the subjects as a "memory task"; very seldom does the subject become aware that some of the elements were presented before. Rather, what we see here is that the subject's memory is showing the effects of its prior exposure to a particular set of words, even though the person is not explicitly trying to recall those words.

The topics that a cognitive psychologist might investigate are discussed in the next section. In the meantime, let's summarize what has been discussed so far. Cognitive psychologists are concerned with questions about the representation of human knowledge and its use as seen in human action. They have developed some terminology to describe both the nature of knowledge used (that is, whether it is declarative or procedural, episodic or semantic) and the nature of the processing used (controlled and explicit processing, or automatic and implicit processing).

Topics of Cognitive Psychology

You may have gotten the impression that cognitive psychologists might study anything they pleased, because practically every human activity requires some sort of knowledge. Technically, you would be right. In practice, however, cognitive psychologists are more likely to investigate some specific sorts of mental events rather than others. Complete agreement will never be reached about which specific mental events should be studied, but at least some consensus exists about those subject matters that are truly cognitive. This section provides an annotated listing of some cognitive topics, along with the questions that cognitive psychologists might ask about those topics. Neither the list of topics nor the questions associated with them should be regarded as complete, but both can be regarded as typical.

> **1. Attention.** We've already looked briefly at the phenomenon of mental focusing. The issue of attention is loaded with practical significance. For example, you've no doubt heard people say that a person can pay attention to only one thing at a time. Yet, various situations commonly demand that we attend to more than one thing simultaneously. For example, in class, I expect my students to listen to me. Yet, at the same time, I expect them to take accurate notes. If the "one thing at a time" theory is correct, I'm doing my students a disservice that compromises their ability to learn the material.

On the other hand, maybe the students are so practiced that these two tasks—listening and writing—no longer require attention. The cognitive psychologist is often interested in the attentional demands that a task makes on a person. If a task is sufficiently demanding, do we pay attention to that task alone, or can we always divide our attention among a variety of tasks?

2. **Pattern recognition**. Survival often depends upon our ability to correctly interpret ambiguous sensory input. While driving home in the fog, we have to pay attention to the road so that we can correctly categorize, and evade, anything that suddenly looms out. However, this process of making sense out of sensory input goes on even when the situation is not life threatening. For example, while writing this book, I made numerous typing errors. In my case, detecting typing errors involves looking at my computer's screen and determining whether the patterns of pixels (points of light) are the appropriate ones. In other words, I have to determine, from the sensory input, whether the pixels have been organized in the right way.

Cognitive psychologists are interested in how this pattern recognition is done. What information do the letters have that can be preserved in a neural and cognitive code? As discussed, pattern recognition of letters is simply a specific example of a far more general problem. What information must be present in the world to enable our sensory and cognitive systems to detect and categorize it? Perhaps, as some cognitive psychologists reason, the problem should be turned around. What sort of cognitive programs exist in our minds that enable the detection and categorization of information in the world?

3. **Memory**. We observe regularities in our own behavior as a function of the experiences that we have had. This simple fact implies that we (and others in whom we observe similar regularities) must possess a means of keeping copies of those experiences; otherwise, our experiences would be of no benefit to us. Many questions about memory fascinate cognitive psychologists, and so the list of questions here is by no means complete. Cognitive psychologists are interested in the nature of the organization of knowledge in memory. How does the memory of our personal experiences fit in with what we have learned about the world in general? Are procedural and declarative knowledge organized similarly in our memories? What has happened to forgotten memories? Are they still present somewhere in our minds, or have they truly been lost?

4. **Organization of knowledge.** Related to questions of memory storage are questions about the *form of the stored material*. If we maintain that this stored material is knowledge, then the question we are asking here comes down to describing the form of knowledge. Going back to a distinction we made earlier, psychologists have been interested in describing the forms of both procedural and declarative knowledge. At this point, cognitivists do not have much in the way of clear ideas about how procedural knowledge is stored, or even how to write a formal theory showing how it *could* be stored. But the situation is a lot different for declarative knowledge. Here, cognitive scientists have developed several theoretical perspectives using both the information-processing and connectionist approaches.

5. **Language**. As we shall see, the phenomenon of language has been subjected to an intense scrutiny from cognitive psychologists. There are many obvious issues to be studied here, including the role of experience in acquiring language, the course of normal and abnormal language develop-

ment, and so on. Apart from these developmental issues, there are many unresolved controversies concerning the very nature of language. We have a great deal of linguistic knowledge, and some of this knowledge (e.g., knowledge of pronunciation, knowledge of word order) seems to be expressible in the form of rules. Does this mean that the linguistically competent adult possesses a set of rules that governs pronunciation and word order? Some linguists have argued that this is so. In addition, some have claimed that the organization of such rules is itself subject to certain inherent limitations of our mental capabilities. According to such a view, therefore, a discovery of the rules of language is equivalent to a discovery of the rules of thought itself. It's interesting here to imagine what might be going on if it turns out that our cognitive systems do not follow linguistic rules. For example, it's just possible that, although our linguistic knowledge may be *described* as following a system of rules, our language use may not actually be *governed* by those rules, or by any other set of formal rules. This distinction, that of rule-describable versus rule-governed actions, pervades much of cognitive psychology. We'll explore its implications in several chapters.

6. Reasoning. You may have taken a course in logic only to find that the principles of correct reasoning often were not intuitively obvious, and in some cases were downright confusing. To the extent that your experience is a common one, what does this say about naturally occurring human reasoning? Are people inherently illogical? This state of affairs would be unsatisfying, and such a proposition seems illogical itself. If it couldn't put two and two together, what would be the good of having a great cognitive system capable of accurate pattern recognition, vivid imagery, and amazingly complex verbal reports? Our experience with logic tells us that people are not necessarily intuitively logical, but our experience in the real world tells us that people are not inaccurate reasoners either. This evidence suggests that people are perhaps using some other (nonlogical) system of reasoning that produces the correct outcome frequently enough to be useful in the real world. This leads to a question: If naturally occurring human reasoning is illogical, then what is its nature?

7. Problem solving. Playing chess and changing a car tire have some elements in common. In both cases, we recognize that the existing situation needs modification (the opposing king hasn't been checkmated; the tire is flat). Also, in both situations, we have an idea of the pattern we seek. We are capable of forming a plan, that is, a mental event that seems to specify a sequence of actions, which if done correctly, might produce the desired outcome. How might we describe the knowledge that enables us to generate such a plan? The whole question of strategy use in problem solving is interesting. What are strategies? If I were to show you a problem that you've never seen before, your solution attempts wouldn't be unorganized for long. We would quickly see the emergence of some actions that indicated you had some plan in mind. How are people able to generate plans and strategies for problems they have never encountered before?

Mental events can be viewed in many other ways, too. For example, one could look at the roles that others play in the formation of one's own mind. Similarly, an investigator could study dreams and other phenomena that seem to have a strong mental component. However, cognitive psychologists usually don't take social factors into account in their study of cognition, nor do they usually study dreams. Further, cognitive psychologists have tended to de-emphasize individual differences in mental events. Of all the variables that might be considered cognitive, cognitive psychologists usually consider only a small part. This raises a question: What factors were responsible for molding the field into its existing shape? Answering this question requires delving into psychology's history.

THE ROOTS OF COGNITIVE PSYCHOLOGY

Speculation about the nature of mental events has existed for at least 2,000 years, but not until the formal beginnings of academic psychology in the last century were such investigations treated from an empirical standpoint. When Wilhelm Wundt (1832–1920) founded a psychological laboratory in Leipzig in 1879, he was determined to carry out a program of research designed to establish psychology as a natural science (Hilgard, 1987). Although Wundt referred to his theoretical position as voluntarism, in the United States his theoretical orientation became known as **structuralism.**

Describing mental events as having structure implies that mentality or awareness can be viewed as a set of organized elements, and Wundt adhered to this position. According to Wundt, the mind was an active agent involved in combining or, more accurately, synthesizing basic mental elements. Wundt had fond hopes for the "new science" of psychology: He hoped to show that basic mental processes could be observed and recorded.

Accordingly, Wundt trained his human subjects in an exacting technique known as *introspection*, which literally means "looking into." The introspectionist was supposed to look into her own mind. In practice, the introspectionist was to report verbally the first associations that entered her awareness when a stimulus word or image was presented. Ideally, these reports were to be expressed in words that were as close to the raw sensory input as possible. Wundt hoped that, through analysis of the subjects' reports, the laws of mental operation could be discovered.

What happened? When asked to introspect about the idea *dog*, Wundt's subjects reported generalized doglike images, often accompanied by kinesthetic sensations such as the feel of holding a dog on a leash, running away from a ferocious dog, or even being bitten by a dog. From a series of such reports, Wundt became convinced that the technique of introspection could be used, if liberally supported by other more "behavioral" measures, as a sort of window on the active, synthetic mental processes that underlie all other mental activity. It's important to keep in mind that the stimuli used in Wundt's experiments tended to be fairly "simple" ones that usually produced only a brief and fleeting experience. Second, we should recognize that the introspective technique invariably produced imagery.

One aspect of Wundt's work that was to have fateful implications for cognitive psychology was his decision to divide the subject matter of psychology into two classes. Wundt believed that the development of mental life was influenced by culture and language to such an extent that "higher" mental processes, such as thinking, which depend upon language and culture, could not be studied successfully using the fairly limited observational techniques of the laboratory (Leahey, 1987). Accordingly, Wundt did not investigate what we might call "thought processes" in the lab. Rather he believed that the higher mental processes could best be studied by observation of the mental products of an entire culture or society, as such a society had developed over time. For this Wundt argued that a historical, or anthropological viewpoint, rather than the experimental approach, would be called for. So, for Wundt the study of thinking processes per se was included in the study of what he referred to as *Volkerpsychologie* ("folk psychology"). Wundt undertook such an enterprise toward the end of his career (Wundt, 1900–1920).

Although Wundt's influence on the new science of psychology was considered strong, a group of researchers in the university town of Würzburg soon began to chafe under the constraints imposed by the Leipzig school. The Würzburgers, led by Oswald Kulpe, began to apply the experimental technique to the problem of thought. Consider the following "problem" and introspectionist report:

> Poem. In what larger category does it belong?
> Once again, immediately a full understanding of the [question]. Then again an intensive glance, the symbolic fixation of that which is sought: then at once, the flitting memory of art, poetry, and so on appeared. The word *art*, I think, in auditory-motor terms. Then the thought that I cannot subsume poetry under art but only under artistic production. With this, I am certain, no words and images: then I said, "work of art." (Humphrey, 1963, p. 137)

Although the style of the report and its terminology are somewhat old-fashioned, the introspectionist seems to be using controlled processes ("an intensive glance") to describe some knowledge that many of us would regard as procedural rather than declarative. That is, most of us would have a hard time telling somebody what exactly had been going on in our minds when we categorized a stimulus. Regarding Wundt's structural position, the important implication of this report is that its author is certain that no images were involved in its production. From reports such as this one, Kulpe and his circle went on to develop the doctrine of *imageless thought*. This position refers to the idea that some mental events could not be classified according to any accompanying sensory content. The issue of the underlying form of thought is still very much with us, as we shall see in the chapters on memory.

From this brief description of Wundt's work, and the response it drew, it's hard to see how such reports could form the basis of modern cognitive psychology. Yet, although Wundt focused on certain topics and ignored others, much of the work of contemporary cognitive psychologists is clearly related to Wundt's ideas. For example, Wundt realized that attention was an important component of cognition. He also recognized that mental events could be described as concepts that were formed through experience. Studies in concept formation have been one of the foundations of modern cognitive psychology. Wundt's notion that mental events were related to one another also foreshadowed modern work in an area known as *semantic memory*. In retrospect, it seems clear that the experimental psychology developed by Wundt and challenged by the Würzburgers had a number of commonalities with contemporary cognitive psychology.

The train of thought that Wundt initiated jumped the track in this country, however. American psychologists were dismayed that Wundt's methods produced findings that were neither reproducible nor observable—two characteristics that seemed necessary for any science of psychology. American psychologists soon turned to behaviorism as their principal theory. For the first fifty to sixty years of this century, many—perhaps most—American psychologists strongly believed that this theory was essentially the only correct approach to erecting a science of behavior. Renewed interest in mental events began to take place in the United States around 1960. The next sections describe some of the events that led American psychologists to question their behavioristic beliefs.

Human Factors Research During World War II

The field of human factors research deals with the problems of human-machine interactions, particularly with regard to improving human skills and performance. This field emerged during World War II when it became clear that the advanced technology then being developed required improvements in the layout and design of instrumentation. Nowhere was the problem of human use of instrumentation more critical than in the area of aviation.

Broadbent's Studies   In his work at the Applied Psychology Research Unit, Donald Broadbent noted that human workers were guided by the information, or "feedback" as it was called, given to them by machines. In the case of pilots, Broadbent observed that not all of the information being displayed was used by the pilot to fly the aircraft. Rather, certain instruments were monitored more diligently than were others. Broadbent also found that, oftentimes, too much information was displayed; the pilots were unable to attend to all of it at once. Instead, the pilots had to focus their attention on successive gauges—a process that required a substantial amount of time.

Broadbent's work has several implications. First, he countered the idea that humans wait passively for stimuli to impinge upon them. Rather, he found, the pilots and other technical personnel actively sought out information, a finding that was somewhat troublesome for the then-popular behaviorist theories. Second, human information processing seemed quite similar to the *servomechanisms* (automatic devices) controlling the complex machines. That is, as each servomechanism responds to a particular kind of information and in a particular way, so can the human information-processing system be thought of as a collection of such mechanisms. For the individual human operator, one key problem then became the allocation of attention to direct the information processing of such mental servomechanisms. The title of one of Broadbent's postwar papers, "A Mechanical Model for Human Attention and Immediate Memory" (1954), is indicative of how far this new approach to human performance could be taken.

Computing Machinery

The discussion of Broadbent's work alluded to the concept of **information.** Broadbent's interest in this term was typical given the spirit of the times. Shortly before World War II, several thinkers—notably Shannon—attempted to define the concept of information mathematically. Shannon reasoned that the function of information was to reduce the uncertainty of particular future events. Specifically, if we imagine future possible events as occupying a range, or space, and then find out that this range has been constrained by exactly half (that is, half of the future events are no longer possible), then our uncertainty about these future events has been reduced. We know that half of them cannot take place, so we have to worry only about the remaining half. How much information have we received? Shannon defined a bit of information as the amount needed to reduce the number of possible outcomes by exactly half. Let's consider an illustration. Suppose Maria tells Bill that she's thinking of a particular square on a chessboard, and Bill's task is to determine which square Maria has in mind. To determine which square Maria is thinking of, Bill is allowed to ask her questions about the chessboard that can be answered with a yes or a no. Further suppose that Bill is trying to figure out the correct square with the minimum number of questions.

How would he proceed? A chessboard has sixty-four squares, so to get one bit of information, Bill needs to ask a question that eliminates thirty-two squares from further consideration. One way for Bill to do this is to ask if the square is in the top half of the board. If Maria said yes, Bill would restrict his search to the top half of the board. If she said no, Bill would know that the square was in the bottom half of the board, and he would begin to search there. Subsequent searches would consist of dividing the appropriate half of the board into halves again, and so on. If Bill did this efficiently, determining the square Maria had in mind would require that Bill ask six questions.

As Shannon phrased it, representing a particular square on a chessboard requires six bits of information. Phrased in a slightly different way, a string of six Y's or N's like this—YYNYYN—represents a particular square on a chessboard. Moreover, every square on the chessboard could be represented by some such string. Shortly after World War II, it became clear to a number of thinkers, including John von Neuman, that a machine capable of creating and storing such strings also would be capable of symbolically representing a wide variety of phenomena. With the publication of *Cybernetics* by Wiener in 1948, the information theory of Shannon was formally welded with the servomechanism theory of Broadbent, and the development of general-purpose computers was just around the corner. Some computing hardware was developed in the late 1930s, although the real power of the digital computer was not exploited until the development of programming languages such as FORTRAN, which took place in the early 1950s.

Psychologists were fascinated with the digital computer for several reasons. First, computers showed that complex actions could be broken down into a series of yes or no decisions. This capability was important because it indicated that, theoretically, no matter how complex a human's knowledge or information, it could be represented by a code that was simply **binary.** When used as an adjective, *binary* refers to information that is expressible in two elements. If a computer could be given correct feedback as it worked its way through each step of a binary code, then a computing machine could (again, theoretically) duplicate the behavior of a person, no matter how complex that behavior. This led psychologists to develop models of behavior based on the ideas of feedback and binary operations. One of these systems was developed by Miller, Galanter, and Pribram (1960) in their famous book *Plans and the Structure of Behavior.* They conceived of human action as being represented by components they called TOTE units. TOTE stands for Test Operate Test Exit.

Figure 1.1 shows the workings of a famous TOTE unit; this one is designed to drive nails. In the first stage of the process, the nail is *tested.* If it sticks up, then the process must *operate* by swinging the hammer down on the nail. After the operate stage, the process must again test the nail. If the nail head is now flush with the surface, then the process may exit, going on to something else.

The beauty of this system is that TOTE units can be built upon one another in a hierarchical fashion, with increasingly general TOTE units near the top of the hierarchy. For example, a building contractor might be endowed with an extremely general TOTE unit for house construction, which might consist of several more specific TOTE units for wall construction, each of which might contain a nail-driving TOTE unit like the one just described. Imagining that humans are governed by such TOTE units does not furnish proof that humans *are* made up of them. Nevertheless, *Plans and the Structure of Behavior* was extremely persuasive because it demonstrated that the feedback and mechanism approach to

FIGURE 1.1
....
A TOTE unit.

Source: (From *Plans and the Structure of Behavior* (1st ed.), by G. Miller, E. Galanter, & K. Pribram. © 1960 by Holt, Rinehart & Winston.) Reprinted by permission of E. Galanter.

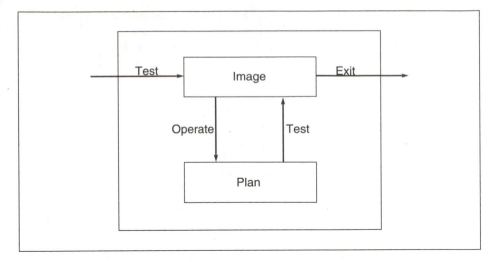

human actions could have tremendous explanatory power—power that was strong enough to challenge the behavioristic account.

Psychologists became fascinated with computers for another reason, too—one that you may have already guessed. From a certain perspective, computers could be thought of as nothing more than gigantic collections of vacuum tubes. The computer's power was awesome, but each vacuum tube couldn't do much: It was either on or off. The machine's power was derived from its speed in altering the on-off pattern of the vacuum tubes and from the fact that it had so many of them. Given what was known about neurology at that time, it seemed reasonable to compare the activity of the vacuum tube with the *action potential,* or firing of the individual neuron. If the analogy were continued, it seemed clear that the complexity of human action depended on the speed of neural events (the action potential could take place one thousand times per second) and on the fact that humans were endowed with billions of such neurons. In retrospect, it's not surprising that early computers were often referred to as "giant electronic brains." This name reflects the fond hope of many early computer scientists that the machines would do more than simply mimic the action of the nervous system; they would duplicate it.

Linguistics

Almost all our utterances have a purpose: to communicate something. For thousands of years, scholars have been interested in both what people say and when they say it. In the past century or so, the study of speaking and listening has become decidedly psychological in tone. That is, many thinkers have realized that speech and hearing acts are closely intertwined and that both acts are influenced by the distinctly psychological process of perception. However, language is not always studied from a psychological perspective. Linguistics is the discipline that studies the structure of language. **Psycholinguistics** is the study of language from a psychological rather than from a linguistic perspective. Rather than focusing on the processes of speech and hearing per se, the linguist attempts to understand the *organization* of language, its regularities that seem more or less universal. Language seems intimately bound together with thought. The linguist hopes that, by discovering the organizing principles of language, the laws of thought also will be revealed.

Skinner's Book and Chomsky's Rebuttal   One classic problem in the study of language is its acquisition. How do children learn to comprehend speech and produce grammatically correct utterances? The behavioristic perspective in psychology was firmly established by the time B. F. Skinner undertook a behavioristic analysis of language acquisition in 1936. Skinner created a phonograph record consisting of random groupings of sounds. The record had been made by recording natural speech and then editing the utterances so that the placement and ordering of the sounds were no longer typical. Skinner played this record—known as a verbal summator—for his subjects, and he noted that people read into the sounds, interpreting them as actual words. This phenomenon impressed Skinner. The verbal summator demonstrated that there was nothing inherently special about linguistic sounds, and, Skinner argued, that meant language sounds could be studied as examples of operant behavior. Skinner reasoned that the same laws that governed the learning of other operant behaviors should govern the learning of language.

Consider the case of a child who makes a request of a parent, which is followed by the parent's response. A behavioristic theory of language would state that this particular verbal behavior was learned, because the parent reinforced the child for producing the utterance by complying with it. If a one-year-old holds up his cup and says "More!" the parent is reinforcing the child's utterance by providing him with more apple juice. Skinner called this function of language the **mand function.** Manded utterances are reinforced through compliance. Children must learn when to make the appropriate mands and what particular mands will be followed by a reward. According to Skinner, this latter problem boiled down to a case of discrimination learning. That is, the child plays a sort of naming game with the parent, during which words gradually become restricted to their appropriate referents. For example, the child might point to a red book and say "Red?" to which the parent might respond affirmatively. If the child then points to a blue book and says "Red?" the parent will respond with a no, and, presumably, the child will learn that the operant *red* does not apply to the shape of the object but rather to some other feature. Proceeding in this way, the child eventually learns what cues must be present before the operant *red* will be rewarded, namely that *red* refers to the color of an object. The child is in a position similar to that of Skinner's pigeons, which would be reinforced for doing a particular behavior under some conditions but not under others. For the child as well as for the pigeon, the task consisted of discriminating the relevant features that signaled when a particular behavior would be reinforced. Skinner referred to this recognition of the appropriate discriminative cues as the **tact function** of language.

As Skinner understood the problem of language acquisition, children go on tacting and manding their way through the first several years of their lives, gradually improving in emitting linguistic utterances. The publication of these ideas in Skinner's book *Verbal Behavior* (1957) was not well received by linguists, however. Noam Chomsky (1959) published a detailed and relentlessly critical review that seemed to devastate Skinner's claims.

First, Chomsky noted the problem of creativity in language. Some people have estimated that the number of humans that have ever lived is 40 to 50 billion. This number being so large, you might think that everything you could say has already been uttered by somebody, somewhere, sometime. This assumption is wrong. Constructing a completely novel remark is easy:

Sophomores are limiculous.

Limiculous is an adjective referring to creatures whose habitat is mud. I'm sure that no one has ever applied that adjective to sophomores before. The problem for the behaviorist is explaining what enabled me to construct the remark. Because I've never created that remark before, no reinforcement could have existed for my constructing it. Simply put, the mand function of language does not appear powerful enough to explain novel remarks.

Chomsky also noted problems with the tact function. Skinner uses the tact function to explain particular responses to particular stimuli, such as when we respond to a piece of music by saying "Beethoven" or respond to a building by saying "Wright." In such situations, we have learned to discriminate when to emit particular verbal behaviors, namely in the presence of particular stimulus characteristics of the music or of the building. For example, when we see a painting and respond "Dutch," we are responding to particular characteristics of that painting—that is, particular stimuli that presumably exist in the world. But Chomsky maintains:

> Suppose instead of saying "Dutch" we said "Clashes with the wallpaper, I thought you liked abstract work, never saw it before, tilted, hanging too low, beautiful, hideous, remember our camping trip last summer?" or whatever else might come into our minds when looking at a picture. . . . Skinner could only say that each of these responses is under the control of some other stimulus property of the physical object. . . . But the word *stimulus* has lost all objectivity in this usage. Stimuli are no longer part of the outside physical world: They are driven back into the organism. We identify the stimulus when we hear the response. It is clear from such examples, which abound, that the talk of *stimulus control* simply disguises a complete retreat to mentalistic psychology. (Chomsky, 1959) (Emphasis in original.)

In this instance, Chomsky points out that the behavioristic account of language is no more scientific that the mentalistic accounts it had supplanted a half century earlier. The behaviorist's frustrating problem is that the tact function is not powerful enough to explain why particular utterances are produced at particular times. The notion of stimulus control is no help because, as Chomsky points out, it's not possible to specify what the stimulus is until we hear the subject's response. In other words, the idea that characteristics of the world signal us to produce specific remarks seems false, because it's not possible to specify in advance what characteristics of the world did the signaling.

Neurocomputing

Earlier, I mentioned that many psychologists of the immediate post–World War II period were impressed with the apparent similarity of computing machines to the human nervous system. It was during this time period that D. O. Hebb (1949) put a novel slant on this comparison by reversing its usual direction. Rather than think of the ways in which a computer might be like a nervous system, Hebb wondered about the ways in which a nervous system could compute things. Hebb theorized that "learning" could be defined as a succession of changes in the neurological states that a given brain could enter, or compute, as a function of its experiences with certain types of stimuli. That is, as a brain processed certain types of stimuli (and remember, each such processing event means that the brain must represent the stimuli as some sort of pattern of neural firing, or neural code), the activities involved in this processing resulted in structural changes in the brain. What are structural changes? Structural changes are essentially changes in the connections among neurons—that is, changes in the number and nature of the neuron's synapses with other neurons. Specifically, Hebb formulated the following principle that describes how these changes might occur:

> When an axon of cell A is near enough to excite a cell B and repeatedly or persistently takes part in firing it, some growth process or metabolic change takes place in one or both cells such that A's efficiency, as one of the cells firing B, is increased. (Hebb, 1949, p. 50).

Put in rather simplistic terms, if two ideas become associated in your mind, then, according to Hebb, some rather large collection of neurons has now achieved some synaptic connection with some other large collection of neurons.

The next person to explore this idea was Rosenblatt (1958). In his viewpoint, the nervous system could be divided into three "layers." The first layer consists of neurons whose job is to bring information in from the physical world. These are the sensory neurons. Rosenblatt used the term *retina* to describe the sensory neurons, because he was most interested in describing visual information processing. But the same logic applies to all sensory systems. The sensory neurons communicate with the neurons in the next layer, and these neurons are called *association cells*. If you've taken a course in physiological psychology, you probably remember that neurons can have many different "styles" of communicating. In some cases, we say that a particular neuron can have an excitatory connection with an adjacent neuron. This means that when the first neuron "fires" or sends its electrochemical impulse along its axon, the second neuron, which receives this impulse, has a tendency to "fire" also. But, there is another style of communication among neurons too. In some cases, when the first neuron fires, it produces a chemical reaction in the second neuron that makes the second neuron *resist* firing. We refer to this type of connection as inhibitory. So, the firing of some neurons can produce firing in adjacent neurons (this is the type of relationship that Hebb discussed), but neurons also can exert an inhibitory relationship on other neurons.

Understanding this concept is important in understanding the activity of the association cells. In Rosenblatt's view, some of the sensory neurons had excitatory connections with a particular association cell, but other sensory neurons might have inhibitory connections with the same cell. Under these circumstances, the association cell becomes a kind of "decision maker." If you put yourself in the place of the association cell, you'll see what I mean. As the association cell, will you "fire" your impulse in response to the activity of the sensory cells that are communicating with you? It depends on how many of the cells have excitatory connections and how many have inhibitory connections. Of all the cells communicating with you, if there are more excitatory sensory neurons than inhibitory cells, then you would "decide" to fire your impulse. But if there were more inhibitory cells than excitatory cells, then you would refrain from firing your impulse.

Now we have one more layer of cells to discuss: the response cells. Just as the sensory neurons communicate with the association cells in either excitatory or inhibitory styles, so too the association cells can have excitatory or inhibitory connections with the response cells. This means that the response cell is a decision maker too. Just as the association cell listens (metaphorically) to all of the sensory neurons that communicate with it and decides if the sum of all the sensory inputs is excitatory or inhibitory, so too the response cells keep track of all the association cells communicating with them. If the net response (that is, the sum of all the excitatory and inhibitory connections) is positive (more excitatory than inhibitory), then the response cell fires, but if the net reponse is negative (more inhibitory than excitatory), then the response cell remains silent.

The discussion so far has pointed out the similarities of the association cells and the response cells, but there is one important difference between them. The association cells have no influence on the firing of the sensory cells, but the response cells *can* influence the firing of the association cells. The specific pattern goes like this: When association cells activate a response cell, the response cell in turn has excitatory connections back to the association cells that activated it. But with any association cell that did not contribute to the activation of the response cell, the response cell has *inhibitory* connections. What function does this serve? This pattern of excitatory and inhibitory connections from the response cell back to the association cell means that the response cell functions as a kind of "amplifier": It has excitatory connections with cells that have excitatory connections with it. Rosenblatt named such a system of artificial neurons a *perceptron*. The perceptron was the first attempt to develop an abstract model of the nervous system that showed how a system with neural characteristics could actually compute things. Although subsequent research (Minsky & Papert, 1969) showed that our nervous system must be much more complicated than Rosenblatt's analysis indicated, this first attempt was nevertheless important.

We've explored four historical antecedent areas—human factors research, computer technology, psycholinguistics, and neurocomputing—to find the roots of modern cognitive psychology. In the 1960s, the strands of research and intellectual activity suggested by these roots came together. In 1967, Ulric Neisser published his eagerly awaited book *Cognitive Psychology*, which was a synthesis of many of the ideas that had been percolating in different areas up until that time. In 1970, further synthesis occurred when the academic journal *Cognitive Psychology* began publication. These publications marked the reemergence of cognition as a fixture of the American psychological landscape.

CONTEMPORARY COGNITIVE PSYCHOLOGY

Two Approaches to Cognition

At a couple of different points in this introduction, I've alluded to the "approaches" that a cognitive psychologist might use in studying some specific problem. This section will discuss the two main approaches: the **information-processing approach** and the **connectionist approach**. As you'll see, each approach has clear links with the historical roots that we have covered. For example, the information-processing approach is squarely rooted in the emergence of the computing machine; in fact, information-processing psychologists sometimes argue that the mind works like a computer. The information-processing approach can also trace its lineage back to the work in human factors. This research demonstrated that humans actively seek information about the world, and that the nature of the plans and goals that humans formed for the world was based on the information they sought and found. Like adherents of the information-processing approach, connectionists also seek to develop computational models of cognition, and in this sense, they can also trace their intellectual ancestry back to the early workers in computer science. However, unlike the approach taken by information-processing adherents, connectionists' work is intimately linked to historical roots in neurocomputing and therefore is very much neuronally inspired. Hence, connectionists, it is said, have adopted the "brain metaphor" whereas information-processing psychologists have adopted the "computer metaphor." In the next sections, we'll explore these distinctions further.

Information-Processing Approach The information-processing approach is frequently described as an abstract analysis. What this means is that neural events are not described explicitly in information-processing accounts. Mental or cognitive events are abstract in the sense that, although they depend upon neural events, they are not neural events per se. Moreover, some cognitivists believe that cognitive events may in principle be untranslatable to neural events. For example, suppose I ask you to imagine the house in which you grew up. I'm sure that you are able to scan a mental image of your house in response to questions such as "How many windows did the house have in front?" Are your mental actions (imagining, scanning, deciding on an answer) accompanied by some activity in your brain? The answer to that question is almost certainly yes. But do any of these mental actions correspond to specific neural events? This question requires a more complicated response than the previous question did. It's true that there is always the possibility that specific relationships may be found between specific neural activities or locations, and particular mental events. In fact, as we'll see in the language chapters, a few such relationships have been discovered. However, despite this, cognitive psychologists working in the information-processing tradition maintain that there are no guarantees that a specific, discoverable neural code underlies all specific mental events. Moreover, these cognitivists make several points to buttress their contention. First, they argue, we have to be aware that our brains are not identical, and this means that specifying what is similar about the *function* of, let's say, my brain vis-à-vis yours may be impossible. Now, it may be the case that my brain obeys certain functional laws that relate my neural events to my cognitive events, and this state of affairs may be true for your brain as well. But there may be no principled (i.e., rule-based) way to relate the functioning of my brain to the functioning of yours. That is, the only operative principle may be "Each person's brain coordinates the functioning of that person's neural events to that person's mental events."

The second issue raised by cognitivists working within the information-processing approach has to do with translatability. Information-processing psychologists use certain language to talk about mental events, and the language they use is necessarily different from the language neurologists use to talk about neural events. It may be the case that the reality of the phenomenon in question (be it neural or cognitive) is simply bound into the language used to describe it and thus cannot be translated into other terms. Let me give you an example of this phenomenon. In your studies of mathematics, you may have encountered the imaginary number, i, the square root of minus one. Mathematicians use this number all day long as a valid mathematical object, and so its existence can hardly be doubted. What would happen if you approached a mathematician and asked him or her what number i would be if i were a real number instead of an imaginary one? The mathematician might reply unkindly that it's a silly question. Imaginary numbers are valid and real in their realm, but they have no reality outside that realm. Despite our intuitions to the contrary, it might be exactly this state of affairs that governs neural and cognitive events. The validity of each type of event may be unimpeachable within its realm, but each type of event may have no validity outside that realm.

From the information-processing standpoint, the cognitive psychologist who wants to describe mental events has something in common with a computer programmer. The programmer's task is to devise a recipe (more or less) that will get the machine to carry out a particular series of computations. In writing the program, the programmer is not concerned about electron flow within the machine nor with many other aspects about the machine as a piece of *hardware*. Rather, the programmer thinks perhaps of data structures and operations upon them. The recipe, or program, that is eventually concocted is a piece of *software* that, generally speaking, is independent of the machine. Adherents of the information-processing approach are in a similar situation. They are not too interested in specifying the neural activity underlying a cognitive or mental event—that's a hardware problem. Basically, then, psychologists of this orientation focus on the software side of the equation, on the description of the cognitive processes that operate on the information within us.

What sort of information is it that we have within us? Earlier, this chapter described Neisser's definition of cognitive psychology, and we saw that, in his definition, cognition begins with sensory input. This sensory input forms the basis of the information studied by many cognitive psychologists. At the moment of sensory pickup, it becomes appropriate to think of two systems coming on line simultaneously. One system is the neural system, and we can, of course, describe the fate of the sensory information that we pick up as a succession of transformations made upon this initial neural code. The other system is the cognitive system. Using this system, we can still describe the fate of the initial sensory information as a succession of transformations, not transformations of the actual, physical, neural energy, but rather as a succession of transformations that involve abstract events. The concept of an abstract event is rather challenging for many students, so perhaps an example will help.

Suppose I ask you to watch a videotape and tell me exactly what you see. You watch the tape and observe two toddlers in a room with toys. At irregular intervals the toddlers address each other, they hand each other toys, they run around, perhaps they fall down and cry, and so on. If you were to give me a precise list of these activities (i.e., "Four minutes and eight seconds into the tape, Child A moved two feet to his left, extended his right hand holding a small truck to Child B, who extended her right hand to grasp the truck . . .," etc.), we would accept this as a valid description of what took place. But suppose you reported that the tape depicted two children playing. This is also a valid description, even though "play," as an event, is an abstraction; that is, "play" represents a way of talking about the children's movements, gestures, vocalizations, and so on, without explicitly describing any of these things necessarily. The information-processing viewpoint takes a similar position when it uses terms like *short-term memory* and *long-term memory*. That is, we can describe the two successive transformations of a "memory code" without explicitly talking about what the nervous system is doing to carry out these transformations.

Further, information-processing psychologists typically assert that these transformations often occur serially—that is, one step at a time. **Serial processing** can be contrasted with **parallel processing,** which refers to transforming more than one cognitive code simultaneously. When we discuss the connectionist approach, we'll have more to say about the issue of parallel processing.

Cognitive psychologists usually divide the human information-processing system into components, as shown in Figure 1.2. This differentiation is based in part on the supposition that some cognitive acts seem quite different from others.

The first component of the information-processing system is the sensory system, where the cognitive code is created. In this system, specific aspects of the environment are detected and their organization is begun. After the cognitive code is created by the sensory system, it is passed on to the memory. As Figure 1.2 shows, cognitive psychologists make a distinction between the permanent memory, sometimes referred to as the inactive memory, and the working memory. The permanent memory can be considered as a vast depository of both declarative and procedural knowledge. The permanent memory is a storehouse not only of facts but also of skills and motor programs that enable us to move and speak. Under some conditions, the central processor allocates attention to the working memory. When this is done, elements that have been passed into the permanent memory become activated, and at this juncture the cognitive code can be elaborated and modified.

Working memory is a kind of workbench for cognitive codes. As Figure 1.2 shows, working memory is the site where goals can be established. These goals will sometimes include the modification of a cognitive code. For example, in problem solving, the cognitive code might consist of representations of both possible solutions and possible operations that might be done to produce a solution. When solving problems, the central processor might use the working memory as a site to systematically match up possible solutions with possible operations to see if a fit can be achieved and the problem solved. The task of the central processor is to

·············· **FIGURE 1.2   An overview of the human information processing system.**

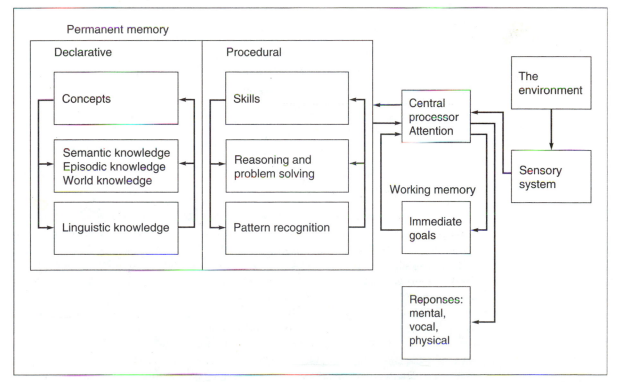

formulate goals. Once the goal is formulated, the central processor must develop a plan to accomplish the goal. In situations in which the central processor is dealing with multiple goals (which is probably the case for most real-life situations), a priority listing of goals must be established. When this has been done, the central processor must allocate attention to the cognitive processes involved to monitor their progress. The central processor uses working, or active, memory to keep track of its place in the plan, and from this site in the working memory, the response system is controlled.

Let's use Figure 1.2 as the basis for an everyday example, that of hitting a forehand drive in tennis. First, the environment offers the tennis player information about the flight of the ball—information that would be picked up primarily by the visual and auditory systems (top tennis pros like Andre Agassi listen to the sound of the ball as it leaves the racquet's strings). Presumably, the player's central processor has allocated attention to processes that recognize and categorize the opponent's shot. This categorization is important; it lets the tennis pro know where to go to be in position for the return. A second function of the categorization is that it affords the pro an opportunity to determine what kind of point is being played. If the ball is hit short, the pro has knowledge of the various patterns of play (a drop-shot return, a cross-court volley, and so on) that can be attempted from a short ball. Following the categorization, the central processor begins to allocate attention to the opponent's movements. Here, the goal is to determine an effective placement for the return shot. Is the opponent coming to the net? If that's the case, then a passing shot down the line could be the right response. While this has been going on, several automatic processes have been initiated. The pro uses automatic and procedural running programs stored in her permanent memory to move quickly from her present position to the desired position on the court. Once there, the pro attempts to hit the forehand drive, and for this she uses the procedural knowledge program that was described earlier in this chapter.

We can sum up this discussion of information-processing systems by listing and describing the principles underlying the information-processing approach (Massaro & Cowan, 1993; Palmer & Kimchi, 1986). In general, the information-processing approach to cognition emphasizes the following five qualities:

1. Informational description
2. Recursive decomposition
3. Flow continuity
4. Flow dynamics
5. Physical embodiment

Let's go through these terms one at a time. Informational description simply means that, according to information-processing theorists, both the environment in which we live and our mental processing of it can be characterized by the amounts and types of information they contain. Recursive decomposition means that cognitive processes can be thought of as consisting of simpler cognitive processes (which can be thought of as still simpler cognitive processes). The idea underlying recursive decomposition is that our cognitive processes are hierarchically arranged, and by clever and careful experimentation, we may be able to discern the nature of this hierarchy. The flow continuity principle asserts that information goes forward in time; whatever input information is needed to carry out a particular cognitive process can be found in the outputs of those cognitive processes that feed into it. The principle of flow dynamics asserts that, because mental and cognitive processes are coexistent with the chemical and electrical events of the neural system, and because these neural events take time, then no mental process can occur instantaneously. All mental or cognitive processes must involve the passage of some amount of time, even if that amount of time is only a few thousandths of a second. The physical embodiment principle refers to the idea that all cognitive processes take place in a physical system—in the case of humans, a neural system. This last principle has an important implication, and it's one that is easily overlooked by people who are just beginning their study of cognition. Let's phrase the implication as a question: If cognitive processes are abstract, then how can something abstract be housed in a physical system? The answer is that the information in the system must be represented by physical events. For example, in the case of the word "boat," the knowlege you have about what the word "boat" means is abstract, but this knowledge must be represented in the cognitive and neural system by a pattern of specific neural events. Thus, the knowledge that we have must be housed in the physical system in the form of "representations."

Connectionist Approach   Whereas the information-processing approach to the study of cognition is described as an abstract analysis, connectionists emphasize the neural and mathematical bases of their approach (Churchland, 1989). What this means is that connectionists do *not* see their models as necessarily abstract; in fact, they frequently maintain that connectionist models (sometimes equivalent expressions such as "distributed" or "neural-network" are used) are "neurally inspired" (Rumelhart & McClelland, 1986). This doesn't mean that connectionists spend their days rooting around in nervous systems; the neural systems they study often are idealized nervous systems that are expressed in the form of mathematical and computerized models. But it's also true that connectionists usually make a strong attempt to show that the actual nervous system could carry out computations that are similar to their idealized systems, thus suggesting that the actual nervous system may behave in ways congruent with the idealized systems.

As you might figure, connectionists don't always agree with some of the positions raised by information-processing theorists. For example, if you look back to Figure 1.2, you'll see that information-processing psychologists may talk about "control" of the system housed in some "central processor." But this is all Greek to a connectionist. If the central processor controls the cognitive system, can the central processor do this without having some sort of control system within itself? And if it does, does this control system within the central processor have its own central processor? To a connectionist, saying that the cognitive system is controlled by a central processor isn't much of an answer, because it just pushes the problem of control one step deeper into the system. In addition to noting this logical conundrum, connectionists also say that the nervous system doesn't work in the way that information-processing theory would imply. You can look all you want for the kinds of control structures implied by information-processing theory, but you'll seldom, if ever, find them. As connectionists point out, there are no executive neurons that "know" more than other neurons and hence direct their underlings' activity. In fact, the central nervous system, in many ways, is not a hierarchy at all. Neurons sometimes facilitate, sometimes inhibit the activity of other neurons, and the pattern of neural activity thus produced may change dramatically with a change in the stimuli presented to the system. Where there was a facilitative relationship, there may now be an inhibitory one and vice versa. Our view of neural activity suggests that there are few, if any, "boss neurons."

Connectionists also point out problems with the serial-processing assumption made by information-processing theorists—the idea that cognitive processes occur one step at a time. Connectionists point out that many significant cognitive operations can be accomplished in one second or so (Feldman, 1985). But if we consider that the basic neuron takes several milliseconds to operate and that the operating speed of these units is the "speed limit" of the brain, then we see that the cognitive system must accomplish its goals within a relatively few number of "time steps"—one hundred or so steps has been the suggested number (Feldman, 1985). As the connectionists point out, the problem here is that it's extremely difficult to write a computer program that is able to accomplish in only one hundred serial elementary operations what our cognitive systems are routinely capable of doing. For the connectionists, this means that any attempts to model the cognitive processes of the human must be based on *parallel,* not serial, processing. In other words, our brains and our cognitive systems must routinely do more than one thing at a time.

What can we say in summary about these two approaches to cognition? We can see that the information-processing approach to cognition emphasizes an abstract, serial analysis of cognitive processes. The information-processing approach implies that some cognitive processes direct other processes hierarchically and that the cognitive system as a whole has a "modular" organization. That is, it has parts, or subunits, that seem to be more or less separate from one another. The connectionist approach emphasizes a neuronally based, parallel-processing view. The connectionist approach maintains that neurons do not typically stand in a hierarchical relationship with other neurons. Moreover, connectionists argue that the cognitive system is not actually modular either, meaning that it really can't be broken down into parts. In each cognitive act, the neural and cognitive system works as entire units, not as systems of cooperating components. Describing how the neural and cognitive systems work as units requires a lengthier discussion than we have time for here. Suffice it to say that throughout the book we'll pose many examples of both approaches in operation.

Methods in Cognitive Psychology

We've seen something of the topics discussed in cognitive psychology, and we've received an orientation to the terms and background of the field. One more task remains for us to accomplish in this chapter: to understand something of the methods and techniques used by cognitive psychologists.

Throughout the textbook are cited studies from which cognitive psychologists infer the characteristics of our cognitive functioning. Cognitive psychologists often use an experimental approach to their subject matter, which involves the manipulation of some independent variable and observations of changes produced in a dependent variable. The listing of things that have served as dependent variables in psychological studies is endless, but cognitive psychologists have become fond of two classes of events for this purpose: patterns of errors and reaction times to complex stimuli.

Consider the case of a person who wishes to say the phrase "a current argument" as part of an utterance but says instead "an arrent curgument." This error, which is authentic (Fromkin, 1971; Garrett, 1982), tells us a great deal about the cognitive processes involved in speech. How would we describe what has taken place? First, we would say that a syllable switch has taken place. The first syllable of "current" has been switched with the first syllable of "argument." From this observation, we might conclude that the human mind builds words by assembling them on a syllable-by-syllable basis. We might go on to theorize that, before being completely assembled, each planned word is held in a group of slots marked First Syllable, Second Syllable, and so on. To assemble the word, a cognitive program draws the contents of the first slot and follows it with the contents of the second slot, and so on. If a mistake is going to occur, presumably it's because this particular program can't recognize which slots go with which other slots. Consequently, this particular program can't tell if an error is being made in the assembly process, because it apparently doesn't know the meaning of the words. This is what seems to be happening here, because there's no such thing as a "curgument."

In English, we use the indefinite article *a* before consonants and *an* before vowels. Although the person in our example intended to use *a*, the assembly error has resulted in a vowel sound being placed where the consonant sound had been intended. We notice that this error has been rectified in the actual utterance: The *a* has been changed to *an*. What can we conclude from this switch? Apparently, the program that determines the sounds of our utterances must operate after the program that assembles the syllables. If the program that determined the sound of utterances went first, then the person would have said "a arrent curgument"; but such errors do not occur.

A second common approach consists of measuring reaction times to the presentation of stimuli. The work of Meyer and Schvaneveldt (1971) offers a good illustration of this approach. They hypothesized that conceptually related words would be recognized as words faster than unrelated words would be recognized. To test this assertion, they presented their subjects with pairs of related and unrelated words. They also presented their subjects with pairs of nonwords. The subjects' task was to decide as quickly as possible if both elements of a pair were words, and, if so, they were to say yes. If an element of the pair was a nonword, subjects were instructed to say no. Table 1.1 shows the findings. The positive pairs (those in which the subject was to respond yes) are of particular interest. When the words were related, subjects responded 85 msec faster than they did when the words were unrelated. Although this difference may not seem like much (and we would probably not be *aware* of such a difference), a 10 percent difference in processing time is usually accepted as substantial by many cognitive psychologists. If one group requires about 1,500 msec to carry out a particular task, and a second group requires about 1,550 msec to carry out some variation of the task, such a difference wouldn't pique our curiosity. If the 50-msec difference between the groups occurred against a base rate of 500 msec, however, then we would be curious.

What can we gather from the Meyer and Schvaneveldt findings? From the substantial difference in processing time, we might state that recognition of a word seems to facilitate the recognition and reading of a related word. Such a finding tells us that words are probably recognized at least in part by their *context*.

A third method, one used by both information-processing theorists and by connectionists, is the use of computers to model or simulate cognitive and neural processes. This approach has certain advantages. For one thing, it forces the theorist/researcher to be explicit about his or her theory. For many years, psychological theories have been plagued with a fuzziness resulting from the reliance on natural language. But when a psychological theory is embodied or translated into a computer program, this fuzziness is immediately exposed because fuzzy programs don't run. A second advantage stems from the intriguing fact that sometimes cognitive tasks that appear to be very different from one another can be simulated with programs that seem rather similar in terms of the program's data

·············· **TABLE 1.1**   Examples of the pairs used to demonstrate associative pairing

| POSITIVE PAIRS | | NEGATIVE PAIRS | | |
Unrelated	Related	First Nonword	Second Nonword	Both Nonwords
Nurse	Bread	Plame	Wine	Plame
Butter	Butter	Wine	Plame	Reab
940 msec	855 msec	904 msec	1,087 msec	884 msec

Source: Meyer and Schvaneveldt, 1971. (Copyright 1971 by the American Psychological Association. Adapted by permission of the publisher and author.)

structures and basic operations. What this fact may (repeat, *may*) suggest is that the cognitive processes and operations underlying these different tasks are actually similar. This could prove to be advantageous because, from a scientific perspective, such a finding might enable cognitivists to entertain some hopes of producing something like a "unified" theory of cognition. A unified theory of cognition would mean that when a system, human or artificial, did something requiring knowledge or intelligence, we would expect to see similarities in its operation because a unified theory implies that there is only one form of intelligence or knowledge, and this form is always expressed in programs having certain features. This would be a dramatic breakthrough, if it occurred.

Let's go through some of the steps involved in building such a program. First, data are gathered from human subjects on some task that requires cognitive operations. Typically, the data are gathered from humans who are relatively new to the task, although sometimes data are gathered from experts. The data can be of the types that we have seen, that is, either error patterns or reaction times. In building a program, the researcher may gather data by asking the subjects to verbalize, or "think out loud," as they do the task. A tape recording is made of each subject as he or she engages in the task, and this tape, called a protocol, is then analyzed intensively to observe commonalities in storing, retrieving, or using data in the task. The commonalties observed in the protocols are then used as a basis for program writing.

As an example of this methodology, let's consider some work of Larkin (1989). Larkin was interested in the cognitive processes underlying the solving of algebra equations such as the following:

$$-3 - 4(2x - 9) = 7 + 5x$$

Larkin's program, the Display-Based Solver (DiBS), solves these kinds of problems by first putting each of the terms into a certain relationship with other terms. This setting of relationships is called a "data structure," and the DiBS data structure for this problem is shown in the first part of Table 1.2. This won't be too meaningful at this point, but notice that the data structure does have a goal. It lists where we "want" the terms of the equation to wind up ultimately—on the left or on the right side. The second part of Table 1.2 is a listing of the operations that the program goes through; this listing is called the "trace" of the program. The data structure that has been created enables DiBS to treat certain sets of variables as groups. For example in operation 4, DiBS gets ready to take apart the group $-4(2x - 9)$. Operation 3 has shown that DiBS has represented this group of elements, called p2, as two subgroups (p3 and p4), and the subgroup p4 is in turn

·············· **TABLE 1.2**   Trace of DiBS' Solution of a Linear Equation

(A) THE INITIAL DATA STRUCTURE

Name	Type	Value	Below	Want__below
p1	term	−3	lhs	rhs
p2	term		lhs	
p3	factor	−4	p2	rhs
p4	factor		p2	
p5	term	2	p4	lhs
p6	term	−9	p4	rhs
p7	term	7	rhs	rhs
p8	term	5	rhs	lhs

(B) TRACE OF THE SOLVING PROCESS

p1		p3	p5		p6		p7		p8
−3	+	−4	(2x	+	−9)	=	7	+	5x

1. put__an__object__where__it__wants__to__be__alg
   p1, value −3 wants to be below rhs
   moving p1 below rhs

2. combine__add
   combining terms of value −3 and −7 on rhs

3. put__an__object__where__it__wants__to__be__alg
   p8, value 5 wants to be below lhs
   moving p8 below lhs

	p2		
		p4	
p8	p3	p5 p6	p7
−5x +	−4	(2x + − 9)	= 10

4. uncover__alg
   taking apart the mixed term p2 with coefficient −4 and
   number 2 and x__term −9

p8		p5		p6		p7
−5x	+	−8x	+	36	=	10

5. combine__add
   combining terms of value −5 and −8 on lhs

6. put__an__object__where__it__wants__to__be__alg
   p6, value 36 wants to be below rhs
   moving p8 below rhs

7. combine__add
   combining terms of value −36 and 10 on rhs

	p5		p7
	−13x	+	−26

8. last__x__term
   dividing both sides by −13

9. done__alg
   all variables are below lhs
   and all numbers are below rhs only two terms remain
   therefore done

Source: Larkin, 1989. (Copyright 1989 by Lawrence Erlbaum Associates, Inc. Adapted by permission of the publisher and author.)

broken down into two elements (p5 and p6). Representing the data this way tells DiBS that in order to break down this group, you have to multiply (−4) by (−9) to get (positive) 36. So, in other words, this data structure enables DiBS to duplicate human knowledge of the role of parentheses in equation solving. But suppose the novice human didn't understand yet that the group, −4(2x−9), had to be treated in this way. That is, suppose that such a person simply understood the equation to be a string of symbols that had no higher relationships to each other?

It turns out that one of the errors that novices frequently make in this type of problem is the following (Sleeman, 1982):

From the initial equation $-3 - 4(2x - 9) = 7 + 5x$

novices get $-3 - 4(2x) = 5x + 16$

or $-3 - 4(2x) = 5x - 2$

The error that is made depends on whether the human literally just takes the −9 across the equal sign, or whether the human incorrectly adds +9 to both sides of the equation. We've seen that DiBS can get the right answer, but can it duplicate these errors? Yes, if some changes are made in the initial data structure, then DiBS treats the equation as simply a string of symbols, rather than as symbols that must be grouped in certain ways, and when this is done, then DiBS makes the same errors that human novices do.

Ecological Validity

Although cognitive psychologists usually bring their subjects into the laboratory for study, during the 1970s a movement was afoot to increase the **ecological validity** of research in cognition. This term, which was popularized by Neisser (1976), refers to the quest for theories of cognition that describe people's use of knowledge in real, everyday, culturally significant situations. Although this quest doesn't restrict the researcher's use of the laboratory, the emphasis on ecological validity does mean that the contemporary cognitive psychologist seeks to gather data and findings in ways that mesh naturally with the sorts of things that people actually use their cognitive systems to accomplish. In other words, memorizing a list of words, when done in a cognitive psychologist's laboratory, may not tell us much about some of the really interesting capabilities of human memory, because memorizing lists of unrelated words is a kind of task that humans do only under highly constrained or unnatural situations. What we'd like to know is how people go about using their memory systems for things that are believed to require the use of memory. Thus, for example, a contemporary cognitive psychologist may be much more interested in how a person goes about trying to study, learn, and remember a textbook chapter than he or she would in learning how many words a subject can remember from a list that was presented once.

The emphasis on ecological validity has a special implication for the nonspecialist reader. It means that much of what you are about to read should be useful to you. I can't promise that you'll be able to use everything that you read in this book, or that the applications will be obvious. But my hope is that, after you study human reasoning, for example (Chapter 11), your reasoning will improve. Perhaps after you study the material on problem solving (Chapter 12), you'll become more successful at detecting and avoiding some of the pitfalls that hinder creative thinking. Similarly, after you study memory (Chapters 4 and 5), I'm optimistic that you'll be able to use the material to improve your retention and retrieval. As long as you keep in mind that the theories presented are the current best guess about their respective phenomena and are not absolute truths, I'm confident that your studies in this book will be rewarded with both practical skills and a deeper appreciation of your mind's complexity.

 ## CONCLUDING COMMENTS AND SUGGESTIONS FOR FURTHER READING

At the end of each chapter, I'll offer some commentary on the material that was presented in an effort to foster your integration and learning of it. In addition, I'll present titles of some books and articles that you might wish to read if you're interested in learning more about the topics that were covered in that chapter.

If you wish to learn more about the methodology of research in cognition, try *Methods and Tactics in Cognitive Science*, Kintsch, Miller, and Polson (1984). If you are particularly interested in the computer applications in cognitive science, try the chapter by Aitkenhead and Slack (1985). Students who would like to find out more about the nuts and bolts of the information-processing approach would benefit by reading the excellent collection of chapters edited by Klahr and Kotovsky (1989). The chapter by Massaro and Cowan (1993) is also a very good overview of the information-processing approach. The research on connectionism in the last few years could fill a good-sized library all by itself. Anderson and Rosenfeld (1988) have edited a good collection of basic papers (many of them are very difficult to read). The books edited by Grossberg (1988) and by Nadel, Cooper, Culicover, and Harnish (1989) have a strong connectionist and biological orientation. Clark (1989) covers the information-processing and connectionist viewpoints from a philosophical perspective.

KEY TERMS

Neural code
Cognitive codes
Declarative knowledge
Procedural knowledge
Semantic knowledge
Episodic knowledge
Controlled processes
Automatic processes

Explicit memory
Implicit memory
Structuralism
Human factors research
Information
Binary code
Psycholinguistics
Mand function

Tact function
Information-processing
   approach
Connectionist approach
Serial processing
Parallel processing
Ecological validity

FOCUS ON RESEARCH
....

What Is the Subject Matter of Cognitive Psychology?

Asking that cognitive psychologists agree on the appropriate subject matter of their field is not an unreasonable request. After all, how can cognitive psychology exist unless the researchers agree on what it is? The issue, however, is far more complicated than this. Understanding the problem is easier if you have some background in the philosophy of science.

Some cognitive psychologists believe that their field has entered a period of *normal science*— one that is governed by the information-processing approach (Lachman, Lachman, & Butterfield, 1979). Normal science refers to the idea that scientific findings are supposed to build on one another. In this way, knowledge accumulates. For example, suppose researcher A does a study on the retention of digits in memory, and then researcher B finds that the number of digits retained depends in part on which digits the subjects are asked to retain. This is normal science. The second study modifies the general conclusion of the first, but its conclusion is nevertheless an elaboration of the earlier finding. Moreover, the methods used in both cases are the same. Science doesn't always proceed normally. For a variety of reasons, researchers sometimes go off in new directions, and the findings produced by such studies do not build upon previous work. Indeed, a fundamental dissatisfaction with previous work is what often propels researchers into new areas. Kuhn (1962) has described this phenomenon as a *paradigm shift*. A paradigm shift is a radical change in a field's approach to its subject matter, its methods, and its interpretation of findings. In looking at the history of science, Kuhn argues that a given field is characterized by cyclical periods of revolutionary paradigm shifting, followed by more stable periods of normal science. The recent history of psychology is sometimes characterized this way. The change

from a behavioristic to a cognitively oriented viewpoint represents a shift in paradigms. Since the revolution, psychology has settled down into a new period of accumulating findings.

If this is true, then some consensus should exist among researchers concerning the appropriate topics for a cognitive psychologist to investigate. White (1985) explored this question in an interesting way. He examined the reference lists of seven introductory cognitive psychology textbooks, all of which were published in 1979 or 1980. He reasoned that, if cognitive psychologists are in agreement about the topics of their field, then they should describe and cite the same studies in their introductory textbooks. The seven texts cited more than 3,200 references. Of these, just 19 publications were cited in all seven texts, and only 144 were cited in at least four of the seven books. Of the 3,200 references, 2,620 appeared in only one book. These findings strongly suggest that the writers of these books were not in basic agreement about the important findings of the field.

Recently, Dale and Cochran (1989; Adler, 1990) analyzed the second editions of five cognitive psychology textbooks; these editions were published between 1985 and 1988. Dale reasoned that if cognitive psychology is indeed maturing as a science, then we should see some convergence in the citations of the "second wave" of books. But this convergence was not observed. Despite the fact that 1,236 reference citations were added to the second editions, there were still just 19 publications that were cited in all five second editions. Just as White found, fully 80 percent of the articles that were cited appeared in only one of the five books. Has cognitive psychology assumed the status of a normal science? Both White and Dale suggest that the answer is no.

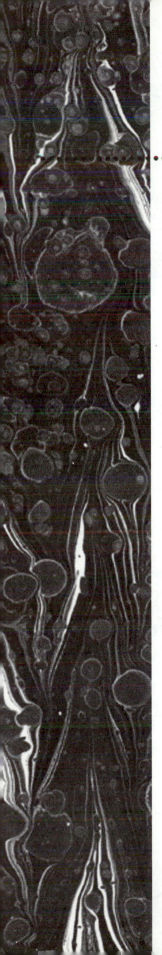

PART **2**

• •

PERCEPTION

Cognitive psychologists refer to a large number of cognitive processes as "perceptual," and many of them are basic to your understanding of the rest of this book. Perceptual processes are those that take sensory input and transform it into a more abstract code. We know that our senses respond to particular forms of physical energy. In our nervous systems, a code is created in which aspects of the physical energy are preserved. For example, you probably remember from your introductory psychology class that the rods and cones in our retinae preserve certain aspects of electromagnetic radiation. But I'm not aware of what my rods and cones are doing; in describing the visual world, I use terms like *light* and *color*. These are psychological terms that correspond to, but are not equivalent with, the sensory information. What does this mean? It means that some other intervening processes have taken the sensory code—the neurological information being relayed by the rods and cones—and converted it into another code that gives rise to my awareness of the psychological experiences of light and color. These intervening processes are perceptual.

Cataloguing all such processes would be incredibly lengthy, but we know about some of them intuitively. For example, we know that we can direct our sensory capabilities, which is referred to as the phenomenon of attention. To a certain extent, we can aim all our senses at sensory stimulation by turning our heads to look or by reaching out and touching. We can even get ready to hear something. Whenever we aim our senses, perception seems to occur faster. We also recognize that perceptual processes sometimes seem to occur in a sequential order. This implies a sort of hierarchy of processing. For example, in order to read, we must organize groups of lines into letters, groups of letters into words, and groups of words into meaning. This kind of hierarchy suggests that some perceptual processes occur earlier than others in the processing of information. After all, how can we know the meaning of a sentence before we know the letters of the alphabet?

As important as sensory information is for perception, it can't be the whole story. If I look out into the parking lot on a bright day, my rods and cones nicely pick up reflected radiation from an object, which my perceptual processes elaborate until I recognize the pattern as a car. But I can still recognize the car on a foggy day or at night, when my rods and cones are not providing my perceptual processes with the same quality of information. How can this be? You may have already guessed the answer. In addition to using sensory information to perceive, I also use my knowledge of the world to make inferences about what sensory information I can expect to encounter. What else would be in the parking lot, if not a car?

We see, then, that perception involves two distinct types of cognitive operations. Perception is achieved by a combination of cognitive processes—some that begin by elaborating the sensory code and others that are inferential and begin with our knowledge of the world. Keep this interplay in mind as you read the next two chapters.

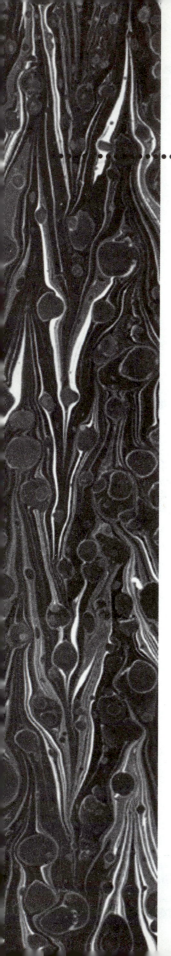

CHAPTER 2

ATTENTION AND PATTERN
RECOGNITION

OVERVIEW

You may have had an experience similar to this one. One morning I was driving to school over an almost deserted rural highway, when the radio station I was listening to began playing one of my favorite symphonic pieces. I was enjoying every minute of it, turning up the radio louder and louder to get the full effect. Everything was going fine, until something flickering in my rearview mirror caught my eye. To my horror, I suddenly discovered behind me the flashing red lights of the sheriff's patrol car! I was going almost 70 miles per hour!

When I thought about the episode later, in a calmer frame of mind, I realized that the incident revealed several characteristics of our information-processing system. For example, it's possible for us to concentrate our senses on particular sources of stimulation to gather information about them, but this concentration is always partial and never total, no matter how intense our concentration seems. Consequently, when other sources of stimulation present themselves, our concentration may shift to these new stimuli and leave the old ones behind. So when I finally saw the flashing red lights in my rearview mirror, I stopped hearing the music—despite its overpowering volume. However, not every new stimulus that presents itself provokes this shift of concentration. As I blasted along the highway, deaf to everything but the music, I didn't bother shifting my attention to count the number of crows perched on the fenceposts. Why did I notice the flashing red lights but not the crows? In other words, what do some stimuli have that enable them

to provoke the shift of concentration that other stimuli don't have? This question is not adequately answered by responding that familiar stimuli don't provoke the shift whereas terrifying stimuli do. This answer is unacceptable because, presumably, I didn't know that the patrol car *was* the patrol car, and therefore it was not terrifying until *after* I had shifted my concentration to the rearview mirror. As you can see, the episode is considerably more complicated than it appears to be initially.

This chapter examines the concept of attention—a mental phenomenon that cognitive psychologists have used to describe and explain concentration and its shifts. We'll review several studies of **selective attention** and we'll consider several theoretical models that have been erected to explain the findings of such studies. Generally speaking, we can divide the research into two phases. In the first phase of theory building, which took place in the 1950s, attention was commonly thought of as a bottleneck in the information-processing system. According to this concept, stimuli cannot fully processed unless they are attended to, and our attentional mechanisms are limited to processing only a small amount of all the stimulation bombarding us. In the second phase of theory building, which has taken place in the last twenty or so years, this conception has been supplemented with a view of attention as the allocation of resources. We'll consider this position and examine one of its implications—namely that highly overlearned tasks require the allocation of a few cognitive resources. When such a state of affairs exists, cognitive processes can take place without conscious guidance; this is referred to as automatic processing.

The function of attention is to bring cognitive processes to bear on external stimuli so that information can be gathered about them. In our attempt to gather information about the stimuli, one of our first tasks seems to be a determination of what sort or what kind of stimuli we're dealing with. Broadly speaking, we do this by discerning what *patterns* might be present in the stimulation. The perception of certain patterns in stimulation is used as the basis for recognizing and categorizing it. Going back to the patrol car once again: Once my attention was focused, I detected characteristics in the stimuli (the lights and their color) that enabled me to recognize and then categorize the vehicle. This chapter closes with a discussion of the role of context, or surrounding stimulation, as it influences the process of pattern recognition. One final point: After the officer pulled me over and asked me why I was going so fast, I told him the truth, and he let me off with a warning. I resolved to pay more attention to my driving and less to the radio.

 ## THE NATURE OF ATTENTION

Definition

Providing a concise definition of attention is difficult because the term has been used in so many ways. For example, when you take a test, you have to attend to it, which implies that you have an ability to focus your mental effort on specific stimuli while excluding other stimuli from consideration. One important aspect of attention, therefore, is its **selectivity.** If a professor advises you to pay particular attention to a certain question and you do, your actions indicate that you have an ability to shift the focus of mental effort from one stimulus to another. In this case, you were able to change the focus of your efforts from one question on the test to another, and this ability seems to be under your control. That is, the shift in attention doesn't seem to be demanded by the stimulus alone (because you could choose to ignore your professor's instructions). Such facts tell us that, not only is the focus of mental effort shiftable, but also some cognitive process must decide the timing and direction of the shift. If you go to a bar after the test to debrief with your friends, you might pay attention to their conversation and watch an episode of your favorite soap opera at the same time. This ability indicates that we apparently can maintain more than one focus of mental effort simultaneously. The focus of mental effort not only is selective and shiftable but also can be divided into parts. As a general definition, therefore, attention refers to the concentration and focusing of mental effort (Matlin, 1983)—a focus that is selective, shiftable, and divisible.

Problems with Definitions of Attention

When we focus mental effort on a task, the action seems to be under our conscious control. That is, we consciously decide which stimuli will be selectively focused upon and which will be excluded. Understanding attention would be much easier if all such selection decisions were made consciously, but unfortunately that doesn't seem to be the case. For example, if a friend takes a long car trip with you, you will pay attention to your friend's speech. This effort is a conscious decision to focus mental effort on particular stimuli. At the same time, you will continue to drive the car appropriately, which involves focusing mental effort selectively on continually changing highway conditions. But this sort of focusing, although ongoing, is probably not done with any awareness of the many decisions that are being made.

The role of awareness seemingly creates problems for the definition of attention. Why is this so? If awareness is not required for selection and shifts of mental effort, then attention is not under conscious control, because such shifts and selections would take place without any decision making that we were aware of. On the other hand, if awareness *is* required for attention, then attention is not selective, because in order to shift attention under those circumstances, we would already have had to be aware of all the stimuli around us.

A couple of difficult questions can now be formulated. Under what circumstances is attention truly under conscious control, and under what circumstances is it truly selective? To arrive at a preliminary answer to these questions, we'll explore the results of several **dichotic listening** studies that made up the first wave of research in this area.

Studies of Selective Attention

Early studies of selective attention often involved the dichotic presentation of material. The subject wore stereo headphones, and into each ear a different message was transmitted. The subject was told to attend to only one ear and to make sure this instruction was carried out; the subject was requested to *shadow* the attended ear. **Shadowing** involves listening to the message in the attended ear and repeating it aloud as soon as possible after hearing it. Assuming the subject makes no errors in shadowing the attended ear, the technique seems to be a good way of ensuring selective focusing on a particular message.

Using the dichotic listening procedure, Cherry (1953) found that subjects had remarkably little difficulty with the shadowing technique. They made few errors in shadowing the attended ear. Cherry was also interested in what the subjects remembered about the message in the *unattended* ear. He found that the subjects could accurately report whether the unattended message had been a human voice or a noise, and they could also report whether the voice had been a man's or a woman's, apparently on the basis of pitch. In other words, the subjects seemed to have some knowledge of the physical or acoustic properties of the unattended message. However, they seemed to have little knowledge of the *meaning* of the unattended message. For example, the subjects were unable to detect the language used by the voice in the unattended ear, and they were not able to recognize words that had been presented in the unshadowed ear thirty-five times (Moray, 1959).

Thirty years ago, such studies were widely interpreted as indicating the highly selective nature of attention. We became conscious of what was attended to. Moreover, the focus of attention was thought to be consciously directed so that little unattended information could enter our consciousness. According to such a viewpoint, subjects would have difficulty doing two demanding tasks simultaneously because, as they focused on one task, they were no longer conscious of the events taking place in the second task. Consequently, some information would be lost no matter how quickly the subjects attempted to alternate between the two tasks, and so their performance on both tasks would inevitably decline.

Mowbray's (1953) study supports this position. Mowbray instructed his subjects to attend to two messages simultaneously. The subjects heard one story while silently reading a second story whose content was unrelated to the story presented aurally. Subjects then took a test measuring comprehension of both stories. The subjects almost always comprehended one of the stories substantially better than the other; the subject's poorer score was usually at the chance, or guessing, level.

 ## BOTTLENECK THEORIES OF ATTENTION

Filter Theory

Broadbent (1958) developed a theory of attention that attempted to account for the findings of Cherry and Mowbray. Broadbent proposed that the focus of attention is determined by three components: a **selective filter,** which led to a channel of limited capacity, which in turn led to a detection device. These components are represented in Figure 2.1.

The sensory register, or sensory information store, is discussed more fully in Chapter 4. Basically, this register is a memory of stimuli that have recently been presented. Stimuli are stored in sensory memory in one of several channels, each channel corresponding loosely to a different sensory modality. Although the duration of this memory is brief, its contents are thought to be exact representations of the original stimuli. While they are stored in the sensory register, the stimuli are subjected to a **preattentive analysis** (Neisser, 1967), which determines some of their physical characteristics, such as pitch, intensity, and so on. As a result of this preattentive analysis, the selective filter determines which stimuli will undergo further processing. Those stimuli that are not selected are essentially tuned out; no further elaboration of them takes place.

Following their selection, the stimuli are shunted along a limited capacity channel to the detection device. The channel's relatively limited capacity has important implications for the human information processor. If asked to pay attention to several demanding tasks simultaneously, the shunting channel lacks the capacity to carry all of the incoming information simultaneously to the detection device. Instead, the selective filter switches as rapidly as possible among the channels in the sensory register, in each case taking the information that has been loaded into that particular channel and transferring it to the shunting channel. This process explains why Broadbent's viewpoint is referred to as a *bottleneck* theory. A great deal of information can be stored in the sensory channels simultaneously, but evacuating information from the sensory register is a laborious process that must be done serially—that is, one channel at a time.

Information in the shunting channel is transferred to the detection device, where an analysis of the information's *meaning* is carried out. According to Broadbent's position, we "know" only about stimuli that make it past the selective filter. Information that was stopped at that stage is subjected only to a preattentive analysis, which is incapable of determining the stimuli's meaning.

This theory provides a reasonable account of Cherry's and Mowbray's findings. Recall that Mowbray (1953) found that subjects could apparently extract the meaning of only one story when two had been presented–one visually, the other aurally. In this case, the decrement in performance was produced by the selective filter's inability to switch between the auditory and visual channels rapidly enough. While information from one channel in the sensory register was extracted and loaded into the shunting channel, information in other channels of the sensory register could not be evacuated. As we'll see in Chapter 4, the sensory storage has a large capacity; however, material in sensory storage has an extremely short "shelf life." If the information stored there is not extracted within a short time, it begins to decay. This is why the subject could not answer questions about

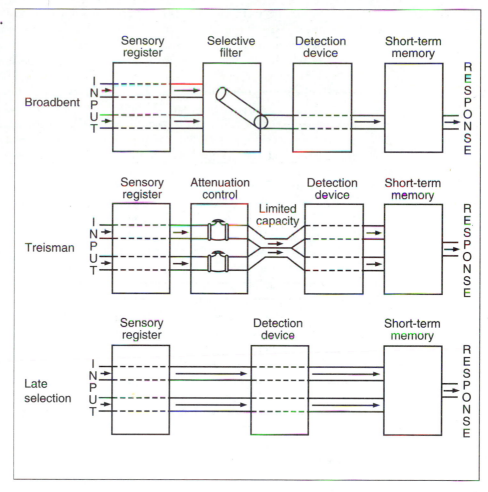

the information stored in the unselected channel. By the time the shunting channel was switched back to this information, it had decayed. Because the subjects gave the information in the blocked channel only a preattentive analysis, they were unable to answer questions about the passage's meaning.

Regarding Cherry's findings: The filter is tuned to accept information from the shadowed ear; this information is loaded into the shunting channel and ultimately processed for meaning by the detection device. Material that is presented in the nonshadowed ear has a different fate. Because the filter is never opened to the nonshadowed ear, none of this material is transferred to the shunting channel and detection device. Consequently, the subjects in Cherry's study were able to report only the physical characteristics of the nonshadowed message. These characteristics were determined by the preattentive analysis.

However, it's possible to demonstrate that Broadbent's theory of attention, although convincing, cannot be completely correct. Moray (1959) found that subjects sometimes recognized that their name had been uttered in the nonshadowed message. According to Broadbent's theory, this recognition should not have happened. Names are meaningful to their owners, but the analysis of meaning is supposedly carried out by the detection device, which nonshadowed material never enters.

Similarly, Treisman (1960) reported that subjects could shadow the semantic content (i.e., the meaning) of a message even when the message was played into the nonshadowed ear. Treisman instructed her subjects to shadow a particular ear into which was played a meaningful message. The nonshadowed ear received a random string of words. At some point in the delivery, the semantic content switched ears, as shown in Figure 2.2. At the same time, the random words were switched into the shadowed ear. Although the subjects had been instructed to shadow a particular ear, many of them ignored this instruction and shadowed the meaningful *message* instead. This finding indicated to Treisman that the subjects must have had some knowledge of the semantic content of the nonshadowed message.

In other studies, Treisman (1964a, 1964b) demonstrated that the analysis of a message's semantic content is accomplished fairly early on in the human information-processing system. Treisman used the dichotic listening procedure once again, telling her subjects to shadow a message. The message in the nonshadowed ear was to be ignored. Unknown (initially) to the subjects, the messages were identical. The nonshadowed message was started either slightly ahead of or slightly behind the shadowed message, and over the course of the presentation, the nonshadowed message was speeded up or slowed down to synchronize it with the shadowed message. The critical variables were whether the subjects detected that the two messages were the same and, if so, what the time interval between the two messages was when detection occurred.

Treisman found that all the subjects detected that the two messages were the same. When the shadowed message led the unshadowed message, detection occurred when the messages were still 4.5 seconds apart. When the unshadowed message led the shadowed message, detection did not typically take place until the messages were much closer, about 1.4 seconds apart. The difference in times probably reflects the extent to which the material has been processed. The shadowed message is processed by the detection device and is passed on to the short-term, or working, memory. Consequently, a fairly durable representation is created that enables the subject to compare and match the contents of the working memory with the nonshadowed ear even when the messages are 4.5 seconds apart. However, the nonshadowed message presumably never leaves the sensory register, and its representation is far less durable than that of the shadowed message. When the nonshadowed ear leads the shadowed ear, the

FIGURE 2.2

. . . .

An illustration of Treisman's (1960) shadowing study.

(From *Cognition* by Margaret Matlin, Copyright © 1983 by Holt, Rinehart and Winston, Inc., reprinted by permission of the publisher.)

subject probably won't be able to detect that the two messages are identical until the shadowed message is brought within the memory span of the auditory channel of the sensory register. This span has been estimated as being about 1 or 2 seconds long. This finding seems to indicate that a semantic analysis of the sensory register is carried out, which is contrary to the predictions of Broadbent's model.

Attenuation Theory

Accordingly, Treisman proposed a modification of the basic theory, which is known as the **attenuation model.** According to this theory, incoming stimuli might undergo three different kinds of analysis, or tests. The first test analyzes the physical properties of the stimuli. For auditory stimuli, the physical properties are equivalent to acoustic properties such as pitch and intensity. The second test determines whether the stimuli are linguistic and, if so, groups the stimuli into syllables and words. The final test recognizes the words and assigns meaning to them. All three tests are not necessarily carried out on all incoming stimuli. Rather, the processing is continued until the competing stimuli can be disentangled from one another.

Disentangling competing stimuli sometimes requires little processing. If you're talking to a man at a party, and the people standing and talking nearby happen to be women, the stimuli can be sorted out on the basis of the first test. Under these circumstances, you would probably not become aware of the semantic content of the women's speech, because their conversation wasn't processed to that point. If the first test fails to disentangle the stimuli, then a second-level test must be carried out. For example, a friend called one day to tell me about the breakup of his latest romance. Unfortunately, he called in the middle of an exciting football game. Because the acoustic differences between the two messages were minimal, a second-level test based on syllables and words had to be carried out to separate the two messages. In this case, I *did* become aware of some of the words used in both messages. That is, my subjective report of the incoming stimuli was something like the following:

So then she says to me Washington, first and goal on the two!

According to Treisman, what takes place in such circumstances is not a complete tuning out of the nonshadowed message, à la Broadbent, but rather an attenuation (turning down) of some messages that have been sorted out following the results of the tests. Reference to Figure 2.1 shows a graphic comparison of Treisman's model with Broadbent's.

The attenuation model differs from the filter model in two ways. First, the filter model postulates that the basis of selective attention is a fairly crude analysis of the physical characteristics of the incoming stimuli. The attenuation model maintains that the preattentive analysis is much more complex and may even consist of semantic processing. Second, the filter in the filter theory is an all-or-none affair. What is not selected is tuned out completely. However, the attenuation model supposes that nonselected channels are not completely shut off but are simply turned down or dampened.

These distinctions are consistent with the findings of Cherry and Kruger (1983), who studied the selective attention abilities of learning-disabled (LD) children. In their task, children aged seven to nine years were required to point to the appropriate picture of a word that was presented in one channel of stereo headphones. In the other ear, the children were presented with one of three distractors: a nonlinguistic, nonsemantic sound called *white noise* (a hissing sound); backward speech, which is linguistic but nonsemantic; or forward speech, which is both linguistic and semantic. When subjected to a distractor, the performance of the LD children was substantially worse than the performance of normal-achieving children. The discrepancy in performance between the exceptional and normal children was greatest when the semantic distractor was used.

Treisman would argue that this finding indicates that the LD children's preattentive analysis includes a semantic analysis of the nonshadowed message. Also, such a finding suggests that LD children's problems stem at least in part from an apparent inability to control the attenuation of nonshadowed messages. The LD children apparently can't completely damp down the nonshadowed (and unwanted) competing stimuli. Incidentally, the Cherry and Kruger study is a good way to demonstrate how a cognitive analysis might help in understanding and possibly treating a practical problem.

Late Selection Theories

Although Treisman's theory provides a good account for many of the phenomena associated with selective attention, it has a serious shortcoming. Specifically, it seems too complicated. The theory postulates that the preattentive analysis is almost as complete as the attentive analysis. If that's so, then what's the point of doing the preattentive analysis in the first place? A simpler alternative to the Treisman position was originally proposed by Deutsch and Deutsch (1963).

These theorists argued that the bottleneck in selective attention occurs later in the processing of information than the Treisman theory proposed. Whereas Treisman maintained that the preattentive analysis determines what information is selected for further processing, Deutsch and Deutsch argued that almost all the incoming stimuli are sent on for further processing. When the information reaches working memory, selection for further processing takes place at that site. This viewpoint is referred to as the **late selection** position because the selection for further processing is made in working memory rather than earlier, in the channels of sensory memory. Figure 2.1 shows a comparison of the late selection position with the models of Broadbent and Treisman.

The late selection model predicts that all incoming stimuli are processed. Consequently, subjects should recognize information under almost any circumstances, even when information is presented to a nonshadowed ear. This assertion was tested in a study by Lewis (1970). In a dichotic listening task, subjects were told to shadow words that were presented in one ear and ignore anything presented in the nonshadowed ear. Words also were presented in the nonshadowed ear. These words were sometimes semantically unrelated to the words being shadowed, while on other occasions the nonshadowed words were synonyms of the shadowed words. Lewis measured the latency between the presentation of the shadowed word and the subject's vocal response. He found that the presentation of a nonshadowed synonym produced a delay in the subject's response, which was not observed when the nonshadowed stimulus was an unrelated word.

This finding is not consistent with either model of early selection. If the filter theory was completely correct, the nature of the word should not have increased the latency of response, because the nonshadowed ear is supposedly completely tuned out. The attenuation model argues that nonshadowed words are turned down. Although the meaning of nonshadowed words might sometimes intrude on the shadowed message, semantic relationships such as synonymity should not. In Lewis's study, the subjects had recognized that a semantic relationship existed between the messages in the nonshadowed and shadowed ears.

As explained by Norman (1968), the late selection model operates in the following way. All information is transmitted to the working memory, but the nature of this transmission is different from that proposed by Broadbent or Treisman. Rather than describe the transmission as a serial (one step at a time) process, the transmission is thought to be in parallel (all at once, as shown in Figure 2.1). Because the capacity of the working memory is limited, parallel transmission strains the operation of working memory. Not all of the information sent there can be stored. In working memory, a judgment is made about the material's importance (this point is discussed later in the chapter). Material that has been judged important is elaborated more fully, which in turn creates a more durable representation of the information that may eventually enter permanent memory (Watanabe, 1980). What is not important is not elaborated or rehearsed, and is consequently forgotten. According to this view, the act of shadowing per se is not what determines what we attend to and consequently become aware of. Rather, the patterns that are formed and recognized in our working memory are what become the basis of our awareness.

A study by MacKay (1973) illustrates these points. The subjects were told to shadow sentences that were grammatically correct although semantically ambiguous. For example, the subjects might shadow the sentence "They were throwing stones at the bank." This sentence could refer to individuals who were standing beside a river throwing stones into it, or it could refer to individuals who were throwing stones at a financial institution. A word that might steer the subject toward a particular resolution of the ambiguity was presented at the appropriate time in the subject's nonshadowed ear. In this case, when the subject shadowed *bank*, either *money* or *river* was presented in the nonshadowed ear. After a series of such sentences, the subjects were given a memory task in which they were asked to recognize the sentences they had shadowed. In some cases, the subjects were given forms of the sentence that were congruent with the word that had been presented in the nonshadowed ear. In other cases, the forms of the sentences were not congruent with the word presented in the nonshadowed ear.

You can probably predict the findings of this study. Subjects tended to remember having shadowed sentences that were congruent with the word presented in the nonshadowed ear. In the previous sentence, for example, the subject might remember having shadowed the sentence "They were throwing stones at the financial institution" if the word *money* had been presented in the nonshadowed ear. But the subject would not remember this sentence as previously shadowed if *river* had been presented in the nonshadowed ear.

Another finding from the MacKay study might be more difficult to predict. When the subjects were asked to indicate which words had been presented in the nonshadowed ear, they could not remember which words they had heard. This finding is somewhat curious. The meaning of the nonshadowed words had been processed, although apparently only a fragile code had been created—so fragile that it no longer survived by the end of the presentation. The subjects therefore did not remember the nonshadowed words on the memory test.

Earlier I referred to the importance of the information entering the working memory. A major implication of the Deutsch and Deutsch (1963) and Norman (1968) position is that working memory can be preset to determine the value of incoming stimuli, and the evaluation of the incoming material can be consciously controlled even if unimportant information does not itself enter consciousness.

Space cadets.

These contentions were explored in a complex and provocative study by Johnston and Heinz (1978).

These researchers argued that humans could control the extent to which unattended stimuli are processed by carrying out different sorts of tests on the material in working memory. They also reasoned that some tests should be carried out before others. Specifically, it's sensible to assume that a subject would carry out a sensory (or physical) analysis before carrying out a semantic analysis. Why? Because in many ways, a semantic analysis is much more effortful than a sensory analysis. A semantic analysis is more effortful because more knowledge is required to carry it out. If you think about this for a minute, you'll see what I mean. I can carry out some physical analyses of foreign languages, but I can't carry out a semantic analysis, because my knowledge is too limited. Johnston and Heinz argued that, if the sensory tests provided enough information to disentangle the competing stimuli, the subjects would be unwilling to engage in the semantic test. So far, this reasoning should remind you of Treisman's theory. However, Treisman described these tests as ways of attenuating unwanted stimulation, whereas Johnston and Heinz had a different objective. They maintained that the processing capability of working memory is limited. Consequently, if the subject were required to carry out several tests to recognize and categorize incoming information, the subject would have little processing capability left over to deal with another ancillary task, and his or her performance on this secondary task should thus be poor. Remember, however, that the nature and extent of the evaluation are thought to be under conscious control. If the subject determines that incoming stimuli can be categorized without a complete semantic analysis, some of the working memory's processing capability should be available for executing the secondary task. In that case, performance on the ancillary task should be reasonable. To sum up, performance on some ancillary task should be poor if the primary task requires a semantic analysis. However, performance on the ancillary task might not be poor if the primary task does not require a semantic analysis. Let's see how this reasoning was enacted in the Johnston and Heinz (1978) study.

Subjects were asked to shadow messages that differed from the nonshadowed message in either physical characteristics, semantic aspects, or both. Messages of low physical discriminability were produced by having the same male voice recite both messages. Messages of high physical discriminability were created by use of a male voice to recite one message and a female voice to recite the other. Semantic aspects varied in two ways. Messages of low semantic discriminability were created by reciting lists of items drawn from the same category. For example, two different lists of types of furniture might be played into the channels of stereo headphones. Messages of high semantic discriminability were formed by reciting lists of items drawn from different categories (such as a list of furniture types and a list of fruits). While subjects were shadowing one message in the familiar dichotic listening task, they were also required to detect and respond to changes in a light's brightness. This was the ancillary task.

The researchers were interested in whether changes in the nature of the shadowing task affect the subject's ability to detect and respond to changes in brightness. If the subject does not have control over the nature of the incoming stimuli's analysis, the differences in physical or semantic aspects of the messages should have no effect on the subject's ability to do the ancillary task. Why? Because if the subject has no control over the analysis, the entire analysis must be carried out regardless of whether the analysis is necessary. Whatever the processing demands of the full analysis, they would be constant across all the different combinations of physical and semantic discriminability, and hence the subject would be left with a constant amount of processing ability to carry out the secondary task.

If the subject does have control over the analysis, however, a different prediction follows. For example, if the messages were discriminable on the basis of sensory characteristics, we might expect that the subject wouldn't bother carrying out the semantic analysis. If the semantic analysis were not carried out, the processing capabilities of working memory would not be as taxed, and the subject would be able to devote some of these capabilities to processing the ancillary task. If the messages were of low physical discriminability, the subject would be compelled to carry out the effortful semantic analysis to keep up with the to-be-shadowed message. In that case, we would look for a decrement in performance on the ancillary task.

The results of the study supported Johnston and Heinz's reasoning. Regardless of the messages' semantic discriminability, the subjects' reaction times on the ancillary task were much faster in the high physical discriminability condition than they were in the low physical discriminability condition. That is, when the messages had high physical discriminability, the subjects were able to rapidly detect and respond to changes in the light's brightness even when the messages were semantically similar. When the full (i.e., semantic) analysis had to be carried out, Johnston and Heinz found that the subjects had little processing capability left over to carry out the ancillary task. This decreased capability was reflected in their slower reaction times and reduced shadowing accuracy in that condition. In other words, when the messages were of low physical discriminability and the subjects had to engage in the semantic analysis, they became slower at detecting and responding to changes in the light's brightness.

Conclusions from the First Phase of Theory Building

The last several pages have dealt with several bottleneck theories of attention, each seeming to supplant its predecessor. Along the way, many findings have been mentioned. Now is the time for us to try to organize these findings into a coherent picture.

We have seen that Broadbent and Treisman thought of attention as a filter that operated in the earliest stages of human information processing to screen out stimuli. In particular, Treisman argued that a complex preattentive analysis was carried out early in the processing of information. Surviving information was sent serially along a limited capacity channel for recognition. Late selection theorists such as Deutsch and Deutsch postulated that all information is sent on in parallel to a recognition device. This change in viewpoint paved the way for another major change in our conceptualization of attention, namely that we can consciously control the nature of attentional analysis even though the results of such analysis might not enter our consciousness (MacKay, 1973; Johnston & Heinz, 1978). As these researchers have pointed out, the subject's intention can be critical in determining what material we become conscious of, which means that we have to consider what strategic factors might be involved in the subject's processing (Lowe & Mitterer, 1982). Paradoxically, however, the intention to process incoming information doesn't ensure that we will become aware of that material for any meaningful length of time. According to the late selection view, we will process to whatever extent necessary to disentangle the competing stimuli. When the stimuli have been sorted out, we'll elaborate the material we wish to keep, thus creating a more durable representation. What is not elaborated will be forgotten.

These findings superficially suggest that attention can be compared to a funnel—a constricted point in the information-processing system through which all incoming material must pass. More recent studies suggest, however, that such an analogy is somewhat misleading. Rather, we might think of attention as a spotlight that comes equipped with a controllable lens. Because this lens is under our control, we can narrow the beam to a pencil point of light, and, in that case, the object of scrutiny comes under an intense and highly focused illumination. On the other hand, we can open up the lens and illuminate several objects at once, although less intensely than before. Notice that the wattage of the light does not change. What changes is the way in which we apply the light's power.

These "spotlight" effects have been explored in a series of studies by Palmer (1990). Palmer's subjects viewed stimuli consisting of one, two, or four horizontal lines that were presented for 100 msec; when four lines were presented, they were always presented in the same spatial location relative to the subject's viewpoint. These horizontal lines are referred to as the "study stimuli"; that is, the subject was supposed to inspect and "study" them while they were on view. The number of lines presented in the study stimulus is referred to as the "set size." For example, when only one line was presented, we say the set size was 1. After seeing the lines, subjects waited a 2,000-msec interstimulus interval after which a test stimulus appeared for 100 msec. The test stimulus consisted of a single horizontal line appearing in the same location as one of the lines in the study stimulus; when the study stimulus consisted of only a single line, the test stimulus's single line appeared in the same location as the single line of the study stimulus. The subject's task was to determine if the test stimulus was longer than the corresponding line of the study stimulus. This task was not "speeded"; the subjects could take as long as they wanted to make up their minds. The dependent measure in this study was basically the difference in line length between study and test stimuli required for the subject to accurately detect any differences in the two lines. Given the research that we have gone over, we might expect that, if indeed the spotlight is weaker when we are forced to examine a greater number of stimuli, then we might expect that the discrepancy in line length would have to be made correspondingly greater when the set size was 4, compared with when it was only 1, in order for the subjects to detect the difference in length between study and test stimuli. Notice that this study also has an interesting memory component because, in addition to paying attention to the lines of the study stimulus, the subjects had to remember how long each line was for 2,000 msec in order to respond accurately.

Palmer (1990) found that set size had a very reliable and pronounced effect on the difference in line length required for detection. For example, when the set size was 2, subjects required about a 40 percent greater discrepancy in line lengths between study and test stimuli to detect the length difference, compared with that required when the set size was 1. When set size 4 was compared with set size 1, the difference was about 100 percent. In other words, if subjects could detect a difference in line lengths with a certain accuracy when the set size was 1, increasing the set size up to 4 would mean the difference in line lengths would have to be doubled in order for the subjects to detect the difference with the same degree of accuracy. Palmer's studies show us just how much weaker in intensity the attentional spotlight gets when the number of stimuli in the input condition is increased.

ALTERNATIVES TO FILTER THEORIES: CAPACITY MODELS

The second phase of theory building in the area of attention began with a reconceptualization of the problem, which occurred with the publication of Kahneman's (1973) book *Attention and Effort*. Partly from everyday examples such as driving a car and carrying out a simultaneous conversation, Kahneman argued that the location of the bottleneck in selective attention tasks seemed less important than understanding what the task itself demanded of the person. For example, because driving and talking are usually not highly demanding tasks, we can do both of them simultaneously. However, driving in heavy traffic is more demanding than driving on the open interstate, so we would expect that conversation might break down during heavy traffic conditions.

Rather than talk about funneling stimuli along some limited capacity channel, Kahneman maintained that attention could be understood as a set of cognitive processes for categorizing and recognizing stimuli. These processes, or **cognitive resources,** were limited. To fully recognize a stimulus, resources were required; and if the stimulus was complex, a large number of resources would be required. If several complex stimuli were presented simultaneously, the resources might be quickly used up; and if additional stimuli were presented to the person whose resources were used up, these newcomers would go unprocessed (and unnoticed). But the situation need not be so bleak. Kahneman postulated that incoming stimuli don't grab the resources all on their own. Instead, the cognitive system features a stage in which resources are allocated to process incoming stimuli. As Johnston and Heinz (1978) pointed out, the allocation of cognitive resources is flexible and under our control. Rather than being slaves to incoming stimuli, we are able to shift limited resources onto important stimuli.

Figure 2.3 is a depiction of Kahneman's model. Notice that Kahneman's model does not assume that the number of resources is completely fixed. Rather, the total pool of resources that are available at any one time is determined in part by the individual's arousal level. The greater the level of arousal, the greater the pool of resources, at least up to a certain point. Beyond that point, increases in arousal may result in a decrease in the number of available resources. Which incoming stimuli have resources devoted to them is determined by the system's **allocation policy.** The allocation policy is set by enduring dispositions and momentary intentions. *Enduring dispositions* are tendencies that many creatures have to process loud noises, sudden motions, bright colors, and other unusual events. One enduring disposition of mature humans is the tendency to process our own names. *Momentary intentions* are situational dispositions to allocate cognitive resources to a particular source of incoming stimulation.

The **cognitive capacity** model makes several predictions, which we'll attempt to deal with. First, the capacity model assumes that the interference produced by competing sources of stimulation is nonspecific. That is, any problems that we might have in doing two things at once are not produced because the tasks interfere with one another, but rather because the tasks require more resources than we have available. Accordingly, the capacity model predicts that we will be able to do two things at once as long as these activities don't exceed the number of available resources. The second prediction follows from the first: Performance on one task will decline if we try to do a second task simultaneously when the sum total of the processing demands exceeds capacity. The third prediction states that the allocation policy is flexible and can be altered to suit the demands of the incoming stimuli. We have already looked at one study that bears on the third prediction. Recall that Johnston and Heinz (1978)

FIGURE 2.3
······················
**A capacity model
for attention.**

(From Daniel Kahneman,
Attention and Effort, ©
1973, p. 10. Reprinted by
permission of Prentice-
Hall, Inc., Englewood
Cliffs, New Jersey.)

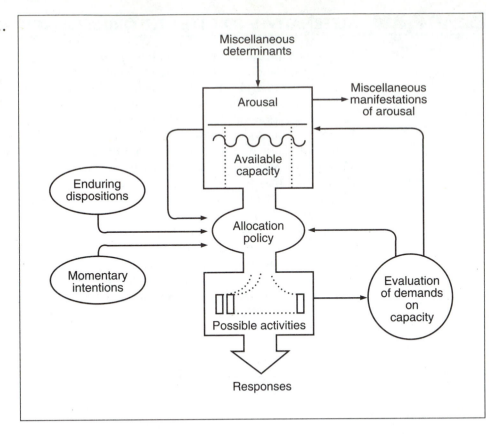

demonstrated that their subjects would tailor their analyses of incoming information to the minimum depth necessary to shadow the message. If the subjects could shadow the message by using only a sensory analysis, which presumably requires fewer cognitive resources than the semantic analysis, then that's what they would do.

A study by Posner and Boies (1971) provides support for the first two predictions. Their subjects were required to do simultaneous tasks. The primary task (the one to which the subjects were told to devote their attention) was a letter-matching task. Following the visual presentation of a warning signal, the subjects were shown a letter, such as a *T*, for a brief (50-msec) interval. After a 1-sec delay, the subjects were shown a second letter, and their task was to indicate as quickly as possible whether the second letter was the same as or different from the first. The subjects indicated their responses by pressing one of two buttons. If the second letter was the same as the first, subjects were supposed to tap a button with their right index finger. If the second letter was different from the first, subjects used the right middle finger to tap.

The second task was an auditory detection task. On some trials, a tone was presented via stereo headphones. Here, the subjects were told to tap a key with their left index finger as quickly as possible when they heard a tone. I'm sure you've already figured out that the procedure leaves a little to be desired, because the handedness of the subjects influences their ability to respond quickly to the tone. Consequently, we'll have to be extra careful in interpreting the findings of this experiment.

Figure 2.4 shows the sequence of stimuli presentation and the results of the study. Point (1) shows the average response time on the tone detection task when the tone was presented prior to the warning signal. This point serves as a basis for comparison when the tone is presented later in the sequence. If the tone is presented before any of the letters are shown to the subjects, a reasonable assumption is that the subjects can devote all of their resources to processing the tone. Consequently, any increases in response time to the tone when it is presented later are apparently the result of the subject's allocation of resources to the primary task. Notice from Figure 2.4 that the response time to the tone decreased somewhat during and immediately following the warning signal. One function of the warning signal is to increase the subject's alertness and arousal, which produces a corresponding increase in the available resources. At point (4), the graph of the response time is at its lowest point. However, this occurs immediately after the first letter has been presented and recognized.

FIGURE 2.4

The procedure and the results of the experiment on simultaneous letter matching and tone detection: *a,* the sequence of events in a single trial (the numbers designate the points at which tones were presented intermittently); *b,* the time required to detect the tones at various points during the trials.

(From Posner & Boies, 1971. Copyright 1971 by the American Psychological Association. Adapted by permission of the publisher and author.)

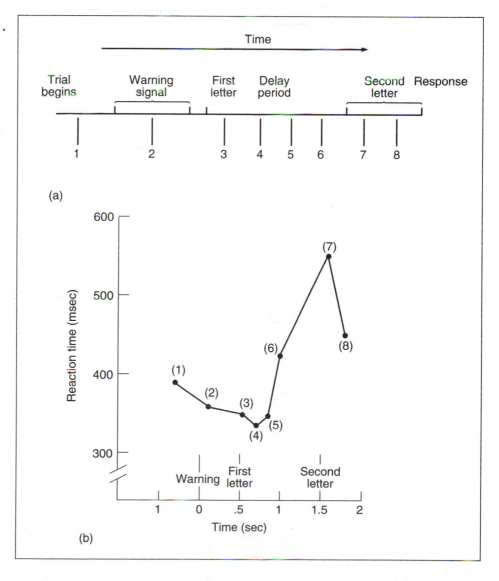

This finding substantiates the first prediction of the Kahneman model: The subjects were able to process competing stimuli when the total demand did not exceed the available capacity. The arousal effects of the warning signal are not durable, and during the delay period, the subject must extract the first letter's code from sensory memory and develop a more durable representation in working memory. This accounts for the increase in reaction time seen at point (6). However, the greatest increases in reaction time are seen at points (7) and (8). At those points, the second letter has been presented, and the subject is occupied with categorizing, recognizing, and judging it. These activities soak up most of the subject's available resources, leaving too few to process the tone quickly. This finding substantiates the second prediction of Kahneman's model: Performance of the auditory detection task declined when the processing demands exceeded capacity.

Some Questions Concerning Capacity Models

Kahneman's capacity model is designed to supplement rather than supplant the bottleneck position. Whereas the bottleneck position postulates that incoming stimuli always compete for space on the shunting channel and therefore always interfere with each other, the capacity model assumes that the demands made by stimuli do not compete. That is, as long as sufficient resources are available, all the incoming stimuli can be accommodated. One question that arises at the outset in comparing the two approaches concerns the interactions of incoming stimuli: Do they compete, or don't they? At this point, cognitive psychologists have hedged their bets. A reasonable assumption is that some stimuli do interfere with each other, meaning that some tasks are truly incompatible. In those cases, some version of the bottleneck viewpoint is necessary to explain the processing. However, as Posner and Boies (1971) demonstrated, simultaneous tasks can be comfortably handled in some situations. In those situations, the capacity model seems to be a reasonable explanation of events.

A second question is more problematic and concerns the nature of the resources: Exactly what are they? No one knows the answer to this question with any certainty. However, some researchers have maintained that the resources are basic and elemental operations of the nervous system. Several researchers have attempted to establish a link between these operations and cerebral architecture.

For example, Dawson and Schell (1982, 1983) had their subjects shadow a list of unrelated words presented via stereo headphones. A separate list of semantically unrelated words was presented over the nonshadowed channel. Occasionally presented in the nonshadowed ear was one of a series of words that had previously been paired with a painful electric shock. We would expect such words to be processed even when they were presented on the nonshadowed channel, because we have an enduring disposition to process events that may signal the onset of pain. Dawson and Schell found this to be the case. Certain skin responses known as **electrodermal responses** (EDRs) were elicited by the presentation of shock-associated words in the nonshadowed channel. But now the plot thickens in an intriguing way. You probably know that the cortex of the brain is divided into two hemispheres. Each hemisphere controls one side of the body. However, hemispheric control over the body is *contralateral*, or opposite sided, meaning that the left hemisphere controls the right-hand side of the body and vice versa. In most people, one hemisphere—typically the left—is dominant.

Dawson and Schell found that, when shock-associated words were presented to the right ear (whose neural pathway winds up in the left hemisphere), EDRs were observed only on those trials in which the subject showed independent indications of attentional shifts. These independent indications included errors in shadowing and increased latency in shadowing the attended word. However, when the shock-associated words were presented to the left ear, EDRs were observed even on trials in which no independent indications of attentional shifts were shown. What to make of this? The hemispheres apparently differ in the resources available to them, or differ in their allocation policies. For the dominant hemisphere, processing the significant word may require more of its resources, thus overloading capacity and producing increased latency in shadowing the attended channel. For the nondominant hemisphere, perhaps fewer or different resources are required to do the same thing. Indeed, Dawson and Schell (1983) have hypothesized that each hemisphere may have a partially independent pool of processing capabilities.

This contention has been explored in a study by Mathieson, Sainsbury, and Fitzgerald (1990). Their subjects participated in a dichotic listening task in which the subjects heard lists composed of either consonants (i.e., speech sounds), emotional nonspeech sounds (e.g., crying), or combinations of both of these. After hearing pairs of such stimuli, subjects were asked to state the ear in which a specific stimulus had been played. The researchers noted that the subjects were more accurate when nonspeech sounds were played into the left ear and when speech sounds were played into the right ear, regardless of whether the list heard by the subject was composed of just speech sounds, just nonspeech sounds, or both classes of stimuli. Although the findings of Dawson and Schell and Mathieson et al. have not gone unchallenged (Walker & Ceci, 1983), it may nevertheless be the case that each hemisphere has a pool of resources that work in a way that is consistent with what we know about laterality effects.

Demanding Stimuli: What Grabs Our Attention?

The capacity model of attention that we've been considering over the last few pages seems to emphasize the control that we have over our attention. And certainly we do have quite a bit of control; for example, I can decide to start paying attention to a source of stimulation, an I can decide to stop. I can even "get ready" to pay attention to something. But the experiences that we have in the world tell us that there are many times when our attention is not so much allocated as it is grabbed: Advertisers seem to know how to create arrangements of stimuli that refuse to stay in the background. Like it or not, these stimuli manage to get into the "spotlight" of our attention and stay there for at least a little while. What are the characteristics of these attention grabbers?

We need a little background information first. Cognitivists have known for some time that when humans are asked to search for a previously specified target (such as a letter) in a field of similar objects (such as other letters), then increasing the number of letters in the field that must be searched produces an increase in the length of time that people need to find the target. This is referred to as the *display-size effect*. And this makes sense: If you're searching for a specific letter, and the display contains only two letters, you should be able to determine whether or not the target is present in that field much faster than if the display contains 100 letters. And why is this? The answer is that, even though we can allocate attention to tasks that we want to do, making the judgment about each letter in the display size apparently must take place serially, or almost serially; it's certainly a processing-intensive task. So when several potential targets are added to an array, we must allocate some attention to scanning each of them and to making a separate decision for each.

But sometimes the display-size effect is not observed. Consider the case when the target differs from all the other objects in the display field on some very salient dimension, such as color. Suppose you're instructed to search for a particular letter, and this target letter is shown to you printed in red ink. Then you are shown the display containing both the target and the distractors. If the target is printed in red ink and all the distractors are printed in green ink, two findings are observed. First, the target is not hard to find, and, second, the display-size effect is negligible. A target that differs from all the distractors on some salient dimension is referred to as a *featural singleton* (Yantis, 1993). A featural singleton seems to "pop out" of the display without any apparent allocation of attention. Now a *featural singleton* actually has two things going for it. First of all, the featural singleton is the target, or contains the target. Second, the featural singleton is different from all the other stimuli. This raises a natural question: What happens when there is a stimulus that is different from all other stimuli, but is nevertheless not the target?

Theeuwes (1992) has shown that, under some circumstances, people have a difficult time not allocating attention to a featural singleton, even when the singleton does not contain information about the target. Figure 2.5 shows the materials that Theeuwes used. The subjects were told to report the orientation of the line (horizontal or vertical) inside the circle. All the other lines in the display were surrounded by diamonds. This means that the circular shape was a reliable form singleton that would presumably pop out, enabling the subjects to quickly report the orientation of the line contained inside it. On half the trials, all of the diamonds were the same color (green). But on the other half of the trials, one of the diamonds was red. This condition was called the distractor condition. Therefore, on the trials in which a distractor was present, there were two singletons: the helpful form singleton that we've already described, and the irrelevant, and useless, color singleton that the subjects might as well ignore if they could. What we want to know is whether the presence of an irrelevant featural singleton (the single red diamond) slowed the subjects in reporting the orientation of the line in the circle. As the bottom half of Figure 2.5 shows, this is exactly what happened. When an irrelevant color distractor appeared in the array, the subjects' reaction time increased significantly. In addition, you can see the beginning of a display-size effect in the distractor conditions. That is, when the display-size consists of nine geometric forms, the subjects are slowed by the irrelevant distractor to a significantly greater extent than they are when the irrelevant distractor appears in a display size of only five geometric forms. What this means is that, when observers search an array for singletons, their attention is apparently grabbed by any area of the array in which a singleton exists.

In all the studies we have talked about so far, the subjects knew that there would be a singleton of some sort, and they knew that at least some singletons are helpful. This knowledge implies that the singleton becomes part of the subjects' attentional set. What happens in those situations in which the subjects do not know if processing the featural singleton will be helpful or harmful? That is, what happens when the singleton is not part of the subject's attentional set? Jonides and Yantis (1990) investigated this by presenting their subjects with arrays of letters, one of which was different from all the other letters in either color or brightness. However, in this study the singleton, whether a different colored singleton or a brighter singleton, was no more likely to be the target than any of the other letters in the array. In this study, the display-size effect returned: Now, when the subjects had to search among many letters, the time required to find the

FIGURE 2.5
· · · · · · · · · · · · · · · · · · · ·
Effect of irrelevant singletons when the target is a singleton.
Top: Sample displays from the form condition of Theeuwes's visual search task, which requires the observer to report the orientation of the single nonoblique line segment. Green lines are shown as solid, red lines as dotted. The target line segment is always inside the green circle, which is a form singleton here. In the left panel, there is no distractor singleton, In the right panel, there is a red distractor singleton. Bottom: Reaction time as a function of display size for the distractor and no-distractor conditions. Reaction time is slower when there is a color distractor than when there is not, suggesting that the color singleton cannot be ignored.

Source: J. Theeuwes, Perceptual selectivity for color and form, *Perception & Psychophysics, 51,* 599–606 (1992).

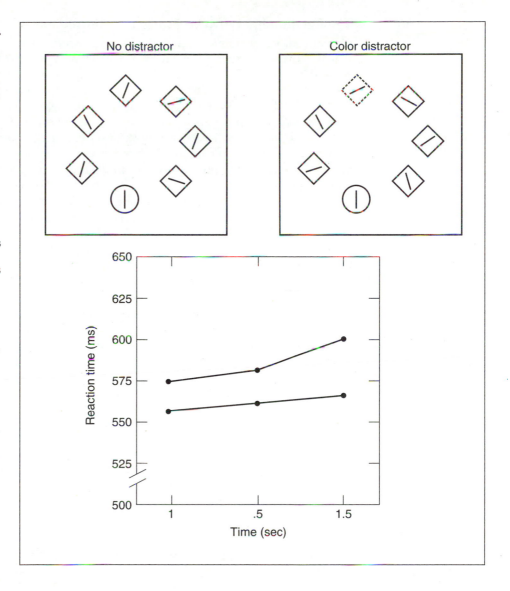

target increased, even in those situations in which the target was a singleton! The conclusion is that salient singletons can capture attention, but only when the singletons are somehow relevant to the perceiver's goals. When the singletons are not relevant, then they don't necessarily grab any more attention than do other stimuli in the array. It's as if people can "tune" their cognitive systems to meet their goals in an efficient way. Thus, when people know that the singleton may be helpful (because the target is always a singleton), then singletons are processed "first," and the display-size effect is not seen. But the mere presence of singletons is not enough to grab attention. In this situation, it's as if the cognitive system is saying, "All right, sometimes there are unique stimuli in this array, but I'm not going to bother processing them first, because they are not necessarily helpful." Under these circumstances, the display-size effect makes its return.

The Relationship Between Practice and Attention

Our first efforts at doing a complex task often seem clumsy and uncoordinated, regardless of the resources we allocate to them. When my tennis teacher first showed me the correct service grip, stance, and movement, my initial thought was, I'll never do it right. Indeed, my first attempts were not promising. Thousands of serves later, I still don't have it right, although I've improved dramatically and, in some objective sense, my serve is reasonably decent. This little tale is more than another illustration of practice-makes-reasonably-decent, however. As I practiced this task, I became aware that I no longer had to allocate all of my attentional resources to monitoring kinesthetic sensations from my body and coordinating them with the toss of the ball. To use terms described in Chapter 1, my tennis serve has gradually become both procedural (I no longer remember the steps of serving that my teacher made me memorize) and somewhat automatic as well. That is, although I'm aware of when it's time to serve in a match, I'm not in conscious control of running off the service program in my brain.

This everyday example has some important implications for cognitive psychologists because it suggests that practice on a given task leads to a reduction in the number of resources needed to process the stimuli associated with doing the task. If practice were continued indefinitely, the performance not only would improve but also would become more automatic, requiring fewer and fewer cognitive resources. As fewer resources were allocated to the task, the subject's awareness would play a smaller and smaller role in the initiation and execution of the task. At the endpoint of such a process (which is probably only seldom reached in everyday life), performance on the task would become truly automatic, requiring virtually no resources and leaving no conscious trace of its execution. This point is important. Recall from our discussion of the capacity model of attention that several different sources of stimulation can be processed simultaneously as long as their demands do not exceed the supply of resources. Now we see that one way of solving the problem of attending to different sources of stimulation is to practice attending and doing one of the tasks involved, thus reducing the number of resources needed to process the task and leaving the remaining resources free to be allocated among the other tasks.

A second and perhaps controversial point is this: If practice reduces the number of resources needed to process incoming stimuli, then there are no demanding tasks, only unpracticed ones. In other words, if the attentional demands of a task can be reduced by practice, then what limits our ability to attend to different sources of stimulation is not our cognitive resources, but rather the time in which we have to practice the tasks. The next section considers the question of automatic processing.

AUTOMATICITY

As Hasher and Zacks (1979) have commented, two pathways lead to automatic processing. One is heredity, the other is learning. One implication of this position is striking: Hasher and Zacks argue that physical activities and mental events share the same pathway to **automaticity.** That is, mental actions, such as those involved in perception and memory, can be treated as though they were similar to motor skills. The same sort of repetition and drill that produce improvements in motor skills should produce improvement in cognitive skills as well.

Schneider and Shiffrin (1977; Shiffrin & Schneider, 1977) have shown that complex but highly practiced perceptual analyses can be done automatically. They also have demonstrated that such analyses will become automatic with practice even if they are not initially done that way. Schneider and Shiffrin (1977) gave their subjects a set of letters or numbers that they called a memory set and instructed their subjects to determine if any of the elements of the memory set appeared on a set of slides that were presented for brief periods. This set of slides was varied in two ways. The slides might have one, two, or four characters printed on them—a factor called "frame size." The relationship of the characters on the slides to the memory set characters was the second variable. In the varied mapping condition, the subject was given a memory set that consisted of one or more letters. All the to-be-searched characters were also letters. In the consistent mapping condition, the subject was given a memory set that consisted of numbers. However, the elements to be searched through were still all letters, unless the memory set number appeared on one of the slides. If one of the memory set numbers did appear, it was the only number present in the entire set of twenty slides. If after scanning the set of slides, the subjects had detected an element of the memory set, they were told to respond yes. If the subjects believed that no elements of the memory set were presented, they were instructed to respond no.

Figure 2.6 shows two examples of their trials. A good way to encode this study is to remember that, in the varied mapping conditions, the subject is searching for a letter among other letters, and in the consistent mapping condition, the subject is searching for a number among letters. Schneider and Shiffrin were interested in how quickly subjects could scan this set of slides while maintaining 95 percent accuracy—that is, saying yes or no and being correct 95 percent of the time.

The findings of this study are shown in Figure 2.7. Examine them and make your own interpretation. Considering the hits (trials in which the subject correctly said yes), we see that subjects could quickly scan the slides in the consistent mapping condition and still maintain 95 percent accuracy. That is, when looking for a number among letters, subjects required only 80 msec per slide to accurately process the information. Indeed, apparently the only variable in the consistent mapping condition that affected the subjects was frame time—the time in which subjects were allowed to view each slide. However, in the varied mapping condition, such was not the case.

Let's compare the same presentation (memory set size = 1, frame size = 2) across the two mapping conditions. As we've seen, subjects could achieve the accuracy criterion when viewing the slides for only 80 msec in the consistent mapping condition. However, subjects required 200 msec to achieve the same accuracy in the varied mapping condition, that is, when they were looking for a letter among other letters. Schneider and Shiffrin reasoned that the processing of letters during the search for a number is automatic, requiring virtually no allocation of resources. However, searching for a letter among letters is not automatic. This process is controlled and requires attention. If this reasoning is accurate, we would expect that frame size should not affect processing speed in the consistent mapping condition. That is, if you're looking for a number among letters, how many letters there are on each slide doesn't matter, because the recognition processes are automatic and fast. But frame size should affect processing speed in the varied mapping condition. To maintain high accuracy levels, the subjects must scan each letter individually, and the more letters there are, the longer this process is going to take. This hypothesis was substantiated. Increases in the frame size had little effect on the subject's processing time in the

··············· **FIGURE 2.6**   The two detection conditions in Schneider and Shiffrin's experiements: the varied mapping condition and the consistent mapping condition. On each trial the sequence of events was: *1,* presentation of the memory set; *a,* a fixation point; *b,* three dummy frames that never contain the target; *c,* distractor frames; *d,* frame containing the target; *e,* more distractor frames; *f,* dummy frames that never contain the target.

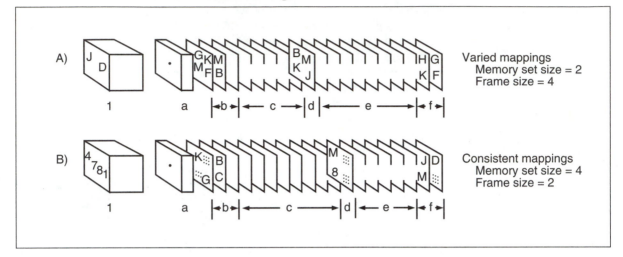

(From Schneider & Schiffrin, 1977. Copyright 1977 by the American Psychological Association. Adapted by permission of the publisher and the author.)

consistent mapping condition, but similar changes produced substantial increases in processing speed in the varied mapping condition.

However, Shiffrin and Schneider (1977) demonstrated that the search for a target letter in an array of letters can be done automatically if this task is practiced. Subjects were given a target letter that was always drawn from a particular set (B, C, D, G, F, H, J, K, L), and they were asked to scan a series of slides in which the distractor elements were always letters drawn from a different set (R, S, T, V, W, X, Y, Z). Although it took more than two thousand trials, the subjects nevertheless eventually performed as well on this ~~varied~~ mapping task as they did on the consistent mapping task in the previous experiment. This finding supports a point made earlier regarding the demands made by difficult tasks. As discussed, practice can tame difficult or time-consuming recognition tasks. Practice not only smooths the performance of motor and cognitive tasks but also reduces the number of resources needed to be allocated to process the information.

A similar point was made by Hirst, Spelke, Reaves, Caharack, and Neisser (1980). Their two subjects attempted to read and take dictation simultaneously. During the reading-only trials, the subjects read short stories, which were followed by tests of reading comprehension. This procedure was done to establish a baseline for reading rate and ability. The dictation task consisted of writing down short sentences, such as "The dog got free," that were slowly (thirty words per minute) presented to the subjects. During the reading-dictation trials, the subjects simultaneously read and took dictation. In the initial trials, the dictation task interfered with reading, resulting in slower speeds and poorer comprehension. After approximately one hundred sessions, the subjects were able to take the dictation without its interfering with their reading. Their scores during the reading-dictation trials equaled the reading scores earned during the reading-only trials. Other evidence suggests that the subjects also comprehended the dictated sentences even though they had not been instructed to try to remember them.

FIGURE 2.7

Results of Schneider and Shiffrin's experiments. Subjects' performance in the varied mapping condition showed the effects of frame time, frame size, and memory set size. In the consistent mapping condition, performance was affected only by frame time.

(From Schneider & Shiffrin, 1977. Copyright 1977 by the American Psychological Association. Adapted by permission of the publisher and the author.)

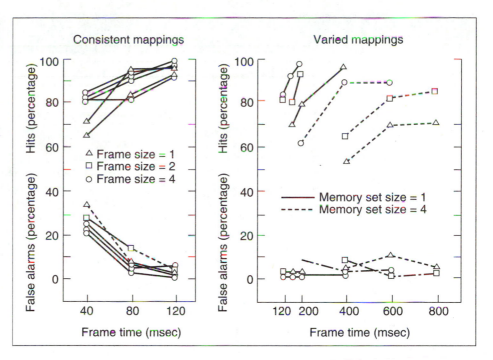

This second finding suggests that the two individuals in the study were carrying out two semantic analyses simultaneously.

One of the interesting and important questions raised by these studies concerns the length of time or, more accurately, the amount of experience with the stimuli, required for a cognitive process to be run automatically. Let's consider what might be involved. Logan (1990) has made an analogy between automaticity, generally speaking, and children's knowledge of addition facts. Asking an adult for the sum of 9 plus 6 produces a fast, effortless, and correct response, but small children must laboriously compute the answer. Now, suppose each time the child works that particular problem, a residue, or trace, of the answer is left in the child's memory, and moreover, suppose residues accumulate with each solving of a particular problem. From a standpoint of the child's cognitive system then, answering the question "What is 9 plus 6?" initiates a sort of race between the computational procedures and memory processes that look at the residues and try to figure out the answer from them. At first, the computational procedures will win this race every time, but with each time the race is run, the residual trace gets stronger and stronger. Eventually the memory processes become faster than the computational procedure. According to this view, every instance of a response adds to the memory trace, and this view suggests that we set foot on the pathway to automaticity as soon as we begin to make the same type of response to specific stimuli.

To support these contentions, Logan (1990) carried out a series of studies using lexical decision tasks as the basic paradigm. In a lexical decision task, a stimulus, either a word or a nonword, is presented to the subject visually. The subject is asked to decide as quickly as possible whether the stimulus is a word or a nonword, and the subjects indicate their choices by pressing keys. It's been known that when a stimulus in a lexical decision task, either a word or a nonword, is presented a second time, the subjects respond faster than they did to the first presentation. This phenomenon is called repetition priming. What

USING YOUR KNOWLEDGE OF COGNITION

In this section, I'll present a question whose answer we might explore using a demonstration or mini-experiment. Using the knowledge that you have gained from the relevant sections of the text, you'll be able to follow along to see how cognitive scientists go about investigating and explaining various phenomena. In this section we'll explore some questions concerning the function of attention: What does paying attention do for us anyway?

To see how attention works, and what it might do for us, prepare the following materials, and then try them out on a friend. First, get a couple of markers of clearly distinquishing colors—let's say red and blue. Then, on a plain sheet of paper, make one blue straight-line letter, like *T*, one red curved-line letter, such as *S*, and one red *T*. Then on a second sheet, scatter around the following stimuli: One blue *T*, 14 red *S*'s, and 15 red *T*'s. Then, ask a friend to locate the blue figure on each page as quickly as possible and notice if there seems to be a time difference. If your friend did as expected, there was no time difference in either version of the task; the blue figure seems to "pop out" (Treisman & Gelade, 1980) whether it is placed in the context of two or twenty-nine distractors. According to Treisman and her colleagues (Treisman & Gelade, 1980; Treisman and Gormican, 1988; Treisman, 1990), this demonstrates that isolated features, such as color, are processed in parallel (that is, simultaneously) without any focusing of attention. This kind of processing results from the same sort of preattentive analysis that we saw in Treisman's earlier work. Now, prepare the following materials and try this next task on a

friend. Make a third display consisting of one blue *T*, 9 red *T*'s, 10 blue *S*'s, and 10 red *S*'s. Now ask a friend to try to find the blue *T* on the first sheet of paper, and then on the third sheet of paper. Observe the amount of time required to do these tasks. If your friend does as expected, it will take him or her substantially longer to find the blue *T* on the third piece of paper, compared with the first display, even though both pieces of paper have the same number of distractors (29). How come? According to Treisman, the increase in time results from the fact that searching for a blue *T* on the third piece of paper involves looking not just for a single feature, but for a combination, or conjunction, of features. That is, the "blueness" is a feature, and the "*T*-ness" is also a set of features. In Treisman's terminology, this means that on the third piece of paper, you must search for the blue *T* at the object level, rather than at the featural level. Searching at the object level requires that the features, which are processed separately in the preattentive analysis, be combined or integrated. According to Treisman, this requires a second analysis in the form of selective attention that integrates or "glues" (that's Treisman's metaphorical term) the separate features together. Selective attention operates serially, not in parallel, which means that selective attention will require more time than the preattentive analysis. That's why there can be no "pop out" phenomenon when the search is at the object level instead of the feature level. So, what does attention do for us? By paying attention to stimuli we integrate otherwise separate features and are therefore able to distinguish and search for stimuli at the object level.

happens when words and nonwords are presented several more times? Logan (1990) found that while the initial decision time for nonwords was in the neighborhood of 670 or so msec, the decision time after two repetitions was 70 to 100 msec less, and after ten presentations had declined by about 150 msec compared with the initial response time. Given that there were 340 words and 340 nonwords used as the stimuli in this study, it's clear that the subjects were not getting faster simply because of a "response set." That is, the number of stimuli in the study rules out the idea that the subjects were getting faster because they were saying to themselves something like, "I just have a hunch the next stimulus is going to be a nonword." Logan's findings suggest that automaticity is not some binary condition (we either have it or we don't) nor is it a terminal state (we're as automatic as we're going to be on some tasks). Rather, findings like these suggest that automaticity is a matter of some degree, and they also suggest that as soon as we begin to make the same class of response with regard to some stimuli, we have begun to attain a measure of automatic processing.

Conclusions from the Second Phase of Theory Building

In the second phase of theory building, Kahneman and others have advanced the idea that attention consists of a group of cognitive processes that can be allocated systematically to deal with incoming information. Demanding tasks require a greater number of resources than do less demanding tasks, but this is true only for unpracticed demanding tasks. With practice, the mental effort required to do demanding tasks decreases, and if practice is continued, the processing of a task may become automatic.

Capacity models should be thought of as complementing the bottleneck theories. Although, as we have seen, in many instances humans seem to be able to process competing stimuli simultaneously, parallel processing cannot be done in some situations. An obvious example is that purely physical limitations, resulting from the way in which your body is constructed, make it impossible to simultaneously attend to visual stimulation in front of you and behind you.

At this point, it is simply not known to what extent incoming stimuli compete for allocation of resources. To the extent that they do compete, bottleneck theories seem to be good accounts of the fate of victorious stimuli— those that make it aboard the shunting channel. In the numerous cases in which competition seems to be absent, the capacity model seems to be a reasonable explanation. Another way of viewing this distinction was offered by Norman and Bobrow (1975). Certain difficult tasks were described as being data limited. For example, we've all had the experience of trying to tune in a faraway radio station. Trying to catch the station's signal against the background of static tends to consume many of our resources as we try to make the fine discriminations necessary to tune in the station. Our processing of this auditory stimulus is limited by the poverty of the data: The signal is weak. We tend to become single-minded as we fiddle with the tuner. An appropriate description is that the signal passes through a bottleneck into a detection device, where we'll try to extract as much information as possible from it. **Data-limited processes** can be contrasted with **resource-limited processes.** As the name implies, tasks must have resources allocated to them before they can be processed, and when we're out of resources, we're out.

PATTERN RECOGNITION

The initial objective of our information-processing system is to recognize and categorize incoming stimuli. The result of this processing is the creation of a cognitive code that can be placed in some sort of context, or background. Against this background, the code can be elaborated and stored. This section describes two explanations of pattern recognition: the **template-matching theory** and the **feature detection theory.**

Template-Matching Theory

When I was a small child, one of my favorite playthings was a stencil that allowed me to trace various geometric objects and letters. To my juvenile eyes, the traced capital letters looked far better than the irregular letters I produced freehand. I was much impressed with the timelessness of such letters. The A that I traced one day was identical to the previous day's A, which could easily be verified by putting the stencil over the traced A and noting that only the correct A parts were visible.

Some researchers have proposed that human pattern recognition is achieved in a similar fashion. To recognize a particular pattern, such as the letter *T*, incoming information is compared with stored codes, called *templates*, until a good fit between the incoming information and the stored codes is found. Presumably, the best fit will be achieved when the incoming information matches the template for *T*. At that point, the incoming information will be recognized and labeled *T*.

Figure 2.8 shows a template-matching system engaged in a series of hits and misses for the letter A. Early proponents of this view were cheered by the news that such a system could recognize letters. For example, if you take out your checkbook and look at the computer digits printed at the bottom of each check, you'll notice that they have been made highly distinguishable from one another. These differences are apparently necessary to permit the digits' recognition by machine.

FIGURE 2.8
....

Examples of template-matching attempts: *A* through *C*, successful attempts; *D* through *H*, failed attempts.

(Adapted from Neisser, *Cognitive Psychology*, 1967. Reprinted by permission of Prentice-Hall, Inc., Englewood Cliffs, NJ.)

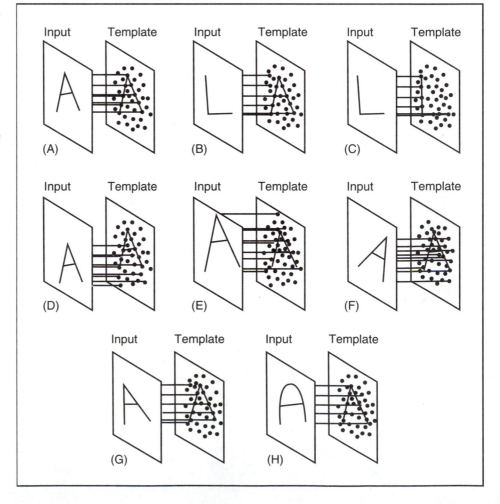

The template-matching theory has two strikes against it. First, such a system is inefficient. Banking firms care little if their recognition machines slap (figuratively) as many as ten different templates onto each digit before recognizing it, because only ten different digits exist, and the machines can rapidly compare the input with the templates. Humans, however, must be able to recognize an infinite variety of patterns, and they don't have the luxury of waiting until a match is achieved.

Second, template-matching systems are extremely inflexible, but human pattern recognition is successful in the face of great diversity of input. Notice from example (*H*) of Figure 2.8 that the input is clearly recognizable as an *A*, but the template system fails to recognize the stimulus because this particular *A* isn't the right kind of input. That is, strictly speaking, the template recognition device can recognize stimuli only when their size and orientation permit a match. This method of recognition has its limitations. If I showed you an upside-down *A*, you would no doubt recognize it as a perfectly good example of an *A* despite its being upside down. However, a recognition device endowed with only a template-matching analysis would draw a blank. These concerns have proved fatal for template-matching theories. Fortunately, a promising alternative exists.

Feature Detection Theory

Earlier I mentioned that, as a child, I was never completely happy with the block letters that I drew freehand. I was dissatisfied with their irritating variability. Perhaps my annoyance was misplaced, because my ability to judge letters as being of one or another type indicates that I had detected that each example of a particular letter had something in common with all the other examples of that letter. The question is, what did each letter have in common with other examples of that letter?

Consider the letter *H*. It has two approximately vertical lines that are about the same length. Both of these vertical lines begin and end more or less in the same place, relative to the border of the page. An *H* has a horizontal line that intersects the two vertical lines, more or less at their midpoints. I have just provided a sort of checklist of things that an *H* must have. This list is not an exhaustive list; the relative lengths of the horizontal and vertical lines probably have additional stipulations. Nevertheless, a system endowed with the checklist just mentioned could scan a particular character, noting which items on the checklist the character had and which it did not. If a given character had all the items on the checklist, the system would conclude that the character was an *H*. Thus, characters like these:

ㄅ ㅓ ㅄ

would not be called *H*s.

Feature analysis is the name given to this approach to the problem of pattern recognition. The basic assumption is that all complex stimuli are composed of distinctive and separable parts known as *features*. Pattern recognition is accomplished by counting the presence or absence of the features, and comparing the count with a tabulation of the features associated with different labels. Naturally, the success of the approach hinges on the decomposability of stimuli. As Gibson (1969) has demonstrated, a tabulation of features can apparently be accomplished, at least for letters.

Figure 2.9 shows the listing of presumed critical features. Notice that letters similar in appearance, such as *E* and *F*, share many features. This leads to the expectation that, when errors in letter recognition take place, letters should be mistaken for letters with which they share features. This hypothesis has been confirmed many times (Geyer & DeWald, 1973; Garner, 1979). Other support for the feature analysis model has been supplied by Neisser (1964). Neisser gave his subjects blocks of letters such as those shown in Figure 2.10. The subjects were told to scan the blocks as quickly as they could to find the target letter, *Z*. Try it. Like most of Neisser's subjects, you probably located the *Z* much more quickly in block (1) than you did in block (2). Let's consider the implications of this finding.

The basic premise of the feature analysis position is that cases of mistaken identity should occur among letters that share features. Thus, one might expect a greater number of such confusions when searching for *Z* in block (2), because the letters in block (2) share features with *Z*. Consequently, we should expect reductions in the accuracy of performance when subjects seek a target in feature-similar backgrounds as opposed to feature-dissimilar backgrounds. However, Neisser reported faster performance when the subjects searched for a target located in a feature-dissimilar background than when they sought the same target in the context of letters with similar features.

The implications of this point have not been lost on cognitive psychologists, who contend that this distinction indicates that the analysis of features must take place in a series of steps, or stages. That is, in the first stage, the features are extracted from the stimulus and noted. After this step is accomplished, the count, or comparison of the target letter with the background letter, is carried out. If the number of features in common is large, then the component of the system that is doing the counting will require more time, as Neisser noted. This is another reason why the feature analysis model is a more persuasive account of pattern recognition than the template-matching theory. Template matching is an all-or-

FIGURE 2.9

Critical features of letters.

(Adapted from Eleanor Gibson, *Principles of Perceptual Learning and Development*, © 1969, p. 88. Reprinted by permission of Prentice-Hall, Inc., Englewood Cliffs, New Jersey.)

Features	A	E	F	H	I	L	T	K	M	N	V	W	X	Y	Z	B	C	D	G	J	O	P	R	Q	S	U
Straight																										
Horizontal	+	+	+	+		+	+								+				+							
Vertical		+	+	+	+	+	+	+	+	+				+		+		+				+	+			
Diagonal /	+							+	+		+	+	+	+	+											
Diagonal \	+							+	+	+	+	+	+	+									+	+		
Curve																										
Closed																+		+			+	+	+	+		
Open V																				+						+
Open H																	+		+						+	
Intersection	+	+	+	+			+	+					+			+						+	+	+		
Redundancy																										
Cyclic change		+							+			+				+									+	
Symmetry	+	+		+	+		+	+	+		+	+	+	+		+	+	+			+					+
Discontinuity																										
Vertical	+		+	+	+	+	+	+	+					+								+	+			
Horizontal		+	+			+	+								+											

FIGURE 2.10
....

Lists used to study
feature analysis in a
high-speed search
task.

(From "Visual Search" by
U. Neisser. Copyright 1964
by Scientific American,
Inc. All rights reserved.)

ODUGQR	IVMXEW
QCDUGO	EWVMIX
CQOGRD	EXWMVI
QUGCDR	IXEMWV
URDCQO	VXWEMI
GRUQDO	MXVEWI
DUZGRO	XVWZEI
UCGROD	MWXVIE
DQRCGU	VIMEXW
QDOCGU	EXVWIM
(1)	(2)

none theory. If the incoming stimulus matches some template, recognition is accurate and complete. If the incoming stimulus does not match some template, then the recognizer would presumably be left completely in the dark. The power of the feature analysis point of view lies in its ability to explain both accuracy as well as latency of recognition. Incidentally, Neisser's subjects practiced tasks of this type for ten days. By now, you should be able to predict what changes had taken place in the subjects' performances by the tenth day.

A whimsical stage model of feature analysis was offered by Selfridge (1959). Called Pandemonium, his system described pattern recognition as taking place in a series of stages that were carried out by highly specialized cognitive processes. Each process was referred to as a demon. In the first stage, the image demons are responsible for converting the physical stimulus into some sort of cognitive representation acceptable to the other demons. Next, the feature demons analyze the representation, with each one looking for her particular feature (horizontal lines, intersections, and so on). Next, the results of the feature count are posted for the cognitive demons. Each cognitive demon looks for his particular array of features. With every appropriate feature that a cognitive demon sees posted, his noisemaking increases a notch. Finally, the decision demon listens to the resulting pandemonium and judges which demon is shouting the loudest; presumably, that is the incoming stimulus.

Independent Confirmation of Feature Analysis

Lines of evidence that are not purely behavioral also suggest that pattern recognition is frequently accomplished by feature analysis. Some of this evidence is biological (this is discussed later in the chapter). Other evidence has been produced from the field of artificial intelligence (AI). AI is concerned with the development of software that enables computing machines to act with intelligence. In this regard, several AI researchers have been concerned with computer vision. That is, they have attempted to determine what it takes to get a machine to "recognize" scenes such as the one shown in Figure 2.11. Waltz (1975) has argued that this simple task requires vast knowledge.

Some of what people do spontaneously, however, can be accomplished by a computer programmed to extract certain features from the array. First, the machine analyzes the bright and dark regions of the array. Although the variations in the intensity of reflected light are not shown in Figure 2.11, they are present in real life. After this analysis has been carried out, the machine computes locations that seem to border the various light and dark regions. In Figure 2.11, points J14 and J15 are examples of such points. From points such as J14 and J15, the machine goes on to recognize other types of intersections, such as L's and

FIGURE 2.11

A scene and the features that might be used to analyze it.

(Adapted from D. Waltz, "Understanding Line Drawings of Scenes with Shadows." Copyright 1975 by McGraw-Hill.)

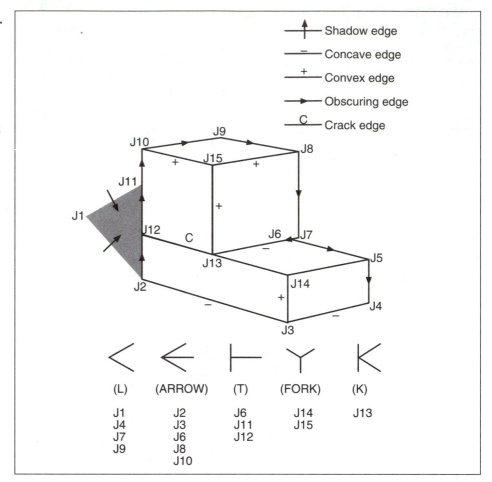

arrows. Finally, the program assembles the patterns of intersections. That is, much like the cognitive demons in Pandemonium, who added up the features they had observed and started shouting if they detected their pattern, Waltz's program adds up the pattern of intersections and attempts to determine what kind of shape it must be.

Waltz's program has been able to handle the scenes shown in Figure 2.12 in the times shown. That is, the machine can label the lines with names that are consistent with what humans see when they look at these drawings. This kind of analysis is important, not because it proves that human pattern recognition is accomplished by feature analysis, but because it demonstrates that a nonbiological information-processing system is nevertheless capable of feature analysis. Consequently, cognitive psychologists have been able to argue that information-processing systems, whether or not biological, seem to share certain characteristics, one of which is the ability to recognize patterns by abstracting features from an array.

Biological Contributions   Other researchers have demonstrated that, although you don't have to be made out of cells to do feature analysis, your biology nevertheless plays a role in feature detection. You probably know that, even when we gaze directly at an object, our eyes are not held perfectly still. Instead, the eye

FIGURE 2.12
....
**Some visual arrays
and their processing
times.**

(Adapted from D. Waltz,
"Understanding Line
Drawings of Scenes with
Shadows." Copyright 1975
by McGraw-Hill.)

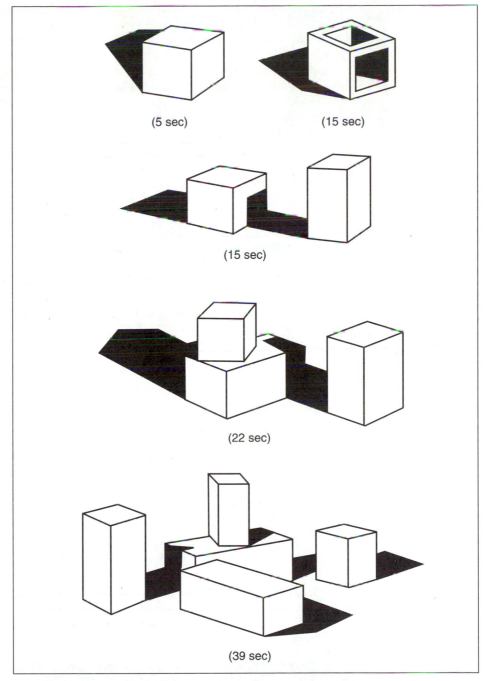

(5 sec)   (15 sec)

(15 sec)

(22 sec)

(39 sec)

continues to move in a variety of actions known as *physiological nystagmus*. Some
of these motions have small amplitudes but high frequencies. For example, the eye
jiggles around in a visual angle of 20 seconds of arc (1/180 of a degree), thirty to
seventy times per second (Lindsay & Norman, 1977). Other movements have
lower frequencies but larger amplitudes. These motions are apparently necessary
for visual perception. Their probable function is to give the retinal receptors
adequate time to refresh themselves. Incoming visual stimuli can be stabilized on

the retina using a system of mirrors (Riggs, Ratcliff, Cornsweet & Cornsweet, 1953). The stimulus to be seen by the subject is first projected onto a small mirror, which has been cemented to a contact lens worn by the subject. This image is then picked up from this screen and bounced around a set of mirrors before finally being projected to the subject's eye. The result is that, no matter how the subject's eye moves, the same set of receptors is stimulated by the incoming image.

Something interesting happens to the subjects in this situation: They become functionally blind within a few seconds. Perhaps even more interesting is that the stimuli don't disappear all at once. Rather, they fade away in pieces, and these pieces resemble the features described by Gibson and Selfridge. Figure 2.13 shows drawings of the stimuli that were used; these appear on the left. On the right are succeeding disintegrations of these stimuli as reported by the subjects (Pritchard, 1961). This finding suggests that feature analysis, which I have been describing as a cognitive process, has its basis in neurology. Implied here is that biological importance probably plays a role in determining what sorts of stimuli can serve as features.

This reasoning impelled Lettvin, Maturana, McCulloch, and Pitts (1959) to examine the retina of the frog. They argued that the frog is a primitive animal that uses its visual system to achieve two important biological ends: acquiring food and avoiding turning into someone else's food. A sensible assumption was that the visual system would support biological needs by extracting those features of the visual array that seemed particularly important to meet those needs. Using advanced technology, Lettvin et al. were able to insert tiny wires known as *microelectrodes* into individual cells in the frog's retina. Lettvin et al. found that the eye of the frog had four kinds of feature detectors:

1. **Edge detectors,** which respond strongly to the border between light and dark regions

2. **Moving contrast detectors,** which respond when an edge moves

3. **Dimming detectors,** which react when the overall illumination is lowered

4. **Convex edge detectors,** which respond when a small, circular dark dot moves about in the frog's field of vision (Lindsay & Norman, 1977, p. 192).

The fourth detector is a highly specialized ability to detect features that are associated with flying insects—something that frogs like to eat. The other detectors are concerned with notifying the frog about the arrival of predators either on the ground (as dark shadows that move) or from the air (as shadows that would lower the overall illumination).

FIGURE 2.13
....
Disintegration of stabilized retinal images.

(From R. M. Pritchard, "Stabilized Images on the Retina." Copyright 1961 by Scientific American, Inc. All rights reserved.)

Context

Despite the persuasiveness of the preceding account, it's nevertheless fairly easy to demonstrate that not all our pattern recognitions could be based on feature analytic theory. For example, if we consider each letter as having five features, and a page of typed text as having about 300 words of five letters each, then reading each page requires about 7,500 feature detections (an example modified from one appearing in Anderson, 1980). A typical reader can read at the rate of 250 words per minute, which would necessitate more than 100 feature detections per second. When you recall the varied mapping condition of the Schneider and Shiffrin (1977) study, the notion that individual letters can be processed that fast seems unlikely. Then how can we read, and accomplish other sorts of pattern recognition, so quickly?

The best answer to this question is that we probably don't process each letter on a feature-by-feature basis. Rather, we use other surrounding letters as a basis for inferring what the intervening letter must be. An example of this use of **context** can be seen in Figure 2.14. Notice that the features of the ambiguous character are not as informative as those of the surrounding characters when making an interpretation. The contrast between feature analysis and contextual analysis is sometimes described by cognitive psychologists as data-driven versus conceptually driven processing (Lindsay & Norman, 1977). **Data-driven processes** operate from the bottom up, gathering and processing information in small pieces, which are later assembled in working memory. **Conceptually driven processes** operate from the top down and can be considered as expectations or plans. Conceptually driven processes gulp in large amounts of information while making deductions and filling in the gaps. In the case of letter recognition, conceptually driven processes are generated from our general knowledge of which letters are likely candidates to begin words, which combinations of letters are likely, and so on.

The effects of context on letter recognition have been known for some time (Reicher, 1969; Wheeler, 1970). The basic finding, known as the **word superiority effect,** is that subjects are more able to identify a letter accurately when it appears in the context of a word than when it appears by itself or in the context of a string of random letters. For example, Wheeler (1970) gave his subjects a brief presentation of a letter or a word. Following this, they were shown either two letters or two words, and were asked to determine which had been presented earlier. A letter trial consisted of showing a letter (*D*) and then two letters (*D*, *G*). The word trial consisted of a word (*WIND*) and then two words (*WIND*,

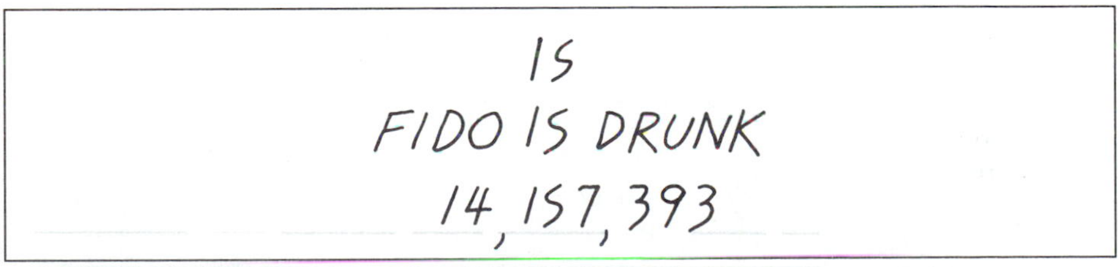

FIGURE 2.14

The stimulus above the handwriting can be interpreted as either "15" or "is," depending on its context. The meaning of a stimulus is often determined in part by its context.

(From *Psychology Today* (3rd ed.). Copyright 1975 by Random House, Inc.)

WING). Wheeler found that recognition was about 10 percent better in the word condition, meaning that subjects were better able to discriminate D from G when these letters appeared in the context of a word.

This finding has been interpreted as showing the existence of some "higher-order unit" (Purcell, Stanovich & Spector, 1978)—a unit of knowledge in which conglomerations of individual features have been associated through repeated presentation. According to such a view, the recognition of some features permits the inference of associated features. Rumelhart and Siple (1974) have explained the word superiority effect in these terms. Suppose the subject in the word condition just described recognizes the letters WIN. The remaining letter is limited to few possibilities: E, D, G, K, O, or S. If the subject has detected even a single feature from the fourth letter (such as the vertical line), then enough information is present for the subject to guess WIND in the recognition task. However, the possession of only a single feature is not very helpful in the letter trials, because no letters can be recognized from a single feature alone.

This explanation, although appealing, has fallen on hard times. Solman, May, and Schwartz (1981) have stated that the word superiority effect has two possible sources. One of these sources is sensory memory. A possibility, they argued, is that some elements—particularly words—are retained in sensory storage longer than are nonwords. Because the words are stored longer, the subject could be "reading" them better on the recognition task. The second explanation is similar to that of Rumelhart and Siple (1974): The subjects could be using word knowledge to make sophisticated guesses on the recognition task.

Figure 2.15 shows the stimuli that Solman et al. used in their study and how they were presented to their subjects. Subjects were first shown fragments of words or nonwords. After a delay of 0 to 150 msec, subjects were shown the second series of fragments. The two sets of fragments could be combined to form a nonword (IESR), a low-constraint word (RISE) in which many letters could be substituted for the S, and a high-constraint word (WISH) in which only a few letters are acceptable in the third position. Following the presentation of the two fragments, the subjects were shown two letters (S and T) and were asked to determine which they had seen. The word superiority effect was again demonstrated: Recognition was better for the S when it appeared in a word as opposed to a nonword combination of letters. If the subjects were using word knowledge to guess about the S's identity, we would expect that recognition would be better in

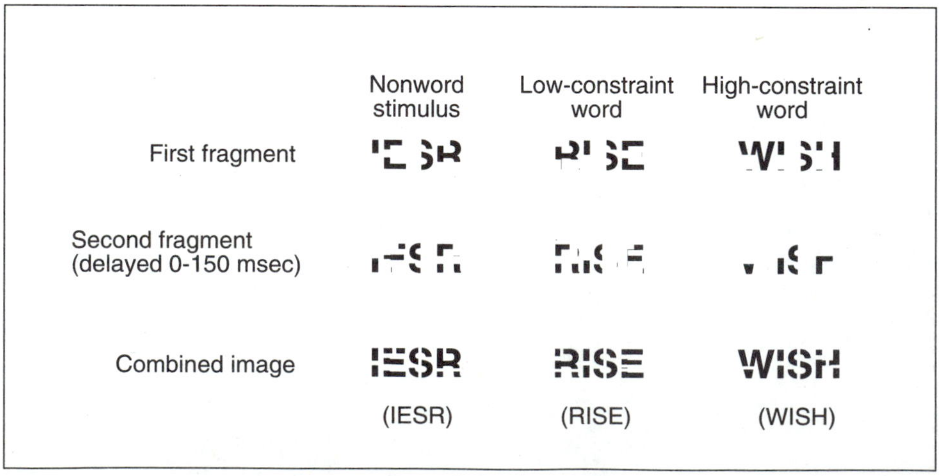

FIGURE 2.15
....

The word superiority effect: setup for Solman, May, and Schwartz (1981) study.

(Copyright 1981 by the American Psychological Association. Adapted by permission of the publisher and author.)

	Nonword stimulus	Low-constraint word	High-constraint word
First fragment	IESR	RISE	WISH
Second fragment (delayed 0-150 msec)	IESR	RISE	WISH
Combined image	IESR	RISE	WISH
	(IESR)	(RISE)	(WISH)

the high-constraint condition. In the high-constraint condition, even the recognition of a single feature would allow the subject to pin down the S, whereas similar knowledge wouldn't be as helpful in the low-constraint condition. However, the performance of the subjects was the same in both word conditions. Similarly, the delay between the presentation of successive fragments had no effect on recognition.

Unquestionably, the effects of context on pattern recognition are powerful. Explaining exactly how these effects are produced has been troublesome for psychologists, at least as far as letter recognition is concerned. Subsequent chapters look again at data-driven and conceptually driven processes and consider some of the cases in which these processes interact.

CONCLUDING COMMENTS AND SUGGESTIONS FOR FURTHER READING

I began this chapter by posing a question about the qualities that the stimulus must have to provoke a shift of attention. As you now know, phrasing the question this way was slightly misleading on my part. First, ascribing to the stimulus all of the power to provoke an attentional shift is incorrect, because in addition to data-driven processes, there also are conceptually driven processes. As the influence of context on the ambiguous figure showed us, pattern recognition is often propelled by our expectations. Things are seen or not seen, heard or not heard, depending upon whether they are congruent with the expectation in force. Second, to speak of shifts of attention is sometimes misleading. Over the last decade and a half, many cognitive psychologists have adopted the position that attention consists of resource allocation. It's unlikely that any action would be so engrossing that all processing resources would be allocated to it (strategically speaking, smart systems always keep a reserve). This means that some resources will be allocated to processing many of the stimuli surrounding us. Will we necessarily become aware of the stimuli we process? As we have seen, the answer to this question appears to be no. The processing of stimuli depends in part upon certain enduring dispositions of the cognitive system. Many of these dispositions are under conscious control in that the nature of the incoming information's analysis can be altered. The results of the analysis, however, may not necessarily enter awareness. As Shiffrin and Dumais (1981) have pointed out, the relationship between attention and awareness is problematic. The results of automatic processing frequently don't enter consciousness, and even the results of controlled processing may not enter consciousness under all circumstances.

Regarding pattern recognition, feature analysis is apparently a powerful method for detecting regularities in stimulation. The elements of stimulation that serve as features are at least partly constrained by biological need and neuronal architecture.

The student who wishes to pursue these topics further should read Kahneman's (1973) book, which contains an excellent review of the literature constituting the first phase of theory building. The original papers by Broadbent (1958) and Treisman (1960) are classics. A good outline of the second phase of theory construction can be found in Posner and Snyder (1975). Advanced state-of-the-art work in this area can be found in the series of monographs called *Attention and Performance*. A first-rate summary of the findings on automaticity can be found in Shiffrin and Dumais (1981), and also in Schneider, Dumais, and Shiffrin (1984).

Lindsay and Norman (1977) provide a readable account of pattern recognition by humans; Horn (1986) covers the question of pattern recognition by machines.

The chapter mentioned that learning-disabled children may have attentional deficits of some sort. There has been some movement to link several childhood disorders, including hyperactivity, learning disability, and some forms of organic brain dysfunction, to an underlying attentional problem called attentional deficit disorder (ADD). Koppel (1979) presented an early view on this topic. This movement has apparently sparked a lively controversy among diagnosticians and theorists. For example, Kuehne, Kehle, and McMahon (1987) argue that ADD children can be differentiated from children with specific learning disabilities. In other words, ADD is just that—an attentional problem, not a catchall category. However, other researchers have argued that hyperactivity is a frequent companion disorder with ADD. Cantwell and Baker (1987) present evidence arguing for two forms of ADD: those that also include hyperactivity (ADDH) and those without such an involvement. However, Lorys, Hynd, and Lahey (1990) have not found any evidence that this distinction can be supported on the basis of neurological and cognitive tests.

KEY TERMS

Selective attention
Dichotic listening
Shadowing
Selective filter theory
Preattentive analysis
Attenuation model
Late selection
Cognitive resources

Allocation policy
Cognitive capacity
Electrodermal responses
Automaticity
Data-limited processes
Resource-limited processes
Template-matching theory
Feature detection theory

Context
Data-driven processes
   (bottom-up)
Conceptually driven processes
   (top-down)
Word superiority effect

FOCUS ON RESEARCH

Automaticity, Skill, and Awareness

The distinction between automatic and controlled processes is a matter of degree. As we improve a skill, the process of automatization proceeds gradually, and the amount of control required gradually recedes.

The course of skill acquisition has been known to psychologists for a long time. Snoddy (1926) studied the acquisition of skill on a mirror-tracing task. This task usually involves subjects guiding a pencil through a geometric shape while watching the reflection of their hands in a mirror. The subjects improved, but the rate of improvement is

what's particularly interesting. If we plot the time required to do the task as function of trials (holding errors constant), we would expect to see a decline. Snoddy plotted the *logarithm* of time as afunction of the *logarithm* of the number of trials. When this log-log plot was created for individual subjects, Snoddy observed that the line of best fit was a perfectly straight line! Figure 2.16 shows how the log-log plot would look for a hypothetical subject.

—*Continued*

FIGURE 2.16 Learning in a mirror-tracing task (log-log coordinates).

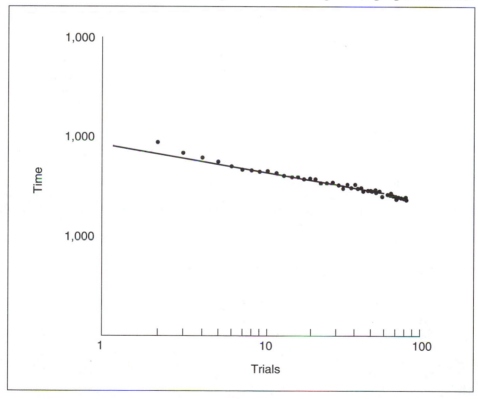

(Redrawn from Snoddy, 1926.)

FOCUS ON RESEARCH
....

Automaticity, Skill, and Awareness

—*Continued*

You should note two important points here. First, the subject's improvement continued across the whole set of trials; there was no endpoint at which improvement ceased. Second, if you consider the amount of improvement (in time) from any one point on the X axis to any other point, you know that, in the future, ten times as many trials will be required to produce a similar improvement.

Cognitive psychologists have since demonstrated that this log-log law holds not only for motor or perceptual skills but also for higher cognitive processes. For example, Newell and Rosenbloom (1981) studied the acquisition of skill in a solitaire card game called Stair. Here are the rules:

> Stair involves laying out all 52 cards face up from a shuffled deck, in 8 *columns* (four with 7 rows, four with 6 rows). There are also four *spots* (initially empty), each of which can hold only a single card. The aim is to build four stacks, ace to king, one for each suit, by moving cards around under typical solitaire constraints. A card in a spot or at the bottom of a column may be moved: (1) to a spot, if it is empty; (2) to a stack, if the card is the next in order building up; or (3) to the bottom of another column, if the card is the next lower in the samesuit (e.g., the six of spades ap-

pended to the seven of spades). (Newell & Rosenbloom, 1981)

You might wish to try playing this game a few times while charting your progress. Notice that this is a game of perfect information. Although aperceptual component is involved (a player might overlook a particular card) and a weak component of motor learning, this game is nevertheless primarily one of intellectual skill. That is, the subject's ability to analyze the initial layout is what determines victory. Newell and Rosenbloom's subject played five hundred hands of Stair. He got better, winning about 28 percent of his initial hands and about 40 percent of his final hands. In addition, the log-log law held for the time involved in playing (regardless of whether the hand was won or lost). For winning hands, the subject started out requiring about 1,000 seconds. By the end, five hundred hands later, this time had been reduced to about 550 seconds. All intermediate points fell close to the straight line established by the two end points, when the log of time was plotted as a function of the log of hand number.

Although playing this intellectual game had not become automatic, it was apparently on its way to becoming so. The implication of this finding is extremely interesting: With enough practice, the most challenging intellectual tasks could become automatic, requiring little or no awareness.

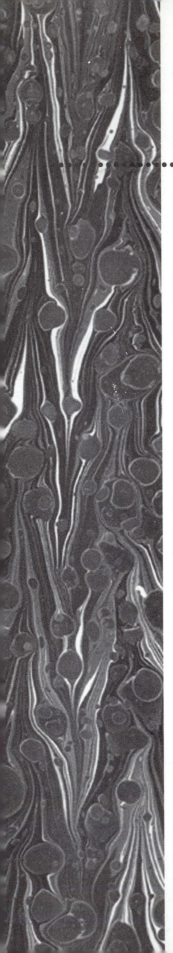

CHAPTER **3**

HIGHER COGNITIVE PROCESSES IN VISION

CHAPTER OUTLINE

OVERVIEW

One day when I was an undergraduate, a friend and I decided to take the afternoon off and go for a drive in the country. We wound up on the huge estate of a wealthy family, an estate that was known both for its beauty and for the secretive and allegedly turbulent history of its owners. According to the local lore, the family members, in an effort to keep their vast holdings and wealth in the family, had married among themselves. After some generations of doing this, their gene pool had become so inbred that many of the family's offspring were mentally defective and physically deformed. Instead of placing these individuals in an appropriate facility however, the ruling members of the family allowed their handicapped brethren to roam at will around the estate. I'm not saying that my friend and I believed any of these stories, for which there was not a scrap of objective evidence, but we knew all the tales.

After a while, we stopped the car and got out to walk down a deserted lane on the property. Here the forest pressed right up to the narrow dirt pathway, and the lowering sun created a shifting, dappled pattern of light on the leaves of the trees, making it difficult to see very far into the woods. As we walked along, we told each other the stories that we knew about the owners, and also about other macabre or gruesome events that were alleged to have taken place in the area. Finally, it was getting late in the day, and we decided to turn back. But then we heard a twig snap in the woods. As we strained to make out the source of the sound, all we could see was the indistinct outline of something in the woods. "Do you see that?" I asked my friend. She nodded, but said that she couldn't make it out. I looked closely and then saw that it was not one, but actually a band of, well, very small men who were alternately hiding and running from tree to tree. Sometimes instead of running, the men got down on the ground and sort of rolled or tumbled from tree to tree. They were wearing shoes that had pointed toes that curled up, like those a jester might wear. As I described each of these features to my friend, she agreed, saying that's what she saw too. And we also noticed the little men were getting closer. "Let's get outta here!" I shouted, and we took off down the road. I had taken no more than a few steps when I realized that no one would believe us, and that we had better verify what we saw. So we stopped and looked around once more. Only now, instead of the little men in their jester's shoes, we saw what had actually been there: A herd of small deer had taken sanctuary inside the estate and were grazing on the plants of the forest floor.

How could I have mentally converted the harmless deer into the menacing band of minute tumblers? How is it that my friend also saw them? Thinking about it much later, I could see that there were two main elements. First, both of us were in a highly suggestible state after telling each other weird stories all afternoon. Second, the light was failing, creating a situation in which the stimuli had become hard to interpret. Putting these two elements together I could see how I had misjudged the evidence from my senses.

For cognitive psychologists, such judgments and misjudgments are informative, because they tell us much about the factors that are involved in making sense out of sensory information. This chapter considers the two basic positions. The **constructivist theory of perception** (also called the transactional position, Ittelson & Cantril, 1954, and the computational position, Ullman, 1980) maintains that sensory stimulation is inadequate by itself to produce perception. Through experience, the brain learns how to interpret sensory cues, which themselves are inherently ambiguous. According to this view, the brain's interpretive activity is critical in perception. That is, the brain is not simply processing neural events that are straightforward alterations of physical energy. Rather, the brain is adding information of its own based on knowledge that has been built up from previous perceptual activity.

The alternative position is referred to as the **direct theory of perception.**

Simply put, direct theorists argue that, at least for vision, all the information we need to perceive is already contained and presented in the light that strikes our retinae. Also, this light is not random or chaotic, but instead is highly organized by the surfaces from which it has been reflected. Thus, the brain needn't add to or spruce up the incoming sensory stimulation. This stimulation is far from unorganized, according to the direct theorists. Instead, a highly accurate depiction of the world-as-it-is becomes available for us whenever we choose to bring our receptors to bear on it. Also implied by this position is the idea that our perceptual machinery has evolved to fit into, or mesh with, the types of information that are available on this planet.

This chapter considers the evidence favoring these two perspectives and offers a possible synthesis.

TWO VIEWPOINTS ON PERCEPTION

Over the next several pages, we'll explore two of the main perspectives that cognitivists have used to guide their research on perception: the constuctivist position and the direct position. As we've seen in the overview, constructivist theorists emphasize the role of the cognitive and neural system in taking information from the world and changing it, perhaps adding information, to produce our perception and our awareness. We should say from the outset that the constuctivist position is congruent with both the information-processing and the connectionist approaches that we looked at in Chapter 1. Constructivist theorists of the connectionist stripe tend to emphasize the role of neurology in perception, or at least emphasize the concept that our neural systems must somehow compute our perceptions from the external stimuli. Information-processing constructivists, on the other hand, are more likely to discuss the "stages" of perception, emphasizing the abstract nature of the computation, rather than its neural underpinnings. The direct position is rather different from the constructivist position. Direct theorists downplay the overall amount of analysis, whether neural or abstract, that must be done by the human in order to perceive. Consider a reflexive action, such as pulling your hand away from a hot stove. Obviously, there is some neural transmission and analysis going on here, but it seems at least intuitively clear that there is less neural "work" to be done in acting by reflex than in, say, solving a calculus problem. Without trying to overstate this, the direct theorists might argue that much of our perception, although certainly not reflexive by any means, is nevertheless not very intensive from a computational standpoint. You may be thinking that, if the direct theorists are not connectionists, and if they are not information-processing theorists necessarily, then in what sense are they cognitivists at all? As you may have surmised, the answer is that the direct viewpoint does indeed downplay the role of cognition of any sort in perception. That is, while direct theorists clearly acknowledge the role of neurology in perception, they nevertheless maintain that much of the information in the physical world is simply "given" to our senses without any extensive organization taking place at the neural level, and to that extent, direct theories are not really cognitive theories.

THE CONSTRUCTIVIST POSITION

This section details the constructivist account of perception, starting with a historical problem in psychology and going on to see how the constructivist position deals with the phenomenon of illusions.

The Höffding Step

Having sensory mechanisms means that certain cells in our bodies respond to particular forms of physical energy. Some of these sensory mechanisms are quite sophisticated in that they are capable of creating a code in which many aspects of the physical stimulation are retained. We can do more than simply encode physical energy, however; we can *recognize* it as well. That is, a pattern of neural events can produce within us an awareness and an understanding of the physical object that has been neurally encoded. I can *see* my wife as soon as the ambient light reflected from her strikes the receptors in my retinae. But I won't *recognize* her until something more than this happens. In other words, the simple creation of a neural code may be the basis of recognition, but the actual recognizing must be accomplished by subsequent neural processes.

How might this take place? According to associationism, a doctrine that was popular during the 1870s (Weimer, 1977), the linkage between a physical object and the naming of a physical object was direct, meaning that the neural events representing some physical object could be equated with the neural events involved in saying the name of the object. Harald Höffding (1891) demonstrated that such a view could not be correct. Consider Figure 3.1. The left side of the figure is a schematic representation of the activities shown on the right-hand side. Thus, A represents the physical object as it stands in the world. For recognition to take place, this object must be sensed, that is, represented neurally as in *a*. However, before the object can be named (either overtly or covertly), it must first be recognized, which requires additional neural activity of a different sort than that involved in sensation. The sensory code is just a neural representation of an object; it carries no information with it regarding categorization. This second kind of neural processing is represented in *b*—the perceptual neural events that categorize the object and allow us to name it. According to the associationists, the route from A to B was a straight line. Höffding showed that the path was not nearly so simple. The **Höffding step** is the step between sensation and perception, and with it, a question is produced. How do sensory neural events get changed over, that is, converted into perceptual neural events that give rise to our awarenesses and understandings?

Before the answer to this question is examined, two points should be noted. First, the Höffding step is quite general. Although the previous example involved vision, each sense creates its own sensory code and consequently produces its own Höffding step. This means that enterprising psychologists who solved the

FIGURE 3.1

. . . .

The Höffding step in the process of pattern recognition or perception.

(From Weimer, 1977. Copyright 1977 by the Lawrence Erlbaum Associates, Inc. Publishers. Adapted by permission of the publisher and author.)

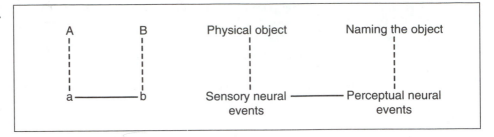

Höffding step for vision might be at a loss to solve the analogous Höffding problem for audition. That is, they might be unable to specify how speech sounds are recognized so that meaning is extracted from them. Second, no psychologist, cognitively oriented or otherwise, has ever offered a solution to the Höffding problem that has proved satisfactory to everyone. At the risk of oversimplifying, the constructivist solution to the Höffding problem involves taking it head-on by specifying the laws that govern the transformation of retinal images into perceptual experiences. Against this, the direct position can be seen as a kind of end run. Rather than laboriously solve the Höffding step for each sense, direct theorists hope to get rid of the Höffding step by completely recasting the problem of perception.

The Constructive Nature of Perception

The constructivist position begins with the premise that retinal events are inadequate to specify how objects are perceived. This proposition may seem unlikely to you, particularly if you believe that the retina transmits an amazingly detailed and accurate picture of the outside world to the brain. But actually, there is probably an abundance of information surrounding you right now that might be persuasive in convincing you otherwise.

In some situations, retinal signals can be ambiguous. First, although the retina has spatial extension, the space is only two-dimensional. It's not too hard to imagine how the retina might send the brain a code that specifies two of an object's three dimensions. But where does the third dimension come from? Our awareness includes knowledge of depth, and the constructivists argue that this awareness of depth could not have been produced at the retina. Rather, the brain must interpret aspects of the retinal code and, as a result of its interpretation, generate the third dimension. In other cases, the retinal code produces certain inaccuracies in our awareness of the external world.

For example, my office is in a wing that juts out at right angles to the main axis of a large building. The facade of the building is basically columnar, but the column effect has been softened by the placement of horizontal brick and concrete patterns. In architecture, such a horizontal effect is called a stringcourse. Viewed from the front of the building, the stringcourses are perfectly horizontal. But from my perspective, on the ground floor and looking across the face of the building, the second story stringcourse seems to be angled somewhat to the ground. The third story stringcourse is more sharply angled yet, and the fourth floor stringcourse appears very steeply angled. I know the stringcourses are horizontal; nevertheless, what I see is not what's out there. My awareness, which is presumably the result of retinal and central nervous system events, is of slanted stringcourses. If questioned, I would answer that they are not slanted, but only because I also have some other knowledge that dominates my awareness. I know the stringcourses are really not slanted; they just look that way.

According to the constructivists, this other knowledge must be added to the retinal code to specify the object as it really is in the outside world. What is this other knowledge, and where did it come from? I've seen the building from a variety of perspectives, and in each case, my recognition of the building has been accompanied by an awareness of how the various parts of the building (including the stringcourses) look from that particular perspective. Even if I remember only some of these views, eventually I'll acquire enough experience with the building to know how the building's appearance will change as a function of my perspective on it. According to the constructivist position, the other knowledge referred to previously is a memorized representation of the building produced by experience. This internal representation may or may not be imaginal. The internal representation doesn't necessarily have to be based on direct sensory experience. For example, if I were placed beside some building I had never seen before, I would still be able to answer questions accurately about it even though I had seen the building only from one perspective. This ability suggests that the internal representation that is added to the retinal code is abstract; it is generated by sensory experiences but is not limited to particular experiences.

Illusions   The constructivist position is cognitively oriented. This means that the constructivists frequently try to specify the successive alterations of sensory stimulation in terms of an information-processing model. Moreover, they may attempt to describe that knowledge that results from this processing of information in terms that were used in Chapter 1. This sort of knowledge hinges on the *experiences* that we've had in the world. That is, the computational procedures used by the nervous system may be more or less independent of our experiences, but the knowledge produced by such procedures is strongly anchored on events that have happened to us. This connection is important for the constructivists because they argue that our perception of things is a function of our experience. Consequently, whenever we misperceive a stimulus, constructivists are interested in the nature of the misperception. If the misperception is congruent with our experiences, then the constructivist might feel more confident in saying that we don't necessarily perceive things as they are, but rather we perceive things according to the way we have previously experienced them. This is why the constructivists have historically been interested in the problem of illusions: What factors make us sometimes misinterpret sensory stimulation?

Psychologists have used a wide variety of illusions in their studies, but none are more famous than the **Müller-Lyer illusion** depicted in Figure 3.2. The horizontal bar between the fins-out segments is the same length as the horizontal bar between the fins-in segments. To most people, the fins-out bar looks longer than the fins-in bar. What factors produce the illusion?

Strictly speaking, the retina does not seem to play a large role in the creation of the illusion per se. For example, it has been known for some time that no eye movements are required to produce the illusion (Yarbus, 1967). But some more recent evidence (Petersik, 1982) has suggested that people do make inappropriate eye movements in scanning the Müller-Lyer illusion. Petersik asked his subjects to estimate the extent of their eye movements in scanning the fins-out horizontal bar, the fins-in bar, and a finless bar. Estimates for the finless and fins-in bar were similar and accurate. However, the subjects overestimated the extent of the eye movement necessary to scan the fins-out bar. Because eye movements are not required to produce the illusion, one way of interpreting

FIGURE 3.2
....
The Müller-Lyer
illusion.

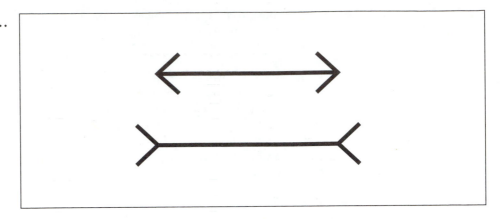

Petersik's findings is that the subjects were *misled*. That is, the faulty estimates were produced by the subject's previous experiences. This interpretation suggests that it was the subject's brain, which directed the eye movements, that was the locus of the illusion.

This interpretation is strengthened by the findings of Gilliam (1980). In this research, the horizontal bars of the Müller-Lyer illusion were briefly presented to one of the subject's eyes while the fins were presented to the subject's other eye. The separate retinal signals were combined, or fused, by the central nervous system, and when this took place, the subjects still showed the illusion's effects. The image of the fins-out bar looked longer to the subjects than did the image of the fins-in bar. This finding suggests that the previous experience of the Müller-Lyer illusion, represented in the subjects' memories, misguided their perceptual processing. But you're probably already aware of a potential snag in this reasoning. Surely some of the subjects had never seen the Müller-Lyer illusion before, so how could they have been misled by previous experience?

As Figure 3.3 shows, the world frequently presents us with stimulation in which some of the characteristics of the Müller-Lyer illusion are embedded. The vertical bar in each of the panels of Figure 3.3 is the same length. You know from your experience in the world that the vertical bar in the right-hand panel highlights the closest part of the doorway to you. Similarly, the vertical bar in the left-hand panels highlights the part of the doorway that is farthest from you. If these bars are the same size, then you know the doorway on the left must be bigger than the doorway on the right. When you look at the Müller-Lyer illusion, your experience in judging the sizes and distances in our highly angular world is what misleads you (Gregory, 1966).

Support for these contentions can be found in various cross-cultural studies of the Müller-Lyer illusion. For example, the Zulus of Africa live in a decidedly noncarpentered world. Although they build shelters, these are usually conical and windowless. If the Müller-Lyer illusion is produced by our experiences in a right-angled world, then it seems reasonable to expect that people such as the Zulus, who have little or no experience in such a world, would not fall prey to the illusion. This assumption seems to be accurate. Deregowski (1972) has reported findings showing that the Zulus don't perceive the Müller-Lyer illusion and other illusions that are thought to be based on experiences with right angles. As is the case with almost any cross-cultural study, some objections can be raised. First, pictorial representations could be among the things with which the Zulus are

FIGURE 3.3
....
Müller-Lyer effects
in everyday life.

(Adapted from transparency 28 from *Overhead Transparencies for Introductory Psychology*. Copyright 1983 by Random House. Adapted by permission of the publisher.)

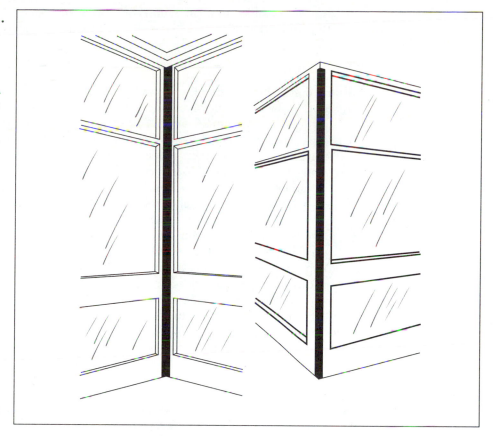

unfamiliar. Looking at and correctly interpreting pictures are skills that other cultures may not foster. Second, in this type of study, language problems are almost inevitable. That the Zulus understood what was being asked of them is not clear.

Initial Summary of the Constructivist Position   The constructivist position is an inherently cognitive one that can be clearly expressed as an information-processing model. That is, it's easy to conceive of perceptual activity as involving the elaboration of a more or less primitive retinal code by successive stages of processing within the central nervous system. In many ways, the processing of this code appears to be serial.

What remains for us is specifying the outcome of this information processing. Our objective in the next section is to detail what sort of knowledge is built up from successive interactions with the world.

Prototypes

Many cognitivists argue that the perception of people, events, and objects proceeds by extracting from these stimuli their distinctive features. As we saw in Chapter 2, humans seem to have developed specialized neural and cognitive mechanisms whose purpose is to analyze complex worldly events by breaking them down into their constituent elements: their features. However, these features are not left in an unorganized state in the cognitive system. The features are in turn assembled into larger units of knowledge—larger in that the principle that organizes the features is extensive. Once developed, these large units of knowledge guide, or channel, subsequent feature extraction. One of the terms used to describe such large units of knowledge is the **prototype.**

Abstraction of Prototypes   Posner and Keele (1968, 1970) conducted a series of studies to show how such large units of knowledge are formed. First, they created a set of four random nine-dot patterns, three of which are shown in Figure 3.4. These patterns were called the prototypes. Next, for each prototype, Posner and Keele created distortions by moving some of the dots slightly, in different directions. Figure 3.4 shows four of the distorted dot patterns. The distortions are not as random as they might look. Although the rule used in producing the distortions is complicated, each dot in the distortion was moved, on the average, the same distance from its position in the prototype. In this way, the *average* position of each dot in the distortion was the same as the prototype.

Posner and Keele presented their subjects with four distortions of each prototype. The prototype was never presented, nor were the subjects told how the distortions were created. Subjects had to learn to associate each of the distorted dot patterns with a name. The subjects underwent a training period in which they learned how to categorize the sixteen distorted dot patterns into four piles reflecting the category names. After the subjects were able to do this perfectly, they were given a test in which they had to sort both old and new stimuli into piles. The old stimuli included the previously studied distortions. The new stimuli included the prototype as well as two previously unlearned distortions. The subjects made errors 20 percent of the time in classifying previously studied distortions. Their error rate for the prototype was 32 percent even though they had never seen it before. The subjects made errors 50 percent of the time when categorizing previously unstudied distortions. If the subject had simply been guessing, the error rate would have been 75 percent (i.e., chance of guessing which stimulus belongs in which pile is only one in four). Notice that the error rate for the prototypes is low and close to that of the previously studied distortions. Clearly, the subjects had learned about the prototypes even though they hadn't studied them explicitly. This implication was supported in another study by Posner (1969). Using a paradigm similar to the one just outlined, Posner gave his subjects a memory task in which they were asked to recognize various dot

FIGURE 3.4
. . . .
Sample stimuli from Posner and Keele's (1968) study of the acquisition of prototypes.

(After Posner, 1973. Copyright 1968 by the American Psychological Association. Reprinted by permission of the publisher and author.)

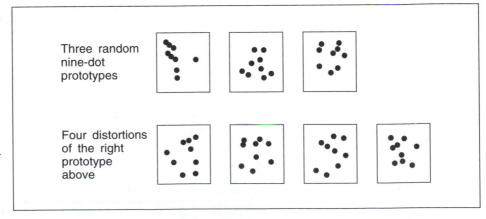

Three random nine-dot prototypes

Four distortions of the right prototype above

patterns as either old (previously studied) or new (never seen before). Even though the prototype had never been presented along with the other distortions, subjects were more likely to categorize it as an old stimulus than as a new one. This finding was not observed for other previously unstudied distortions.

Another interesting finding concerns the variability of the distortions. When the subjects are given only low-variability distortions during the training period (i.e., distortions that have been produced by only small movements of the dots), their ability to categorize or recognize previously unstudied high-variability distortions is impaired. However, if subjects are given only high-variability distortions during the training period, their ability to classify previously unstudied low-variability distortions is unimpaired. Although the presentation of high-variability distortions during the training period does not necessarily produce better recognition of the prototype, it does seem to produce better knowledge of the width or the boundaries of the category names (Homa, 1978; Homa & Vosburgh, 1976).

Other studies have focused on the role of feedback in the formation of prototypes. Fried and Holyoak (1984) presented their subjects with distortions of prototypical "artwork" created by two artists, "Smith" and "Jones." Figure 3.5 shows the prototypes and some of the distortions of each artist's work. The diagrams were shown one at a time to the subjects, who had to classify the designs into one of two piles by pressing a button. Subjects in one half of the group were informed about the correctness or incorrectness of each guess as soon as the choice was made. The other subjects were not given this information. Each subject continued sorting the designs until ten correct consecutive choices were made or until two hundred designs were presented. Although neither group of subjects was ever shown the prototype, and one group of subjects received no information concerning the correctness of this sorting, both groups did equally well on the sorting task. Although this fairly surprising finding has drawn fire (Homa & Cultice, 1984), this work nevertheless has an interesting implication. The Fried and Holyoak findings suggest that the corrective feedback given by adults to children who misclassify objects is probably not essential in enabling the children to form a prototype.

Bomba and Siqueland (1983) tested the validity of this assertion in a study involving the presentation of distorted dot patterns to babies aged three to four months. The researchers made use of a habituation paradigm to assess the formation of prototype knowledge of three geometric dot patterns: a square, a triangle, and a diamond. **Habituation** refers to our tendency to stop attending to, or noticing, stimuli as they become familiar. A variety of methods can be used to determine when habituation has taken place in infants. For example, the frequency and length of gazing, changes in heart and respiration rates, or even actions such as the intensity of sucking on a pacifier, have all been used to determine that an infant has lost interest in, and habituated to, a particular stimulus. Bomba and Siqueland found that the babies studied showed no initial preference for the prototypical geometric forms over their distortions. However, the babies did show habituation to the previously unseen prototype following the presentation of six distortions of each of the three prototypical forms. That is, the babies seemed to recognize that the prototype was similar to the six distortions that they had already seen, and therefore was not as interesting as a truly novel stimulus. Considered together, the Fried and Holyoak and Bomba and Siqueland studies suggest that the process of prototype abstraction emerges early in the life span and seems to operate independently of linguistic feedback. As discussed in

FIGURE 3.5
••••••••••••••••••••
Prototypes and
distortions of
designs by "Smith"
and "Jones."

(Copyright 1984 by the
American Psychological
Association. Adapted by
permission of the publisher
and author.)

Prototype A (Smith)   Prototype B (Jones)

7% distortion of A   7% distortion of B

15% distortion of A   15% distortion of B

Chapter 11, substantial evidence supports the idea that natural concept formation proceeds by stages, the first of which is formation of prototypical instances (Whitney and Kunen, 1983).

Accounts of Prototype Formation   We have seen that, in successive encounters with the environment, people systematically build up organizational principles of knowledge that are used to help channel or categorize future transactions with the world. As we've seen, people seem to be able to do this from a very early point in their lives. Moreover, corrective feedback need not be given for the process of prototype formation to occur.

Cognitive psychologists have typically described the buildup of organized world knowledge as being dependent upon the abstraction of relevant stimuli from objects present in the world (Posner, 1969). According to this view, people are sensitive to perceived regularities among the stimuli in the world (Howard, 1983). Moreover, people are able to make use of the fact that certain stimuli seem to occur in the presence of certain other stimuli and from this they learn about the "correlational" structure of the world (Rosch, 1977)—the fact that certain qualities have a high probability of occurring together. Prototypes then can be thought of as simply one variety of cognitive structure—one that enables the owner to answer questions about the similarity among stimuli by comparing the stimuli to the most central members of various categories.

This position on the influence of experience in perception is both common (Hull, 1920; Reber, 1967) and plausible. However, the position has not gone unchallenged. Brooks (1978) has argued that it is not feature abstraction per se that occurs during successive interactions with the environment. Instead, Brooks hypothesized that each object we encounter is stored intact in our memories, meaning that the object's features are not abstracted from it and stored separately. In dealing with new stimuli, the questions we ask ourselves concern the similarity between the new stimulus and the memory of previously encountered stimuli. A person categorizes novel stimuli by constructing an analogy: What old stimulus is this new stimulus most like?

Although limitations of space preclude a complete detailing of his work, Brooks has found that people perform well on some sorting tasks that seem to require multiple prototype formation according to the feature abstraction view-point. The simultaneous formation of multiple prototypes should require greater cognitive effort than the formation of a single prototype, and consequently we should expect a greater number of classification errors on such a sorting task. However, Brooks (1978) observed that sorting performance under such conditions is not degraded, which suggests that the feature abstraction viewpoint may not be the whole story. As Brooks notes, the two viewpoints are not necessarily contradictory. Some situations may exist in which either method of prototype formation works effectively. Given that, what we may be seeing here is another example of a situation in which a person can exert some strategic control over the method of prototype formation, or perhaps the method of prototype formation is driven by certain characteristics of the environment.

Prototypes and Schemata   The prototype has been defined as a hypothetical, "most typical" instance of a category (Anderson, 1980). Comprehending this definition might be easier if you think of membership in a category as involving the passage of a series of tests. The more tests that are passed, the closer a given instance is to becoming a central, or prototypical, member of that category. For example, consider the category *college professor*. Beyond certain formal qualifications for this role, what can we say about the informal characteristics of college professors? Some of the qualities that come to my mind are maleness, a slight obesity, being middle-aged, going bald, having a beard, and "tweediness." One could be a college professor without possessing any of these qualities, but with the possession of more of these qualities, a given professor becomes more typical and, with the possession of all of them, becomes prototypical.

Whereas the term prototype refers to a specific instance of a category member, and is thus fundamentally a perceptual term, cognitive psychologists sometimes speak of other units of knowledge that are assembled form separate stimuli. The term **schema** (or sometimes just "scheme," the plural forms are schemas or schemata) refers to a unit of knowledge that consists of linked actions or decisions. For example, a group of otherwise separate actions or events may be linked together because such actions are all taken to reach the same goal. When this is the case, we may talk of an event schema, or an event scheme.

In this sense, a schema is fundamentally a memory term, rather than a perceptual term, because the schema is something that must be retrieved, rather than perceived. Schemas have at least two interesting properties. First, the schema may have a prescriptive component: The schema tells us what to expect in the future as the events guided by the schema unfold. Second, the schema may have a corrective component, and this means that the knowledge of the schema may help us get back on track if some nonschematic event occurs to derail us from the schema.

Implications for Other Areas of Psychology   Until this point, the constructivist position has been described as though it were relevant only to the problem of interpreting information that is primarily visual. The constructivist argument is in reality far broader than that. This section provides a brief account of the ways in which the constructivist view of perception has affected other areas of psychology. The objective here is to show that the processes of **feature abstraction** and prototype formation are omnipresent aspects of our mental lives. These processes influence our knowledge of other people as well as our self-knowledge.

As Fiske and Taylor (1984) have pointed out, the concept of the schema has been fruitfully applied to social psychology, wherein the term denotes organized generic prior knowledge that enables us to function in a social world that would otherwise be of paralyzing complexity (Fiske & Taylor, 1984, p. 149). In other words, varieties of schemata allow us to organize incoming information about our social world in an efficient way. *Social cognition* describes this particular type of cognitive activity in which the psychological question of knowledge in human relationships is treated from the standpoint of the information-processing model. Table 3.1 shows several types of schemata that have been postulated as guides of human social interactions. For example, the **self-schema** is a complex cognitive structure into which information about the self is accepted and organized. As Markus (1977) has demonstrated, almost everyone is *schematic* regarding certain personal qualities, meaning that one's self is defined as possessing certain qualities, and information about these qualities presented by the world will be attended to.

·············   **TABLE 3.1**   Types of Schemata in Social Cognition

A schema is a cognitive structure that contains knowledge about the attributes of a concept and the relationships among those attributes. All types of schemata guide perception, memory, and inference in similar ways, toward schema-relevant information, and often toward schema-consistent information. Disconfirming or incongruent information requires more effort to process than congruent information; if that effort is made, it may be well remembered.

Person schemata: People's understanding of the psychology of typical or specific individuals, composed of traits and goals, helps them to categorize others and to remember schema-relevant behavior.

Self-schemata: General information about one's own psychology makes up a complex, easily accessible, verbal self-concept that guides information processing about the self.

Role schemata: Intergroup perception and stereotyping are affected by role schemata that describe the appropriate norms and behavior for broad social categories, based on age, race, sex, and occupation.

Event schemata: People's prior knowledge of the typical sequence of events on standard social occasions helps them to understand ambiguous information, to remember relevant information, and to infer consistent information where it is missing.

Content-free, or *procedural, social schemata:* A rather different kind of social schema consists entirely of rules for linking content but not much content; it guides information processing toward schema-relevant information.

Source: Fiske & Taylor, 1984. From *Social Cognition* by Susan T. Fiske & Shelley E. Taylor. Copyright © 1984 by McGraw-Hill, Inc. Reprinted by permission of the publisher and author.

In that regard, schematic qualities are those that people have decided are important about themselves. Suppose, for example, I regard myself as frugal. Assuming that this is one of my schematic qualities means that I will pay attention to how others describe my actions in financial matters, and I will likely respond if someone tries to assert that I am a spendthrift. In contrast with schematic qualities, the self has many other potential characteristics about which we care little and, consequently, to which we pay little attention. On these dimensions of the self, we are *aschematic*. If asked whether I am political, I may not know how to respond; I don't think of myself in those terms. Consequently, I'm not inclined to think of this characteristic of myself as very important.

The possession of schematic qualities exerts a predictable effect on certain self-judgments. Bargh (1982) presented his subjects with a variety of adjectives; the subjects were told to respond, as quickly as possible, whether or not the adjectives were true about them. Subjects who were schematic on independence (referred to as independence schematics) responded quickly—almost automatically—to adjectives related to independence. However, they did not respond quickly to adjectives related to dependence. Independence aschematics, on the other hand, did not respond quickly to adjectives related to independence or dependence. Being schematic on a particular dimension confers an advantage to the person who is that way, because it allows that person to rapidly process particular kinds of information. Highly schematized individuals (those who are schematic on many dimensions and who consequently have a highly differentiated sense of self) might fare better in social situations than less schematized individuals, simply because they are more able to organize incoming information about the social setting. Thus, highly schematized individuals are more likely to know where they stand in a group.

Other evidence (Markus & Sentis, 1982) has suggested that people use their self-schemata to evaluate the characteristics and behavior of others. That is, we interpret the characteristics of others according to characteristics that we believe we possess. This finding has at least two implications. First, a person who is schematic on a given dimension tends to group what appear to be isolated behaviors on the part of others into some coherent (schema-relevant) characteristic. Thus, if we imagine a person for whom body weight is a highly schematic dimension, then we would predict that such a person would group the idiosyncratic actions of others into a larger, schema-relevant picture. If the weight schematic observes another person having dry toast and grapefruit for breakfast and plain yogurt and fruit for lunch, swimming laps in the pool that afternoon, and drinking Perrier at a party that evening, then the weight schematic might assume that the other person is engaged in exercise and avoidance of high-calorie foods and beverages because the other person is dieting. Someone who was weight aschematic would not be inclined to link together all of these separate actions (Fong & Markus, 1982). However, someone who was weight aschematic but who *was* schematic on some other dimension might notice all the actions but assemble them into a different picture. Suppose a woman, having discovered she is pregnant with her first child, becomes quite concerned with nutrition and exercise. If the person whose behavior just described was a woman, the pregnant woman would assume that the person described was also pregnant.

The second implication is based on the origin of the self-schema. As we saw earlier, the prototype is apparently produced by abstracting the distinctive features from a set of stimuli. The self-schema is formed similarly. From the barrage of comments that are directed toward us and from those comments directed toward others that we overhear, we abstract those terms that are used in relation to us, either much more or much less frequently than they are used in relation to others. For example, we probably wouldn't abstract and build into our self-schemata the term *sloppy* unless we heard our actions described that way substantially more often than we heard the behavior of others described that way. Such terms denote characteristics that are thought by others to be distinctive features of our personality. As you are probably aware, this means that the abstraction and assignment of distinctive personality characteristics is highly dependent on the context in which such abstraction occurs.

Consider the case of a child who is told by others that he is bright. That kind of message is not given out randomly. To be described that way, the child must behave in some ways that are not characteristic of his peers. Under what sort of contexts are such performances likely? For the child who is able to do bright things against a background of normal children, such actions are distinctive and will be labeled so. If the development of the self-schema goes as expected, such a child would likely come to consider himself as being smart. However, if the same performances occur against a background of children who are all bright (i.e., capable of similar behaviors), then the child's actions would not be distinctive and the child would probably not be told that he is bright. Children raised under such circumstances would probably not incorporate the term *intelligent* into their self-schemata, even though in some objective sense they might be just as bright as the people who do regard themselves as intelligent.

Because the self-schema is so heavily dependent on context, using the self-schema as a predictor of one's actual personality is terribly problematic (Fiske & Taylor, 1984). As discussed previously, someone might be aschematic on some trait that is true about that person. Similarly, an individual might be schematic on some traits that are not accurate descriptions about her. People of moderate intellectual ability might think of themselves as bright if they were raised against a background of relatively low intellectual achievement. This means that no inherently obvious relationship exists between self-schemata and our "true" personality. Most people think they know themselves. But the research on self-schemata suggests that there is no necessary correlation between being schematic on a particular dimension and being correct about its authenticity as a component of one's personality (Fiske & Taylor, 1984).

According to the constructivist argument, the self-schema is a product of the same perceptual mechanisms that generate the rest of our mental lives. Consequently, to the extent that these other aspects of our mental lives are fabrications produced by our experiences, to that extent the self-schema is similarly fabricated. This type of reasoning is in opposition to traditional personality theories whose general objective is to uncover some enduring and stable characteristics of individuals that exist despite the apparent randomness of their behavior. Nevertheless, the cognitive standpoint on personality maintains that traditional approaches are not likely to bear fruit, because they overlook the fact that our dispositions are not necessarily anchored on reality, no matter how strongly we believe that to be the case.

Summary and Evaluation of the Constructivist Position

The constructivist position emphasizes the role of cognition in perception. That is, perception is thought to consist of a series of operations, beginning with a transformation of physical energy. The constructivist viewpoint takes a strong position with regard to the role played by the central nervous system in perception. Essentially, constructivists argue that perception would not be possible without the extensive computations performed by our brains. In other words, the position assumes that the events that are out there in the world aren't very informative *by themselves*. The various kinds of perception that we do (categorizing, for example—being a kind of perception) are possible only because the brain adds some information to these stimuli.

In the position's strongest sense, the stimuli truly become informative only *after* the central nervous system has added its own processing into the recipe. In that sense, the categories we perceive as being out there in the world aren't necessarily out there. This means that the categories we perceive as being real tell us far more about how our brains work than they do about the factual nature of the world. In this sense, too, the constructivist position strongly implies that our awareness of the world is not necessarily accurate. The stimuli in the world are inherently ambiguous and could be organized in any number of possible ways by the brain, with the result that how we look at the world and what we recognize would be markedly different. Awareness might be understood as a representation of worldly events, but it is almost certainly not a copy of them. According to the constructivists, learning plays an extremely important role in perception. Through our experiences with the world, large, well-organized units of knowledge, called prototypes and schemata, are abstracted and assembled on the basis of distinctive features. Once assembled, these units of knowledge channel subsequent information processing; that is, their influence is top-down. If correct, the constructivist view of perception has strong implications for the areas of social psychology and personality theory.

It's possible to criticize the constructivist account on several grounds. The beginning of the chapter described the historical problem of the Höffding step and stated that the constructivist position tried to take this problem head-on by specifying how sensation was converted into perception. When I say that I perceive something, I'm really saying something about the contents of my mind. For example, if I tell you that I see my tennis racquet in the corner of the room, this is not true, strictly speaking. I can't "see" my tennis racquet because my retinae, which do the seeing, don't know anything about tennis racquets. At some point in time, presumably after my retinae did their work, other aspects of my cognitive system categorized the stimulus as a tennis racquet, and only then did these perceptual processes produce the term *tennis racquet* that finally entered my awareness as their output. The contents of my mind, then, seem to consist of categories into which stimuli can or cannot be fitted. The question for the constructivists is to specify how these contents got there in the first place. Saying that I abstracted the features of the tennis racquet and compared the abstracted list with a prototypical racquet won't do. After all, how many features does a tennis racquet have? Before I ever saw a tennis racquet, how did I know which features to abstract so that I'd be able to mentally build a prototype of one?

A second objection to the constructivist argument is grounded in evolutionary theory. The physical structures of animals and their actions often show adaptation to changing environmental circumstances. What advantage is conferred on an animal that constructs its world rather than responds to the real world?

Although being able to perceive the world in a variety of ways is useful, it's reasonable to assume that being firmly anchored in the real world is generally *more* useful. Because our awareness of events and people is only one way of representing those things, and not necessarily the most faithful way either, the constructivist position implies that we may be divorced from the reality of the world in a fundamental way.

A related problem is that the constructivist approach to perception doesn't deal well with some basic empirical findings. For example, if I look at a book sitting on my desk, it's obvious to me that the book and the desk are two separate things. I can focus on the book, and the other objects in my visual field become the background against which the book is seen. Alternatively, I can turn the relationship around by focusing on the desk and letting the book recede into the background. The ability to make figure-ground distinctions of this sort does not seem to require any extensive experience with the world. This was shown in early experiments with congenitally blind individuals whose cataracts were removed during their adult years (von Senden, 1960). For the constructivists, the problem is to specify how events that are very close to one another in the retinal code become so distinct from one another in our awareness even when previous experience with the stimuli is ruled out as an explanation. Without elaborating this too much, a corresponding problem also exists. Sometimes events that are not nearby one another at the retinal level are nevertheless grouped together in our awareness.

For these and other reasons, not all cognitive psychologists have accepted the constructivist argument in its strictest sense. Some have moved to a modified constructivist position, and others have shifted to viewpoints that are radically different from the constructivist account. Some cognitive psychologists have disagreed with the fundamental belief of the constructivists, namely that physical energy in the world is inherently ambiguous. In other words, these cognitive psychologists have emphasized the basis from which feature abstraction takes place, rather than emphasize the process of abstraction itself. The next section describes such a viewpoint.

DIRECT THEORIES OF PERCEPTION

The direct approach to the problem of visual perception is typically associated with its originator, J. J. Gibson. Gibson's work is based on one central thesis: The light that strikes our retinae is highly organized and informative as is, and doesn't require extensive interpretation and elaboration by the central nervous system in order for it to become meaningful (Gibson, 1966, 1979). Our sensory systems are well-matched with information that the environment offers us. Rather than discuss any sort of fundamental separation between awareness and reality, Gibson believes that, because our sensory systems have developed to pick up information as it is from the environment, our awareness is not particularly tricky.

The Ecological Approach to Visual Perception

During World War II, Gibson worked as an officer in the Army Air Corps. One of his duties was to develop training films depicting the problems in taking off, landing, and navigating aircraft (Reed & Jones, 1982). Gibson quickly realized that what was known about such matters was inadequate for training purposes. He began to investigate the nature of the information that was available to the pilot, hoping that his investigation might prove useful in making teaching materials.

Consider the display in Figure 3.6 (*a* and *b*). What do the placement and length of the arrows tell you about the way these scenes might look to a pilot?

FIGURE 3.6
. . . .
Radial expansion
patterns: *a,* retinal
motion perspective
looking ahead;
b, retinal motion of
gradients during a
landing glide.

(From Reed & Jones,
1982. Copyright 1982 by
the Lawrence Erlbaum
Associates, Inc. Publishers.
Adapted by permission of
the publisher and author.)

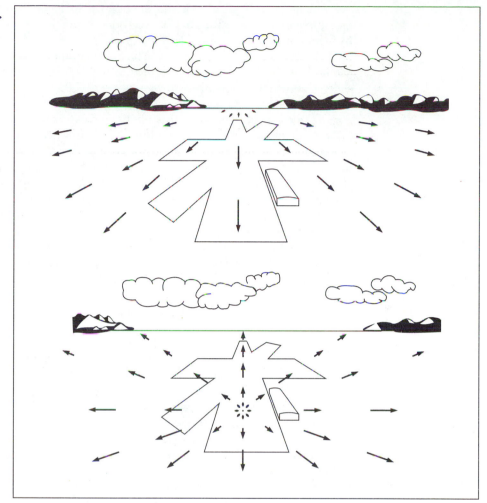

According to Gibson, the arrows are a way of showing how information in the world unfolds to the eyes of a pilot in a moving plane. Specifically, information seems to emanate, or emerge, from the point toward which we are moving. In Figure 3.6 (*a*), if we focus our eyes on the imaginary spot from which the arrows seem to be emerging and imagine that the arrows are actually moving past us, then we might get some idea of what Gibson was driving at. The arrows are short near the point of emergence, indicating that, as faraway objects come into view, their apparent motion toward us is at first slow. The arrows are progressively longer near the bottom of the scene.

This phenomenon corresponds to another we're familiar with. As we move toward objects, they seem to rush at us faster and faster until they become a blur as we finally move past them. If we were to keep track of the time involved in an object's emergence from the center of expansion at the top of the scene until its apparent disappearance at the bottom of the scene, then we would know something about own our velocity. That is, the shorter the time required for that process, the faster our velocity. Notice also that the information seems to expand radially outward from the point toward which one is moving. In Figure 3.6 (*a*), this fact tells us that we're moving toward the horizon and, consequently, horizontal to the earth's plane.

Contrast this view with the one shown in Figure 3.6 *(b)*. Here we see a radial expansion pattern similar to the one depicted in Figure 3.6 *(a)*. However, in Figure 3.6 *(b)*, the center of the expansion is not at the horizon but rather is located near the end of the runway. The arrows pointing back to the horizon don't get progressively longer as they approach the top of the scene; indeed, they get shorter and shorter. But the arrows pointing to the bottom of the scene do get longer and longer as they approach the bottom.

To get an idea of what this phenomenon means, imagine that you are a pilot, bringing in a plane for a landing on this runway. As you approach the point of contact with the runway, the bottom of the runway will appear to stretch out under you as you get closer and closer. Moreover, the rate of such apparent stretching will increase as you get closer to the runway. The top of the runway will appear to be stretching, too, but it will be stretching away from you, toward the horizon. Its rate of stretching will get slower and slower as you come in to land. Taken together, the arrows at the top and bottom of the runway are intended to show a pattern of emergent information that the pilot could use to gauge the rate and slope of descent during a landing attempt.

The arrows are simply a convenience but nevertheless indicate something important. As we move through the world, the visual field changes in highly predictable ways. At different points in time, as we move through space, some aspects of the visual array will change, while others will not. The aspects of the visual array that don't change are sometimes called its **invariant features.** For example, one of the invariant features of the visual array is the fact that the center of expansion is always the point toward which we're moving. This pattern of changing and invariant features of the visual array is referred to as the **optical flow pattern.** Optical flow patterns provide pilots with information about their direction, velocity, and altitude. But even those of us who are earthbound can use such patterns in navigation, as Figure 3.7 shows. Notice here that the pattern of radial expansion can still be observed even though terrestrial movement is in two rather than in three dimensions.

Also important is realizing that these patterns of change and invariance pointed out by Gibson were believed to be truly available to anybody who took the time to look for them. In other words, these invariances were not added in by the central nervous system, or inferred by our cognitive system on the basis of our experiences in the world. Instead, Gibson maintained that such invariances were truly seeable and seen. Gibson believed that the optical flow pattern was simply one type of invariance that was present in the world and immediately available to the perceiver. He also maintained that other sorts of invariances were similarly available. He called these **higher-order invariances** (i.e., the optical flow pattern is one type of higher-order invariance). Determining exactly how many higher-order invariances there are is impossible, although Gibson did describe various other kinds. For example, in Figure 3.8, the apparent distance between the successive ridges of the windblown sand decreases close to the horizon. Moreover, the detail in the drawing diminishes as you move your eyes from the bottom of the page to the top. The drawing seems to possess depth because it has retained elements of the world that are useful in judging depth. Gibson referred to such an invariance as a **texture gradient.** Certain details of the surface on which we stand diminish and become indistinct as their distance from us increases, and because the loss of clarity is progressive and orderly, we can use such facts about the surface to make judgments about depth and space. What is invariant about texture gradients is the fact that all surfaces display them. You can test the reality of this assertion for yourself using Figure 3.8. You most likely recognized right

FIGURE 3.7
....
The flow of the environment as seen from a car speeding across a bridge toward point A. The flow (shown by the arrows) is more rapid closer to the car (as indicated by the increased blur) but occurs everywhere except point A, the point toward which the car is moving.

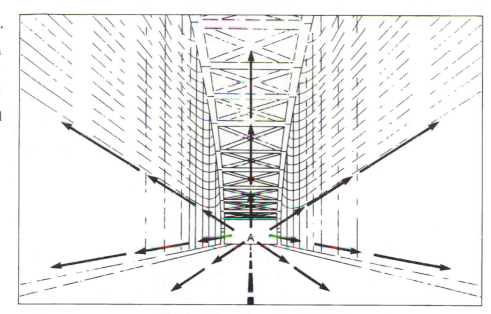

FIGURE 3.8
....
A texture gradient made up of ridges in the sand. If viewed from above, the distance between each sand ridge appears approximately equal; however, when viewed from the ground, the ridges appear to be spaced closer and closer together as distance increases.

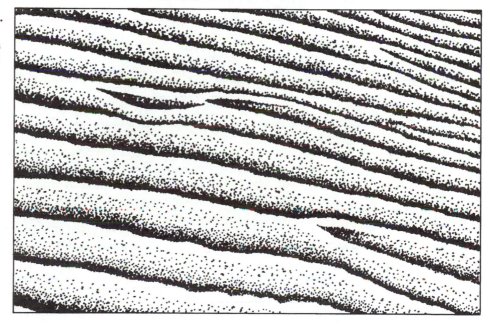

away what was depicted in the drawing because, in part, the texture gradient that was visible on the earth's surface when the drawing was made is still visible. But you can easily destroy the texture gradient by simply inverting the book. The drawing won't look like an upside-down desert but instead may look like an abstract painting of wavy lines. This effect means that the texture gradient is not a property of the drawing but rather a characteristic of the earth's surface. Consequently, as you move over the earth's surface, a continual presentation of information tells you about depth, that is, the distance between you and other objects or points on the surface. Like the information presented by the optical flow pattern, the information in the texture gradient is truly visible to the observer, rather than being constructed by the observer's brain.

In the 1950s, Gibson developed the notions of the texture gradient and optical flow pattern to counter the traditional idea that the product of retinal processing—the so-called **retinal image**—was inadequate by itself to produce perception. His attack focused on the retinal image, whose adequacy or inadequacy Gibson thought was irrelevant. He argued that, because we don't see retinal images anyway, debates about their functions weren't going to lead anywhere. Instead, Gibson maintained that the basis of visual perception was not the retinal image but rather a set of invariants such as those outlined previously. In so doing, Gibson completely reformulated the problem of perception (Mace, 1974, 1977). Whereas earlier, the problem of perception had consisted of specifying the cognitive mechanisms by which we process the inadequate stimulus, now the problem involved the development of a theory that specified, or described, all of the information that was already present in the visual array. Processing mechanisms were consequently de-emphasized.

Gibson's theory, therefore, is *not* an account of how retinal images are spruced up by the brain so they can become the basis of perception. Instead, his theory deals with accurately describing the pattern of information that is present in the world and directly available to the perceiver (Neisser, 1976). Perhaps you can now see why Gibson's theory is called a "direct" theory of perception. The perceiver is in direct contact with the real world. He is considered to be on intimate terms with the visual information in the world, rather than being separated or isolated from this information by several stages of cognitive processing. Rather, the information in the light is simply given to the perceiver (Gibson, 1960).

For Gibson's account to be correct, the light that strikes our retinae must be truly informative and complete; it cannot be chaotic or unorderly. This point leads to a question. Gibson assumes that the light that strikes our eyes is highly organized and well-structured. How did the light acquire this organization? Gibson's answer is straightforward. The light that strikes our eyes has been reflected from objects on the ground, and the light carries information from these objects. In other words, the light is altered as it is reflected from objects. Some aspects of this alteration (i.e., changes in intensity and wavelength of the light) had long been known. However, Gibson believed that the nature of the alteration was more extensive than that. Because the objects on the ground were themselves organized and well-structured, and because the reflection of light was also orderly, then the light took on the organization of the properties of the objects from which it had been reflected.

To direct theorists, this answer meant that the role of learning in perception should be de-emphasized. According to them, we don't have to learn how to interpret the ambiguous information in the environment, because the information isn't ambiguous. Gibson's theory does not completely rule out the usefulness of experience in perception, but he and other direct theorists differ sharply from the constructivists in their beliefs about the role of experience. Whereas constructivist theory argues that the perceiver must learn how to see objects in the world by learning how to interpret retinal images, direct theorists maintain that the perceiver learns how the higher-order invariants are produced by motion through the world. In particular, such motion produces knowledge of the texture of geometrical surfaces such as edges, corners, convexities, and concavities (Gibson, 1960). This knowledge of geometrical shapes was referred to by Gibson as the **layout of perceivable space.**

All perceivable spaces had layouts, and knowledge of them was enhanced by attempts to move through them. This principle enabled Gibson to answer some of the criticism aimed at his theory for its apparent position on illusions. According to constructivist criticism, Gibson's theory could not explain illusions. If the perceiver is assumed to be in direct contact with the information in the light that is given, then why is the perceiver sometimes mistaken about that information? Why do we fall prey to illusions? The direct response to this criticism has two parts. First, Gibson notes that most illusions are static displays of information. However, the perceptual systems of most animals are designed to pick up visual information by movement through the world. Gibson argues that we shouldn't be too surprised if the invariants we usually detect are not picked up in this static and therefore artificial situation. In other situations, a person may misperceive because she has not yet learned to extract the invariants that specify the layout (Gibson, 1977). The information that is directly available to us is always in potential, but not necessarily actual, form. The person who approaches a glass door and, thinking it's open, tries to go through it may be doing a good job of perceiving some of the invariants of texture and optical flow. However, some of the other aspects of the layout, such as the highlights in the glass or dust on its surface, must also be detected if the collision is to be avoided.

To summarize, the **ecological approach to visual perception** is concerned with specifying the layout of perceivable space, with an emphasis on the word *layout*. Gibson's theory is not about the perception of space per se but rather how light is organized by its reflections from surface and objects on the ground.

What the Environment Affords Us

Gibson developed the notion of the **affordance** in an attempt to further specify the properties of the environment that are present in reflected light. An affordance of anything is a specific combination of the properties of its substance and its surfaces taken with reference to an animal (Gibson, 1977, 1979). Note that the definition refers to a combination of properties. Most objects, because they have a variety of properties that can be combined in a variety of ways, will also have a variety of affordances. Also, the affordance is uniquely related to the animal being considered (Gibson, 1977). For example, my cocktail table has a number of affordances. It affords support, its glass top affords transparency, and its chrome legs afford reflectance. Some of the affordances are related to particular animals. For me, the cocktail table has the affordance of color, but it doesn't have this affordance for my cat. On the other hand, the surface of the cocktail table affords walking for my cat but not for me.

Table 3.2 is a listing of affordances that Gibson (1976) described in a talk given to a meeting of architects. Some of the items in this listing provide a clue for getting a more intuitive understanding of the affordance. We might say that an affordance is a bundle of properties about some specific object that provides us with an opportunity to perceive something specific or to move through the world in a specific way. An affordance, then, is an opportunity to see something or to move in a characteristic way.

Saying that affordances are related to the perceptual system of an animal implies that the nature of an animal's awareness is highly dependent upon the matchup that is achieved between its sensory apparatus and the information available to be picked up. From all the invariants offered by reflected light, our sensory apparatus has become, over time, tuned to accept certain invariants but not others. The accepted invariants are the affordances. Because our sensory apparatus is unique, Gibson's theory raises the possibility that some affordances are uniquely human. To the extent that we are aware of these affordances, we can

·············· **TABLE 3.2**   Some Natural and Artificial Affordances

1. A solid horizontal surface affords *support*. A water surface does not.
   —A surface of support affords *resting* (coming to rest).

2. An extended surface of support affords *locomotion*, for a terrestrial animal.

3. A *vertical* solid surface stops locomotion and affords *mechanical contact*. It is a *barrier*.
   —A rigid barrier surface affords injury by abrupt contacts, i.e., collision. It is an *obstacle*. Deceleration is necessary to achieve contact without collision.
   —A *nonrigid* barrier surface can avert injury by collision.

4. A vertical *double surface*, that is, a wall or screen, affords *hiding behind*, that is, being out of sight of observers on the other side. This is true if the double surface is *opaque*.

5. A double surface at sufficient height above the ground affords *getting under*. It is a *roof*.

6. Any layout of surfaces that encloses an appropriate volume of air affords *shelter* (from the wind, cold, rain, snow). A cave, burrow, or hut.
   —An enclosure affords being out of sight of observers in all directions ("privacy") and thus it affords protection from predators. (All animals sometimes need to *hide*.)

7. An aperture or gap in an enclosure affords *entry* and *exit*.
   —It also affords *vision* within the enclosure by admitting illumination (sunlight).
   —It also affords *looking through* (both looking *out* and looking *in*).
   —It also affords long-term *respiration* (breathing fresh air).
   —Note that all the complexities of doors, windows, shutters, grilles, and panes of glass, etc. get their utilities from these basic affordances (e.g., the misperception of a glass door is a real danger in modern buildings).

8. A horizontal surface at about knee height above the surface of support affords sitting, a *seat*.

9. A horizontal surface at about *waist height* above the ground affords support for objects and facilitates manipulation of objects, e.g., tools, and materials for writing and reading, a workbench, desk, table.

10. A large drop-off in the surface of support affords injury by falling off, a "brink." But a railing affords protection from falling off (like a fence, which is a barrier to locomotion).
    — A *small* drop-off in the surface of support affords stepping down without injury.
    — A series of "steps" in a *stairway* affords ascent or descent of a cliff by a pedestrian.
    — A *ladder* affords ascent or descent.
    — A *ramp* affords a different mode of ascent or descent.

Source: From Gibson, 1976. (Copyright 1982 by the Lawrence Erlbaum Associates, Inc. Publishers. Reprinted by permission of the publisher and author.)

describe our mental lives as being channeled or, more accurately, canalized by our sensory system. Saying that our mental lives are canalized means that, to a certain extent, the content of our minds is influenced and bounded by the nature of our perceptual systems (Turvey & Shaw, 1979).

Some evidence supports the idea of unique human affordances and hence the **canalization** of mentality. As you may know, a substantial body of literature demonstrates the universality of human facial expressions (Izard, 1971). Despite the variations in milieu, facial expressions are produced in similar ways, and photographs of them can be accurately recognized by people of different cultures. Bassili (1978) investigated this phenomenon using a somewhat unusual approach. Tiny lights were attached to the faces of professional actors who were instructed to portray certain emotions. These portrayals took place in a darkened room so that only the lights were visible. The resulting patterns of light movements were filmed, and subjects watching the films had no difficulty in correctly categorizing the expressions even though the actor's face was not visible.

A similar approach was used by Cutting and his colleagues (Barclay, Cutting & Kozlowski, 1978; Cutting & Kozlowski, 1977; Cutting, Proffit & Kozlowski, 1978). In these studies, lights were attached to various joints and body parts of a subject, who was then invited to walk through a darkened room. The pattern of light movement was once again filmed. Although individual slides and line tracings (similar to the pattern of lines created by head- and taillights of cars in a long-exposure photograph) were not recognizable to people viewing them, if the entire pattern was seen, it was recognizable. People were highly capable of classifying the pattern of movement as being produced by a walking person. Viewers also were able to accurately categorize the walkers as men or as women. They were even able to recognize the distinctive gaits of their friends.

Such studies exemplify the spirit of Gibson's work. Perceptual systems are designed to extract information from objects as those objects move about in the world, or from the nature of the changes in the world as we move through it. The human perceptual system appears to be particularly tuned in to certain kinds of motion, probably because the recognition of these motions is adaptive.

Evaluation of the Direct Theory

Perhaps Gibson's greatest contribution is that his work produced a radical departure in what psychologists thought of as the stimulus for visual perception. Prior to Gibson, psychologists had contented themselves with the description of retinal images, but now some consensus exists that the light reflected from objects must be organized in some way. Second, Gibson demonstrated that depth perception does not seem to require elaborate processing by the central nervous system. Instead, Gibson argues that depth can be picked up directly by a perceptual system that moves. Although Gibson's work has gained some currency among cognitive psychologists, this result is paradoxical because the theory is *not* cognitive. Gibson downplayed the role of information processing in perception, and he similarly de-emphasized physiological accounts of the brain's role in perception. From Gibson's perspective, the historical problem of the Höffding step simply fades away. Sensory neural events don't have to be converted into perceptual neural events, because perception is direct. The same neural machinery responsible for sensation also subserves perception.

Despite these solutions, some problems remain with Gibson's account. First, Gibson did not use the established vocabulary among psychologists of his era. Because he thought the standard vocabulary was incorrect, he decided to develop his own terminology. However, this special terminology makes his work hard to understand. More than one psychologist has made an earnest effort to come to grips with Gibson's work, only to wind up being somewhat baffled by it.

In addition, the empirical support for Gibson's theory is mixed. The findings of some studies seem to support Gibson's conclusions, while other findings tend to refute them. For example, a study by Larish and Flach (1990) supports the Gibsonian perspective. Their subjects viewed one of the two types of displays shown in Figure 3.9.

These patterns were presented to the subjects on a computer screen. In both cases, the display was animated by moving the elements of the display, either the grid texture or the dots, from the top of the screen to the bottom, thus suggesting that the observer was flying over the area depicted in the display. The subjects were instructed to make an estimate of their apparent speed. Before talking about the findings, let's analyze the two displays. In the grid display (*a*), the subject has an opportunity to see the horizontal lines move down the screen and then out of sight. If we were to fix our gaze at a particular point on the side of the display, we might be able to use the rate at which the horizontal lines seem to pass this point as a rough indication of our speed. It seems that humans do use this sort of "edge

FIGURE 3.9
. . . .
a: Grid texture display representative of those used in Experiment 1.
b: Dot texture display representative of those used in Experiment 1.

(Copyright 1990 by the American Psychological Association. Adapted by permission of the publisher and author.)

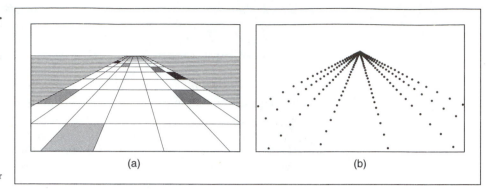

(a)   (b)

rate" information in calculating their velocity in a number of situations. For example, Denton (1980) experimented with putting pavement stripes at closer and closer intervals as the distance to a traffic signal decreased. To the person in a car approaching these stripes, apparent edge rate increases (because progressively more of the stripes seemed to be going past the fixed reference point of the car). Denton (1980) found that drivers reduced their speed considerably more when they approached traffic circles equipped with such pavement stripes, compared with when the pavement was not equipped with them. Now consider the second of Larish and Flach's two displays, the dots-only display (b). As you can see, there are no edges here; consequently, the subject cannot base a speed estimate on edge counting, but must base the speed estimate on some sense of optical flow, as the dots emerge from the top of the screen and fan out toward the bottom. We might predict, then, that if subjects require some sort of computation to make an estimate of speed (as the constructivist view would have it) then the subjects' perception of speed would be influenced by changes in the edge rate, as generated by the computer. If, on the other hand, optical flow is enough to produce a sensation of speed, then the subjects' perception of speed should be relatively uninfluenced by the nature of the display, whether it consists of a texture grid or just dots. Larish and Flach (1990) found that subjects were influenced by changes in the edge rate: The faster the horizontal lines moved past a fixed point on the screen, the higher the subjects rated their speed, suggesting that subjects do engage in a kind of edge counting. However, there were no differences in this effect between the two displays. Subjects were just as likely to increase their ratings of speed when the dot pattern's motion was increased as when the texture grid's motion was increased. This finding is consistent with Gibson's position: He maintained that texture gradients and optical flow patterns are present on every surface and that they're all we need to perceive speed and direction.

On the other hand, a study by Toye (1986) does not support the Gibsonian position. His subjects viewed a set of thirteen metal stakes situated around a 70-ft circular stimulus area. The subjects had several tasks, including judging the distance between all seventy-two possible pairs of the thirteen stakes, and drawing a map of the array. All subjects completed these tasks twice. Half of the subjects made both sets of judgments from the same position; the other half made their second set of judgments after moving 90 degrees to a new spot on the field. Let's consider what's involved in making such estimates. From any point on the periphery, some of the stakes appear to be "beside" one another, and not so much behind or in front of each other. That is, the stakes are in the same depth plane but are in different locations in the breadth plane. Other stakes appear to be in front of or behind other stakes. Such stakes are in the same breadth plane but are in different depth planes. According to the constructivists, the neural computations that produce depth are of a different class altogether than those that are responsible for height and breadth in the visual field—the latter dimensions may be computed from retinal locus. What happens as a viewer moves 90 degrees around the periphery of a scene? What was the breadth plane becomes the depth plane, and vice versa. The constructivist might predict, therefore, that, because the neural machinery is different in each of these cases, the scene should look different to a viewer who moves to a new spot. However, the direct view maintains just the opposite: Because the invariant affordances should be common to all scenes, making judgments about the scene should not be influenced by movement around the periphery, only by movement through the array (none of the subjects were permitted to do that however). However, Toye's findings, which are shown in Table 3.3, indicate that, contrary to the Gibsonian position, subjects who made a second set of judgments after moving around the periphery were influenced significantly by this movement to a new vantage point. Notice that the subjects who move tend to reduce their estimates of the distances that were in the breadth plane and are now in the depth, or radial, plane. Such distances appear foreshortened to us, and the constructivist position argues that the foreshortening is the result of difficulties in computing distances in the depth plane. The Gibsonian argument however states that, because the texture gradient is equally available from any position around the edge of the flat grassy field, and because, theoretically, it is such gradients that are used in making judgments of depth, the subjects should not have been influenced by their movement. Thus, the changes in the subjects' perceptions tend to support the constructivist, rather than the direct, viewpoint.

Although Gibson said that texture gradients are present at all times, in some situations they have been difficult to locate empirically (Goldstein, 1984). Also, Gibson's work is essentially a **sufficiency analysis.** This term refers to an analysis that shows how something *could* be accomplished, but not how it necessarily *is* accomplished. This means that, while texture gradients and optical flow may be available to the perceiver, it is another matter altogether to show that these invariants are really what the perceiver uses in moving. Similarly, the direct theory postulates that depth is directly visible through motion, but this doesn't deal adequately with the fact that depth is not lost when we are motionless. A good deal of consensus exists among cognitive psychologists that Gibson under-

·············   **TABLE 3.3**   **Difference Between Subjective Distance Estimates Across Replication for 35 Interobject Distances**

CONDITION	ABSOLUTE DISTANCE JUDGMENTS	RELATIVE DISTANCE JUDGMENTS*	MAP DRAWINGS
No position shift	−34.14 cm (−1.12 ft)	−0.08	1.94 mm
Position shift	−245.36 cm (−8.05 ft)	−0.91	−12.94 mm

Source: Copyright 1986 by the Psychonomic Society, Inc. Adapted by permission of the publisher and author.
*Rank order difference.

Note: Each number represents a difference between judgments when the distance is horizontal and when it is radial for the position-shift group. Each number represents a difference between judgments made in replications 1 and 2 for the no-position-shift group.

USING YOUR KNOWLEDGE OF COGNITION

Can you see texture grids and optical flow patterns if you look for them? Try this exercise to see if these invariants might become more visible under some circumstances. The best place to try this is in a fairly long corridor of a building, but it should work anywhere. First, look at the ceiling directly over your head. Perhaps it's acoustic tile of some sort, and the little holes or squigley shapes are probably quite distinct. Now look at a section of the ceiling that's distant. Notice that the ceiling's surface now seems much smoother and any irregularities are hard to discern. If the ceiling is acoustic tile, the holes become impossible to see, and the tile takes on a uniform white or grey. Intermediate sections of the ceiling offer intermediate levels of detail. We observe a similar phenomenon if we look at the floor. There's definitely texture present on the surface of the ceiling and the floor. Now, begin to move forward. If there are light fixtures in the ceiling, have you noticed how they seem to advance toward you and then glide over your head? Take a look at the walls. You may find that, if the walls are made of ceramic tile, or any sort of lined material, one of the horizontal lines separating the tiles is just about at your eye level. Now, as you walk, deliberately change your "altitude" by ducking your head down a foot or so. (If people are looking at you, simply explain that you're taking a class in cognitive psychology, and this is something that students of cognition do all the time.) As you duck down, notice that now a different horizontal line is at eye level, and the previous eye level line is slanted downward. Return to your normal cruising altitude, and keep your eye on the horizontal lines as you do so. Did you observe the orderliness of the return? Now, the lower line is slanted upward. If you continue to experiment a little bit, and observe, I'm sure that you will see other regular or invariant features too. This demonstration shows us that texture and optical flow can be found on many surfaces and that information from these surfaces can be used to tell us something about direction and speed in locomotion.

rated the difficulty in detecting and using the invariants he proposed (Marr, 1982). Finally, some question has arisen concerning the role of the individual in his own perception: Learning about the layout of perceivable space must involve some sort of information processing (Heft, 1982; Heil, 1979).

 ## A SYNTHESIS

We've considered two overarching perspectives on perception, and apparently neither the constructivist nor the direct account seems complete— a result that has led some theorists to develop treatments that emphasize the positive features of both theories. This section describes one such attempt (Neisser, 1976).

Neisser considers perception a cyclical activity that can be couched in an information-processing theory. Unlike most such theories, however, which assume a definite starting and concluding point, in Neisser's model, perception is never finished because the components of the model are arranged in the form of a loop. Figure 3.10 shows the **perceptual cycle** as it is embedded in large units of knowledge shown as **cognitive maps.** According to this model, perception is indeed a constructive process. For the sake of convenience, we'll say that the process begins with certain schemata of the present world. These schemata are similar to the ones discussed earlier; they represent knowledge that has been assembled from previous experience. The schemata have an important function: They act as plans or expectations that guide subsequent information processing.

FIGURE 3.10
....
Schemata as embedded in cognitive maps.

(From *Cognition and Reality* by Ulric Neisser. Copyright 1976 W. H. Freeman and Company. Reprinted with permission.)

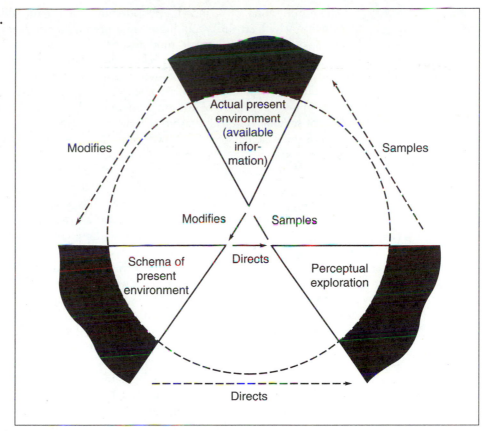

In this way, the schemata let the perceiver construct anticipations of what information is about to become available.

Exploration refers to the application of our perceptual systems, as well as any orienting movements of the head and eyes. As Figure 3.10 shows, the perceptual exploration is rooted in the larger activity of locomotion and action. This concept is consistent with Gibson's idea that the purpose of direct perception is to allow the organism to move through the world efficiently. The function of such exploration is to sample, that is, pick up information from the world. This sampling is assumed to be direct. Notice that information about the immediate object is embedded in knowledge of the actual world that is potentially available. This means that the information picked up by the perceiver can be processed in several ways or, one might say, on several levels. If the perceptual system we are using is vision, then the information we pick up directly will be optical. But because the optical information has been picked up from an object that occurs in some context in the world, we can go beyond the merely optical pickup to analyze the information in other ways. We have to keep in mind, however, that such analyses won't be direct.

The example Neisser gives concerns a person's smile. Reflected light from the person's face can be picked up directly, affording us knowledge of the color and shapes of the person's teeth and the movement of her lips (Neisser, 1976). Because smiling occurs in certain contexts, we might use the optical information to infer something about the person's mood: Is she happy or just being polite? Making such evaluations will involve the use of different perceptual cycles. That is, determinations of a mood might require calling up different anticipatory schemata, which in turn would channel different sorts of explorations. Information picked up from the world modifies the schemata in use. The two aspects of this modification are *corrective* and *elaborative*. The corrective aspect refers to the fact that information from the world can be used to infer that the wrong anticipatory schemata have been called up initially. That is, the perceiver might realize that the pickup of information might be more efficient if guided by a different schema. The elaborative aspect refers to the fact that the coherency and depth of the schema are built up with use. In this sense, the nature of the schema is similar to that of the prototype. As we saw earlier, when people are given highly variable distortions during the training period of prototype acquisition, such training seems to improve their knowledge of the prototype's boundaries (Homa, 1978; Homa & Vosburgh, 1976). Neisser has suggested that experience can produce a similar improvement in schematic knowledge.

An example might help to show how these components fit together. Before I moved to the Midwest, I didn't know that the county seats of rural areas in that part of the country were all so incredibly similar. Almost invariably, the town is built around a central square fringed with shops forming the town's principal shopping location. On the lawn of the square is a reasonably imposing courthouse, and peppered around the lawn are monuments. Without fail, one of these monuments is dedicated to the townsmen who lost their lives in the Civil War.

When my travels take me through an unfamiliar county seat, I notice that Neisser's account of my perceptual process is persuasive. First, I look around and then call up certain anticipatory schemata. (Is there a square? A courthouse?) Then I pick up information in the world that confirms these expectations and suggests others. (Where's the monument?) When I see the monument and begin to walk toward it, other schemata are brought into play. I begin to pick up information about the monument itself: its typical granite base, the weathered statue of the Civil War soldier standing on top. Even the statue is characteristic: The soldier stands ready, holding his musket with its curiously long bayonet, wearing the typical slanted cap of the period, the kepi. As I detect these aspects of the object, still other anticipatory schemata surface. I expect to see a plaque on the base of the monument that lists the names of the fallen. As I get closer and see the plaque, I expect some of the listings to conform to the naming practices of the period. That is, some of the men will have first names inspired by classical literature, such as Horace or Virgil.

So far, all my anticipations have been corroborated by my experiences in these towns. But suppose someday, in an as-yet-undiscovered town, I approach the plaque expecting to read "In honor of . . .," but instead find only the words

GENERIC
CIVIL WAR
MONUMENT

In that case, my schemes for monuments and county seats—even for the Midwest— must undergo dramatic revision. As long as my various schemata are accurate in guiding information pickup, there is no need to modify them. With new information, however, the horizon of my knowledge will be expanded. What was formerly only potential knowledge will become actual. In this case, future attempts to pick up knowledge in those situations must proceed much more cautiously. (After all, midwesterners may have introduced bogus monuments in other towns as well.)

Neisser's account of perception is an effective combination of the constructivist and direct points of view. It has a constructivist component in that the schema is a cognitive structure that guides information processing. But it also has a direct component that emphasizes that the visual array provides humans with some information with a minimum of cognitive processing. According to Neisser, each of the component accounts is incomplete because it fragments a normally fluid and ongoing activity. Perception is not a static and isolated event but rather a cyclical process.

IMAGERY

Up until this point, we've been concerned with perceptual processes that deal with stimuli that originate outside our bodies and are picked up by our sensory apparatus. But what about stimuli that don't originate there? If you drove to school today, where did you park your car? As you read the previous sentence, did a mental image pop into your head, and did the mental image show your car in one of your typical parking places? If that happened, then you're aware that the mental image seemed to have some striking visual properties. Of course, there was no actual visual experience involved in the generation of the mental image, but several questions nevertheless occur. When such a mental image is present, can we inspect it as we might a visual event arising from actual physical stimulation? And if we do try to inspect the image, does it really contain all the information that the actual physical stimulation might have? Finally, if we inspect such images, and succeed in extracting some information from them, does that mean that we are using cognitive processes that are similar to those that we use in actual visual perception (Shepard & Podgorny, 1978)? These are some of the issues that we'll address in this section.

Visual/Spatial Representation

How many ways of representing information does the cognitive and neural system have? As we'll see in later chapters, some theorists believe that the system has only one way of representing information. But other theorists argue that cognitive representations may change with the nature of the stimulation they are representing. For example, in the case of verbal material, the cognitive system may make both an acoustic (sound-based) representation, and a semantic (meaning-based) representation. In the case of visual material, some theorists maintain that our nervous system is capable of forming an **analog representation.** An analog representation is one in which the elements of the stimulus are represented by the nervous system in a way that preserves many of the relationships observed among those elements in the natural world. Think of your TV screen: As you watch a movie on TV, you can see that some characters appear to the right or to the left of other characters. Presumably, a character who appears to be standing to the right of another on TV was actually standing to the right when the movie was being filmed. The shapes on the TV screen are only electronic representations of actual people, but they are electronic representations that nevertheless have some things in common with the stimuli they depict. Basically, the analog representation is thought to have the same visual/spatial properties of the object it represents. This doesn't mean that the image of a basketball is actually a round image. But the theory does suggest that, just as an actual basketball takes up space in our visual field, so too does a mental basketball take up an analog of space in our mind's eye.

Dynamic Properties of Images

In this section we'll look at one of the implications of the analog viewpoint, namely that people seem to be able to manipulate images that they have generated and maintain in their short-term or working memory.

Shepard and Metzler (1971) presented their subjects with pairs of abstract objects such as those shown in Figure 3.11. The subjects' task was to look at the pairs and, as quickly as possible, determine whether the drawings showed two different views of the same object or two different objects. Part *a* of Figure 3.12 shows two views of the same object: The right-hand view has been rotated 80 degrees from the left-hand view. Part *b* also shows two views of the same object. In this case, the right-hand view also has been rotated 80 degrees from the left-hand view, but the nature of the rotation is different from that in part *a*. In part *a*, the circles could be cut out from the page, placed on a surface, and physically rotated until they looked identical. This is referred to as a rotation in the picture plane. Part *b* shows a rotation in depth. The left-hand view has to be turned "into the page" to get it to match the right-hand view. Part *c* shows two views of two different objects. No rotation either in the picture plane or in depth will produce a congruence. If the two views were of the same object, the subjects were to respond "same"; if the objects shown were different from one another, the subjects were to respond "different." The time it took the subjects to make correct judgments was recorded.

One question Shepard and Metzler were concerned with was the rate at which these forms could be rotated. A moment's thought reveals why. If the subjects accomplish this task by generating, holding, and "watching" one of the views rotating mentally, this mental rotation would have to proceed slowly enough to permit the subjects time to see if the two views were going to match. If the two views of the objects were drawn so that there was a greater **angular disparity** between them, let's say 120 degrees instead of 80, it should take the subjects a longer time to give the correct answer.

Figure 3.12 shows the study's findings. On trials in which the subject's correct response was "same," notice that the required time for response is linear as a function of initial angular disparity. Not only do the subjects require more time to make the correct decision as a function of angular disparity between the two views, but also the increased time is proportional to the increase in angular disparity. The subjects were apparently rotating the mental image at a fairly constant rate—about 50 to 60 degrees per second. Another remarkable fact about these data is that the slope of the line for picture plane pairs is virtually the same as that of the depth pairs. The depth pairs were no more difficult to rotate than were the picture plane pairs. From these findings, Shepard and Metzler drew yet another conclusion about the nature of the imaginal code in working memory. When subjects engage in retrieval of information from an active imaginal code, the operations they engage in appear to be analogs of perceptual operations on actual objects in the visual field. Thus the subjects almost universally reported that they did the task by watching the mental rotation of an image. But Shepard and Metzler's findings go beyond this. Their findings argue that the subjects were not simply watching an image while other, perhaps nonanalog, cognitive operations or processes were "really" doing the computations that enabled the subjects to give the answer. Instead, the findings strongly suggest that the real computa-

FIGURE 3.11
....

Samples of the three-dimensional stimulus pairs that Shepard and Metzler used in their study of mental rotation: *a*, a pair differing by an 80-degree rotation in the picture plane; *b*, a pair differing by an 80-degree rotation in the depth plane; *c*, a pair that differs by a reflection as well as by a rotation. Subjects were to respond "same" to pairs like *a* and *b*, and "different" to pairs like *c*.

(From "Mental Rotation of Three-dimensional Objects," by Shepard and Metzler. *Science* vol. 171, p. 701. Copyright 1971 by the American Association for the Advancement of Science.)

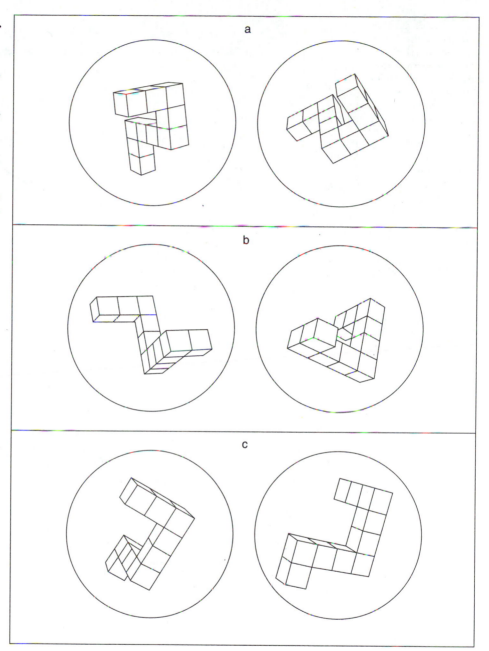

tional work was being done by the cognitive operations that rotated the images. All the subjects had to do was look at them.

This conclusion was extended in a study by Metzler (1973). One argument was that subjects in the original study were not getting the correct answer by watching a continuously rotating image. Perhaps the subjects were engaged in some other sort of computation that enabled them to get the correct answer. According to this view, the subjects required a greater amount of time to do the task when the angular disparity was greater because this task had greater computational difficulty, not because the image required more time to rotate. Metzler's (1973) study was designed to counter these criticisms.

FIGURE 3.12
....
Data from the Shepard and Metzler study of mental rotation.   They depict the mean reaction time to determine that two objects have the same three-dimensional shape as a function of the angular difference in their portrayed orientations. Notice that the slopes for these two kinds of rotation are identical.

(From "Mental Rotation of Three-dimensional Objects," by Shepard and Metzler. *Science* vol. 171, p. 702. Copyright 1971 by the American Association for the Advancement of Science.)

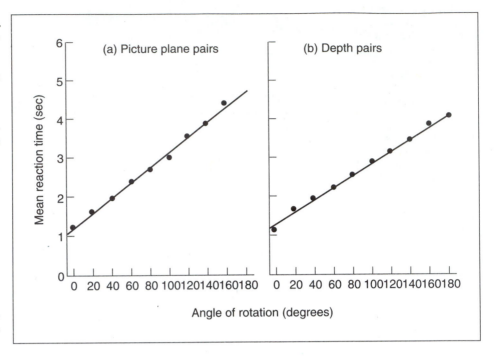

If we give subjects a series of objects to be rotated mentally and compute the average latencies for a variety of angular disparities on a subject-by-subject basis, we can determine an individual's average mental rotation velocity. For example, suppose a particular subject required three seconds more time to determine that two forms were the same when they were presented at 180 degrees difference than when they were presented with 0 degrees difference. We could then conclude that this subject was rotating the image at a rate of 180 degrees in three seconds, or 60 degrees per second.

Metzler used this information to determine the effects of the initial angular disparity on the subject's reaction time. She presented her subjects with an abstract form and instructed them to begin rotating it in a specified direction. After a time interval, Metzler presented the subjects with a second stimulus that had been rotated several degrees from the first stimulus. The subjects were told to judge whether the two stimuli were the same or different. The length of the time interval between the two presentations was determined by the degrees of rotation between the two stimuli and by the individual subject's velocity. For example, if the angular disparity between the stimuli was 180 degrees and the subject's rate of rotation was 60 degrees per second, then the stimuli were presented three seconds apart. The logic is that, if the subject is continuously rotating a mental image throughout this three-second interval, not much additional time should be required to make the judgment of "same," because the subject has already rotated the mental image to the point where it matches the second stimulus presentation fairly closely.

The stimuli's initial angular disparity had almost no effect on reaction time. That is, subjects required approximately one second to judge that the stimuli were the same regardless of whether they were initially presented with 45 degrees of angular disparity or with 270 degrees. This finding has some implications for the latencies observed by Shepard and Metzler (1971). For subjects who show consistency in speed of rotation (and not all subjects do), most of the time involved in making "same" judgments when the stimuli start out far apart is spent watching the stimulus rotate, and only about one second of the total time is spent making the "same" judgment.

These findings have since been confirmed by Cooper (1976). In this study, Metzler's procedure was again used. This time subjects were required to make judgments about irregular polygons. Like Metzler, Cooper found that the reaction time function was flat. The imagery effects we have examined are apparently not limited to the block figures used in the Shepard and Metzler studies.

Mental Rotation of Letters   We have considered the mental rotation of abstract shapes—those that have no obvious reference to real-world objects. As the literature on mental rotation accumulated, researchers began to wonder if people also were capable of rotating shapes that were meaningful to them. Such findings could be interesting. For example, familiar objects are usually meaningful. However, familiar objects acquire their familiarity in part because they usually occur in standard orientations. Consequently, meaningfulness could be a hindrance in mental rotation, especially if the subject does not know how to rotate objects that typically occur in some standard orientation. Finding that meaningfulness was a hindrance to mental rotation may be an embarrassment to analog theorists. After all, if the subject is doing the imagery tasks by generating and watching an imaginal code, the subject should not have to know (in advance) what the object looks like upside down in order to carry out the task. The subject should simply be able to rotate the analog and inspect it.

Like Shepard and Metzler (1971), Cooper and Shepard (1973) argued that most of the time spent in making "same" judgments was taken up with rotating the mental image. They wondered if the preparation time could be reduced by supplying the subjects with certain kinds of information before they rotated the image. Three letters (R, J, and G) and three digits (2, 5, and 7) were used in their study. The stimuli appeared in one of two ways: normal or mirror image reversal. The stimuli were presented in one of six orientations: upright or 60, 120, 240, or 300 degrees from upright.

Part *a* of Figure 3.13 shows how R might be presented. The subjects' task was to determine if a stimulus had been presented in the normal or mirror-image format. To accomplish this task, the subject would apparently have to rotate the letter to its upright orientation and then analyze its features. The farther away from upright that the letter was presented, presumably the longer the subject's reaction time. This expectation was confirmed. As Part *b* of Figure 3.13 shows, subjects in the "no information" condition required the greatest amount of time to make the "same" or mirror-image judgment when the stimulus was presented 180 degrees from upright. Notice that the distribution of reaction times is almost perfectly symmetrical about 180 degrees. This means that the subjects did not rotate the stimuli in only one direction. The direction of rotation was determined by the subjects, who rotated the letters clockwise or counterclockwise depending upon which direction was closer to upright.

Other conditions of Cooper and Shepard's study were designed to assess the role played by prior information. In condition C, the "combined" condition, the subjects were informed simultaneously about both the identity and the orientation of the to-be-judged image. This was accomplished by showing the subjects an outline of the letter that would appear on the next trial. In addition, this outline was shown in the orientation (i.e., degrees of tilt) in which it would appear on the following trial. The outline was shown for two seconds, followed by a one-second blank interval. The subject was then shown the letter again and was asked to

FIGURE 3.13
••••••••••••••••••••
a: Cooper and Shepard showed subjects characters and reversed characters in six orientations defined by their angle to upright. Subjects were to decide as quickly as possible whether the characters were normal or backward. *b:* Reaction time was a function of stimulus orientation when the subjects were not given any previous information to help them prepare an image (This is the top line, labeled "No information" in the Figure). In the B conditions, subjects were shown an outline of the test stimulus in its upright form, followed by an arrow showing the orientation of the to-be-presented test stimulus. The longer the arrow was shown (100 msec, 400 msec, etc.), the more time the subjects had to prepare an image, and consequently, the faster their reaction times to the test stimulus. Finally, in the C condition (labeled "combined information" on the Figure), the subjects were given test stimulus and orientation information simultaneously.

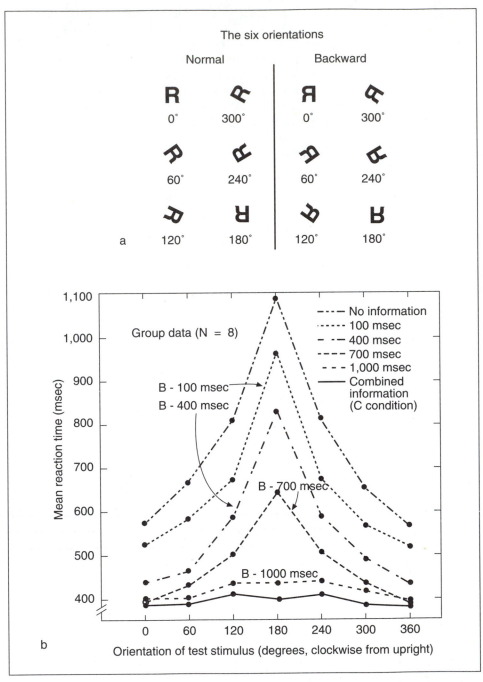

(From Cooper & Shepard, 1973. Copyright 1973 by the Psychonomic Society, Inc. Adapted by permission of the publisher and authors.)

respond ("normal" or "mirror image") as quickly as possible. We would expect that the three seconds' preparation should be plenty of time to allow the subject to rotate and orient the letter. Consequently, reaction times should be brief and uninfluenced by degrees of rotation required to make the letter upright. As the findings in the "combined information" line of Figure 3.13 show, this hypothesis was supported.

We have seen that, if the subjects are given combined identity and orientation information and ample preparation time, the effects of angular disparity seen in the "no information" condition can be completely wiped out. What would happen if the subjects were given separate (rather than combined) identity and orientation information, and perhaps less than adequate preparation time? The B conditions were designed to answer this question. In these conditions, the subjects received the identity and orientation information sequentially, rather than simultaneously as they did in condition C. In these trials, the subjects saw an upright outline of the to-be-judged letter for two seconds. This was followed by an arrow showing the orientation of the soon-to-appear test stimulus. The directional arrow was shown for either 100, 400, 700, or 1,000 msec. Next, the test stimulus appeared, and the subject responded as quickly as possible.

Figure 3.14 is a schematic representation of these events. The B-1,000 condition can be compared with condition C. Recall that, in condition C, the subjects were given combined identity and orientation information, and the subjects essentially had three seconds to prepare for the test stimulus. The B-1,000 condition is similar: The subjects get identity information (they know what the test stimulus is going to be), and they get orientation information (in the form of the directional arrow). However, in the B-1,000 condition, the subjects get these facts sequentially, rather than simultaneously as they do in condition C. As Figure 3.13 shows, the B-1,000 findings are indistinguishable from the condition C findings. When the subjects know in advance what the test stimulus is going to be, then 1,000 msec is enough time to rotate the letter into the same orientation as the test stimulus. In this sense, familiarity is no hindrance to mental rotation. Looking at the reaction time for the 180-degree stimulus in the B-1,000 condition, we see that subjects required only about 450 msec to respond. This finding indicates that the subjects were apparently rotating the letter at a rate far faster than the 50 to 60 degrees per second rate observed by Shepard and Metzler (1971). Knowing that 1,000 msec is apparently enough time

FIGURE 3.14

. . . .

In the B conditions, the information about the name and angle of rotation of the test character was presented sequentially before the presentation of the test character.

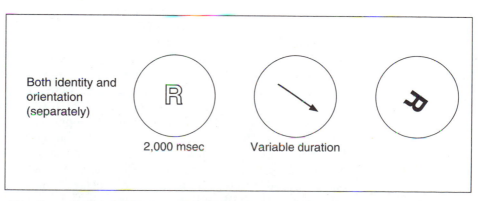

(From Cooper & Shepard, 1973. Copyright 1973 by the Psychonomic Society, Inc. Adapted by permission of the publisher and authors.)

to rotate the image, Cooper and Shepard next examined the other three B conditions.

In the B-700 condition, the subjects saw the directional arrow for 700 msec. As Figure 3.13 shows, this was almost enough time to enable the subjects to rotate the image. Except for the 180-degree point, most of the other reaction times are close to the B-1,000 curve. With 400 msec, there is an intermediate level of preparation; 100 msec offers hardly any advantage to the subjects. In that case, the reaction times are close to those observed in the "no information" condition.

Scanning Imaginal Environments

The research that we have reviewed suggests that people can carry out a cognitive analog of motion using imagined stimuli. In this section, we'll take this phenomenon one step further and ask whether people can set up imagined environments and reorient themselves within this imagined environment, while maintaining the appropriate spatial relationships.

Before we look at this research, though, we need to examine the elements of the physical world that must be encoded by the cognitive system in order to engage in imagined movement. The standard orientation of a person viewing the world is upright, and this implies that the three-dimensional perceptual world of the observer has two horizontal dimensions and one vertical dimension. The sole vertical dimension, height, can be defined in terms of an external phenomenon, namely, gravity. The fact that gravity pulls things in only one direction means that there is an asymmetry regarding height: Gravity will assist your movements in one direction, but will resist your movements in the opposite direction. There is a similar asymmetry regarding one of the two horizontal dimensions, that of front/back. An observer in the standard orientation can see, pay attention to, and move toward things in the frontal direction more easily than in the backward direction. But the final horizontal dimension, left/right, has none of these asymmetries, and is defined in the most arbitrary terms. Perhaps for these reasons, the directions left and right are frequently confused for one another: Very seldom does someone say "up" when they mean "down," but people frequently say "left" when they mean "right."

Given these facts, a person who is asked to reorient himself in an imagined environment must first construct an internal representation of the environment, and this internal representation must allow the perceiver to recompute changes in the location of objects relative to changes in the observer's orientation. In a study of these effects, Franklin and Tversky (1990) gave their subjects vignettes to read in which the subject was asked to imagine that he or she was in a particular environment (e.g., at an opera house). In this environment, there were various easily visualized objects on display, and each object was located in a particular spatial slot relative to the observer (e.g., "There is a beautiful bouquet of flowers on a shelf directly to your right"). The subjects were told to read these vignettes for comprehension, and were told that they were to try to learn the spatial organization of the objects in the environment. In the next phase of the study, subjects were presented with sentences on a computer screen corresponding to the vignette they had read. At various times, the subjects were instructed to (mentally) turn their bodies to various different orientations, and, while mentally fixing their gaze on an object now before them, they were asked a question about one of several directions ("front," "left," "below," and so on). The subjects were told to press the keyboard's space bar as soon as they had accurately determined which of the objects they had read about occupied the spatial slot being referred to. The direction of the subject's reorientation had a large effect on the speed with which this computation could be made. Subjects were quicker to respond to questions involving "above" (1.59 sec) or "below" (1.55 sec) than they were in responding to either "ahead" (1.75 sec) or "behind" (1.98 sec). Additionally, subjects responded to "ahead" or "behind" more quickly than they did to either "left" (2.20 sec) or "right" (2.22 sec). These findings are exactly congruent with what we would expect, given the previously described asymmetries that make some dimensions easier to describe than others. These findings also offer an interesting counterpoint to some of the imagery findings that we looked at earlier. There, we saw that the degree of angular disparity strongly influenced the subjects' reaction times, with greater degrees of disparity resulting in longer reaction times. Here we see that subjects basically can compute a 180-degree reorientation ("behind") more quickly than they can compute a 90-degree reorientation ("left" or "right"). Do these findings contradict the earlier work? Not necessarily. Scanning an image in which an external object is changing its orientation (for example, by rotating) is different from scanning an image resulting from a change in the perspective of our mind's eye—precisely because the spatial dimensions involved require different descriptions. I can mentally rotate an object by saying to myself, "It's rotating *this way*," without computing "left" or "right." Obviously I can't rely on this simple expedient when I'm asked to reorient myself mentally to the left, because I first must mentally compute, "Which way is left, anyway?" before I begin my reorientation.

CONCLUDING COMMENTS AND SUGGESTIONS FOR FURTHER READING

At this point, it's impossible to see how the issue of direct versus constructivist accounts is going to turn out. An interesting point is that cognitive psychologists who aren't particularly interested in the problem of vision almost always adopt some information-processing approach—that is, constructivist approach—to understand whatever problems they're working on. In the area of vision research, however, it seems that cognitive psychologists have been strongly influenced by Gibson's work, even though his theory is not inherently cognitive.

Those students who wish to get a good general introduction to the problems of perception could read Rock's (1983) book *The Logic of Perception*. The volume by Dodwell and Caelli (1984) is a good interdisciplinary approach to the problem of form perception. Marr's (1982) book on vision is relevant here, as are books by Bruce and Green (1990) and Humphreys and Bruce (1989).

The issues of perception, knowledge, and awareness have proved to be tough nuts for psychologists to crack. Dretske's (1981) book *Knowledge and the Flow of Information* represents the viewpoint of a philosopher (this book is not nearly as pro-Gibson as the title might lead you to believe). Dretske (1983) has written a synopsis of this book in the journal *Behavioral and Brain Sciences*. Those students who want to get a good introduction to Gibson's work should start with Goldstein (1984). Each of the volumes by Weimer and Palermo (1982) and McCabe and Balzano (1986) has several chapters with a Gibsonian influence. Reed and Jones (1982) have produced a collection of Gibson's essays with commentary, and Lombardo (1987) puts Gibson's thinking into its historical context.

Those students who want to find out more about the opposition to Gibson's theory (of which there has been more than a little) should start with Ullman (1980). Neisser's attempt at reconciling the two perspectives can be found in

Cognition and Reality (1976). Recently, Bruce and Green (1990) have written a comparison of the two views, which they refer to as "computational" and "ecological."

Social cognition is a growing field of research, and I recommend four books that will provide a solid foundation in this area. Fiske and Taylor (1984) have written an informative and lively account of the research. Hampson's (1982) book is also quite good, as is the book by Wegner and Vallacher (1977). The issue of person perception has been treated in a book by Cook (1984). Some of the latest research in social cognition is discussed in Srull and Wyer (1988).

KEY TERMS

Constuctivist theory of
  perception
Direct theory of perception
Höffding step
Müller-Lyer illusion
Prototype
Habituation
Schema
Feature abstraction

Self-schema
Invariant features
Optical flow pattern
Higher-order invariances
Texture gradient
Retinal image
Layout of perceivable space
Ecological approach to visual
  perception

Affordance
Canalization
Sufficiency analysis
Perceptual cycle
Cognitive maps
Analog representation
Angular disparity

FOCUS ON RESEARCH

Facial Perception in Infants

For most cognitivists, the focus of research is on the cognitive processes of adults, but there are nevertheless many developmental cognitivists who have wondered about the cognitive processes of infants. Although we'll discuss this topic in greater depth later in the book, it is appropriate to discuss some aspects of visual perception of infants here.

It has been known for some time (Fantz, 1961) that children as young as six months old seem to prefer looking at depictions of human faces. In Fantz's (1961) study, six-month-olds gazed at drawings of human faces, some of which were scrambled by moving the facial features around to unusual places on the face. Children of this age looked longer at the normal depictions than they did at the scrambled faces, suggesting that babies of this age can certainly discriminate a natural face from a scrambled one, and perhaps that infants like to look at human faces. However, there are some facts that complicate this interpretation. There are lots of things, other than their humanity, about faces that might capture the attention of a baby. Human faces have relatively high contrast (for example, babies often look at a person's hairline). In addition, there are other characteristics of human faces that could complicate Fantz's inter-

pretation. Faces are basically symmetrical. They also move and make noise.

Dannemiller and Stephens (1988) designed a study whose purpose was to rule out some of these confounding effects. Their subjects were six- and twelve-week-old babies who saw the stimuli shown in Figure 3.15. Adults tend to see A in Figure 3.15 as being substantially more "facelike" than B, even though the only difference between them is the fact that A is a "positive" image, while B looks more like a photographic negative. Six-week-old infants had no viewing preference between A and B, but by twelve weeks of age, babies showed a clear preference for A. However, these same children showed no preference for C over D, showing that their preference for A wasn't simply the result of a preference for figures with dark edges and bright interiors, but rather because the twelve-week-olds genuinely seemed to like looking at faces and facelike stimuli. In addition to whatever implications it might have about preference, we can also conclude from this study that the cognitive systems of three-month-olds seem to be able to compute just what it is about faces that makes them facelike, and this too is an impressive achievement.

·············· **FIGURE 3.15   Stimuli presented to infants by Dannemiller and Stephens (1988).**   Despite A and B being identical except for the reversals of the black and white shading, A looks more facelike to adults and attracts more attention from twelve-week-olds. The same infants had no preference between C and D, indicating that their preference for A was due to their perceiving its facelike quality, rather than generally preferring stimuli with dark borders and light interiors.

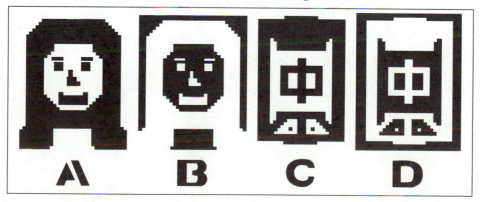

(Copyright 1988 by the Society for Research in Child Development. Adapted by permission of the publisher.)

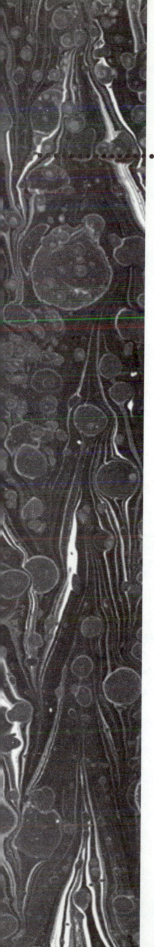

PART 3

MEMORY

If we were to ask a sample of cognitive psychologists to list the core topics of their field, we would see substantial disagreements. But almost all cognitive psychologists would include the topic of memory, regardless of how short their lists might be. When academic experimental psychology began in Europe over a century ago, memory was one of the phenomena it began studying. And in this country, the study of memory has continued apace, regardless of what other theoretical doctrines dominated the psychological landscape.

You shouldn't conclude, however, that the study of memory has continued without any disruption, either from without or from within. In this country, research on memory was heavily influenced by the work of learning theorists and also by the findings of one of the original European investigators of the last century, Hermann Ebbinghaus. Ebbinghaus was preoccupied with finding out how much well-learned verbal material would be saved (i.e., retained) by his memory over various periods of time. The Ebbinghaus tradition in memory research thus approaches memory with the basic question, *How much* is retained? However, other Euro-

pean researchers were more concerned with other issues. For example, Bartlett (1932) was interested in how memories *change* over time. The focus here is not necessarily on what has been lost, but rather on how the retained material has been altered. The Bartlett tradition in memory research thus begins with the question, *What kind* of material is retained? Over the next two chapters, we'll see elements of both of these traditions play their roles.

You should be aware of another distinction as you read the memory chapters: the distinction between structure and process. The structural approach to memory focuses on the organization of memories, their properties, and their relationships to one another. The process approach deals with the operations that can be used to transform memories, abbreviate them, or elaborate them. Both structure and process are (or should be) involved in every theory of memory, but the emphasis placed on these aspects differs from theory to theory. As you read, you might want to periodically ask yourself which of these components seems to be more important for the issues at hand.

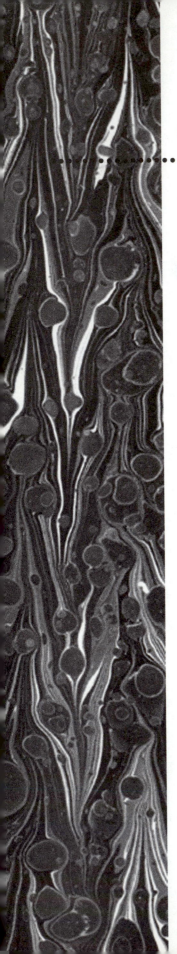

CHAPTER **4**

STRUCTURAL ACCOUNTS
OF MEMORY

CHAPTER OUTLINE

OVERVIEW

All of us forget things. Sometimes we're irritated by our forgetfulness, but many other times, it doesn't seem to bother us. For example, I don't remember what I had for dinner last night, and I don't care a whit. Why am I not irritated with my memory failure?

I have no reason to be irritated, because I wasn't *trying* to remember my dinner. I'm irritated only when I forget things I want to remember. Forgetfulness is not what we mind so much; what we find frustrating is our occasional lack of control over our memories. This loss of control shows itself in at least two ways. First and most obvious, there are unintentional *losses* from memory. Second, there are unintentional *intrusions* into our memories. For example, as I typed the previous sentence, I had, without my calling for it, an astonishingly clear image of the boardwalk in Ocean City, New Jersey. I haven't been there in over twenty years, and during the times I was there, I can't recall ever having thought, "I must remember this." How did this image get into my memory, and what made it reappear? Have I been storing this image in my memory all these years? If I have been storing it, I should be able to recover the image from time to time. But my previous experience has been that such unasked-for images often make a one-time-only appearance.

Cognitive psychologists have been interested in these and other questions, and this chapter considers some of their answers. Much of the material in this chapter is based upon the information-processing theory of memory. This viewpoint maintains that memory can be thought of as a system of components that have both structural and process aspects. By "structural aspects," we mean that memories seem to differ markedly in their nature and organization. For example, consider the *duration* of a memory. If I'm distracted while trying to memorize something unfamiliar to me, the memory will seem to evaporate. The memory is fragile. Other memories seem to be much more permanent. It's as if different memories are stored in different locations, and the properties of the memory seem to reflect the properties of the storage location in which the memory is housed. We can hang onto a memory stored in the permanent location, but it seems as if the memory has to go through a temporary location first. By "process aspects," we mean the cognitive operations that transferred and altered the memories stored in different locations.

The information-processing viewpoint has undergone a great deal of theoretical development over the last twenty-five years, meaning that the emphasis on structural or process aspects of memory has shifted back and forth as new findings have come to light. This chapter examines some of this shifting and attempts to point out why cognitive psychologists have decided to modify some aspects of the basic theoretical account. A good grounding in the theoretical issues will help us to understand what some of the research battles have been fought over. As a result of the intense effort by many cognitive psychologists to refine and advance knowledge in the area of memory, our understanding of this complex topic has increased dramatically.

THE INFORMATION-PROCESSING POSITION

Approximately twenty-five years ago, an information-processing theory of memory was developed (Atkinson & Shiffrin, 1968; Waugh & Norman, 1965), and this section provides an overview of its basic parts. The theory considers memory as a system of interrelated components. Each component, called a storage, is capable of processing particular types of cognitive codes. The theory also holds that cognitive codes can be transferred from storage to storage using control processes. One of the storages is known as the sensory register, where our feature detection and pattern recognition processes rapidly produce a cognitive code that can be stored for a brief period. The operation of the sensory register does not depend on resource allocation, meaning that a person does not have to pay attention to incoming stimuli in order to have a cognitive code in sensory storage; it happens automatically. One implication of this position is that the sensory register's capacity must be large, because all incoming stimulation is assumed to be stored at least briefly. The sensory register is also thought to be modality specific. This term means that part of the storage is devoted to visual stimuli, part to auditory stimuli, and, presumably, other parts devoted to each of the remaining senses. The duration of material in sensory storage is short. Visual stimuli remain there for about 250 to 300 msec, and auditory stimuli are kept for perhaps ten times that duration. Material stored in the sensory register is affected by the passage of time. Within the durations just mentioned, codes in sensory storage simply decay. *Decay* is a term that memory theorists use to refer to the loss of cognitive codes whose disappearance is produced strictly by the passage of time. To transfer the cognitive code from the sensory register, a person must allocate some resources to evacuate the information before it fades.

Information-processing theorists believe that cognitive codes are next transferred to a component called the short-term storage. Short-term storage (STS) differs from the sensory register in several ways. First, the capacity of STS is assumed to be quite limited (Miller, 1956). Second, information in STS is organized in a cognitive code that is acoustic, verbal, or linguistic. This organization applies even when the incoming information (i.e., the material evacuated from sensory storage) has been presented visually. Third, material can reside in STS much longer than it can in sensory storage. The duration of unrehearsed material in STS is about 30 seconds. STS and the sensory storage are similar in one aspect, however. In both cases, material that is not elaborated and transferred decays.

Codes stored in STS can be transferred to a long-term storage (LTS) whose capacity, like that of the sensory register, is extremely large. The control process that permits the transfer of coded material between these two storages is called rehearsal. *Rehearsal* is a term with many meanings in cognitive psychology, but for the time being, let's restrict its meaning to those cognitive operations that seem to have the following two functions. First, rehearsal refers to procedures that maintain the vitality of the code in STS. As long as the STS code is occasionally refreshed by rehearsal, it can apparently reside there for long periods. Second, rehearsal refers to operations that build up a corresponding code of the STS material in LTS. In a sense, then, information in STS is not transferred intact to LTS. Instead, rehearsal operates by duplicating a representation of the STS material in LTS. We're familiar with the subjective experience that often accompanies rehearsal. When we try to retain an unfamiliar bit of knowledge, we often say it to ourselves over and over again. Whether rehearsal depends upon this kind of subvocal speech is currently controversial (Klatzky, 1980). Once stored in LTS, the code is believed to be permanent. Failures to retrieve information that has been transferred to LTS are the result of other codes that seem to have a blocking or inhibiting effect on the memory we're searching for. In other words, cognitive codes can sometimes interfere with one another. In STS, cognitive codes are organized on the basis of acoustic or verbal properties. In LTS, the organization is different. Once there, material is organized semantically—that is, by its meaning. Figure 4.1 summarizes the relationships between these storages.

This introduction to the information-processing theory has pointed out that the storages differ in their capacities, durations, and operating characteristics. The sections that follow describe each of these storages in greater depth and examine some of the evidence for the claims made in the introduction. Criticism is withheld until a later section so that we might appreciate the theory's strengths.

Sensory Storage

Sperling (1960) has conducted some of the classic studies in the area of sensory storage. These studies demonstrate that humans seem to have an extremely

FIGURE 4.1
....
Structure of the memory system.

(From Atkinson & Shiffrin, 1968. Copyright 1968 by Academic Press. Adapted by permission of the publisher and author.)

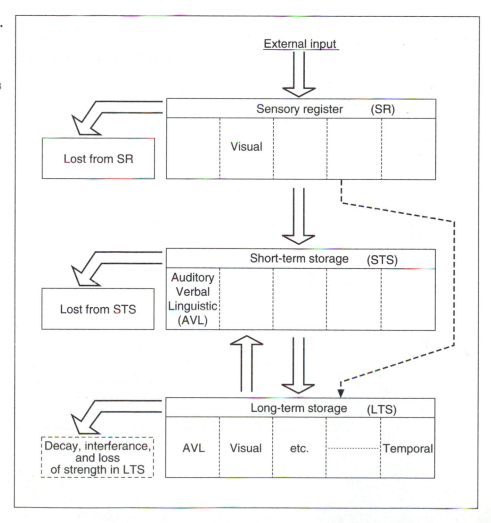

accurate and complete memory for visual stimulation, although this memory's duration is brief. Sperling found that, if four or fewer letters were tachistoscopically presented (a tachistoscope is a device used to present visual stimuli briefly) for 50 msec, subjects' retrieval of the elements was good, often approaching 100 percent. Moreover, Sperling found that the way in which the stimuli were arranged on the tachistoscope slide didn't seem to have any effect on the subjects' retrieval. For example, it didn't matter if six elements were presented in a single row or in two rows of three elements. In either case, the subjects retrieved an average of four elements. Similarly, the number of elements in the array didn't seem to produce any effect on retrieval. When the array had nine or more elements, subjects still retrieved only about four of them. Finally, even when exposure time was increased dramatically, up to about five-tenths of a second, the number of elements retrieved stayed constant. This last finding indicates that the upper limit of retrieved items was not imposed by any difficulty in *seeing* the items—half a second is plenty of time for that. Instead, the finding suggests that the difficulty in reporting elements from arrays of greater than four was produced by memory loss. This raises a question: What was the nature of memory deficit? Was it one of capacity (the initial storage being overloaded by more than four items) or one of duration (the items not remaining in the initial register long enough to get them out and into more durable storage)?

To settle these issues, Sperling abandoned the **whole-report technique,** in which he had asked the subjects to retrieve as much as they could from the array. In his next series of studies, Sperling substituted the **partial-report technique.** The subjects were now required to report only certain elements of the preceding display. The display consisted of an array of letters and digits arranged in three rows of four elements each. The subjects had to report only one row. However, unlike the whole-report technique, in which the subjects could begin responding as soon as the slide had been presented, in the partial-report technique, the subjects could not begin responding until they heard a musical tone, which signaled the row that was to be reported. A high-pitched tone was the signal for subjects to report the top row of the array, a medium-pitched tone was the signal for the middle row, and so on. Since the order of the tones was presented at random, the subjects could not know which of the three tones would be heard on any particular trial. From a subject's perspective, the order of events went something like the following. First, the subject saw the array for 50 msec. Then the array was turned off, and the subject waited until the tone was heard. This interval—called the inter-stimulus interval—was originally set at 50 msec. During this time, the subjects relied upon their memories to hang onto as much of the original array as they could. Finally, at the end of the inter-stimulus interval, a tone was sounded and the subject began responding. Sperling found that the subjects' accuracy was good: Most could retrieve all four of the signaled elements. This finding may seem predictable for the results of the whole-report studies, but there is a difference. In the partial-report procedure, the subjects did not know in advance which row they would have to report. That subjects were accurate in reporting any signaled row strongly suggests that they had all twelve elements of the array stored in their memories across the inter-stimulus interval.

Sperling's next task was to determine how long the elements were stored. To determine this, he increased the inter-stimulus interval, and he found that retention was good until the interval was increased to about 250 msec. When the interval was increased to 300 msec, the subjects seemed to be guessing. If they correctly anticipated which row would be signaled, they were able to report it. However, if they misjudged the to-be-signaled row, they weren't able to say much about what had been presented. Sperling's interpretation of this finding was straightforward. The information-processing system seemingly held all incoming visual stimulation in a memory or buffer for an ultra-brief period. This memory was considered complete in that all the aspects of the original stimulation were present in the storage. In addition, the contents of the storage were considered *precategorical* (Crowder & Morton, 1969; Long, 1980), which means that the information had not yet been transformed into the acoustic or semantic codes that characterize the organization of STS and LTS. Sperling elaborated his original findings by developing a theory of visual perception. He argued that visual information is recognized, elaborated, and rehearsed after the sensory stage. The subjects could not report more than four or five letters from the initial array because subjects must recognize and transfer the contents of the sensory memory to a more durable location from which they can be reported. Clearly, some time is required for this process, and the transfer problem is made worse by the items being apparently transferred serially. By the time four items have been extracted from the sensory register, the remaining contents have decayed.

In 1967, Neisser developed a name for this brief visual memory: the **icon.** The sensory register is not restricted to visual events alone. The **echo** is the appropriate name given to auditory stimulation stored in the sensory register. Presumably, each sense contributes an accurate copy of the recent stimulation of sensory storage, although the icon and the echo have been investigated more than the other sensory memories.

The Nature of the Icon   One of Sperling's other studies addressed the precategorical nature of the icon. In this study, subjects were shown a typical matrix of letters and digits, but instead of signaling the subjects to report a row, Sperling cued the subjects to report one category (letter or digit) of the elements. Let's consider the implications of these instructions. If the icon is truly precategorical, its elements have not yet been encoded into any meaningful format, such as letters. Consequently, we would not expect this type of signaling to be very helpful. Sperling found that this expectation was confirmed. Using the partial-report technique, he discovered that if he gave his subjects a letter or a digit cue, they had no more of the array's elements available to them than if he had used the whole-report procedure. This finding seems to indicate that the material in the sensory register is stored without any attempt at pattern recognition.

Sperling found that the icon's durability was strongly influenced by the adaptive state of the viewer's eye (Haber, 1983). When the presentation screen was illuminated at normal reading levels, so that the presentation of the stimulus didn't bring with it a change in the energy level of the visual field, the icon lasted for about one-quarter of a second. However, if the viewer's eyes were dark adapted, and thus more sensitive to light, then the presentation of the stimulus was also accompanied by a change in the overall energy level in the visual field. The icon then might persist for as long as four or five seconds. Sperling observed something far different when the prestimulus and poststimulus fields were much brighter than the stimulus. The icon then became much harder to "see," and its durability was lessened substantially.

Short-Term Storage

The studies just reviewed have suggested that visual information that is presented for less than 200 msec is held until a more durable cognitive code can be made. Short-term storage (STS) is the name given to this more durable storage.

Our STS is often compared to a mental workbench (Klatzky, 1980). Items from other storages can be transferred onto this workbench, where they can be "worked on," meaning that the material can be elaborated or transformed in a variety of ways. The workbench analogy has other implications, too. Like a real workbench, our short-term memories have limited space, implying that we can work only on a few things simultaneously. Just as a real task on a workbench requires our concentration, working on material in STS also seems to require the allocation of cognitive resources (Atkinson & Shiffrin, 1968). For these and other reasons, the contents of the short-term store have sometimes been equated with the boundaries of our consciousness.

Basic Findings   The classic study of short-term storage was conducted by Peterson and Peterson (1959). First, the Petersons demonstrated that subjects could retrieve a three-consonant trigram (e.g., MBN) after thirty seconds with no difficulty. Then the Petersons carried out the next phase of the study. Subjects were asked to recall only a single trigram, but during the retention interval, the subjects had to perform a distractor task. There are a variety of such tasks. The one used by the Petersons involved counting backward out loud by threes, starting from a three-digit number given to the subject right after the trigram. From the subject's perspective, each trial involved hearing the trigram, then hearing a three-digit number, let's say 987, then counting backward as quickly as possible, 987, 984, 981, 978 . . . until a retrieval cue was given. At that point, the subject attempted to recall the trigram. Figure 4.2 shows the findings of this study. Note that the probability of retrieving the trigram decreases to about 10 percent after a period of only fifteen to eighteen seconds. This probability of retrieval is far less than that observed when the subjects were not given a distractor task. Clearly, the distractor task prevented the subjects from carrying out an important operation on their "workbenches"—namely, rehearsal.

As discussed earlier, rehearsal seems to refresh or regenerate the contents of STS, and without it, the material disappears. Because the distractor task seemed to prevent rehearsal, it was reasonable for the Petersons to interpret the retrieval failures as being produced by decay.

This finding was a landmark one, because cognitive psychologists had known for some time that decay was not necessarily a major reason for retrieval

FIGURE 4.2

Results of the experiment on forgetting in short-term memory, showing that recall decreases as a function of the retention interval.

(From Peterson & Peterson, 1959. Copyright 1959 by the American Psychological Association. Reprinted by permission of the publisher and author.)

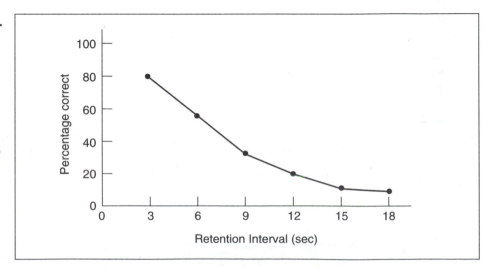

failure over long intervals (Jenkins & Dallenbach, 1924). Now, with the demonstration that simple decay was responsible for retrieval failures when the retention interval was short, the argument that two different storages must exist had a firm basis. The basis for this argument was the mechanism that produced forgetting. Decay produced forgetting from short-term storage, but forgetting from long-term storage was caused by **interference.** Interference refers to the blocking effect that some memories can have on other memories. This line of reasoning also explained some aspects of the well-known **serial position effect.**

Suppose we present a list of forty common nouns to our subjects at the rate of one noun per second. Immediately after the presentation, we ask the subjects to recall as many of the nouns as they can. Would you expect the recall probability of each noun to be equal? As you may know, that's not what happens. When a lengthy list is presented using such a free-recall procedure, the subjects' responses are predictable. Nouns that were presented first and those that were presented last tend to be recalled with greater frequency than those that were presented in the middle (Deese & Kaufman, 1957; Murdock, 1962). A noun's position in the sequence of presentation affects the likelihood of its being recalled. The serial position effect has two components. The **primacy component** refers to the fact that the nouns presented first (and whose memory is therefore the oldest) are recalled better than items whose presentation occurred in the middle of the list. The **recency component** refers to the greater likelihood of an item's retrieval when its serial position is near the end of the list. These effects are observed because the subjects are retrieving the words from separate storages. When the subjects began seeing or hearing the list, their short-term storages were basically empty, and consequently, a great deal of rehearsal could be spent on each word as it entered the storage. Because the initial words were thoroughly rehearsed, we would expect that they would develop into a more permanent representation in long-term storage. However, as the short-term storage gradually became loaded to capacity, the subjects had less time to rehearse each new incoming word, and the probability of a permanent representation being made was correspondingly diminished. Because material had to spend some time in the short-term storage before it could be transferred to LTS, the most recently presented nouns should be found in STS. This account suggests that subjects might not retrieve the material in the same chronological order in which it was presented. Instead, the subjects might spill the contents of their STS first, because it was prone to decay. Indeed, if you ever get a chance to observe the behavior of the subjects in a free-recall situation, you'll see that their response pattern is characteristic. When the list has been presented and the cue is given to recall as many words as possible, the subjects first write down the words that have just been presented, then they retrieve the words that were presented first, and finally, they jot down whatever else they can retrieve from the middle of the list.

If this retrieval pattern truly reflects storage in two different, independent locations, then apparently it should be possible to design an experiment that influences the retrieval from one, but not the other, location. Such a study was carried out by Postman and Phillips (1965). In one group of conditions, lists of ten, twenty, or thirty words were presented at the rate of one word per second. Recall was measured immediately after presentation. The top part of Figure 4.3 (labeled "0 seconds") shows the findings from this phase of the study. Notice that the serial position effect is much stronger when the list is twenty or thirty words long than when it consists of only ten words. For the ten-word list, the probability of recalling the middle words approached 50 percent, which is a preliminary indication that the capacity of STS must be almost that size. The reasoning here is that, if we made the list so short that all of it could be fit into STS, then we would expect the retrieval in the free-recall procedure to be good—in the 70 to 80 percent range. The observed retrieval probabilities for the middle words are close enough to those figures to enable us to infer that they've only recently been dropped from STS and begun their decay.

In the second phase of the experiment, Postman and Phillips conducted a variation of the procedure used by Peterson and Peterson. The words were presented as before; however, the subjects were not permitted to recall the words immediately after the presentation. Instead, the subjects were given a three-digit number from which they had to count backward by threes. After thirty seconds of this process, the subjects were given the recall cue. What should we expect? The theory predicts that the distractor task should affect the contents of STS but not LTS. We would expect that the subjects would have some difficulty dumping the contents of their STSs, because after thirty seconds of decay, those contents should be long gone. However, the distractor task should not affect the contents or the retrieval of any words that had already been transferred to LTS. Consequently, if the subjects are truly retrieving the words from two separate storages, we should expect that the distractor task would affect the recency component but not the primacy component. As shown by the bottom half of Figure 4.3, this effect is exactly what Postman and Phillips found, and it has been replicated on several occasions (Atkinson & Shiffrin, 1968).

The Nature of the Code in Short-term Storage   As discussed earlier, the contents of the sensory register have no real organization, meaning that they are more or less untransformed by the cognitive system. The sensory register is simply a copy

---

FIGURE 4.3
....

Probability of correct recall as a function of serial position for free verbal recall with test following zero seconds and thirty seconds of intervening arithmetic.

(After Postman & Phillips, 1965. Copyright 1965 by Lawrence Erlbaum Associates Publishers. Adapted by permission of the publisher and author.)

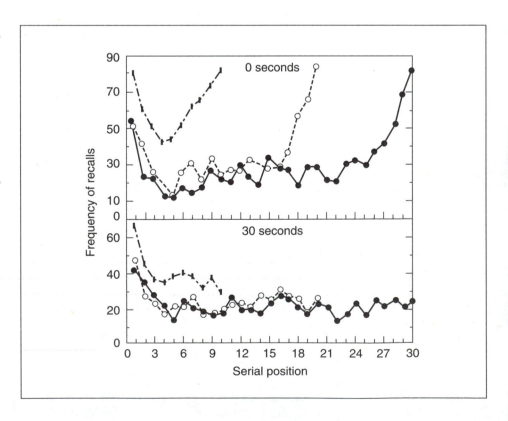

of the stimuli in close to their raw form. The contents of short-term storage, however, are highly transformed, or coded, by the cognitive system. What is the nature of this code?

Wickelgren (1965) aurally presented his subjects with a series of letters, and the subjects' task was to remember as many letters as they could. When the errors were analyzed, Wickelgren found that the subjects tended to substitute letters that sounded like the letters they had forgotten. For example, a *D* might be substituted for a *T*, and an *A* for a *K*. Notice that these substitution errors are not based on alphabetic proximity, nor are they visual confusions. This finding suggests that the nature of the code in STS is acoustic.

This finding was reinforced in a study by Conrad (1964), who wished to make a more explicit test of the acoustic cue hypothesis. In this study, the letters were presented to the subjects visually as well as aurally. Conrad found that, even when substitution errors were made for letters that had been presented visually, the nature of the error indicated the confusion had been acoustic. In other words, a *V* might be substituted for a *B* but not for a *U*.

This basic finding was complicated somewhat by the work of Hintzman (1965, 1967), who maintained that such errors were not acoustic per se, but rather were produced by the kinesthetic feedback the subjects got as they articulated the letters subvocally during the retention interval. His analysis of substitution errors, which were made against a background of white noise, indicated that such errors were explainable by the letter's voicing qualities (whether or not the vocal chords vibrate during the letter's production) and by place of articulation (where the tongue points during sounding). These qualities are closely related to the letter's sound, but Hintzman's findings suggest that the nature of the code in STS is verbal or linguistic rather than simply acoustic. Clearing up this issue has proved to be difficult (Atkinson & Shiffrin, 1968), which is why STS is sometimes referred to as the AVL storage. The nature of the code seems to be acoustic, verbal, or linguistic.

The Capacity of Short-term Storage   Determining the capacity of STS has proved to be difficult. Before examining some of the studies bearing on this issue, we should note one point. Pinning down a storage's capacity has been a tricky task partially because different theorists mean different things by this term (Craik & Lockhart, 1972). For example, we can discuss the *storage capacity* of some memory location, which means we're trying to describe how much information that component of the system can *hold*. On the other hand, we can discuss the *attentional,* or processing, capacity of storage, in which case we're focusing on *how much can be done* on the information storage (Zechmeister & Nyberg, 1982). Going back to the workbench analogy, storage capacity refers to how many items can be physically placed on the workbench, whereas processing capacity refers to how many separate operations (like nailing things together or painting them) can be done on those items in some unit of time. Establishing which factor is dominant in limiting the capacity of STS is hard because we never see the "workbench" except in the form of the subject's verbal reports or other behaviors.

However, regardless of which definition of capacity we adopt, we know that the capacity of STS is limited. In his famous paper, Miller (1956) suggested that the capacity of the short-term store was seven, plus or minus two items. However, exactly what constitutes an "item" can be debated. For example, suppose you are given a list of unrelated digits at the rate of one per second, and you are asked to repeat the list in the original order. If you're like most college students, you'll show high accuracy in repeating a list of about seven or eight digits. This experiment is an easy way to demonstrate the so-called memory span and is the basis for Miller's "magic" number seven. However, suppose the list you're given is the following:

1, 4, 9, 2, 1, 7, 7, 6, 1, 9, 4, 1

Because this list has twelve digits, technically we shouldn't expect good retrieval. But, if you're an American, you'd probably have no trouble remembering all twelve digits, because they can be grouped into three clusters of four digits each. Each cluster represents a year in which a historical event significant to Americans occurred. The name of this process is **chunking.** A chunk is a unit of information organized according to a rule or correspondence to some familiar pattern. A substantial body of evidence indicates that chunks are the items that fill up STS (Zechmeister & Nyberg, 1982).

Murdock (1961) demonstrated that three words would decay in STS about the same rate as three letters. But during the same time period, one word would show relatively little decay. If individual letters were the relevant items in short-term storage, then three letters should show more decay than one word. Similarly, three words should decay much more quickly than three letters. Murdock's findings indicate that the organizational unit in STS is the chunk. When three unrelated letters are entered in STS, they are stored as three chunks. When the letters are related because they constitute a word, then the word becomes the organizational unit and occupies one chunk.

Long-Term Storage

This section considers two lines of evidence that have traditionally been used to support the idea of a long-term storage, or LTS, which is the ultimate repository of our knowledge. First, we know that the nature of the memory code seems to change as a function of its time in the memory system. Second, evidence from the neuropsychological literature points to a distinction between STS and LTS.

Semantic Codes in Long-Term Storage   If we show subjects a list of words and ask them to recall the words several hours later, we'll see that subjects typically make what are called intrusion errors—they recall words that were not on the list. These intrusions are interesting. The relationship between the intruding word and left-out word is almost always *semantic*, that is, based on shared meaning. In other words, if the original word on the list was *boat*, the intruder is much more likely to be *ship* than *bud* or *boar* (Baddeley & Dale, 1966). These intrusions are far different than those that occur in STS, which tend to be acoustic.

Neuropsychological Findings   When a person suffers a painful shock induced by physical, electrical, or chemical stimuli, it's likely that the person will be unable to recall the events that took place immediately before the trauma (Russell & Nathan, 1946). In extreme cases, memory for events that happened up to an hour before the trauma occurred may be absent. From the time the person regains consciousness, his memory appears to function normally; events occurring after the accident are processed typically. The person usually regains the formerly wiped out memories, and this occurs in a characteristic fashion. The oldest wiped out memories (those that were farthest "in front" of the accident) are recovered first. Subsequently, the individual recovers memories that are closer and closer in time to the accident. The name for this type of memory loss is **retrograde amnesia.** What produces it?

If memories are transferred from STS to LTS, then we would expect the memory code to be particularly fragile at the time of transfer. Memories that had just been transferred, or were just about to be transferred, would be particularly likely to be disrupted. Those whose transfer had already occurred might be a little hardier and more able to survive the traumatic shock.

These concerns were addressed in an experiment by Chorover and Schiller (1965), who studied passive avoidance conditioning in rats. Their study was set up in the following way. The animal was placed on a small platform that was raised several inches from the cage's floor. When the animal stepped onto the floor, it received an electroconvulsive shock (ECS). Chorover and Schiller varied the time delay between the animal's stepping down and the ECS. They reasoned that, if the memories were truly being transferred, and were thus disruptible, then the rat should show poor avoidance learning when the time interval between stepping down and ECS was brief. This reasoning also implies that avoidance learning should improve if the delay between stepping down and ECS were increased, because the rat's memory system would have already transferred the memory into LTS and secured it. After exposing their animals to the ECS, Chorover and Schiller returned the rats to the experimental chamber twenty-four hours later for a memory trial. Their hypotheses were supported: If the ECS had been administered within ten seconds of the rat's stepping down on the learning trial, then the rat showed a significantly shorter step-down latency in the memory trial than rats that were shocked more than ten seconds after stepping down, or rats that hadn't been shocked at all. The interpretation seems to be that the rats that were shocked early (within ten seconds) were more likely to have the memory of stepping down wiped out by the ECS. Consequently, when they were placed in the experimental chamber twenty-four hours later, they duplicated their error and stepped down again. The rats that were shocked late knew better than to do this. They were more likely to remember what had happened to them twenty-four hours ago, and so they were cautious about stepping down from the platform. Chorover and Schiller concluded that the retrograde amnesia gradient was about ten seconds, during which the transfer of memories from STS to LTS could be disrupted.

Summary of the Information-Processing Position

Memory can be thought of as a system of interlocking but separate storages. Each of these storages has different capacities, each is organized differently, and the mechanism that produces forgetting also differs. The sensory register is a large-capacity storage that retains sensory stimulation in a raw form, meaning that no apparent code exists for material stored in the sensory register. Material stored here decays. For visual stimuli, the period of decay is about 250 msec. STS is a somewhat more durable storage capable of holding material for approximately thirty seconds. Material here is organized acoustically, and the capacity of STS is limited to about seven chunks. Unrehearsed material in STS decays. LTS contains our permanent memories. Its capacity is extremely large, and it can apparently hold material indefinitely. Material in LTS is organized semantically and is subject to interference by other memories.

EXTENDING AND MODIFYING THE INFORMATION-PROCESSING POSITION

During the 1970s and 1980s, cognitive psychologists continued to develop and modify their basic theoretical perspective on memory. First, a general attempt has been made to establish or refute the notion that the storages are truly distinct from one another. Second, cognitive psychologists have shown a sustained interest in memory processes, particularly those involving encoding and retrieving material. Those processes are examined in greater depth in Chapter 5. The next section considers some additional evidence on the separability of the storages in memory.

The Existence and Importance of a Sensory Register

This section is somewhat misnamed. Although it refers to the sensory register, for reasons of space, the discussion is limited to visual sensory storage. Although nobody seriously questions the findings of the many studies dealing with sensory storage, some debate exists regarding the interpretation and implications of those findings (Haber, 1983; Kolers, 1983). This debate has focused on two issues. First, researchers have questioned certain technical matters such as the nature of iconic organization (Merikle, 1980) and its locus (Adelson, 1978; Banks & Barber, 1977, 1980). Second, some thinkers have expressed a more general concern with postulating the icon as the necessary first step in an information-processing theory of memory or perception (Coltheart, 1980; Neisser, 1967; Turvey, 1977).

To review briefly, Sperling and other researchers thought that the nervous system passively copied information, which it stored in a raw format in sensory storage. The sensory register was therefore said to be precategorical, meaning that the information there was uncoded. Consequently, cuing the subject to report a particular kind of stimulus (e.g., letters or numbers) was ineffective, because the material in the sensory register had not yet been transferred into STS, where the material is coded. However, Merikle (1980) questioned this interpretation, reasoning that the display used by Sperling and others was simply a random series of letters and digits. Because the display itself was unorganized, the subject had only one strategy available when asked to report letters or digits. Each element in the array had to be searched on a one-by-one basis. Under those circumstances, it should not be surprising that the partial-report technique shows no advantage over the whole-report procedure. In effect, the subject was being asked to carry out a full report. Merikle attempted to remedy this problem by varying the spacing and format of the display. Using these modified matrices, Merikle found that poststimulus cuing was as effective for categorical elements (such as letters or digits) as it was for purely physical elements (such as "elements in the top row"). On the basis of this evidence, Merikle argued against the notion of a sensory storage as a separate location in the memory system. Instead, Merikle suggested that different aspects of a stimulus are probably encoded and transformed at different rates by the nervous system. For example, information about a stimulus's location might be encoded first, perhaps followed by a code representing the element's identity. If these codes are assembled by the nervous system quickly enough, then iconic effects can be explained without the recourse to a separate storage.

Other researchers raised some questions concerning the locus of the icon; that is, what part of the nervous system is responsible for creating and preserving it? There are two obvious places to begin looking for the icon's whereabouts: the retina and the brain (Haber, 1983).

A study by McCloskey and Watkins (1978) bears on this issue. They examined a well-known illusion: If a visual stimulus is swung back and forth rapidly behind a narrow slit, subjects perceive the stimulus as being compressed in such a way that the whole stimulus is thought to be on view simultaneously through the slit. This effect is an illusion because the subject never sees the whole stimulus simultaneously. McCloskey and Watkins therefore named the effect the "seeing-more-than-is-there" phenomenon. In their study, fairly complex forms were oscillated behind a narrow slit at a rate of sixty-four cycles per minute. The subject's task was to draw the oscillating stimulus as accurately as possible. Figure 4.4 shows some examples of the target figures and subjects' subsequent attempts to draw them. Notice that the subjects saw the complete figure compressed in the narrow space of the aperture, even though at no point in the target figure's cycle was such a view available.

In their interpretation, McCloskey and Watkins commented that such findings seem to necessitate some type of iconic storage. The subject seems to be holding one part of the target stimulus in the sensory register and incorporating additional information into her perception as it appears, as more of the target stimulus crosses the slit. For two reasons, such effects are not likely produced by the photoreceptors alone. First, it's hard to imagine how one set of photoreceptors could hold on to visual stimuli in some memorized format while simultaneously responding to additional incoming information. Second, the effect is produced even when the subject does not move her eyes. With eye movements, it's possible

FIGURE 4.4
. . . .
Target figures actually presented and subjects' reproductions of what they saw. The size of the target figures is shown relative to the size of the slit behind which they oscillated. In the experiment, subjects could see only what is revealed in the space between the two lines.

(From "The Seeing-More-Than-Is-There Phenomenon: Implications for the Locus of Iconic Storage," by M. McCloskey and M. J. Watkins. In *Journal of Experimental Psychology: Human Perception and Performance*, 1978, 4, 533–565. Copyright 1978 by the American Psychological Association. Adapted by permission of the publisher and author.)

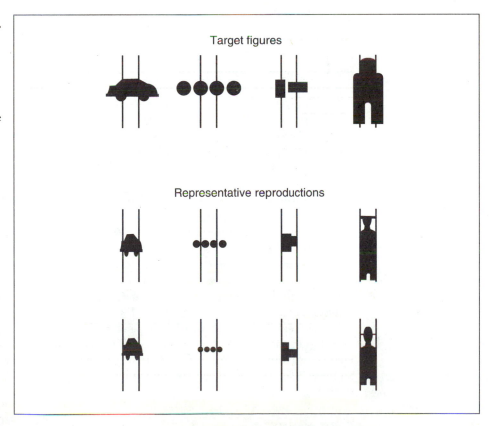

Target figures

Representative reproductions

to conceive of a way in which the subjects might overcome the first objection mentioned. But without eye movements, it seems as if the subject is asking the photoreceptors to do two highly complex tasks (perceive and remember) simultaneously. McCloskey and Watkins argue that the illusion must be at least partially produced by the central nervous system, which suggests that the locus of the icon must be there, too.

Even if the definitive study were to appear that pinned down forever the icon's nature and its location in the nervous system, some thinkers have wondered how important the sensory storage would be in any case. Even Neisser, who bestowed the icon with its name in 1967, later felt that the icon must play only a small part in everyday vision and memory (Neisser, 1976). Other thinkers have echoed this belief. Turvey (1977) reasoned that theories of perception and memory that are initiated by pictures or picturelike entities such as the icon have been called into question by Gibson's account of perception (see Chapter 3), which postulates no such devices and yet is able to explain perception. The real problem here seems to be the nature of Sperling's task, which is highly artificial: In what sense does normal vision correspond to looking at something in a tachistoscope? The answer is, not much. Tachistoscopic viewing is heavily dependent upon our ability to detect highly discrete stimuli that have been presented for brief segments of time. Such viewing heavily weighs on our ability to differentiate the chronological order of visual events—something most people are not very good at doing. In everyday vision, such an ability doesn't seem to be necessary. This leads to a question: Why would our cognitive system depend on a component in whose use we aren't very skillful and which isn't very useful anyway (Haber, 1983)?

All these findings suggest a modification of the basic position on sensory storage. The effects of sensory storage studies are reliable, so the nervous system clearly does have the capability to make highly accurate copies of sensory stimulation for short time periods. However, the copy made by the nervous system is not completely raw, or primitive, but rather has some code or organization. We know this because the central nervous system is implicated in the icon's formation. Also, the icon may be useful in some situations, but also clear is that the existence of the icon is not critical for accurate perception or memory. This evidence suggests that the boundaries around the sensory register—its limits— may be much fuzzier than was once thought.

The Distinction Between Short- and Long-term Storage

The distinction between separate storages beyond the sensory register is based on several lines of evidence (Wickelgren, 1973), only some of which are reviewed here. First, there is the coding issue. As we saw earlier, the information-processing theory describes short-term storage as acoustically organized, whereas long-term storage is semantically organized. Second, we have the mechanism of forgetting issue. Material in STS decays, whereas retrieval failures in LTS are produced by interference. This raises a question: Do situations exist in which material in working memory interferes with other material residing there? Third, there is the question of capacity. Is the capacity of STS much more limited than that of LTS? Finally, we have to contend with neuropsychological evidence. The following sections deal with each of these concerns.

Semantic Codes in Short-term Storage   Shulman (1971, 1972) demonstrated that people do have semantic information about material being stored in STS. His subjects underwent a series of trials, each of which had the following format. First, the subjects saw a list of ten words that were presented for 500 msec each. The tenth word was followed by the probe word, and the subjects had to tell whether the probe matched a word on the ten-item list. However, the nature of the match varied from trial to trial. On some trials, the term *match* meant that the subject had to report if the probe was identical to one of the words appearing on the list. On the other trials, a match would be achieved if the probe word was a synonym of one of the words appearing on the list. The subject did not know in advance which trials would be synonym trials and which would be identity trials; the nature of the trial was signaled by flashing an *S* or an *I* just before the probe word appeared.

Before we go on to the findings of this study, let's review some of the implications of this procedure. If the subject has only acoustic information available in STS, then there should be no confusions about the probe word when it has only a semantic relationship to the words on the list. That is, we would not expect subjects to mistake the probe word as having been identical to a word on the list when it was a synonym of one of the words on the list. If such confusions are observed, they must be based on a semantic, not an acoustic, similarity, which means that the subjects must have some semantic knowledge available to them in STS. Figure 4.5 shows the findings of this study. When an identity match was signaled, and the probe was a word that was not semantically related to the words on the list, the proportion of errors was .11. However, when an identity match was signaled, and the probe was a word that was a synonym of one of the words on the list, the proportion of errors increased dramatically to .19 (this is the line on the graph labeled "IS"). Notice, too, that the proportion of such errors as a function of serial position in presentation remained constant. If an acoustic code dominated, or even existed alongside, the semantic information, we would expect to see a reduction in errors when the probe was a synonym of the three or four most recently presented items. Presumably, these items would be the most likely to be coded acoustically and therefore the most resistant to confusion. The fact that such a reduction was not observed suggests that the semantic information was more than simply available to the subjects. Rather, it suggests that the subjects had coded the words on the list on the basis of their semantic properties.

It's important to note that Shulman's subjects were not left to their own devices in the formation of a code. The nature of the task must have encouraged the subjects to form a semantic representation of the list. Indeed, ample evidence suggests that, when subjects are left to their own devices on a short-term task, the nature of their representation is likely to be acoustic to some extent (Drewnowski, 1980). Drewnowski and Murdock (1980) have presented findings showing that intrusion errors for monosyllabic words stored in STS are primarily acoustic (echoing Conrad, 1964). However, when dissyllabic words were presented either visually or aurally, the intrusion errors could not be well explained on a purely acoustic basis. Instead, Drewnowski and Murdock found that the intrusions were made on the basis of the syllabic stress pattern, the phonemic class of the initial and final syllables, and the identity of the stressed vowel. Recall Atkinson and Shiffrin's comment concerning the difficulty of separating acoustic from linguistic codes. The Drewnowski and Murdock findings seem to amplify the idea that a variety of codes are produced early on and perhaps nearly simultaneously by the cognitive system. Because of this, many cognitive psychologists are reluctant to use coding differences as a basis for establishing separate long- and short-term storages, and have taken instead to studying the emergence and transformation of these various codes (Horton & Mills, 1984).

FIGURE 4.5
....

Proportion of correct identity matches *(II)* and synonym matches *(SS)*, as well as proportion of times subjects mistakenly said yes to a synonym when an identity match was requested *(IS)* as a function of serial position.

(From "Semantic Confusion Errors in Short-Term Memory," by H. G. Shulman. In *Journal of Verbal Learning and Verbal Behavior*, 1972, 11, 221–227. Copyright 1972 by Academic Press, Inc. Adapted by permission of the publisher and author.)

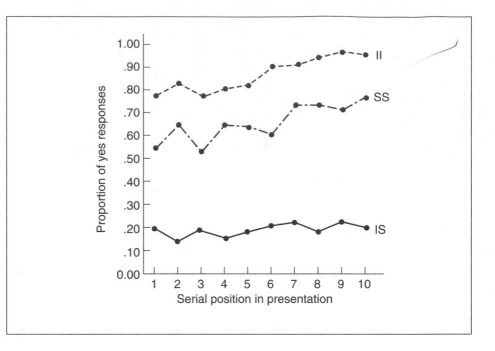

The Mechanism of Forgetting The difference in forgetting mechanisms—decay in STS, interference in LTS—has also been used as a basis for claiming that these storages are truly separate. Unfortunately, this distinction has been under a cloud for some time. Early critics of the original Peterson and Peterson finding noted that the possibility of interference from trial to trial had not been completely controlled for. According to this argument, the act of storing one trigram in STS may have interfered with the ability to store the trigrams that were presented on later trials. As more and more trigrams were presented on successive trials, a reasonable supposition was that the interference from one trial to the next might increase. If this putative explanation were correct, then the results observed by the Petersons were not produced by decay but rather by the interference of earlier trials on later trials. The Petersons defended themselves against this charge by saying that, if this explanation were true, then the subjects' performance should get worse on successive trials of the counting backward task. But it didn't. Performance on the first trial and the Nth trial were essentially the same. This rebuttal seemed sound until Keppel and Underwood (1962) read the Petersons' procedure section closely and noticed that the Petersons had given their subjects two practice trials. Keppel and Underwood wondered if interference might have been induced on those trials. When the study was replicated without the practice trials, they noticed that a buildup of interference occurred across trials. Retention was better on trial 1 than on trial 2, which was in turn better than retention on the third and subsequent trials. Keppel and Underwood's study concluded that at least some interference seems to be involved in forgetting from STS.

Capacity Differences Between Short-term and Long-term Storage In a previous section, we've seen that one of the foundations of the information-processing viewpoint of memory rests on apparent differences in capacity between STS and LTS. Specifically, the theory argues that STS has a rather small capacity, while LTS has a large, or perhaps even infinite capacity. But is this distinction valid? In this section, we'll take a closer look at the phenomenon of chunking, and we'll see that both the existence of chunking, and the relative case with which chunking is done by most people, may argue against the idea of necessary differences in the capacities of STS and LTS. That is, it's possible to learn to chunk information rather well, so well in fact, that apparent capacity of STS balloons to rather large dimensions.

In the literature on memory, this effect is perhaps seen most clearly in the case of S.F. (Ericsson, Chase, & Faloon, 1980). S.F. was an undergraduate with normal memory abilities who agreed to participate in an extended study of memory skills. Three to five times per week, for approximately an hour each session, S.F. was read sequences of random digits at a rate of one digit per second. S.F.'s task was to recall the sequence. If he succeeded, he was read another list, this list being one digit longer than the preceding list. Over the course of approximately 1½ years, S.F. logged 230 hours hearing and recalling random digit sequences. During this period, S.F.'s memory span (the number of random digits he could recite correctly) increased from a very typical 7 digits to a phenomenal 80 digits! It happened that S.F. was a talented distance runner who used his knowledge of this sport as a particularly effective mnemonic device to organize 3- and 4-digit groups of numbers as times that might be achieved in particular races. Thus, for example, the sequence 3492 might be encoded as 3 minutes, 49.2 seconds—a near record time in the mile. The power of this mnemonic is seen in a demonstration that Ericsson et al. carried out after S.F. had about two months of practice. At that point S.F. was presented with a sequence of digits that could not be easily coded as race times. When this was done, S.F.'s performance dropped almost to his beginning level. On the other hand, when a sequence of digits was given that could all be easily represented as running times, then S.F.'s performance increased by a dramatic 22%.

S.F.'s impressive memory performance raises a question: By chunking, is it possible to keep up to 80 distinct elements in short-term storage? Ericsson and his coworkers don't think so. To show why, the researchers analyzed the structure of S.F.'s recall. First, it's important to realize that in retrieving the digits, S.F. did not recite them at a constant rate or speed. Rather, S.F. seemed to retrieve a certain number of digits very quickly, then pause before reciting another group of digits. Based in part on the amount of time that S.F. hesitated between retrieving digits, Ericsson et al. determined that S.F. used a three-level hierarchy in retrieving the random strings. This structure is shown below:

444 444   333 333   444   333   444   5

What this means is that S.F. began by grouping the digits into groups of four, and this was the first level of organization. So, for example, if a string began with the digits "8", "3", "3", "2", these digits were grouped together, and are represented by the very left-most 4 in the structure above. Then he used units of this sort to form a group of three such strings (that accounted for the first set of 4s). This was the second level of organization and accounted for the first 12 digits. Then after a short pause, he produced another set of 12 digits in the same way. These first 24 digits constituted a "super group" and made up the third level of organization. Then after a longer pause he grouped the next set of 18 digits into a super group that was based on subgroups of 3, rather than 4 digits. He continued with this pattern, using groups of 3 or 4 digits as the basic unit of organization.

There are two interesting observations about this organization. First, the basic size of the groups was always 3–5 digits, which is well within the traditional memory span limit. Second, S.F. made use of his "normal" short-term storage. You can see this in the group of 5 digits occurring at the end of the sequence. These five digits were not translated into running times; they were simply left in S.F.'s rehearsal buffer in an acoustic format. It might appear as if S.F were maintaining 80 items in his short-term memory, but according to Ericsson et al., he really wasn't. Rather S.F. was using a mnemonic device to impose a hierarchical organization on this material. Findings like those produced by S.F. tell cognitive psychologists that we really can't use memory span as a good indication of STM capacity.

Neuropsychological Evidence   Finally, we have considered the phenomenon of retrograde amnesia and its implications for the transfer of memories between STS and LTS. Recall that Chorover and Schiller (1965) demonstrated that, in a passive avoidance procedure, ECS delivered within ten seconds of stepping down seemed to partially eradicate the memory of the punishment. This finding seems to indicate the existence of a ten-second retrograde amnesia gradient during which memories in STS are transferred to LTS, where they are consolidated. Unfortunately for proponents of the information-processing view, several other interpretations are consistent with the findings. First, the ECS may disrupt the storage of memories rather than their transfer. For example, memories may be transferred in an extremely brief time, let's say less than a second. ECS given within the ten-second interval following this transfer may simply scramble the contents of the memory, making it hard to locate the memory at a later time. On the other hand, the ECS may disrupt the retrieval of a memory that has been successfully stored and transferred. The memory itself might be intact, but the ECS might disrupt the operation of certain retrieval processes whose job is to pull the appropriate file at a later time. Although space limitations preclude a complete discussion, another difficulty with the retrograde amnesia gradient stems from the fact that ECS sometimes does not completely prevent the formation of a memory (Miller & Springer, 1972; Quartermain, McEwen, & Azmitia, 1972; Schneider, Tyler, & Jinich, 1974).

So What Is Short-Term Memory?

If you're like me, you probably have a strong intuition that you have two memory systems: one system for the stimuli that are currently present, but out of your immediate focus, and a second system for information that you had to learn, but whose learning took place long ago. This won't be the last time in the course of going through this book that we see that our intuitions about our cognitive system may not be completely correct. The fact is that it is not necessary to postulate two separate systems to account for the overwhelming majority of memory phenomena. There are no data that mandate the two separate memory systems that seem, intuitively, to be so obvious. This conclusion leaves us with a question though: Is it possible to describe what it is that the cognitive and neural system is doing when it produces the events that seem to us like STM or LTM retrieval?

As several theorists have noted (Cowan, 1993; Crowder, 1993), the cognitive and neural system must be doing something different when it retrieves briefly stored material than when it retrieves information that has been held for a long time. Let's consider what the central nervous system might be doing when some stimulus is being held in short-term memory. According to many views, when stimuli are being held in short-term memory, the central nervous system maintains a consistent pattern or arrangement of neural activity—we might call this pattern of neural activity the "posture" of the brain. Obviously, you cannot maintain this posture forever, if only for the simple reason that new incoming stimuli constantly demand to be processed, and doing so requires the instantiation of a new pattern of activity congruent with the encoding of these new stimuli. In effect, the brain goes on to a new posture with the processing of these incoming stimuli. According to this view, as long as the brain is maintaining a certain posture, the stimuli that produced that posture, whether they are still currently visible or not, are nevertheless still being represented and thus can still be retrieved. To store something for a longer period of time, the implication is that your brain must achieve a different configuration or pattern of neural activity. Whatever the pattern of neural activity, this view implies two different brain "postures" for stored material: one posture that occurs immediately as the material is converted to a neural code, and a second posture that reflects a more durable neural coding. If such a view is accurate, the first posture represents that brain activity that gives rise to our experience of short-term memory, whereas the second posture refers to the brain activity that produces our experience of long-term memory.

Cowan (1993) apparently had in mind a similar view of the STM-LTM distinction. Cowan refers to STM as a hierarchical concept containing at least two components. The first component refers to those elements of LTM that are currently activated. This may mean that such elements are reconverted from whatever "posture" the neural system uses for durable storage back into the "posture" the brain used to represent those elements when it first encoded them. A second component of STM refers to those activated elements that are currently the focus of attention. It is this second component of STM that may provide us with our subjective experience of STM—namely, that STM consists of those things that we are currently "thinking of" or that are currently "on our minds." At this point, there is no way that I can comment on the accuracy of this viewpoint; obviously more time and research will be needed before we completely understand the relationship of the cognitive to the neural system.

Modifying the Information-Processing Theory: A Summary

Let's sum up the literature we've reviewed. First, we've seen that, in the intervening thirty years since Sperling's initial studies of visual sensory memory, cognitive psychologists have learned a great deal about the icon. They now know that the icon does have some sort of organization; it is truly a cognitive code. The information is not simply stored in a raw, or precategorical, format. The capacity of visual sensory storage is not infinite. Cognitive psychologists have also discovered that information can be evacuated from sensory memory at different rates, depending on an individual's material and strategic choices. Moreover, cognitive psychologists have realized that a sensory register or buffer may not be essential to an information-processing theory of memory.

Second, we've seen that researchers have gotten progressively more sophisticated concerning the contents of STS and LTS. Earlier, we believed that the structural aspects of the storage affected its contents. In other words, we would see acoustic errors when we asked people to retrieve material from STS, because STS organized material by sound. We now recognize that stimuli can be coded in a variety of ways at any point in their processing by the memory system. This means that the rigid division of the memory system into two separate locations is probably an overstatement of the situation. If people are left to their own devices, the sequence they go through in coding material apparently has some fairly reliable phases, including an acoustic and a semantic phase. This phenomenon does not necessarily mean that material is being transferred from one location to another—and we know that now.

The tone of the literature we have just reviewed may seem negative and perhaps has given you the impression that the information-processing approach is bad or wrong. This impression isn't accurate. True, most cognitive psychologists would probably be unwilling to endorse the notion of separate memory structures that correspond to either features of our brains or our cognitive systems. But despite its apparent retreat from its initial theoretical position, the information-processing approach validated the notion of memory processes that create and transform memory codes in ways that facilitate or inhibit their retrieval.

The Dual-Code Position

Judging from the account of the memory system given in the first part of this chapter, you may have gotten the impression that the memory system treats all incoming stimulation in the same fashion. However, some theorists have argued that such a conclusion is not warranted. Specifically, these theorists have maintained that the memory system deals with visually presented material in a different way than it deals with verbal material. According to such a view, the nervous system is capable of creating two sorts of representations. In the case of verbal material, as we have seen, the incoming representation may first be stored in a sensory register before being held in a short-term memory where an acoustic representation of it is made. Finally, the acoustic code is transformed again by our cognitive system into a semantic, or meaning-based, code. But in the case of visual material, the theory maintains that our nervous system is capable of forming an analog representation.

This reasoning is summarized by a theory called the dual-code position (Paivio, 1969, 1971). This position argues that the memory system will work better when both verbal and analog systems are brought to bear on a specific memory. Thus, it argues that pictures should be better remembered than words, because pictures can be represented both visually and verbally. For words that are concrete, and hence easily visualized, the apparent superiority of the pictorial format should be reduced, although elsewhere Paivio (1978) argues that the visual or analog code may have some inherent superiority over the verbal code. There are some striking experimental findings supporting these contentions.

Frost (1972) used reaction-time methodology to show the effects of the imaginal format. She showed her subjects a series of sixteen drawings such as those in Figure 4.6(a). Fifteen minutes after the series of drawings were presented, subjects saw a stimulus and had to determine as quickly as they could by pressing one of two keys if the drawing was of an object that had been presented earlier. The subjects were instructed to respond to the object being depicted, not to the exact form of the drawing. So, for example, to both of the drawings in Figure 4.6(b), the subjects should respond "yes" as quickly as possible. Now, if the meaning of the objects is what is stored, the subjects should respond equally quickly to either one of the drawings in Figure 4.6, because both of them have the same meaning: They are depictions of an elephant. If, on the other hand, people store stimuli in an imaginal format, the subjects should respond faster to the drawing that is identical to the test stimulus. This is what Frost observed. Subjects responded to identical drawings 180 msec faster than they responded to the different drawings of the same object.

FIGURE 4.6
....
Part *a* shows an example of a drawing subjects studied in the first phase of Frost's (1972) experiment. Part *b* shows two test stimuli.

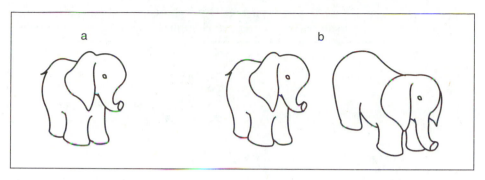

(From N. Frost, "Encoding and Retrieval in Visual Memory Tasks." *Journal of Experimental Psychology*, 1972, 95, 317–326. Copyright 1972 by the American Psychological Association. Adapted by permission of the publisher and author.)

Dual-coding issues also may be at the bottom of an intriguing finding reported by Erdelyi and Kleinbard (1978). Their subjects were presented with sixty pictures of common objects (e.g., a watch) or with the names of the objects. Each stimulus was presented for five seconds. Subjects were asked to recall the objects (by writing them) several times over a period of approximately one week. Their findings are shown in Figure 4.7. When the subjects recalled stimuli that had been presented as words, their performance did not improve as a function of repeated recollections. But the subjects who recalled stimuli that had been presented as pictures showed continued improvement across the 160-hour interval! We'll discuss theories of retrieval in greater detail in Chapter 5, but, for now, we'll take as a given that subjects use a generate and recognize strategy in free-recall tasks. That is, when asked to retrieve, the subject first internally generates candidates that may have been on this list and then compares these candidates with an internally computed "recognition criterion." If the internally generated candidate exceeds the recognition criterion, the subject reports the stimulus as being on the list, and if the candidate does not exceed the criterion, the subject rejects it. Let's see how this applies to the subject who is trying to retrieve words. Over time, the subject will generate progressively more targets, some of them more than once. As the subject generates targets and becomes more familiar with them, it will become progressively more difficult for the subject to distinguish between generated targets that were really on the list and targets that have been generated previously but didn't pass the recognition criterion. However, for the subject who is trying to retrieve pictures, a different story unfolds. According to the dual-code theory, stimuli stored in the analog format are more discriminable than words. Consequently, as time passes and the subject generates progressively more candidates in the imaginal format, it will be relatively easy to tell whether the generated candidates were actually on the list or whether they were simply candidates that had been previously generated. Presumably, self-generated targets that were actually on the list are also more likely to pass the recognition criterion and hence be recalled.

Episodic Memory and Semantic Memory

As we've seen, there seems to be a semantic component in our permanent memories, but we have not yet considered how our permanent memories may be organized. We'll spend a great deal of time describing this semantic memory

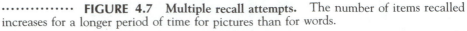

·············   **FIGURE 4.7   Multiple recall attempts.**   The number of items recalled increases for a longer period of time for pictures than for words.

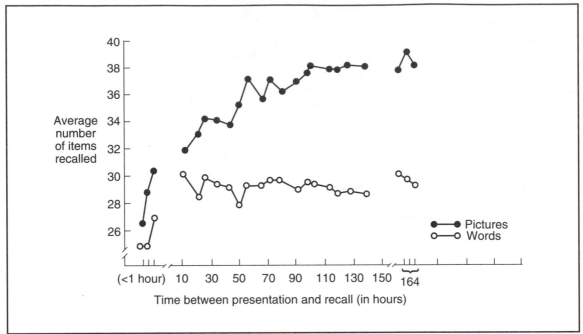

(From Erdelyi, M. H., and J. Kleinbard, 1978. "Has Ebbinghaus Decayed with Time?: The Growth Recall (Hypermnesia) over Days," *Journal of Experimental Psychology: Human Learning and Memory* 4:275–289. Copyright 1978 by the American Psychological Association. Adapted by permission of the publisher and author.)

component in Chapters 6 and 7. At this point, however, our objective will be to understand more about this semantic component in the context of other systems theorized as residing in permanent memory.

Tulving (1972, 1983) proposed a distinction between two types of permanent memory. **Episodic memories** were autobiographical, personal, and sensitive to the effects of context. These memories were organized by time and place of occurrence and could frequently be described in terms of their perceptual characteristics. Episodic memories could be contrasted with **semantic memory,** which housed general, encyclopedic knowledge of the world and language. Semantic memory was organized on the basis of class membership and other abstract principles such as sub- or superordination. In other words, semantic memory seemed to consist of facts that could be organized hierarchically. For example, I know that dogs and cats are both mammals, but they can be grouped together in a superordinate category—chordates— along with other animals that are not mammals. Semantic memory was composed of knowledge that had no specific temporal or spatial referent, and was therefore not sensitive to the effects of context. Although, as Tulving (1972) pointed out, these two systems do interact with each other, Tulving felt that each system probably has its own encoding, storage, and retrieval laws.

There is some evidence to support Tulving's contentions, at least to a degree. Kihlstrom (1980) reported episodic and semantic memory dissociation for normal subjects who were in a hypnotic state. The subjects were hypnotized and then memorized a list of unrelated words. Following the learning session, the subjects were given a posthypnotic suggestion, telling them that they would not be able to remember the memorized list until a specific retrieval cue was given. Following that, the subjects were told that they would now have to supply free associates to words given by the experimenter. These priming words were deliberately chosen because they had a high probability of eliciting the list words that the subjects had memorized. Subjects performed well on this task, indicating that the hypnotic state had not affected their general (i.e., semantic) knowledge of the words' meanings. However, even after they had recited many of the words on the list, the subjects maintained that they were unable to retrieve the studied items. Yet, when the retrieval cue mentioned in the posthypnotic suggestion was finally given, the subjects' retrieval was close to perfect.

Salasoo, Shiffrin, and Feustel (1985) investigated semantic and episodic effects in word recognition. Recognition of words that have been briefly presented would appear to involve semantic memory, and, true to expectations, subjects typically identify, name, and make decisions about actual words faster than they do for pronounceable nonwords. However, there are also episodic effects. For example, consider the identification of a grammatically acceptable, but completely novel, nonword. Presumably, such a stimulus has no representation in semantic memory because the subject has never encountered it before and it doesn't mean anything anyway. It has been shown though that the identification of such a stimulus is enhanced upon its *second* presentation, even when the delay between the initial and the second presentation is quite lengthy. This effect, known as the repetition effect, is clearly the result of episodic memory. Salasoo et al. wondered about the contributions of the two memory systems to each of these phenomena: How many episodic presentations were necessary before the identification of a grammatically correct nonword equaled that of a familiar, semantically based actual word? They found that approximately five such presentations were required to enable subjects to identify a nonword as accurately as they did a word. They also found that these episodic effects were quite durable. They brought their subjects back into the lab one year after the original study. Subjects still showed the effects of repetition: Their identification performance for previously seen nonwords, previously seen words, and new words was similar and superior to their performance for new nonwords.

Autobiographical Memory   One form of episodic memory that cognitivists have begun to research recently is autobiographical memory—retrieval of events that have happened to you. How are these events organized, and what principles govern their retrieval?

A study by Reiser, Black, and Abelson (1985) explores the type of knowledge structures people use in making such judgments. They propose that the events in autobiographical memory are organized by the knowledge structures that guided the comprehension of the event as it was being experienced. Specifically, they propose two types of such cognitive structures. As you can probably infer, these structures are closely related to the schemas that we have already examined. One such structure they call an *activity*. An activity is a sequence of deliberate actions designed to achieve a goal. For example, *shopping in department stores* and *going to the movies* are activities. Each of these events can be decomposed into other events that represent subgoals of the activities. For example, the action *making reservations* is a component of the activities *playing indoor tennis, going to a nightclub,* and *eating at restaurants.* Reiser et al. refer to these components as general actions. Although activities are composed of general actions, they argue that general actions per se are not the basic elements of autobiographical memory. In one study, their subjects were asked to retrieve a personal experience, and the subjects were given an activity/general-action prompt. Reiser et al. found that retrieval was faster when the subjects were given the activity prompt first rather than the general-action prompt. In addition, when subjects were given just an activity as a prompt, retrieval was faster than when the subjects were prompted with only a general action. So in other words, given the prompt "Think of a time when you were playing tennis and had an injury," subjects retrieved an autobiographical memory faster than when they were simply prompted to think of a time when they had an injury. This is a curious finding. Surely the number of times that a person received an injury must be greater than the number of times that he or she received an injury playing tennis, yet the latter cases were retrieved faster. This finding suggests that it is such particular activities that are the basic building blocks of our personal memories.

One recent study bears on this issue. Wagenaar (1986) recorded events that happened to him over a period of six years. These events were described in several ways, including who and what the event was about, where it occurred, and, of course, when it happened. In addition, Wagenaar made estimates at the time of recording (which usually occurred at the end of the day) about the event's pleasantness, his emotional involvement with the event, and its salience (how frequently such events typically occur, from once per day to once in a lifetime). At the end of the test interval, Wagenaar was prompted by a colleague to recall the recorded events. Recall was attempted for approximately five events per day of the 1,600 events that had been recorded during the test interval. There were several interesting findings. First, Wagenaar noted that the accessibility of memories that were prompted by nonspecific cues dropped off much more precipitously as a function of age than did memories that were prompted by cues that were unique for a certain event. This finding seems to suggest an agreement with one of the findings of Reiser et al. Autobiographical memory does not seem to be organized in terms of classes of general actions, even though these are clearly involved in all such memories. This interpretation seems to be buttressed by Wagenaar's analysis of cuing efficiency. By cuing efficiency, Wagenaar was referring to the likelihood of retrieval as a function of which particular prompt (who, what, where, or when) was used. In this regard, the time prompt "when" was almost useless as a cue: the likelihood of retrieving the autobiographical memory in question was only about 2 percent when this cue was used. In contrast to this, when the prompt "what" was used, the likelihood of retrieval was approximately 60 percent. Salience had a predictable effect as well. The more out of the ordinary the event, the greater the likelihood of its being retrieved with the passage of years. Finally, Wagenaar discovered something interesting about the emotional tone of his memory. Unpleasant events were less likely to be retrieved than were pleasant memories, but this effect was observed only for those events that had taken place within the last year. After a year had elapsed, pleasant and unpleasant memories faded away together at a more or less equal pace.

As Wagenaar's study has shown us, the prompt "when" is not particularly effective in cuing autobiographical memories. But this does not mean that no aspect of time is encoded in such memories. The intriguing effects of time in autobiographical memory are seen in a study by Friedman (1987). Employees at the college where Friedman worked were asked to retrieve, as accurately as possible, the hour, day, date, month, and year in which a mild earthquake had occurred in the college's vicinity some eight months previously. The subjects also were asked to indicate the things that they thought of in trying to remember the timing of the earthquake and to rate their confidence in their varying estimates. As you might expect, most of the subjects could retrieve the year accurately and were reasonably confident that their recollection was accurate. But estimates of the date, the month, and the day of the week varied widely from subject to subject and were not significantly different from what we would expect by chance. This gives us some reason to believe that the subjects were just guessing about those elements of their memories. However, the time of day estimate did not vary as widely as did estimates of the other components, and the subjects also reported greater confidence in their time of day estimates than in their estimates of any other component. This might seem odd until we realize that the earthquake began at approximately 11:50 A.M., shortly before the traditional noon lunch hour for most of the school's employees. A detailed analysis of the things that the subjects thought of in trying to answer the questions makes it clear that many of the subjects associated the earthquake with their normal lunch time preparations. This tells us that some aspects of time may be encoded in autobiographical memory, specifically when an autobiographical memory occurs in the context of a stereotypical activity usually occurring at a specific time. *(say "lunch that day")*

Flashbulb Memories   Flashbulb memories are those that result when we find out that a highly unexpected and emotionally charged event has taken place (Winograd & Killinger, 1983). They have been described as examples of extreme episodic memories (Houston, 1986). In some ways, such memories seem to obey the normal laws of retrieval. For example, they can seldom be cued by a chronological prompt. Can you retrieve one newsworthy event that happened in, let's say, January 1986? Most people can't. However, in other ways, these memories are unusual. One curious thing about them is the amount of detail they seem to contain. For example, where were you when you learned of the *Challenger* space shuttle disaster? Who were you with? How did you find out? Many people can provide answers to these questions, and they believe that their answers are quite accurate. (This event took place in January 1986, by the way.) Some have argued that it's the highly charged emotional flavor of flashbulb memories that gives them their seemingly indelible, accurate nature. On an intuitive level, this account is appealing, but the scientific literature simply doesn't support it. First as Wagenaar's findings show, pleasant and unpleasant memories do show differential retrieval probabilities, but only for a year or so. After that, very pleasant memories were no more likely to be retrieved than were neutral or very unpleasant memories. Now it may be the case that the emotionally charged memories *appear* to be indelible and accurate, but probably we use the same fallible inferential retrieval strategies with both emotional and nonemotional memories.

Neisser and Harsch (1992) demonstrated this in a study of people's memory of the *Challenger* disaster. While the rest of the nation sat transfixed and disbelieving in front of their TVs, Neisser and Harsch got busy and developed a questionnaire, which they administered to 106 subjects the very next morning. Among other things, the subjects were asked to answer five questions concerning their hearing of the news, including where they were, what they were doing, who told them, what time that occurred, and so on. Thirty-two months after the incident, forty-four subjects agreed to complete the questionnaire again. When the results of the follow-up were compared to the answers on the original questionnaire (which were presumably accurate), it became clear that the subjects' memories for the incident had dimmed. Of the 220 potentially recallable facts produced by the subjects the morning after the explosion, the subjects' later recall efforts were at least partially wrong on more than 150 items. Fully 25% of the subjects misremembered all five attributes on their original questionnaires. It's important to note that the accuracy of any specific subject's memory was not correlated with his or her confidence in that memory. In some cases, subjects were quite confident of the accuracy of an incorrect retrieval.

At this juncture, it may be worthwhile to comment briefly on some of the implications of autobiographical memory (or "everyday" memory as it's sometimes called). From the standpoint of ecological validity (Neisser, 1978), research on flashbulb memories and autobiographical memory generally is healthy because it anchors the scientific study of memory on our everyday experience. Such a viewpoint implies a natural linkage between the scientific enterprise and our everyday lives: The scientific study of memory *should* help us answer questions about why we remember or forget what we do. On the other hand, some cognitivists have maintained that an emphasis on ecological validity leads to studies that must have very low generalizability (Banaji & Crowder, 1989). That is, they argue that asking subjects about the *Challenger* disaster, for example, might answer questions about the accuracy of memory for that incident, but such an approach tells us next to nothing about what people remember in some general sense. Banaji and Crowder (1989) go on to suggest that only laboratory studies (which are frequently rather low in ecological validity) can provide theories and findings that are generalizable.

Another important point concerns the precision of the terms "episodic memory" and "autobiographical memory." As they are being used here, autobiographical memory is described as a kind of episodic memory, and this implies that all autobiographical memories are episodic in nature. However, this does not mean that all episodic memory is autobiographical in nature. In fact we can be pretty sure that there are many episodic memories that are not, and will not, become autobiographical memories. Nelson (1993) makes this point by comparing what she had for lunch yesterday with the first time that she delivered a research paper at a scientific conference. You may be able to retrieve (today) what you ate for lunch yesterday, but it's unlikely that you will be able to do so for an extended period of time into the future, unless your lunch yesterday was something very special. On the other hand, you probably will be able to retrieve a personal milestone like the memory of your first job interview for a long time thereafter. This distinction implies that autobiographical memories might start out being "normal" or everyday episodic memories. But unless something occurs to somehow "elevate" them, such memories will not become part of our personal life story.

For the student, what we can say at this point is that the findings from autobiographical, or everyday, memory studies are interesting, and that cognitivists are still sorting out the relationship of such findings to "mainstream" laboratory results.

Episodic and Semantic Memory Reconsidered   In addition to the studies described above, other researchers (Herrmann & Harwood, 1980; Klatzky, 1984; Shoben, Wescourt & Smith, 1978) also have reported evidence favoring the distinction between semantic and episodic memory. However, not all cognitivists think the distinction is a valid or useful one (Anderson & Ross, 1980; McCloskey & Santee, 1981; McKoon & Ratcliff, 1979). Hannigan, Shelton, Franks, and Bransford (1980) have concluded that both memory systems must be involved in performance on every memory task. That is, although it's theoretically possible to disentangle the contributions made by each system to a person's performance, in practice, disentangling these contributions has proved difficult.

In the Hannigan et al. research, subjects were presented with a long list of unrelated sentences. Some subjects were supplied with an organizing framework

USING YOUR KNOWLEDGE OF COGNITION

Ask some of your friends to determine, as best they can, the month and year that the United States and its Coalition partners launched the ground attack against Iraq known as Desert Storm. (It was in February 1991.) Ask them to "think out loud" as they try to retrieve the date. There are several strategies that a person could use to make this determination. Let's consider a couple. A person may respond to the question as follows: "Approximately how many years ago was that? Four or five? Then I was still probably a senior in high school, and taking a physics class. Is that right? Who was in that physics class with me? Do I remember talking to them about Desert Storm?" Let's contrast that approach with the following retrieval attempt: "Let's see, I remember that I talked about it with this one person—he was in a physics class that I had my senior year in high school, so that would have been five years ago." Do you notice any difference in the two hypothetical approaches?

Using the first strategy, the person makes an estimate of the time that the event occurred and then treats this event as a hypothesis for which evidence can be gathered either to support or refute it. Using the second strategy, the person relies on his or her memory to retrieve an image or a moment, and then the person attempts to place this moment chronologically. Although each of these strategies is theoretically plausible, if you do this exercise, I think you'll find that very few people use the first strategy. Instead people seem to overrely on the accuracy of their memory in retrieving a specific conversation, or reaction, "observing" this memory, and finally dating it.

for these sentences, and other subjects were not. The memory task was slightly similar to the shadowing studies examined in Chapter 2. The subjects heard various sentences presented against a background of white noise, and their task was to repeat them out loud as accurately as they could. The performance of subjects who had been presented with the sentences was compared with a control group who had not. Subjects familiar with the sentences outperformed the control group.

This finding indicates an episodic memory effect. Even when the subjects had no organizing framework for the sentences, the fact that they had encoded and stored them conferred an advantage over subjects who didn't have that experience. The subjects who had been provided with a framework, however, outperformed all other subjects on the task. This finding demonstrates the effects of semantic memory. The subjects who had an organizing schema to guide the encoding process were apparently able to elaborate the sentences more completely, which in this case meant associating the sentences with previously stored general knowledge.

This effect was demonstrated in another way, too. During the white noise test, the subjects were also presented with new and unfamiliar sentences that were nevertheless appropriate to the framework. What might we predict about the subjects' performance on such sentences? Clearly, the control group should have no particular advantage in repeating such sentences, nor should the nonframework subjects, because their episodic encoding shouldn't contain much general knowledge that might be helpful in guiding the processing of sentences partially masked by the white noise. However, the framework subjects should have an advantage in processing these ambiguous stimuli. That is, the framework might help the processing of these sentences by at least constraining the range of guesses that the subjects might consider when they are forced to conjecture.

Thus, the Hannigan et al. study offers a good demonstration of the *combined* effects of semantic and episodic memory. But, overall, it seems that those researchers who have gone hunting for a scientific foundation on which to base the distinction between episodic and semantic memory have not found it (Dosher, 1984; McKoon, Ratcliff & Dell, 1985; Neely & Durgunoglu, 1985; Watkins & Kerkar, 1985). For his part, Tulving (1985, 1986) has modified his original position, now suggesting that episodic memory is a subsystem of a larger semantic memory unit. This idea will certainly be scrutinized in the future.

CONCLUDING COMMENTS AND SUGGESTIONS FOR FURTHER READING

This chapter has examined the basic information-processing theory of memory, some of its modifications, and some alternative accounts. Along the way, we've received an introduction to some of the basic techniques and findings of the memory literature. What have we come up with so far?

First, what happened to the information-processing model could be approached as a case study of cognitive science in action. The original theory as erected by Atkinson and Shiffrin was a first-rate summary and interpretation of the huge memory literature that cognitive psychologists and their predecessors had painstakingly worked on. However, other findings accumulated, and the theory has had to undergo fairly extensive modifications over the last twenty or so years. These changes are to be expected and should be taken as a sign of vitality. A fair statement is that most cognitive psychologists would still endorse some version of the information-processing theory of memory, but perhaps not exactly as written by Atkinson and Shiffrin. What has changed? First, the operation of the sensory register has been downplayed. In light of the recent findings, the evidence suggesting that sensory storage is necessary for further information processing no longer seems as compelling as it once did. If you read this chapter closely, you'll know the reasons for this.

Second, the distinction between STS and LTS has blurred over the last decade or so. Again, our intuitions tell us that we have both a working memory and a permanent memory, and countless reports in the literature indicate that these intuitions are essentially correct. What has changed over the years is the characteristics of these storages. I've used the words *distinct* and *separate* several times in the chapter to describe the border between STS and LTS. However, the recent findings have indicated that the characteristics of the memory code are not determined as it moves rather passively through our information-processing system. Instead, the evidence seems to indicate that people have great flexibility in how material is encoded, stored, and retrieved. Again, if you read this chapter closely, you'll know why cognitive psychologists are not likely to endorse the notion of completely separate short- and long-term storages.

Students who would like to find out more about these matters could probably start with the Atkinson and Shiffrin (1968) article. Two good technical reviews of iconic storage are Coltheart (1975) and Holding (1975). More recent (and more critical) reviews can be found in Kolers (1983) and Haber (1983). I didn't discuss echoic storage in any depth, but Crowder (1976) has written a first-rate review that points out the issues.

For students who might like to read reviews of the current status of memory theorizing and research, I would say that the chapters by Schacter (1989) and

Hintzman (1990) would be good choices. Students who would like a good grounding in the episodic/semantic memory distinction would be well served by reading Tulving's own writings (1983, 1985, 1986). To see how Tulving's theory can be converted into a practical research program, see Harris and Morris (1984) for a good collection of articles on episodic and autobiographical memory. Regarding autobiographical memory, I commented on the rather negative view-point of Banaji and Crowder (1989), and their cogent article makes for interesting reading. In the January 1991 issue of the *American Psychologist,* a series of rebuttals appeared, and, along with a book by Neisser (1982), these readings will offer the student an opportunity to hear both sides of this issue. Also worth reading are the edited volume by Neisser and Winograd (1988) and an introduction to the literature on autobiographical memory by Conway (1990).

 **KEY TERMS**

Storage
Cognitive code
Control processes
Sensory register
Capacity
Modality specific
Decay
Short-term storage
Long-term storage

Rehearsal
Whole-report technique
Partial-report technique
Inter-stimulus interval
Icon
Echo
Interference
Serial position effect
Primacy component

Recency component
Chunking
Retrograde amnesia
Dual-code position
Episodic memory
Semantic memory
Backward masking

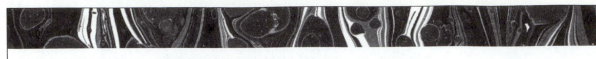

FOCUS ON RESEARCH
How Much Is an Icon Worth?

The subjective experience of seeing an icon is powerful. Indeed, most people cannot tell precisely the point at which the physical stimulation stops and the icon's existence begins. This inability is what has led many researchers to wonder about the icon's perceptual properties. The same processes that are used to extract information from actual physical stimuli are apparently also used to extract information from the icon. But is this true? Is the information stored in the visual sensory register so raw that it can be accessed by perceptual processes? This question was addressed in a study by Loftus, Johnson, and Shimamura (1985). The reasoning and methodology used in this study were clever. Let's assume that looking at an icon is like looking at the physical stimulus. If the rate of information extraction is equal (and if the same processes are involved, it should be), then the subject who first sees a target stimulus and then sees an icon should have an advantage in recognizing the stimulus over a subject who sees only the target but no icon.

Loftus et al. formulated the problem in this way. Let's assume that a picture is presented to a subject for some base duration of *d* msec. Let's also assume that we let the subject have an icon. Finally, let's suppose that we later test the subject's recognition memory for the picture. We can formalize her performance as being helped by two components: the base duration and the icon; and we can let $p(d, i)$ stand for this performance. Contrast this approach with the situation in which we let the subject have the actual physical stimulus for a period of *a* msec over and above the base duration.

In the natural course of events, this situation would also lead to the formation of an icon. But suppose we find a way to prevent the icon's formation? Then we would be in a position to compare subjects' performance when they had both the physical stimulation and the icon as opposed to just having more of the physical stimulation. There is a way to prevent the formation of an icon. It has been known for some time that, when a second visual stimulus is presented within approximately 100 msec of an initial visual stimulus

that has been on display for 50 msec, people have an extremely difficult time retrieving any information from the first stimulus. In fact, people are typically likely to report that the initial stimulus was never presented at all, despite the fact that, if not followed by a second stimulus, the initial stimulus is very perceivable. This phenomenon has an obvious name: **backward masking.** The formation of an icon can be blocked by presenting a second visual stimulus that interferes with the normal processing of the initial stimulus. On the recognition task, from Loftus et al., we could symbolize the subject's performance with the term $p(d + a, -i)$. That is, in this case, the individual has had access to more actual physical stimulation but no icon, as opposed to the first hypothetical subject who had less physical stimulation but who also had the icon to look at. So the question we're asking is this: How long does the *a* interval have to be before the two performances are even? In other words, what does *a* have to be to make the following equation hold: $p(d,i) = p(d + a, -i)$?

The subjects saw 144 complex pictures, which were presented in durations ranging from 62 to 1,050 msec. The mask consisted of a jumble of black and gray lines. In some cases, the mask was presented immediately after the target picture; in other cases, a 300-msec delay occurred. Other subjects were not shown the mask at all. In the recognition test phase, the subjects were shown the pictures in a different order and were asked to indicate whether or not they had seen them before. The results indicated that *a* was about 100 msec. What does this mean? Suppose a picture had been presented for 270 msec. If this picture was not masked, the subjects formed an icon of it. In the recognition test, subjects correctly recognized pictures presented for that duration about 69 percent of the time. Their hit rate was therefore .69. However, if we compare this performance with that of subjects who were not permitted to form an icon, we find that a duration of 370 msec was required to achieve a hit rate of .69. In other words, having an icon was worth about 100 msec of additional physical stimulation.

CHAPTER 5

HUMAN MEMORY: A PROCESSING VIEW

CHAPTER OUTLINE

"Don't you remember?" the student was asking me. "You said I could take the test later." "Well," I responded, "I can't remember saying that." "No, really," she said, "It was right after class, and I think it was the last class before we left for Thanksgiving break. I had two other finals the same day as yours, and you said I could take your test later. Don't you remember that?" she said. Now I thought I detected a slight but rising panic in her voice because she thought I would make her take a test for which she was unready. "No," I said, "I can't remember having that conversation, but it's ok. If you have two other finals the same day as ours, then you can reschedule the final in this class." The student was visibly relieved as we set up an alternative time for her to take the final.

Unfortunately, I have retrieval failures like that all the time. When students intercept me after class and tell me about some special circumstances that necessitate a change in procedures for them, I almost always agree to the change. And so I wind up saying yes to a lot of things, but, because of the sheer numbers of these requests, I tend to forget the specifics of each encounter. So, the fact that I couldn't remember this case in particular wasn't unusual or interesting. But I found the episode interesting for other reasons. First is what the student did to prompt my recall. Clearly, although the student may not have thought of herself as a memory theorist, she did have a practical theory of memory nevertheless. She had the idea that if she told me an increasing number of specific facts about the circumstances of the original conversa-

tion, then the likelihood of my retrieving the memory would be increased. From this perspective, the student's prompting ("Don't you remember?") was her way of saying, "Have I given you enough retrieval cues to enable your obviously faulty cognitive system to retrieve this important fact?" On one hand, the student's theory of memory is probably correct: the more context she gave me, the more likely it was that I would retrieve the conversation. But the student really had no way of knowing that I had built up a "student-asking-me-permission-for-something" scheme over my years as a professor (we'll learn more about the term "scheme" in this chapter). Unfortunately for her, such schemes really don't seem to retain very much information about specific encounters.

Another interesting part of the student's theory had to do with something we'll call the "copy theory" of memory. The copy theory, in one form or another, dates back to antiquity. Although it is not now an acknowledged theory of memory, I think that most people believe some form of it to be true nevertheless. It's called the copy theory because, according to this view, my memory is a stored "copy" of my experiences. For example, according to the copy theory, somewhere inside my cognitive system is the memory of my conversation with the student; all I have to do is "look for" the memory in the right way, or in the right spot, and I'll retrieve it. The copy theory says retrieval failures come about for the same reason that books sometimes cannot be located in a library: The book is in there somewhere, but it's been misshelved. Nobody knows where in the library the book might be. According to the copy theory, the same holds true for our memories: Each memory still exists inside the cognitive system, or inside our brains, or inside something, but the memory has gotten out of its proper location in the system. This view has a nice explanation for the recovery of "repressed" memories too. The recovery of a repressed memory is something like the finding of a long-lost book in some unusual place in the library: It's been there all along, but the library had just lost track of it. But could the "copy theory" be a correct theory of memory? Are my memories of things actually "stored" anywhere in my cognitive system? I don't want to use this overview to bias you, but I will say at the outset that it is difficult to see how the cognitive system could "store" anything in this way. One of the problems seems semantic: Given that the cognitive system is really just an abstract depiction of the neural system, it is difficult to see how the cognitive system has anything "inside" or "outside" it. Abstractions like the cognitive system don't have any spatial qualities like "inside" or "outside." But even if you drop down to the neural level, there are still problems: What would it mean to say that the neural system keeps a copy of something?

Let's go back to the conversation I had with the student for one more point. It's clear that, following her prompting and contextual information, the student expected me to experience an event called "remembering" something. This event is sort of hard to put into words, but basically, when you remember something, you "feel" like you're remembering something. This suggests that there are two apparent parts to many retrievals: one part carries the content of the memory; the other part carries the "feeling" of having retrieved it, that is, the conscious experience of having retrieved the memory. For example, yesterday there was a special deal available at a local fast-food place (two for $2), and so I had two barbecued hamburgers for lunch. The content of the memory is the knowledge of what kind of burgers they were, and the conscious experience is the feeling of remembering ordering, looking at, eating, and cleaning myself up after the burgers. But this second part raises an interesting question: Is this feeling of remembering a critical part of my remembering something? Could I remember something that was not accompanied by this conscious experience of retrieval? In a certain sense, the answer to this question has to be "yes, you could, and it's a good thing too." Why this response? Well, think about it for a minute: Every time you put your foot on the gas at a green light, you do so because the cognitive system "remembers" that you go on a green light. That's the "content" of that particular memory. But what would it be like if you had to have a conscious experience of remembering this every time you wanted to go? It would be cumbersome to put it mildly. This suggests that the "feeling" of remembering, or the conscious experience of remembering, is not a critical component in remembering something. That is, the cognitive system may demonstrate that it can retrieve information, without producing a conscious experience of having done that retrieval. How might such retrievals be demonstrated? We'll take a look at that issue too in this chapter.

In the previous chapter, we considered memory from the standpoint of the organizational characteristics that are apparent in its retention. In this chapter, we'll examine what people seem to be doing with their cognitive system when they want that system to be able to retain and retrieve something. That is, we will look at memory from the standpoint of what people do to get their memories to work; these are the processes and procedures of memory.

For cognitive psychologists, there are at least three discernable memory operations that need to be discussed.

These are **encoding, storing,** and **retrieving.**

Encoding refers to a transformation of the stimulus into a format that can be retained by our cognitive systems. In this sense, encoding a stimulus means preparing it to be stored (Klatzky, 1980). This preparation in turn involves organizing the stimuli in some particular way. When we encode stimuli, we prepare them for our memories by organizing them in certain ways. Next, there is the *storage operation*. Like most people, you probably assume that, when you store something in your memory, a change takes place in your brain; that is, your central nervous system is somehow physically altered by the activities involved in storing things. This belief is valid to a certain extent. We know that the destruction of particular neural tissue produces disturbances in memory. Moreover, the relationship between the tissue destroyed and the memory deficit produced is often predictable. But nobody knows exactly what takes place in the brain when you store something in it. Finally, after encoding and storing the material, in order to use your memory, you must *retrieve* the information.

One other point should be noted. This chapter is divided into three principal sections, and some passages may imply that encoding, storing, and retrieving are three memory processes that are always truly separable from one another. That implication is not completely true. The three processes almost always influence each other and are not to be understood as separate stages. Separating them is basically a teaching convenience to provide some landmarks in what might otherwise be confusing terrain.

ENCODING

Chapter 3 described a debate that has arisen among cognitive psychologists concerning the organization of stimuli. Direct theorists believe that some stimulation—light in particular—is inherently organized as a result of its reflection from objects in the world. These theorists also typically believe that humans have evolved with a sensitivity to this type of organization. In other words, direct theorists believe that people are inherently tuned into the organization of stimuli in the world, and consequently, little cognitive work is required to encode much of the stimulation surrounding us.

Most memory theorists, however, would probably be reluctant to accept this position. Instead, they would argue that most of the stimulation impinging on us is ambiguous in that it can be encoded, or organized, in a variety of ways (Wickens, 1970). For example, consider the word *grounds*. What does it mean? "Meaning" implies "synonym" but *grounds* can be a synonym for *property*, for *reasons*, or for the sediment left in the coffeepot. The point here is that the word *grounds* doesn't have much meaning by itself. Yet, to remember this word, it must be encoded (i.e., organized), and for that purpose, some meaning must be assigned. This section considers some of the variables that influence encoding. We'll see that the nature of the encoding has a powerful influence on the ease or difficulty of retrieval.

Levels of Processing

As you'll recall, by the end of the last chapter we had seen that cognitive psychologists were becoming convinced that a complete understanding of memory would not result from a specification of the characteristics of the separate memory buffers. Indeed, cognitivists were instead trying to understand the many ways that it might be possible to encode a stimulus. Craik and Lockhart (1972) were among the earliest researchers to express this viewpoint. They rejected the idea that memory's location determined its characteristics. Rather than think of the to-be-remembered stimulus as a fixed object with distinct properties that were altered as it moved through a rigid system of storages and buffers, Craik and Lockhart maintained that the stimulus could be processed in a variety of ways. For example, an individual could bring sensory processes to bear on a stimulus and extract its physical characteristics from it. On the other hand, the person had control over other cognitive processes capable of extracting and encoding acoustic or semantic features of the stimulus. Craik and Lockhart viewed this as a continuum of progressively deeper cognitive processing—deeper in the sense that more background knowledge is required to carry out a semantic analysis of a word than to carry out an acoustic analysis. Material stored in memory—the memory code—acquired its semantic or acoustic properties not because it was being stored in certain locations but because it had been processed in particular ways that were under the person's control. The nature of the memory code is therefore a record of the cognitive processes that have been performed on it. In summary, each approach to processing produced a cognitive code that could be evaluated along a continuum of depth. Generally, the greater the semantic analysis (the more meaning extracted from the stimulus), the greater the **depth of processing.**

Craik (1979) has stated that the levels of processing model has two central postulates. First, a semantic analysis results in a deeper code, and thus a more meaningful one, than does a nonsemantic analysis. Second, the deeper the code, the more durable the memory. This means that forgetting is simply a function of depth of processing: We forget things that we have not processed semantically. To these central postulates I'll add some corollaries. First, you should be aware that we're not dealing with a multiple storage model. That is, there is no notion of the transfer of memories from one storage location to another. Second, and correspondingly, there are no capacity limitations. Evidence that seems to indicate the need for different storages with differing capacities (such as the phenomenon of memory span) can be interpreted in terms of processing limitations. Another implication is that the durability of a memory is somewhat independent of the time spent processing. A great deal of time spent processing material at a nonsemantic (shallow) level will probably not produce a more durable memory than would a short time processing at the semantic level (Craik & Watkins, 1973; Rundus, 1977).

A study by Parkin (1984) illustrates the basic depth of processing effect. His subjects were given a word, about which they had to make a semantic-orienting or nonsemantic-orienting decision. The orienting decision refers to a particular kind of judgment about the word. For example, a semantic-orienting decision might involve a category or synonym judgment. A nonsemantic task might involve making a judgment about how many vowels the word contained or whether it had been printed completely in capital letters. Following a series of such trials, the subjects were given a surprise free-recall test. The subjects who had been semantically oriented recalled significantly more of the target words than did subjects who were nonsemantically oriented. This result suggests that semantic processing produces a more durable memory code than does nonsemantic processing.

A study by Jacoby, Craik, and Begg (1979) supports this interpretation. Their subjects were given pairs of common nouns (e.g., *horse–goat*) and were told to evaluate the size of the difference between the objects on a 1 (not much difference) to 10 (vast difference) scale. In some cases, the difference between the named objects was relatively small, whereas in other situations, the difference in size was large. After the subjects had made these evaluations, they were given an unexpected memory test in which they were asked to recall as many of the objects as they could. Jacoby et al. found that an inverse relationship existed between the size of the difference between the objects and the likelihood of their recall. The subjects were more likely to recall the objects when the difference between them was small than when it was large. As Jacoby et al. explained, the task required a semantic analysis of the objects' properties. However, when the objects were approximately the same size, a deeper analysis was required, thus producing a more durable memory code. Notice that the subjects were not aware that a memory test was forthcoming when they made their evaluations of size differences. But the fact that they engaged in a semantic analysis of the words facilitated their retrieval. The implications of this finding are clear: Your chances of retrieving a memory depend on the type of processing you do to remember it, not on how *hard* you try to remember.

These effects were shown in a study by Hyde and Jenkins (1973). The subjects saw a list of twenty-four words, which was presented at the rate of three seconds per word. Each subject had one of two tasks. In one condition, the subjects simply had to check whether each word contained an *a* or a *q*. In the second condition, the subjects had to rate the pleasantness of the word, which presumably required a deeper level of processing than simply looking at the word's physical characteristics. This study had a second variable. Half of the group of subjects was told that a memory test would be given after the words were presented, and these subjects were encouraged to learn the words. This group was called the intentional learning group. The other half of the group was uninformed about the subsequent memory test, and any knowledge they retained about the words was therefore incidental.

Table 5.1 shows the findings of this study. Notice that there is a strong depth of processing effect. When the subjects carried out the semantic analysis, their recall was dramatically enhanced. Notice, too, that intentionality had only a small effect on the proportion of the words recalled. The levels of processing viewpoint is thus able to account for something that vexed multiple storage models. Our memories are not controlled directly by our intentions (which makes the Atkinson and Shiffrin term *control processes* somewhat misleading) but rather by the type of processing we do.

Maintenance Rehearsal and Elaborative Rehearsal   To help make these processing effects clearer, Craik and Lockhart (1972) distinguished between two kinds of rehearsal. Type I rehearsal, sometimes called **maintenance rehearsal,** refers to the continual repetition of analyses that have already been carried out. It does not lead to stronger or more permanent memories; its principal function is to retain

....   **TABLE 5.1**   Percentage of words recalled as a function of orienting task and whether subjects were aware of learning task

Learning Purpose Conditions	ORIENTING TASK	
	Rate Pleasantness	Check Letters
Incidental	68	39
Intentional	69	43

Source: Hyde and Jenkins, 1973. (Copyright 1973 by Academic Press, Inc. Adapted by permission of the publisher and author.)

the availability of an item in memory. Maintenance rehearsal tends to emphasize the phonetic aspects of a stimulus (Wickens, 1984). Type II rehearsal, also known as **elaborative rehearsal,** refers to successively deeper processing of the stimulus and does produce more durable memories. It emphasizes the semantic aspects of a stimulus. Both types are under the person's control: They operate on material in working memory, and they compete for cognitive resources with other tasks.

Craik and Watkins (1973) demonstrated that the nature of rehearsal, not how much, is what determines a memory's durability. The subjects in their study were presented with a total of twelve lists, each containing twelve words. The subjects were told to rehearse these words consciously. Moreover, they were told that the last four words of each list were especially important and that these should be remembered at all costs. To emphasize this point, the last four words of each list were printed in block letters. The study had two retrieval conditions. Subjects were asked to recall the list either immediately or following a twenty-second delay. If recall was delayed, the subjects were told that active rehearsal of the list was permitted. When all twelve lists had been presented, Craik and Watkins sprang a surprise: they asked the subjects to recall as many of the entire set of 144 words as they could. The findings are shown in Figure 5.1.

As the top graph shows, the subjects took advantage of the opportunity to rehearse the last four items of the lists during the twenty-second delay. As the

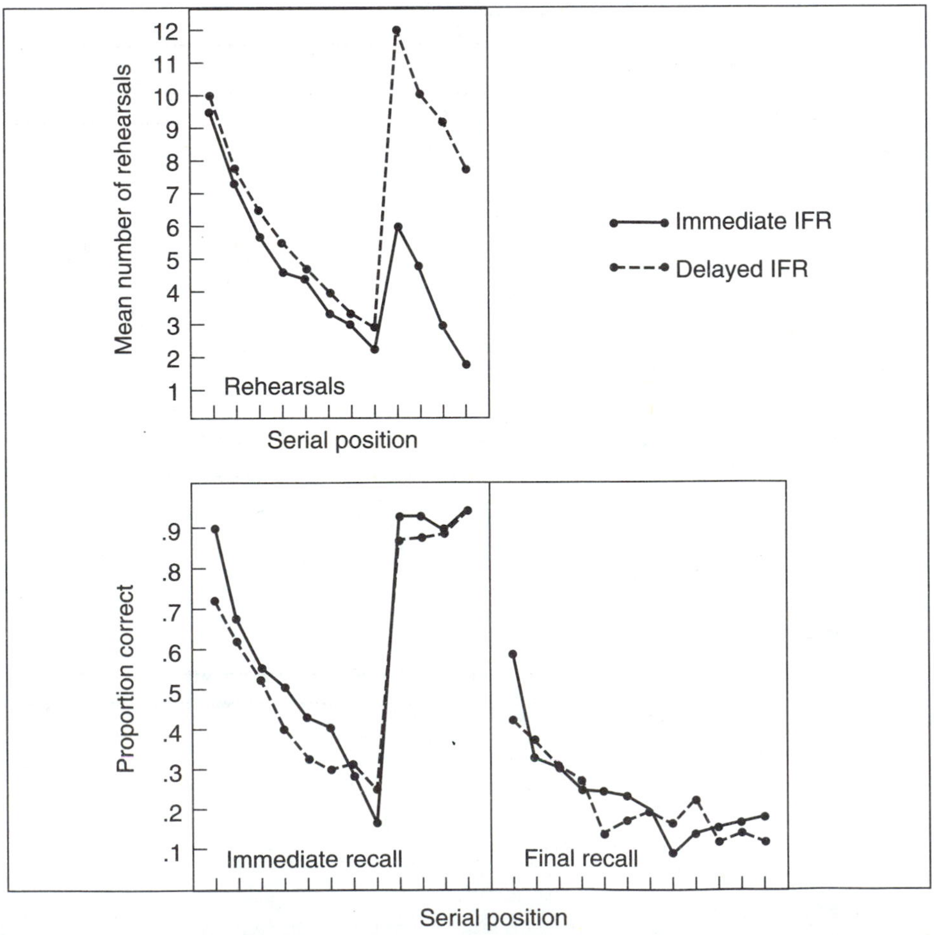

FIGURE 5.1

Average number of rehearsals (top graph), proportion correct on the immediate free-recall test (lower left graph), and proportion correct on the final recall test (lower right graph) as a function of serial position. The two lines in the graphs show the results for groups that recalled after no delay or after a twenty-second delay in the immediate free-recall test.

(From "The Role of Rehearsal in Short-Term Memory," by F. I. M. Craik and M. J. Watkins. In *Journal of Verbal Learning and Verbal Behavior*, 1973, 12, 599–607. Copyright 1973 by Academic Press, Inc. Reprinted by permission.)

lower left graph shows, an expected recency effect occurred when the words were recalled immediately after presentation or after the twenty-second delay. The lower right graph shows the effects of the surprise. Even though the last four items of each list were rehearsed far more frequently than were the other items, and even though an immediate recency effect occurred, there was virtually no long-term effect. In the final recall test, words that had been presented in one of the last four serial positions were not recalled with any greater frequency than were words presented in other serial positions. Even though the last four words had been rehearsed more than the others, this was maintenance rehearsal, which did not necessarily lead to more durable memories (Craik & Watkins, 1973).

The distinction between elaborative and maintenance rehearsal sounds plausible, and the results obtained by Craik and Watkins make sense. However, this position implies that *all* semantic processing is equal and thus should create memories of equal durability. But does it?

To answer this question, Craik and Tulving (1975) presented sentences and words tachistoscopically to their subjects. The words and sentences were shown concurrently, and the subject's task was to decide whether the word would meaningfully fit into a blank left in the sentence. The semantic complexity of the sentence was varied, too. The following three examples show the increasing semantic complexity of the sentences:

> Simple: She cooked the _____ .
> Medium: The _____ frightened the children.
> Complex: The great bird swooped down and carried off the struggling _____ .

After sixty judgments (twenty of each complexity level), Craik and Tulving sprang the by-now-familiar surprise: a memory test was given. A cued-recall format was used in this test. The subjects were given the sentence and asked to recall the word that had been shown concurrently. This time the surprise was on Craik and Tulving: Subjects remembered more of the complex sentence fill-ins than the simple sentence fill-ins. Considering only yes responses, those in which the word could be meaningfully used in the sentence, the subjects recalled about twice as many from the complex sentences as they did for the simple sentences. But how could this have occurred? In all cases, semantic processing had been carried out, which is the deepest level according to the theory. Therefore, there should not have been any differences in retrieval as a function of the sentence's complexity. Why, then, did Craik and Tulving observe these differences? The answer must lie in the nature of the elaborative rehearsal *and* the larger cognitive structure into which the elaborated code was being fed. In other words, the semantic processing done by subjects on the complex sentences seems to have accessed other cognitive codes whose nature was richer or more elaborate than those accessed in the simple sentences.

Some Problems with "Levels" of Processing   Although the levels of processing account is persuasive, it has been dogged by a few problems. First, the approach has the problem we just touched on—that of contradictory findings. Nelson and McEvoy (1979) reasoned that, if words have been processed at the semantic level, then providing a semantic cue should produce better retrieval than a nonsemantic cue. But as it turns out, presenting nonsemantic cues (such as the cue *IME* for the list word *DIME*) is just as effective as presenting semantic cues (such as "an American coin" for *DIME*). Further, Hunt and Elliot (1980) have demonstrated that words with an irregular and distinctive orthography (like *phlegm*) are retained better when they are processed as part of a list containing words with both regular and irregular orthographies than when a list is made up totally of such distinctive words. Even when the task requires a semantic analysis, some nonsemantic information—in this case orthographic distinctiveness—seems to be retained.

A second problem with this approach involves an independent definition of depth of processing. Usually, the level of processing is operationally defined by the nature of the orienting task that the subject is given to do. For example, if the subject is given a task involving checking letters or producing rhymes, this processing is considered nonsemantic. But if the subject is required to produce a synonym, then the subject must be processing the material at the semantic level. As many commentators have pointed out (Nelson, 1979; Postman, Thompkins, & Gray, 1978), this operational definition is barely adequate. It's hard to say exactly what the subject is doing when he is instructed to process the material in a particular way. Furthermore, it's hard to see a way around the problem of defining depth. Linking depth of processing to *time* spent processing is irrelevant by definition, and asking the subjects to self-report their own depth of processing is fraught with difficulties (Seamon & Virostek, 1978).

Yet another problem concerns the relationship between depth of processing and automaticity. As we saw earlier in the book, highly overlearned tasks become progressively more automatic; that is, they can be executed without heavy demands on cognitive processes. What if subjects become highly practiced at making semantic decisions? According to the levels of processing view, the subjects should show good retention of this material because it has been deeply processed. However, according to the automaticity viewpoint, the subjects should show little or no retention of such material. Fiske and Schneider (1984) pitted these viewpoints against one another. Their subjects were extensively trained to categorize certain materials automatically. Categorization is an orienting task that is usually thought of as semantic. But Fiske and Schneider found that their subjects, who had done well at the categorization task, showed little recognition memory for the categorized materials. This finding is contradictory to the levels of processing approach.

A problem can also be found in the concept of maintenance and elaborative rehearsal. For example, at least in some cases, maintenance rehearsal does improve memory (Glenberg & Adams, 1978). That kind of finding has suggested to many students of memory that a categorical view of rehearsal strategies is probably not correct (Craik, 1979; Jacoby & Craik, 1979). Rehearsal strategies can probably be graded along a continuum of elaboration. This formulation will almost certainly be assessed in future work.

Transfer Appropriate Processing   Perhaps the biggest complication for the levels of processing position comes from a classic study done by Morris, Bransford, and Franks (1977). In this study, the experimenter read aloud thirty-two sentences, each having a missing word. In the shallow processing condition, the experimenter might read a sentence such as the following: "Blank rhymes with legal." After hearing this sentence, the subjects heard an additional word called the target word, and their task was to decide if the target could be substituted appropriately for the blank. For example, in this case the subjects should say "yes" if the target word were "eagle" but "no" if the target word were "peach." In the deep processing condition, the task was similar but was modified slightly to demand semantic processing by the subjects. Now, the experimenter might read a sentence such as, "The blank has a silver engine." Hearing the target word "eagle" after this sentence should produce a "no" from the subjects, whereas hearing the target word "train" should be answered "yes." At test time, half of the group of subjects was given a standard recognition task: Each of the target words was presented along with some additional words that functioned as distractors. The subject's task was to pick out the target word. Consistent with the levels of processing position, the subjects did a better job of recognizing target words that had been presented in the semantic version of the task than those presented in the rhyming version of the task. But a different fate awaited the other half of the group. These subjects were given a rhyming recognition task. In the rhyming recognition task, the subjects were presented with a series of words and asked to pick out which word in that series rhymed with a target word that had been seen before. So, continuing the example above, if the original target word had been "eagle," the subject might see a series containing the word "regal," and if the original target word had been "train," the subject might now see a series including the word "brain." Now something surprising happened: The subjects did a better job of picking out rhyming words of targets that had originally been presented in the rhyming condition than they did for rhyming words of targets that been presented in the semantic condition. This finding is exactly the opposite of that predicted by the levels of processing position; here, when subjects engaged in the shallow, rhyming task, they did better than when they had engaged in the deep, semantic task. How come?

Morris et al. used the concept of **transfer appropriate processing** to explain these effects. Transfer appropriate processing refers to the idea that the cognitive processes that are used in the initial learning or encoding of some material interact with the cognition used at retrieval time. This means that the best encoding is the encoding based on cognitive processes that most closely match the type of cognitive processing that will be used at retrieval time. Simply put, if you're going to have to retrieve something by rhyming, then the best encoding you can make also will involve rhyming. But if you are going to have retrieve some material using semantic processing, then it is probably best for you to use semantic processing at encoding time.

Context

The **context** of a stimulus refers to the other stimuli that have been presented concurrently. As you might imagine, surrounding stimuli can exert a strong effect on the kind of encoding that is done. For example, consider the word *grounds* that I mentioned earlier. *Grounds* would probably be encoded as *property* in the context of *Country Homes* magazine, but an altogether different encoding would be carried out if the term *grounds* appeared in the *Amateur Electrician*. In the encoding of a stimulus, context sets the stage. Context is really another example of top-down, or conceptually driven, processing (Jenkins, 1974). The surrounding stimuli guide the interpretation of the to-be-encoded stimulus.

This issue was explored in a study by Light and Carter-Sobell (1970). Their subjects were presented with sentences in which a specific phrase had been emphasized (e.g., "The boy earned a GOOD GRADE on the test"). The subjects were told that, following the entire presentation of sentences, a memory test would be given in which the subjects would be asked to recognize the emphasized noun but not the adjective. The recognition task had several conditions. In some cases, the noun was presented once again with the same adjective (i.e., "good grade"). In other conditions, the noun was presented with a different, but nevertheless meaningful, adjective. For example, the subject might see the phrase "steep grade." In either case, the subject's task was to report whether or not *grade* had been presented in a sentence.

This manipulation produced a dramatic effect. Subjects correctly recognized the nouns 64 percent of the time when they were presented in their original context. But the recognition accuracy was only 27 percent when the nouns were presented in a different context. Light and Carter-Sobell also found that recognition accuracy was superior even when the noun was presented with a never-before-seen adjective, as long as it established the same context as the original adjective. Recognition accuracy was not substantially diminished when the noun was shown in a context such as "bad grade."

This study is important for several reasons. First, as we saw in the levels of processing literature, it demonstrates that a stimulus such as a word is not a rigidly fixed thing that can be encoded in only one way (Hulse, Deese, & Egeth, 1975). Instead, almost every stimulus apparently has many properties, from which we choose the ones that will be used as a basis for the encoding. Second, the study demonstrates that the context produces its biasing effects, even though the context itself is apparently not encoded. In other words, the subjects were obviously influenced by the semantic content of the adjectives even though they were told that the adjectives weren't important and no apparent attempt was made to encode them.

One implication of this point is that the physical environment, which after all is the ultimate context in which all encoding takes place, influences the subject's representation even though aspects of the environment are not them-selves encoded. These effects were explored in two studies. Smith, Glenberg, and Bjork (1978) had their subjects study lists of paired-associate words under different physical conditions. In the first condition, the subjects learned the lists in a large but windowless room, which was located off campus. The experimenter was dressed in a jacket and tie, and the lists were presented visually. In the second condition, the subjects learned the lists in a small room on campus. The experimenter (who was the same person in both conditions) was dressed informally, and the lists were presented on a tape recorder. The day after the subjects learned the lists, a memory test was administered in which the subjects were given one of the paired associates and were asked to recall its mate. Half of the subjects took the memory test in the same room where they learned the list; the other half of the subjects tried to recall the paired associates in the other room. The results were impressive. When the subjects were tested in the same room in which they had learned the list, they recalled 59 percent of the paired associates. When they were tested in the other room, however, their recall dropped to 46 percent.

We should be somewhat cautious in our interpretation of these findings, because further research by Glenberg indicates that, although context can be an important factor in retention, its importance can be mitigated by the presence of other retrieval cues. In short, the situation is more complex than originally thought. The study nevertheless makes an important point: If the subjects had been graded on their performance, their drop-off would have meant the difference between an A and a B, which leads to another important and practical point: If teachers are serious about getting optimal performance from their students, then tests and finals should always be given in the same classroom in which the class meetings took place.

A study by Godden and Baddeley (1975) makes a similar point. Their subjects were scuba divers who learned a list of forty words in one of two conditions: ashore or under water. The subjects then had to recall the list in one of two environments. Half of the subjects recalled the list in the learning environment (i.e., either ashore or under water). The other half of the subjects recalled the list in the other environment. Recalling words under water might seem difficult to you, but the subjects who learned and recalled the words under water performed about 50 percent better than subjects who learned under water and recalled on dry land.

The effects of context are not limited to the physical environment's influence. The mood of the subject who is learning some material is also part of the context, and the probability of retrieval is enhanced if the subject can reestablish the same mood at recall time (Bower, 1981; Bower, Montiero, & Gilligan, 1978). This effect is related to a phenomenon known as **state-dependent learning.** For example, if people learn something while intoxicated with alcohol, they are somewhat more likely to retrieve the material if they are under the influence of alcohol (again) than if they are sober (Overton, 1972; Parker, Birnbaum, & Noble, 1976). Eich, Weingartner, Stillman, and Gillin (1975) have reported similar state-dependent memory effects from marijuana smoking.

Effort and Encoding

There are two issues to be addressed in this section. As the previous sections suggest, each stimulus is a malleable thing that will be encoded in a number of ways depending in part on the individual's strategic choices and in part on other information that surrounds the stimulus. The first issue that we have to deal with concerns people's knowledge of these facts. Can humans take advantage of the fact that the cognitive system is flexible by redirecting their encoding efforts depending on the nature of the memory task they face? The second issue concerns the effort that is expended in making a cognitive code. If I exert a great deal of effort in semantic coding, will my memory be more durable than that of someone who also engages in semantic coding, but who, for some reason, doesn't put as much effort into it as I have?

In answer to the first question, there is some evidence to suggest that people do know, in some sense, that their cognitive systems are flexible. Moreover, this evidence also suggests that people encode things differently depending upon the nature of the memory task. You'll recall that, in Chapter 4, we looked at the work of Frost (1972) who showed her subjects pictures such as those shown in Figure 4.6. Subjects demonstrated that they had coded the pictures visually because they recognized the object faster when it was presented in the same form that they had seen before than they did when the object's drawing was presented in a different perspective. In another study, Frost (1972) used the same series of drawings, and she told one group of subjects that they would be tested in a recognition paradigm (thus implying that it was to the subject's advantage to make a visual encoding of the drawings). However, she deceived a second group of subjects by telling them that they would have to take a free-recall test of the objects' names; in reality, all subjects were tested in a recognition paradigm. Clearly, from the deceived subject's viewpoint, a visual coding would be of no real help. Now, if people truly have some control over their encoding efforts, we should expect that the deceived subjects would *not* make a visual encoding of the drawings. The results confirmed this hypothesis. Only the subjects who expected the recognition task showed the effects of visual coding. Subjects who expected the free-recall test recognized the drawing faster when it was shown from the previously studied perspective than when it was shown in a different perspective.

Given the importance of encoding for retrieval, the person who makes a strong effort to organize material for memory apparently should be more likely to retrieve the material than the person whose efforts are haphazard. The issue here is not the nature of the encoding; the general assumption is that some encoding formats are better than others. Rather, the question we seek to answer here is this: Given a similarity in encoding format, is the person who puts more effort into the encoding better off at retrieval time than the person who doesn't try as hard?

Subjects in a study by Walker, Jones, and Mar (1983) read a series of paragraphs and were later given a cue to recall the last sentence of each paragraph. Each of these last sentences expressed an *anaphoric* relationship with other material in that paragraph. An anaphoric relationship is one in which a particular word in a sentence refers to a word or phrase that occurred earlier in that sentence or in a previous one. For example, if I say, "I like to watch a short tennis match but not a long one," the word *one* refers back to the phrase "tennis match," and the relationship between these two terms in anaphoric. Determining the anaphoric relationship is sometimes difficult. This is especially true when the terms are somewhat ambiguously related or if the text distance between them is lengthy.

The difficulty in understanding the anaphoric relationship was the independent variable in the Walker et al. study. The researchers found that, when the anaphoric relationship was hard to understand, recall of the final sentence was improved significantly. The implication is that the improvement in recall was produced by the greater processing effort required to comprehend the difficult anaphoric relationship. Looked at superficially, this finding might seem to be just another example of the depth of processing effect described earlier. But there's a difference. Walker et al. took some pains to make sure that the material was processed in similar ways, to similar depths, by all the subjects. Assuming that these measures were successful, their findings suggest that the effort involved in encoding material has an effect that is independent of the depth to which the material is processed.

This finding thus seems to agree closely with common sense: The person who puts more effort into semantic coding should be better off at retrieval time than the person who does not. However, some researchers (Hasher & Zacks, 1979, 1984) have maintained that the human nervous system is capable of coding some categories of events automatically, that is, without any effort expended. One such category is that of frequency of occurrence. Hasher and Zacks (1984) found that subjects were capable of coding how frequently certain stimuli were presented even though the individuals' processing of such information was completely automatic. According to Hasher and Zacks, frequency of presentation information is encoded automatically without regard for the effort the subject expends, or his or her age. Moreover, because such encoding is thought to be truly automatic, it is not improved by practice or feedback, nor can it be disrupted by stress or the demands of processing an ancillary task.

Nonstrategic Processing   If people are capable of encoding such information automatically as suggested by Hasher and Zacks, it might help explain some of the mysteries in prototype formation, or language acquisition (Johnson & Hasher, 1987). However, is it likely that people encode and process some information nonstrategically, that is, without any effort? Recent studies have found that the likelihood of encoding frequency information does depend in part upon the age of the subject (Kausler, Lichty, & Hakami, 1984), the nature of the instructional set (i.e., incidental vs. intentional) (Williams & Durso, 1986), and the competing demands of an ancillary task (Naveh-Benjamin & Jonides, 1986).

Similarly, other researchers have found that mental effort comes into play in the encoding of information in other ways as well. For example, Bjorklund and Harnishfeger (1987) inferred the amount of mental effort expended in a free-recall task by looking at interference in an ancillary, finger-tapping task. They compared the effect of mental effort upon memory performance in college students, seventh-graders, and third-graders and found that comparable expenditures of mental effort resulted in better performance for college students and seventh-graders compared with third-graders. In other words, putting out the same amount of mental effort seemed to benefit the older subjects more than it did the third-graders. Next the researchers looked at the effects of an organizational, mnemonic strategy. Seventh- and third-graders were shown some organizational principles that could be used to help them remember a list of words. Both groups of subjects used this strategy and expended comparable amounts of mental effort, as measured by the deterioration in finger tapping. However, surprisingly, only the seventh-graders benefited from the strategy: The performance of third-graders was not improved whether they used the strategy or not. Of course, Hasher and Zacks are not necessarily arguing that a list of words can be encoded automatically. However, the Bjorkland and Harnishfeger findings suggest that mental effort and encoding strategies seem to interact to produce different effects on people of different ages. This finding makes it difficult to infer from a given performance whether mental effort was or was not involved in any particular encoding. Finally, Birnbaum et al. (1987) demonstrated that, whatever else might be true, automatic encoding of frequency information seems to be accomplished only by a nervous system that is in normal operating condition. Subjects who were intoxicated with alcohol were more likely than were sober subjects to misestimate the frequency with which certain words had been presented.

Although some of the initial studies supported the idea that our neural and cognitive system is capable of making automatic encodings of some information, principally frequency of presentation information, later findings haven't always agreed. As Johnson and Hasher (1987) have noted, some of the disagreement may result from the fact that some terms such as *effort, attention, consciousness,* and *automatic* may not have been used or understood by every researcher in the same way. However, despite these definitional and perhaps conceptual problems, the general issue of what type of processing (automatic or effortful) is necessary for various sorts of encodings will probably continue to be investigated in the future (Johnson & Hasher, 1987).

Encoding Specificity

We've seen that context exerts a biasing influence on the encoding process in that the surrounding stimuli, which are used to organize a particular event in memory, also form a mental framework that helps in retrieval. If the same framework can be reestablished at retrieval time, then the ensuing memory search has a good chance of success. As stated earlier, the distinction between encoding and retrieval is somewhat artificial, and that point seems particularly valid here. The kind of encoding that is carried out almost always influences the ease of retrieval, and advance knowledge of the kind of retrieval that will be called for is almost sure to influence the nature of the encoding that the person will do. Another way of expressing this thought is to say that organization in memory is a process that encompasses both encoding and retrieval (Klatzky, 1980). This point is theoretical, but is has some practical implications as well.

For example, as a student you're subjected to a variety of tests. Some of these are probably essay tests or oral exams, whereas others consist of true-false or multiple-choice questions. Essay and oral exams measure a student's ability to recall material from memory, and multiple-choice questions tap the student's ability to recognize stored material. The distinction between recall and recognition often boils down to the number of cues or prompts provided. And as you probably well know, knowing which kind of test you have to face has a strong influence on the way you study. That is, knowledge of the retrieval task influences the nature of the encoding you do.

This point was well demonstrated in a study by Leonard and Whitten (1983). Half of their subjects studied a list of words with the expectation that they would be given a recognition task. The recognition task would be arranged like a multiple-choice test; the subjects would be required to pick out the listed word from among several alternatives. The other subjects studied the list with the idea that they would be given a free-recall test. But these subjects were deceived. All the subjects were tested with the multiple-choice procedure. On some of the items, the previously studied word was presented in the context of semantically related words. On other items, the studied word appeared in the context of semantically unrelated words. Leonard and Whitten found that the performance of subjects who had studied for recognition showed a decrement when the words were presented in a semantically related context, but this effect was not observed in the subjects who had studied for recall.

This finding makes sense when you think about the task from the subject's point of view. Suppose one of the words on the list was *evil*. Subjects who expected a multiple-choice test may have prepared themselves to pick out a word that means "bad," "cruel," or "rotten." Subjects who expected a free-recall test had to do something different. They had to establish some sort of context for *evil* that they could reproduce from scratch at retrieval time. Consequently, when the alternatives were semantically related to the studied word, the subjects who had expected a recognition task apparently had trouble deciding what was the target word and what was the context.

The findings of the Leonard and Whitten (1983) study have several implications. First, they imply that subjects use different retrieval strategies depending on the nature of the memory task. Second, the findings suggest that the subjects know ahead of time that they will use different strategies to retrieve the material depending on the task. (A more complete discussion of this phenomenon awaits us later in this chapter.) Third, the findings suggest that the intended retrieval strategy affects the actual encoding.

Retrieval processes in recognition and recall have been thought to differ in the following way. In a recall test of a list of words, the subject generates candidate items and then makes a decision about each candidate's inclusion or exclusion from the studied list (Hulse, Deese, & Egeth, 1975). In a recognition task, this sort of process need not take place, because the candidates have already been provided by the experimenter. According to this view of retrieval, performance on recognition tasks should always be superior to performance on recall tasks. To recall something, a person has to do two things: generate the candidate and then recognize that it belongs on the list. But to recognize something, a person has to do only one thing: recognize it. The generation stage can be bypassed (Wessells, 1982).

When Recall Beats Recognition A striking series of studies (Flexser & Tulving, 1978; Tulving & Thompson, 1973; Watkins, 1974; Watkins & Tulving, 1975) has demonstrated that under some conditions, recall is superior to recognition and that subjects are sometimes able to recall material that they cannot recognize.

Watkins (1974) gave his subjects lists of paired-associate nonsense words. The pairs consisted of a five-letter A part and a two-letter B part. Although the A and B parts were not meaningful by themselves, the combined seven-letter item was (as in SPANI–SH, or INVOL–VE). After a single presentation of the list, recognition memory was assessed by giving the subjects a list of the B parts they had just seen against the context of other two-letter nonsense syllables. In a later assessment of cued-recall memory, the subjects were prompted with the A part and had to recall the B part of the pair. Recognition accuracy was a dismal 9 percent, while cued-recall accuracy was 67 percent.

This effect was extended in a study by Watkins and Tulving (1975). Their subjects were given a list of paired associates such as HEAD–LIGHT, but they were told that they would be responsible only for the second word of the pair. This word was called the "to-be-remembered" word, or TBR. After the subjects had studied the list, they were given a word and were asked to generate the first four free associates that entered their minds. For example, the subject might be given the word *dark*, and the associates *light*, *night*, *shadow*, and *pitch* might be produced. The words given to the subjects were deliberately designed to elicit the TBR. If the subject spontaneously produced the TBR in response to this prompt, the experimenter then showed the subject the four free associates and asked which one was a TBR (subjects had to choose one of them). In this way, the recognition memory of the subjects was assessed. In the final phase of the experiment, the subjects were given the first word of the paired associates and were asked to recall the TBR. When the subjects gave the TBR as one of the free associates, they correctly recognized it 54 percent of the time. However, in the recall phase, accuracy improved to 61 percent. Perhaps even more startling was that 42 percent of the words that the subjects successfully recalled had not been recognized when the subjects had seen them a few minutes earlier.

These findings are usually explained in terms of the principle of **encoding specificity** (Flexser & Tulving, 1978, 1982). According to this principle, a cue will aid retrieval if it provides information that had been processed during the encoding of the to-be-remembered material (Tulving, 1979). When a prompt is presented that wasn't processed at encoding time, then such a prompt doesn't increase the probability of retrieval. In the Watkins and Tulving (1975) study, the prompts that were presented during the recognition task (i.e., the four free associates) weren't present during the initial encoding. However, because the prompt presented in the recall task was processed at encoding, the probability of successful recall was greater than the probability of successful recognition. We're accustomed to thinking of recall as a harder task than recognition. The Watkins and Tulving study, however, demonstrates that what really determines the difficulty of a memory task is the degree to which the encoding and retrieval contexts match.

More recent empirical and theoretical work in this area has dealt with the strength of the encoding specificity principle. To this end, a mathematical formulation predicting the degree of encoding specificity has been developed (Flexser & Tulving, 1978, 1982). But this formulation has been criticized on several grounds. Bower and Humphreys (1979; Humphreys & Bower, 1980) have maintained that the Flexser and Tulving model doesn't take into account the considerable priming effects of the recognition task on recall. The force of this criticism is that performance on the recall task is spuriously (i.e., artificially) high because, on many of the trials, the subjects had actually seen the TBR when they spontaneously generated it in the recognition phase, which gave the subjects an unfair advantage on some of the recall trials.

Other criticisms have focused on the generality of recognition failure among different types of verbal materials. Recognition failure is more likely to take place among some verbal materials than others, and this differential effect has some implications for encoding specificity (Horton & Mills, 1984). For example, Gardiner and Tulving (1980) performed two experiments in which the paired associates were either abstract nouns (Honor–Anxiety) or number-word pairs (47–Wet). When subjects were given "typical" instructions, performance on the cued-recall task was poor, and consequently, recognition failure of recallable items was also low. However, when the subjects were instructed to "elaborate" the pair so that the abstract terms became somehow related, then cued-recall improved and the number of recognition failures also increased.

This finding tells us that, when the paired-associate terms are abstract or unrelated to one another, they don't provide much context for one another, and the effects of encoding specificity will be correspondingly weaker. However, when the paired-associate terms are strongly related, either inherently or by the subject's efforts, then the effects of encoding specificity become stronger. That is, if the encoding context can be reinstated at retrieval time, the probability of recalling the TBR is high.

Remembering Textual Presentations

If you look at the Table of Contents, you'll see that we're not scheduled to discuss the cognitive processes in reading until Chapter 9. However, it would be very incomplete to discuss memory without talking about one of the things that we are most likely to do with our memories in our everyday lives, namely encode coherent text. This section considers what's involved in organizing such presentations.

Encoding Text   We've discussed the effects of encoding specificity as they apply to single words. These effects are persuasive but also artificial, because in real life we are seldom called upon to remember lists of paired associates. However, we are frequently called upon to retrieve as much as we can from passages of text that we have studied. Cognitive psychologists have tried to determine what encoding effects might be present in such situations.

Thorndyke (1977) had his subjects read different versions of stories such as the one shown in Table 5.2. This tale was manipulated in several ways. In one version of the story, the main point (getting the cow into the barn) was shifted to the paragraph's last sentence. Other versions had the main point eliminated

· · · · · · · · · · · · · ·   **TABLE 5.2   A story used in the Thorndyke study**

A farmer had a cow that he wanted to go into his barn. He tried to pull the cow, but it would not move. So the farmer asked his dog to bark and scare the cow into the barn. The dog refused to bark unless it had some food. So the farmer went to his house to get some food. He gave it to the dog. It barked and frightened the cow, which ran into the barn.

Source: Thorndyke, 1977. (Copyright 1977 by Academic Press, Inc. Adapted by permission of the publisher and author.)

altogether. In still other versions, the sentences were randomly strung together or had the cause-and-effect references deleted. Thorndyke found that these variations produced decrements in the subjects' recall of the passage. This finding is surprising because, in some of the variations, material had been deleted that should have lightened the subjects' load. This finding suggests that subjects had some preexisting idea about how the story should go, which they used as a basis for encoding. The variations used in the Thorndyke study supply us with some hint about the contents of this preexisting idea. Prose passages are seemingly organized on the basis of the cause-and-effect relations among the actors. Chronological order is also an important variable. If a story conforms to certain conventions regarding the motivations of characters and chronological order, it fits into the subject's mental framework better and is consequently well encoded.

Thorndyke explored this idea in a second experiment. The subjects learned two stories. For half of the subjects, the second story repeated the structure of the first but featured new characters. For the other half of the subjects, the second story involved the same characters in a story with a different structure. If the subjects organized the stories on the basis of certain characters, then we would expect recall of the second story to be better when the same characters reappeared. But if the subjects encoded the story on other bases, then this effect would not be observed.

Thorndyke found that the repetition of character names did not facilitate recall. In fact, recall of the second story was worse when the same characters were used in a story with a different structure than when the structure was repeated with different characters. This finding suggests that adults were more sensitive to the organization or structure of the story than they were to the names of the characters per se. As we'll see in a later section, a considerable amount of research has been devoted to understanding the nature of the organization that adults use to encode and comprehend such simple stories.

The Title as an Aid in Encoding   Dooling and Lachman (1971) have investigated the effects of titles on text encoding and retrieval. Their subjects read the passage shown in Table 5.3.

How much of this passage do you think you would remember? What do you think would be a good title for this passage? How about "Columbus Discovers America"? If you review the passage, you can probably see why the subjects who were primed with the title recalled more than subjects who were not so informed. If you're an American, you probably know a lot about Columbus, and in this study, knowledge of Columbus was used to encode the details of the passage. When you hear about Columbus, you expect three ships to be mentioned, so the reference to the "three sturdy sisters," although metaphorical, fits in, as does the description of the stormy ocean ("turbulent peaks and valleys").

Other evidence has suggested that the title must be presented before the text if it is to have a positive effect on encoding and retrieval. Bransford and Johnson (1972) presented their subjects with an ambiguous passage. In one case, the passage was preceded by the presentation of a cartoon that clarified the text. In other cases, the cartoon was withheld until after the subjects had completed their reading. On a subsequent recall test, subjects who had seen the cartoon first outperformed subjects who hadn't. In fact, no difference in recall was noted between subjects who had seen the cartoon after their reading and subjects who hadn't seen the clarifying cartoon at all (Bransford & Johnson, 1972).

The effects of encoding upon retrieval have been investigated by Sulin and Dooling (1974). Their subjects read the passage shown in Table 5.4. Another

············· **TABLE 5.3   The passage used in the Dooling and Lachman study**

With hocked gems financing him, our hero bravely defied all scornful laughter that tried to prevent his scheme. "Your eyes deceive," he had said. "An egg, not a table, correctly typifies this unexplored planet." Now three sturdy sisters sought proof. Forging along, sometimes through calm vastness, yet more often over turbulent peaks and valleys, days became weeks as many doubters spread fearful rumors about the edge. At last from nowhere welcome winged creatures appeared, signifying momentous success.

Source: Dooling and Lachman, 1971. (Copyright 1971 by the American Psychological Association. Adapted by permission of the publisher and author.)

············· **TABLE 5.4   Carol Harris's need for professional help**

Carol Harris was a problem child from birth. She was wild, stubborn, and violent. By the time Carol turned eight, she was still unmanageable. Her parents were very concerned about her mental health. There was no good institution for her problem in her state. Her parents finally decided to take some action. They hired a private teacher for Carol.

Source: Sulin and Dooling, 1974. (Copyright 1974 by the American Psychological Association. Adapted by permission of the publisher and author.)

group of subjects read the same passage, except that the name Helen Keller was substituted for Carol Harris. One week later, all subjects took a memory test in which they were given a series of sentences and were asked to determine whether each sentence had been part of the passage. One of the critical sentences was "She was deaf, dumb, and blind." This sentence is not in the passage, and only 5 percent of the "Carol Harris" subjects claimed that it was. But a full 50 percent of the "Helen Keller" subjects falsely remembered reading the sentence.

This effect is an interesting one. We've seen that having some prior knowledge of the material seems to help in encoding and retrieval, but now we see that prior knowledge can have some unfortunate side effects on memory. In this case, the "Helen Keller" subjects had gotten something into their memories that didn't appear in the passage. One empirical question in this literature concerns the time at which this error was made: Did the subjects falsely encode the passage, or was the error committed at retrieval time? The distinction made here is between material that had been stored in the subjects' memories, which was perhaps retrievable, and inferences that the subjects made about the material when a scan of their memories had drawn a blank.

Several studies (Anderson & Pichert, 1978; Dooling & Christiaansen, 1977; Spiro, 1977) suggest that the latter interpretation is more correct. If the subjects are making inferences at retrieval time, we would expect that the likelihood of such inferences would increase with longer delays between encoding and retrieval. Because the actual encoding is likely to deteriorate with time, consequently, the subjects would be more likely to use their logic, or inference-making abilities, to determine whether the sentence had been part of the passage. This interpretation seems to be accurate. Dooling and Christiaansen (1977) and Spiro (1977) have found that inferential intrusion errors are more likely with increased delays between encoding and retrieval.

Dooling and Christiaansen also used an alternative procedure to substantiate this conclusion. Their subjects read the Carol Harris passage and reappeared one week later to take the memory test. At that point, the subjects were informed that Carol Harris was really Helen Keller. On the subsequent test, the subjects made inferential errors (such as falsely recognizing sentences that pertained to

Helen Keller) at a rate comparable to the subjects who had read about Helen Keller in the first place. The "name switch" subjects had never seen any reference to Helen Keller until test time, and they would not have been likely to make such faulty encodings about Carol Harris.

Scripts

A **script** is a general, content-free mental framework that can be used to organize particular sequences of common and familiar actions (Schank & Abelson, 1977). The implication of the Thorndyke (1977) findings as well as those of Dooling and Lachman (1971) and Sulin and Dooling (1974) is that adults are able to "call up" such mental frameworks to help organize incoming textual material. The implication of this view is that the script has at least two functions in organizing text. First, it offers the adult a way of anticipating which events are going to be discussed next. Second, it offers the adult a way of remembering what was discussed, because the adult can compare the factual content of the incoming material with the factual content specified by the script.

The Influence of Scripts on Encoding   Owens, Bower, and Black (1979) did a study that shows how scripts influence an adult's encoding of textual material. Their control subjects read a short story about a student's fairly routine day. The story consisted of five episodes, one of which follows:

> Nancy arrived at the cocktail party. She looked around the room to see who was there. She went to talk with her professor. She felt she had to talk to him but was a little nervous about just what to say. A group of people started to play charades. Nancy went over and had some refreshments. The hors d'oeuvres were good but she wasn't interested in talking to the rest of the people at the party. After a while she decided she'd had enough and left the party. (Owens, Bower, & Black, 1979)

The other four episodes were also unremarkable. The experimental subjects read the same five episodes, but before they did so, they also read the following preamble:

> Nancy woke up feeling sick again and she wondered if she really were pregnant. How would she tell the professor she had been seeing? And the money was another problem. (Owens, Bower, & Black, 1979)

We might expect that subjects who were primed with this knowledge of Nancy's problem might interpret her actions at the party and in other situations differently from those subjects who had not seen the preamble. Also, to the extent that the episodes described in the story matched scripts stored in the subjects' long-term memories, then we would also expect to see inferential intrusion errors. All subjects were given a free-recall test twenty-four hours after they had read the story. The subjects were encouraged to remember the sentences as precisely as they could. Table 5.5 shows the findings of the study.

Subjects who had been provided with knowledge of Nancy's problem were able to use this fact as an organizational device to aid encoding and retrieval. And it worked: Subjects in the problem condition recalled almost 50 percent more from the story than did the control subjects. However, the side effects were there as well. Subjects in the problem condition made almost five times as many intrusion errors than control subjects did. The nature of the intrusion errors is also interesting. Owens et al. characterized these errors as being of two types. *Script-based errors* resulted from subjects' recall of events that might typically

·············   **TABLE 5.5   Things remembered from the "Nancy" story**

CONDITION	PROPOSITIONS RECALLED FROM TEXT	INTRUSIONS	TOTAL
Problem	29.24	15.20	44.44
Control	20.24	3.76	24.00

Source: Owens, Bower, and Black, 1979. (Copyright 1979 by the Psychonomic Society Inc. Adapted by permission of the publisher and author.)

occur in one of the episodes, even though that particular event was not mentioned. For example, in one episode Nancy makes some coffee for herself, and subjects typically recalled that she "turned on the stove to boil the water." Subjects also committed what were called *interpersonal theme errors*, which resulted from knowledge of Nancy's condition. For example, subjects sometimes recalled that Nancy didn't talk to the professor because she "was feeling miserable" or "felt depressed." The intrusion errors of control subjects were almost completely script-based. The intrusion errors of problem subjects were almost equally divided between the two categories.

It's important to realize that when a script has been selected to guide information processing, certain details that may have gotten encoded if a different script had been selected will go undetected. Some of these effects are seen in a study by Foti and Lord (1987). Their subjects watched a videotape of a five-person board meeting. Subjects were given one of two observational purposes: Some subjects were told to try to remember the interactions of the board members as well as they could. Other subjects were instructed to pay attention to their impressions of the personalities of the board members. Subjects who were given the instructions to remember the interactions apparently used a script, but those who were given the second observational purpose used what Foti and Lord called a leader-prototype schema to organize the meeting events. That is, these subjects apparently computed and encoded the difference between a given person's actions and those of a hypothetical person who had a prototypical leader's personality. These two encoding strategies had some predictable effects. When the subjects using the meeting script were asked to recognize whether particular events had taken place, their responses took longer and were less accurate as the typicality of the event was increased. On the other hand, subjects who used the leader-prototype schema to code the material made similar sorts of errors when asked about leader behavior. Subjects who used the script may not have encoded much about the leadership of the participants, but what they did encode tended to be less subject to the sorts of intrusions that victimized the subjects using the leader-prototype schema. Here we see that the choice of a script influences what gets noticed and, consequently, what gets encoded about various events.

A study by Yekovich and Walker (1986) makes a similar point. Their subjects read script-based stories containing nouns that were central to the script, as well as those that were peripheral. After they had finished reading, subjects took a noun recognition task. One version of the task included unread but script-relevant nouns. Here, the false recognition of unstudied but central nouns was high. The intake of information according to a perceived script enabled subjects to encode and retrieve central nouns that were actually present faster and more accurately than they responded to peripheral nouns. However, the subjects apparently had some difficulty in detecting whether central concepts had actually been presented. Using the script helped the subjects encode central script-relevant concepts that had actually been presented, but the subjects were also likely to be misled by the presentation of central script-relevant nouns that had been absent. The script apparently suggested that such concepts "should" have been presented.

Encoding Events

Loftus and her colleagues have carried out an important series of studies (1975, 1977, 1979b, 1979c; Loftus & Palmer, 1974) showing what sometimes happens when subjects encode and retrieve events they have witnessed. The typical paradigm for these studies consists of showing the subjects a film of some event (often a car accident), followed by a series of questions designed to influence the subject's encoding. In the final phase of the study, the subjects are asked to retrieve the event.

This procedure was used by Loftus and Palmer (1974). After seeing the film, the subjects were asked to fill out a questionnaire in which they made several judgments about what they had seen. One of the questions asked, "How fast were the cars going when they _____ each other?" Subjects saw one of five verbs in the blank space: smashed, collided, bumped, hit, or contacted. Loftus and Palmer found that the verb definitely influenced a subject's judgment. Subjects who read the verb *smashed* estimated that the cars were traveling at 40.8 MPH. But subjects who read the less violent verb *contacted* estimated that the cars were only doing 31.8 MPH—a big difference! It's important to realize that Loftus and Palmer maintained that this sort of leading question truly changed the nature of the subjects' memories. That is, no matter how the subjects may have encoded the event when it was visible, after the researchers had biased the subjects with a particular verb, that original encoding was no longer available; it had been written over by the new encoding.

If the new encoding were really successful in **overwriting** the original encoding, then we would expect that the subjects would also "know" things about the event that were consistent with this new encoding. That is, we might expect the subjects to make intrusion errors similar to the ones observed by Owens et al. (1979).

In a second experiment, Loftus and Palmer (1974) tested this idea. Subjects saw a four-second film in which two cars collided. The subjects were then administered a questionnaire containing the critical item about the cars' velocities. One group read the verb *smashed*, a second group, *hit*, and for the third group, this item was deleted. All the subjects returned to the lab one week later to answer additional questions about the film. One of these additional questions was critical: "Did you see any broken glass in the film?" Although no broken glass had appeared in the film, 32 percent of the subjects who had read the verb *smashed* said that they remembered seeing broken glass. Only 14 percent of the subjects who had read the verb *hit* responded that way, as did 12 percent of the subjects who had not made an estimate of the car's speed.

This demonstration that the subjects' memories have been overwritten seems convincing. Once subjects read the verb *smashed*, their memories were altered, and consequently at retrieval time, they were "accurately" retrieving something they believed to be true: If the cars were traveling at 40 MPH, then some broken glass would likely be visible.

Although the Loftus and Palmer paradigm seems convincing, critics argued that the subjects were not misled by the questions and that their memories were not altered. Instead, they argued, the subjects had simply figured out what the experimenters wanted them to say and were responding to these **demand characteristics** (Orne, 1962).

Evidence for Overwriting   Loftus, Miller, and Burns (1978) developed what they hoped was a telling rebuttal to these criticisms. Their subjects viewed a sequence of thirty slides, which showed a red Datsun hitting a pedestrian after turning a corner. Half of the subjects saw a slide that showed the Datsun stopping at a stop sign before turning the corner. The other half of the subjects saw a slide that showed the Datsun stopping at a yield sign before proceeding. After viewing the slide set, the subjects were given a questionnaire. Half of the subjects saw a question that asked, "Did another car pass the red Datsun while it was stopped at the stop sign?" For the other half of the subjects, the question was worded so that it mentioned a yield sign. These conditions were completely crossed. That is, half of the subjects who had seen the stop sign got a consistent question (it also mentioned the stop sign). The other half of the subjects who had seen the stop sign got an inconsistent question—one that mentioned a yield sign. Subjects who had seen the yield sign also got consistent and inconsistent questions.

Twenty minutes after the subjects saw the slide set, they were given a memory test. In this test, the subjects were shown a series of slides in pairs and were asked to pick out which slide of the pair had been presented earlier. All the pairs were of the same format. In each case, one slide had been presented earlier, and the other slide was designed to closely resemble an actual slide. The critical pair showed the red Datsun at a stop sign and at a yield sign.

Before I reveal the findings, let's think about the implications of this procedure. If the subjects are truly compliant, and they have an accurate memory of what was presented, then they should be able to pick out the slide that they had seen, because that's what they have been asked to do. If, however, the inconsistent question has produced a distortion in the subjects' memories, then no matter how compliant they are, the subjects will show some decrement in performance when asked to pick out the previously seen slide. This procedure seems to rule out whatever effects the demand characteristics may have had.

Now the results. When the subjects were asked a question that was consistent with what they had seen, they picked out the correct slide 75 percent of the time. However, when the subjects were given a question that was inconsistent with what they had seen, their performance was indeed lowered to 41 percent accuracy. This demonstration seems to effectively show that the earlier inconsistent question overwrote the encoding that was made when the subjects saw the slide. One further finding seems to anchor this interpretation. In a follow-up experiment, Loftus et al. asked the subjects point-blank if they had been given any misleading information in the questionnaire. They found that, of the subjects who had been misled—that is, given an inconsistent question—only 12 percent recognized that the misleading had been done. The overwhelming majority of the subjects did not detect the inconsistent question, which strongly suggests that their memories of the slide had been irretrievably altered.

However, convincing as it may be, Bekerian and Bowers (1983) contested Loftus et al.'s interpretation. Arguing that the reinstatement of the encoding context at retrieval time would show that the memories had not truly been overwritten, Bekerian and Bowers adopted a simple expedient. Rather than ask the subjects questions about the witnessed incident in random order, Bekerian and Bowers organized the questions to match the chronological order in which the events were witnessed. When they did so, they found that the subjects were not nearly so likely to be misled by any information that had been presented between the viewing of the incident and their attempt to retrieve it. This conclusion was supported in a study by Kroll and Timourian (1986). Their subjects were "returned to the scene of the crime" by being permitted to see the slides showing the incident again, after they had gone through the recognition task one time. After seeing the slides again, even though they were subjected to a similar set of misleading instructions, the subjects performed substantially better on a second recognition task. Notice the implications of these findings for the overwriting hypothesis. If the memory were truly being overwritten by misleading questions given before the recognition task, then the overwriting process should work just as completely the second time as it did initially. The fact that it didn't tells us that we probably need to reevaluate the overwriting hypothesis. There are a variety of alternative interpretations possible, but probably the most plausible one is that the misleading questions interact with, but do not completely replace, the previous memory.

Summing Up the Encoding Issue

Probably the three key words here are *flexibility, organization,* and *context*. When we looked at the literature on levels of processing, we saw that people are not rigidly bound by any particular constraints regarding the type of encoding they are obligated to do. Moreover, in Frost's studies, we saw some evidence that indicates that people are perhaps aware of the demands of particular memory tasks. Thus, if the task calls for visual encoding, then people seem able to do that. However, if verbal coding is called for, then people can shift gears. We also saw that context or surrounding information seems to play a role in the nature of the encoding that people engage in. What this means is that people don't actually take in just the stimulus they are trying to encode, but rather they take in that stimulus as well as some of its surrounding information. This fact is the basis of the encoding specificity principle. When the same context that was encoded can be reinstated at retrieval time, the context or surrounding information functions like a set of additional retrieval cues. Although people are flexible in their encoding, whatever encoding system people use imposes an organization of some sort on the material. Depending on the type of organizational principles used, people may encode, and thus be able to retrieve, only a particular type of information about the stimuli that were presented to them. It's also important to realize that the imposition of some type of organization (i.e., the use of some sort of script, schema, or category knowledge) seems to be necessary in order to be able to retrieve anything at all. It may be the case that the human nervous and cognitive system is capable of automatic coding of a few unpracticed tasks, but for the overwhelming majority of human memory tasks, mental effort seems to be required.

 ## STORING

A common tendency is to think of our memories as vast warehouses into which things have been put away. We recognize that this is a metaphor, but nevertheless it's a metaphor with a point. Most of us believe that our brains are able to make some kind of neurological copy of our experiences and that this copy is retained in some magical way. To complete the metaphor, many of us also believe that, when we remember something, we direct some other part of our brain to look for the neurological copy and somehow reinstate it, which then reproduces the cognitive events, that is, the experiences that have been encoded.

Brain writing (Dennett, 1981) is a phrase that describes the idea that the brain makes and stores a physical trace of our experiences. Researchers who have looked for this physical trace (Babich, Jacobson, Bubash, & Jacobson, 1965; McConnell, 1962; Tate, Galvan, & Ungar, 1976; Ungar, Desiderio, & Parr, 1972) are apt to make a comparison between brain storage and computer storage.

For example, when I created this text on my computer monitor, my monitor "experienced" this text for the first time. Later, when I stored this writing on a diskette, a copy of the writing in some coded form was retained. Later, when I came back to resume writing, I retrieved this file, which means my computer got the code from the diskette, allowing my monitor to "reexperience" it.

The prior example implies that the memory code created by our experiences is somehow independent of the brain that has produced the code. This is also true of my microcomputer. For example, I can store something on a diskette and send it to my brother, who has the same brand of computer that I do, and then his monitor can "reexperience" something that perhaps it has never projected before. But does the truth of disk writing really imply the truth of brain writing?

I'm not trying to imply that there isn't some relationship between your memory system and your brain. The next section of the book describes some of the classic findings in this area. But for those of you who may be waiting for a pill in which all of the information in, say, this book is already encoded for you, the news from the front is disappointing.

The Work of Karl Lashley

Karl Lashley was born in 1890 and earned his Ph.D. in zoology from Johns Hopkins University in 1914. He had studied there with John B. Watson, whose research on learning had developed from the ideas of Ivan Pavlov. Pavlov had produced a fairly specific notion of the neurological changes underpinning learning. Specifically, Pavlov believed learning was accompanied by certain structural changes in the brain. Parts of the brain that had not communicated neurally prior to learning were associated during learning, and this association took the form of a physical, neural connection. Once formed, the association could not be uncoupled; however, the association did depend upon the continued integrity of the neural connection. If the connection were destroyed, whatever had been learned would be lost.

Lashley (1929, 1950) set out to prove this theory. His method was simplicity itself. Rats were trained to run one of a set of mazes varying in difficulty from easy to hard. After the rats were proficient at running the mazes, Lashley systematically cut the cortex of each rat; the cuts were made in a different location in each rat's brain. Lashley's thinking was that some of the cuts should interrupt the critical connections in the rats' brains, and the rats should show memory deficits on the mazes. But Lashley's expectation proved inaccurate. No matter where the cut was made, the rats still performed up to par, regardless of the maze's difficulty. Although Lashley may have missed the critical connection in every animal, this possibility is remote. Far more likely is Lashley's conclusion, namely that learning and memory don't seem to involve specific connections in the brain.

A second experiment underscored this point. Lashley once again trained his rats to run complicated mazes. Some of the rats had had various amounts of their cerebral cortexes removed prior to the training. The remainder of the rats' brains were intact. The learning rate of the brain-damaged rats was indeed slower than that of the intact rats. Moreover, the extent of the performance decrement was more or less proportional to the amount of the brain tissue that had been removed. Again, the location from which the tissue had been taken was not relevant. When lesions were made in the brains of the intact rats, Lashley observed that their performance was similar to that of the original brain-damaged group.

From these and other studies, Lashley formulated two principles of brain organization:

1. **Mass Action.** "The efficiency of performance of an entire complex function may be reduced in proportion to the extent of brain injury" (Lashley, 1929). **Mass action** means that the brain works en masse. If a small amount of brain tissue is removed, the brain can cope; but if a lot is removed, deficits will occur.

2. **Equipotentiality.** **Equipotentiality** means that all parts of the brain are created equal, at least as far as learning and memory are concerned. No one part of the brain seems to be more important than another for memory storage.

We can summarize Lashley's findings by saying that, regarding memory per se, the amount of brain tissue removed is far more important than the location of its removal. That is, if a small amount of tissue is removed, the location doesn't matter, and no apparent memory loss will probably result. If a large amount of tissue is removed, the location still doesn't matter, and memory loss will probably result.

Do not assume, however, that the location of damage in the brain is unimportant. A relatively small amount of damage to language or to vision centers can produce an irretrievable disability. In other words, the principle of equipotentiality may be true for humans up to a certain point. However, some areas of specialization within the human brain do exist. If these areas are destroyed in an adult, complete recovery is almost impossible.

H. M. and Anterograde Amnesia

Lashley approached the problem of memory storage from an experimental perspective. Although his efforts failed to find any trace of memories in specific cerebral locations, other experimental research (Mair, Warrington, & Weiskrantz, 1979; Mishkin, 1978) has determined that various subcerebal structures—in particular, the hippocampus and the amygdala—have been associated with memory loss in monkeys.

This finding substantiates a relationship that has long been suspected by clinical neuropsychologists who have observed a coincidence of memory deficits and hippocampal trauma in humans. One case is particularly well known (Milner, 1959; Penfield & Milner, 1958; Scoville & Milner, 1957). H. M. (referred to in this way to protect his privacy) is a man who developed an incapacitating form of epilepsy, which was intractable to all forms of treatment, including the anti-epileptic drugs then in use. His physicians decided that psychosurgery might be beneficial, and several brain structures, including his hippocampus, were removed. The operation was successful in some ways. The severity of the disorder was lessened, and H. M. showed no apparent disturbances of thought or mood. However, a severe impairment did result. H. M. showed an inability to remember anything that had happened since his hippocampus was removed. This form of memory loss is known as **anterograde amnesia** and can be distinguished from retrograde amnesia, which was discussed in Chapter 4. As it turned out, H. M. showed little or no memory loss for events that had taken place prior to the operation, nor was his working memory particularly impaired (Milner, 1959). However, if H. M. was distracted during any short-term memory task, his performance was poor. H. M. is institutionalized for good reason: His life has almost no continuity of events. As H. M. describes it, life seems as if he were constantly awakening from a dream.

Cognitive Neuropsychology of Memory

In several places in the book, I've referred to the "neural and cognitive system," obviously implying a strong relationship between the two. But, with the exceptions of the literature on anterograde amnesia, and electroconvulsive shock in the last chapter, I have not yet spelled out the relationship between the neural and memory systems in great detail. In this section, I'll try to make this relationship more explicit.

In the last chapter, we discussed Paivio's (1971) dual-code theory, a position maintaining that there are two basic coding systems, verbal and visual, available to the human memory system. Looking at patients with unilateral damage to the temporal lobes, Moscovitch (cited in Paivio and te Linde, 1982) found some neurological evidence for the dual-code theory. The subjects were shown sixteen pictures of objects that could be coded in two obvious ways. Some of the objects possessed similar spatial, but different categorical, features: They looked similar but were of different categories. Other objects were members of the same category but were not similarly shaped. The location of the patient's lesion had an effect on the encoding strategy used. Subjects who had lesions in the right temporal lobe relied upon category membership to encode the pictures, apparently indicating that the ability to engage in visuospatial encoding is dependent upon having an intact right temporal lobe. However, those subjects who had lesions in the left temporal lobe relied upon shape (a visuospatial dimension), suggesting that verbal codes cannot be formed, or can be formed only with difficulty, when the left temporal lobe is damaged. This finding suggests that for amnesics like H. M., who had portions of both medial temporal lobes removed in addition to his hippocampus, the basic difficulty is that of encoding. This conclusion has been investigated in a number of studies, including one by Cermak, Butters, and Moreines (1974).

Before learning about this study, you need some background information. In the last chapter, do you remember going over the work of Keppel and Underwood (1962)? These researchers demonstrated that performance on the Peterson and Peterson trigram retention task got progressively worse as the subject participated in successive trials. Keppel and Underwood interpreted this progressive performance deficit as the result of a particular type of interference. Specifically, when an item encoded earlier interferes with the retrieval of an item encoded later, we refer to this sort of interference as proactive interference (PI). For example, suppose a friend and I sign up for computer classes to learn a language with which we are unfamiliar. Suppose, in addition, that I already know a particular computer language, but my friend knows none. If my friend finds learning the language very easy, but I find myself getting confused over the differences between the new and the old languages, I can claim to be the victim of proactive interference: My old memory is interfering with the formation of a new memory. When a subject is given a series of Peterson-and-Peterson-type trials, his retrieval performance across the series invariably worsens, *unless the subject is given a different type of stimulus to encode after a few trials*. For example, if the subjects in a short-term memory task are given trigrams to encode for four trials, their performance worsens, presumably as PI from the previous trials builds up. On the fifth trial, if the subjects are given yet another trigram to encode, their performance continues to deteriorate. If, however, on the fifth trial, subjects are given a stimulus from a different category, for example, a word, retrieval performance suddenly zooms up on that trial, as if the subjects have been "released from PI" (Wickens, 1972). Additional research found that a wide variety of stimulus shifts, including numbers to words, different taxonomic categories, different sense impressions, even different languages (for bilinguals), will produce a release from PI (Tarpy & Mayer, 1978).

This phenomenon has some implications for explaining the problems suffered by amnesics. First, the existence of PI itself indicates that encoding is obviously taking place: The encoding of previous memories interferes with the encoding of current memories. Second, the release from PI is another example of the by-now-familiar context effect. When subjects are given a stimulus to encode that has been drawn from a different category than previous stimuli, the category membership can be used as an aid in both encoding and retrieving. Consequently, it seems clear that, if amnesics suffer from encoding problems, such individuals should show relatively little buildup of PI from trial to trial. In addition, however, whatever PI does build up from trial to trial should hold the amnesic subjects in its grasp: If the amnesic subjects' difficulties result from encoding deficits, changing the context of the encoding should not help such people. Basically then, if the memory problems of amnesic individuals are produced by encoding deficits, we should not observe release from PI among such subjects.

This was the logic followed by Cermak et al. (1974). They had their amnesic subjects engage in a typical series of short-term memory trials. They found that, contrary to expectations, there was some deterioration of performance across trials, indicating the buildup of PI. Shifting stimuli from letters to digits produced a release from PI in amnesic subjects. However, shifting stimuli from animals to vegetables or vice versa did not produce a release from PI in amnesic subjects, although it did so among the normal subjects who made up the control group. How should such findings be interpreted?

First, the findings do not provide unequivocal support for the idea that the amnesic's problems are the result of encoding difficulties. If that were so, then there shouldn't have been a buildup of PI in the first place. There are at least two other difficulties. It may be the case that the amnesic person has encoded the material appropriately but at retrieval time is confused. Kinsbourne and Wood (1975) have suggested that this might be the case. In their study, amnesic subjects were prompted *at recall time* with the appropriate category names. Performance nevertheless deteriorated across a series of short-term memory trials, but, importantly, the amnesic subjects did show a release from PI under these circumstances. If the amnesics' problems were solely the result of encoding deficits, prompting them at recall time would not have produced the release from PI. The second difficulty stems from the subjects themselves in the Cermak et al. study. The amnesia suffered by these subjects was brought on by prolonged alcohol abuse, and it is almost certainly the case that, in addition to their temporal lobes, other parts of their brains also were damaged.

It's intriguing to note that Moscovitch (1982), who studied the memory processes of people who had damage to only their frontal lobes, found that such people show failure to be released from PI, but also do *not* suffer from amnesia. Thus, there is at least the possibility that release from PI is not the most appropriate vehicle with which to measure encoding deficits in amnesics whose disorder is the result of alcoholism because the failure to be released from PI may be produced by damage in other parts of the brain that are not directly involved in encoding.

Beatty and Butters (1986) investigated this matter among amnesics whose disorder was not produced by alcoholism, but by Huntington's disease. This is a genetically controlled disorder that produces a loss of neurons in a subcortical forebrain structure known as the basal ganglia, resulting in memory losses, difficulties in moving, and delusions. These individuals showed a comparable buildup and release from PI in short-term memory tasks when compared to normal subjects.

Given these difficulties, it's not surprising that theorists and researchers began to look at the retrieval, rather than the encoding, processes of amnesics. The leading proponents of this view are Warrington and Weiskrantz (1973; Weiskrantz & Warrington, 1975). They have argued that the amnesic's problems begin at retrieval time when they have difficulty sorting out responses that have actually been seen, from those that have simply been internally generated. All of us have this problem from time to time, but this sort of response competition is unrelenting for the amnesic. This argument is based upon three principal findings. First, although the performance of amnesics is inferior to that of normals on free-recall or recognition tasks of verbal materials, their performance when given partial information (such as a word's initial letter) is not much worse than that of normals (Warrington & Weiskrantz, 1970). This finding is consistent with the response competition hypothesis. If the amnesics are given a little help sorting out the correct answer from the competing stimuli, their performance is close to normal, indicating that they had successfully encoded the material but just couldn't get it back again.

Second, amnesics make more intrusion errors than do normals on a wide variety of memory tasks (Warrington and Weiskrantz, 1978). Specifically, Meudell, Butters, and Montgomery (1978) have demonstrated that amnesics made four times more prior list intrusions than did controls. In their study, 66 percent of all the amnesics' errors were prior list intrusions, whereas only 43 percent of the controls' errors were of this type. This demonstration of response competition is probably the clearest. The amnesics seem to be unable to sort out the current list from previous lists.

Third, amnesics are sometimes no worse than normals on tasks that require memory but that are also relatively uninfluenced by prior learning. For example, Brooks and Baddeley (1976) have demonstrated that amnesics are fairly good at learning and retaining knowledge of mazes and jigsaw puzzles.

As we saw for the encoding hypothesis, however, counterarguments can be mustered against the response competition theory. First, some of the spatial learning effects have been difficult to replicate. For example, H. M. can do the same jigsaw puzzle over and over again without any recognition that he has done it before (and without any improvement in performance). There is also a theoretical problem in sorting out the effects of response competition from other explanations. For example, it may be the case that contextual information decays more rapidly for amnesics than it does for normals. If this hypothesis is true, the greater occurrence of intrusions among the amnesics may simply be a result of their "weaker" storage capabilities rather than a result of any specific retrieval deficits (Meudell & Mayes, 1982).

What About Storage?

Most memory losses seem to be the result of encoding failures or inadequate retrieval strategies, although some recovery failures are apparently the result of a "trace loss" (Begg, 1979). In some ways, this finding represents an embarrassment to cognitivists and neuropsychologists who have been at a loss to determine how the brain records a physical trace of experience. Beyond that, cognitivists have been unable to agree that such brain writing is even necessitated by their theories of memory. This ambiguity at both the empirical and conceptual levels partially explains why storage is the unwanted stepchild of the memory literature (as opposed to encoding and retrieval, which are areas of intense interest).

Although cognitivists who have looked for storage locations in the brain largely come away empty-handed, a pervasive feeling nevertheless persists that some pure storage theory must be right. Loftus and Loftus (1980) surveyed the memory beliefs of 169 people, 75 of whom had advanced training in psychology. The others were occupied in a wide variety of other fields. They asked their respondents to indicate which of the following two statements came closer to expressing their opinion about memory:

1. Everything we learn is permanently stored in the mind, although sometimes particular details are not accessible. With hypnosis, or other special techniques, these inaccessible details could eventually be recovered.

2. Some details that we learn may be permanently lost from memory. Such details would never be able to be recovered by hypnosis, or any other special technique, because these details are simply no longer there. (Loftus & Loftus, 1980)

Eighty-four percent of the psychologists agreed with the first statement, 14 percent agreed with the second statement, and 2 percent were noncommittal. Of the nonpsychologists, 69 percent agreed with the first statement, 23 percent were in accord with the second statement, and 8 percent were undecided. A substantial majority of the people surveyed agreed with the proposition that memories last forever. The strange aspect of this finding is that psychologists were somewhat more likely than nonpsychologists to hold this belief. This aspect is strange because, presumably, psychologists should be more aware than nonpsychologists that such beliefs rest upon extremely shaky empirical ground.

 ## RETRIEVING

We've looked at the issues of encoding and storing, and we've seen that the way in which these operations are done critically influences the likelihood of keeping the memory. However, all the encoding and storing in the world are useless unless we are able to retrieve what has been stored. In other words, retrieval is what makes having a good memory practical, and, in a sense, the only time we really use our memories is when we retrieve a stimulus that is no longer present.

We'll cover retrieval phenomena in two principal sections. In the first section, I'll present a model of working memory and show how its retrieval operations are conducted. Then we'll turn to the issue of retrieval from permanent memory.

Retrieval from Working Memory

In chapter 4, we looked at memory from a structural viewpoint, and we found that many cognitive psychologists would not endorse the concept of a short-term memory that is structurally distinct from long-term memory. In this section, we'll consider a processing-based alternative to short-term memory, namely that of working memory. "Working memory" is not just a different name for short-term memory. The two concepts differ in a number of ways, with working memory being viewed as a set of several different active search processes scanning a group of allied, but somewhat independent, storage registers.

Baddeley (1982, 1983 1990; Baddeley & Lewis, 1981) has developed a model that typifies this thinking. Figure 5.2 is a diagram of his approach. The central executive functions like a limited capacity attentional system, similar to those discussed in Chapter 2. This system is responsible for directing the activities of the various "slave" systems, two of which are shown. Baddeley makes it clear that future research may carve some additional peripheral systems away from the executive function. But for now, the two subsystems shown—the **articulatory loop** and the **visuospatial scratch pad**—are the only ones about which much is known.

The articulatory loop is a component of working memory consisting of two parts: a phonological input store, and an articulatory rehearsal process that may involve something like subvocal speech. The phonological store operates like the acoustic-verbal-linguistic storage that we saw in the Atkinson-Shiffrin model. Essentially, incoming verbal material is coded and stored by its sounds, or its articulatory (oral-motor) properties. However, as conceived by Baddeley, the articulatory loop can explain various retrieval facts that were problematic for previous viewpoints. Consider the following phenomenon. It has been known for some time that retrieval of visually presented items such as numbers can be degraded by the simultaneous presentation of spoken text. This degradation occurs even when the subject is told to ignore the spoken material. The semantic properties of the text are uninfluential (nonsense syllables are just as disruptive as

FIGURE 5.2
....
A simplified representation of the working memory model.

(Copyright 1983 by The Royal Society. Adapted by permission of the publisher and author.)

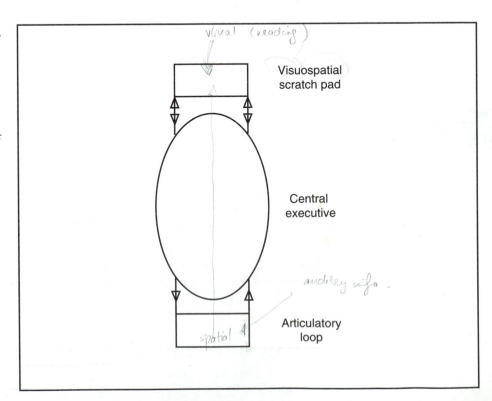

speech). But phonological properties are critical: a blast of ignored white noise doesn't have nearly the degrading effect that ignored speech does (Salame & Baddeley, 1982). This phenomenon is referred to as the **unattended speech effect.** Now, if subvocal rehearsal is prevented by requiring the subject to repeat the same word over and over, then, mysteriously, the unattended speech effect disappears. The subject's memory for visually presented letters is then not impaired by the simultaneous presentation of a spoken text, but only if the subject repeats a word over and over while the spoken text is being presented.

The model explains this effect in the following way. All spoken material has a direct access to the phonological storage. Typically, when material is presented visually, it is recoded, or transformed, into a phonological representation and is thus able to take advantage of the phonological store. Thus, the visual materials are recorded into a phonological representation in the normal course of events, thus aiding their retrieval. However, when the subject is exposed to the spoken text, this material makes its way into the phonological store, thus taking it out of action for the recoded visual stimuli. Thus, retrieval of the visual material is hampered. However, the repetition of the word blocks the spoken text's obligatory entry into the phonological store. This in turn paves the way for the executive to recode the visual material into the phonological store, thus enhancing retrieval of the visual material.

Figure 5.3 shows a task that was originally developed by Brooks (1967) to study the effects of spatial working memory. The subject was given the series of statements and was asked to repeat them. When the subjects were given the spatial statements, those on the left, they were able to recode them into a path through the matrix of cells, and hence the statements could be remembered as a visual pattern. The nonspatial statements contained the same amount of information as did the spatial statements, except that they could not be recoded so easily. Brooks found that the spatial statements were retained better when presented auditorily rather than visually, whereas the reverse was true for

FIGURE 5.3

The task for studying spatial and verbal memory coding, devised by Brooks (1967).

(Copyright 1983 by The Royal Society. Adapted by permission of the publisher and author.)

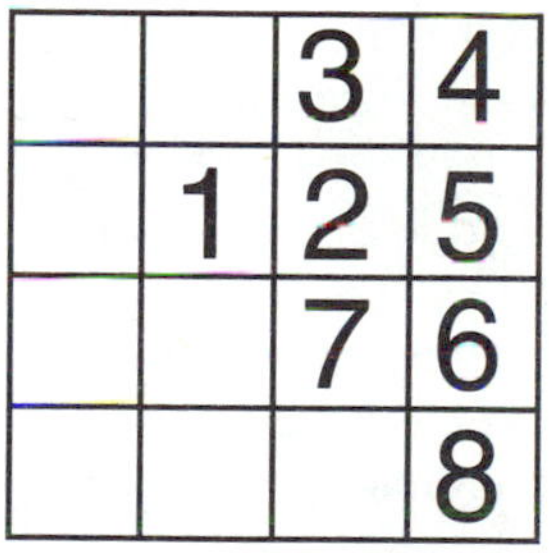

		3	4
	1	2	5
		7	6
			8

Spatial material
In the starting square put a 1.
In the next square to the right put a 2.
In the next square up put a 3.
In the next square to the right put a 4.
In the next square down put a 5.
In the next square down put a 6.
In the next square to the left put a 7.
In the next square down put an 8.

Nonsense material
In the starting square put a 1.
In the next square to the quick put a 2.
In the next square to the good put a 3.
In the next square to the quick put a 4.
In the next square to the bad put a 5.
In the next square to the bad put a 6.
In the next square to the slow put a 7.
In the next square to the bad put an 8.

nonspatial sequences. Brooks suggested that representing the spatial sequence relies upon a visuospatial coding that interferes with processing visual stimuli such as written text. Moreover, the interference is bidirectional: processing visual stimuli interferes with the visuospatial coding of a spatial sequence. Baddeley and his colleagues further theorized that the nature of the interference is produced by spatial conflicts: Reading text requires the involvement of the scratch pad in a spatial task, namely that of directing the eye movements in order to encode the text into working memory. Of course, the spatial statements also demand a spatial encoding, thus producing a conflict because the two tasks are both trying to make their way into the scratch pad's storage register.

In an experiment designed to test these ideas, Baddeley and his colleagues had their subjects engage in the memory task just described while simultaneously visually tracking a target on a computer's screen. In one condition, the target was actually moving in a sine-wave pattern on the screen. In a second condition, the target was stationary, but the background was moving, creating the illusion of target motion. In another condition, both the background and target were moving. Given that the stimuli in the retention task were presented auditorily, we would expect that the subjects would perform better on the spatial version of the task, and this expectation was confirmed. When the subjects' eyes were fixed (i.e., when the background alone was moving), they retained 70 percent of the spatial sequences and 68 percent of the nonsense sequences. However, when the subjects' eyes were moving, with or without a moving background, the subjects retained only 52 percent of the spatial sequences while retaining 63 percent of the nonsense sequences. In other words, moving one's eyes while doing the nonsense version of the task knocked performance down only 5 percent. But eye movements produced an 18 percent performance decrement on the spatial version of the task.

To summarize, Baddeley's work has indicated that our working memory is probably not simply a passive, single register. Rather, retrieval from working memory involves the application of several different cognitive processes, extracting material from related, but somewhat independent, registers.

Retrieval from Permanent Memory

Theories of Retrieval   When we talk about retrieval, we're actually talking about two kinds of activities: recognition and recall. Typically, recognition and recall are defined in terms of each other. In recognition, the subject must choose from among elements present, detecting which ones have already been encoded and stored. Thus, in most recognition tasks, the subject is attempting to determine if he or she has a copy of a currently present stimulus stored in memory. In recall, on the other hand, these cues are not present, and the person is responsible for (perhaps) producing his or her own cues internally. This implies that the two retrieval tasks are based on two different cognitive operations, the first one generating the internal cues, the second choosing from among the internal cues that have been generated. Thus, recall is typically thought to be the more difficult of the two retrieval tasks because the subject must engage in both operations to recall something. However, recognition is generally thought to involve only the second cognitive process, that of comparison. This sort of thinking underlies most of the theories on retrieval, and such theories are usually categorized as **generate and recognize models.**

Thus, in accordance with the theory, subjects who consciously use a generate and recognize model seem to outperform subjects who don't. Rabinowitz,

Mandler, and Patterson gave their subjects lists of fifty words organized around five meaningful categories (e.g., kinds of animals). One group of subjects was given explicit instructions to use the generate and recognize model to learn the list. That is, these subjects were told to retrieve the categories, then generate plausible elements of that category, and finally check to determine if they thought the generated element had actually been on the list. A second group of subjects was not given these instructions. A recall task was given next. As expected, subjects who used the generate and recognize model recalled more words than did subjects who received no explicit instructions. When the subjects were given a recall test one week later, the subjects who had been given the generate and recognize instructions still outperformed the other subjects, although the difference between the two groups was smaller than it had been. If you think about it, you'll see that the reduction in the instructional group's advantage must have been produced by recognition deficits. In other words, with time, we wouldn't necessarily lose our ability to generate plausible targets (provided we could recall the category names!), but we would expect difficulty linking the internally generated target to a previously stored copy.

However, it has been demonstrated that the generation process can be influenced by the presence of certain retrieval cues. J. Brown (1968) asked his subjects to recall as many states' names as they could. (Incidentally, most Americans find it difficult to recall all fifty states in five minutes—try it.) For one group of subjects, the names of twenty-five states were read out loud just before the recall attempt. A second group of subjects did not get the benefit of this recitation. There was no surprise in one of the study's findings: subjects who had heard the names of twenty-five states recalled more state names than those subjects who didn't. However, subjects who had heard the list recalled fewer of the twenty-five states whose names they hadn't heard than did those subjects who hadn't heard the recitation. Notice that this finding cannot be well accounted for by recognition deficits: the implicit (and, one hopes, still valid) assumption here is that all Americans can recognize the names of all fifty states. Given that assumption, we must conclude that hearing the names of twenty-five states apparently inhibited in some way the ability of the subjects to generate the names of the twenty-five nonread states. This suggests that the internal generation of possible candidates may bring forth more associations than does simply hearing a possible item. The Brown finding also suggests a second intriguing possibility: the number of possible responses that can be made to any cue, whether internally generated or not, is limited.

When a person seeks to recall elements belonging to a familiar category such as states or animals, success will be enhanced if the individual is able to generate elements that might work as additional recall cues. For example, if someone were to ask me to recall all the animals I know, I might start by first thinking of chordates, with the idea that I would generate the names of some mammals and some reptiles. In this way, "chordates" functions as an additional recall cue. Of course, it's also possible that particular chordates might function as recall cues for additional chordates. So, in thinking of "leopard," I might also recall "cheetah." These recall cues are referred to as **secondary recall cues.** Some research has shown that a person's skill in generating secondary recall cues has a strong influence on performance in a free-recall task.

Gruenewald and Lockhead (1980) asked their subjects to recall as many elements of a category as they could in either 15 or 30 minutes. The resulting protocols are interesting for a number of reasons. First, and this has been shown in other studies as well, the response rate tends to be a negatively accelerated curve. What this means is that the subject generates a large number of responses at a fast rate early in the 15- or 30-minute session, but the response rate tends to taper off as the session proceeds. Second, the subjects apparently use generated members of the category as secondary recall cues because the responses are almost always clustered in some recognizable fashion.

Figure 5.4 shows the items produced by one subject during a portion of the allotted time. Notice the clustering effect. For example, after saying "wart hog," the subject paused briefly and then quickly generated several animals' names that have an obvious relationship to wart hogs: pig, boar, sow. The subject paused again and then produced a new cluster with an obvious relationship to pigs—farm animals.

Although the subjects generated a few clusters that contained ten or more elements, most of the clusters contained only one or two elements. A question emerges: Did the subjects' productivity decline because they filled up the clusters with fewer and fewer elements as time went on, or did productivity decline because the subjects got worse at generating the cluster names? The second alternative is the correct one. The average cluster size was less than two elements, regardless of the timing of the cluster's generation. However, the subjects produced fewer and fewer clusters as time went on. Gruenewald and Lockhead accounted for these findings in the following way. Assume, they stated, that the subject has a finite number of animals stored in memory and uses secondary recall cues to generate the elements which are in turn recognized. Suppose, moreover,

FIGURE 5.4
. . . .
Items produced in a portion of the 30-minute animal recall task.

(From Gruenewald & Lockhead, 1980. Copyright 1980 by the American Psychological Association. Adapted by permission of the publisher and author.)

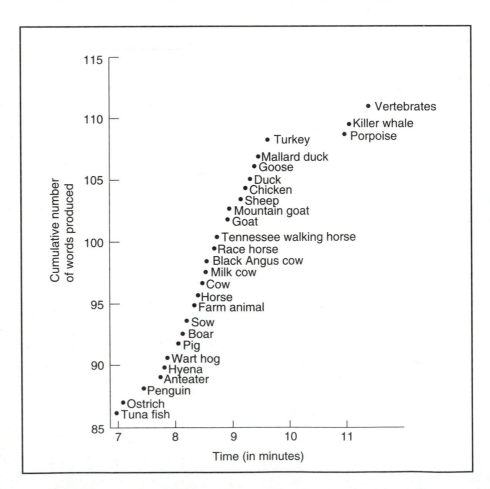

that these secondary recall cues are generated by the subject at a constant rate. Initially, because no animal names have yet been generated, any secondary recall cue will generate some clusters of animal names. However, with the passage of time, the recall of additional secondary cues is progressively more likely to generate additional clusters of animal names that have already been listed. Consequently, because the subject has to wait equal amounts of time in between the generation of secondary cues, we would expect the latency between clusters to gradually increase, as the subject waits longer and longer for a cluster containing names that have not yet been listed. Going back to Figure 5.4, notice how the subject waited more than one full minute between the clusters containing "turkey" and "porpoise."

Recognition Memory   The foregoing discussion may give you the impression that recognition is perhaps an easy retrieval task. Actually, explaining recognition has proved to be fairly difficult. Let's think about the prototypical recognition task, the multiple-choice test. What happens when we recognize the correct alternative? We usually have the feeling that the item looks familiar to us, suggesting to us that we have seen it before. Thus, if a particular alternative provokes a strong feeling of familiarity, we might be likely to say we recognize it. If the alternative does not provoke a strong feeling of familiarity, suggesting to us that it is a new or unstudied alternative, and not the correct one, we might say that we don't recognize it. Finally, if the alternative provokes ambiguous feelings of familiarity (we may or may not have studied it), we must initiate a slower, but perhaps more intensive, search of our memories. According to Johnston et al. (1985), this analysis suggests that recognition, like retrieval more generally, might be accomplished by a two-process model. One process is used to make an assessment of the item's familiarity, whereas the second process is a self-directed search. Moreover, they theorized that the first process was influenced by what they called an item's **perceptual fluency.** Perceptual fluency is usually defined in terms of how easy it is to recognize a particular element under poor presentation conditions. For example, if I am able to identify a tune playing softly over a shopping mall's sound system while I'm surrounded by the distracting noises of the shoppers and their transactions, I might say that I have perceptual fluency for that tune.

Johnston et al. went on to make an intriguing claim about perceptual fluency. Specifically, they stated that people use their perceptual fluencies to judge the familiarity of objects and hence to influence their likelihood of recognizing them. According to this view, when the subject detects perceptual fluency for a particular item, the subject concludes that the item must be familiar and hence is likely to say, "I recognize it." On the other hand, if the subject detects little or no perceptual fluency, the subject is fairly unlikely to say that the item has been recognized, unless the second set of processes, the search processes, indicate that the item has indeed been encoded. It's important to realize that, unlike many of the other theories that we've discussed thus far, Johnston et al. theorize that these two processes work in parallel fashion rather than sequentially. That is, the search processes don't necessarily wait to begin until the perceptual fluency processes either succeed or fail in producing a recognition judgment. Rather, both sets of processes are ongoing at the same time.

Johnston et al. assessed the influence of these factors in the following way. Their subjects read a list of fairly uncommon words that were presented on a computer screen. After reading the list, the subjects were informed that there would be a test. The subjects were then told that they would see obscured words on the computer screen and that they should attempt to identify the word as quickly as they could by speaking it out loud. After the subjects identified the word, they were asked to determine if the word was an "old" one (one from the list they had read) or a "new" (previously unread) word. In the test phase, the words were obscured by the presence of 300 randomly positioned dots. One dot was removed from the display every 20 msec, thus gradually clarifying the word. The subject's latency in identifying the word was therefore a measure of perceptual fluency: the shorter the response latency, the greater the perceptual fluency.

Before going on to talk about their findings, let's consider some possible outcomes and their meanings. Remember, the subject's basic task is to recognize old words. If the subject judges an old word to be an old word, we can describe this successful outcome as a "hit." If the subject judges a new word to be a new word, we can describe this successful outcome as a "correct rejection." However, when the subject calls an old word new, this is a mistake that we can call a "miss," and when a new word is called old, this is a second kind of error called a "false alarm."

How might these outcomes be related to the operation of the two recognition processes? First, perceptual fluency should obviously be greater for old items than for new items, and if the subjects are using perceptual fluency as a cue in recognition judgments, we should expect latencies of hits to be faster than latencies of correct rejections. In addition, we should expect the accuracy of the subjects to be greater for hits than for misses. However, we also need to take the false alarm rate into account. If perceptual fluency is used to make recognition judgments, it should tend to be greater for items that are simply judged old, regardless of their actual status, rather than for items that are simply judged new. So, for example, if the subject has some awareness that he or she has a rapidly developing feeling of recognition for a particular item, and the subject is using this information to make a recognition judgment, the subject should show a tendency to call such an item an old item, regardless of whether it actually is one. What this means is that, if perceptual fluency is truly being used as an internal cue in recognition, the subjects should show greater perceptual fluency for false alarms (again, shorter latencies and greater accuracy) than they should for correct rejections. Table 5.6 shows Johnston et al.'s findings. As you can see, the latency of hits was shorter, and the subjects' accuracy greater, than was true for correct rejections. Moreover, the same was true for false alarms: subjects' latencies for false alarms were shorter than they were for correct rejections, and the subjects' recognition of false alarms was more accurate than it was for correct rejections.

· · · · · · · · · · · · · ·   **TABLE 5.6** Identification latency and percent accuracy for each recognition outcome in experiment 1

ACTUAL STATUS	JUDGED STATUS	RECOGNITION OUTCOME	IDENTIFICATION LATENCY[a] (MEAN)	% ACCURACY (MEAN)
Old	Old	Hit	3807	.76
Old	New	Miss	3875	.68
New	Old	False alarm	4022	.70
New	New	Correct rejection	4167	.65

[a]Only correctly identified words are included.

Source: Copyright 1985 by the American Psychological Association. Adapted by permission of the publisher and author.

Both of these findings support the notion that the subjects were indeed using perceptual fluency as a cue to make recognition judgments.

However, Table 5.6 also contains some evidence that the subjects were using a directed search process in addition to the fluency factor. If perceptual fluency had been the only factor used by the subjects in making recognition judgments, the perceptual fluency should have been greater for all words judged old than for any words judged new. Thus, latency for false alarms (a new word judged old) should have been shorter than it was for misses (an old word judged new). However, this wasn't the case. Subjects responded to misses about 150 msec faster than they did to false alarms. The facts that some old words were perceived with high fluency but still misjudged to be new, and that some new words were perceived with low fluency and still misjudged to be old, suggest that some search factor was operating in addition to perceptual fluency.

To test this hypothesis, Johnston et al. carried out a second study. In this study, some of the words were converted to pronounceable nonwords by letter switching. The reason for this manipulation was to reduce the usefulness of the search process. In other words, it makes sense to think that we can search our memories for codings of actual English words, but it doesn't make much sense to think that we routinely search our memories to find previous encodings of nonwords. This manipulation had a predictable effect. With the usefulness of the directed search diminished by the letter switching, the subjects were forced to rely more heavily on the familiarity factor as indicated by perceptual fluency. Under these circumstances, the latency for false alarms was 93 msec shorter than that of misses, and the accuracy of the false alarms was 6 percent better than that of misses. Taken together, Johnston et al.'s studies suggest that recognition memory can be seen as the result of two different cognitive processes operating in parallel.

Search of Associative Memory: A Formal Model of Recall and Recognition   One of the goals of cognitive science is to develop formal, mathematical descriptions of certain phenomena, and, as we'll see over the next couple of chapters, this approach has been quite prevalent in the memory literature. In this section we will look at a highly simplified "teaching" version of the search of associative memory (SAM) model for describing memory processes (Raajmakers & Shiffrin, 1981). According to SAM, the "memory" for any particular thing, such as the memory for a particular word appearing in a list of words, is stored in interrelated pieces. One of these pieces corresponds to contextual information, meaning any other element or variable that was present at the time of encoding. A second piece contained in the memory corresponds to the item itself. Finally, part of the information stored relates to associations that the subject makes at the time of encoding.

For example, let's say that a subject in a study is given a list of paired-associate words like "boat-dog," and the subject is asked to learn and remember the word "dog." The subject's memory for this word will consist of several pieces or components. These will include whatever the subject manages to encode and store about the context, the word "dog" itself, the associations that are present, including the association to the paired-associate "boat," and whatever other associations he or she formed to any other words on the list. The entire memory for "dog" is stored as what is called a memory "image." (But don't fall into the trap of thinking that there is anything visual about this representation; "image" just happens to be the word chosen to describe what is stored.) The following example shows how the memory image for "dog" might be represented in SAM. In showing this representation, and in the operation of the model, I've changed some notation, and procedures, in the hope of making this concept more understandable to someone just beginning their study of cognitive psychology, but the flavor of the model is still here.

S(CT—Wdog)
S(Wboat—Wdog)
S(Wl—Wdog)
...
S(Wn—Wdog)

The top element shows whatever has been stored (S) about the association between the context at retrieval time, or "test time" (CT), and the word (W) the subject is trying to remember (in this case, "dog"). The next element shows what has been stored specifically about the association between the words "boat" and "dog." The next elements show whatever associations may have been stored relating "dog" to each of the other words on the list. Here the remaining words on the list are shown as "l" through "n." In an actual study, the subject would have as many images as necessary to account for the words on the list, and that could easily be twenty or more items. We're making the assumption that each paired associate produces exactly one image, but this may not always be the case. Some studies have shown that, under some circumstances, an image might represent considerably more information than is contained in a single word (Shiffrin, Murname, Gronlund, & Roth, 1989).

As we've seen earlier in this chapter, almost all accounts of retrieval talk about the importance of cues, and SAM is no exception. What types of cues drive retrieval, and how are they represented? Let's consider the following set:

[C Wl W2.....Wn]

Here, C might represent the context at encoding time. Each of the rest of the terms represents one of the prompt words on the list, with one of those words representing our prompt "boat." To show the effect of these prompts on the images, I'm going to make up some numbers that will show the differing "strengths" of the various associations. In the actual model, the strength of the association varies as a function of both the encoding strategy and the amount of time that the subject spent working on the encoding in his or her working memory. For our example here, we'll use numbers from 0 to 9, with 0 representing essentially no association, and 9 representing a maximally strong association. Also, we'll set this problem up so that two cues are being used to activate the images stored in memory, and we'll assume that we are going to consider the effects on only three of the images in a list. Just keep in mind that all of the images are effected when cued, not just three or any other arbitrary number. Now, a preliminary question: How can we show the effects of cuing on the images representing the memory of words on a list? One way we can do that is to use matrix algebra: By premultiplying each of the images with a subset of all the cues that could be given, we get a product that might represent the "activation level" of that image. If the activation level of an image is higher than some preset threshold, then we say that the system has "retrieved" that image, and this is analogous to human retrieval of a memory. Our hypothetical example, with two cues from the cue list and three images stored in memory, might look like this:

$$[9\ 0\ 0\ 0\ 1]\qquad \begin{vmatrix} 4 \\ 1 \\ 1 \\ 1 \\ 2 \end{vmatrix}\quad \begin{vmatrix} 2 \\ 3 \\ 3 \\ 1 \\ 3 \end{vmatrix}\quad \begin{vmatrix} 0 \\ 1 \\ 1 \\ 1 \\ 9 \end{vmatrix}$$

Using the cues to multiply the first image we get: $[(9 \times 4) + (0 \times 1) + (0 \times 1) + (0 \times 1) + (1 \times 2)]$ which equals 38, and this becomes the strength of the activated image in memory. Treating the other two images in just the same way, we get activation strengths of 21 and 9. Does this mean that the system would "remember" the first image? The answer is yes, if an activation strength of 38 is higher than whatever the system's preset threshold criterion is. So, if that criterion were set at, let's say, 30, then the system would retrieve the first image. Of course, if the criterion were set below 20, then the system would retrieve two images, but it's certainly possible to imagine an outcome like this. For example, the subject might hear the cue "boat" and retrieve its correct paired associate, "dog." But the subject might also retrieve another word (maybe "tree") and recognize that "tree" also appeared somewhere in the list of words. In looking over the numbers I made up to illustrate SAM, you may get the idea that I stacked the deck in the sense that the "same" image would always be retrieved no matter what the numbers were. But, if you play around with the numbers a little bit, I think you'll see that it's possible for any specific image to be retrieved under the right circumstances. Remember, we used a sample of only two cues from a listing of cues, substituting zeros for the cues that weren't being used. If we had used a set of different cues, ones that may have had different associative strengths, then we very likely may have gotten the system to retrieve a different image.

I admit that I find SAM, and models like it, fascinating, but sometimes my students are a little skeptical about the usefulness of such formal models. They argue that it is not possible to test or verify them. I appreciate the skepticism, but I think that SAM, and many similar models, can handle that criticism. Can you think of some of the implications of this model that we could actually test? One implication is that the more cuing information a subject has, the more likely it is that the subject will select a cue that has a large associative strength with some specific part of the image that he or she is trying to retrieve. In other words if we go back to some actual human data, SAM should lead us to expect that the larger the number of cues that are given from a list of paired associates, the greater the likelihood of a person's retrieval of a specific word. It's true that the more cues that are given, the higher the activation of all the images in memory (because each cue that's given has an independent effect on each image that has been stored). But it's also the case that, all things being equal, a greater number of cues increases the likelihood that one of those cues will have a high associative strength with some element of the image that a person is trying to retrieve. Hence, that image would stand a greater chance of being retrieved as a result of prompting with a greater number of cues. And basically, this is the phenomenon that we observe in human cued recall—a phenomenon that can be well accounted for by SAM.

This discussion of the effect of various numbers of cues also leads to a discussion of phenomena of which the basic model has a harder time explaining. Can you think of some phenomena that SAM might not be able to account for? Let's consider what might happen if, for example, all the cues were present simultaneously. In such a case, you would expect retrieval to be optimal. That is, if you gave subjects all the cues that were present at encoding time, you might expect them to be able to retrieve whatever it is that was stored with a high degree of accuracy. Yet, we can be pretty sure that this isn't the case: The number of effective cues eventually diminishes. In other words, while it's true that presentation of two cues almost always produces better retrieval in cued recall than does a presentation of a single cue, it's not necessarily the case that, let's say, the presentation of nine cues always leads to better retrieval than does seven cues. As the number of cues gets larger, their effect does not seem to accumulate in the same way that it does when the number of cues is smaller.

The Bartlett Tradition

We've been discussing theories of retrieval from a "bottom-up" perspective, emphasizing the factors that enable a specific stimulus to trigger the recall or recognition of another stimulus. However, it is also possible to discuss recall from a "top-down" perspective. This involves looking at the knowledge people use to guide their recall efforts. Modern accounts of this approach are based directly on the work of F. C. Bartlett, whose major findings are now more than fifty years old. Whereas most psychologists of that period asked *how much* learning was retained in memory, Bartlett asked *what kind* of learning had been retained (Hulse, Deese, & Egeth, 1975). In other words, Bartlett was interested in qualitative changes in memory as well as quantitative ones, and he was interested in how a given person's knowledge influenced his or her recall efforts.

In 1932, Bartlett published *Remembering,* which was an account of his findings using both his friends and Cambridge undergraduates as subjects. Since Bartlett was interested in studying the storage and retention of meaningful material, his subjects studied a potpourri of folk tales, fables, American Indian hieroglyphics, and so on. The subjects were given a brief time to read or study the material; then after a fifteen-minute break, they were asked to retrieve it. Bartlett often used the method of serial reproduction, which means that a subject might be asked to retrieve the same material over and over again. The retention intervals were often irregular depending upon when Bartlett was able to prevail on one of his friends to attempt another retrieval. Some of Bartlett's friends were long suffering: In a few cases, his subjects tried to retrieve material that they had studied ten years earlier. With the method of serial reproduction, Bartlett hoped to measure the progressive nature of the deteriorations and distortions in the subject's memory. Bartlett's most famous story is titled "The War of the Ghosts" and is reproduced in Table 5.7.

To get the same experience as one of Bartlett's subjects, read the story twice, take a fifteen-minute break, then try to write the story from memory as accurately as you can. Having done that, you might be interested in comparing your efforts with those of Bartlett's subjects. Those results are shown in Table 5.8.

Bartlett was perhaps most interested in the subjects' errors. In this case, the subjects' errors offer strong evidence that they were reconstructing the story during their retrieval attempts. The effects of this reconstruction can be seen in many ways. The story is altered so that it becomes more consistent with knowledge that Cambridge undergraduates might have. For example, the canoe is remembered simply as a boat, and the natives are remembered as occupied with fishing. This second error is particularly telling. If one assumes that the activity was encoded in terms of abstract but related facts such as "requires a boat," "is done on a lake," and "is done to get food," and one asks an English student what activity this is, the student might well respond with what, in England, is easily the most plausible answer: fishing. Bartlett noted that many of the transformations and distortions the subjects made were attempts to make the story more coherent and rational—at least from the standpoint of British culture.

Schemas   This kind of error is reminiscent of the script-based errors described earlier; certain similarities are present. The script is a unit of organized knowledge

·············· **TABLE 5.7**   The "War of the Ghosts" story

Read the following American Indian folk tale, take a 15-minute break, and then attempt to reproduce the story by writing it down from memory.
One night two young men from Egulac went down to the river to hunt seals, and while they were there it became foggy and calm. Then they heard war-cries, and they thought: "Maybe this is a war-party." They escaped to the shore, and hid behind a log. Now canoes came up, and they heard the noise of paddles, and saw one canoe coming up to them. There were five men in the canoe, and they said:
"What do you think? We wish to take you along. We are going up the river to make war on the people."
One of the young men said: "I have no arrows."
"Arrows are in the canoe," they said.
"I will not go along. I might be killed. My relatives do not know where I have gone. But you, " he said turning to the other, "may go with them."
So one of the young men went, but the other returned home.
And the warriors went on up the river to a town on the other side of Kalama. The people came down to the water, and they began to fight, and many were killed. But presently the young man heard one of the warriors say: "Quick, let us go home: that Indian has been hit." Now he thought: "Oh, they are ghosts." He did not feel sick, but they said he had been shot.
So the canoes went back to Egulac, and the young man went ashore to his house, and made a fire. And he told everybody and said: "Behold I accompanied the ghosts, and we went to fight. Many of our fellows were killed, and many of those who attacked us were killed. They said I was hit, and I did not feel sick."
He told it all, and then he became quiet. When the sun rose he fell down. Something black came out of his mouth. His face became contorted. The people jumped up and cried.
He was dead.

Source: Adapted from *Remembering*, F. C. Bartlett, Cambridge University Press.

about actions and can be used to encode incoming information about actions. However, Bartlett invoked the notion of the **schema** to describe the subject's errors. For Bartlett, the schema was "an active organization of past reactions or past experiences" (Bartlett, 1932). The schema was used in learning about new material, in the same way that a script might be used, but it was also used in retrieving facts. As Bartlett understood it, the subject was more or less unable to separate encoded facts from the previously existing schema at retrieval time. Consequently, schema-based facts were "remembered" at retrieval time along with whatever was left of the actually encoded facts.

Many contemporary theorists echo these views (Brewer & Nakamura, 1984; Thorndyke, 1984). For example, it's common for cognitivists to maintain that a particular episode will be encoded in terms of its theme, a few important or atypical details, and the schema. At retrieval time, the schema, which is basically an organized cluster of generic knowledge, is retrieved initially and is used to guide the retrieval of additional, specific facts. However, it's also true that some recent research (Abbott, Black & Smith, 1985) has suggested that schemas may not always be used quite as inflexibly as this. It now seems that people may be able to "tailor" the application of a schema to specific situations, even if those situations are unfamiliar to the people encoding and retrieving them. First, more emphasis is now placed on what we might call specific-event schemas. Second, additional research has focused on higher-level, and perhaps even more abstract, organizing structures that are capable of assembling schemas as needed from basic building blocks sometimes called "scenes" (Schank, 1982).

Retrieving What We've Read   Bartlett's work seems to indicate that the storage and retrieval of text is an "effort after meaning," implying that the subject is

·············· **TABLE 5.8** Attempts by one of Bartlett's (1932) subjects to reproduce the "War of the Ghosts" story

First recall, attempted about 15 minutes after hearing the story:

Two young men from Egulac went out to hunt seals. They thought they heard war-cries, and a little later they heard the noise of the paddling of canoes. One of these canoes, in which there were five natives, came forward towards them. One of the natives shouted out: "Come with us: we are going to make war on some natives up the river." The two young men answered: "We have no arrows." "There are arrows in our canoes," came the reply. One of the young men then said: "My folk will not know where I have gone"; but, turning to the other, he said: "But you could go." So the one returned whilst the other joined the natives.

The party went up the river as far as a town opposite Kalam, where they got on land. The natives of that part came down to the river to meet them. There was some severe fighting, and many on both sides were slain. Then one of the natives that had made the expedition up the river shouted: "Let us return: the Indian has fallen." Then they endeavored to persuade the young man to return, telling him that he was sick, but he did not feel as if he were. Then he thought he saw ghosts all around him.

When they returned, the young man told all his friends of what had happened. He described how many had been slain on both sides.

It was nearly dawn when the young man became very ill; and at sunrise a black substance rushed out of his mouth, and the natives said one to another: "He is dead."

Second recall, attempted about 4 months later:

There were two men in a boat, sailing towards an island. When they approached the island, some natives came running towards them, and informed them that there was fighting going on on the island, and invited them to join. One said to the other: "You had better go. I cannot very well, because I have relatives expecting me, and they will not know what has become of me. But you have no one to expect you." So one accompanied the natives, but the other returned.

Here there is a part I can't remember. What I don't know is how the man got to the fight. However, anyhow the man was in the midst of the fighting, and was wounded. The natives endeavored to persuade the man to return, but he assured them that he had not been wounded.

I have an idea that his fighting won the admiration of the natives.

The wounded man ultimately fell unconscious. He was taken from the fighting by the natives.

Then, I think it is, the natives describe what happened, and they seem to have imagined seeing a ghost coming out of his mouth. Really it was a kind of materialization of his breath. I know this phrase was not in the story, but that is the idea I have. Ultimately the man died at dawn the next day.

Third recall, about 6½ years later:

1. Brothers.
2. Canoe.
3. Something black from mouth.
4. Totem.
5. One of the brothers died.
6. Cannot remember whether one slew the other or was helping the other.
7. Were going on a journey, but why I cannot remember.
8. Party in war canoe.
9. Was the journey a pilgrimage for filial or religious reasons?
10. Am now sure it was a pilgrimage.
11. Purpose had something to do with totem.
12. Was it on a pilgrimage that they met a hostile party and one brother was slain?
13. I think there was a reference to a dark forest.
14. Two brothers were on a pilgrimage, having something to do with a totem in a canoe, up a river flowing through a dark forest. While on their pilgrimage they met a hostile party of Indians in a war canoe. In the fight one brother was slain, and something black came from his mouth.
15. Am not confident about the way the brother died. May have been something sacrificial in the manner of his death.
16. The cause of the journey had both something to do with a totem, and with filial piety.
17. The totem was the patron god of the family and so was connected with filial piety.

Source: Adapted from *Remembering*, F. C. Bartlett, Cambridge University Press.

literally working hard to make some sense out of a passage. If Bartlett's main point is accurate, we would expect that people would have little memory for what was actually printed or spoken, as opposed to the passage's intended meaning. Bartlett's own work suggests that this expectation is true. His subjects seldom wrote down verbatim what they had read. This doesn't prove that they didn't have the material stored verbatim. In spite of Bartlett's instructions to write down what they remembered as accurately as possible, the subjects may have gotten fatigued or lost interest and, consequently, didn't transcribe all the details stored in their memories.

Retrieval of Meaning and Retrieval of Wording

However, a study by Sachs (1967) examines this issue directly. Her subjects heard a recorded passage such as the one shown in Table 5.9. At some point, subjects were given a test sentence and were asked to determine whether or not the test sentence had been presented verbatim in the passage. If it had been, the subjects were to respond yes; if not, no. In one condition, the test sentence was presented immediately (0 syllables) after a particular sentence—called the base sentence— had been heard. In other conditions, the test sentence was presented either 80 or 160 syllables after the base sentence had been heard. The test sentence was presented to the subjects in one of several forms. In the *identical* condition, the test sentence was presented exactly as it had been heard in the passage. In our example, the identical form of the test sentence would be "He sent a letter about

USING YOUR KNOWLEDGE OF COGNITION

Does simply seeing a stimulus over and over again insure that it will enter your memory? Before looking at Figure 5.5, you might try drawing the head side of a penny, nickel, dime, and quarter. It might also be fun to get some of your friends to try this task too. Were your drawings and those of your friends accurate? If you're like most people, there were probably numerous errors in your depiction of the coins.

Rubin and Kontis (1983) asked their subjects to do this task. Figure 5.5a shows how the coins actually appear; Figure 5.5b shows how the subjects typically drew the coins. If you look at the mistakes in the drawings, you'll see that the subjects tend to make the same kind of errors in drawing each of the coins. For example, all the heads are drawn as facing the left; this orientation is generally true to the actual coins, except that Lincoln faces to the right on the penny. Similarly, subjects seem to think that each American coin says "In God We Trust" at the top of the head

side, but actually, only the penny shows this inscription there. For the rest of the coins, the "In God We Trust" inscription appears in various places on the coin's head side. Finally, subjects tend to remember each coin as listing its denomination ("Five Cents") at the bottom of the head side, but actually no American coins have this feature. Rubin and Kontis (1983) suggest that Americans have a very strong coin schema, or general concept, of American coins. At retrieval time, it is this schema that is accessed, and it is this schema that tells us how coins "ought" to look. Rubin and Kontis (1983) checked this hypothesis by asking subjects to design hypothetical 20-cent coins. The subjects' designs of hypothetical coins corresponded almost exactly with their recollections of actual coins, suggesting that the schema, rather than the subjects' actual experience with the coins, was providing the information for the retrieval.

············ **TABLE 5.9**   The Galileo story

There is an interesting story about the telescope. In Holland, a man named Lippershey was an eyeglass maker. One day his children were playing with some lenses. They discovered that things seemed very close if two lenses were about a foot apart. Lippershey began experiments and his "spyglass" attracted much attention. *He sent a letter about it to Galileo, the great Italian scientist.* (0 syllable test here.) Galileo at once realized the importance of the discovery and set out to build an instrument of his own. He used an old organ pipe with one lens curved out and the other curved in. On the first clear night he pointed the glass towards the sky. He was amazed to find the empty dark spaces filled with brightly gleaming stars! (80 syllable test here.) Night after night Galileo climbed to a high tower, sweeping the sky with his telescope. One night he saw Jupiter, and to his great surprise discovered with it three bright stars, two to the east and one to the west. On the next night, however, all were to the west. A few nights later there were four little stars. (160 syllable test here.)

Source: Sachs, 1967. (Copyright 1967 by the Psychonomic Society, Inc. Adapted by permission of the publisher and author.)

it to Galileo, the great Italian scientist." In the *formal* condition, the form of the test sentence was different from the base sentence, but the meaning was preserved: "He sent Galileo, the great Italian scientist, a letter about it." For the *voice* condition, the base sentence was changed from active to passive voice so that the test sentence became "A letter about it was sent to Galileo, the great Italian scientist." Finally, in the *semantic* condition, the meaning of the base sentence was altered so that the test sentence was phrased "Galileo, the great Italian scientist, sent him a letter about it."

This study has two independent variables. First, time has been manipulated, which allows us to make an inference about the duration of the subject's representation. Second, the test sentence conditions enable us to say something about the kind of representation that the subject had stored. The dependent measure was the percentage of correct responses, and the findings are given in Figure 5.6.

When the test sentence was given immediately after the base sentence, the subjects were readily able to correctly respond yes to the identical form and no to all the other forms. The implication here is that the subjects had good memory for both meaning and wording for at least a brief period. However, the picture changed when 80 or 160 syllables had intervened between the test and base sentences. The subjects were still holding at about 80 percent correct responses in the semantic condition, but performance in the other conditions had fallen close to chance levels. Apparently, the subjects were able to retrieve the meaning of the base sentence after time, but the specific wording was gone.

We might expect, then, that as long as material can be held in working memory, the subject may have access to specific phrasings. However, as this material is elaborated and incorporated into permanent memory, larger cognitive structures are brought into play, which guide both encoding and retrieval. Support for this notion can be seen in a study by McKoon (1977). Subjects studied a passage that had a hierarchical organization: Its most general points appeared near the beginning, and the rest of the passage consisted of fleshing out the main argument. Subjects were tested either immediately after study or twenty-five minutes later. We might expect that subjects who were tested immediately would have more knowledge of specific phrasings than would subjects who were tested later. Those were the results. Subjects who were tested immediately didn't respond any faster to low-level statements from the passage than they did to high-level

FIGURE 5.5
························

a: **Actual coins now in use.** *b*: **Modal coins constructed from recall data.**

(From Rubin and Kontis, 1983. Copyright 1977 by Academic Press. Adapted by permission of the publisher and author.)

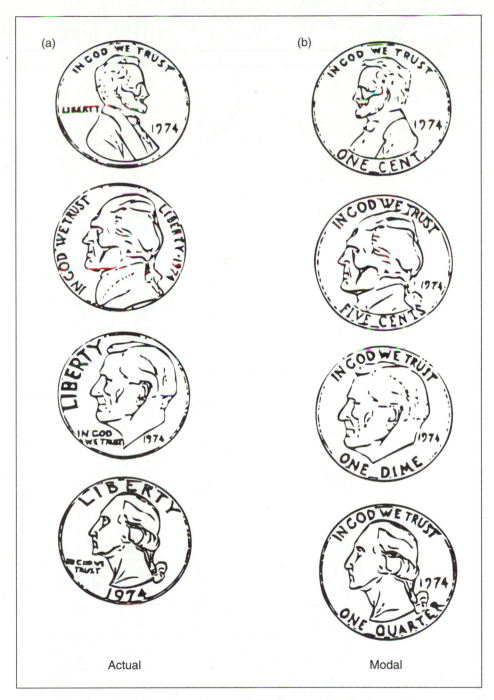

Actual   Modal

ones. But the subjects who were tested after twenty-five minutes answered high-level questions faster than they did low-level questions.

A practical point should be made here. Because professors usually test for main ideas rather than for specific facts, test performance might be enhanced if students could be induced to elaborate incoming material by associating it with material in permanent memory (Palmere, Benton, Glover, & Ronning, 1983). The findings also suggest that you're not necessarily helping yourself by keeping your textbook open until the last possible minute before a test—unless you're interested in retaining low-level facts.

FIGURE 5.6
· · · · · · · · · · · · · · · · · · · ·
The findings of the
Sachs study.

(From Sachs, 1967. Copy-
right 1967 by the Psy-
chonomics Society, Inc.
Adapted by permission of
the publisher and author.)

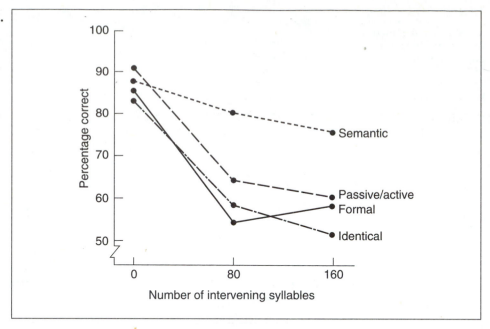

Although retrieval from permanent memory generally recovers a highly schematized version of the meaning of a passage, some verbatim data are nevertheless retained. Anderson and Paulson (1977) used a Sachs-like procedure in their study. However, they developed an ingenious way to estimate the length of time the subject had access to verbatim knowledge of a sentence. First, they measured the time it took the subject to say "true" when the test sentence was identical to the base sentence. Next, they measured the time involved in saying "true" when the test sentence was a formal but not a semantic change of the base sentence. Then they subtracted the first measure from the second. Logically, no difference should occur in these times unless the subject has retained verbatim knowledge. In other words, if the subject has extracted only the meaning of the sentence and not the exact wording, then the response should be just as fast in either condition, as long as all we ask the subject to do is verify meaning. If the subject has retained verbatim knowledge, however, then we would expect the subject to respond faster to the identical sentence than to the formally changed sentence. In other words, the subject with verbatim knowledge should respond faster to a request to verify an identical sentence. If time differences are noted between these two conditions, they can be used as an estimate of the amount of verbatim knowledge remaining in the subject's memory.

A second variable in Anderson and Paulson's study was the effect of the time delay between the presentation of the base sentence and the test sentence. In their study, this variable was measured by the number of intervening sentences. Figure 5.7 shows their findings. Notice that the difference in response time declined steadily in the interval from zero to three intervening sentences, but no further decline occurred thereafter. More important, even with fifteen intervening sentences, the difference in response time is still present. This finding means that the subjects were still responding faster to the identical sentence than to the formally changed one, which indicates that some verbatim knowledge was still retained.

FIGURE 5.7
. . . .
**Difference in re-
sponse times to true
test sentences that
were identical or
changed from origi-
nal sentences.**   The
measure is shown as
a function of delay
(in terms of inter-
vening sentences).
The measure de-
clines with delay but
does not reach zero.

(After Anderson & Paul-
son, 1977. Copyright 1977
by Academic Press.
Adapted by permission of
the publisher and author.)

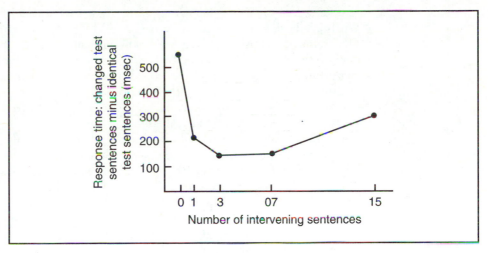

Other findings have suggested that verbatim knowledge of voice is retained
in some circumstances. Anderson and Bower (1973) used Sachs' procedure and
replicated one of her findings: subjects did not retain verbatim knowledge of voice
for very long. However, when Anderson and Bower repeated the procedure using
unrelated sentences, they found that subjects were sensitive to that difference.
Other researchers (Anisfeld & Klenbart, 1973) have pointed out that, when
grammatical form seems important to understanding the meaning of a sentence or
utterance, then the grammatical form is often retrievable.

In summary, people are generally capable of retrieving verbatim material for
only a fairly limited period. As information is elaborated in permanent memory,
its meaning is abstracted and stored, which results in a loss of ability to retrieve
specific phrasings. However, people are nevertheless capable of retaining specific
phrasings, and they encode and store this information in situations in which the
specific phrasing is important to understanding meaning.

Implicit Memory

We're often conscious of using our memory, either to encode and store information, or to retrieve information, but is this conscious experience necessary for
retrieval? Just a moment's thought will probably tell you that it isn't: There must
be many circumstances in which our cognitive system retrieves, or recomputes,
some previously encoded information without our being aware of it.

The effects of *memory without awareness* can be seen in the following study.
Jacoby and Dallas (1981) showed their subjects sixty words; three different
subgroups processed the words at several levels (by looking for certain letters in
the words, by rhyming the words, or by determining the meaning of the word).
Later, the subjects were presented with a test list of eighty words; sixty of these
were the words that the subjects had seen before, and twenty of the words were
new. For half of the group of subjects, the test list was presented using a
conventional procedure that is used in memory labs all over the world: The
subject was given each of the eighty words one at a time and simply asked to
determine if the word had been on the study list or if it hadn't. This is a
straightforward recognition task—a typical memory test. For the other group of
subjects, each word on the test list was presented for a brief 35-msec interval. The
subject's task was to correctly identify the word on the basis of this brief

presentation. Here, the subject is placed in a perceptual identification task, and technically this is not a memory task at all by most conventional definitions of the term. If I'm asked to identify briefly presented words, there is no reason to believe that I would be helped by consciously using my memory of anything. But, surprisingly, Jacoby and Dallas found that a word's status on the study list definitely had an influence on the likelihood of the subject's identifying the word: 80% of the words on the study list were correctly identified, but only 65% of the new words were correctly identified.

Being skeptical, you might be thinking that these results don't really provide very compelling evidence of memory without awareness, because the subjects could be using conscious retrieval attempts to help them answer in the perceptual identification task. Suppose the word "king" is on the study list, and I happen to correctly identify it after a brief presentation. Then, suppose I realize it was on the study list, thus (now) recognizing the word as well. If this happens a few times, I may be inclined to mentally "check" words whose identity I'm not sure of to see if they might correspond to words that I remember from the study list. And if I were doing that, that certainly seems that I'm using my conscious memory retrieval strategies to help me with the perceptual task. But this criticism seems much less valid when we look at the findings of the recognition task. Here, Jacoby and Dallas found that the orienting task given to the subjects when the study list was presented (looking for letters, rhyming, etc.) had a clear influence on the likelihood that the subjects would correctly recognize the words during the recognition test phase. Specifically, when a subject was asked about the meaning of a word on the study list, there was a 95% chance that the subject would correctly recognize that word when it appeared on the recognition test. This likelihood declined significantly when the subject was asked to rhyme a word on the study list (likelihood of correctly saying yes = 72%) and declined significantly yet again when the subject had hunted for certain letters in the words on the study list (likelihood of correctly saying yes = 51%). Thus, it looks like we have a basic "depth of processing" effect going on in the recognition task: the deeper the subjects processed the words on the study list, the greater their likelihood of being correct when they said "yes" to a word on the recognition task.

Now why is this finding relevant to the outcome of the perceptual identification task? If the subjects were using conscious memory processes to influence their responses on the perceptual identification task, then the depth of processing manipulation, which produced an obvious and clear effect on the recognition task, also should produce an effect on the perceptual identification task. But the depth of processing manipulation had no effect on the perceptual identification task. Regardless of whether the subjects had processed the words on the study list at a deep or at a shallow level, their correct identification of previously seen words in the perceptual identification task remained the same, that is, 80%. What conclusion can we draw? Essentially, the Jacoby and Dallas study (1981) supports the idea of memory without awareness because the subjects in the perceptual identification task were clearly influenced by their cognitive system's prior processing of the words on the study list, even though the subjects were not aware that this prior processing was influencing the accuracy of their current identifications.

These ideas also are seen in a study by Eich (1984). Eich's study involved a shadowing task, similar to those discussed in Chapter 2. The subjects wore stereo headphones; they were told to shadow an essay that would be heard in one ear. In the nonshadowed ear, pairs of words were played, with the second word of each pair being a homophone of some other English word. Homophones are words that sound alike but have different meanings. The pair or words "meet" and "meat" are homophones of each other. In the Eich study, the first word of each pair was a contextual word that could bias the interpretation of the homophone, just as the word "red" might do in the example above. Subjects heard sixteen such word pairs. In half the cases, the contextual word biased the homophone toward one of its meanings (such as "red-meat"); in the other half of the cases, the contextual word was chosen to suggest the other meaning of the homophone (such as "track-meet"). The subjects were not instructed to learn these word pairs. At the conclusion of the procedure, the subjects were asked to summarize the essay they had shadowed, and this was done just to make sure that the subjects had actually been following directions. Then the subjects were given a recognition task: Eight of the sixteen homophones of each word pair were read to the subjects, who were instructed to rate the word on a scale of 1 (definitely old, i.e., presented in the nonshadowed ear) to 6 (definitely new, i.e., not presented in the nonshadowed ear).

Take a minute to figure out what the effects of having heard the words in the nonshadowed ear might be on this task. If you reasoned that this rating task is basically a recognition memory task, similar to the one used by Jacoby and Dallas (1981), and therefore having heard the words in the nonshadowed ear should not influence the rating of the word as old or new, then give yourself a small reward. That was the finding. Subjects were not any more likely to rate the previously heard words as "old" than they were to rate new words as "old." But then Eich gave the subjects an additional task. Now the subjects were asked to spell a series of words, and some of these included the homophones that the subjects had heard in the nonshadowed ear. Consistent with the findings of Jacoby and Dallas, the subjects were inclined to spell homophones in a way that was consistent with the bias induced by the contextual word. In other words, the subject who may have heard "track" in the nonshadowed ear was more likely to spell the homophone "meet" than "meat."

Schacter (1987) used the term **implicit memory** to describe the sorts of phenomena that we've seen in the Jacoby and Dallas (1981) and Eich (1984) studies. Implicit memory refers to those situations in which it is clear that a specific previous experience influences a current performance without the performer's awareness of either the specific previous experience or a retrieval attempt. Implicit memory can be contrasted with **explicit memory**. In the case of explicit memory, the performer uses his or her memory and becomes aware of certain aspects of this use; the performer may be aware of actively searching his or her memory, comparing a current stimuli with whatever can be retrieved about specific previous ones in an effort to retrieve something not currently available.

One of the dominant themes in the literature on implicit memory consists of the demonstration that variables or manipulations that influence explicit memory have little or no effect on implicit memory. That is, we frequently observe a dissociation of performance when the effects of specific experience are measured in an explicit memory task vs. an implicit one. For example, in the literature on explicit memory, there is a well-known effect produced by having a subject actually generate or produce a to-be-remembered stimulus. Namely, subjects who, for some reason, actually generate materials that are to be retrieved later show better explicit memory for those materials than do subjects who are simply shown the same materials. Superior retention of self-generated stimuli is referred to as the **generation effect**. But the question before us concerns the way the memory is measured: Do generated materials show the same superior retention when they measured by implicit methods?

A study by Jacoby (1983) explores this question. Some of Jacoby's subjects were given words to read in a variety of conditions. One group read a single presented word (e.g., "cold") aloud, whereas other subjects read the word in the presence of some not very informative letters (such as "xxx-cold"). Together, these groups made up the "No Context" condition. Another group of subjects read the word in the context of an antonym, such as "hot-cold." Finally, a third group did not actually read the words used in the study. These subjects were told that they would see a stimulus such as "hot-????" and their job was to produce (generate) a word that came to mind. Obviously, the target word is "cold"; that is, the study just won't work unless the "generate" subjects produce on their own the same words that the other subjects had read. But the good news is that this manipulation was quite successful; the subjects generated the target words perfectly. After this procedure, the subjects were placed in either an explicit or implicit memory task. The explicit memory task was the familiar recognition memory procedure. These subjects were shown words and were asked to make a judgment if the word in question had been read or generated previously. In this case, the dependent measure is the likelihood of correct recognition. The implicit memory task will also be familiar: This was the perceptual identification task that we've seen before. These subjects were simply asked to identify the briefly presented words they saw. Here, the dependent measure is the degree of priming by the previously read or generated word. If the specific previous experience of seeing or generating the word influences implicit memory, then we should expect to see a large priming effect, meaning that the specific previous experience of reading or generating the word facilitates the speed of perceptual identification. Figure 5.8 shows the results of this study. If you look at the top panel (labeled "recognition"), you'll see the expected generation effect. The words that the subjects generated from an antonym cue were recognized significantly better than words that had been read in context, which in turn were recognized significantly better than were words that had been read out of context. But now look at the bottom panel, labeled "perceptual identification." On the Y axis is a measure of the amount of priming or facilitation. As the graph shows, the priming effect for generated words was quite small. Putting it another way, the bottom panel shows that the words that had been generated were identified significantly more slowly than were words that were read in context, which in turn were identified significantly more slowly than were words read out of context. The pattern of findings in perceptual identification (once again, this is a measure of implicit memory) shows exactly the opposite ordering of the pattern for recognition (or explicit memory)—very interesting findings indeed!

Now, our next task is to try to explain such dissociations in performance. Some researchers (Schacter, 1989) have suggested that performance differs between explicit and implicit memory measures because different areas of the brain are involved in explicit and implicit memory.

Processing Accounts of Implicit Memory Dissociations

Other researchers have adopted a different perspective on the nature of implicit and explicit memory. Roediger (1990) has developed an idea known as **transfer appropriate procedures** to account for these dissociations, and, as you might guess from the name, this idea is clearly based on the concept of transfer appropriate processing that we examined earlier in the chapter. The idea of transfer appropriate procedures is based on four assumptions. The first assumption is that

FIGURE 5.8
....
The study manipulation produced opposite results on recognition memory (an explicit test) and on primed perceptual identification (an implicit test).

(From "Remembering the Data: Analyzing Interactive Processes in Reading," by L. L. Jacoby, 1983, *Journal of Verbal Learning and Verbal Behavior*, 22, 493. Copyright 1983 by Academic Press, Inc. Adapted by permission of the publisher and author.)

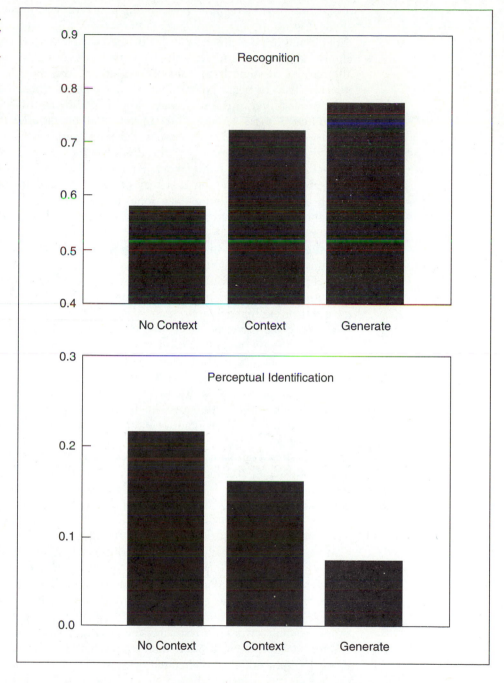

at test time, retrieval will be better to the extent that the same cognitive operations that were used to encode the material in the first place also are involved in the retrieval. Thus, if I used a rhyming scheme to encode some material, then my retrieval will be helped to the extent that I use a similar rhyming scheme in an effort to retrieve the material, rather than using some other type of procedure. The second assumption is that tests of explicit memory and tests of implicit memory frequently require either different types of retrieval operations, or they require access to different types of information. As you think about this assumption, think back to the way in which retrieval was measured in explicit and implicit memory tasks. In the case of explicit memory, the task was almost always recognition, which is basically a decision-making task. The alternatives are directly in front of you; all that you have to do is decide which item was seen or heard before. But in the studies we looked at, implicit memory was not measured in the same way. Now, according to this second assumption, if the different tasks require different retrieval operations, then these retrieval operations will succeed to the extent that they overlap with the original encoding operations. This explains how the dissociations between explicit memory and implicit memory may come about: At retrieval time, different cognitive operations are called into action that may or may not take advantage of the way in which the original encoding was done. If the retrieval operations are a good fit with the operations used to encode, then retrieval will be good. But if a somewhat different retrieval task is used, then different retrieval operations will be called for, and these might not make a good fit with the cognitive operations used at encoding time; hence the retrieval effort will suffer.

The third and fourth assumptions of the transfer appropriate procedures view are extensions of the second assumption. The third assumption states that measures of explicit memory, such as recognition, tend to produce retrieval of semantic, elaborative, or conceptual information. So, in other words, if you're a subject in a study of explicit memory and you are shown four words and asked to recognize which one of them appeared on a previous list, you probably will try to think about the meaning of each alternative to see if you may have stored a similar meaning when the list was first presented. You probably wouldn't think about the number of letters or syllables or typeface of each alternative. On the other hand, the fourth assumption states that measures of implicit memory, such as ultrabrief word presentations, tend to produce retrieval based on perceptual characteristics. For example, implicit memory is influenced by the senses that are used to encode and retrieve the material. So, if a stimulus is presented auditorily, then implicit memory is negatively influenced if the retrieval measure is visual word identification. But this kind of switch does not influence explicit memory as greatly.

Now, the next question concerns the usefulness of these four assumptions: Can we use them to help explain the dissociations in performance that we see between explicit and implicit measures of memory? Let's go back to the Jacoby (1983) study. In the explicit memory condition, you'll recall that the subjects who generated a word from its context outperformed the other subjects. This is because generating information leads to greater conceptual elaboration than simply reading a word. At test time, the attempt to recognize a word also leads to greater conceptual elaboration than simply reading a word, so we would expect that the subjects who generated the word "cold" from its context would outperform the subjects who simply read the word. And this is what was found. What about the subjects in the implicit task? Here, we would expect that subjects who read a word engaged in greater perceptual processing than did subjects who generated the word. (In fact, the "generate" subjects didn't really see the word at all, so there was very little perceptual processing here compared to the "reading" groups.) Now at test time, the subjects are given an identification task that calls for them to read the words again. Now we would expect that the group that read the words in the first place would outperform the subjects who simply generated the word, and this is what was found on the perceptual identification task.

CONCLUDING COMMENTS AND SUGGESTIONS FOR FURTHER READING

After I reviewed this literature, three words came to mind: sensitivity, flexibility, and frustration. In looking at the work on encoding, I was struck by the incredible sensitivity of the cognitive system in its use of so many contextual details as it prepares material to be stored. These contextual effects seem strong enough to warrant my statement that we really can't remember only one item. Efforts to store something necessarily store other things as well. Indeed, Alba and Hasher (1983) have commented that the final result of the encoding process is an event they call "integration," in which a holistic, unified, mental representation is created, incorporating aspects of the stimulus, its context, and previous knowledge.

I have often shared the frustration that my students experience when they are confronted with the tantalizing mystery of the central nervous system and its relation to the cognitive system. As closely allied as these two systems seem, some time will pass before cognitive psychologists will achieve a clear enough perspective on memory to suggest that the central nervous system must operate in certain ways. I also think that some substantial amount of time will elapse before neurologists inform psychologists of precisely which theory of memory is mandated by neuropsychological findings.

When we look at some of the scientific findings regarding retrieval, the words that come to my mind are flexibility and directionality. Here's what I mean. We can use some operating characteristics of our memory system to generate and recognize things that we are trying to retrieve. On the other hand, we can call up and use an apparently wide variety of top-down schemes to suggest directions for memory search, and otherwise guide retrieval efforts. This fact gives us great flexibility in long-term storage. For example, we saw that we typically cannot retrieve the exact wording of messages that we hear or read. This, however, is not an inherent limitation of our memory systems, but more likely the typical outcome of how the resources of those systems are typically deployed. If we wish to use the resources of our memory systems differently, then yes, we will become much more successful at retrieving specific wordings, particularly in those cases in which specific phrasing is critical to the extraction of meaning.

Students who want to find out more about encoding processes might start with either of two introductions to memory by Gregg (1986) or Stern (1985). Regarding specific encoding issues, Loftus (1979a) summarizes her work quite well. Mandler's (1984) book examines the script concept. Klatzky (1984) has written a lucid and somewhat speculative account of the relation between memory and awareness that covers many of the ideas dealt with in this chapter.

Cognitive neuropsychology is dealt with in a book by Ellis and Young (1987). Regarding the cognitive neuropsychology of memory, Mayes (1987) has written a review of some recent findings and has suggested a categorization of the various memory disorders. Parkin (1987) offers a book-length treatment of amnesia. Students who want background information on neuropsychology should read Beaumont's (1987) text.

The development of the levels of processing viewpoint can be traced in a series by Craik and Lockhart (1972), Craik and Tulving (1975), and Jacoby and Craik (1979). For critical reviews of this approach, consult Nelson (1977), Baddeley (1978), and Postman, Thompkins, and Gray (1978).

For students who might like to go a little deeper into the retrieval literature, Bartlett's (1932) book is probably a good place to begin because almost all modern theories of retrieval from permanent memory are in some way based on that work. Also in a historical vein, Houston (1986) has written a clear exposition of the development of interference theory in the Ebbinghaus tradition. Readers who would like to see how modern psychologists have handled the Ebbinghaus tradition, with its emphasis on interference, might look at a collection of articles edited by Gorfein and Hoffman (1987).

Baddeley (1990) has written a clear, general introduction to the memory literature. Watkins (1990) presents an interesting thesis that argues that memory research in general is going nowhere because it continues to focus on the concept of an underlying "memory trace," a physical basis of our recollections. While many cognitivists might disagree with this assessment, it remains important to pay attention to the critics of current research as well as to its supporters.

KEY TERMS

Encoding	Script	Unattended speech effect
Storing	Overwriting	Generate and recognize models
Retrieving	Demand characteristics	Secondary recall cues
Depth of processing	Brain writing	Perceptual fluency
Maintenance rehearsal	Mass action	Schema
Elaborative rehearsal	Equipotentiality	Implicit memory
Transfer appropriate processing	Hippocampus	Explicit memory
Context	Anterograde amnesia	Generation effect
State-dependent learning	Proactive interference	Transfer appropriate procedures
Encoding specificity	Articulatory loop	
Inferential intrusion errors	Visuospatial scratch pad	

FOCUS ON RESEARCH
Memory Deficits in Alzheimer's Disease

Alzheimer's Disease is a type of dementia; that is, it is an organic disorder that produces a deterioration of various cognitive functions. In the case of Alzheimer's, the person suffering from the disease becomes progressively more disoriented and out of touch with reality. In addition, the victim frequently suffers losses of language and memory functions. The memory lapses associated with Alzheimer's are first noticed as an annoying forgetfulness, but these lapses increase until the amnesia is quite general. This disease occurs in approximately 5 percent of the population over the age of 65. The specific cause of the disorder is not known, but some of its effects on the brain have been discovered. The disease results in a loss of cells in the hippocampus and in the frontal and temporal lobes, so much so that the brains of Alzheimer's victims show up in CAT scans as noticeably smaller than the brains of normal people. Autopsies of the brains of Alzheimer's victims typically show neuritic plaques; these are abnormally shaped axon terminal buttons whose synaptic functioning is clearly degraded.

Victims of the disorder show pronounced deficits in working memory, with both verbal and spatial memory being impaired. Performance on Peterson-and-Peterson–type short-term retention tasks is also poor. Consistent with our discussion of retrieval from working memory, we might raise a question concerning the cause of such deficits at the cognitive level: Are they produced by specific failures of the visuospatial scratch pad or articulatory loop, or perhaps are such problems produced by more general failures of the central executive in working memory? Baddeley, Logie, Bressi, Della Sala, and Spinnler (1986) investigated these effects in the following way. Three groups of subjects—young people, normal elderly people, and Alzheimer's victims—were trained to certain error-rate criteria on a visual/motor task called a "pursuit rotor." On a pursuit rotor, a machine produces a small spot of light that travels in a circular direction, and the subject must keep a light-sensitive wand in contact with the point of light as it moves around. If contact between the wand and the point of light is broken, a buzzer goes off, telling the person that he or she has to move the wand faster to catch up. The speed of the light source was slowed down for the Alzheimer's victims, so that when measured by the total amount of time that the wand was in contact with the light (called time on target, or TOT in the experimental psychology business), all three groups were performing equivalently. Next, a traditional digit span task was given to the subjects, and once again, the number of digits given to the Alzheimer's victims was less than for the other groups. When measured by error rate, all three groups performed equivalently on the verbal task. Finally, all three groups were asked to perform both the visual (pursuit rotor) and verbal (digit span) task simultaneously. The young people and the normal elderly people were able to do both tasks simultaneously, but the Alzheimer's victims showed a severe dropoff in performance when asked to do both tasks simultaneously. Now, what's the interpretation? These findings suggest that, at the cognitive level, the deficit in working memory that is observed in Alzheimer's victims is not the result of deficits in verbal or visual memory per se, but rather such deficits seem to result primarily from the central executive's failure to coordinate sensory and memory codes of two different types.

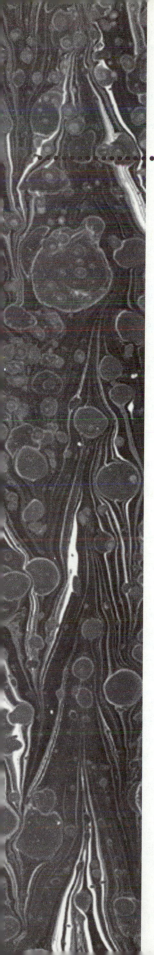

PART 4

THE ORGANIZATION OF KNOWLEDGE

In the previous part of the book, we looked at the theories and findings supporting a cognitive view of memory structure and processes. Although we didn't really discuss it, one of the most striking things about memory is the feeling that the operation of the memory system produces when we use it. So for example, not only can I remember certain fact, but, sometimes at least, I'm very conscious of the instance that was the basis of the memory. So if you ask me what I had for lunch a little while ago, not only can I answer, "I had a ham and cheese sandwich," but I also have the feeling of remembering the specific ham and cheese sandwich that I ate.

In this part of the book, we'll consider a topic that seems clearly related to memory and, yet, seems clearly different as well. To introduce this, consider what happens when I produce an utterance like, "I know that Lincoln was the sixteenth president of the United States." At one level, I know Lincoln's number in the sequence of presidents in just the same way that I know what I

had for lunch today. But, unlike the lunch situation, I have no feeling of remembering anything when I produce the Lincoln fact. In the case of Lincoln's presidency, it just seems more comfortable to me to say "I know" to describe this fact, rather than saying "I remember learning." This suggests that, at least in some cases, I might use words like "I know" to describe what I can retrieve, rather than using words like "I remember." What's the nature of this difference? We'll get into this issue in a little more depth in the upcoming chapter, but, at the intuitive level, the expression "I know" seems to be a better description than "I remember" for things for which we have no conscious recollection of having learned. That is, in a literal sense, my cognitive system is clearly retrieving something about Abraham Lincoln in the utterance that I produced above, but I cannot possibly begin to tell you when I acquired this fact about Lincoln. It's part of my knowledge, but not part of my memories. On the other hand, two weeks from now, I probably won't be able to remember what I had for lunch today (who am I kidding? I probably won't be able to remember it tomorrow.). This suggests that I might use the words "I know" to describe things that are more durable than the things I describe with the expression "I remember."

Over the course of the next two chapters, our focus will be on knowledge: its description and structure. As you have probably surmised by now, there are several perspectives for describing knowledge. These approaches can be broadly categorized as being one of two types. First, we can describe a number of information-processing positions that are basically symbolic in nature. According to the symbolic view, my knowledge of Abraham Lincoln is stored in an abstract format that somehow organizes all the different facts that I might produce about Lincoln, such as the following:

1. Lincoln was president during the Civil War.
2. Lincoln wrote the Emancipation Proclamation.
3. Lincoln was from Illinois.
4. Lincoln was tall.

I suppose I could go on, but you get the idea. I really didn't look up any of the four facts that I just wrote about Lincoln. According to the symbolic view, to write these facts, my cognitive system was able to consult something like a "mental mini-encyclopedia," in which the relevant information had already been collected and organized. The format of the organization is symbolic however, and that means that the cognitive system is using some sort of code to store the information. And what does that code look like? Well, stay tuned, we'll explore that issue in the next chapter.

One alternative to the idea of symbolic organization is offered by connectionism. According to this view, we don't need to talk about an abstract, mysterious language into which the cognitive system's knowledge has been formatted. Rather, proponents of this view argue that the kind of phenomena that are observed when people are asked to retrieve knowledge like the four Lincoln facts above is directly the result of a "brain-style" computation that is not abstract (or at least not very abstract). Instead of suggesting that knowledge is retrieved by looking something up in a mental encyclopedia as the symbolic theorists have it, the connectionist view champions the idea that if a large enough group of "neural-like" entities interact with each other even in very simple ways, then very complex patterns of information can be stored and retrieved in an organized fashion. We'll deal with that perspective in Chapter 7.

As you wend your way through the next two chapters, you should be particularly mindful of two issues; the representation issue and the formalism issue. Briefly, the representation issue has to do with the description we give to our knowledge. This issue is concerned with the properties of knowledge. For example, it's a commonplace thing to say that our knowledge is organized, but what, if any, are the principles of that organization?

We've considered the formalism issue before, when we looked at the retrieval literature. There we examined models that attempted to explain retrieval as a rule-based system. Here we're looking at rules again. But this time, we're not studying the rules governing retrieval; instead, we're looking at the rules that govern knowledge in general. What is the best way to characterize the operation of the knowledge that we have? What rules are being followed in knowledge acquisition, representation, retrieval, and use?

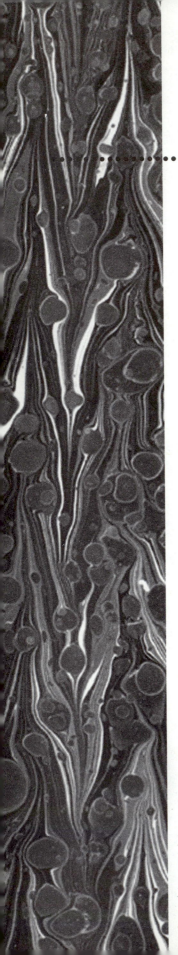

CHAPTER **6**

THE STRUCTURE OF KNOWLEDGE: A SYMBOLIC APPROACH

CHAPTER OUTLINE

OVERVIEW

The road I take to my university passes through some of the most productive farmland in the Midwest. In the spring, when the farmers start to plant, quite a bit of heavy farm equipment can be seen, and I enjoy looking at this equipment, especially at the gigantic tractors. Sometimes I think it would be fun to ride on one of them. Once, I told a colleague about this, and he agreed with me completely, saying that if he ever saw a sign advertising tractor rides for five dollars, he would be the first in line. Then my colleague, who also commuted over the same road, asked if I had ever noticed a particularly huge tractor, the one with twelve wheels, which he said was his favorite. The machine in question, a Steiger, did indeed possess a full dozen wheels: six on each axle, with three on each side of the cab, each wheel's diameter being about six feet. I replied that I had seen it, and that it was one of my favorites too.

One recent morning dawned warm and humid, heralding spring, and I expected that it wouldn't be long before the farmers got busy. Sure enough, on the drive in I saw the Steiger, which I hadn't seen since fall, roaming through a field. And almost with the first sight of the tractor, a mental image of my colleague, who had taken a job at another school some years ago, popped into my mind. Although I had never made any conscious effort to associate my colleague with a tractor, some part of my cognitive apparatus apparently did so anyway.

We usually take for granted our cognitive system's ability to associate two apparently unrelated stimuli, but a moment's thought will show you how remarkable this ability is. For example, a principal technique of psychoanalysis is called *free association*. As practiced by Jung, the analyst supplies a word and the analysand produces the first thing that enters his mind. This technique relies upon the apparently associative nature of our minds, but there's more to it than that. Free association would hardly be a useful technique unless some associations were more or less expected and common, and others were unusual and perhaps deviant. In some sense, then, the success of free association depends upon the existence of some commonality of associations from person to person. If associations are produced by experiences, we must conclude that, even though you and I have had plenty of different experiences in our lives, we must have had enough similar experiences to generate the associations that we have in common. That people generate common associations also suggests that people have organized their different experiences in similar ways. In other words, the organization that seems to be inherent in most people's free associations could be indicative of the organization of their minds.

It is this sort of analysis that is the foundation for the material we'll cover in this chapter. The position is that human knowledge must be organized somehow, and if this organization can be discovered, then it can be described and modeled. This last term refers to one of the main preoccupations of researchers in this area. One of the most important objectives for a cognitive theory of knowledge involves the creation of a mathematical device, or formalism, whose performance seems to mimic the characteristics of human knowledge. We'll explore several such formalisms in this chapter.

THINGS REMEMBERED AND THINGS KNOWN

In the previous two chapters, we described memory structures and processes; in this chapter, I want to begin by drawing a distinction between information that we seem to remember, and information that we seem to know. I won't suggest that these are completely separable issues. They really aren't; knowledge is probably involved in almost any retrieval effort. But nevertheless, you'll see quite a few differences in how we handle the material in this chapter compared with the immediately previous ones. First, in the previous chapter, we talked quite a bit about retention following explicit repetitions of a stimulus. In this chapter, we'll see that subjects may be asked to "respond" to a particular stimulus, rather than to explicitly remember it, and the stimulus may be presented only once. Second, most of the studies that were described in the previous chapter dealt with retention over relatively short time periods (obviously, there were some exceptions). But, in some of the studies described in this chapter, the researchers may ask subjects to respond to stimuli that the subejcts have known for years and years. Third, in most of the cases described in the previous chapters, the subjects were asked to retrieve specific instances—for example, particular words on a particular list. But that won't be true here. Rather than trying to retrieve something about a particular presentation, subjects in the studies in this chapter typically were asked to respond to the general properties of a stimulus.

These differences might be considered in the form of hypothetical studies. Suppose a researcher presents subjects with a list of sentences and tells the subjects that they will be given a recognition task later. One of the sentences appearing on the list is "Lincoln was tall," and when this sentence is presented in the recognition phase, the subjects indicate "yes" (they recognize it) or "no" (they don't). This is a memory experiment. Suppose, on the other hand, the subjects are given a sentence like "The Sears Tower is tall" and are simply asked to state whether the sentence is true or not as quickly as they can. The researcher measures their response times. Suppose, moreover, we find that, for subjects who had already seen the "Lincoln" sentence just before the "Sears Tower" sentence, their response time to the "Sears Tower" sentence is actually faster than it is for subjects who had not previously seen the "Lincoln" sentence. Now, this is just a hypothetical finding, but we have a question nevertheless. What accounts for the faster response time for the "Sears Tower" sentence? Could it be that, having gotten and used one bit of knowledge involving the concept "tall," these subjects are more ready to make another such judgment than are subjects who have not had any immediately prior experience with the concept "tall"? Using this procedure, we might be getting at the structure of the subject's knowledge of "tall things."

Accompanying knowledge and memory are certain feelings too. For example, we may be able to somehow distinguish within ourselves information that we are retrieving from information that we otherwise know. This matter was investigated by Rajaram (1993). In one study, subjects were given a study list of words, and they processed these in two ways. Subjects processed half of the words semantically (that is, the subjects produced semantic associates for these words), whereas subjects produced rhymes for the other half of the words. No doubt you'll remember from Chapter 5 that this is a straightforward "levels of processing" manipulation. However, this procedure is somewhat unusual in that the same set of subjects engaged in both types of processing; in most such studies, some of the subjects engage only in semantic processing and others engage only in rhyming.

Subjects were given 160 such study words, and one hour later they received an explicit recognition task. But subjects had more to do than simply note "yes" if they recognized an item, or "no" if they did not. Rajaram went on to inquire about this recognition. Here the subjects were tasked with telling whether they actually "remembered" the word or if they "knew" that the word had been presented even though they couldn't explicitly remember it. I'll excerpt from the instructions to the subjects to show how these judgments were to be made:

Remember judgments: If your recognition of the word is accompanied by a conscious recollection of its prior occurrence in the study list, then write "R." "Remember" is the ability to become consciously aware again of some aspect or aspects of what happened or what was experienced at the time the word was presented.

Know judgments: "Know" responses should be made when you recognize that the word was in the study list, but you cannot consciously recollect anything about its actual occurrence or what happened or what was experienced at the time of its occurrence.

To further clarify the difference between these two judgments: If someone asks for your name, you would typically respond in the "know" sense; however when asked the last movie you saw, you would typically respond in the "remember" sense, that is, becoming consciously aware again of some aspects of the experience. (Rajaram, 1993)

The results of one study (shown in Table 6.1) revealed a basic and familiar "levels-of-processing" effect: Words that were processed semantically were significantly more likely to be recognized correctly than were words that had been processed as rhymes. But look at the "remember" and "know" judgments. When the correctly recognized words are broken down into the categories of remembering vs. knowing, we see that the basic levels of processing result is very strong for words that the subjects remember. But the opposite pattern of findings is observed in the "know" responses. For words which they had given "know" responses, the subjects gave more "know" responses to the items in the rhyme condition than they gave to words in the semantic condition—just the opposite for the words the subjects remembered!

Let's go through the hypothetical thought processes of a typical subject to get a down-to-earth view of this result. The subject sees a word in the recognition test and thinks, "Yeah, I remember that word; I had to come up with a synonym for that word." Basically, the subjects are telling us that, when they remember a word, they are a lot more likely to have semantically processed it, rather than rhymed it. But for the "know" judgments ("Hmmm, I don't remember it, but I know it was on the study list"), the subjects are more likely to have rhymed the

.... **TABLE 6.1** **Mean proportion of hits and false alarms as a function of study conditions and response type**

| STUDY MANUPULATION | LEVELS OF PROCESSING OF TARGETS | | LURES (FALSE ALARMS) |
	Semantic	*Rhyme*	
Overall Recognition	.86	.62	.16
"Remember"	.66	.32	.02
"Know"	.20	.30	.14

From Rajaram, 1993. Copyright 1993 by the Psychonomic Society, Inc. Adapted by permission of the publisher and author.

word at study time rather than generated a synonym for it. These findings suggest that for most people it is the conscious experience of "reliving" a specific instance that tells them that they are actually remembering something. In the absence of this conscious experience, people may still retrieve something, but then they will tend to make an "I know I saw it response." Notice too that the "know" response is much more likely to be perceptual or even inferential in character rather than a specific reliving: I say that I know something when it seems like I've seen it, or when I think that I must have seen it. This finding tells us something important about the nature of knowledge: It could be the case that what I call my knowledge about something refers to information that has been built up by perceptual or inferential processes, rather than by recomputations based on specific events.

THE INTERNAL LEXICON

Cognitive psychologists who wish to demonstrate that human knowledge is organized face a difficult problem. Because this knowledge is inherently private and internal, what is the behavioral "window" through which we could look to see the underlying structure? What collectible data would show us convincingly what the structure of our knowledge is?

One type of task used by cognitive psychologists for this purpose is known as **lexical access**. If a dictionary is a book that defines words and describes the relationship of words to each other, then we can say that our lexicon is like a mental dictionary. And the basic position is that our lexicon, our knowledge of words, is inherently organized. Cognitive psychologists attempt to find out something about this organization by asking people questions about words and measuring the amount of time needed to respond. If we vary the nature of the words in some systematic way, and then we see corresponding time differences in access, then we can infer something about the organization of our lexicon.

Usually, studies such as the ones that will be reported here involve the subjects making judgments about words that they must read. And sometimes students therefore believe that these studies can tell us something about how people read words. However, these studies really aren't about reading, because reading involves some interpretation of meaning made over an entire set of sentences. Here, our objective is not to learn how people read but how they organize knowledge.

Accessing the Internal Lexicon

Researchers have agreed that there are three enduring lexical access findings. First, there are differences in the availability of lexical units, and these seem to be related to the frequency with which the item appears or is used. Second, a recent presentation of an item speeds subsequent access, and this phenomenon, known as repetitive priming, can be observed for lexical elements that are infrequently presented, as well as for more common ones. Finally, lexical items are made more accessible by the calling up of semantically related elements.

Although such findings are the underpinnings of semantic memory, several researchers have wondered exactly how the lexicon is organized, based on these findings. First, some researchers (Salasoo, Shiffrin, & Feustel, 1985; Ratcliff, Hockley, & McKoon, 1985) have maintained that episodic as well as semantic memory may be involved in many lexical access tasks. In addition, there's been another controversy over the role of context in accessing the lexicon, with some researchers maintaining that the lexicon itself is relatively uninfluenced by semantic context. That is, the organization of our conceptual knowledge is relatively impervious or insensitive to the context in which lexical access is taking place. This view is perhaps most clearly identified with Fodor's (1983) "modularity" approach, which holds that the lexicon is "encapsulated" and therefore resistant to context effects. Other theorists (Glucksberg, Kreuz, & Rho, 1986; Wright & Garrett, 1984) maintain just the opposite, stating that the nature of the lexicon itself, and therefore what you get when you access it, is heavily influenced by events occurring at other levels of linguistic processing, such as the syntax used in the prompting or priming sentence, or the theme established by a group of related sentences.

Disagreements aside, most cognitivists seem to be satisfied that the basic lexical access paradigm remains a satisfactory way to establish the nature of the relationship among elements of our conceptual knowledge.

Semantic Priming

When a particular lexical item is called up by the cognitive system, this calling up facilitates (speeds up) the subsequent accessing of semantically related lexical items. This phenomenon, known as **semantic priming** (Foss, 1982), will come into play at several points in this chapter, so we need to spend some time with this concept. A study by Meyer and Schvaneveldt (1971) illustrates the basic effect. (This study was also discussed in Chapter 1.) Subjects were presented with pairs of elements, and their task was to judge as quickly as possible whether both elements of the pair were words. If both the elements were words, subjects were supposed to respond yes. If either of the elements was a nonword, subjects were told to respond no. Several kinds of trials were used. On positive trials, both elements were words, and in some cases these words were highly associated. On other positive trials, the words were unrelated. On negative trials, one or both of the elements were nonwords. Table 6.2 shows some examples of these trials and the subjects' reaction times.

The response times from the negative trials seem to indicate that the subjects read the top element and made a decision about it before reading the second element. The subjects' decisions were made faster when the nonword was the top element rather than the bottom element. The positive trials demonstrate the effects of semantic priming. When the words were strongly associated, the subjects were able to read and respond much more quickly than when the words were unrelated. This effect wasn't produced by any inherent quality of the words

· · · · · · · · · · · · · ·   **TABLE 6.2**   **Examples of the pairs used to demonstrate associative pairing**

| POSITIVE PAIRS | | NEGATIVE PAIRS | | |
Unrelated	*Related*	*First Nonword*	*Second Nonword*	*Both Nonwords*
Nurse	Bread	Plame	Wine	Plame
Butter	Butter	Wine	Plame	Reab
940 msec	855 msec	904 msec	1,087 msec	884 msec

Source: Meyer and Schvaneveldt, 1971. (Copyright 1971 by the American Psychological Association. Adapted by permission of the publisher and author.)

themselves—*nurse* isn't more difficult to read, nor is it more uncommon, than *bread*. The time difference was apparently produced by the relationship between *bread* and *butter*.

As you can see, these two lexical items share a semantic, or conceptual, relationship. Meyer and Schvaneveldt's findings suggest that when the cognitive system retrieves a particular lexical item, the system also brings into a state of heightened accessibility other lexical items that are semantically or conceptually related to the initial item.

These effects were explored in a study by Ratcliff and McKoon (1981). Their subjects memorized a series of sentences such as "The doctor hated the book." Then the subjects were given a word recognition task in which a series of nouns was presented and the subjects had to determine if the noun had been used in any of the memorized sentences. So, if the noun *doctor* appeared, the subjects were instructed to say "yes." In some cases, prior to being presented with a previously studied noun such as *doctor*, the subjects were given a priming noun that had come from the same previously studied sentence (in this case, "book" would be the priming noun). When the subjects were first given a priming noun, their reaction time to its sentence-mate noun was lowered by approximately 40 msec compared with their performance in those conditions in which the noun was given without a priming stimulus. Let's think about what this finding means. In the Meyer and Schvaneveldt study we saw that certain well-established pairs of words like *bread* and *butter* will produce semantic priming. In the Ratcliff and McKoon (1981) study we see that such priming effects can be shown for words that have been linked together only in the laboratory. In other words, the words don't have to be "really" semantically related: If we provide the subject with the necessary experiences, his or her cognitive system will apparently make the necessary associations. Ratcliff and McKoon went on to look at the effects of various delays between the priming word and the previously studied target word. That is, in some cases, the priming word appeared 50 msec before the target, whereas in other cases, the delay between the two stimuli was as great as 300 msec. Figure 6.1 shows the effects of delay on reaction time; in this case reaction time means the time required by the subjects to respond to the target word. This is a very interesting effect: The reaction time grew progressively shorter as the delay between the stimuli was increased. Basically, this finding means that the greatest effects of semantic priming do not occur immediately. Rather, the effects of semantic priming seem to build over an interval that is at least 300 msec.

In one of the more complex and thorough investigations of the priming phenomenon, Neely (1977) studied the effects of semantic priming on a lexical decision task. In the lexical decision task, subjects are given various strings of letters, and their task is to determine as quickly as possible whether the string is a word. In Neely's version of this task, the subjects were given a prompt in anticipation of the letter string, and it is the relationship of the prompt to the target string that is of interest to us. In one case, Neely told the subjects that, if the target string was indeed a word, it would be an example of the type suggested by the prompt. Thus, for example, if the prompt was BIRD, then if the target string was a word, it might be "robin," or some other bird. In another condition, the subjects were told to expect a categorical shift between the prompt and the target. That is, the subjects might see the categorical prompt BODY, which was their signal to expect a shift to a target representing a part of a building, such as a "door." Or, conversely, the subjects might see the categorical prompt BUILD-ING, which was their clue to expect a target representing a body part, such as "arm." Now things get really interesting. Although the subjects were told to

FIGURE 6.1

....

Difference between primed and control conditions as a function of the interval between priming word and target word.

(Copyright 1981 by the American Psychological Association. Adapted by permission of the publisher and author.)

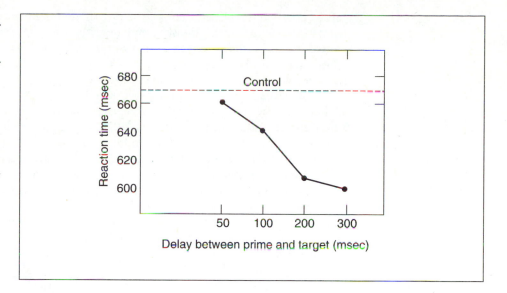

expect a shift in these conditions, sometimes the shift did not occur. That is, sometimes the subject saw the prompt BODY and then a letter string that really was a body part, such as "leg." Finally, in some cases, the subjects were told to expect a shift, and the shift did indeed take place. But instead of going to the expected category, such as from BUILDING to a body part and vice versa, the shift went to an unexpected category, such as from BODY to BIRD.

Before we look at the findings, let's think about what might happen. First, if the subjects are given a prompt such as BIRD and then are actually given a letter string representing a kind of bird, we should expect the prompt to show a priming or facilitative effect. That is, the subjects who see such a prompt should, as a result of semantic priming, be able to identify the letter string as a word faster than those subjects who have not seen any prompt. In addition, for subjects who are given a prompt like BIRD and are *not* told to expect any category shift, we might expect that if the letter string is a word not drawn from the appropriate category, then it should take the subjects appropriately longer to recognize the string as a word. That is, if a subject, is given BIRD and, expecting a bird, actually gets a string like "arm," it should take the subject longer to identify the string than if he or she had not gotten any prompt at all. We would call this an inhibiting effect of the prompt. This reasoning holds for the "shift" conditions as well: If the subject were to get a BUILDING prompt, and then a letter string representing a body part, such as "leg," we would expect to see a facilitative effect of the prompt because the subject had been told to expect a shift. But, we can raise an interesting question about what might happen if we prompt the subject with BUILDING and the expected shift does *not* occur: The subject actually sees a letter string representing a building part such as "window." If the subject had not been in the shift condition, we would expect such a prompt to have a facilitative effect on reaction time because a window really is a part of a building. But, because the subject is in a shift condition, and because the shift does not occur, we would expect to see an inhibitory effect of the prompt. What actually happens? Do the two effects, facilitative and inhibitory, cancel each other out? We'll find out in a minute.

Neely had one other variable that we need to discuss. In addition to the other conditions that have already been described, Neely also varied the time that elapsed between the presentation of the prompt and the presentation of the letter string in the lexical decision task. The latency between these two presentations is referred to as **stimulus onset asynchrony,** or **SOA.** That is, if there was a 100-msec latency between the presentation of the prompt and the presentation of the letter string, then we call this a 100-msec SOA.

Figure 6.2 shows the findings of the Neely study. Looking first at the left-hand side of the figure, we see that the expected priming effects did occur: When subjects were prompted with BIRD, there was a facilitative effect on recognition of letter strings such as "robin." Moreover, the longer the SOA, the stronger the facilitative effect became, an effect that we have also seen in the Ratcliff and McKoon (1981) study. In addition, when the subject was not expecting a shift, the prompt BIRD had an inhibitory effect on lexical decisions involving unexpected elements such as "arm," and this inhibitory effect also got stronger with longer SOA. Now turning to the right-hand side of Figure 6.2, we see that a prompt like BODY did have a facilitative effect on a word like "door," as long as the subjects were told to expect a shift from the body-part category to the building-part category. When the shift went to a member of an unexpected category however, such as to "sparrow," we see that there was an inhibitory effect of the prompt BODY, even though subjects were expecting to shift categories. This finding means that simply telling the subjects to expect a category shift does

FIGURE 6.2
....
Reaction time (RT) to lexical decision targets.

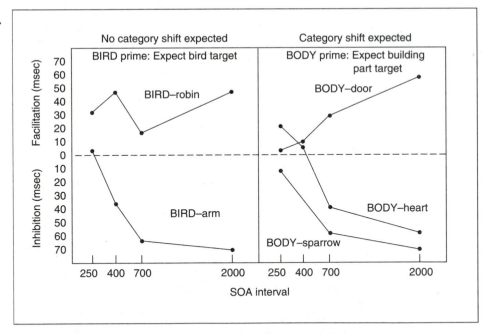

In the left half, subjects saw a prime and did not expect a shift in category; sample stimuli are BIRD–robin for a relevant prime, and BIRD–arm for an irrelevant prime. In the right half, subjects expected the target to come from the part of a building category if they saw BODY as a prime, and from the body part category if they saw BUILDING as a prime. When the shift in category occurred as expected, the RT was facilitated at longer stimulus onset asynchrony (SOA). When the expected shift did not occur, there was facilitation when the prime was relevant (BODY–heart). Inhibition occurred when the shift was completely unexpected (BODY–sparrow).

(From Neely, 1977. Copyright 1977 by the American Psychological Association. Adapted by permission of the publisher and author.)

not prime all the lexical items in every other category—indeed, how could it? Rather, prompting a particular category, while telling the subjects to expect a shift, presumably primes only those lexical items in the category to which the subjects expect to shift. Now, let's consider the last case, that in which the subject is given a prompt like BODY, told to expect a category shift, and then sees a letter string that really is a body part, such as "heart." Here we see that the subject's cognitive/neural system temporarily "overrides" the category shift instruction. At the briefest SOA (250 mscc), the BODY prompt actually does facilitate a body-part letter string such as "heart," even though the subject has been instructed to expect a category shift. However, at longer SOAs, this facilitative effect is no longer seen, and in fact the prompt has an inhibitory effect that is similar to the other unexpected category shift. Here we seem to see an interaction of some conscious and some automatic cognitive processing. At the "automatic" level, subjects know that "heart" is a body part, and at short SOAs this automatic, unconscious processing is likely to occur. However, when the subjects are given two full seconds to think about the prompt BODY, they are probably consciously ready to look for a word in the expected shift category, building parts. It is probably this conscious expectation that must be overcome for these subjects to recognize that "heart" is indeed a word, even though it does not come from the category they expected.

SYMBOLIC NETWORK MODELS OF KNOWLEDGE

In the last section we saw that reaction times in a lexical decision task can be facilitated by prompting the subject with a semantically related word. Moreover, from the pattern of reaction times that we obtain in such studies, we can make some inferences about the underlying knowledge structures in which such lexical information is contained. In this section, we'll expand on the findings that we looked at above in an attempt to specify more completely the nature and function of such knowledge structures. One objective shared by all models of knowledge is to capture or mimic the function of knowledge structures in a formal system. For example, as we have seen, retrieval patterns from permanent memory are not unorganized.

A good theory of knowledge must clarify the factors that make certain retrieval patterns predictable. One frequently adopted tactic consists of developing a formal system (which, by definition, must be organized) and then arguing that the organizational principles of the formal system are analogous to, or even in some sense identical to, the organizational principles of knowledge.

In looking for a philosophical basis for their theories, many cognitive psychologists have found appealing analogies between human and computer memory. In both cases, the processes of encoding, storing, and retrieval seem to take place. The successful storage of information in computers requires that the information be organized in some fashion. Moreover, the computer's retrieval of this organized information depends on a formal system called a *retrieval algorithm.* The questions posed by cognitive psychologists seem straightforward: What is the nature of the organization of human knowledge? Can this knowledge be represented by a formal system? Finally, is it possible to specify a formal retrieval procedure that seems to duplicate human retrieval processes?

One type of formal system that is often used is the **network model.** Network models are so named because the associations among the elements of knowledge are depicted as arrows. Figure 6.3 shows a tiny part of a generic network model.

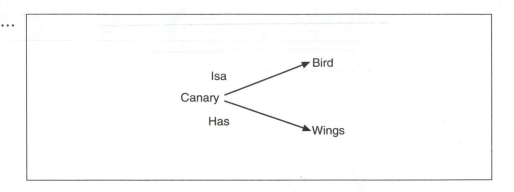

Although Figure 6.3 gives the impression that the elements of knowledge are words, strictly speaking, that isn't the case. In Figure 6.3, the word *canary* stands for the concept of a canary, and this symbolism is true for the other elements of the figure, too. Concepts in network models are generally referred to as *nodes*. Nodes are connected by arrows, but again, this is simply a convention for denoting a particular kind of relationship (or association) among the nodes. Figure 6.3 shows that *canary* and *bird* are ideas that are associated in particular ways, one of which is that a canary is a member of the superordinate, or higher, category *bird*. This association is denoted by the arrow labeled "*Isa*." Although Figure 6.3 specifies the canary node as having only one *Isa* relation, it could have others. Similarly, the *has* relationship is not the only one that could be specified. It's important to realize at the outset that the direction of the arrows sometimes has theoretical significance in these models. That is, the relationship between *canary* and *bird* can be expressed by *Isa*, but that's not true for the relationship between *bird* and *canary*.

Assumptions of Symbolic Network Models

One assumption generally made by network models is that the activity we call "searching our memories" is analogous to a search among the nodes of the model. In this instance, the search refers to a kind of metaphorical movement among the model's nodes, in the direction specified by the arrowhead. This search is considered to proceed node by node—that is, serially—as an unspecified cognitive process that accesses the node and reads out the knowledge contained there. If that knowledge enables the individual to answer a particular question, then the search stops. Otherwise, it continues until the person finds the answer or gives up.

Typically, network models assume that the nature of the associations constrains the extent, or the scope, of the search. Although this point will be clearer when we look at some specific models, for right now we can say that the nature of the associations is usually assumed to govern the nature of the search. It's also important to realize that these models consider themselves representations of knowledge that cannot be completely expressed verbally. Although all the models that we'll look at seem to consist of words and arrows, be aware that the nodes are supposed to represent concepts rather than words. The graphic depictions shown in these pages are just that: representations (not copies) of mental events that surely must be more complex than words alone.

Finally, most network models make what is called a **type-token distinction.** Broadly speaking, this distinction refers to the differentiation we usually make between general categories (types) and particular, familiar examples drawn from that category (tokens). These relationships are expressed in Figure 6.4.

USING YOUR KNOWLEDGE OF COGNITION

The semantic or conceptual basis of our declarative permanent memory becomes very clear in the following demonstration. First look at your watch and give yourself ten seconds to write down all the words you can think of that begin with a certain letter, let's say L. Now, having done that, look at your watch again and give yourself ten seconds to write down as many members of a particular category, let's say, household furniture, that you can think of. Compare the two lists. More items on the furniture list? I'm not surprised. On the letter list, you probably have *like*, or *love*; you may have *letter* or *list*; you may even have *lima bean* (cheating a little). But you probably don't have *lamprey* or *lugubrious* or very many of the other 6,230 words beginning with L in my dictionary (and this is surely a low estimate of all the words in English that begin with L). On the other hand you prob-

ably have *sofa, chair, table, lamp, bed, dresser*, etc. on the furniture list. I really doubt that there are anything like 6,230 household furniture items, and this makes the discrepancy between the lists even more interesting because it means that you recalled a much higher percentage of the elements on the hypothetical furniture list than you did on the letter L list. Why the difference in performance? You probably can foresee the answer: This is a semantic retrieval task. Prompting with a category name semantically primes the lexical items that are part of that category, increases their accessibility, and therefore makes them easier to recall. Prompting with a letter doesn't cause the same thing to happen, because there is no underlying conceptual or semantic relationship connecting the words that begin with the letter L.

FIGURE 6.4
....
Episodic and semantic knowledge in semantic memory.

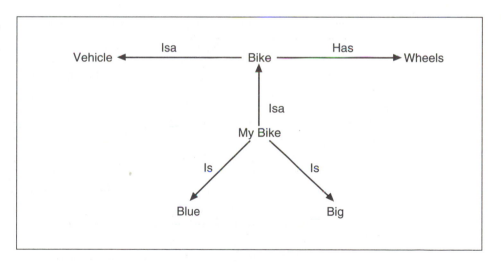

I know that bikes are two-wheeled vehicles, usually designed to carry only one or two people. This knowledge is semantic. Also, I know that my bike "isa" bike; it's blue and has a 27-inch frame to accommodate my long legs. You wouldn't have known this, because this knowledge of my particular bike is episodic. In other words, the type-token distinction affords the theorist a way of separating semantic from episodic knowledge. Stored at the type nodes are the facts that are true about that particular category. The facts define the category and are consequently context-free. Stored at the token nodes are facts that are true for that individual. This knowledge is context-dependent and can consequently be distorted, bypassed in the search, or even, as we saw in the Loftus and Palmer

(1974) study in Chapter 5, overwritten by later episodic facts. If our objective is to develop a theory of conceptual knowledge, why bother incorporating episodic knowledge into the model?

To answer this question, we need to remind ourselves of the findings of the Hannigan et al. (1980) study. You'll recall that they demonstrated that both episodic and semantic memory seem to be involved in almost every act of retrieval from permanent memory. This finding brings us to a related point. People typically use episodic memory as a basis for inference when semantic knowledge is lacking. An example might help clarify this. Suppose I were to ask you, "Could a car's battery fail on a hot summer day?" This question of battery failure involves technical knowledge of battery properties and their relationship to temperature changes. You could get this information from a book, and you might be able to answer without ever having any personal experience with car batteries. However, because most of us don't possess this knowledge, we think about all the car battery failures that we're familiar with. No doubt most, if not all, of them have taken place in the wintertime, so we're inclined to answer no to the original question. To answer the question, we've had to search among the token nodes dealing with battery failures to make a logical generalization about what must be true for the type nodes as well. Because such inferences occur routinely, any theory of knowledge would have difficulty predicting certain responses if it failed to make provisions for episodic knowledge. Having examined these general considerations of network models, let's turn to a specific case.

Teachable Language Comprehender

Teachable Language Comprehender (TLC) is one of the earliest network models and is based on a doctoral dissertation by R. Quillian (1968). Quillian did not set out to build a static model of knowledge. His objective was to demonstrate that language had certain formal properties that could be captured in a formal system—in this case, a computer program. Quillian designed the program to be able to demonstrate some rudimentary comprehension of language. Collins and Quillian (1969) made some modifications and simplifying assumptions and produced a model of knowledge that could be tested empirically.

Assumptions of the Teachable Language Comprehender   Part of TLC's network is shown in Figure 6.5. The concepts, or nodes, in TLC each have two kinds of relations. First, each node has a superordinate relationship to some other node, which determines category membership. Although it hasn't been shown in Figure 6.5, the superordinate characteristic expresses the *isa* relationship. For example, a canary is a kind of bird, which in turn is a kind of animal. Second, each node has one or more property characteristics, which express the *has* relation. A shark *has* the property *can bite*.

TLC also assumes that semantic knowledge can be captured in the sort of hierarchical display shown in Figure 6.5. That is, canaries and ostriches are organized by the more general and more inclusive category BIRD. Birds and fish are in turn characterized by the more general category ANIMAL. TLC also assumes that the cognitive system is characterized by what has been called *cognitive economy*. You know that nearly all animals have skin, but this fact is noted in TLC only once: at the highest—that is, the most general—level. Collins and Quillian designed this model to be stored in a computer and were careful not to tie up too much of the computer's memory by repeatedly storing general animal facts with each specific animal. They reasoned, however, that the cognitive

··············   **FIGURE 6.5**   **An illustration of the memory structure assumed by the Teachable Language Comprehender. One part of the semantic network for animals is depicted.**

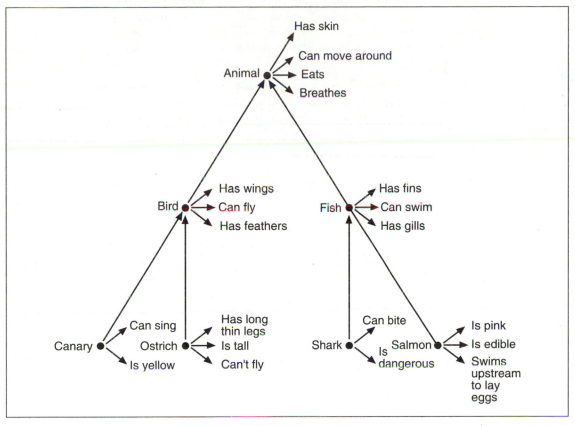

(After Collins & Quillian, 1969. Copyright 1969 by Academic Press. Adapted by permission of the publisher and author.)

system must have similar storage constraints, and consequently, the assumption of cognitive economy seemed plausible.

TLC also assumes that knowledge access is accomplished by an **intersection search**. This type of search specifies that the search process begins from particular nodes and fans out from them. The fanning out is in parallel, meaning that cognitive processes scan all the nodes associated with the entry nodes at the same time. The search is also assumed to have unlimited energy, meaning that the rate of search is not slowed by the number of associations emanating from any particular node. In other words, if the cognitive process fans out to three nodes from the entry node, it accomplishes this process in the same time that fanning out to only one node would take. With each node accessed in the search, the scanning processor leaves an indicator pointing to the node where the search originated. This process is called *flagging*. If the search processes, which have begun their fanning out from different nodes, ever meet one another during the search, an intersection is then noted. When an intersection is discovered, cognitive processes check all the flagged nodes until they determine the pathway linking the nodes from which the search originally began. Once this pathway is determined, TLC can use its inference programs to determine if it indeed "knows" that particular fact.

Let's consider an example. Suppose we give TLC a statement—"A shark is an animal"—and ask it to verify whether this statement is true. The search begins from the *shark* and *animal* nodes and fans out from there. At *fish*, the search processes will intersect, and the nature of the pathway from *shark* to *animal* will then be evaluated. In this case, the pathway goes from one node to a superordinate node to another superordinate node, so TLC would say yes to the statement.

Empirical Findings of the Teachable Language Comprehender   Although the intersection search is assumed to take place in parallel, it nevertheless requires time to move the search process from node to node. Consequently, the greater the semantic distance between the two originating nodes, the more time required by TLC to verify the sentence.

Consider the three following sentences from TLC's perspective:

S0: A canary is a canary.
S1: A canary is a bird.
S2: A canary is an animal.

In the case of S0, little time should be required to verify the sentence, because the search processes should intersect quickly, starting as they do from the same place. However, in the case of S2, the search processes have to fan out across two levels, and so we would predict that more time would be required to verify this sentence. These three sentences deal with superordinate relationships, but we would have the same expectation for property relationships. Consider the following three sentences:

P0: A canary is yellow.
P1: A canary can fly.
P2: A canary has skin.

In the case of P2, the search processes have to fan across two levels. If the mechanism proposed by Quillian and Collins is an accurate depiction of what goes on when our knowledge is searched, then subjects should require more time to verify P2 than P1 or P0.

These predictions were tested in a study in which a large group of subjects was given simple sentences whose truth or falsity had to be determined as quickly as possible. Subjects were given an equal number of true and false sentences. Figure 6.6 depicts the findings of this study. Note that humans performed in a way that was consistent with the theory, lending support to the notion that permanent memory is searched in the manner suggested by TLC.

However, in the tidal wave of research generated by these findings, some problems were also washed ashore. First, Rips, Shoben, and Smith (1973) found that some superordinate relationships are verified faster than others. Consider the following two sentences:

A dog is a mammal.
A dog is an animal.

Collins and Quillian would predict that the first sentence should be verified faster than the second sentence. This prediction is based on their assumption that semantic knowledge is hierarchically organized. Because mammals are nested (subordinate) within the animal classification, the search processes should intersect sooner when verifying the first sentence. However, Rips et al. (1973) demonstrated that the second sentence is verified faster.

FIGURE 6.6
....

The results of Collins and Quillian's (1969) sentence verification experiment.   The data depicted are for true responses only, showing mean reaction time (RT) as a function of the number of levels in the hierarchy that the Teachable Language Comprehender assumes needs to be searched. The sentences shown are only examples, since many sentences were used. Notice that RT increases systematically as the number of levels increases.

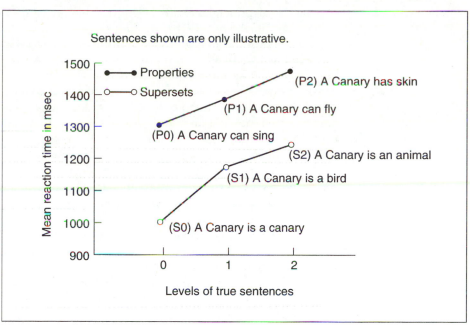

(After Collins & Quillian, 1969. Copyright 1969 by the Academic Press. Adapted by permission of the publisher and author.)

Now consider the following two sentences:

A peach is a fruit.
A watermelon is a fruit.

Each sentence mentions a perfectly good example of a fruit, and each example would be nested one level below *fruit* in TLC's knowledge structure. On these grounds, we shouldn't expect any consistent differences in verification times for these two sentences. But there are consistent differences: People verify the first sentence faster than they do the second (Smith, Shoben, & Rips, 1974). Why is this so?

Each sentence does mention a perfectly good example of a fruit. However, although people recognize that all fruits are equal in some sense, some fruits are apparently considered more typical of the category than others. Knowledge of typical category members seemingly can be accessed and verified faster than knowledge of less typical members (Rips et al., 1973). This concept of typicality is important and is related to the notion of the prototype examined in Chapter 3. That chapter stated that people seem to abstract relevant features from various stimuli in the world and then reassemble these feature lists to form higher-order (i.e., more general) units of knowledge, which can in turn be used to guide future perception. One such unit of higher-order knowledge is the prototype, the most central element of a category. What makes the prototype the most central element of a category? Many theorists believe that the prototype has more of the features that have been abstracted to form the category in the first place—more features than any other single element in the category. The implication of this view is that some fruit comes close to being the prototypical fruit (Chapter 11 will show that this is apparently true). The problem for TLC is that it's too simple to incorporate these effects, meaning that actual human knowledge has other, richer organizational principles than the limited hierarchical ones seen in TLC (Mc-Closkey & Glucksberg, 1978).

Finally, the assumption of cognitive economy seems unwarranted. Recall that Collins and Quillian postulated that specific factual knowledge was stored only once—at the most general possible node. This was why the statement "A canary can sing" required less time to verify than the statement "A canary has skin." Because *skin* is stored only once—at the *animal* node—the search processes require time to fan out and note the intersection. Conrad (1972) questioned this claim, maintaining that the reason for the faster reaction times for the first sentence was simply because the concept *canary* is more strongly associated with the concept *can sing* than it is with the concept *has skin*.

Conrad tested this idea by asking her subjects to describe a series of common nouns, such as *canary, bird*, and *animal*. She found large differences in the properties that were ascribed to particular nouns. For example, canaries were often described as being yellow but hardly ever described as having skin. Conrad next computed a measure of the association strength based on the frequency-of-mention data she had collected. She then gave her subjects a sentence verification task similar to the kind used by Quillian and Collins. She found that the reaction times were predictable from the association strength measure, regardless of how many levels the subjects had apparently searched through. For example, subjects quickly verified statements such as "An orange is edible," even though these terms are separated by at least one level in the hierarchy. Also, subjects required a lengthy amount of time to verify statements whose terms were only weakly associated, even when those terms were adjacent in TLC's hierarchy. Conrad's work was influential in closing the door on a pure and simple hierarchical model.

Spreading Activation Model

As the shortcomings of TLC became more widely recognized, Collins and Loftus (1975) developed an alternative model of conceptual knowledge, one that was not organized hierarchically. Instead, the notion of semantic distance, or semantic relatedness, was used as the organizing motif. Figure 6.7 shows a small part of their network. The lines connecting the nodes indicate that an association exists between those concepts. *Daffodils* are associated with *yellow*, which is in turn associated with *bananas*. However, *bananas* and *daffodils* are not associated.

The **spreading activation model** makes two other assumptions regarding structure. First, the length of the line connecting two concepts is intended to have theoretical meaning. The shorter the line, the more closely associated are the concepts. For example, *car* and *truck* are closely associated, but *yellow* and *bus* are only weakly associated. Second, like TLC, the spreading activation model assumes that superordinate relationships are labeled with an *isa* link. Thus, the linkage from bus to vehicle would be of this type. However, this model represents an advance over TLC in that it also includes some *isnota* links. This means that the model can quickly determine that some strongly associated concepts are nevertheless not superordinate. This point is an important one. Consider what might take place if subjects were given the following sentence:

A school is a bus.

TLC would begin by carrying out a search beginning from the *school* and *bus* nodes, eventually intersecting at some hypothetical *things in the world* node, and finally deciding that the terms were not on a superordinate path. If TLC were a

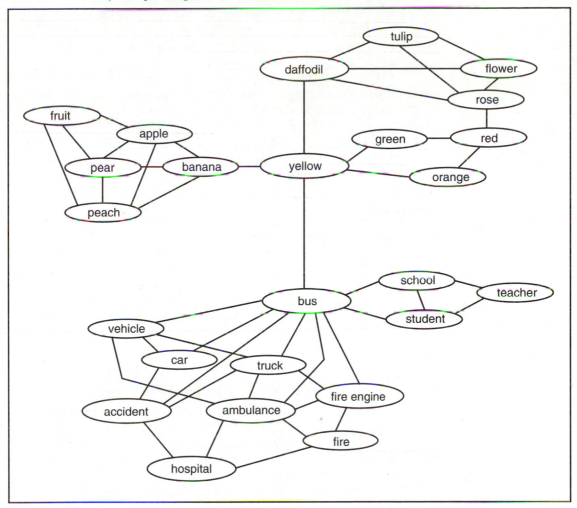

(From Collins & Loftus, 1975. Copyright 1975 by the American Psychological Association. Adapted by permission of the publisher and author.)

completely accurate model of human knowledge, we would predict that the subjects would take a lot of time before determining that this sentence was false. Although these terms are strongly associated, however, subjects are quick to refute the sentence, indicating that a complete search is probably not carried out. Collins and Loftus developed the term **prestored knowledge** to describe such facts that do not require an extensive memory search. Some research (Smith, 1978) has indicated that at least some of our knowledge is like this. Knowledge of certain relations is stored directly in the network, thus obviating the need to scan our memories.

This notion of expert knowledge has important implications, although a fuller development of them is reserved for Chapter 12. Also, you probably already know that prestored knowledge wasn't always prestored: Small children don't know that a bat isn't a bird. The implication is that the organization of our knowledge must be modifiable as people develop. The important point here is that some memory processes must exist that do more than simply search the structure of permanent memory in a somewhat passive way. Some processes must go to work on this structure, modifying it to incorporate new knowledge. That is, on a practical level, Collins and Loftus must shoulder the burden of specifying what experiences produce the *isnota* link in semantic memory. This objective hasn't been done very well in this model. This chapter later considers some proposals that accomplish this objective.

In addition to these assumptions regarding memory structure, the Collins and Loftus model also makes some assumptions about the search process, one of which is particularly important. As nodes are searched, the knowledge stored therein undergoes a change in status. Specifically, the activity of search is thought to activate searched nodes, meaning that the knowledge is brought into a state of heightened accessibility. Which nodes are activated depends upon several factors, including certain strategic decisions of the person searching her own memory. However, evidence suggests that highly associated nodes are activated more or less involuntarily. Having activated one node, the spread of activation radiates outward along strong associative lines to make other nodes more accessible. How far the activation spreads is determined by several factors. The strength of the initial activation, the amount of time since the initial activation, and, of course, the degree of semantic distance between the nodes all play a role in influencing the resulting spread of activation. If an unusual, or remote, concept is the locus of the initial activation, then not many other nodes will be activated. If, however, a concept at the center of a richly interwoven network is stimulated, then many other nodes will be activated.

ACT-R

The theory that we are about to describe has been evolving for many years and so a brief history is warranted. The "ACT" part of ACT-R stands for Adaptive Control of Thought and is pronounced as the word "act." The term "ACT" has been used to designate different versions of an entire family of models that have been developed over the course of the last two decades by cognitive scientist John Anderson and his colleagues. In a book published in 1976, Anderson described one of the most important early versions of the model, known as ACT-E. A later, and improved, offspring of the model, ACT* (pronounced "act-star"), appeared in 1983. ACT-R itself was given birth in books appearing in 1990 and 1993. The "R" in ACT-R stands for "rational," and in his most recent work Anderson has argued strongly for the existence of a "rational level" in cognition, as well as for an accompanying analysis at this rational level. We'll make our way to a discussion of this analysis and its implications in due time.

The early versions of the ACT family had many similarities with TLC and the other spreading activation models that we've discussed. Thus, in ACT-E, for example, nodes representing concepts could be in one of two states: active or inactive. Active nodes represented concepts, or parts of concepts, that had become accessible to the cognitive system. Once a node was activated, activation spread out to other connected nodes, changing them from inactive to active.

In ACT*, the mechanics of activation were changed somewhat. Whereas before the linkages between nodes could exist in only one of two states, now the linkages between concepts could exist at a variety of different levels of activation. A light switch and a rheostat, or "dimmer," can be seen as metaphors for the early and later versions of the theory. In ACT-E, the node is like a light fixture, and its activation is controlled like a conventional light switch: The light is either on or off. In ACT*, the node's activation can be turned up or down depending on the setting of the dimmer.

The Organization of Knowledge in ACT-R

The development in the ACT family that was seen in both ACT-E and ACT* has continued in ACT-R, resulting in many new ideas concerning the organization of knowledge and its representation. ACT-R is further developed than ACT-E and ACT* in that it has different representations for procedural and declarative knowledge. If you think back to Chapter 1, you'll remember we made a distinction between factlike knowledge that you have in your working memory (declarative knowledge) and the action-knowledge that is used when you engage in a skill (procedural knowledge). ACT-R acknowledges these different types of knowledge with two completely different formats for knowledge representation. Declarative knowledge is represented in ACT-R as "chunks," whereas procedural knowledge is represented by "**production systems.**"

Production Systems   A production system consists of a set of production rules. Each production rule can be expressed as an "if-then" rule, or, more formally, as a "condition-action" pair. The "if" part of the rule specifies the "conditions" that govern the rule's use. The following could be an example of a production rule in a hypothetical system:

> IF   it's raining
> THEN   carry your umbrella with you

In other words, under the condition that the weather is rainy, then that's the time to bring along an umbrella. I should add that the number of conditions is not limited to only one; in many cases, the number of conditions might be greater than one. When the number of conditions is greater than one, then the rule applies only in progressively narrower situations, with the result that the action may be taken with less frequency. Consider the following production rule:

> IF   it's raining AND
>   you have to park far from the office AND
>   your raincoat is at the cleaners
> THEN   carry your umbrella with you

For the action of umbrella carrying to be taken here, there are more conditions to be met than was true in the case of the previous production rule. A person who followed the first rule might be seen carrying his or her umbrella quite a lot (every time it rains). But a person following the second rule may park as close as possible to the office on rainy days, turn up the collar of his or her raincoat, and simply run for it, hardly ever bothering with the umbrella.

Production systems are organized by their goals. A given production system may have a set of interrelated goals, but at least one goal must be active at any given point in time. This point can be illustrated by looking at the production system for addition shown in Table 6.3. The goal of the entire system is to arrive at the correct answer to a typical addition problem. This overall goal is in turn broken down into subgoals, with the idea being that when all the subgoals have been solved in a certain sequence, then the overall problem will perforce be solved. Let's take a closer look at the first production rule to be mentioned, NEXT-COLUMN. The "condition" part of this production says that if "cl" is the rightmost column without an answer digit written under it, then the "action" part

············· **TABLE 6.3**   **Production rules for addition***

NEXT-COLUMN
   IF   the goal is to solve an addition problem
            and c1 is the rightmost column without an answer digit
   THEN   set a subgoal to write out an answer in c1

PROCESS-COLUMN
   IF   the goal is to write out an answer in c1
            and d1 and d2 are the digits in that column
            and d3 is the sum of d1 and d2
   THEN   set a subgoal to write out d3 in c1

WRITE-ANSWER-CARRY
   IF   the goal is to write out d1 in c1
            and there is an unprocessed carry in c1
            and d2 is the number after d1
   THEN   change the goal to write out d2
            and mark the carry as processed

WRITE-ANSWER-LESS-THAN-TEN
   IF   the goal is to write out d1 in c1
            and there is no unprocessed carry in c1
            and d1 is less than 10
   THEN   write out d1
            and the goal is satisfied

WRITE-ANSWER-GREATER-THAN-NINE
   IF   the goal is to write out d1 in c1
            and there is no unprocessed carry in c1
            and d1 is 10 or greater
            and d2 is the ones digit of d1
   THEN   write out d2
            and note a carry in the next column
            and the goal is satisfied

Note: *c1, d1, d2, and d3 denote variables that can take on different values for different instantiations of each production.

of the production says to set up a subgoal to add the rightmost column that doesn't have an answer. So, in the case of the following addition problem

$$\begin{array}{r} 35 \\ +46 \\ \hline \end{array}$$

we see that the rightmost column (5 + 6) doesn't have an answer written under it, and so finding this answer would be our first subgoal. Now, where does the production system go from here? The next production rule PROCESS-COLUMN picks up where NEXT-COLUMN left off. The conditions of PROCESS-COLUMN basically say that if you want to write the sum of the digits in cl, then you must add them up and write the answer below the line. Notice that sums like this could be greater than nine (as this one is) or less than ten. If the sum of a column's digits are greater than nine, then the production system goes to the production rule named WRITE-ANSWER-GREATER-THAN-NINE. If a certain column sum is less than ten, then the system goes to a different production rule: WRITE-ANSWER-LESS-THAN-TEN.

  The action that the production system takes from each specific production rule has a lot to do with the specific production rule that the system attempts to implement next. This raises a general question: How does the production system determine the appropriate sequence for specific production rules? How does the system know which rule to apply next? The answer is that after the production system executes a specific production rule, it engages in a process called *pattern matching* to determine which production should be executed next. In pattern matching, the system does two things. First the system examines the contents of working memory and notes what parts of the problem have been solved and what parts still need to be solved. Then the system matches this current state to the production rules that would apply to the parts of the problem that still need to be completed. Basically, this means that the system considers all of the "if" statements, the conditions, to see which ones are currently pertinent.

Sometimes a situation arises in which more than one production rule could apply. For example, suppose it is currently raining, and you had the following two production rules in your personal production system:

IF	it's raining
THEN	carry your umbrella
IF	it's raining
THEN	wear your raincoat

The conditions for both production rules are met, so which production rule would be enacted? In other words, would you carry your umbrella or wear your raincoat, or do both? In such cases, production rules have a system of *conflict resolution* to determine which of these two production rules would be executed. There are lots of ways to accomplish this. Sometimes each production rule is given a priority number and if the conditions for two productions match at the same time, then the production with the higher priority is enacted. Sometimes the system "remembers" which action it took the last time these two production rules were in conflict and executes the rule that it did *not* execute last time. In other words, sometimes the systems are designed to alternate between production rules when the conditions for two rules match. In the most complicated form of the system, the conflict resolution procedure might actually try to evaluate which production rule leads to the system's goal faster.

Two other important terms in production systems are "firing" and "cycle." When the action part of a production rule is enacted, we refer to the production as "firing." The sequence of steps from pattern matching, conflict resolution, through firing is referred to as a "cycle" of activity.

Production systems represent cognitive skills. This means that we probably are not going to have much, or any, awareness of actually "running" the production system as we use it. It is true that the *contents* of each production are deposited in working memory. And that means that the contents of the production system are declarative knowledge. So, as we solve an addition problem, we should be aware of what we are doing (because that represents the contents of the production system), but we might not have awareness, or be able to talk about, how we are solving the problem, because that represents the actual running of the production system.

Sources of Knowledge for Building Production Systems   In the previous section, we introduced some of the basic terminology about production systems, and we described their operation. Now the question we must deal with concerns the origin of such systems: What sort of information could be used as a basis for building a production system? One source of information comes from a technique known as *task analysis* (Anderson, 1993). To do a task analysis, the experimenter asks what knowledge, actions, and conditions for actions are needed to carry out a certain task. Basically, this amounts to writing a program in the form of a production system for a specific task. Although this might seem very open ended, there are some principles that are used in task analyses. First, if the system is to mimic human knowledge, the number of conditions to be matched for each production rule should be reasonable; that is, it should should not exceed the number of conditions that a human could have active in working memory at any one time. Generally, this means that there will be a limit of three to five conditions for each production rule. A second principle concerns the complexity of the conditions mentioned in each production rule. Generally, most successful production systems do not have production rules that would require humans to make complicated inferences to see if the conditions match some existing situation in the world. In most cases, determining whether an existing situation matches the conditions of a particular production rule can be assessed by a simple observation. Bovair, Kieras, and Polson (1990) have found that these types of guidelines are sufficient to produce a good task analysis for certain simple tasks like text editing.

Chunks in Declarative Memory   Production systems deposit their contents in working memory, but ACT-R uses a different representation to describe the actual contents of working memory and permanent memory. This representation is referred to by a variety of equivalent names: sometimes as the "chunk," or sometimes as the "**working memory element**" (**WME,** pronounced wimee). There are several aspects of chunks that are important to know. First, a chunk can be a combination of several stimuli, but only a limited number of stimuli can be combined in a single chunk. ACT-R suggests that three or four elements can be represented by a single chunk. Second, the elements of the chunk are said to have "configural properties." For example, suppose I give you the numbers 1776 and ask you to store them. Now, given that there are only four elements here, you could store these numbers as a single chunk, especially if you are familiar with American history. But once you store them as a chunk, then shifting the elements around to different positions, such as 7617, would not be recognized as the "same" chunk that you had stored. When we say that a chunk has configural properties, we mean that the relationship of the elements to each other within the chunk is important. Third, chunks can have a hierarchical relationship with each other. This means that two separate chunks can themselves be chunked together to make a "super-chunk." And in some cases, we might be able to take two "super-chunks" and put them together to make a "super-super-chunk." There was an example of this phenomenon in Chapter 4. Do you recall the runner who learned how to remember and recite random strings of digits containing up to eighty numbers? If you go back to that discussion, you'll see that the runner became very skillful in developing a strategy that converted many of the groups of three or four digits into a chunk that might stand for a typical time that could be earned in a certain running event.

A Representation for Chunks   There are probably many ways to depict cognitive structures that have the property of chunks; the representation chosen in ACT-R is not very difficult. Table 6.4 shows the representation for the chunks that would be present at the start of the addition problem described above. There are several points that need to be made concerning this representation. First of all, the "name" for the chunk is the word that is not indented, such as "problem1," "column0," and so on. We probably don't really have any awareness of the

············   **TABLE 6.4**   Schema representation of the problem:

$$35$$
$$+46$$

```
problem1
    isa numberarray
    columns (column0 column1 column2)
column0
    toprow blank
    bottomrow +
    answerrow blank
column1
    isa column
    toprow three
    bottomrow four
    answerrow blank
column2
    isa column
    toprow five
    bottomrow six
    answerrow blank
```

"name" of the chunk. Second, beneath each chunk name are no more than three lines representing three features or elements of that chunk. These are the "contents" of the chunk. For example, underneath "problem1" are the statements "isa numberarray" and "columns (column0, column1, column2)". Unlike the name of the chunk, we are aware of the contents of the chunk. So, for example, the problem1 chunk says that, after looking at the problem, in your working memory, you should have the knowledge that this array of numbers represents an arithmetic problem, that it consists of two columns of numbers, and that the answer is currently unknown. The third important point is how the representation shows the hierarchical relationship between chunks. Notice that the problem1 chunk has in its contents the names of the other chunks. This is how this representation shows the hierarchical relationship of the "super-chunk", (problem1) to the normal chunks (collumn0, column1, and so on). The chunk that is higher in the hierarchy contains the names of chunks that are lower in the hierarchy.

ACT-R in Action: The Navigation Studies

Now we're at the point where we can begin to show how ACT-R actually models human knowledge. The logical starting point is to gather some information about how humans perform on a reasonably demanding problem. To do this, Anderson and colleagues designed several navigation tasks, one of which is depicted in Figure 6.8. In this particular task, a subject looked at a computer screen showing the information in panel *a* of the figure and was asked to find a route from the point labeled "start" to the "destination" point. The screen also showed roads (shown as lines in the figure) over which the subject could drive a "car" to several imtermediate locations. As you can see from Figure 6.8*a*, there wasn't any direct road from the start to the destination. When the subject arrived at an interme- diate location, that location turned dark on the computer screen, and all of the pathways radiating outward from it, which previously were not shown on the

FIGURE 6.8
....
The various states
observed by a stu-
dent trying to
navigate.

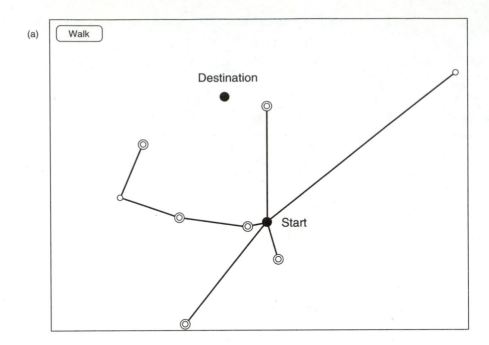

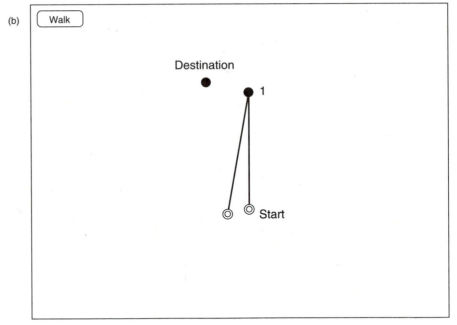

screen, suddenly became visible. Subjects could move from location to location by two means. First, they could "drive" a simulated car along one of the roads. A car moved across the computer screen at a rate of .25 cm/sec. Given that the screen was approximately 24 × 33 cm, you can see that the car moved quite slowly. This low rate of speed was deliberately designed to make the subject think twice about where he or she was going. In other words, just like in real-world navigation, there are costs attached to making wrong turns and other misjudgments. In addition to driving a car to a destination, the subject could "walk." Walking was painfully slow; the subject's velocity across the screen was only one-tenth that of the car's

FIGURE 6.8

· ·

The various states observed by a student trying to navigate.
Continued

Copyright 1993 by
Lawrence Erlbaum Asso-
ciates, Inc. Adapted by
permission of the pub-
lisher and author.

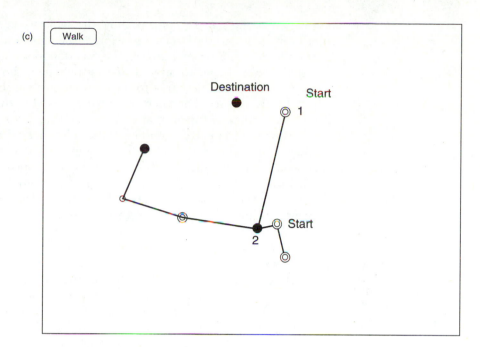

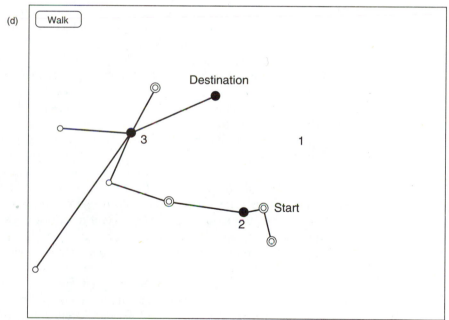

speed, that is, .025 cm/sec. As you can imagine, most subjects made the decision
to start walking only when they were quite close to the goal. Walking was
necessary, however, because not every destination was reachable by car.

Figure 6.8 *b*, *c*, and *d* show the progress of a subject as she attempted to find
her way through this "progressive" map. As these panels show, the subject first
drove to the location labeled "1." This is a reasonable move, as location 1 is
clearly closer to the destination than are the other way points originally shown.
However, as panel *b* indicates, there is no direct linkage from location 1 to the
destination. Moreover, the only two pathways from location 1 take her either
back to the start point, or to another location that is almost as distant from the

destination as the starting point is. Now the subject could have started walking from location 1. But she decided to explore the situation further, driving to the location labeled "2" in panel *c*. Here, the situation looked a little more promising. The subject now began to drive to the farthest point on this set of linkages, a point that was quite a bit closer to the destination than she previously occupied. In panel *d*, we can see that when the subject arrived at this point, labeled "3," a direct connection between that point and the destination became visible, enabling her to complete the journey. Notice also that a definite memory load was imposed on the subject in this task. For example, suppose in panel *d*, there was no direct connection between location 3 and the destination. Our subject may have decided to throw in the towel at this point by driving back to location 1 and walking from there. But from location 3, location 1 was no longer visible because there was no direct connection between those two points. The subject would have had to retrieve her pathway in order to get back to location 1.

Several types of maps were designed. Some maps had only fifteen intermediate locations; these were called "simple" maps. "Complex" maps contained thirty possible intermediate locations that the subejct might drive or walk to. Obviously, not all fifteen or thirty points were on view during the entire time that the subject explored the map, and in some cases, specific locations were irrelevant to finding the solution path. For both simple and complex maps, there were several subtypes. "Easy" maps had a clear subgoal structure in which the subject's arrival at successive locations revealed routes that took the subject progressively closer to the destination. "Long" maps had a similar feature, but the pathway to the goal was roundabout. "Walk" maps involved situations in which the subject had to get out of the car and walk because there was no direct drivable pathway to the destination. Finally, "back-up" maps involved a pathway that led deceptively near, but not directly to, the destination. The subject in this situation was faced with a "walk or explore" decision. The map shown in Figure 6.8 is of the simple back-up type.

Anderson and his coworkers next designed a production system to model the knowledge and action of humans on the navigation task. An English-language version of the production system is shown in Table 6.5. Actually, the last production shown in Table 6.5, "Give Up," was not available to the subjects in the study described here. The subjects *had* to find a solution path.

The production system has several interesting features. As you can see, the production system doesn't seem to be as complex (at least in terms of the overall number of productions) as the addition system that we looked at earlier. Does this mean that the navigation task is not as complicated as addition is? The answer is "no, not necessarily." First, remember that the production system for navigation is a first approximation; it may become more complicated as deeper analysis is done of humans on these types of tasks. Second, the number of productions is influenced, to a certain extent, by the number of different conditions that have to be matched up before an action can be taken. It could be the case that a particular production system contains numerous productions whose conditions are hardly ever matched by stimuli in the real world, and so these productions would "fire" only infrequently. Finally, much of a production system's complexity is the result of its conflict resolution scheme. It could certainly be the case that a production system containing numerous productions might also contain a straightforward conflict resolution scheme that produced very little variation in the system's behavior or performance. On the other hand, a more elaborate resolution scheme might account for much of the complexity in the system's strategy.

············· **TABLE 6.5**   **Productions involved in the navigation task**

COMBINE-ROUTES	
IF	the goal is to find a route from location1 to location2
	and there is a route to location3
	and location3 is closer to location2
THEN	take the route to location3
	and plan further from there.
DIRECT-ROUTE	
IF	the goal is to find a route from location1 to location2
	and there is a route from location1 to location2
THEN	take that route.
WALK	
IF	the goal is to find a route from
	location1 to location2.
THEN	walk
GIVE-UP	
IF	the goal is to find a route from
	location1 to location2
	and you are getting nowhere
THEN	give up.

Copyright 1993 by Lawrence Erlbaum Associates, Inc. Adapted by permission of the publisher and author.

In this case, the production system is designed to "look for" direct routes; these are considered first in this system. In other words, if you are at a location and a direct route lights up between you and the destination, then that's the route you want to take. As might be expected, walking is considered last. Walking will always get you to your destination, but unless you are at a location that is quite close, then walking will probably require more time than driving. Considered in between these, we have the "Combine-Routes" production. Basically, this production looks for locations that are closer to the destination than the current location, with the closest locations being evaluated most favorably. Of course, there's no guarantee that when you actually arrive at such a location, it will contain a further route to the destination. But in the absence of actually knowing a direct route, and given the slow speed of walking, the system will usually try to build a route to the destination by exploring specific segments one at a time.

Now we come to the main question: Does ACT-R do a reasonable job of modeling human knowledge on this type of navigation task? The answer appears to be yes. Table 6.6 compares human performance with ACT-R when ACT-R was run on the navigation problems used in this study (ACT-R's performance is shown in parentheses). As this table shows, there is a good correlation between human performance and that of ACT-R both in terms of the number of moves taken to solve the problem ($r = .94$) and the distance that was traveled to get to the destination ($r = .83$). In comparing ACT-R's performance with the typical human, I think it's interesting to note that the only substantial difference between the two seemed to take place in the back-up problems. Specifically, ACT-R solved both simple and complex back-up problems in fewer moves and less distance than did humans. What might this mean? The difference between ACT-R and humans on these types of problems might suggest that if humans use something like a "Combine-Routes" production in their production systems, they may overvalue the importance of taking a route that gets them closer to the destination, at the expense of exploring further for a direct route. In other words,

·············· **TABLE 6.6**   Summary of behavior in navigation task: average number of moves and units of distance (simulation averages in parentheses)

	Simple (15-point)	Complex (30-point)
Easy	3.80 moves (3.83)	4.87 moves (5.33)
	28.2 cm (28.4)	25.1 cm (26.8)
Long	3.77 moves (3.50)	4.00 moves (4.00)
	33.4 cm (34.7)	26.3 cm (30.8)
Walk	3.87 moves (4.00)	6.4 moves (7.00)
	31.6 cm (31.4)	20.8 cm (21.0)
Back up	3.57 moves (3.00)	7.37 moves (6.50)
	25.5 cm (18.0)	42.7 cm (37.5)

Copyright 1993 by Lawrence Erlbaum Associates, Inc. Adapted by permission of the publisher and author.

ACT-R was not as likely to fall for the "trick" in the back-up problems as humans were.

The "R" in ACT-R

In this chapter, we haven't spoken very much about the "R" in ACT-R, the R that stands for rationality. But we'll try to partially redress that problem here. ACT-R's basic argument here is that the human cognitive system is essentially "economical" (I don't mean "miserly"). The cognitive system is economical in the sense that it attempts to determine the nature and intensity of demands that will be placed on it in the future. Using this estimation of use, the cognitive system devotes as much of its resources to a particular problem as it can "afford."

FOCUS ON RESEARCH
···
Nonsemantic Priming

Are there cases in which a prompt might spontaneously prime another lexical item even if the two elements do not share a semantic relationship? Neely, Crawley, and Vellutino (1990) used a standard lexical decision task with SOAs in the 250- to 600-msec range to first duplicate some well-known priming effects. For example, they found, as expected, that the prompt CAT will facilitate the letter string "kitten" in a lexical decision task—this is to be expected. In addition, they found that these elements do not produce facilitation when they are embedded as the first syllables of unrelated words. For example, the prompt CATALYST does not facilitate lexical decision of "kitten," even though CATALYST obviously contained the prompt CAT. This finding could be interpreted within the standard framework pretty

easily too. It suggests that although we might, in some sense, have the ability to break down a word cognitively and use it to facilitate component words, our cognitive system probably does not typically start the activation process until the entire prompting word (not just its initial syllable) is encoded. However, there may be some cases in which activation is commenced after just the initial syllable is encoded. For example, Neely et al. found that using CATALYST as a prompt does facilitate lexical decision for the word "cat"! Clearly, these words are not semantically related, and they were not episodically related either through repeated presentations in the laboratory. This finding seems to suggest that there might exist some spread of activation over networks whose organization is not semantic.

The cognitive system's rationality emerges as it is successful in predicting, and meeting, future demands, in just the same way that we would expect a rational person to be successful in budgeting his or her financial resources.

Let's look at a somewhat extended example of a rational analysis applied to human memory. Under this view, the memory system tries to estimate the likelihood that a particular unit of knowledge, or memory, will be needed in the future. If the system concludes that there is a high likelihood that the memory will be needed, then a suitable portion of the system's resources will be devoted to encoding and retrieving it. If, on the other hand, the likelihood of a memory's being needed again is low, then our cognitive system may well decide to leave it unencoded. Occasionally the system might not work perfectly: We try to retrieve something and find we can't. When that happens, we may lament our "forgetfulness." But ACT-R invites us to think about the number of times a particular part of our cognitive system, such as our memory, doesn't let us down. For example, you may not be able to remember what you had for lunch exactly two weeks ago today, but I'll bet you can always retrieve your name, your phone number, and your address fairly effortlessly. If you were the "manager" of a vast cognitive bureaucracy called "your memory," you might make the decision to encode or not encode something based on the likelihood that it was going to be asked for at some unspecified time in the future. For any given lunch, you may decide that the need to retain this information is small, because it's unlikely that the memory is going to be needed in the future. But for your name and other personal information, you may decide to encode the information because there is a high likelihood that it is going to be needed again at some point in the future.

CONCLUDING COMMENTS AND SUGGESTIONS FOR FURTHER READING

Let's recapitulate what we did in this chapter. We began by talking about a distinction between things remembered and things known. The literature suggests that our intuitive feelings about remembering vs. knowing something are well founded; there seems to be some dissociation of the cognitive processes that affect memory versus those processes that influence knowledge. In turning to investigate the question of knowledge, we first looked at findings from the literature on lexical access. Here we saw that when a concept is called up by the cognitive system, that process speeds up the access of related concepts. We saw too that the cognitive system can do whatever work is necessary to relate concepts to one another. Findings like these suggest that much of our knowledge can be modeled as a vast network of interrelated concepts. What organizational principles govern the formation and use of these networks? That was the question that occupied us for the remainder of the chapter and took us to an investigation of models such as TLC and ACT-R.

Here's a question to ask yourself about this chapter after you've finished studying: In general, what are formalisms like ACT-R saying about human knowledge? Phrased slightly differently, what sort of position about human knowledge is implied by a model like ACT-R? Think about this for a minute before you read any further. There are many things that could be said here, so if your mental response does not agree completely with what follows, it doesn't mean that your response is wrong. First, we would say that ACT-R and models like it strongly suggest that the cognitive system has organizational principles and that these principles are orderly and describable. If the model had gone no further, a demonstration of just these facts is enough to make most cognitive psychologists giddy. In addition, the organizational principles of any given cognitive system seem to be common enough that we can talk about people sharing them. In other words, we can talk about a specific person as having a typical cognitive system. Finally, the systems that we talked about in this chapter are symbolic representations of knowledge. This is an advanced idea, but let's delve into it. When we say that ACT-R and models like it are symbolic, what we're asserting is precisely the idea that, whatever it is that people have going on in their heads when they use their knowledge, we know that people don't really, literally, have production systems, or chunks. Instead, what we're arguing here is that a production system is an accurate, symbolic representation of the computation the neural system makes when people solve puzzles like the navigation problem. In other words, when we say that a production system is symbolic, we mean that the steps that a production system takes as it computes the next action in a problem are abstract depictions of the steps that the actual neural system takes as it computes the next action in a problem. And when we say that a production system is accurate, we mean that, at some level, in some nontrivial way, the correspondence between the abstract depictions of the production system and the "actual steps" of the neural system is close enough to be convincing that models like ACT-R are correct.

If you'd like to read more about production systems and their uses, a terrific article by Neches, Langley, and Klahr (1987) will help you get started. In fact, the entire edited book (Klahr, Langley, & Neches, 1987) is a very worthwhile collection of applications of production systems. Some comments on production systems also appear in an excellent, although challenging, book by Newell (1990).

The ACT-R model, its precursors, and its applications are fully described in four surprisingly accessible sources. The beginnings of a general rational analysis of cognition are seen in Anderson (1990). Further developments are described in *Rules of the Mind* (Anderson, 1993). Although each book contains some "heavy-duty" mathematical analysis, the writing and compelling logic are lucid and, to a certain extent, can be read apart from the mathematical underpinnings. The same can be said for two articles in which Anderson shows how a rational analysis of memory might proceed (Anderson & Schooler, 1991) and how a general production-system-based model of problem solving and learning might unfold (Anderson, 1993).

KEY TERMS

Lexical access
Semantic priming
Stimulus onset asynchrony (SOA)
Network models

Type-token distinction
Teachable Language Comprehender (TLC)
Intersection search
Spreading activation model

Prestored knowledge
Production system
Working memory element (WME)

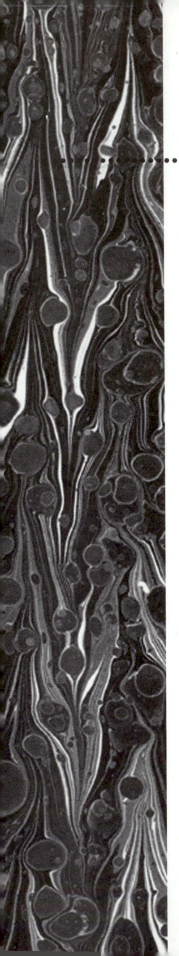

CHAPTER 7

THE STRUCTURE OF KNOWLEDGE: A CONNECTIONIST APPROACH

CHAPTER OUTLINE

OVERVIEW

Let's try solving the following problem (Tank & Hopfield, 1987): Imagine that you are the director of an academic library. Part of your job is to supervise the assistants who reshelve the books that have been returned by the library's patrons. The library's holdings cover many different topics. Each of the assistants is familiar to a greater or lesser extent with all of the topics, but their familiarity influences the speed with which they are able to reshelve the books. And because the assistants are paid on an hourly basis, it's important to assign assistants to areas with which they are familiar so they can reshelve the books quickly. The following table shows the number of books per minute that each assistant can reshelve in each of the topic areas:

reshelve ten books per minute in geology, it's obvious that Sarah should be assigned to this topic. But because Tim's fastest area is also geology, this means that Tim would have to be assigned to his second fastest area, which is physics. But if you do that, then you can't make use of George in physics, and George's rate in physics is two books per minute faster than Tim's. So that seems to result in a dead end. As an alternative approach, you may have realized that the number of possible assignments is finite. Because this number is finite, you could generate all of the assignments, compute the total number of books that would be reshelved per minute using each specific arrangement, and simply pick the arrangement with the highest total. This approach is guaran-

Assistant's Name	TOPIC					
	Geology	Physics	Chemistry	History	Poetry	Art
Sarah	10	5	4	6	5	1
Jessica	6	4	9	7	3	2
George	1	8	3	6	4	6
Karen	5	3	7	2	1	4
Sam	3	2	5	6	8	7
Tim	7	6	4	1	3	2

Now here's the problem: Assuming that you can assign an assistant to only one collection, and assuming that each of the collections must have one person assigned to it, what is the optimal assignment of assistants to topics (where optimal means the highest total number of books reshelved per minute)? It's a nontrivial problem. You may begin by thinking that because Sarah can

teed to work, but it has some disadvantages. Although the number of possible arrangements is finite, it's still a large number, 6! (or 720 different possible assignments). Even if you could generate and examine one possible assignment scheme per minute, it would take you twelve hours to look at all the possibilities, and so it might take you that long to find the optimal assignment. You might like to try some approaches on your own; I can tell you that the optimal assignment would result in forty-four books per minute being reshelved.

If you found an assignment scheme that results in forty-four books per minute being reshelved, congratulations. If you didn't and you want to know the answer, look at the "Concluding Comments" section at the end of this chapter. If you tried working this problem, I'm sure you realize that what is called for here is a technique that somehow *simultaneously* takes into account each assistant's fastest area and the effects of that assignment on all the other assistants (Tank & Hopfield, 1987).

Keeping track of these mutual dependencies seems hard for us to do at a mental level, but at a cognitive and neural level, we must solve problems similar to the reshelving problem all the time. For example, suppose a friend asks you to take a break from studying and join her for a meal. But suppose that you really need to study to earn a decent grade on a test the following day. In resolving this type of problem, which is sometimes called a double approach-avoidance conflict, we can see that your cognitive system is faced with the same sort of incompatibilities that we dealt with in the reshelving problem. Each course of action (studying or taking a break) has positive and negative aspects that must somehow be simultaneously balanced in order to make a decision.

Let's look at one more example. We usually don't think of our visual system as having a "problem" with perception, but in fact, almost all of the visual information from our retinae could be interpreted in numerous ways by our brains. How does your brain come up with a single interpretation from the complicated neural information produced by the retinae? And how does the brain go about making sure that its interpretation is the "right" one? As this last example suggests, our brains are frequently faced with the problem of assembling a single coherent interpretation from sensory data that are conflicting and "noisy." Further, what these examples suggest is that the brain and cognitive system may frequently be faced with complex problems that can be successfully resolved only by simultaneous consideration of many mutual incompatibilities.

What we're going to explore in this chapter are models of cognition that attempt to mimic this simultaneity that we see in many actions of the cognitive and neural system. These models are sometimes called neural network models, sometimes connectionist models, or sometimes distributed, nonsymbolic processing. Regardless of the name used, the approach is characterized by an attempt to produce models of cognition that seemingly have much in common with the operation of the neural system.

SOME BASIC CONCEPTS OF DISTRIBUTED REPRESENTATION

If you look back at Chapter 1, you'll find that we talked about three different levels of psychological analysis: a neural level, a cognitive level, and a mental level. The mental level corresponds to our consciousness or our awareness; it's what you usually think of when you think about your "mind." The neural level is based on a more or less literal description of the activity of the nervous system. But we can describe the activities of the nervous system in more abstract terms too, and when we do this, we arrive at the cognitive level. We might not be aware of all of the activities of our cognitive and neural system, but these levels are nevertheless very convenient ways to describe certain psychological events. When we use the information-processing approach to describe particular events, the degree of abstraction away from the neural system is marked. Think back to the last chapter. We were able to characterize some types of memory search as activating a particular unit or node representing your knowledge of, let's say, your dog. Does this node really exist? The answer is yes: The node exists at the cognitive level of analysis, where activating a node represents the summation of a great deal of neural processing. In contrast to the information-processing approach, the connectionist perspective can be understood as an attempt to produce a model that is considerably "closer" to the neural action than are information-processing models. In other words, although all cognitive models are abstract representations of neural events, the degree of abstraction in connectionist models is thought to be much less than it is for information-processing models. This means that connectionist models use terms and procedures that, at least superficially, seem to have a lot in common with actual neural events.

Actual and Idealized Neurons

Let's consider some of the things that are known about cortical neurons. First, we know that such neurons frequently exhibit a phenomenon called an action potential. Second, each neuron is highly interconnected with other surrounding neurons, and finally, these interconnections between specific neurons might be excitatory or inhibitory. When we say that neurons exhibit an action potential, this is just another way of saying that, theoretically, many cortical neurons continually exist in one of only two states. The neuron may "fire" an electrochemical impulse down the length of its axon, and when it does so, we refer to this firing, or transmission, as the action potential. If the neuron is not currently engaged in an action potential, then it is simply waiting to fire. What causes a neuron to fire? Simply put, if the neuron receives sufficient input of the right sort from other neurons, then the neuron's firing threshold is exceeded, and the action potential is seen.

Each neuron's impulse may be sent to thousands of surrounding cortical neurons. For example, each noncortical Purkinje cell of the cerebellum receives inputs from 100,000 neighboring cells (Kalat, 1984). For us, one of the important facts is that the firing neuron's effects on those thousands of surrounding neurons are simultaneous. This is what we mean when we say that cortical neurons are typically highly interconnected. When a specific neuron fires, it may send its transmission to thousands of other cells, and when a specific neuron receives transmissions, they may come from thousands of surrounding cells. Notice, too, that the strength of the neuron's message is not altered by the number of neighboring cells with which it communicates; the signal is never "diluted" or weakened by virtue of its connections with adjacent cells.

Although the strength of the signal is not diluted, the nature of the signal is not always positive. As you might recall from our discussion in Chapter 1, the work of Rosenblatt (1958) showed that computation among neurons is produced not only by excitatory connections between them, but also by inhibitory connections. What this means is that, in some cases, a neuron's firing might increase the likelihood that a neighboring neuron does *not* fire in response to other input. Each neuron then becomes a kind of "decision-maker" by summing up all the excitatory and all of the inhibitory transmissions from other neurons and firing (or not firing) depending on whether the total input is positive or negative.

So much for actual neurons. How do the idealized neurons of connectionist models compare with actual neurons? Consider Figure 7.1. The three circles

FIGURE 7.1
....
A small neural
network.

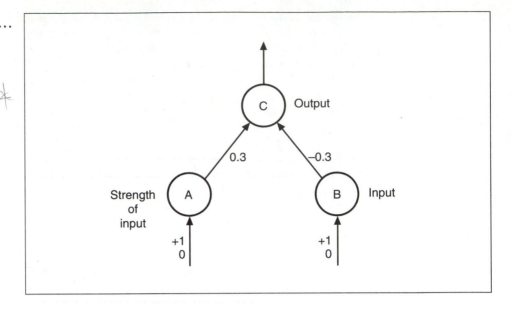

represent three artificial neurons in a tiny neural network. Let's use the term "neurode" to stand for such neurons (Caudill & Butler, 1992). What are the properties of these neurodes? We might say that, somewhat unlike real neurons, these neurodes are arranged in layers. There is a convention used in neural network models that labels the bottom layer as the "input" layer and the top layer as the "output" layer. (As we'll see later, frequently there are layers of neurodes in between these two.) After we get past this initial artificiality however, we begin to some commonalities between neurodes and actual neurons. For example, each neurode in the input layer communicates with the output neurode. It's true that this isn't exactly like the thousands of inputs that occur in the real nervous system, but some neural networks might have a lot more neurodes and connections. Finally, as the positive and negative signs suggest, the input layer does have excitatory and inhibitory connections with the neurode in the top layer. This means that neurode A apparently will have an excitatory influence on neurode C, while neurode B will tend to a simultaneous inhibitory influence on the output.

We haven't seen how an analogue of the action potential works in this sort of network (that will be in the next section), but the concept of the action potential is based on the idea of spreading activation that was discussed in the previous chapter. As you'll recall, in those models the activation of a particular node brought connected nodes into a similar state of activation. Here, the linkages between the neurodes establish the pathways over which activation will flow. If two neurodes are linked by a line, then there is some sort of influence between them. If two neurodes are not connected by a line, then their operation is basically independent of each other.

The Transfer Function

In real neural networks, information often is transmitted among neurons by means of the action potential; in connectionist models this transmission is enacted by a transfer function. So the action potential is to neurology what the transfer function is to neural networks. Basically, the transfer function takes inputs into the system and describes a means of spreading that input throughout the system. In the language of neural networks, we refer to this as propagating that input throughout the system. Let's go back Figure 7.1 and describe this little network in the following way:

1. If Input Unit A is active (has a strength of 1), then Unit A outputs an activation of 0.3.

2. If Input Unit B is active (has a strength of 1), then Unit B outputs an activation of −0.3.

3. If an input unit is not active, then it outputs no activation.

4. The output of Unit C is always the sum of the activation of all input units.

Now let's describe the strength of the connection between the input units and the output units (0.3 or −0.3 in this case) as the "weight" of the connection between two neurodes. We can then express the output of Unit C as follows:

$$\text{Output}_{\text{Unit C}} = (\text{Input}_{\text{Unit A}} \times \text{Weight}_{AC}) + (\text{Input}_{\text{Unit B}} \times \text{Weight}_{BC})$$

If we assume that both inputs shown in Figure 7.1 are active, then we get:

$$\begin{aligned}
\text{Output}_{\text{UnitC}} &= (1 \times 0.3) + (1 \times - 0.3) \\
&= (0.3) + (-0.3) \\
&= 0
\end{aligned}$$

On the other hand, if only Input Unit A is active, then we get:

$$\begin{aligned}
\text{Output}_{\text{UnitC}} &= (1 \times 0.3) + (0 \times -0.3) \\
&= (0.3) + (0) \\
&= 0.3
\end{aligned}$$

To summarize, in this case what the transfer function asserts is that the neural network we have created will have a positive output if Input Unit A and only Input Unit A is active. If Input Unit B and only Input Unit B is active, then the output of Unit C is negative. If both input units are active, then the output of Unit C is zero, meaning that there is really no output under that circumstance.

How can we conceptualize this little network? What does it actually "do"? Essentially, this model neural network works to dampen or diminish the strength of incoming stimulation. In other words, the strength of the input at Input Unit A might be 1, but the output of the system works to diminish this to 0.3. Similarly, if two strong but contradictory inputs are received, their effects are canceled by the network so that no further transmission takes place. The reason why we say that no further transmission takes place is because the output of Unit C is zero under stimulation from both input units. If the output of Unit C were to be fed into an another neural network (and there really is no theoretical limit about how many such "layers" of networks we can create), then Unit C would be silent and hence would transfer no information when both of its inputs were active.

Now we can generalize the transfer function to compute outputs for neurodes with any number of inputs:

$$\text{Output}_j = \sum (\text{Input}_i \times \text{Weight}_{ij})$$

In other words, the output of a given neurode "j" is equal to sum of all the activation of its inputs 1 through "i" times the weight of the connections between the inputs and the output neurode.

 ## DIFFERENCES BETWEEN DISTRIBUTED AND SYMBOLIC REPRESENTATIONS

Typographically, the neurodes that we're talking about in this chapter look quite a bit like the nodes that we covered in the last chapter. And the connections between the neurodes seem quite a bit like the connections between nodes that we've already seen. And it's true that neural networks can represent knowledge and cognitive actions just as well as the symbolic models did in the previous chapter. But there are some important differences in how the two approaches go about representing cognition. For example, even though neurodes and nodes look similar, the neurode is actually quite a bit more "stupid" than are the nodes of a symbolic network. A node is capable of housing quite a bit of information. When a node is activated, a great deal of information can be accessed, perhaps even more than an entire proposition. This makes accessing a node comparable to looking up an entry in an encyclopedia. By contrast, monitoring a neurode would be more like watching a traffic light than looking up something in a book. Each individual neurode just doesn't contain much information. A node is a complicated thing; a neurode is a simple thing.

A second difference between nodes and neurodes stems from this first difference. In the case of symbolic models containing nodes, it's legitimate to ask the question: "Where specifically is the knowledge housed?" But this question is much less legitimate in the case of neural models. To see this, consider Figure 7.2, which contrasts two modes of representing a familiar concept.

FIGURE 7.2

Two depictions of conceptual knowledge, (a) a symbolic depiction and (b) a correctionist depiction.

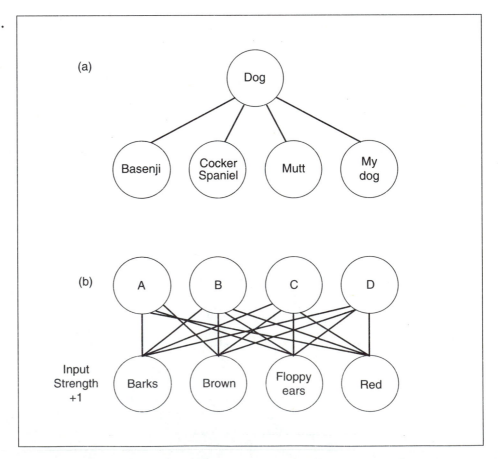

Figure 7.2a shows a typical symbolic representation of the concept "dog." What this model asserts is that if any one of the specific dog tokens is activated, then activation spreads upward from that token to activate the type node, namely "dog" at the apex of this hierarchy. Within each token node, there may be quite a bit of information (you probably know a lot about cocker spaniels) or there may be very little information (the basenji breed is much less familiar to most people).

Figure 7.2b shows how a distributed representation of specific dogs, that is dog tokens, might work. At the input layer, we have a set of neurodes representing unitary distinctive features that may be present or absent in the case of a specific dog. If present, then that specific neurode in the input layer becomes activated with an input strength of "1." If the feature is absent, then that specific neurode is not activated and has a strength of "0." Because this network has quite a few neurodes and connections, I did not put the strength of the connections on the linkages from the input to the output layer, but Table 7.1 shows all sixteen of them.

Suppose, for example, that if the "barks" input were activated, activation would flow to each output unit in the following way: 0.4 to A, 0.1 to B, 0.3 to C, and 0.2 to D (as another simplification, I used only positive numbers in this example). Let's also say that if the "floppy ears" node were activated, then activation would flow to each output unit in the following way: 0.1 to A, 0.3 to B, 0.3 to C, and 0.6 to D. Now what would the output of the network be for a dog that barked and had floppy ears, but was neither red nor brown? We can use the generalized rule for calculating the effects of each feature's activation on each output neurode (remember that the weights are just my own devising; they may not correspond to anything that might actually exist "in reality"). Only two of the input neurodes are going to be active, namely the ones for "barks" and for "floppy ears." Because the other two input neurodes will be inactive, we'll have zeros for their activation. In the equation below, I got the two weights for the effects of "brown" and "red" from Table 7.1. Now, using the generalized rule, we get:

$$\text{Output}_{\text{Unit A}} = (\text{Activation of "barks"} \times \text{weight of "barks" to A}) + \\ (\text{Activation of "brown"} \times \text{weight of "brown" to A}) + \\ (\text{Activation of "floppy ears"} \times \text{weight of "floppy ears" to} \\ \text{A}) + (\text{Activation of "red"} \times \text{weight of "red" to A})$$
$$\text{Output}_{\text{Unit A}} = (1 \times 0.4) + (0 \times 0.2) + (1 \times 0.1) + (0 \times 0.5)$$
$$= (0.4) + (0) + (0.1) + (0)$$
$$= 0.5$$

That is, if the dog barks and has floppy ears, then the Output Unit A is active with an activation level of 0.5. Of course, we would have to do the calculations for the other three output neurodes too. Instead of going through the calculations for each of the other three output neurodes, I'll just list the output of each of the four output units if "barks" and "floppy ears" are the only two active inputs:

· · · · · · · · · · · · · **TABLE 7.1 Strength of Connections in a Hypothetical Neural Network.**

FEATURE	STRENGTH OF THE CONNECTIONS			
Barks	0.4	0.1	0.3	0.2
Brown	0.2	0.6	0.4	0.5
Floppy ears	0.1	0.3	0.3	0.6
Red	0.5	0.2	0.1	0.2
Connection weight with	A	B	C	D

[0.5 0.4 0.6 0.8]

If you look back at Table 7.1, I think you'll be able to see where each of these terms came from. It's not obvious, but it's very important that you realize that this set of four numbers represents a specific dog—in this case a barking dog with floppy ears. Now let's complete this exercise with one more question: Suppose the dog in question had activated the feature "barks" and had been "brown" but did not have "floppy ears"? What would the output have looked like then? Using Table 7.1 and the general rule for summing activation, we get:

[0.6 0.7 0.7 0.7]

As you can see, the output pattern becomes quite a bit different when different input neurodes are activated. In other words, different tokens of dogs are represented in neural networks by different patterns of activation across a set of output units. In contrast to the symbolic representation, in which each node stands for quite a bit of information, in the connectionist approach, the information is not contained in any one neurode, but rather is seen as a pattern of activation across the entire set of interacting neurodes. In response to the question, "Where is the information housed?," the connectionist responds that the information is spread out across the entire network. Sometimes we say that the knowledge is in the connections or in the weights in a neural network.

Some important implications result from this view. According to the symbolic position, the loss of a single node could really incapacitate a system. Just think how disastrous it could be if somehow you lost your "dog" node. But according to the connectionist position, the loss of a single neurode should not bring the system down. In fact, you might have some fun playing with the network above to see what would happen if one of the output neurodes, or even if one of the input neurodes, were somehow lost from the system. As I think you'll find, the loss of a single output neurode leaves the rest of the output pattern intact. According to the connectionist, this finding makes a great deal of sense. However it is that our cognitive system represents and retrieves knowledge, it seems that it should be able to survive the loss of specific, tiny portions of its representation without any particularly noticeable deficit in performance.

Let's summarize the differences that we have discussed. Symbolic models emphasize networks whose nodes contain quite a bit of information. Connectionist models contain neurodes, each of which really can't do much on its own. In symbolic models, it's appropriate to ask at which node in the system certain information is stored, but in connectionist models, knowledge is seen as a pattern of activation across a set of interacting elements. Specific knowledge is not stored in specific locales in connectionist networks. Finally, loss of specific nodes can produce strong decrements in performance in symbolic models, but connectionist models generally are able to survive the loss of some, or even many, of their interacting neurodes before serious decrements in performance are seen.

SOME FUNDAMENTAL NETWORKS AND THEIR COMPUTATIONAL PROPERTIES

There are certain networks that work almost like Lego building blocks. That is, they are simple in themselves, but they can be put together in a variety of ways to form more complicated arrangements. We'll take a look at several such networks in this section.

The Perceptron

The simplest type of building block is the **perceptron,** which was originally developed by McCulloch and Pitts (1943). Figure 7.3 shows this simple network. McCulloch and Pitts defined the transfer function of this neurode as follows:

$$\text{Output}_j = \sum (\text{Input}_i \times \text{Weight}_{ij})$$
$$y = \{+1, \text{ if Output}_j \geq T\}$$
$$\{-1, \text{ if Output}_j < T\}$$

This transfer function is slightly different from the one we considered above. What it does is convert the output neurode's activation into one of two values. If the activation of the output neurode is above a certain threshold (T), then the output becomes +1. If the activation is below a certain threshold, then the output becomes −1. The threshold that usually is used is zero. So the output of a perceptron is always going to be one of two values, +1 or −1. Given this simplicity, you might wonder what a perceptron can actually do.

Rosenblatt (1958) was apparently the first to realize that this single neurode could be "trained," in a sense, to perform a variety of different cognitive computations. We'll be dealing with this notion of training a neural network at several points throughout the rest of this chapter. Informally, the first principle of training a neural network goes something like this: To get a neural network to perform differently, change the weights that connect the inputs to the neurodes in the output layer. Here's the rule that Rosenblatt used to change the weights linking the inputs to the outputs in the perceptron:

$$W_{new} = W_{old} + Byx$$

where W_{new} = the "new" weights to be used in the perceptron; W_{old} = the weights that have been used in the perceptron up until now; B = +1 if the perceptron's answer is correct and −1 if the perceptron's answer is wrong; y = the perceptron's answer; and x = the input pattern.

What this learning rule says is that, if you define the perceptron's output as an "answer," the weights are changed by taking the old weights, adding one to each weight if the perceptron's answer is correct, and subtracting one from the

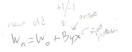

FIGURE 7.3
. . . .
The McCulloch-
Pitts neurode,
shown here with
two input signals.

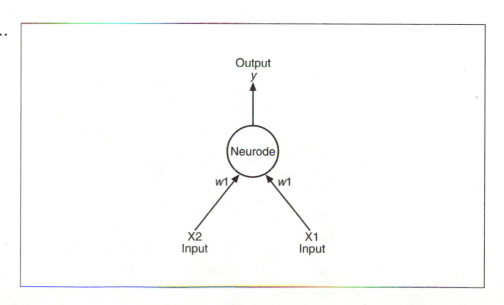

weights if the perceptron's answer is incorrect. In other words, if you treat each computation as an answer that is either right or wrong, and then give the network feedback about whether it was right or wrong, then the network will start to produce the correct output more frequently, in a way "learning" to come up with the correct answer more frequently. Here, the neurode is learning to take an arbitrary stimulus and categorize it as a member of one or another class of things.

We'll go through a conceptual example to show how this occurs. First, imagine that you have a piece of graph paper, and on this paper, you draw a standard Cartesian coordinate system. In this system, you have an x (horizontal axis) ranging from -1 to 1 in increments of 0.1 and a y (vertical axis) with the same range and increments. Next you plot six or eight points in this space, using the conventional (x, y) coordinates. Then you label each of the six or eight points either "A" or "B." You can label any point either A or B, just as long as when you are finished, it's possible to draw a straight line that separates each and every A from each and every B. Then you arbitrarily decide that the correct answer for the A points will be "1" and the correct answer for the B points will be -1. What this means is that if you input the Cartesian coordinates of an A point into the perceptron, and the output of the perceptron is "1," then you will call the output of the perceptron "correct," but if you input the coordinates of an A point, and the perceptron's answer is -1, then you'll call that answer incorrect. You can use almost any numbers between 0 and 1 for the initial weights. Regardless of what values you select for the initial weights, they will be changed as a result of the points that you input and the perceptron's answer. But if you go back to the training rule, you'll see that the weights are changed quite a bit differently depending on whether the perceptron's answer is correct or not.

Now there are several highly interesting things about the behavior of the perceptron. First, as you input more and more of the A and B points, you'll notice that the weights change less and less with each new point. Eventually, you'll get to a point where the weights don't change anymore because the neurode has "learned" all that it's going to learn. Second, you'll notice that the neurode seems to be getting the "correct" answer more and more frequently. Finally, you may have realized that it's not only the various A and B points that can be graphed. The weights of the perceptron are represented by two coordinates as well, and the first weight can be treated as an x coordinate and the second as a y coordinate. So what happens when you graph the weights? Well, if you graph the weights and draw a line connecting that point with the origin of the graph (that is, the point whose coordinates are 0, 0), you'll see that this line gradually "rotates" through the space of the points with each change in the weights of the perceptron. When the line is finally done rotating, because the weights are no longer changing, you'll see that the line neatly divides all the points on the graph paper. All the A points are on one side of the line and all of the B points are on the other. At a concrete level, we might say that the weights of a perceptron define a line segment that bisects two arbitrary sets of points, but in a more abstract sense, we can argue that the perceptron can be trained with feedback to accurately categorize certain stimuli as being of one class or another.

The Pattern Associator

In this section we'll continue to look at neural network building blocks and their operation. Figure 7.4 shows a commonly used neural network known as a pattern associator. Pattern associators are neural networks that can reproduce several particular output patterns when specific input patterns are given. One of the most interesting characteristics of pattern associators is their ability to reproduce several distinct output patterns using the same set of weights. What this means is that different input patterns can be propagated through an identical set of weights to produce output patterns that are uniquely associated with a particular input pattern. This characteristic of pattern associators enables them to be used as neural network models of memory. Here, the idea is that having a memory essentially means having the ability to associate or link a distinct input pattern (as psychologists, we might call this the stimulus) with a distinct output pattern. The output pattern might be an actual response, but it doesn't have to be. For example, it might be the case that the stimulus simply produces an expectation, or a visual image.

The pattern associator that is shown in Figure 7.4 is like this. This pattern associator learns to link certain visual stimuli (such as the sight of a rose perhaps) with the appropriate olfactory impression that we would expect whenever we see a rose (namely, the pleasant fragrance of a rose). Of course, we should expect this same pattern associator also to be able to reproduce the great smell of a barbecued steak from the sight of a T-bone on a smoky grill. We'll go through an example later in this chapter to show how this works.

We've already seen an example of a pattern associator, although it was expressed in a format that is superficially different than the one shown in Figure 7.4. If you go back to the network shown in Figure 7.2 (the "dog" network) and compare it to the one shown in Figure 7.4, you'll see that, although the two networks look different, in a formal sense, they are the same. That is, each network consists of two layers, with both the input layer and the output layer

FIGURE 7.4
. . . .
A simple pattern associator. The example assumes that patterns of activation in the A units can be produced by the visual system and that patterns in the B units can be produced by the olfactory system. The synaptic connections allow the outputs of the A units to influence the activations of the B units. The synaptic weights linking the A units to the B units were selected so as to allow the pattern of activation shown on the A units to reproduce the pattern of activation shown on the B units without the need for any olfactory input.

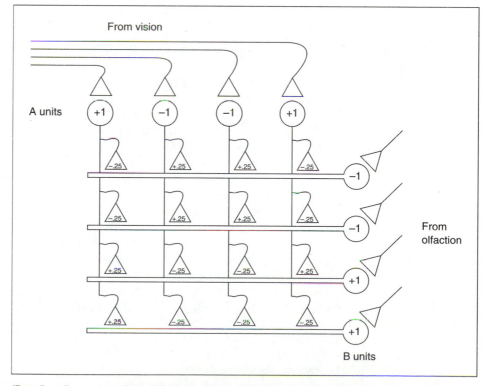

(From Rumelhart and McClelland (Eds.), *Parallel Distributed Processing*, Vol. 1. Copyright 1986 by MIT Press. Adapted by permission of the publisher and author.)

having four neurodes. Moreover, each input neurode is connected with each output neurode. Now, there is a distinction between the two: If you take a closer look at the vision-olfaction network under consideration, you'll see that it has weights whose values are negative. We'll explore the implications of that point a little later in this section.

Vector Encoding   One of the concepts that is most critical in your understanding the operation of neural networks is the idea of **vector encoding.** Informally, a vector is an ordered string of numbers containing at least two elements. For example, the following arbitrary vector has three elements:

[-1 1 1]

Vectors have many interesting mathematical properties, but for cognitive psychologists, one of the most interesting properties of vectors is their ability to encode and represent strings of features. Here's how that might be done. If you look at the representation of speech sounds in Chapter 9, or the representation of alphabetic characters in Chapter 2, you'll see that cognitivists frequently consider a stimulus like a speech sound or a letter to be nothing more than a bundle of discrete "features." In the case of speech sounds, such features may represent the presence or absence of "voicing" or, in the case of letters, perhaps the presence or absence of "vertical line." As long as the system knows which feature is which, it could represent the presence of a feature by a positive 1 and the absence of a feature by −1. After doing that, the system could "read" a vector as a representation for the stimulus in question, just as the checkout machines at the grocery store can read a bar code to come up with the price of the object in question. So, at the risk of getting ahead of the story a little bit, in the case of the vector above, if the first number represented a −1 for "voicing" absence, the second number indicated "bilabial" (i.e., +1 = bilabial, and −1 ="absence of bilabial"), and the third number indicated manner of articulation (let's say +1 = stop), then the sequence of three numbers above, [−1 1 1], would represent a speech sound such as an unvoiced bilabial stop or, in other words, the consonant /p/.

It's true that if we really wanted to make a vector representation of all consonantal speech sounds, more than three numbers would be required, because there are certainly more than three features involved in consonantal perception. But the addition of more features doesn't change the underlying concept; it would just mean that the vector would contain more elements. As it turns out, most real-life, psychologically interesting variables probably do require a lot more than three or four elements to represent them, and it's also the case that the encoding and representation of each feature does require one neurode. So the resulting neural networks could become extremely large. But the size of a neural network becomes much less of a problem if you think back to one of the basic tenets of neural-style cognitive computation. Namely, neurodes, like the neurons they are supposed to represent, are rather "inexpensive," in the sense that your head has a whole lot of neurons, maybe 100 million of them, each of which has to be kept busy on a daily basis. Seen from that perspective, our neurons are really "cheap labor," and we probably shouldn't mind so much that it takes so many of them to carry out psychologically relevant and useful computations. Having said that, I'd like to point out that I certainly don't feel that I have any neurons to spare.

The Pattern Associator at Work   Let's get back to that T-bone steak that we left out on the Webber. What happens when we look at the steak? Looking at Figure 7.4, let the four numbers labeled "A units" be a vector representing a visual encoding of the steak. Moreover, let the four numbers labeled "B units" be a vector representing the aroma of the steak. For our purposes here, the A units will be our input, and the B units will be the output of the network. The connective weights of each A unit to each B unit are shown in the triangles. You'll notice that, at this point, each weight is either +0.25 or −0.25. To operate this network, we convert the visual encoding into a vector, namely [+1, −1 −1 +1], and propagate that encoding through the weights that are shown. To do that, let's begin with the generalized rule to compute the topmost B unit's activation:

$$\text{Output}_j = \sum (\text{Input}_i \times \text{Weight}_{ij})$$
$$\begin{aligned}
\text{Output}_{\text{topmost B unit}} &= (+1 \times -0.25) + (-1 \times 0.25) + (-1 \times 0.25) + \\
&\quad (+1 \times -0.25) \\
&= (-0.25) + (-0.25) + (-0.25) + (-0.25) \\
&= -1
\end{aligned}$$

This is indeed the activation showing on the topmost element of the B units in Figure 7.4. We can use the generalized rule once again to compute the transfer function from the A units to the third-from-the-top B unit (the second-from-the-top is just the same as the one we have just done). We can see from Figure 7.4 that the number we're looking for is +1. If you look closely, you'll see that the weights from the A units to the third-from-the-top B unit are different than they were for the previous computation. Going through this example,

$$\begin{aligned}
\text{Output}_{\text{third-from-top B unit}} &= (+1 \times +0.25) + (-1 \times -0.25) + (-1 \times -0.25 \\
&\quad + (+1 \times +0.25) \\
&= (0.25) + (0.25) + (0.25) + (0.25) \\
&= +1
\end{aligned}$$

And that's the value we're supposed to come up with.

As I mentioned above, one of the most useful characteristics of pattern associators is their ability to represent several such associations in the same network, that is, with the same set of weights. To show how this is done, consider the arrangement of numbers shown in Figure 7.5. Now the left-hand side of this figure, labeled "A," shows the pattern associator that we have been discussing. The row vector on the left under "A" represents the sight of the T-bone steak (you'll see that those numbers are the same as those shown as the A units in Figure 7.4), and the column vector (the numbers that are arranged vertically) represents the aroma of the steak. And once again, you'll see that those numbers

FIGURE 7.5
. . . .
Two simple associators represented as matrices. Note that the weights in the first matrix are the same as those shown in the diagram in Figure 7.4.

(From Rumelhart and McClelland, eds., *Parallel Distributed Processing*, Vol. 1. Copyright 1986 by MIT Press. Adapted by permission of the publisher and author.)

		A						B			
+1	−1	−1	+1			−1	+1	−1	+1		
−.25	+.25	+.25	−.25	−1		+.25	−.25	+.25	−.25	−1
−.25	+.25	+.25	−.25	−1		−.25	+.25	−.25	+.25	+1
+.25	−.25	−.25	+.25	+1		−.25	+.25	−.25	+.25	+1
+.25	−.25	−.25	+.25	+1		+.25	−.25	+.25	−.25	−1

are the same ones that were shown as the B units in Figure 7.4. What about the pattern on the right-hand side, under "B"? This pattern represents a different sight-smell combination, perhaps the sight of a rose and the pleasant fragrance of a rose. That is, if you use the system we have described, you can propagate the row vector under "B" to produce the column vector, where the row vector represents the sight of a rose, and the column vector represents the fragrance of a rose. If you take a look at the weights shown in the boxes in Figure 7.5, you'll notice that they are different from those used in the steak example. But the question is, could we somehow combine the two sets of weights in such a way that exactly the same set of weights will produce the steak aroma from the visual steak input and the rose fragrance from the sight of a rose?

Figure 7.6 shows how this can be accomplished. Figure 7.6 shows only the algebraic sign of the weights (positive or negative). We can get away with this reduced representation in this case because all the weights had the same numerical value. The only thing different about them was their sign. The plus sign linking the two sets of weights shows that the weights can be added algebraically, with +0.25 and −0.25 cancelling each other out to make zero. The resulting arrangement, following the equal sign in Figure 7.6, shows each place in the set of weights being held by either a blank (this will be a zero), two plus signs, or two minus signs. Let's now translate the two plus signs as 0.5 (i.e., 0.25 + 0.25) and two negative signs as −0.5. The resulting arrangement of numbers looks like this:

$$
\begin{vmatrix}
0 & 0 & 0.5 & -0.5 \\
-0.5 & 5 & 0 & 0 \\
0 & 0 & -0.5 & 0.5 \\
0.5 & -0.5 & 0 & 0
\end{vmatrix}
$$

I should be able to take the steak input and get the steak aroma from these weights, while simultaneously being able to get the rose fragrance from the sight of the rose input, without any further changes in the set of weights. Let's try it shall we?

I won't go through the entire computation of both outputs, but let's see if we can get the fourth-from-the-topmost output from the steak example (+1) and the fourth-from-the-topmost output from the rose example (−1). In the case of the steak, we have:

$$
\begin{aligned}
\text{Output}_{\text{fourth-from-top B unit}} &= (+1 \times 0.50) + (-1 \times -0.50) + (-1 \times 0) + \\
&\quad (+1 \times +0) \\
&= (0.50) + (0.50) + (0) + (0) \\
&= +1
\end{aligned}
$$

FIGURE 7.6
. . . .
The weights in the third matrix allow either row vector shown in Figure 7.5 to recreate the corresponding column vector.

$$
\begin{bmatrix}
- & + & + & - \\
- & + & + & - \\
+ & - & - & + \\
+ & - & - & +
\end{bmatrix}
+
\begin{bmatrix}
+ & - & + & - \\
- & + & - & + \\
- & + & - & + \\
+ & - & + & -
\end{bmatrix}
=
\begin{bmatrix}
 & & + + - - \\
- - & + + \\
 & & - - + + \\
+ + - -
\end{bmatrix}
$$

(From Rumelhart and McClelland, eds., *Parallel Distributed Processing*, Vol. 1. Copyright 1986 by MIT Press. Adapted by permission of the publisher and author.)

So it worked there. Let's try the rose example. Now remember, the input will be different from the previous example, but the weights are the same:

$$\text{Output}_{\text{fourth-from-top B unit}} = (-1 \times 0.50) + (+1 \times -0.50) + (-1 \times 0) +$$
$$(+1 \times +0)$$
$$= -0.50) + (-0.50) + (0) + (0)$$
$$= -1$$

This is also the desired value.

The pattern associator shows us that a given set of weights can be constructed to allow a neural network to compute several different outputs from several different inputs. There are some limitations on this ability. You may have wondered how many such associations we could load onto this pattern associator. The answer is that a pattern associator of this type will always compute the right response pattern as long as the set of input vectors has a mathematical property called linear independence. There's no need for us to know what this means mathematically, but, practically speaking, the need for linear independence means that the input vectors must be uncorrelated with each other. In the case that we have been considering, the number of such completely uncorrelated input vectors that could be generated is four. That does put a rather severe limitation on this particular pattern associator as a practical device, because it means that this associator could retrieve only four memories. However, the limitation of this pattern associator as a teaching device in no way implies that our cognitive and neural system could not have extremely large networks that would be capable of storing many more than four memories.

Three-layer Systems

The XOR Problem   Up until now, the building blocks that we've considered have consisted of two layers of neurodes: an input layer and an output layer. Although we've seen that two-layer systems like this possess considerable strength, there are some problems that they cannot handle, regardless of the size of the system. One of these problems is known as the "exclusive-or" problem or, as it's abbreviated, the **XOR problem.** The XOR problem is shown schematically in Table 7.2.

The problem is to construct a neural network such that the input patterns shown can be propagated through a set of weights to come up with their associated output. Let's look more closely at the output patterns. When the system is given the inputs "00," the appropriate output is "0." And when the system is given the inputs "11," the output is exactly the same, "0." We haven't seen anything quite like this before, namely a system that comes up with the same output from different inputs. Further, if you consider the inputs that produce this output, you'll notice that the inputs are highly dissimilar from each other. In other

·············· **TABLE 7.2 XOR Problem**

INPUT PATTERNS		OUTPUT PATTERNS
00	$\rightarrow$	0
01	$\rightarrow$	1
10	$\rightarrow$	1
11	$\rightarrow$	0

Source: Copyright 1989 by the MIT Press. Adapted by permission of the publisher and author.

words, of the four inputs that can be made in this set, "00" and "11" are maximally dissimilar to each other. This is the XOR problem in a nutshell: how to make a neural network produce an identical output when the input conditions don't have anything in common. We'll get to the solution directly, but before doing so, I should point out that the solution to this problem is critical to the ultimate success of neural networks. That is, an inability to handle this type of problem would be a fatal flaw for neural networks, because it's clear that the human neural system, and therefore the human cognitive system, can handle the type of situation that the XOR problem represents.

For example, if I'm driving down the street and the traffic light in front of me turns red, I put my foot on the brake. But I may make the same response if I see a child playing with a ball on the sidewalk. In the second case, I've learned that if the ball gets away from the child, then there's a chance that he or she will dart into the street without looking. Here then is a situation in which my cognitive system computes the same foot-on-brake response from input conditions that are maximally different from each other (traffic signal vs. child playing with a ball).

Hidden Units   The solution to the XOR problem requires the addition of a third layer of neurodes to the neural network. This third layer is placed *between* the input and output layers. The operation of this third layer is never observed as directly as are the input and output layers, and for this reason, the neurodes of the third layer are referred to as **hidden units.**

Figure 7.7 shows a mininetwork that is capable of solving the XOR problem. The numbers inside the single hidden and output units refer to those neurodes' thresholds. If the activation of the neurode exceeds its threshold, then the neurode fires, but if the activation is not up to the threshold value, then the neurode remains silent.

To see how the addition of a hidden unit solves the XOR problem, let's operate the network shown in Figure 7.7. Suppose that the input units are fed with the [0 0] vector as shown in Table 7.2. Each of the input units feeds +1 unit of activation to the hidden unit. Thus, the hidden unit's current activation (+2)

FIGURE 7.7
. . . .
A simple XOR network with one hidden unit.

Copyright 1989 by the MIT Press. Adapted by permission of the publisher and author.)

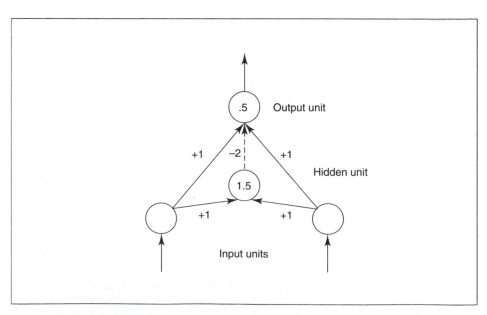

exceeds its threshold, and so the hidden unit fires. Before we go on to examine the effects of the hidden unit's firing however, notice that each of the input units is still directly linked to the output unit. The output unit's threshold is +0.5, which would appear to be exceeded in this case, because each of the input units is sending +1 units of activation to it. But, as we look further, we see that the hidden unit, which also has been activated, has an *inhibitory* influence on the output unit, to the tune of −2 units of activation. This inhibitory influence completely cancels the positive activation sent by the input units, and so the output unit is silent. And the output unit's activation is zero if the input units are fed with a [1 1] vector too. But when the input units are given different levels of activation, either in the form of a [0 1] or [1 0] vector, something different happens. Consider the [0 1] case. Here the hidden unit is not activated because only one input cell is activated and therefore input to the hidden cell is below the hidden cell's threshold. Because of this, the hidden unit does not exert its inhibitory influence on the output unit. However, the output cell still receives activation directly from one input unit. This +1 level of activation produced by the active input unit is great enough to raise the output unit above its threshold, and, because the hidden unit is not doing anything to inhibit it, the output unit is in turn activated and fires. Our examination of the XOR problem has suggested that if the hidden units in a neural network are arranged in a particular way, then almost any independent input vector can be propagated to produce almost any type of output.

Training a Three-layer Network

We've seen that a two-layer system, such as a perceptron, can be trained to make discriminations of specific data points. Three-layer systems can be trained too. When we speak of training a three-layer system, what we mean is that we can modify the weights connecting the various neurodes in such a way that the system becomes progressively better at producing a desired output when a certain input is given. In this section we'll talk about a commonly used procedure for doing this and how it works.

The most commonly used procedure for training three-layer systems is known as the backpropagation algorithm; it's been estimated that this procedure is used in 80 percent of all neural network projects (Caudill & Butler, 1992). Figure 7.8 is a depiction of how the algorithm is implemented in a typical three-layer network.

Before we talk about the algorithm, it's worth pointing out some of the characteristics of the typical network in which a backpropagation algorithm might be used. First, each of the neurodes is connected only with neurodes higher than themselves. In other words, input neurodes are connected only with hidden units; hidden units are connected only with output units. It's possible to design a neural network in which the neurodes are connected with other neurodes at their same level (we'll see one later), and it's certainly the case that our real neural system has such "intralayer" communication among neurons. But implementing a backpropagation algorithm in such a system is not as straightforward as it is here. Notice too that the network shown in Figure 7.8 has no connections from the input layer directly to the output layer, unlike the network that was used to solve the XOR problem. In the case of the network in Figure 7.8, the input neurodes have no direct influence on the output neurodes; all communication must pass through the hidden units. Finally, each of neurodes at a certain level is connected with all the neurodes at the next level. In other words, all of the input neurodes

FIGURE 7.8
· · · · · · · · · · · · · · · · · · · ·
A backpropagation network trains with a two-step procedure. The activity from the input pattern flows forward through the network, and the error signal flows backward to adjust the weights.

Copyright 1992 by MIT Press. Adapted by permission of the publisher.

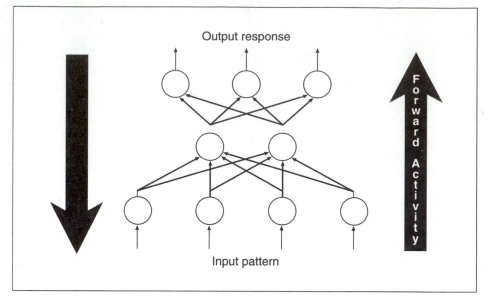

Output response

Forward Activity

Input pattern

are connected with all of the hidden units, and all of the hidden units are connected with all of the output neurodes.

Implementing a backpropagation algorithm in such a network is a two-step procedure. In the first step, an input is given to the system, and this is propagated upward through the system in the conventional way. When the system arrives at an output, this output is compared to the desired or ideal output. This ideal output is called the "teacher" because this ideal output is used to teach the system how to behave.

For example, suppose that some input is given to the network in Figure 7.8, and it produces the following output:

[0 0 1]

But suppose that the following output is actually what we wanted the system to produce when that input was given:

[0 1 0]

It seems that the system has not outputted what we wanted it to, given this particular input, and we call the difference between the actual output and the desired output an "error signal." We then compute the size of the error signal as follows:

$$\text{Error signal} = \text{Ideal output} - \text{Actual output}$$
$$= [0\ 1\ 0] - [0\ 0\ 1]$$
$$= [0\ 1\ -1]$$

At this point we go to the second step of the procedure. Here, we take the error signal and backpropagate this signal through the network by treating the output units as the input units. In other words, instead of going from the bottom up with an input, we take the error signal and move from the top of the network back down to the input level, changing the weights between the output units and the hidden units and then changing the weights between the hidden units and the normal input units as we go. Now you can see why it's important that all the units at each layer are connected with all the units above and below them. It means that the network is symmetrical from top to bottom; any pathway from the input layer to the output layer can be duplicated from the opposite direction. Eventually, as the inputs are propagated forward through the system and error signals are backpropagated, the size of the error signal diminishes and drops to zero. At that point, we say the network is fully trained: It produces the desired output directly from the input without any need for further backpropagation.

Learning Rules and a Bowlful of Error   How does backpropagation work? We won't get into the mathematics of the algorithm, but we'll look at a commonly used learning rule to show how weights are changed under backpropagation. In a highly simplified form, here's a rule, called the **delta rule,** that might be used to train a network under backpropagation:

$$\Delta w_{ij} = \epsilon \, E \, f\,(I)$$

where Δ (delta) w_{ij} means the change in the weights between two neurodes; ϵ (little epsilon) is the "rate of learning" in the system; E is the error; and $f\,(I)$ is the input to a particular neurode. Overall, this rule says that you change the weights between two neurodes depending on how big the error is in relation to the input of a particular neurode and how quickly you want the system to arrive at the target. With ϵ set to a low value (the actual number might be 0.05), the system will take longer to arrive at the target than when ϵ is set to a higher value, such as 0.15 perhaps. Sometimes my students ask why ϵ isn't always set high to maximize the speed of learning. That's a good question. Answering it will be easier if we consider what actually happens to the system when we backpropagate an error signal through it.

Figure 7.9 shows how a weight vector, that is, the connections between a layer of neurodes and a specific neurode above or below that layer, changes when the delta rule is applied. The solid shape hovering in the three-dimensional space is called an **error bowl.** What you have to imagine is that the initial vector represents a line drawn directly down from this error bowl onto the two-dimensional plane below it. If we draw this line from a place high on the error bowl, it means that the initial vector is way off from the ideal vector. As we draw this line from points that are lower and lower on the error bowl, it means that the network is getting closer and closer to the ideal weight vector, which is always located at the bottom of the error bowl. The part of Figure 7.9 labeled "delta vector" shows specifically how much the weights are changed each time we backpropagate the error through the system. As you can tell by looking at the figure, the fastest way to get to the bottom of the error bowl would be to draw a line straight "down" the outside surface of the bowl. But if you look, you'll see that the delta vector is not actually doing this; it seems to be going a little bit "sideways" instead of straight down. This is the effect of setting ϵ either high or low. The bigger the value of ϵ, the more likely that the delta vector will go straight down the outside surface of the error bowl. The smaller the value of ϵ, the more likely that the delta vector will spiral around the surface of the error bowl. So, why shouldn't we set ϵ to a high value and consequently cruise straight down?

The answer is that in real life, because these networks can become very complicated, the actual error bowl might not have nearly so smooth a surface as we see here. Rather it might contain numerous small bumps, ridges, and valleys. The valleys can be especially troublesome. If the delta vector were to enter such a valley directly, the network might be "fooled into thinking" that it had reached the bottom of the error bowl. But it's unlikely that such a valley would extend

FIGURE 7.9

....

The generalized
delta rule is a gradi-
ent descent system.

Copyright 1992 by MIT
Press. Adapted by permis-
sion of the publisher.

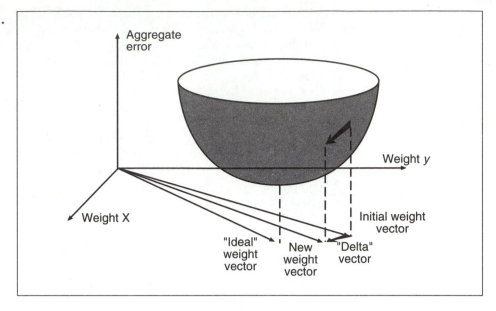

around the entire surface of the error bowl. By moving a little bit sideways as it heads down, the system may avoid getting into one of these local traps. I think a sledding metaphor is appropriate here. You may know of a generally steep hill that nevertheless contains a little valley or trough. If you head into it directly, you might not have enough energy to sled through it and continue going down the hill. But if you head into the trough at an angle, even though you may slow down a little initially, you'll still have enough energy to keep going all the way down the rest of the hill.

KNOWLEDGE REPRESENTATION AND RETRIEVAL

In this section, we'll consider a connectionist model of knowledge organization and memory search. How do such searches work? Typically, you know something about the to-be-retrieved memory, and you use this information as a prompt to help you retrieve the rest of the stored information. So the question becomes: Is there any way that this partial information can be used to establish a pattern of excitation and inhibition in a neural network such that, when a prompt is supplied, the network outputs a vector corresponding to the complete memory?

In response, Table 7.3 shows the characteristics of gang members who might live in a particularly unsavory neighborhood (McClelland, 1981; Rumelhart & McClelland, 1986). Each gang member has a name, an age, marital status, an educational attainment, a gang membership, and a "livelihood." Parenthetically, I would point out that the problems associated with juvenile urban gangs seem much more severe today than they probably appeared when this research was done, and so the almost lighthearted use of names like "Jets" and "Sharks" (inspired by the Bernstein musical) may seem somewhat discordant to us. But the point is to demonstrate how a neural network might organize and retrieve information, so let's agree to accept the materials at face value.

Figure 7.10 shows how the network would be set up. Each irregularly shaped form containing names of gang members, or their characteristics, is called a

·············   **TABLE 7.3**   **Characteristics of members of the Jets and the Sharks**

NAME	GANG	AGE	EDUCATION	MARITAL STATUS	OCCUPATION
Art	Jets	40s	J.H.	Sing.	Pusher
Al	Jets	30s	J.H.	Mar.	Burglar
Sam	Jets	20s	Col.	Sing.	Bookie
Clyde	Jets	40s	J.H.	Sing.	Bookie
Mike	Jets	30s	J.H.	Sing.	Bookie
Jim	Jets	20s	J.H.	Div.	Burglar
Greg	Jets	20s	H.S.	Mar.	Pusher
John	Jets	20s	J.H.	Mar.	Burglar
Doug	Jets	30s	H.S.	Sing.	Bookie
Lance	Jets	20s	J.H.	Mar.	Burglar
George	Jets	20s	J.H.	Div.	Burglar
Pete	Jets	20s	H.S.	Sing.	Bookie
Fred	Jets	20s	H.S.	Sing.	Pusher
Gene	Jets	20s	Col.	Sing.	Pusher
Ralph	Jets	30s	J.H.	Sing.	Pusher
Phil	Sharks	30s	Col.	Mar.	Pusher
Ike	Sharks	30s	J.H.	Sing.	Bookie
Nick	Sharks	30s	H.S.	Sing.	Pusher
Don	Sharks	30s	Col.	Mar.	Burglar
Ned	Sharks	30s	Col.	Mar.	Bookie
Karl	Sharks	40s	H.S.	Mar.	Bookie
Ken	Sharks	20s	H.S.	Sing.	Burglar
Earl	Sharks	40s	H.S.	Mar.	Burglar
Rick	Sharks	30s	H.S.	Div.	Burglar
Ol	Sharks	30s	Col.	Mar.	Pusher
Neal	Sharks	30s	H.S.	Sing.	Bookie
Dave	Sharks	30s	H.S.	Div.	Pusher

Source: "Retrieving General and Specific Knowledge From Stored Knowledge of Specifics" by J. L. McClelland, 1981, *Proceedings of the Third Annual Conference of the Cognitive Science Society*, Berkeley, CA. (Copyright 1981 by J. L. McClelland. Adapted by permission of the author.)

"cloud." For the sake of clarity, only the excitatory connections are shown in this network, and they are shown by double-headed arrows. To see how they work, suppose the system were prompted with the name "Rick" and asked to retrieve everything it could about him. When this stimulus is converted to a vector representation, two things happen. First, this representation has an inhibitory influence on every other name or characteristic in the same cloud. So in other words, the representations of all the other gang members' names (Art, Lance, etc.) are inhibited. Second, this representation has an excitatory connection with any characteristic linked to it with a double-headed arrow. Tracing one such arrow from "Rick" to the cloud in the center of the figure (where the dark dots are), we can see that this representation has excitatory connections with "high school," "Shark," "divorced," "burglar," and "30s." Moreover, each of these characteristics has inhibitory connections with all other characteristics in their clouds. Thus, as "Shark" is activated, its representation tends to inhibit "Jet" from being activated.

There are other aspects of this model that agree well with the literature on human memory. Notice that the approach offers a nice explanation of the effect of additional memory prompts. As additional prompts are brought into play, additional elements in the system are excited or inhibited. When that happens, the system as a unit becomes more likely to wind up outputting certain vectors than others, and these are more likely to correspond to the "correct" or

FIGURE 7.10

Some of the units and interconnections needed to represent the individuals shown in Table 7.3. The units connected with double-headed arrows are mutually excitatory. All the units within the same cloud are mutually inhibitory.

(From "Retrieving General and Specific Knowledge From Stored Knowledge of Specifics" by J. L. McClelland, 1981, *Proceedings of the Third Annual Conference of the Cognitive Science Society*, Berkeley, CA. Copyright 1981 by J. L. McClelland. Adapted by permission of the author.)

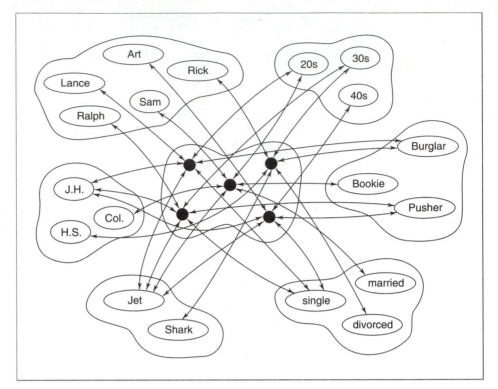

searched-for vectors. As you've probably figured out for yourself, the model offers a reasonable explanation for the cuing efficiency of different memory prompts. For example, if most gang members are married, and if you are prompted to list all the married gang members, that prompt tends to activate the names of all the married gang members, thus driving the system into the desired output states. However, not many of the gang members' names will be inhibited, because relatively fewer of them are single. On the other hand, highly idiosyncratic or individualistic prompts are likely to succeed because their excitatory connections may be linked to only a single element, which in turn drives the other elements in that cloud into their inhibitory states.

SPEECH SOUND ORGANIZATION

I used to have a speech synthesizer loaded onto my computer. It was fun to play with. First, I typed the word that I wanted the computer to pronounce and then clicked on the "Speak" icon. It could handle common words, pronouncing words like "lint" and "mint" correctly. But I never could get it to pronounce "pint" correctly. My assumption was that the speech synthesizer program was just too crude or limited to really know much about English speech sounds. That is, the program didn't know that in the context of *p* and *nt*, *i* is pronounced as a long *i* instead of a short *i*. As it turns out, this kind of contextual knowledge may not be required.

Rosenberg and Sejnowski (1987) produced a connectionist model of pronunciation called NETtalk that is able to pronounce words despite the fact that it does not have any of the contextual knowledge that I just referred to. The elements of the model are shown in Figure 7.11. Here's how it works. Imagine that a particular string of letters is placed into a narrow "window" and centered there. Then NETtalk looks at the letter at the center of the window, reads it, and begins to map this letter onto a standard pronunciation. That is, this center letter is converted to a phonetic representation. The other letters are converted to phonetic representations too, and these phonetic representations are fed forward to a hidden layer of units. As you can probably tell by now, inhibitory and excitatory connections from these hidden units are then fed forward to an output layer. The output layer is a vector representation of phonetic features, which is converted back through a speech synthesizer to produce a spoken version of the word which was read. The connections between the processing units, that is, the matrix of connections, W, was adjusted by implementing a delta rule that gradually, over repeated presentations, "told" the various units how to handle different combinations of letters within a string. The network was thus trained to pronounce 1,000 frequently occurring words. Then a second set of words that the network had never seen before was fed into it: NETtalk's success rate for pronouncing these new words was better than 80 percent. Next, the network was retrained, with the weights adjusted once again based on the experience that the network had acquired with these new words. When the network was given a second set of new words, its performance was truly impressive: Now it could correctly pronounce over 95 percent of the words it had been given.

By just about any standards, NETtalk is a huge system. In one configuration it has 309 processing units (203 inputs, 80 hidden units, 26 outputs, with 18,629 weights to be adjusted during its computation) (Churchland & Sejnowski, 1989). How does such a huge system get sufficiently organized to pronounce words correctly? One way to analyze this problem is to look at the activity of the hidden units as the pattern of activation is fed forward to them. For each string of letters that are read into the system, there is a corresponding pattern of activity among the hidden units. In analyzing the hidden units' activity, we can then look at the average amount of hidden unit activity for each letter-to-sound correspondence. In the case of words like *tuck* or *muck*, for example, we can look at the hidden

FIGURE 7.11

. . . .

Elements of the NETtalk model.

(Copyright 1989 by the MIT Press. Adapted by permission of the publisher and author.)

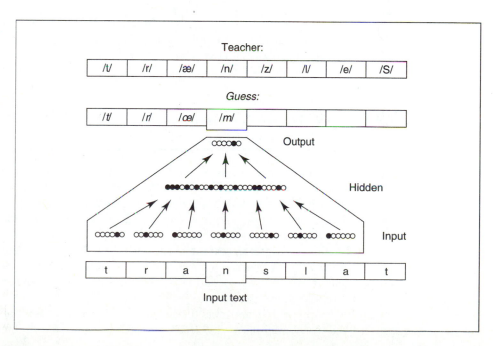

units' activity in converting a letter *c* in the middle of a word to a hard *c* sound. Of the 80 hidden units, most receive little or no activation for most such letter-to-sound correspondences. Typically, about 15 of the 80 units were highly activated for each of the specific letter-to-sound correspondences. This procedure was then repeated for each of the 79 letter-to-sound correspondences that NETtalk knows about. (If you think about it for just a minute, you'll see why we can't have just 26 letter-to-sound correspondences.) What we have then is, from the standpoint of the hidden units' activity, 79 "functional vectors" (Churchland, 1989) that are thus created. Each functional vector basically represents the pattern of hidden unit activity for one letter-to-sound correspondence. Rosenberg and Sejnowski (1987) then carried out an analysis of the similarity among these functional vectors. They went about this by asking, for each of the 79 vectors, which other vector in the set was the most similar, that is, most highly correlated, to it. This procedure resulted in the identification of about 30 pairs of vectors that were very similar to one another. Rosenberg and Sejnowski (1987) continued this analysis by then averaging the vectors in the set of 30 pairs to get a "secondary vector" for each pair. They then proceeded by correlating all of the secondary vectors to find similarities among them. After they identified pairs of secondary vectors that were similar, they in turn averaged these to create tertiary vectors, which were in turn correlated.

The upshot of this procedure is that a hierarchy of vectors was produced that shows the degree of similarity between the activation levels of the hidden units. Figure 7.12 shows this hierarchy. The numbers at the bottom represent the degree of difference between the various vectors. Remarkably, the greatest degree of difference is between consonants and vowels, meaning that that pattern of activation across NETtalk's hidden units is most different when consonants and vowels are being read and pronounced. Within the vowels, all the letter-to-sound correspondences that used the letter *a* were grouped together, as were the letters that stand for the other vowel sounds. Speech sounds that are closely related such as *p* and *b* are also closely related in the diagram, showing a vectoral dissimilarity of less than 1.0. These findings are much more interesting than they might appear initially: NETtalk doesn't have any idea of what a vowel or a consonant is. As Churchland and Sejnowski (1989) have pointed out, this organization that becomes apparent in the fully trained NETtalk is in no way programmed into it. Rather, NETtalk discovers the pattern of activation, in a very real sense programming itself.

 ## CONCLUDING COMMENTS AND SUGGESTIONS FOR FURTHER READING

There are plenty of specific findings in this chapter, but, unlike almost all of the other chapters in the book, there are relatively few human findings in this chapter. You might be wondering why. As you'll recall from Chapter 1, we said that cognitive psychology is simply one of the cognitive sciences, and not all of the allied disciplines rely as heavily as psychology does on human subjects. Perhaps to a greater extent than the other chapters in this book, this chapter reflects the perspective of some of the other disciplines—although I should add that it is extremely difficult to establish the precise borders between cognitive psychology and the other cognitive disciplines.

In the last two chapters, we've looked at two approaches (local networks and distributed networks) that seem to have a common objective: Both of these

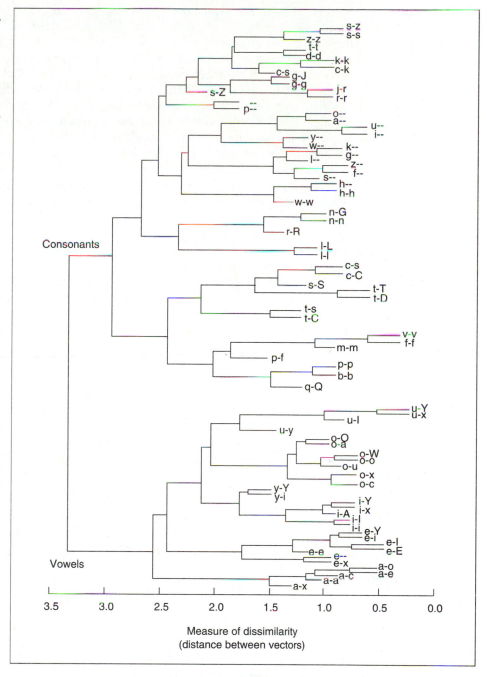

approaches represent computational, formal models of human knowledge representation and retrieval. Sometimes students are curious to know why two approaches are needed, especially when it seems that each approach has been used rather successfully. There are several points I'd like to make in response to this question. First, I would say that each approach is needed to the extent that the human cognitive system itself seems to operate that way. What I mean by this is that cognitive science is fundamentally committed to the idea that cognitive processes can be treated as naturally occurring objects in a natural world. The task of the cognitive scientist then becomes one of understanding the nature of such objects. Thus, to the extent that certain aspects of our cognitive system really do operate in a serial and sequential way, that's the extent to which our models of memory should ultimately reflect this reality.

Readers who would like to find out more about parallel distributed processing approaches might read Rumelhart and McClelland (1986). For those who want a hands-on introduction, a handbook by McClelland and Rumelhart (1988) comes with software that shows how to build your own neural networks. Levine (1990) offers another hands-on approach showing how a number of cognitive phenomena might be modeled using a neural network approach. The volumes of Caudill and Butler (1992) are accompanied by software that allows users to build and modify neural networks. Tank and Hopfield (1987) have written an article-length introduction to distributed networks. Two important articles dealing with connectionism, by Smolensky (1988) and Hanson and Burr (1990), have appeared in the journal *Behavioral and Brain Sciences*. One of the very nice features of articles appearing in this journal is that the "open peer commentary" following each article lets the reader see the points of disagreement and controversy as well as the points of agreement. Books by Nadel et al. (1989) and Churchland (1989) are excellent introductions to this literature. Anderson and Rosenfeld (1988) have collected a large number of historically important articles on connectionism, and it's interesting and instructive to trace the development of the modern connectionistic approach from these historical fonts. Gallant (1993) ties the neural network literature to the literature on expert systems, and the volumes edited by Hanson, Drastal, and Rivest (1994) summarize the more recent developments. My rendition here has been basically supportive of distributed network systems, but parallel processing approaches haven't met with completely universal acclaim. Those who would like to read two critical and very challenging articles might consider Pinker and Prince (1988) and Fodor and Pylyshyn (1988). Besner, Twilley, McCann, and Seergobin (1990) have questioned the ability of such networks to reproduce such empirical outcomes; Seidenberg and McClelland (1990) rebut the questions in the same issue of *Psychological Review*.

Oh, one other thing, I almost forgot: Sarah shelves geology (ten books per minute); Jessica shelves history (seven); George shelves art (six); Karen shelves chemistry (seven); Sam shelves poetry (eight); and Tim shelves physics (six).

 **KEY TERMS**

Perceptron	XOR problem	Delta rule
Pattern associator	Hidden units	Error bowl
Vector encoding		

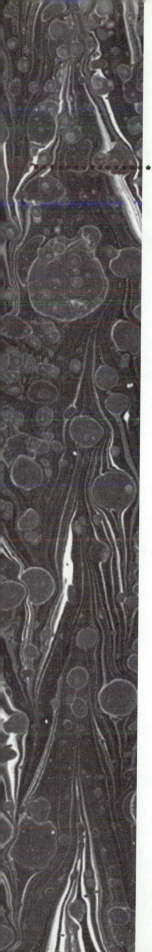

PART 5

LANGUAGE

Understanding and producing language are fundamental aspects of our mental lives and our humanity. Without these abilities, we would be cut off from one another. Language enables us to erect complex social structures and to form intimate social bonds.

These claims may seem like overstatements to you. For example, you might point to colonies of insects, such as termites, which have elaborate social structure without having language. However, one striking finding to emerge from the studies of such creatures concerns the complexity of their communication systems, which seems out of proportion to the complexity of the creatures themselves. Termites, for example, signal one another by drumming their heads against the floor of their nest. This action produces a sound like that of sand falling on paper, but a close analysis of the drumming reveals that it is highly organized and complex. By varying the rhythmic phrasing and duration of the drumming, termites send complex codes throughout the whole colony.

In addition to being an apparently essential part of our social structure, language seems to be a crucial ingredient of our mental lives. Our intuitions support this assertion. When we think, we are often aware of some sort of internal speech that seems to accompany our thought processes.

For a variety of reasons, cognitive psychologists have turned their attention to the phenomenon of language. This part of the book considers some of their discoveries and deals with a number of issues. First, defining language is difficult. Second, expressing the essence of language in a set of formal rules has also proved unachievable so far. Almost all linguists believe that our knowledge of linguistic sounds, word order, and meaning can be rewritten as a formal system of rules, and we'll examine some of the reasons for this belief. Not much is known about these rules, although psycholinguists have a good idea of some of the minimum elements that are required in any proposed theory of linguistic knowledge.

Another issue concerns the origin of language. The concern here is with the role of experience as both a necessary and a sufficient basis for language. As you are probably aware, a number of people believe that experience with language per se is not sufficient to enable the child to learn it. Hence, according to these theorists, the child must be aided in language acquisition efforts by innate linguistic predispositions. We'll cover this question in the next three chapters. We'll also consider some of the cognitive operations that are involved in the comprehension and production of speech, and we'll see that both top-down and bottom-up processes seem to be involved in this form of pattern recognition.

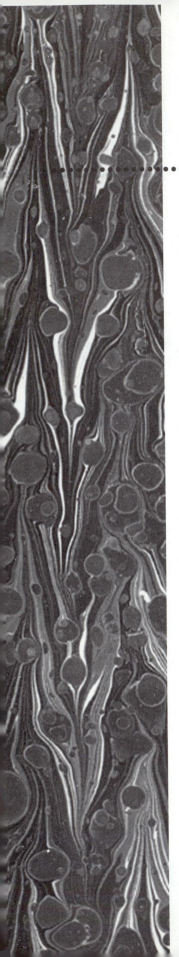

CHAPTER **8**

THE STRUCTURE OF LANGUAGE

CHAPTER OUTLINE

OVERVIEW

Consider the following passage:

> Well, I will tell you. I got a little concern yesterday in the first three innings when I say the three players I had gotten rid of and I said when I lost nine what am I going to do and when I had a couple of my players. I thought so great of that did not do so good up to the sixth inning I was more confused but I finally had to go and call on a young man in Baltimore that we don't own and the Yankees don't own him, and he is doing pretty good, and I would actually have to tell you that I think we are more the Greta Garbo type now from success. (Quoted in Barrows, 1977.)

The great baseball manager Casey Stengel, who uttered these words, apparently used to talk that way all the time. Does the passage make sense to you? We recognize that a wide latitude must be given to individual speakers in matters of word choice and tone. But we would also assert that some commonality must exist among various speakers if any communication is to take place. Does Stengel's speech fall within these boundaries, or does it represent such a substantial departure from standard usage that it can hardly be considered language? Answering this question requires a definition of language, and so far, linguists haven't been entirely successful in coming up with one. This chapter examines some of the reasons why defining language is so difficult.

Perhaps you're thinking that I shouldn't be so hard on the old ballplayer. After all, if read closely, the passage is reasonable enough. Here's my translation: Stengel was worried that some players he had traded were doing pretty well against him, and he obtained the services of a young man who had not signed with any club. Consequently, the team had come out of its tailspin and was now playing pretty well; that is, they were now "the Greta Garbo type from success." I may seem to be stretching things a little, but this last part of my translation is based on several bits of knowledge stored in my memory:

1. Greta Garbo was a popular movie star during the 1930s.

2. Casey Stengel was old enough to have seen Garbo in the movies when she was popular.

3. Greta Garbo was widely regarded as beautiful.

Language comprehension inevitably requires vast knowledge. Moreover, several different types of knowledge are called for. First, speech comprehension requires knowledge of phonology, or linguistic sounds. Second, we must have some models or rules for generating and recognizing appropriate **syntax,** or word order. Finally, language requires semantic knowledge of the type examined in Chapters 6 and 7. Linguists refer to the conglomeration of all this linguistic knowledge as **grammar.**

For at least the past thirty years, syntax has probably been the most intensively studied component of grammatical knowledge. Many reasons account for this intensive study, not the least of which is that Noam Chomsky—perhaps the most important of contemporary theoretical linguists—believed that **semantics,** or meaning, was derived from and secondary to syntax. This chapter examines Chomsky's proposition.

Words and phrases can be put together in many different ways. Yet, all normal children seem to acquire the appropriate knowledge despite their immature intellectual abilities. How can this be? How can children learn language—an extremely complex ability—when they are still more or less incapable of other, similar intellectual feats? The realization of this paradox has led some theorists (Chomsky among them) to argue that children are helped in their linguistic quest by innate predispositions that make them sensitive to certain regularities in linguistic sounds and phrases. This chapter examines some of the evidence supporting that proposition and contrasts it with the alternative viewpoint—namely, that no innate abilities are required to learn language.

 ## WHAT IS LANGUAGE?

Whenever I ask the question, "What is language?" in my classes, students usually seem content to let the following equation express their beliefs:

Language = Communication.

Students who hold this opinion are (perhaps unwittingly) asserting that the *intention* of the gesturer determines whether language is being displayed. That is, if I make a gesture (broadly speaking, sounds should be considered gestures), and if the gesture is seemingly made in the context of a deliberate mental event, then my students are willing to say that this gesture is linguistic and that my other gestures are probably linguistic, too.

This view of language is sometimes called the **continuity theory** (Aitchison, 1983). According to this perspective, human language is a sophisticated calling system that is not fundamentally different from animal cries and calls. Proponents of this position often describe the work of Struhsaker (1967). Struhsaker studied the cries of vervet monkeys in the wild. Vervet monkeys use substantially different vocalizations for different dangerous animals. For example, a *chutter* is used to signal the arrival of a cobra, but if an eagle appears, the monkeys produce the *rraup* sound. The argument that these sounds are one step removed from words doesn't seem too farfetched. That is, among our primitive ancestors, similar danger calls may have been used, and these calls gradually came to represent the animals themselves; they became the animals' names.

The continuity theory suffers from several problems. First, the vervet monkeys may simply be responding to the intensity of the danger rather than to anything specific about the stimulus. That is, the chutter may be used for something extremely dangerous, the rraup for a less frightening stimulus, and so on. This interpretation has been empirically supported; vervet monkeys sometimes chirp at the sight of an eagle. This call is usually given in response to a lion and suggests that the vervet monkey considers lions and eagles equally threatening. The implication is that the apparent specificity observed (heard?) in animal cries doesn't necessarily indicate that such animals have specific referents in mind.

A second problem with continuity theories is that the attribution of intentionality is often difficult to make in practice. Whale songs are one of the better-known illustrations of this problem. As you may know, certain species of whales produce sounds that have definite rhythm. These songs change in predictable ways. Over the course of a lengthy migration, certain themes are introduced, become dominant, and are eventually supplanted. Nobody knows why the whales produce these sounds; consequently, nobody knows whether these sounds are communicative.

Although my students might be willing to assume that regularity of gesture is an indication of both specificity of referent and intentionality (and therefore language), we might do well to modify the equation initially proposed: Language is communicative—at least potentially—but simple communications aren't necessarily linguistic. This statement suggests that, to be considered truly linguistic, a set of gestures must have other properties besides the simple intent to communicate.

Design Features

Hockett (1963) has proposed a list of essential characteristics that seem to be required in any definition of language. Although many linguists believe that this approach is the only valid way to define language, we should first be aware that such an approach nevertheless has some problems. Even if Hockett had managed to isolate just those features of communication that determine the essence of language, such a listing wouldn't make clear how those features were *related* to one another. Yet, the relationship among such design characteristics may be the sine qua non of language: We are not necessarily interested in the parts that make up language; we are interested in how those parts have been put together.

Figure 8.1 is a pictorial representation of some of Hockett's **design features.** Some of these features are obviously more important than others. For example, use of the *vocal-auditory channel* is a desirable but not essential feature of language. Speaking and hearing are more or less nondirectional senses, which means that our eyes and limbs can be trained on other stimuli while we converse.

Broadcast transmission and *rapid fading* are also aspects of the physics of sound. We are amazingly able to locate the source of sounds, which can be an aid in communication. Typically, speech is an extremely transitory event. Although having linguistic codes that are more durable is sometimes advantageous, the transitory nature of speech can also be beneficial. Because this type of communication fades rapidly, privacy is enhanced. The rapid fading of speech also permits duplicity (telling different people different versions of something), but this isn't all bad, because at times, editing the content of certain messages is desirable. Rapid fading also implies a social function. To talk to someone, you have to get relatively close to him.

With *interchangeability*, we move closer to a characteristic of language that could be called essential. This design feature refers to a competent speaker's ability to reproduce any message that she can understand, and the content of that message is left undisturbed by this process. This ability isn't true for all animal communication systems. In some systems, particular gestures are sometimes strongly associated with sex roles and can't be reproduced by the opposite gender.

Total feedback refers to the fact that we hear everything we produce. *Specialization* is a term that linguists use in several ways. In this context, the term means that the usual purpose of human speech is to communicate. The sounds that we make are not simply incidental to some other purpose. In the case of some animal vocalizations, such as whale songs, this property is not obviously present. *Semanticity* and *arbitrariness* are related and refer to the fact that in language no inherent relationship exists between the linguistic sounds and their referents, even though the linguistic sounds clearly mean something.

FIGURE 8.1
·····················
A pictorial view of Hockett's design features.

(From *The Origin of Speech,* by C. F. Hockett. Copyright © 1960 by Scientific American, Inc. All rights reserved.)

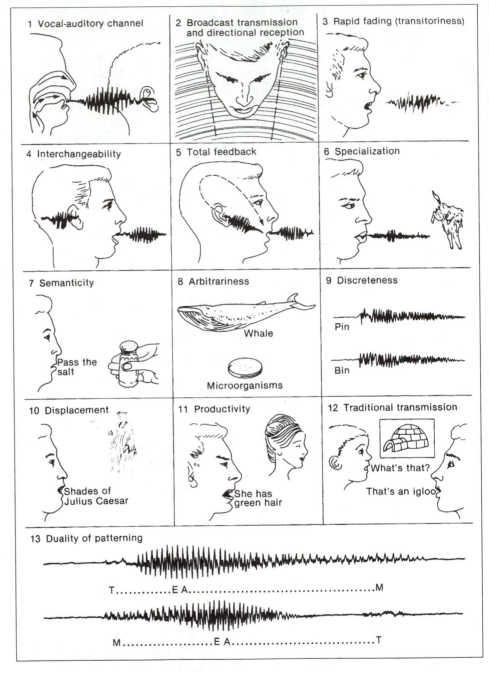

1 Vocal-auditory channel

2 Broadcast transmission and directional reception

3 Rapid fading (transitoriness)

4 Interchangeability

5 Total feedback

6 Specialization

7 Semanticity

Pass the salt

8 Arbitrariness

Whale

Microorganisms

9 Discreteness

Pin

Bin

10 Displacement

Shades of Julius Caesar

11 Productivity

She has green hair

12 Traditional transmission

What's that?

That's an igloo

13 Duality of patterning

T.............E A.........................M

M....................E A.......................T

Discreteness refers to the idea that language consists of small, separable units of sound, called **phonemes,** each of which has an identity. Typically, only a small number of different phonemes are used in any given language. For example, the English language has about forty different phonemes. Standing alone, phonemes have no meaning. They can, however, be combined in a wide variety of ways. The combination of phonemes according to the rules of a particular language results in the creation of a **morpheme,** the basic unit of meaning. In the English language, morphemes are usually words, but not all morphemes are words. For example, the suffix *ly* is a morpheme.

Duality of patterning describes this process of creating an infinite number of meaningful words from a small set of phonemic building blocks. This ability is not unique to humans. For example, bird songs are made up of a series of notes, each of which is meaningless by itself. Whatever meaning the song might have is conveyed only by the entire sequence.

Traditional transmission refers to the idea that many (perhaps most) of the elements of language are handed down from one generation to the next; some sort of experience within a culture is necessary to acquire language. Children reared in isolation almost invariably seem to show deficits in linguistic ability, some of which seem permanent (Lenneberg, 1964). Traditional transmission is a hallmark of language; the role of experience doesn't seem nearly as clear in animal communication. For example, certain bird songs, such as that of the thrush, appear to be completely innate. For such animals, the presence or absence of other members of the same species has little or no effect on the acquisition or nature of the call. Incidentally, it's important to avoid thinking of these innate abilities in categorical—that is, either-or—terms. Other birds, such as the chaffinch, seem to hatch with the basic song pattern built in. Details of the song's pitch and rhythm, however, are acquired by experience (Thorpe, 1961, 1963).

Displacement refers to a feature of language that humans use and take for granted every day. We often refer to things that are far removed in time and place, but such talk seems acceptable to our listeners. Thus, a movie might begin with the narration "A long time ago, in a galaxy far, far away"—which doesn't strike us as unreasonable. So common is this feature that we seldom stop to think about its implications. Although the cries of animals might be truly communicative, can they communicate about things that are no longer present? Your dog might bark at an intruder—perhaps might even emit a particular bark—but can the dog bark at the memory of last year's intruder?

Only a very few cases of bona fide displacement have been seen in animal communication, and even these are far more limited than human displacement. For example, von Frisch (1967) clearly demonstrated that bees have arbitrary communicative gestures, which have the property of displacement. When a bee discovers a source of nectar that is distant from the hive (i.e., at least 200 yards away), she returns to the hive and does a dance (von Frisch's term), which shows the appropriate direction of flight from the hive. Following that, the scout does either a "round dance" or a "waggle dance"—the former if the source is relatively close by, the latter if it is far away. The vigor of the scout bee's dance indicates something about the quality of the nectar. When the nectar is plentiful and good, the scout bee's dance is energetic. When the rest of the colony emerges from the hive to gather the nectar, they fly en masse to the indicated spot. This behavior is an impressive demonstration of displacement in animal communication. However, von Frisch (1954) also demonstrated the limitations of this system. A hive of bees was placed near the bottom of a radio tower. As the scout bees emerged, they were collected and taken to a container of sugar water, which had been placed on the top of the tower. Then the scouts were released. They dutifully returned to the hive and energetically reported (via the round dance) that a good source of nectar was nearby. When the rest of the colony emerged, they flew in all directions except up, because the communication system of the bees denotes only horizontal, not vertical, distance.

This failure on the part of bees highlights an extremely important aspect of human communication. We have the ability to use our language in novel, creative ways. If we were confronted with the bees' plight, making up a word (or, I should say, a dance) that communicated the idea of altitude would be relatively

············· **TABLE 8.1**   **A comparison of eight systems of communication**

	A MEMBERS OF THE CRICKET FAMILY	B BEE DANCING	C STICKLEBACK COURTSHIP
1. Vocal-audition channel	Auditory, not vocal	No	No
2. Broadcast transmission and directional recognition	—a	—	—
3. Rapid fading (transitoriness)	Yes, repeated	?b	?
4. Interchangeability	Limited	Limited	No
5. Total feedback	Yes	?	No
6. Specialization	Yes?	?	In part
7. Semanticity	No?	Yes	No
8. Arbitrariness	?	No	—
9. Discreteness	Yes?	No	?
10. Displacement	—	Yes, always	—
11. Productivity	No	Yes	No
12. Traditional transmission	No?	Probably not	No?
13. Duality of patterning	?(Trivial)	No	

Source: *The Origin of Speech,* by C. F. Hockett. Copyright © 1960 by Scientific America, Inc. All rights reserved.

Note: Eight systems of communication that possess in varying degrees the thirteen design features of language proposed by Hockett.
a A line indicates that the feature cannot be determined because another feature is lacking or indefinite. bA question mark means that it is doubtful or not known whether the system has the particular feature.

easy for us. This sort of creativity takes place every day. When actor Lee Marvin's live-in lover sued him a few years ago, the word *palimony* was created by an anonymous wag, and all of us knew exactly what it meant, even though we hadn't thought of it ourselves. This creativity in language is referred to as **productivity.** Unlike animals, whose vocalizations seem to be largely stimulus bound, we can decide what we want to say and when we wish to say it.

Table 8.1 compares language with several other phenomena in terms of the presence or absence of specific design features. As Table 8.1 shows, only language has all the design features that have been described. Moreover, the least shared (and therefore the most essential) aspects of language seem to be displacement, productivity, and duality of patterning. This point is important, because these three features seem to be related. Duality of patterning and productivity in language indicate that the nature of linguistic rules must be general and abstract. For example, in the English language, the rules specifying the production of morphemes from phonemes are not dependent in any principled way on the nature of the phonemes themselves. Certain combinations are not permitted in the English language (no English word begins with *mg*), but most combinations are permitted, although the patterns thus created are far from random. Similarly, novelty in language is commonplace and is often comprehensible to our listeners. Recall that I demonstrated this by creating a novel sentence in Chapter 1. Demonstrations such as these show that patterns of morphemes we produce are not dependent in any rigid way on the morphemes that we may have already uttered. If they were rigidly dependent, we would never be capable of producing a creative utterance. Can you see why? Once we had picked a particular morpheme to begin our comment, that choice would rigidly constrain our subsequent choice, which in turn would rigidly constrain the next choice, and so on. The number of producible utterances would be large, but it would be finite.

·············   **TABLE 8.1**   (continued)

D WESTERN MEADOWLARK SONG	E GIBBON CALLS	F PARALINGUISTIC PHENOMENA	G LANGUAGE	H WESTERN INSTRUMENTAL MUSIC (SINCE BACH)
Yes	Yes	Yes	Yes	Auditory, not vocal
—	—	—	—	Yes
Yes	Yes, repeated	Yes	Yes	Yes
?	Yes	Largely yes	Yes	?
Yes	Yes	Yes	Yes	Yes
Yes?	Yes	Yes?	Yes	Yes
In part?	Yes	Yes?	Yes	No, in general
If semantic	Yes	In partYes, often	—	
?	Yes	Largely no	Yes	In part
?	No	In part	Yes, often	—
?	No	Yes	Yes	Yes
?	?	Yes	Yes	Yes
?	No	No	Yes	—

But we know this isn't true: The number of producible, and therefore creative, utterances is infinite.

Still, not all novel strings of morphemes are comprehensible to our listeners. Presumably, the reason why some novel strings of morphemes are comprehensible whereas others aren't has something to do with our adherence to some general rules in the former and our violation of them in the latter. Together, the features of duality of patterning and productivity combine to allow us to expand our ability to refer to objects that are remote. In the most extreme case, these features allow us to refer to things that are, strictly speaking, never present anywhere; here I'm referring to ideas such as truth or beauty.

Hockett's work suggests that the design features that are truly essential to language are those dealing with creativity and flexibility. For some time, a common tendency among linguists has been to think that people's grammatical knowledge can be expressed as a series of rules that are specific enough to permit the production of well-formed words and sentences but general enough to permit unlimited creativity.

GRAMMAR AND LINGUISTICS

Encountering the heading "Grammar and Linguistics" in a book about cognitive psychology may seem odd, but good reasons exist for discussing the theories and modus operandi of linguists.

First, as noted in Chapter 1, linguists were among the first to mount a successful attack on behavioristic psychology. In the 1950s, when this criticism first appeared, psychologists became highly interested in the work of theoretical linguists, and the discipline known as psycholinguistics was born. Psycholinguists and linguists have different but complementary ways of doing research. Whereas the psychologist is likely to design experiments that test fairly limited hypotheses about language comprehension in a fairly rigid way, the linguist is much more likely to study sentences that have actually been produced by speakers in a natural context. In some cases, the linguist may even compose sentences, which are then studied in light of the linguist's intuitions concerning the sentence's structure and what that structure might indicate about the nature of grammatical knowledge.

The second reason for studying theoretical linguistics is based on one of its stated objectives. Linguists are concerned with the discovery of **linguistic universals.** These universals are general principles of language that are thought to be embodied in every language. The evidence supporting linguistic universals is currently unclear; nevertheless, the linguist makes an interesting claim about them. You are no doubt aware that language and thought seem intimately bound together. For this reason, it is often thought that these linguistic universals reflect some underlying rules of thought. That is, linguists have maintained that, by understanding fully the nature and organization of language, it will be possible to understand the nature and organization of the human mind.

Early Views on Grammar

Work in experimental linguistics began about thirty years ago when various thinkers realized that language has obvious regularities. For example, in the sentence:

Would you please pass the _____?

the blank is more readily filled with "salt" than it is with "chilled monkey brains," and the entire sentence becomes somewhat ambiguous when the blank is filled with "skyscraper." This phenomenon occurs in many sentences and has suggested to some thinkers that the rules for syntax (word order) could be written in the form of a left-to-right grammar. Such grammars were governed by finite state rules, meaning that the next word choice at any point, or state, in the sentence was determined by consulting a finite number of candidates and picking one of them. In other words, the choice made at the left-most word in the sentence constrained the choice made at the next left-most word, and so on, until the sentence was completed.

What's implied by such a system of syntax? First, this view implies that human grammar consists of constraint rules that limit the word choices that can be made at any point in the production of a sentence. Second, this system implies that humans produce sentences on a word-by-word basis. That is, having chosen one word, the person consults some mental list of acceptable choices and produces one of them. Having made this choice, the person consults the mental list to see what choices are available for the next word, and so on, until the utterance is completed.

Early research with these types of grammars was impressive. Miller (1958) showed his subjects strings of letters, some of which were generated by the finite state system shown in Figure 8.2. The transition rules are indicated under the figure. For example, one of two paths can be taken from the node marked O. The system could move through N to node 1, or through S to node 3. From node 1, the system could move through N to node 3 or through G to O', the finish node. These pathways aren't the only ones through this network, but you can see how the strings were created. How many different strings could be created by this primitive system? Because the finite state rules permit a **recursion** at node 3, an infinite number of different strings could be generated. All strings produced by these finite state rules have some things in common: They all begin with either an N or an S, and they all end with a G.

FIGURE 8.2
· ·
Diagram of a finite state generator. A string is any sequence of letters generated by starting at state O and finishing at O'. A letter is added to the string by taking the path labeled by that letter from one state to another.

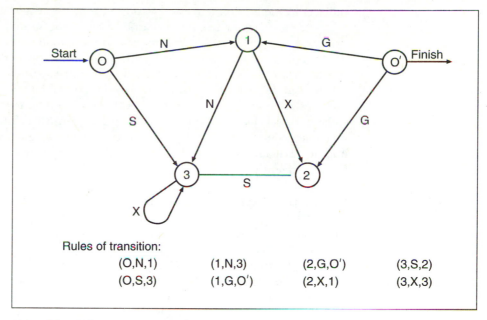

Rules of transition:

(O,N,1)	(1,N,3)	(2,G,O')	(3,S,2)
(O,S,3)	(1,G,O')	(2,X,1)	(3,X,3)

(Adapted from Miller, 1958.)

Miller next used the same four letters to create another set of strings. This time, however, the strings were created by using a random numbers table to determine which letter should come next, the only constraint being that each of the random strings had to be of the same length as one of the grammar-generated strings. Table 8.2 shows the two sets of strings, which look similar. If you hadn't been reading the text up to this point, determining exactly what is different about the two sets of lists might be difficult for you.

The adult subjects attempted to learn all nine strings in two of the lists by looking at each string in the list one at a time. After looking at all nine strings, the subjects tried to write them down. Each such pass through the list constituted a trial. Subjects studied the list for ten trials or until they reproduced all nine strings without error. Figure 8.3 shows the findings of this study. Notice that the

· · · · · · · · · · · · · · **TABLE 8.2**   **Lists of redundant and random strings used in an experiment on the learning of structure**

STRUCTURED (REDUNDANT)		RANDOM	
L_1	L_2	R_1	R_2
SSXG	NNSG	GNSX	NXGS
NNXSG	NNSXG	NSGXN	GNXSG
SXSXG	SXXSG	XGSSN	SXNGG
SSXNSG	NNXSXG	SXNNGN	GGSNXG
SXXXSG	NNXXSG	XGSXXS	NSGNGX
NNSXNSG	NNXXSXG	GSXXGNS	NGSXXNS
SXSXNSG	NNXXXSG	NSXXGSG	NGXXGGN
SXXXSXG	SSXNSXG	SGXGGNN	SXGXGNS
SXXXXSG	SSXNXSG	XXGNSGG	XGSNGXG

Source: Adapted from Miller, 1958.

subjects learned the grammatical strings at a much faster rate than they learned the random strings. These effects carried over to the second list that the subjects learned. Having learned a grammatical list originally seemed to facilitate the learning of random strings. To see this, compare the performance of the *LR* subjects with the *RR* subjects. Those who had first learned a grammatical, or *L*, list tended to outperform the *RR* subjects (who had learned a random list previously) on each successive trial. Although the differences in the lists appear to be fairly subtle, the subjects were extremely sensitive to the regularities of the grammar-generated lists. At the time, psychologists were willing to interpret these findings as a demonstration that syntactical knowledge was formally equivalent to a **finite state grammar.**

Objections to Finite State Grammars   As theories of grammar acquisition, finite state systems fit in nicely with the general stimulus-response theories of learning then in vogue. The pronunciation of each word in a sentence is a response. But because we have total feedback and hear each word we say, the hearing of a word acts as a discriminative stimulus, which cues us to produce the next word in the sentence. At the end of the sentence, we are reinforced by our listeners' compliance. This approach reduces the learning of a sentence to a much simpler problem—that of learning a chain of stimulus-response associations. Because researchers had demonstrated many times in laboratories all over the world that animals could learn lengthy stimulus-response chains, and because children must surely be capable of learning anything that a rat could learn, finite state grammars were thought to be the definite answer to the problem of syntax acquisition.

FIGURE 8.3

The mean number of letters correctly recalled in free recall of random (R) and redundant (L) lists of letters.   Notice that, on the second list, those exposed to *L* lists at first performed better than those exposed to *R* lists.

(Adapted from Miller, 1958.)

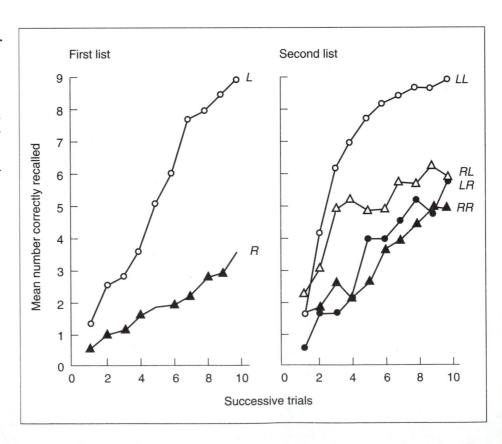

Finite state systems, however, suffer from a number of theoretical problems, some of which are worth reviewing. First, a competent speaker can embed any syntactic structure into an already formed sentence. We can do this with utterances, too, as demonstrated in Chapter 1. This ability means that the central premise of finite state systems—that a particular word choice is constrained by previous word choices—is false. Reviewing Figure 8.3, we see that we really don't have to move to any particular word in a sentence as a function of the words we have already uttered. We can move from any node to any other node if we wish to. Now we may *typically* produce utterances in accordance with finite state rules, but we are not obligated to follow them. Because we are not obligated to follow such rules means that our knowledge of syntax must consist of more than simple chaining rules. In other words, we apparently know how to do a lot more than we typically do when we speak. A complete theory of grammar should specify our capabilities as well as typical usage.

Second, according to finite state grammar, judgments of grammaticality would be dependent on the frequency with which individual words have been paired in the past. Grammatical sentences would be those that contained a large number of words that had been paired (that is, placed adjacent to each other in previous sentences), whereas ungrammatical sentences would not have this property. This idea is also wrong, however. Subjects sometimes judge sentences as grammatical, even though they contain words that probably have seldom been paired together. Consider one of Chomsky's most famous demonstration sentences:

Colorless green ideas sleep furiously.

Most respondents judge this sentence to be grammatical (although meaningless). Notice that the sentence is grammatical in spite of its violating the assumptions of finite state grammar. It's safe to say that not many of us have ever seen the pairs "colorless–green," "green–ideas," and so on, yet the sentence seems well formed. On the other hand, it's also possible to construct a sentence out of words that have frequently been paired together. Miller and Selfridge (1950) composed the following:

Was he went to the newspaper is in deep end.

Although the words of the sentence can be grouped together in a series of high-frequency pairs (e.g., "was–he," "he–went," and so on), the sentence has no meaning and isn't judged to be grammatical. This result demonstrates that people probably do not form sentences on a word-by-word basis. Instead, sentences are apparently composed and understood in units that are larger than pairs. This suggests that we look at such large units, called clauses, as the unit of grammatical knowledge. The contribution of finite state system, although negative, was nevertheless important because it pointed linguists and psychologists toward a path that has been much more productive.

Phrase Structure Grammars

Phrase structure grammars were originally developed by the linguist Leonard Bloomfield near the turn of the century. Unlike finite state grammars, which operate on a left-to-right basis, phrase structure grammars are organized hierarchically—that is, from the top down. Probably the easiest way to show this hierarchical organization is by analyzing a particular sentence:

The boy will hit the ball.

As you recognize, this is a grammatical string of words. But what exactly might that mean? When we looked at the finite state grammars we saw that the grammaticality of a sentence does not seem to have anything to do with the associative links between specific words. So where does that leave us in our search for the meaning of "grammatical"? *Grammatical* is a word that may mean many things, but one of the things that it might mean is that each of the words in this string is a legitimate part of speech in English. So, our initial pass at understanding the grammar underlying the sentence may consist of mapping each of the words onto its part of speech (Burt, 1971). Then we get: "The," which is a kind of article called a *determiner*; "boy," which is a noun; "will," which is an auxiliary to the verb "hit"; another determiner; and then the final noun, "ball." Laying this out against the sentence, we have:

> The boy will hit the ball.
> Det noun aux verb det noun

From this perspective, it appears that the expressions "Det noun" form larger units, which we can call "noun phrases" (*NP*). And we can use these noun phrases to begin to build the hierarchical structure that I referred to earlier.

Noun phrase			Noun phrase
Det noun	aux	verb	det noun
The boy	will	hit	the ball

This diagrammatic approach implies that equivalent expressions can be substituted for each other and this operation will maintain grammatically. Let's test this assertion by substituting the second noun phrase for the first one. We then get the sentence

> The ball will hit the boy.

Obviously, this second sentence means something completely different from the first sentence, but this second sentence is nevertheless grammatical, indicating perhaps that we're on the right track in our attempt to understand something of the structure underlying these sentences. That is, by mapping each of the words in the sentence onto a part of speech, and then by grouping certain parts of speech into higher, or more general units, we seem to be getting a clue about the sentence's structure. Now let's go back to the original sentence and take the next step. Just as we grouped two parts of speech together to make a noun phrase, we can also group the verb and the second noun phrase together to make a "verb phrase." Taking another step, we recognize that the entire string of words can be grouped into another level which we could call the "sentence." Showing both of these steps diagrammatically we have

		Sentence		
Noun phrase		Aux	Verb phrase	
			Verb	Noun phrase
Det noun				Det noun
The boy		will	hit	the ball.

Finally, we can convert this diagrammatic structure to a treelike depiction called a phrase marker. Figure 8.4 shows the phrase marker for the sentence we have been dealing with. The expressions "verb phrase" and so on appear above the specific words of the sentence. We call these expressions *nonterminal nodes*, and we say that nonterminal nodes dominate the terminal nodes, or the specific lexical entries. The nonterminal nodes make up the "natural" parts of a sentence; we call these natural components of a sentence its **constituents.** In fact, what we

FIGURE 8.4
· · · · · · · · · · · · · · · · · · · ·
This entire diagram is called a *phrase marker*, or *tree*, and the labels *S, NP, Det, N, Aux, VP,* and *V*, which appear above or *dominate* other nodes of the tree, are referred to as *nonterminal* nodes. The words *the, boy, will, hit,* and *ball*, which are not connected by any lines to lower nodes, are called *terminal* symbols.

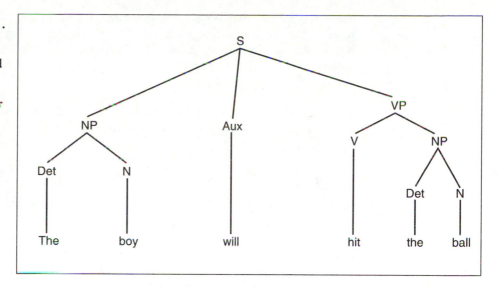

have just done with this sentence is a form of constituent analysis: mapping the sentence onto its parts of speech and then grouping, and regrouping, the components into increasingly more general units.

As we saw in this analysis, equivalent constituents can be substituted for each other, and this suggests that part of the grammatical knowledge of adults consists of rules that specify how constituents can be substituted or "rewritten" for each other. These rewrite rules have the form $X \rightarrow Y$, which specifies when a particular constituent symbol, Y, can be substituted for a constituent symbol X. To see how this works, consider the following sentence (Clark & Clark, 1977):

The likable general collapsed.

This sentence could be divided into two constituents: an *NP* (noun phrase) standing for "the likable general" and a *V* (verb) designating "collapsed." The *NP* can be represented with the following formula: $NP = ART + ADJ + N$. However, if you think about it for a minute, you might detect the limitations of such a formula. Although the formula is a perfectly good representation of some noun phrases, it does not represent all noun phrases. Some well-formed noun phrases could be cooked up with the following formula: $NP = ART + N$. And indeed, the phrase "The officer" could be substituted for the noun phrase in the "likable general" sentence (Clark & Clark, 1977). To fully represent the grammatical knowledge of adults, then, we need a series of rewrite rules showing under what circumstances an *NP* of the *Y* type can be rewritten as an *NP* of the *X* type.

You may have noticed that I have been describing phrase structure grammars as representations of or as expressions of the grammatical knowledge of adults. This description is intentional on my part. Linguists don't necessarily claim that people actually use phrase structure grammars to produce or plan their utterances. Rather, they intend to state only that phrase structures are good ways to characterize the regularities observed in language and *describe* the features that grammatical sentences have in common. If this little proviso can be accepted, phrase structure grammars offer many powerful advantages over finite state grammars.

First, phrase structures account for judgments of grammaticality. If the phrase structures and rewrite rules are specified adequately, then all the sentences generated by the phrase structure grammar will be judged as grammatical, and none of the sentences thus produced will be judged as nongrammatical. Second, phrase structure grammars have a tidy explanation of ambiguity. What is the meaning of the following sentence?

They are cooking apples.

The interpretation of the phrase "cooking apples" is the problem. This sentence cannot be mapped onto just one phrase structure; rather it can be decomposed into two:

They   are cooking   apples.
They   are   cooking apples.

Figure 8.5 shows the two phrase structures that result from the "cooking apples" sentence. In the first case, "cooking" would be a part of speech called a participle, and when it is included with "are" as a copula, the two words make up the verb of the sentence. In the second case, "cooking" maps onto the adjectival role and consequently is part of the final noun phrase of the sentence. Thus, when a sentence cannot be mapped successfully onto any phrase structure, it is judged to be nongrammatical. When it maps successfully onto just one phrase structure, the sentence is judged to be grammatical and meaningful. However, when the sentence maps onto two phrase structures, it is judged to be grammatical but ambiguous. In such cases, the explanation of ambiguity harmonizes nicely with the notions of constituent analysis and phrase structures.

A third advantage concerns the abstract nature of the phrase structures themselves. The possession of knowledge expressed as phrase structures allows its owner to do at least two things. First, he can accept as grammatical any sentence that maps onto a phrase structure, regardless of whether that sentence has been heard before. Second, the general nature of the phrase structure permits some creativity in utterances. For example, I can generate the following sentences (assuming that all of the words are in my vocabulary):

Rainey parked the car.
Britain ruled the waves.

These sentences don't mean the same thing, but they can be mapped onto the same phrase structure. This has some implications for children, who are trying to learn appropriate syntax. According to finite state theories, children build up their knowledge of syntax on a pair-by-pair basis. That is, children learn to associate two words in a particular order. Once formed, this association could be used as a basis for learning successively longer strings. According to this

············· **FIGURE 8.5** Two phrase structures.

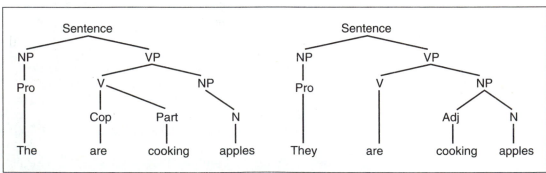

viewpoint, the child acquires syntax in the same way that a tourist in a foreign country might operate, that is, by encoding and storing a series of stock phrases that could be helpful in a variety of situations. However, given what we know of children's memories, that children could acquire syntactical knowledge that way seems unlikely.

According to the phrase structure position, the task of the child is simplified somewhat. Phrase structure grammar proposes that, instead of a series of specific word orderings, children learn general rules that can be used as formulas to generate a wide variety of sentences. This simplifies the child's task because, presumably, there are fewer rules to learn than there are specific word orderings. In other words, whereas the number of sentences in the English language is infinite, the number of phrase structures probably isn't. However, this simplification is purchased at a price. Unlike specific phrasings, the phrase structures themselves are never heard directly. Instead, they must be inferred from all the utterances that the child hears. Given that the inference-making abilities of children are no better than their metamemories, phrase structure theory's explanation of syntax acquisition is far from complete.

Some other problems also prevent our adopting phrase structure theory wholesale. First, although not infinite, the number of different phrase structures is surely large. Is the expectation that children somehow infer this large number of rules a reasonable one? Other criticisms are founded on the idea that phrase structures don't tell us the whole story about a given sentence. According to the phrase structure position, sentences that have different phrase structures should be judged as dissimilar. The meaning of a sentence depends upon the constituent analysis that is carried out upon it. If this analysis points to two different phrase structures, the meaning of the sentence should be accordingly altered. But this phenomenon is not always observed, as the following trio of sentences shows:

1. Rainey parked the Renault.
2. It was the Renault that was parked by Rainey.
3. Americans won the gold.

Sentences 1 and 2 don't share the same phrase structure, but sentences 1 and 3 do. Yet, most of us would say that sentences 1 and 3 are more dissimilar than sentences 1 and 2, because the first two sentences share the same *meaning*. This response indicates that the meaning of a sentence is only partially dependent upon the results of a constituent analysis. The trio of sentences also shows that we must have some linguistic knowledge that is not expressed in the phrase structure rule.

A third problem with phrase structure grammars is their inability to explain some types of sentence ambiguity. For example, the sentence

Visiting relatives can be tiresome.

is ambiguous. What's tiresome—the visits from one's relatives or the act of visiting one's relatives? According to phrase structure grammars, ambiguity arises because a particular sentence can be mapped onto more than one phrase structure. However, both meanings of the prior sentence can be mapped onto the same phrase structure:

Visiting relatives   can be   tiresome.

Technically, this sentence should not be ambiguous, because its constituents can be divided up in one and only one way. The fact that the sentence is ambiguous amplifies one of our earlier conclusions. Namely, our linguistic knowledge must have more than what is expressed in phrase structure grammars.

Transformational Grammar

Transformational grammar is an extension of Bloomfield's ideas and is strongly associated with its originator, Noam Chomsky. In his (1957) book *Syntactic Structures*, Chomsky detailed the limitations of both finite state and phrase structure grammars and proposed an alternative that attempted to represent more of the linguistic knowledge that we must have.

Chomsky reasoned that no single-level theory of grammar would ever account for all observed ambiguities in sentences, because these ambiguities were of at least two fundamentally different types. For example, the "cooking apples" sentence is ambiguous because it can be mapped onto more than one phrase structure. To resolve the ambiguity, all one has to do is ask whether the "cooking" goes with "apples" or with "are." However, the "visiting relatives" sentence is not ambiguous for that reason and can't be resolved by asking a question about which word "visiting" should be grouped with. The grouping is obvious, but the meaning isn't. Chomsky maintained that these two kinds of ambiguities were evidence that grammatical knowledge is organized in two levels.

He referred to the first of these as **surface structure.** This term denotes a level of grammatical knowledge that is seen in the superficial appearance of the sentence and is instantiated in the rewrite or transformational rules that I alluded to earlier. **Deep structure** denotes a level of grammatical knowledge that is closely related to the meaning of a sentence and is instantiated in the phrase structure rules that we have already examined. Both kinds of rules are required for a complete description of our grammatical knowledge. Let's see how these terms are enacted in Chomsky's theory.

First, we should understand that transformation grammars are said to be generative. This means that, because such grammars specify the relationship of the constituents to one another, an individual who knows explicitly the formal properties of the grammar (the rules in which it is embodied) should be able to apply these rules to a particular sentence. And an individual who could do that could, in a sense, "prove" that a particular sentence must be grammatical—that none of the explicit rules had been violated. Such a generation of a grammatical proof of a sentence is referred to as a derivation (Carroll, 1986). The mathematical connotations of this term are not wholly farfetched. That is, although we've seen that our linguistic intuitions seem accurate in creating tree structures such as the one we made from the "boy" sentence, we'd like to have a more formal specification of the basis for such breakdowns.

To begin, consider the following sentence:

The charming professor escorted the visiting dignitary.

We know that we could use our linguistic intuitions to break down this sentence in a hierarchic way. However, here our task is to find a set of rules, called phrase structure rules, that can be applied to this sentence and, by their application, show how such a sentence could come to be generated. Table 8.3 shows a very simple set of such phrase structure rules. (This table is modified from one appearing in Carroll, 1986.) For example, PS 1 (phrase structure rule 1) states the S (a sentence) can be rewritten as an *NP* (or noun phrase) and a verb phrase. PS 2 means that a noun phrase can be rewritten as an article and a noun. Adjectives are optional, and if they are included, they must be placed between the article and

············ **TABLE 8.3**   **A simple set of phrase structure rules**

PS 1:	S (sentence)	⟶	NP + VP
PS 2:	NP (noun phrase)	⟶	ART + (ADJ) + N
PS 3:	VP (verb phrase)	⟶	VP + NP
PS 4:	N (noun)	⟶	professor, dignitary
PS 5:	V (verb)	⟶	escorted
PS 6:	ADJ (adjective)	⟶	charming, visiting
PS 7:	ART (article)	⟶	the

the noun. Phrase structure rules 4 through 7 are referred to as lexical insertion rules. These rules describe which elements in our lexicons may be inserted into the slots called for in the first three phrase structure rules. Armed with this set of rules, we might derive the sentence above in the following way.

Applying PS 1 to the sentence we would get:

$$NP + VP$$

Next, we can apply PS 2 to the noun phrase (*NP*), rewriting it as:

$$ART + (ADJ) + N + VP$$

Then, we can apply PS 3 to expand the verb phrase (*VP*) as follows:

$$ART + (ADJ) + N + V + NP$$

Then we can reapply PS 2 to the noun phrase denoting the object of the sentence:

$$ART + (ADJ) + N + V + ART + (ADJ) + N$$

Finally, we can apply the lexical insertion rules; we apply PS 7 first:

$$THE + (ADJ) + N + V + THE + (ADJ) + N$$

Then we can apply PS 6, the adjective insertion rule:

$$THE + CHARMING + N + V + THE + VISITING + N$$

Following that, we can apply PS 4 and insert the nouns:

$$THE + CHARMING + PROFESSOR + V + THE + VISITING + DIGNITARY$$

Last, we can apply PS 5 and insert the verb:

$$THE + CHARMING + PROFESSOR + ESCORTED$$
$$+ THE + VISITING + DIGNITARY$$

But although such rules make the logic underlying the tree structure clearer, they cannot account for all our linguistic knowledge. Consider the "visiting relatives" sentence that we looked at earlier. Our problems in extracting the meaning of this sentence were not the result of inappropriate phrase structure selection, and consequently a derivation of this sentence in the same manner as the "charming professor" sentence would not clear up its ambiguity. Rather, the ambiguity of the "visiting relatives" sentence is produced because certain elements or constituents of the sentence's deep structure have been (optionally) deleted from the sentence's surface form. With the departure of these elements, the sentence is rendered ambiguous. The rules that operate on the phrase structure in this fashion are known as transformational rules. There is another important distinction between phrase structure rules and transformational rules.

Whereas phrase structure rules operate on only a single constituent, transformational rules operate on entire strings of constituents. This will be made clearer by taking a look at a particular transformational rule, one known as the particle-movement transformation (Carroll, 1986).

Let's consider the following sentence:

Billy picked up his date.

We know that this sentence is roughly synonymous with the following, "Billy picked his date up," and we can see that the particle "up" has indeed been moved around with no loss of meaning. Specifically, we see that the particle has been moved around the noun phrase "his date." How can we go about expressing this movement? We could simply add two phrase structure rules to our previous list that cover such rewrites. For example, we might write the following two rules:

$$PS\ 8: VP \rightarrow V + (PART) + NP$$
$$PS\ 9: VP \rightarrow V + NP + (PART)$$

These rules would permit us to derive both forms of the "Billy" sentence, but the problem is that there is nothing in these two rules that expresses the fact that the two forms of the "Billy" sentence are clearly related to one another. To show the relationship, let's concoct the following transformational rule:

$$T\ 1: V + PART + NP \rightarrow V + NP + PART$$

What this rule states is that both forms of the "Billy" sentence share the same deep structure and have consequently been built from the same phrase structure rules. After the initial construction, the particle movement rule was applied to the initial format to create the second form of the "Billy" sentence, which is superficially, but not meaningfully, different from the first form. Notice also that the particle movement rule always operates to move the particle around the entire noun phrase, regardless of how that constituent might itself be rewritten. Thus the following pairs of sentences can all be derived:

Billy picked up his attractive date.
Billy picked his attractive date up.
Billy picked up his mysterious, but nevertheless intriguing, date.
Billy picked his mysterious, but nevertheless intriguing, date up.

Let's examine some of the implications of these transformational rules. Consider these sentences:

He bit her.
Himself bit her.

The first is grammatical but the second one isn't (Fromkin & Rodman, 1978). But why shouldn't the second sentence be grammatical? Its subject is a pronoun, but this is true for the grammatical sentence too. The only difference is that the subject of the first sentence is a "standard" pronoun, but the subject of the second sentence is a reflexive pronoun. We recognize that reflexive pronouns cannot be the subjects of sentences, but how do we make our grammatical rules reflect this? The problem here is that pure phrase structure grammars have no way of making a distinction between these two different kinds of pronouns: As far as they are concerned, there can be distinctions only among specific lexical entries. In other words, to pure phrase structure grammars, a pronoun is a pronoun.

But the existence of transformational rules operating in concert with phrase structure rules offers us a way out of this problem. Fromkin and Rodman (1978) have explained the solution this way. Let's say that lexical insertion rules never consider putting reflexive pronouns into a sentence. Rather, each sentence is generated according to the well-defined phrase structure rules that we have already considered. Now suppose that after the string of words has been completely generated by the phrase structure rules, an entirely different kind of rule "looks" at the whole structure that's been created. If these different rules detect that two identical noun phrases in the same sentence refer to the same individual, then these rules change the second noun phrase to a reflexive pronoun that agrees with the first in person, number, and gender.

Figure 8.6 shows what these transformational rules do to the underlying phrase structure.

For example, to construct the sentence "The girl cheats herself," we would first derive the sentence "The girl cheats the girl." Then looking at the entire sentence, the transformational rule that we've been discussing alters the phrase structure by inserting the reflexive pronoun "herself." As Figure 8.6 shows, the effect of these transformational rules is dramatic: Their effect is to alter the underlying phrase structure, the one used to derive the sentence in the first place, into a different phrase structure, one that is used to produce the surface form of the sentence.

And with this discussion, we come to what is perhaps Chomsky's most essential insight, namely that phrase structure rules can be used to generate a tree structure representing meaning, and to this deep structure, transformational rules

FIGURE 8.6 This reflexive rule changes or transforms one phrase-structure tree, which the phrase-structure rules specified by the methods discussed earlier, into a different phrase-structure tree. It changed the NP, which was specified as *Art + N* (and as *the girl* after the lexical-insertion rules), into an NP specified as *Pro* and finally as *herself*.

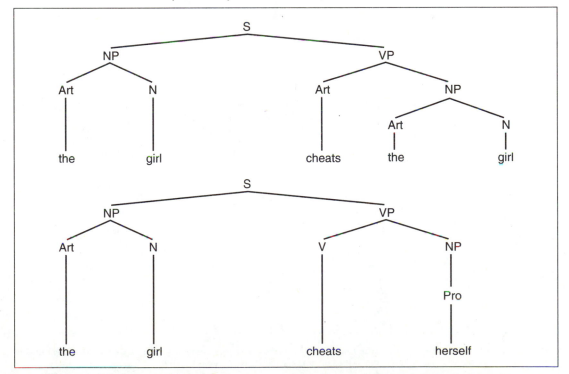

(Copyright 1978 by Holt, Rinehart, Winston. Adapted by permission of the publisher and author.)

then can be applied to create the specific form of the sentence. This is a radical view because it implies that a speaker cannot have an intention to communicate meaningfully without the recruitment of some phrase structure rules. These phrase structures then may be operated on by transformational rules to produce the specific form of the actual utterance, but these sorts of modifications affect only the surface structure of the sentence, not its underlying meaning which is embodied in the phrase structure rules.

These relationships are expressed in Figure 8.7 which shows the general format of transformational grammar. At the risk of redundancy, Figure 8.7 shows that, according to Chomsky, the syntactic component of grammar occupies center stage. Consequently, for Chomsky, it's impossible to study meaning without also studying syntax and, in fact, it's impossible to understand the phonological structure of language without also understanding how syntax shapes these surface considerations. Thus, Chomsky's position is said to espouse what is called the *centrality of syntax*—the idea that syntax is the central ability underlying other grammatical competencies and can therefore be studied more or less in isolation. The rationale underlying this argument has been outlined by DeJong:

> Native speakers have syntactic competence: they can judge the syntactic well-formedness of natural language utterances. Furthermore, their syntactic judgments seem to be purely recursive. That is, both membership and nonmembership in the class of syntactically well-formed utterances is decidable. Or, put another way, there is an effective procedure that always halts and assigns an acceptable or unacceptable status to every finite input string of words. Such syntactic competence will

············· **FIGURE 8.7** Overall form of standard transformational grammar.

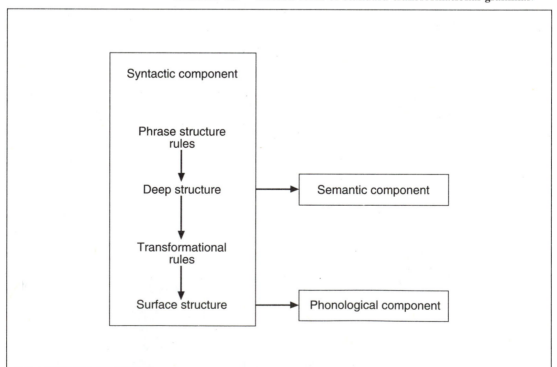

necessarily be a part of any complete natural language competence. Thus, it may be studied more or less in isolation and later, after the other components have also been worked out, the various pieces can be connected together in whatever way then seems appropriate. (DeJong, 1982, p. 35)

Although DeJong admits that this statement is an oversimplification of the position, the tenor of the passage is crystal clear. According to transformational grammarians of whatever stripe, syntactic knowledge can be studied on its own. This has an important implication for psychologists: If Chomsky is correct, no syntax-free grammars could exist. The study of semantics would always be subordinate to the study of syntax.

Origins of Grammatical Knowledge

Where does grammatical knowledge come from? Clearly, experience must play a crucial role in its acquisition. We saw earlier in this chapter that traditional transmission seems to be one of the most essential of Hockett's design features. Nevertheless, Chomsky believes that much of our grammatical knowledge is based on innate predispositions that guide and channel experience, and which make us sensitive to the regularities of phonology, syntax, and discourse. Let's explore this idea further.

A child, states Chomsky, who is trying to acquire grammar is in a position similar to that of a scientist who is trying to understand a phenomenon. Like the scientist, the child observes the events around her and looks for orderly patterns. After observing, the child, like the scientist, makes a hypothesis about the rule or law presumed to be underlying those patterns and producing them. This hypothesis is almost certain to be incomplete. As the child continues to observe and record linguistic events, her next hypothesis will be more accurate, the succeeding hypothesis still more accurate, and so on. Ultimately, the child winds up with a hypothesis about language that is purely recursive and quite accurate.

But some substantial differences also exist between a child and a scientist. First, scientists are trained to formulate hypotheses; without that training, they aren't very good at it. Yet, even though the child doesn't receive any explicit training in syntax hypothesis formulation, he seems to do just fine. Second, the child accomplishes syntax acquisition in a short period of time. Third, a great deal of variation exists among the theories of scientists. Often (perhaps too often), a group of scientists can observe the same phenomenon and generate a large number of plausible and undisprovable hypotheses about it. But the opposite situation is true for children. They hear a wide variety of sentences and from it generate identical grammatical knowledge. This effect is astonishing: A theoretical linguist, working with exactly the same information a child has, can't duplicate that feat. Nobody has ever written a complete theory of grammar for any naturally occurring language, yet all children (and all of us) know what that grammatical knowledge is. How can children accomplish this?

Chomsky's answer is that the child is aided in the process of grammar acquisition because certain kinds of information about language are already built into the child's mind. That is, the child has innate knowledge about the general form that languages can and cannot take. These innate predispositions are called linguistic universals. Linguistic universals can be thought of in two ways. First, they are features that all languages have in common. Second, they act as boundaries or constraints around the permissible forms that specific languages can take on. These linguistic universals guide the hypothesis making of the child

USING YOUR KNOWLEDGE OF COGNITION

We've seen that a transformational grammar has rules that "operate" on the initial phrase structures that are used to derive a sentence, thus creating a surface form of the sentence. So we would use this reasoning to say that the sentence:

Betty expects to feed herself.

is "really" (at the phrase structure level) the sentence:

Betty expects to feed Betty.

You can thus understand the first sentence because your cognitive system knows that the first sentence, with "herself" in it, is really just the second sentence, which has "spent some time in the shop" being worked on. And the meaning of the second sentence is clear. But we can use the following demonstration sentences to show that your cognitive system can be fooled: It's not always able to recover the underlying structure by working backward from the final surface form. Ask your friends to tell you what this sentence means:

Which one of the older women is it that Betty expects to feed herself?

Is it that Betty, as opposed to someone else doing it, expects to feed one of the older women, or is it that Betty expects one of the older women to be able to feed herself? Your friends were probably confused. And even if they can come up with an interpretation (and most people can), they nevertheless admit that the other interpretation is plausible. Look what happens if we try to work backward to figure out what noun has been substituted for:

1. Which one of the older women is it that Betty expects to feed Betty? (This doesn't make much sense.)

2. Which one of the older women is it that Betty expects to feed the older woman? (This suggests that there is really only one way to understand the sentence.)

3. Which one of the older women is it that Betty expects to feed one? (This is ambiguous and hard to comprehend, but casts some doubt on the correctness of the interpretation of 2.)

By trying to go backward from the final form of the sentence to the underlying phrase structure, we can get at least a partial handle on why the clause "Betty expects to feed herself," which is clear by itself, becomes ambiguous in the presence of the complete sentence. Essentially, your cognitive system is unable to determine which of the three nouns in the original sentence has been pronominalized by the reflexive pronoun, "herself."

within fairly narrow boundaries, ensuring that the final hypothesis generated by the child is indeed equivalent to the grammar of that particular language. This state of affairs is shown in Figure 8.8.

Implications of Chomsky's Theory

Many ideas in Chomsky's work have implications for cognitive psychology, but space precludes our dealing with more than few of them. First, there is the notion of linguistic universals. If these truly exist and are discoverable, they might possibly represent a quantum leap in our understanding of the basic rules of language and thought. Second, Chomsky has argued that children cannot possibly acquire grammatical knowledge on their own—they must be helped by innate predispositions.

The third implication concerns the basic premise of Chomsky's theory. Is our linguistic knowledge based fundamentally on syntax? If this is so, we should be able to find evidence for deep and surface structure in human judgments of grammaticality. In addition, the case of Chomsky's theory would be strengthened

·············· **FIGURE 8.8** The relationship of linguistic universals to grammar, as assumed in Chomsky's theory.

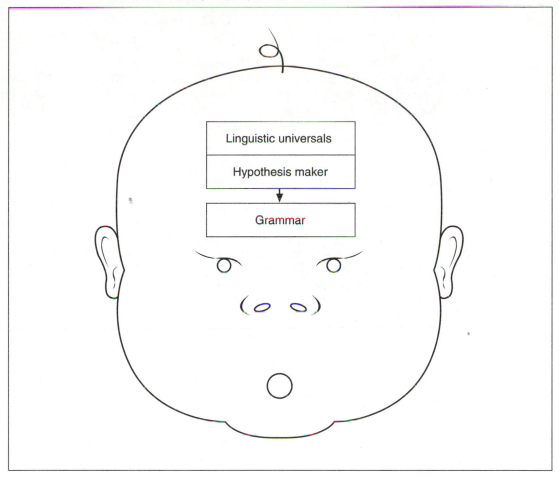

The Articulate Mammal: An Introduction to Psycholinguistics, 2d ed., by Jean Aitchison. © 1976, 1983 by Jean Aitchison. Reprinted by permission of Universe Books, New York.)

if we could identify some evidence indicating that phrase structure and transformational rules are a valid form of representing our syntactic knowledge. These issues are dealt with next.

Empirical Support for the Deep-Surface Structure Distinction

Click Studies   A classic and controversial study by Garrett, Bever, and Fodor (1966) seemed to demonstrate that the division of a sentence into constituents is based on its structure rather than on its sounds. The researchers composed two sentences:

1. In order to catch his train George drove furiously to the station.
2. The reporters assigned to George drove furiously to the station.

In each case, the sentence contains the words "George drove furiously to the station." However, in the first sentence, "George" is the subject of the sentence, and in the second sentence, the subject is "reporters." To understand the sentences, they must be parsed in the correct places:

1. In order to catch his train—George drove furiously to the station.
2. The reporters assigned to George—drove furiously to the station.

That is, in the first case, the break occurs before "George"; in the second case, it occurs right after it. Garrett et al. made recordings of these two sentences and devised an ingenious way to ensure that the utterance's sound would not cue subjects about the correct place to make the division. They cut each of the tapes right before "George" and then connected each "George" clause onto the *beginning* of the other tape:

1. In order to catch his train George   drove furiously to the station.
2. The reporters assigned to George   drove furiously to the station.

The spliced tapes were then played for the subjects, who heard them via stereo headphones. In one ear, the subjects heard one of the spliced sentences; in the other ear, the subjects heard a click. The click was timed to occur in the middle of "George." What was the purpose of the click? If the subjects were busy allocating cognitive processes to understand the sentence, they would not likely have enough processing capability left over to precisely determine the placement of the click. In that case, the subjects could misperceive the timing of the click. If the timing of the click was misperceived, the researchers were interested in knowing when the subjects thought it had occurred.

After hearing the sentence, the subjects were asked to indicate exactly where the click had occurred. Subjects tended to misperceive the location of the click, and their errors were predictable from an analysis of the constituents. In the first sentence, subjects tended to think the click had occurred earlier than it actually had. In the second sentence, they thought the click had occurred after it had actually been presented. These effects can be shown with arrows:

1. In order to catch his train George drove furiously to the station.

2. The reporters assigned to George drove furiously to the station.

Notice that, in both cases, the click was moved closer to the border of the constituent in which "George" was included. Also, the basis for this movement could not have been the sounds of the sentences, because Garrett et al. had controlled for that effect by cutting and editing the tapes. The implication is that the constituent analysis is derived from the structure of a sentence, not from its sounds.

Other studies using the click displacement paradigm have also supported Chomsky's position. Bever, Lackner, and Kirk (1969) used sentences such as the following:

The corrupt police can't bear criminals to confess quickly.
The corrupt police can't force criminals to confess quickly.

These sentences have the same surface structures but different deep structures. Aitchison (1983) has suggested a good way to demonstrate that the two sentences have different deep structures (apart from simply realizing that they have different meanings). Try converting each sentence into the passive voice. You'll find that conversion is easy for the second sentence with no loss of meaning, but the first sentence cannot be converted without becoming ungrammatical:

> Criminals cannot be borne by the police to confess quickly.
> Criminals cannot be forced by the police to confess quickly.

If the two sentences had the same deep structure, they could both be converted into the passive voice with equal ease. Via a set of stereo headphones, the subjects heard the sentence in one ear and heard a click occurring at "criminals" in the other ear. The results were intriguing. For the first of the two sentences, the subjects displaced the click forward, congruent with Chomsky's theory that a deep structure break should occur after "bear:"

> The corrupt police can't bear   criminals to confess quickly.

But in the second sentence, the click was not displaced in either direction. The explanation of this lack of movement can be seen in Aitchison's representation of the deep structure of the second sentence, which is shown in Figure 8.9. As Figure 8.9 shows, the deep structure representation includes "criminals" in both clauses. This representation suggests that the click was not displaced because, in effect, it was being pulled in both directions by the occurrence of "criminals" in both clauses:

> The corrupt police can't force criminals   criminals to confess quickly.

These findings are suggestive, but we must be cautious in our interpretation. On the one hand, these findings are consistent with some aspects of Chomsky's theory, namely that a sentence is parsed on the basis of its constituents, and that this parsing is apparently consistent with the rules of surface and deep structure. However, although these findings are consistent with Chomsky's theory, they don't necessarily *substantiate* it, because other theories of grammar may make the same predictions. On the empirical level, there are several reasons for caution in interpreting the basic findings. First, Reber (1973) has pointed out that clausal boundaries are almost always confounded with other aspects of the sentence, such as serial position and intonation pattern. The tape cutting of Garrett et al. doesn't appear to control for all of these effects.

Second, the typical subject is not completely naive with regard to constituents. If she is in doubt about where a click occurred, she must have a strong temptation to push the click toward the direction of the nearest clause boundary.

FIGURE 8.9
∙∙∙∙∙∙∙∙∙∙∙∙∙∙∙∙∙∙∙∙∙∙
A representation of deep structure.

(From *The Articulate Mammal: An Introduction to Psycholinguistics*, 2d ed., by Jean Aitchison. © 1976, 1983 by Jean Aitchison. Reprinted by permission of Universe Books, New York.)

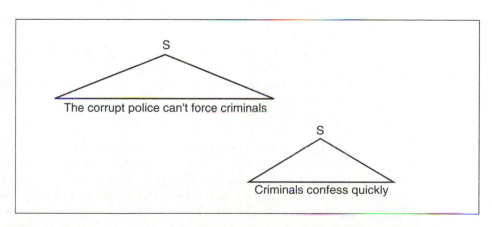

Reber and Anderson (1970) demonstrated this effect in a startling way. They used the standard click displacement procedure but added a twist. They also told their subjects that the experiment involved subliminal perception and that, in some cases, the click would be almost inaudible. In reality, no clicks of any kind were presented in some of the sentences. Yet, the subjects tended to say that they heard a click, and its location was usually at clause boundaries.

Phoneme Detection Studies   Other implications of the theory have also had a checkered history in the literature. For example, according to Chomsky, the meaning of a clause is not extracted until the clause boundary has been reached and the clause has been mapped onto a base marker in deep structure. If a word or part of a word has two meanings, this duality of meaning is thought to have an effect on the extraction process, because the ambiguous term cannot be clearly assigned to one particular deep structure. This type of ambiguity, known as *lexical ambiguity*, is not resolved until the clause boundary is reached (Olson & MacKay, 1974); and presumably, only the information from that particular clause is used to resolve the ambiguity. If all this is true, then both meanings of the lexically ambiguous term are activated, and they stay activated until the clause boundary is reached and one particular meaning can be assigned.

These theoretical points have been studied using a so-called *phoneme detection* paradigm. Recall that a phoneme is a term referring to a basic unit of linguistic sound. In this paradigm, a subject first hears a phoneme in isolation, called the *target phoneme*. Next, the subject listens to a sentence in which the phoneme may or may not occur. If it occurs, the subject is supposed to respond as quickly as possible. When lexically ambiguous words occur right before the target phoneme, the detection latency is usually increased (Cairns & Kamerman, 1975; Danks & Glucksberg, 1980). This finding makes sense, given what we know about activation in permanent memory and the allocation of attention. Apparently, the subject waits until the clause boundary to disambiguate the troublesome lexical item, and consequently, substantial processing efforts are expended on that task at the clause boundary. When the target phoneme occurs there too, the subject doesn't have quite as many cognitive resources to allocate to processing the target phoneme, and the detection latency increases. Moreover, prior context—that is, information from previous clauses that could be used to resolve the ambiguity—typically does not eliminate this effect. These findings have been interpreted as supporting the idea that a lexical analysis is carried out on a clause-by-clause basis.

However, more recent studies have muddied the water in this area, too. Mehler, Segui, and Carey (1978) have argued that previous work did not control for all possible contaminating variables such as the phonemic composition of the words occurring immediately before the target phoneme. Blank and Foss (1978) and Swinney and Hakes (1976) did control for these and other variables and found that information occurring before the clausal boundary could indeed reduce the phoneme detection latency. Such findings argue against a strict interpretation of Chomsky's theory.

Summary   On an intuitive basis, the distinction between surface and deep structure seems valid and necessary. Also, Chomsky has bolstered this intuitive argument by composing sentences demonstrating that, rationally, we must have two levels of grammatical knowledge. Although Chomsky's theory has generated an impressive number of studies, the empirical findings are, however, mixed. If surface and deep structure are truly represented by different sets of abstract grammatical rules, these rules apparently don't behave in ways that are consistent with other aspects of the information-processing viewpoint. Similarly, regarding Chomsky's claims for transformational rules that bridge deep and surface structure, several researchers (Fodor, Bever, & Garrett, 1974) have noted the absence of any strong empirical reason for supporting a belief that Chomsky's position is the correct one.

In retrospect, it seems that this failure to find empirical support for Chomsky's theory was quite predictable: Chomsky has all along maintained that his is a theory of linguistic competence, not linguistic performance. That is, he has stated that transformational grammar is a formal device for creating grammatical strings of English words, and for expressing in a formal sense what it is that's similar about sentences that people judge to be similar. He has been careful not to suggest that this theory has any necessary implications for the cognitive operations that humans actually engage in when they speak to one another. Hence, we can see that the term *grammar* does double duty for Chomsky: Not only does it describe a formal device for generating linguistic strings, but also it describes the knowledge about those strings in the minds of humans, knowledge that can never be tapped directly (Johnson-Laird, 1987).

But we needn't be so glum. It may be the case that people do use their grammatical knowledge indirectly as a series of "strategies" (Clark & Clark, 1977) that might aid them in understanding and producing sentences. For example, you might adopt the following strategy to help you process sentences:

Strategy 1: Whenever you find a function word, begin a new constituent whose length is larger than one word.

A function word is any lexical element that has an almost purely syntactic rather than content function. In the constituent "the green boat," "green" and "boat" are content words, "the" is a function word. One other kind of function word is the category of relative pronouns such as "that," or "which." We may now write one of the many variations of strategy 1 that we could possibly erect and use to help us process sentences:

Strategy 1a: Whenever you find a relative pronoun (a kind of function word), begin a new clause.

How could this strategy help us? Consider two more sentences:

The man that the dog bit bought the house.
The man the dog bit bought the house.

Which is easier to understand? If you're like most people, you probably thought that the sentence with the relative pronoun in it was easier to comprehend than the sentence from which it was missing. If you are using Strategy 1a, this difference is easy to understand. Strategy 1a tells the user that it's time to create a new clause when you hear the "that," thus giving you a good clue to the surface structure that is being used in the sentence. However, for the sentence with the relative pronoun missing, even though it's grammatical, listeners must struggle because they don't get the clue to open a new clause. Instead the second determiner "the" tells them only to open a new noun phrase. Consistent with this interpretation, Fodor and Garrett (1967) found that sentences with the relative pronoun intact were easier to process than those with the pronoun missing. These effects are made even clearer when another clause is embedded within the first:

The man that the dog that the cat enraged bit bought the house.
The man the dog the cat enraged bit bought the house.

Sometimes my students try to tell me that the second sentence of this pair isn't even grammatical, even though they'll all acknowledge that, without the "cat" clause, it is. Some researchers (Hakes & Foss, 1970) failed to replicate the Fodor and Garrett findings with sentences having two embedded clauses, suggesting perhaps that even strategies like 1a will fail to help if the person's memory system is overloaded by the processing demands of the sentence.

This lack of empirical support has caused some cognitive psychologists to wonder if syntax-based grammars might not have run their course (Smith, 1982), which brings up the inevitable question, "What's the alternative?" In the last few years, psycholinguists have been likely to turn to semantically based grammars as possible solutions. For example, Charniak (1983) has proposed the beginning of a theory of grammar founded on a type of spreading activation model such as those considered in Chapter 6.

ASPECTS OF LANGUAGE ACQUISITION: IS KNOWLEDGE INNATE?

When we looked at Chomsky's theory, we saw that innate predispositions are assumed to play a major role in language acquisition. The main theoretical division is along these lines. On the one hand, we have a group of theorists who argue that language is learned—and learned in a way similar to other behaviors. According to this group, there is nothing particularly special about language; the same conditioning principles that seem to explain the acquisition of other behaviors can be fruitfully applied to language as well. On the other hand, we have a group of theorists who, although not exactly proposing a clear alternative, argue that theorists of the first group have simplified things dramatically. This second group maintains that language cannot be acquired simply by learning it. Consequently, the acquisition of language must at least be partially dependent on innate knowledge.

Arguments for Innate Knowledge

There is a substantial body of literature suggesting that our linguistic knowledge is based on innate predispositions. Once again, Chomsky was among the recent protagonists in the controversy; he argued that the evidence in favor of this position was overwhelming. These claims have often been misunderstood. First, to argue that Chomsky espouses an innate position doesn't necessarily mean that all his opponents are non-innatists. Almost everybody agrees that most skills—even cognitive ones—are based in some way on innate predispositions. The question really is, "Are there innate *linguistic* predispositions?"

Second, what Chomsky means by *innate* has also been misunderstood. Aitchison has expressed his position quite well:

> By innate, Chomsky simply means "genetically programmed." He does not literally think that children are born with language in their heads ready to be spoken. He merely claims that a "blueprint" is there, which is brought into use when the child reaches a certain point in her general development. With the help of this blueprint, she analyzes the language she hears around her more readily than she would if she were totally unprepared for the strange gabbling sounds which emerge from human mouths. (Aitchison, 1983, p. 31)

The evidence supporting this contention comes from diverse sources. First, we'll consider some of the biological adaptations of our bodies that seem to have no purpose other than to support language. Second, we'll consider some of the specializations in our brains. We'll also take a look at human infants' abilities to recognize speech sounds early in their lives.

Anatomical and Breathing Specializations

Aitchison (1983) has noted a number of characteristics of the human vocal tract that are somewhat unusual. For example, human teeth are different from those of other animals. The teeth are approximately the same height and typically have no spaces between them. The degree of overlap between the upper and bottom set is usually small. These features are not required for eating but are helpful—perhaps necessary—for speech. Certain sounds (e.g., *sh*, as in *shut*, or *th*, as in *thin*) are possible only because the flow of air can be controlled fairly precisely, which wouldn't be possible if air escaped through our teeth. The human tongue is relatively short, thick, and mobile compared with the tongues of monkeys. This characteristic is helpful in changing the size and shape of the vocal cavity, which is necessary to produce vowel sounds.

In all primates, the larynx contains the vocal cords, but the human larynx is different and, oddly, simpler than that of other primates. Such simplification is sometimes an indication of biological specialization. For example, birds don't have teeth, which enables them to consume their typical diet quickly because they don't have to chew it. In humans, the simplified larynx enables the air to flow through the vocal tract without impediment, permitting great control and flexibility. However, this simplification presents a disadvantage. Other primates can close off their mouths from their tracheas, which enables them to breathe while they eat. Humans can't duplicate this feat; and if they try, they risk getting a piece of food stuck in their tracheas. No self-respecting monkey would ever choke to death while eating, but for humans, that's an unfortunate possibility. This point is a telling one though. Evolution would not likely favor a dangerous development unless the advantage conferred were very great.

Breathing is a natural act, but in some cases, humans need breathing instructions. For example, in learning to play a wind instrument, such as the flute or oboe, the student needs to learn the proper breathing techniques. Similarly, in swimming, the usual impediment to going more than a lap or two is the oxygen debt that builds up from improper breathing. We don't think about it, but speech also imposes breathing demands. While speaking, the number of breaths per minute is reduced. Inhalation is accelerated, while exhalation is slowed (Aitchison, 1983). If we try to do other things that involve altering our natural breathing rhythm, we must be taught how to do them, or else we quickly get into trouble. Although speech also significantly alters our breathing rhythm, we can talk for hours without ever "coming up for air."

Specializations of the Brain   Pioneering work in brain specializations was done by the great French researcher Paul Broca in the 1860s. Broca discovered that, if a certain area of the cortex was damaged by a stroke, an **aphasia,** or language disorder, was produced. This area is located in the frontal lobe and is now usually referred to as Broca's area. Broca also discovered that the aphasia appeared only if the stroke had taken place in the left hemisphere of the brain. Damage to the corresponding area in the right hemisphere did not produce language deficits. These findings confirmed what other researchers had suspected: that a specific location in the brain seems to be responsible for the production of speech. In most cases, this language center seems localized in the dominant (i.e., left) hemisphere.

Broca's area is adjacent to the area of the brain that controls muscular movement in the face, and damage to Broca's area usually is accompanied by partial paralysis of the right side of the face. However, Broca ingeniously demonstrated that the aphasia was not simply the result of this paralysis by asking his patients to sing. Surprisingly, singing ability was unimpaired. The muscles that wouldn't cooperate in order to speak would work together to sing, suggesting that singing ability was controlled by another area of the brain.

People who suffer damage to Broca's area speak only with a great deal of difficulty. Their speech is slow and telegraphic, meaning that some words are left out. The pronunciation of verbs and pronouns is often impaired. Geschwind cites the following example of this aphasia. In this case, a person was asked about an upcoming dental appointment.

> Yes ... Monday ... Dad and Dick ... Wednesday nine o'clock ... ten o'clock ... doctors ... and ... teeth. (Geschwind, 1980, p. 209)

This type of aphasia isn't the only kind. In 1874, Carl Wernicke identified another type of language disorder. This aphasia was the result of damage to a location in the temporal lobe of the left hemisphere, posterior to Broca's area. People with damage to this location (now known as Wernicke's area) produce speech that is fluent and often syntactically sound. However, the content of the utterance is often meaningless. The following is an example of this disorder. The patient was asked to describe a picture that showed two boys stealing cookies behind their mother's back.

> Mother is away here working her work to get her better, but when she's looking the two boys looking in the other part. She's working another time. (Geschwind, 1980, p. 209)

Although not known to Broca and Wernicke, the two areas named after them are connected by a band of tissue called the *arcuate fasciculus*. This area has suggested a view of the brain's role in speech production that has gone more or less unchallenged in the past century. The meaning of an utterance, or its underlying structure, is first produced in Wernicke's area. This code is next transferred via the arcuate fasciculus to Broca's area, which is responsible for formulating a more detailed speech plan. This plan is next sent on to the motor area of the cortex, which activates the appropriate muscles of the lips, tongue, larynx, and so on.

These findings are easily interpretable as evidence that our linguistic ability is "wired into" our brains. We shouldn't be too hasty with that interpretation. In some cases, the hemispheric organization differs from the usual, and these people have no trouble speaking. Also, ample evidence suggests that Broca's and Wernicke's areas are simply centers for activity that can be taken up by other structures in the cortex. In most cases following a stroke, people make a substantial recovery of their language abilities. Neural tissue adjacent to that which was destroyed is apparently capable of taking on the functions of the original areas.

Categorical Perception of Speech Sounds   The human vocal tract is capable of making a wide variety of sounds, only some of which are linguistic. Moreover, babies are exposed to a wide variety of sounds, both linguistic and nonlinguistic. These facts put babies in somewhat of a bind. If babies are going to learn to speak, they must be able to distinguish linguistic sounds from nonlinguistic ones and must distinguish the linguistic sounds from each other. These are large problems, but babies seem to know the basis for distinguishing linguistic sounds from nonlinguistic ones. For example, babies imitate the sounds of human speakers, but they don't imitate other sounds (such as that of the refrigerator) that might be present at the same time. Similarly, they stop crying if someone speaks to them but not if someone rings a bell. The ability to make this discrimination appears to be present early—perhaps by two weeks of age (Wolff, 1966). Babies also seem to know how to distinguish linguistic sounds from one another. This ability has been demonstrated in a classic study of Eimas, Siqueland, Jusczyk, and Vigorito (1971).

Before discussing the study, some background information is necessary. The speech sounds *b* and *p* are produced by closing the lips, then opening them, releasing air. In producing *b*, the vocal cords begin vibrating as soon as the air is released. For *p*, a short latency occurs between the release of air and the slight vibration of the vocal cords. Speech sounds that involve vibrations of the vocal cords are called *voiced phonemes*. Listeners use the latency between the release of air and the beginning of the vibrations as a cue in determining whether the *b* or *p* sound has been produced. This cue is called *Voice Onset Time*.

Research with adults has demonstrated that Voice Onset Time has a major influence on how certain sounds will be heard. Lisker and Abramson (1970) were able to program a computer to produce acoustic information that corresponded to the *p* and *b* sounds. In this way, the buzzing sound associated with *b* could be produced separately from the acoustic information heard in *p*. Armed with this technology, they were able to systematically vary the timing of the voicing. The Voice Onset Time was varied from −150 msec (i.e., the voicing began 150 msec before the simulated release of air) to +150 msec (the voicing began 150 msec after the simulated air release). Lisker and Abramson found that subjects were unanimous in their judgment that the sound was a *b* unless the Voice Onset Time was 10 msec or greater, at which point a rapid shift in opinion occurred. At that point, the subjects began to hear the stimulus as *p*, and if the Voice Onset Time was extended to about 30 to 40 msec, the subjects were once again unanimous that the sound being produced was a *p*. The perception of speech sounds is called **categorical perception,** because subjects don't seem to be aware of any gradual fading away of the "*b*-ness" of the sound as the Voice Onset Time increases. Instead, the subjects seem to be fairly confident that the sound is a *b* until the critical Voice Onset Time is reached, at which point the subjects are sure that it's a *p*. Clearly, the subjects are imposing a fairly definite mental organization on the somewhat ambiguous speech sounds. This phenomenon is interesting enough, but researchers also wanted to know the age at which categorical perception of speech sounds begins.

To assess this, Eimas et al. used a procedure that relies on the infant's ability to become familiar with certain stimuli and to stop responding to them. In this procedure, the infant is given a pacifier that contains a device that measures the infant's rate of sucking. A sound is then played repeatedly for the infant until the sucking rate is constant. At that point, a new sound is played. If the baby notices anything different about the sound, this interest is translated into a heightened level of activity, which is expressed by a sudden increase in the rate of sucking for a short period of time. After the baby gets used to the new sound, the rate of sucking gradually declines.

Eimas and his colleagues presented one-month-old babies with a variety of synthetic speech sounds with differing Voice Onset Times. They found that the infants' perception of the speech sounds was indeed categorical. Moreover, the boundary between *b* and *p* was about the same for infants as it was for adults: approximately 20 msec. In other words, if the babies had gotten used to a sound in which the Voice Onset Time was 60 msec, and they heard a new sound in which the Voice Onset Time was 80 msec, the rate of sucking did not increase. Apparently, the infants did not consider these sounds to be different from one another. However, if the babies had gotten used to a sound in which Voice Onset Time was 0 msec, and then heard a sound in which Voice Onset Time was 20 msec, their rate of sucking increased. The infants seemed to regard these sounds as different from one another.

Infants don't know a *b* from a *p* in the sense that they can refer to these sounds with linguistic labels the way more mature humans do. For this reason, Eimas et al. (1971) maintains that humans must have some built-in system that is sensitive to the acoustic properties of speech (Clark & Clark, 1977).

 ## CONCLUDING COMMENTS AND SUGGESTIONS FOR FURTHER READING

Two overarching points should be made about this chapter. The first point concerns the nature of linguistic knowledge, and the second has to do with its foundation in the human mind. Regarding the first point, we've seen that it's extraordinarily difficult to specify the knowledge that enables us to speak and comprehend the utterances of others. Nobody has written a complete account of the grammar of any naturally occurring language. Indeed, specifying any part of this knowledge is extremely difficult. For example, nobody has written an account of grammar that specifies how people make decisions about acceptable syntax. Yet, the cognitive processes involved operate reliably and quickly. We know this because we quickly make judgments about appropriate syntax, and the consensus about such judgments is good. Perhaps the main point of Chomsky's work is that such knowledge cannot be expressed by a set of rules that work on just one level. For the reasons that we reviewed in the chapter, grammatical knowledge must exist on at least two—perhaps more—levels. As we saw in the chapter, extracting the nature of this knowledge has proved extremely difficult for cognitive psychologists and linguists. This difficulty, too, is puzzling. Over the last two decades, researchers have acquired more facts about mentality than they did in the entire previous history of psychology. Yet, despite the overall yielding of many bits of knowledge in many areas, the cognitive operations underlying language have proved frustratingly resistant to the research techniques that have been brought to bear upon them. Why?

Responding to this question brings me to the second of the chapter's main points. Many cognitive psychologists have come to believe that the mental operations underlying language will remain obscure precisely because they are not assembled from simpler information-processing routines, as are many of the other cognitive events we have studied. In other words, because the degree of innate knowledge involved in language seems greater than for other mental events, the operation of this knowledge is correspondingly more obscure. To a certain extent, how strongly you believe this is probably partially dependent upon on how persuasive you found the material on innate predispositions. If you found this evidence convincing, you are probably willing to believe that language will remain forever mysterious. On the other hand, some cognitive psychologists don't find this sort of evidence particularly convincing. They maintain that, although it's obvious that some sort of innate influences affect the course of language development, the application of the correct research technique, the correct angle on the existing findings, or whatever, will demonstrate that language is not necessarily different in kind than the other cognitive processes we have studied. This issue is sure to be surrounded by more debate in the years ahead.

Students who want to learn more about these topics must realize that they cannot be approached by any particularly easy route. Hudson (1984) has written a pragmatic introduction to linguistics. Chomsky (1972) has written an introduction to his thinking, which is intended for an educated but nonprofessional audience. Some of his more recent work (Chomsky, 1979) might also be a good starting point. Chomsky (1983) also has contributed a chapter to a volume edited by Mehler and others, and other chapters in this book also make a contribution to Chomskyan theory. Chomsky's formulation is not the only generative grammar system. Horrocks (1987) describes two other generative grammatical systems, Generalized Phrase Structure Grammar and Lexical-Function Grammar, as alternatives to the traditional transformational approach. For those adventuresome souls who want to tackle some of Chomsky's professional writing, try *Aspects of the Theory of Syntax* (1965). One of the issues raised by Chomsky's work is the concept of linguistic universals. This notion has been explored in a recent book (Hawkins, 1988).

Students who want to learn more about language acquisition could start with any of several excellent books. Clark and Clark (1977) have written a comprehensive introduction to psycholinguistics, as have De Villiers and De Villiers (1978). Aitchison's (1983) book is easy to read and informative, and her more recent book (1987) could also be read profitably in connection with this chapter. Ellis and Beattie (1986) have written a general, more recent introduction to the cognitive operations involved in communicating. The edited volume by Franklin and Barten (1987) covers a variety of topics from a developmental perspective including children's understanding of discourse and metaphor. Another edited volume (Kessel, 1988) also covers developmental aspects of language.

KEY TERMS

Syntax	Duality of patterning	Phrase structure
Grammar	Displacement (as a design	Constituents
Semantics	feature)	Surface structure
Continuity theory	Productivity	Deep structure
Design features	Linguistic universals	Specializations for language
Phoneme	Recursion	Aphasia
Morpheme	Finite state grammar	Categorical perception

FOCUS ON RESEARCH

....

Language Acquisition in Feral Children

This chapter discussed categorical perception of speech sounds by infants, and the research suggests that at least the basis for discriminating speech sound seems to be inborn. But this doesn't mean that children have speech sounds built into their brains. Clearly, some sort of experience with language is necessary to become fluent. But exactly what experiences are necessary, and how much of them are necessary? Perhaps this question is what prompted many theorists to wonder what would happen to a child who wasn't talked to.

Over the years, many cases of so-called feral children have occurred. Feral children are abandoned children who have fended for themselves in the wild, and they invariably have linguistic deficits. Usually, it's not clear how long such children have been left on their own. Neither is it typically known to what extent they were cared for prior to their abandonment. For these reasons, it's difficult to know the extent to which the language deficits were produced by the social deprivation. For obvious ethical reasons, a controlled experiment cannot be done to answer this question, but sometimes the world offers illuminating cases.

Genie was born in April 1957 and was reared under the most abject conditions:

> From the age of twenty months, Genie had been confined to a small room . . . She was physically punished by her father if she made any sounds. Most of the time she was kept harnessed into an infant's potty chair: Otherwise she was confined in a home-made sleeping bag in an infant's crib covered with wire mesh. (Curtiss, Fromkin, Krashen, Rigler, & Rigler, 1974, p. 529)

Genie was fed by her blind mother in a highly routinized way; little or no conversation took place between them. Apparently, her father and older brother never spoke to her. Genie was almost fourteen years old when she was discovered; at that time she could not speak at all. Since then, researchers have followed the course of her language acquisition with interest. Soon apparent was that, in most areas, Genie's development proceeded at a pace much slower than that of other children. For example, normal children begin expressing negatives by simply putting the word *no* in front of already established utterances ("No want go"). Genie also used this form. However, whereas normal children typically pass through this stage quickly, Genie used this primitive form of negation for two years. Normal children begin asking "Wh——" questions ("Where mommy?") around two years of age. However, Genie never mastered this ability, and her attempts were ungrammatical. She did excel in the acquisition of vocabulary. Although her overall language competence seemed to be that of a three-year-old, her vocabulary was much larger than that of a typical three-year-old.

Curtiss (1977) later wrote a follow-up account of Genie, who by then was eighteen years old. Curtiss noted that Genie spoke in short sentences whose grammatical forms were fairly primitive. However, Genie's knowledge of speech, including her knowledge of English word order, seemed fine. Although her production of syntactically correct sentences is limited (and Curtiss apparently believes that these effects are permanent), Genie's comprehension is more or less unaffected by her years of deprivation.

Apparently, some innate linguistic predispositions can survive a traumatic and deprived upbringing. But other specializations, including those that enable people to acquire syntax, can apparently be destroyed if the individual doesn't have adequate opportunities to use them.

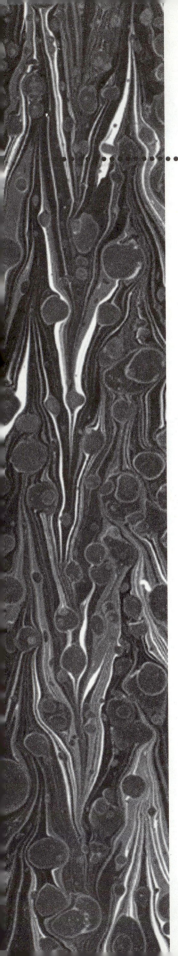

CHAPTER **9**

••

COGNITIVE PROCESSES IN SPEECH AND LANGUAGE PERCEPTION

CHAPTER OUTLINE

OVERVIEW

Recently, my wife bought a series of tapes whose purpose was to teach the listener how to understand and speak Italian. Our thinking was that we could listen to these tapes when we took trips in our car, thus doing something productive during the drive. I had never studied Italian, but I had studied Latin, so I thought I would be able to follow along right from the start. I was wrong about that: I got absolutely nowhere in my initial attempts at understanding the typical tourist-ordering-in-a-cafe conversation. If you've studied a foreign language, then you have an idea of what I experienced: a profound confusion at what seems like a totally formless babble. The sounds are different, the sequences of sounds are unpredictable, the beginnings and endings of words cannot be discerned, and of course, the meaning is completely lost. But then, after listening for a while, and with a little coaching from the tape, something interesting began to happen. The foreign speech began to take form. I was somehow able to begin to "tune into" the different sounds and they started to make some sense. For example, when I first heard a speaker say "ahranjhadah" (that's what it sounded like), I didn't know what to make of it, except that it didn't sound like an Italian word. Then when I found out that it meant "orangeade," I was able to mentally accomplish a sort of deliberate equivalence, "orangeade" = "ahranjhadah." But then when it dawned on me that the Italians pronounced every vowel, including what for us is a silent *e* at the end, I had a new level of comprehension in which "ahranjhadah" sounded like a perfectly natural word for orangeade.

This chapter considers some of the numerous issues involved in perceiving and using speech. Let's consider what's required. First, the comprehension of speech requires an ability to perceive the speech sounds of a particular language. This question is one of feature detection and pattern recognition. What are the features of speech sounds? This chapter tries to answer that question.

Even after the speech sounds are correctly detected and categorized, the listener's work is far from over. The sounds must be organized into words. This means that the listener must quickly produce a cognitive code that maintains the order in which the sounds were heard. Further, the speaker must have some way of determining the boundaries between the words. This is no easy trick. We seem to be naturally aware of the pauses between words, but most of the pauses we hear are really not there. We'll examine some of the factors that enable native speakers to determine word boundaries in ongoing speech.

We can not only comprehend speech but also produce it. We'll examine speech production, which seems to be accomplished in a series of stages, each consisting of a cognitive code that is modified by successive cognitive operations. Some of these cognitive operations can be glimpsed by analyzing errors in speech production. We'll study and interpret some common errors.

As you read this material, keep in mind the top-down–bottom-up distinction first raised in Chapter 2. Probably nowhere else in cognitive psychology is the interplay of these two modes more intertwined. Understanding and producing speech requires a knowledge of how top-down and bottom-up processes interact. Keep your eyes open for this interaction as you read the chapter.

PERCEPTION AND COMPREHENSION OF SPEECH

Speech sounds are not naturally distinct from one another; they usually have no readily distinguishable boundaries between them. Moreover, the pauses that we seem to hear between words and phrases are often illusory. For these reasons, Clark and Clark (1977) have noted that the problems involved in comprehending speech are similar to the difficulties we would have extracting a signal from a warbling siren. This section describes some of the problems of speech perception and comprehension, and discusses some of the approaches various disciplines have taken to understand them.

Why Speech Perception Is Such a Problem: The Stream of Speech

Clark and Clark (1977) have written of the problems posed by speech perception, and my account is based largely on theirs. Illustrating a complex problem is sometimes best accomplished by analogy—even though the analogy might be incorrect. That's the case here.

Let's suppose that speech could accurately be represented by letters. That is, let's assume for a moment that the letters of a sentence such as:

Jim is a hero.

each stood for a particular unit of sound, or **phoneme.** If this state of affairs were true, then speech comprehension would be easy to understand. Why? Because in that case, each phoneme would be distinct from the phonemic segments that preceded and followed it. Assuming that each phoneme is a distinct acoustic event with distinct acoustic properties, the perceiver would simply engage in the following sequence of events: (1) map the acoustic signal onto his knowledge of phonetics, (2) determine which phoneme had been signaled, (3) store this representation, and (4) add onto it the next phoneme that was detected, and so on.

Although comparing speech to print seems natural, the resulting "theory" of speech perception thus implied is unfortunately almost completely wrong. First, speech is ongoing. Letters are discrete, separable stimuli. But speech sounds are not discrete and separable. The stream of speech is hardly ever marked by periods of silence. Second, unlike letters, phonetic segments are usually influenced by their location within a word. Consider, for example the /m/ sounds in *Tim* and *mink*. The letter *m* is used to designate this sound in both cases, and we truly hear the same sound at the beginning of *mink* and at the end of *Tim*. Yet, the acoustic properties of the /m/ sound are markedly different in these two cases. In other words, although we hear these sounds as the same, their pronunciation is different. You can readily see the problem here. The symbol /m/ denotes some regularity in our perception of sounds. But this regularity in perception seems to be independent of any particular regularity in the acoustic patterns themselves.

Third, the opposite problem sometimes emerges: We perceive as different speech sounds that aren't different at the acoustic level. For example, consider the words *writer* and *rider*. Like most people, you probably hear a difference between the /t/ and /d/ sounds. Consequently, it seems reasonable to look at the speech stream with an eye to finding what the person does with her mouth to make the /t/ as opposed to the /d/ sound in this situation. But your search would be in vain: In this case, the two sounds have no phonetic distinction per se. The only pronunciation difference between the two words is the length of time the vowel

/ay/ (this is the way this sound is designated) is held. The /ay/ in *rider* is held slightly longer that the /ay/ in *writer*.

These difficulties are not the only ones that cognitive psychologists must face in grappling with speech perception; they are also faced with the order problem. To identify the word *pill*, a person not only must identify the phonetic segments /p/, /i/, and /l/ but also must keep their order straight. If this process weren't done, the person would be unable to distinguish *pill* from other words made up of the same phonetic segments arranged differently (such as *lip*).

Warren, Obusek, Farmer, and Warren (1969) played sequences of sounds such as a hiss, a vowel, a buzz, and a musical tone for their subjects. They found that the subjects could not accurately report the order of the sounds if they were played at a rate of 1.5 segments per second or greater. However, speech typically proceeds at 12 phonetic segments per second and is intelligible at rates of up to 50 segments per second. There are two ways of accounting for this finding. First, the appearance of a particular phonetic segment may constrain the range of phonemes that might appear next. If this were true, then hearing a particular phoneme might enable the perceiver to shrewdly guess which phonemes were likely to appear next, thus narrowing the range of phonemes that would have to be processed. On the other hand, the possibility exists that phonemes are not processed sequentially but rather in bunches. This process could be accomplished if each phoneme included an acoustic clue about the phoneme or phonemes that were upcoming. This would mean that phonemes are never produced in isolation—they always contain information about the phoneme to come, which results in their own pronunciation being altered. This second interpretation seems to be the more likely explanation of the Warren et al. findings.

How Speech Sounds Are Categorized

Phonetics and Phonology   The last section examined some of the reasons why speech perception is so complicated. This section deals with the attacks on the problem. Understanding the basics of speech perception is almost impossible without some background in **phonetics** and **phonology.** Phoneticians try to describe the nature of linguistic sounds. There are two varieties of phoneticians. *Acoustic phoneticians* analyze the physical characteristics of speech sounds. *Articulatory phoneticians* try to specify the nature of linguistic sounds by determining the patterns of tongue placement, airflow, and vocal cavity changes that characterize different sounds. Table 9.1 shows the symbols phoneticians have developed to represent linguistic sounds.

Phonology is a branch of linguistics that attempts to determine the rules, or principles, that characterize the production and comprehension of speech sounds. Phonologists don't deal with the sounds directly, in the same sense that linguists are not necessarily interested in the production of specific sentences. Rather, the phonologist is interested in the more abstract aspects of speech sounds—the general knowledge a person has that enables him to formulate specific utterances. For example, consider the word *electric*. The final *c* sound, symbolized with a /k/, is a "hard" sound. When we change the adjective to a noun (i.e., *electricity*), we know that the hard sound softens to an /s/. Knowledge of this rule also enables the speaker to pronounce the noun derived from *egocentric*, even if she has never seen or heard that noun before. As this example suggests, both phonetic and phonological knowledge seem to be required for successful speech comprehension and production.

·············· **TABLE 9.1**   Phonetic symbols

CONSONANTS				VOWELS		DIPHTHONGS	
p	pill	θ	thigh	i	beet	ay	bite
b	bill	ð	thy	ι	bit	æw	about
m	mill	š	shallow	e	bait	cy	boy
t	till	ž	measure	ε	bet		
d	dill	č	chip	æ	bat		
n	nil		gyp	u	boot		
k	kill	l	lip	U	put		
g	gill	r	rip	»	but		
η	sing	y	yet	o	boat		
f	fill	w	wet	e	bought		
v	vat	ʌ	whet	a	pot		
s	sip	h	hat	·	sofa		
z	zip			ɨ	marry		

Source: Clark and Clark. (Copyright 1977 by Harcourt, Brace, Jovanovich. Adapted by permission of the publisher and author.)

Articulatory Phonetics   The articulatory gestures involved in speech can be divided into two broad classes: those gestures that produce vowel sounds and those that produce consonants. Producing consonants usually involves a constriction of the oral cavity, which is generally accompanied by movement of the tongue. Vowel sounds are considerably more open and static; little movement is involved during vowel production. Speech proceeds by the production of syllables, which are constructed by embedding a vowel sound or sounds within a string of consonants (Clark & Clark, 1977). During the initial part of the syllable's production, movement and constriction of the vocal cavity occur. In the middle of the syllable's production is a short period during which the vowel is sounded; this sound is heard as a "constant" sound. Finally, in the last part of the syllable, the ending consonantal sound is produced, again with movement and constriction. Given that the consonants apparently include information about the sounds to come, the pronunciation of the consonant must somehow change to reflect the identity of the upcoming vowel. This process is vividly expressed in the following passage:

> Consonants are pronounced as the tongue and mouth move from the vowel of one syllable to the vowel of the next. The consonants hang off one or both sides of each vowel, so to speak, and depend for their very existence on the pronunciation of the vowel. (Clark & Clark, 1977, p. 180)

Consonants can differ in three ways. First, the **place of articulation** describes which part of the mouth is constricted to produce the consonant. In the English language, this constriction can take place at any of seven points, as shown in Table 9.2. Notice that the table shows constriction points from the front of the mouth to the back; the constriction can occur at various places from the lips to the throat.

Consonants can also differ in their **manner of articulation**—the way in which the constriction is produced. On this basis, consonants can be classified into one of six categories: *stops, fricatives, affricatives, nasals, laterals,* and *semivowels*. Stops are formed by completely closing the vocal cavity at the point of articulation. For example, producing /b/ involves a brief but complete closure of the lips, followed by a release of the pressure that has built up during the closure. Fricatives are the result of less complete closures. For example, in producing the

·············· **TABLE 9.2   The seven places of articulation**

1. The two lips together (called *bilabial*)
2. The bottom lip against the upper front teeth (*labiodental*)
3. The tongue against the teeth (*dental*)
4. The tongue against the alveolar ridge of the gums just behind the upper front teeth (*alveolar*)
5. The tongue against the hard palate in the roof of the mouth just behind the alveolar ridge (*palatal*)
6. The tongue against the soft palate, or velum, in the rear roof of the mouth (*velar*)
7. The glottis in the throat (*glottal*)

Source: Clark and Clark. (Copyright 1977 by Harcourt, Brace, Jovanovich. Adapted by permission of the publisher and author.)

consonant /s/, you're probably aware that the tongue is touching but is not completely pressed against the alveolar ridge. Affricatives are produced in two steps, involving both a complete closure and a fricativelike turbulence. Affricatives, such as /j/ as in *judge*, are combinations of stops and fricatives. Nasals, naturally enough, involve the nose. For example, in producing /m/, the tongue is pushed up against the soft palate, closing it. The air is then expelled through the nose. Shutting the nose makes it impossible to produce nasals accurately (if you don't believe me, try humming something while you have a cold). The lateral /l/ is produced by flattening the tongue and letting the air flow around its sides. In contrast, the semivowels involve folding the tongue in the middle and letting the air flow through it. If you contrast the pronunciation of /l/ with /r/, you'll feel how the shape of the tongue (rather than its placement, which is the same in both cases) contributes to the difference in perceived sound.

One other way of distinguishing consonants is based on the degree of **voicing** present. Voiced consonants are accompanied by vibration of the vocal cords; voiceless consonants are not (recall that we briefly examined this distinction in Chapter 8). In the English language, voicing is the only way that some pairs of consonants, such as /d/—/t/, can be distinguished. Table 9.3 shows a classification of the phonetic symbols that denote the English consonants.

The information in Table 9.3 can tell us a lot about speech perception. If, for example, a speech pathologist asked a client to say "cake" and the client's production sounded something like "take," he could readily interpret the client's difficulties. Table 9.3 shows that /k/ is a velar, voiceless stop, and /t/ is an alveolar, voiceless stop. In other words, the child who says "take" for "cake" is "fronting" a "back" consonant, suggesting a breakdown in the articulatory program, which is shown in a front-back confusion.

·············· **TABLE 9.3   A classification of consonants**

	BILABIAL	LABIODENTAL	DENTAL	ALVEOLAR	PALATAL	VELAR	GLOTTAL
Stops	p b			t d		k g	
Fricatives		f v	θð	s z	šž		h
Affricatives					čj		
Nasals	m			n		ŋ	
Laterals				l			
Semivowels	w			r	y		

Source: Clark and Clark. (Copyright 1977 by Harcourt, Brace, Jovanovich. Adapted by permission of the publisher and author.)

Note: Symbols on the left side of each column are voiceless. Those on the right side are voiced.

Unlike consonants, which are produced by altering the nature and degree of constriction, vowels are regulated by curvature of the tongue. This curvature can vary in two ways. First, the degree of tongue curvature is referred to as its height in the mouth. Tongue placement can be high (as in *bit*), middle level (as in *bet*), or low level (as in *bat*). Second, the part of the tongue that is held highest can also vary. For example, the pronunciation of *bit* requires that the front of the tongue be held highest. In the pronunciation of /ɨ/ as in *marry*, the middle of the tongue is held highest. Finally, in the pronunciation of some vowels such as the /u/ in *boot*, the back of the tongue is highest. The results of this two-way classification of vowels are seen in Table 9.4.

If you pronounce the word *sofa* and pay attention to your tongue movements, you'll probably become aware that little muscular movement seems to be required to produce the second vowel sound. Indeed, the /ə/ sound, called the *schwa*, never appears in accented syllables, almost as if it can't be pronounced with stress. This phenomenon tells us something about the relationship of tongue movements and accents within a word. Some amount of muscular tension is apparently required if the syllable contains an accented vowel. That is, the muscles involved must pull the tongue away from its central position (see Table 9.4) if the syllable is to be stressed. Without such muscular tension, the tongue returns to its unstressed position, which is used to produce the schwa. If the stops are the most consonantal of the consonants, then the schwa is the most vowel-like of the vowels.

Distinctive Features in Speech For the past forty years, linguists have maintained that the *organization* of speech sounds is what enables us to distinguish them from one another. According to this view, the articulatory gestures form the basis for a number of characteristics called **distinctive features,** some of which can be used to distinguish phonemic segments from one another. Some of these features are closely related to the articulatory gestures we've examined. For example, one of the features is voicing. If a consonant is voiced, it is indicated this way [+voice]. If the consonant is unvoiced, it is designated with a minus sign in the brackets: [−voice]. Rather than thinking of the phoneme as an articulatory gesture or acoustic energy, we may grasp the problem of speech perception by thinking of phonemes as bundles of features.

If you produce a speech sound and your vocal cords vibrate in the production of that sound, then this vibration will produce a change in the acoustic energy coming out of your mouth. Apparently, we have certain cognitive processes that are tuned in to detect whatever has changed about the acoustic

.... **TABLE 9.4** Two-way classification of English vowels

| Height of Tongue | PART OF THE TONGUE INVOLVED | | |
	Front	Central	Back
High	i beet	ɨ marry	u boot
	ɩ bit		∪ put
Mid	e bait	ə sofa	o boat
	ɛ bet		ɔ bought
Low	æ bat	ʌ but	a pot

Source: Clark and Clark. (Copyright 1977 by Harcourt, Brace, Jovanovich. Adapted by permission of the publisher and author.)

code. If the vocal cords are vibrating, then the cognitive processes tuned to speech note a [+voice] feature on that particular segment of sound. The features are based on articulatory and acoustic aspects of speech sounds, but they are psychological categories nevertheless because they are detected and assigned by cognitive processes. Each phoneme is distinctive because it has a unique pattern of distinctive features.

Chomsky and Halle (1968) performed such an analysis of English speech sounds. They argued that all consonants and vowels can be categorized using thirteen distinctive features. This categorization is shown in Table 9.5. Some of the distinctive features require explanation. All true consonants are [+consonantal] and [−vocalic], just as all true vowels are the opposite. However, the liquids /l/ and /r/ have properties of both consonants and vowels, making them somewhat ambiguous. Similarly ambiguous are the semivowels /y/ and /w/, which don't have the properties of either consonants or vowels. The anterior feature results when the phoneme is made at the front of the mouth ([+anterior]) or elsewhere ([−anterior]). Similarly, if the phoneme is produced in the top center of the mouth, it is designated [+coronal]. If a feature is [+continuant], it is produced with a continuous sound. For example, all the fricatives are [+continuant]. Phonemes without this quality are marked [−continuant]. Stridency is based on the buzzing quality associated with some phonemes. For example, the vibrations associated with a fricative such as /f/ are apparent; this phoneme is also marked [+strident]. We've already discussed voicing, and nasality is self-descriptive.

The features consonantal and vocalic reappear to distinguish the vowels. The other elements of the cardinal vowel diagram shown in Table 9.4 also

·············· **TABLE 9.5** **The distinctive features of consonants and vowels**

CONSONANTS AND LIQUIDS																				
Distinctive Feature	*p*	*b*	*t*	*d*	*č*	*ǰ*	*k*	*g*	*f*	*v*	*θ*	*ǒ*	*s*	*z*	*š*	*ž*	*r*	*l*	*m*	*n*	*ŋ*
Consonantal	+	+	+	+	+	+	+	+	+	+	+	+	+	+	+	+	+	+	+	+	+
Vocalic	−	−	−	−	−	−	−	−	−	−	−	−	−	−	−	−	+	+	−	−	−
Anterior	+	+	+	+	−	−	−	−	+	+	+	+	+	−	−	−	−	+	+	+	−
Coronal	−	−	+	+	+	+	−	−	−	−	+	+	+	+	+	+	+	+	−	+	−
Voice	−	+	−	+	−	+	−	+	−	+	−	+	−	+	−	+	+	+	+	+	+
Nasal	−	−	−	−	−	−	−	−	−	−	−	−	−	−	−	−	−	−	+	+	+
Strident	−	−	−	−	+	+	−	−	+	+	−	−	+	+	+	+	−	−	−	−	−
Continuant	−	−	−	−	−	−	−	−	+	+	+	+	+	+	+	+	+	+	−	−	−

VOWELS AND GLIDES																
Distinctive Feature	*ɨ*	*ɪ*	*e*	*ε*	*æ*	*i*	*ə*	*ʌ*	*a*	*u*	*U*	*o*	*ɔ*	*y*	*w*	*h*
Vocalic	+	+	+	+	+	+	+	+	+	+	+	+	+	−	−	−
Consonantal	−	−	−	−	−	−	−	−	−	−	−	−	−	−	−	−
High	+	+	−	−	−	+	−	−	−	+	+	−	−	+	+	−
Back	−	−	−	−	−	+	+	+	+	+	+	+	+	−	+	−
Low	−	−	−	−	+	−	−	+	+	−	−	−	+	−	−	+
Round	−	−	−	−	−	−	−	−	−	+	+	+	+	−	+	−
Tense	+	−	+	−	+	−	−	−	+	+	−	+	−	−	−	−

Source: Clark and Clark. (Copyright 1977 by Harcourt, Brace, Jovanovich. Adapted by permission of the publisher and author.)

reappear in somewhat altered form. The height feature has been broken down into two opposed features: high and low. For example, the phoneme /i/ (the vowel sound in *beet*) is marked [+high] and [−low]. The other dimension from Table 9.4 was the front-back distinction, which reappears in Table 9.5 as the features back and round. For example, the vowel /u/, as in *boot*, involves the back of the tongue and is designated in the chart as [+back]. The final feature is tension. Tension is difficult to get a subjective feeling for, but it is related to the amount of muscular effort that is needed to produce the vowel. One of the last vowel sounds to emerge as children acquire speech is /i/, apparently because of the movement involved. Predictably, this vowel is marked [+tense], whereas a lax vowel such as the schwa is marked [−tense].

Table 9.5 can tell us a lot about the nature of speech perception. Notice that most of the phonemes have more than one feature distinguishing them. For example, /b/ and /t/ are phonetically distinguishable by their place of articulation. According to Table 9.5, this difference translates into a difference of two distinctive features. That is, /b/ is [−coronal], and /t/ is [+coronal]. Also, /b/ is [+voice], and /t/ is [−voice]. This may raise a question in your mind. Why are /b/ and /t/ different in two dimensions, when, technically, a difference on just one dimension should be enough to tell one sound from another? The answer is that some redundancy appears to be built into the speech recognition system. That is, in a sense, we're giving our speech recognizers two chances to make the discrimination between /b/ and /t/. If these recognizers miss the coronal difference, recognition will still be accurate as long as they catch the voicing difference between the two sounds. This also implies that the acoustic information in speech must be fairly subtle. If the features were more perceptible, we probably wouldn't see so much redundancy built into Table 9.5. This fact has some other implications for speech recognition, too. If Table 9.5 is an accurate depiction of speech features, we would expect that, if subjects misperceive speech sounds, their confusions should be between sounds that have only one distinguishing feature between them. The following section examines a well-known study that addresses this matter.

Comprehension of Isolated Speech Sounds   Miller and Nicely (1955) have answered many of the basic questions about comprehension and confusion of speech sounds. Their five subjects listened to a series of sixteen consonants, each of which was followed by the vowel /a/, the vowel sound in *pot*. In many of the cases, the sound was masked by white noise. The loudness of the white noise was held constant throughout the study, but the loudness of the speech signal was varied. Seven levels of speech loudness were used, ranging from one-twelfth as loud as the white noise (−18 decibels when expressed as a signal-to-noise ratio) to twelve times louder than the white noise (or +18 decibels). The subjects' task was to correctly identify the consonant. Their dedication brings tears to the eyes of all but the most hardened researchers: Miller and Nicely asked their subjects to make almost seventy thousand consonant identifications over a period of several months.

In their original form, the findings were difficult to summarize, but this task has been eased by Shepard (1972), who developed the tableau shown in Figure 9.1.

The array in Figure 9.1 might seem bewildering at first, but its interpretation is quite straightforward. Consonants that are depicted as physically close together are more likely to be confused for one another than are consonants that are shown with distance between them. For example, /k/ was very likely to be

·············· **FIGURE 9.1**   **Representations of the effect of signal-to-noise ratio on confusions among Miller and Nicely's sixteen consonants.**

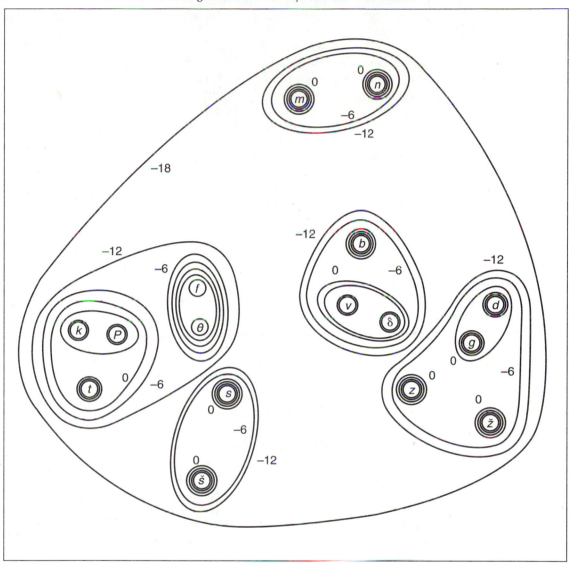

(From R. N. Shepard, "Psychological Representation of Speech Sounds." In *Human Communication, A Unified View.* E. E. David, P. B. Denes, eds, © 1972 by McGraw-Hill.)

confused with /p/. The lines around the consonants show the intensity at which the speech signal had to be transmitted before the consonant in question could be correctly identified. Each contour line is labeled numerically, with the negative numbers showing greater intensity of the masking noise relative to the speech signal. When the speech signal was only one-twelfth as loud as the masking noise (−18 decibels), all the consonants were confused with one another. Consequently, the line labeled "−18" encircles all the consonants in the display. However, when the intensity of the speech signal was boosted up to −12 decibels, certain clusters of consonants could be distinguished from one another. For example, the cluster /s/š/ could now be distinguished from the adjacent cluster /f/θ/k/p/t. Looking within this latter cluster, when the speech signal's intensity was again boosted up, this time to −6 decibels, a further discrimination could then be made. The consonants /k/p/t/ could be distinguished from /f/θ/.

Analyzing the contour lines in this way produces the following clusters of confusion:

m − n f − θ v–ð p − t–k d − g s − š z − ž

That is, these groups required that the speech signal be boosted up to at least the same intensity as the noise (0 decibels) before the elements of the group could be discriminated from one another. Referring to Table 9.5, you can verify that, considered pairwise, the members of these groups do tend to differ from one another on only one distinctive feature.

The Need for a Phonological Level   Students sometimes wonder why knowing about phonology is important to understanding speech perception. After all, they reason, don't the findings of Miller and Nicely tell us what features of speech are attended to, encoded, and used as the basis of perception? The answer to this question is yes and no.

Miller and Nicely's work points out that the articulatory features as conceived by phoneticians would probably be inadequate to enable speech perception by themselves. Rather, the speech signal seems to contain more information than those voicing and articulation features shown in Table 9.3. Instead, Miller and Nicely have suggested that something like five channels of speech perception pick up as many as thirteen different kinds of binary-opposed features as suggested by Chomsky and Halle (1968).

This view is not without its problems, however. First, Miller and Nicely's work clearly implies that the speech signal must have something invariant across a variety of situations, or we would never be able to comprehend speech. That is, they claim that speech must have some invariant acoustic features, which are capable of being detected by some type of feature analyzers. However, when the acoustic information in the speech signal is analyzed, numerous situations exist in which people perceive different sounds in acoustic events that are identical (Liberman, Cooper, Shankweiler, & Studdert-Kennedy, 1967). Other research has also suggested that consonant perception must be strongly vowel driven. Blumstein, Tartter, Nigro, and Statlender (1984) artificially enhanced some of the acoustic information in a series of stopped consonants. Next, these consonants were synthesized on a computer and played for subjects. If the subjects are using acoustic information to perceive speech, such enhanced consonants should be easier to detect than they are in natural speech. This hypothesis was not supported, however. Neither normal individuals nor aphasics found the lengthened consonants any easier to recognize.

Generally speaking, the search for "context-independent" features in speech perception has not met with much success (Remez, 1979, 1980). What's the alternative? One way of approaching the problem of relativity in speech sounds is to look for what are called "context-dependent" features (Pisoni, 1978). These are not invariant features that permit immediate recognition in all situations for all speakers. Instead, they are features whose acoustic coding changes depending on the phonetic context in which the sounds appear. According to this view, speech perception proceeds by mapping the acoustic code onto some abstract set of rules flexible enough to adjust for the contextual influences that have distorted the speech sounds away from some idealized pronunciation.

Linguists have argued that these rules are phonological in nature. Phonological rules are based on the notion of distinctive features, but here this term is used somewhat differently from the way I've used it so far. For the phonologist, a sound is made up of distinctive features—features whose presence is *not predictable from the other features in the immediate vicinity*.

For example, consider the word *spin*. It has four phonetic segments, corresponding to each of its letters. Referring to Table 9.5, we can see that looking up each segment's list of features is easy. This has been done in Table 9.6, which also shows the phonological representation for *spin*.

Notice that the phonological representation doesn't have many features; indeed, the initial segment /s/ has only one: [+consonantal]. How can the presence of just one feature enable someone to identify the speech sound in question? The answer lies in the two-consonant rule: Whenever a phonetic segment is detected that is [+consonantal] and it's followed by a segment that is [+consonantal] and [−vocalic], then the first segment must also be marked [−vocalic], [+anterior], [+coronal], [−voice], [+continuant], [−nasal], and [+strident]. If you refer to Table 9.5, you will see that this is exactly the set of features that specifies the phonetic segment /s/. If this explanation seems too abstract, the two-consonant rule has a down-to-earth alternative phrasing: If an English word begins with two true consonants (i.e., [+consonantal] and [−vocalic]), then the first one must be an /s/. When I first came across this rule, I was astonished by its implications. I thought some exception must exist—but it doesn't. Try it yourself. Take any true consonant from Table 9.5 and imagine it in the second position of some to-be-generated word. Then, given that situation, try to come up with a word that has anything other than an /s/ in the initial position.

Phonological rules are to speech perception and production what syntactic rules are to sentence comprehension and generation. Just as syntactic knowledge enables us to know what sequences of words are legitimate in our language, phonology enables us to judge which sequences of sounds are legitimate words. From an empirical standpoint, it's easy to see how the existence of such phonological rules aids speech perception. For example, the two-consonant rule means that, if a word begins with two consonants, the feature analyzers have to pick up only one feature from the initial consonant, [+consonantal], to identify it as an /s/. This means that the acoustic signal need not specify all the features of the sound in question. We can rely on our prestored knowledge of phonology to fill in information missing or undetected from the stream of speech.

·············   **TABLE 9.6**   The phonetic representation of *spin* and its underlying phonological representation

	S	P	I	N
Underlying phonological representation	+Consonantal	+Anterior −Coronal −Continuant −Strident	+High −Back −Low −Tense	+Anterior +Coronal +Nasal
Final phonetic representation	−Vocalic +Consonantal +Anterior +Coronal −Voice +Continuant −Nasal +Strident	−Vocalic +Consonantal +Anterior −Coronal −Voice −Continuant −Nasal −Strident	+Vocalic −Consonantal +High −Back −Low −Round −Tense	−Vocalic +Consonantal +Anterior +Coronal +Voice −Continuant +Nasal −Strident

Source: Clark and Clark. (Copyright 1977 by Harcourt, Brace, Jovanovich. Adapted by permission of the publisher and author.)

Stages of Speech Perception: From the Bottom Up

Let's review some of the elements that appear to be required in any theory of isolated speech sounds before we go on to examine the perception of continuous speech.

Speech perception seems to take place in a series of independent stages (Pisoni, 1978), each of which modifies and elaborates the code produced by the preceding stage. How much of this processing is sequential and how much is done in parallel has been a topic of controversy (Pisoni & Sawusch, 1975). However, a reasonable consensus seems to exist about the basic components involved.

1. Auditory Stage.   At the auditory stage, the acoustic signal is converted into a neurological representation that preserves various features of the physical signal. For example, feature analysis at the auditory stage is presumed to encode the sound's fundamental frequency, as well as some details of its harmonic structure. In addition, in the auditory stage, a code representing the signal's overall intensity and duration is produced. This code is presumed to be stored in some form of sensory storage, and for this reason, the code at the auditory stage is sometimes called "raw." At this point, no phonetic or phonological information has been extracted from the signal.

2. Phonetic Stage.   The main purpose of the phonetic stage is to name the speech sounds correctly, that is, to assign phonetic labels to the speech signal that are congruent with the speaker's intentions. Here, the listener faces a major difficulty known as the segmentation problem, which was alluded to in an earlier section of this chapter. The segmentation problem can be stated this way: Because speech resembles a warbling siren, with hardly any pauses, how is the listener supposed to know where to put the boundaries around phonetic segments to identify them? Fortunately for us, speech is constructed by syllables. This means that the influences that vowels have on the production of consonants will probably be most often limited to a range of one syllable. The implication is that some perceptual mechanism must be set, or tuned, to look for patterns of alternating constriction and openness, which are then categorically boxed into syllables whose phonetic names are subsequently determined.

3. Phonological Stage.   At the phonological stage, the phonetic segments that have just been identified are mapped onto underlying (more abstract) phonological rules that extract the true essence from the phonetic segment. This true essence refers to information about the phoneme that permits its other features to be computed from knowledge of phonological rules. As we saw, for example, knowledge of the two-consonant rule enables a person to compute the identity of the first consonant in a two-consonant sequence. Thus, if /s/ happened to be misidentified as /š/ in the phonetic stage, then cognitive processes in the phonological stage would correct this error if the next segment identified was another true consonant.

Phonological rules are inevitably language specific, meaning that the rules of English can be used only to discriminate sounds that make a difference in meaning in English. To understand this point, say *pit* out loud, and pay attention to the /p/ as you do so. Next, contrast the /p/ of *pit* with the /p/ in *spit*. What's the difference? You were probably aware that the /p/ in *pit* is accompanied by a little puff of built-up air, but the /p/ in *spit* wasn't pronounced that way. Linguists refer to the first /p/ as *aspirated* and the second one as *nonaspirated*. The different /p/

sounds in these two cases are said to be *allophones* of each other. Allophones are variations in pronunciation that don't signal any difference in meaning. *Pit* is still *pit,* regardless of how much air pressure you happen to build up during its pronunciation. Since we don't use aspiration to signal any difference in meaning, phonological rules in English don't have anything to say about aspiration. But in other languages, aspiration signals a difference in meaning. For example, in Thai, /p^{h}aa/ (aspirated) means "split," whereas /p°aa/ (nonaspirated) means "forest." Allophonic variations are resolved at the phonological stage. For a speaker of English, during the phonological stage, both /p^h/ and /p°/ are mapped onto the same underlying phonological segment, /p/, before any further /p/ rules are applied. However, in Thai, this difference is preserved because some phonological rules presumably apply only to the aspirated or nonaspirated /p/.

Perception of Continuous Speech: From the Top Down

The discussion of speech perception so far has focused on those elements of speech that must be extracted more or less directly from the speech signal. However, even if all the bottom-up mechanisms go awry, we can still use larger units of speech to help us comprehend the message. For example, if you hear someone say,

> "She did really well on the test—in fact, she got the highest grade in the whole _____ ."

you know the missing word is *class,* or *section,* or something to that effect. Even before the last word occurs, you can predict what it's going to be. The sentence is so redundant that much of the speech signal can be left unprocessed without much loss in meaning. It's not clear what proportion of the speech signal is typically processed this way, but Pollack and Pickett (1964) have produced some surprising findings. They covertly recorded people in spontaneous conversations. The participants gave no indication that they misunderstood one another; the replies to questions, jokes, and so on were all appropriate to the situation. Pollack and Pickett then cut the tapes to make recordings of isolated words. The tapes were played for the subjects, who were asked to identify the word. The subjects were successful on 47 percent of the trials—a fairly low percentage. Pollack and Pickett then asked an interesting question: How much context is necessary for a listener to accurately identify a word? As they added larger and larger segments of the original tape to the single words, they found that identification accuracy slowly improved until a certain critical point was reached. At this critical point, accuracy dramatically improved. The self-reports of the subjects were congruent with these findings. The word seemed more or less unintelligible until "all of a sudden" it seemed perfectly clear.

Other research (Sitler, Schiavetti, & Metz, 1983) has clarified the role of context in speech perception. Sitler and his colleagues had twenty hearing-impaired speakers pronounce isolated words and the same words in sentences. Recordings of these pronunciations were then played for one hundred normal-hearing subjects, whose task was to write down what they understood of the words and sentences. As expected, the subjects performed better when they heard sentences rather than isolated words. However, this effect was limited to speech produced by the more skilled among the hearing-impaired speakers. When the words were produced by poorer speakers, the subjects did no better in the sentence condition than they did in the isolated word condition. This result indicates that it is not simply more sound per se that enables a person to comprehend continuous speech better than isolated words. To establish a meaningful context, the acoustic signal cannot vary outside some—presumably wide—boundaries.

A phenomenon that's related to these findings is called the **phonemic restoration effect** (Obusek & Warren, 1973; Warren, 1970; Warren & Obusek, 1971; Warren & Warren, 1970). In the original study, Warren presented twenty subjects with a tape on which the following sentence had been recorded:

> The state governors met with their respective legi*latures convening in the capital city.

The asterisk marks the point where .12 second was chopped out of the original speaker's utterance and the recording of a cough substituted in its place. Warren asked his subjects if they detected any sounds missing from the recording. Nineteen of the subjects said no, and the remaining subject misidentified the expunged sound. The subjects did detect the presence of the cough, but they were unable to locate it correctly. Later studies found that a substantial part of a word could be removed without destroying the illusion. In addition, Warren found that a tone or a buzz could be substituted for the /s/ without subjects noticing that any sounds were missing. However, subjects were quick to detect a silence, and they were also accurate in reporting its placement. This finding tells us something about the nature of the illusion. The subjects perceived the sentence as coexisting alongside some extraneous nonspeech sound. Only when the chopped-out sound was not replaced with something else did subjects realize that a gap had occurred in the speech signal.

The fact that subjects were quick to detect a silence, and that they were able to correctly place this silence, suggests that subjects' top-down analysis of speech may not occur at the expense of, that is, in place of, an analysis of the acoustic information. Rather, it may be that this is an example of parallel processing, in the sense that the acoustic analysis may occur at the same time as the top-down analysis.

These effects were seen in a study by Samuels (1981), who showed that acoustic as well as contextual information plays a role in the phonemic restoration effect (and presumably therefore in continuous speech). There were several variables in the study. In some cases, a particular phoneme was expunged from the word and its gap replaced with white noise. In other cases, the white noise was simply added to the speech signal. A second variable was the familiarity of the words altered by the first variable: Some words were familiar; others were somewhat more obscure. In addition, the length of the word was a variable: Some words were relatively short; others were longer. Finally, Samuels noted the particular phonetic segments within the words that were replaced or augmented with white noise. In some cases, the replaced phoneme was a fricative; in other cases, a stop was replaced. These manipulations were designed to produce different effects. The addition of white noise affected the acoustic information, and in addition the particular phoneme involved had acoustic implications. For example, an /s/ or a /z/ is more acoustically similar to white noise and consequently should be more influenced by it than would a stop consonant such as /b/ or /t/. However other manipulations were designed to influence contextual information and, hence, top-down processing. Thus, the familiarity of the word, or its length, affects contextual information, in the sense that a longer word provides more context than does a shorter word. The dependent variable was the degree of phonemic restoration these variables produced, that is, the extent to which the subjects continued to hear the expunged sound as being present.

Samuels found that both classes of variables were involved. The greatest degree of restoration (that is, the greatest tendency to say that speech was present when in actuality it had been replaced with white noise) was observed for longer and more familiar words. In Samuels' interpretation, these words provided more context, thus revealing the expected top-down effects. However, Samuels also found acoustic or bottom-up effects. A strong degree of phonemic restoration was observed for words in which the expunged phoneme was a fricative, rather than a stop.

However, a study of Remez, Rubin, Pisoni, and Carrell (1981) showed that, whatever the nature of the acoustic information in continuous speech, it might be more complex than what we've seen. Describing the study requires at least a rudimentary understanding of the physics of sound, and of speech sounds in particular.

Speech is a complicated waveform consisting of several components. In every speech sound, there is a fundamental frequency corresponding to the basic frequency at which our vocal folds are currently vibrating. (This is usually in the range of 250 Hz for males and 450 Hz for females.) The fact that the fundamental speech frequency of two different people may be the same may produce a question in your mind: What enables us to differentiate two singers from one another when both are singing the same note? The answer to this question involves the other components of the wave. Everybody is physically unique, and, as a result, our physiques uniquely enhance or de-emphasize certain aspects of the fundamental frequency produced by our vocal folds. These enhancements also can be depicted as separate waves whose frequencies are higher than the fundamental frequencies. The waveform of speech then typically consists of the fundamental frequency and usually two or three additional components. When this signal is displayed visually on a special machine, the concentrations of acoustic energy representing the four sound wave components, which are called **formants,** are clearly visible and, to the untrained eye, look like elongated and rather shapeless blobs. However, closer inspection of the formants reveals that they do indeed vary somewhat as a result of the particular speech sounds produced, and the fact that there is such variation suggests that the formants do bear the acoustic information that we use in our bottom-up analyses of speech.

Remez et al. recorded a natural utterance of the sentence "Where were you a year ago?" and subjected the resulting speech signal to an electronic analysis that substantially altered the formants. Put simply, the amount of acoustic information in the speech signal was reduced in the following way. Whereas the normal formant is a concentration of acoustic energy spread over a particular frequency range (thus giving them their "bloblike" shape), the formants as altered by Remez et al. were constricted to a narrow line, showing only the changes in central frequency of the three formants as the utterance was produced. Obviously, a large measure of the acoustic information normally contained in ongoing speech was sacrificed by this procedure. Remez et al. sought to determine if people could still discern the message despite the impoverishment of the acoustic information in the speech code.

Subjects who were not told what the sounds represented were not aware that the sounds represented altered speech and, consequently, were wildly inaccurate in identifying the sounds (subjects frequently reported that the sounds resembled computer beeps and chirps or "science fiction sounds"). However, when other subjects were told that they would hear a sentence reproduced by a computer and that their task was to try to identify it, recognition accuracy improved substantially, even though, obviously, there was no change at all in the signal at the acoustic level. Let's summarize and interpret the findings of Samuels, and Remez et al. Samuels demonstrated that both top-down and bottom-up processes are involved in the perception of continuous speech, suggesting that parallel processing of the speech code was taking place. Remez et al. showed that, whatever sort of acoustic information was processed, its nature was complex. Moreover, the findings of Remez et al. suggest that, to engage in top-down analysis of the acoustic information, people require a fairly lengthy sample of speech sounds, perhaps as long as that produced in a typical sentence.

Analysis by Synthesis: Interaction of Top-Down and Bottom-Up Processing

We've covered a great deal of terrain in the last several pages. Let's catch our breaths before winding up the story on speech perception. We've seen that the stream of speech is an extremely ambiguous signal. This stream offers some acoustic information that is quickly analyzed and categorized into its configuration of features. Probably at the same time these bottom-up cognitive processes are at work, top-down processes commence their operation, helping the individual infer, or fill in, missing or undetected speech information. These ideas have been lucidly expressed by Liberman:

> Some of the distinctive features that specify each phonetic segment probably can be determined from the available acoustic signal. Other distinctive features cannot be uniquely identified. The listener therefore forms a hypothesis concerning the probable phonetic content of the message that is consistent with the known features. However, he cannot test this hypothesis for its syntactic and semantic consistency until he gets a fairly long segment of speech into his temporary processing space. The speech signal therefore remains unintelligible until the listener can successfully test a hypothesis. When a hypothesis is confirmed, the signal abruptly becomes intelligible. The acoustic signal is, of course, necessary to provide even a partial specification of the phonetic signal. However, these experiments [Pollack & Pickett, 1964] indicate that in many instances the phonetic signal that the listener "hears" is internally computed. (Liberman, 1967, p. 165)

This passage implies that speech is analyzed by first synthesizing (hypothesizing) a guess about the utterance's meaning. This synthesis is based on information extracted from the acoustic events and context-based inferences made by the perceiver. Almost all existing theories of speech perception are based on a version of this **analysis by synthesis model** originally proposed by Halle and Stevens (1964). The essential idea of analysis by synthesis is that the bottom-up processes that act on the acoustic signal cannot do the whole job of speech perception by themselves. Based on an analysis of the context in which the incompletely specified speech signal occurs, the person internally computes (synthesizes) a likely candidate for the missing phonetic segment. The missing segment thus generated will next be checked to make sure that it conforms to phonological, syntactic, and semantic rules.

As we've seen, the analysis by synthesis model is a way of summarizing the interaction of two different pathways to pattern recognition. Because the acoustic events are so complex, the human perceiver must rely on some top-down, or inferential, processing. On the other hand, the top-down processes must have something—however ambiguous—to work with. At this point, the bottom-up processes come into play.

Pragmatics: Coherence in Speech

Suppose that a casual sports fan watched the final game of the NCAA men's basketball tournament and then the next day said to a colleague, "Great game yesterday, wasn't it?" But suppose the colleague was an avid sports fan who was aware not only of the NCAA final, but also of a closely contested ice hockey game in which a team was eliminated from playoff contention, a professional basketball game decided in overtime, and a no-hitter pitched on the last day of spring training. The colleague might then come back with "Which one?"

We might say that the communication process suffered a temporary breakdown here, but notice that the problem was not caused by an ambiguous grammatical formulation. Rather, in this situation, and every time we speak, our task is to use such structures coherently to establish a linkage between our intentions and our utterances. Notice also that such linkages are established inferentially based on an internal analysis that tells us how much information we have to give our listeners to enable them to make the connection between what we have actually said, and what it means. The basis of such an analysis is frequently to be found in societal conventions. For example, suppose that the initial speaker above had known that his listener was a passionate sports fan. Then the first speaker may have reasoned that the listener probably had heard or watched several games on the previous day and that therefore greater precision was required to specify the one the speaker was talking about. Had the first speaker made such an analysis, he may have opened the conversation with, "The NCAA final was super last night, wasn't it?" **Pragmatics** refers to the social rules underlying language use and the strategies used by speakers to establish coherence across several sentences.

Direct and Indirect Speech Acts   The relationship between a speaker's intention and his or her actual utterance was explored by Austin (1962) who made several important distinctions. Austin described the actual utterance of the speaker as the locutionary act, the interpretation of that utterance by a listener as the illocutionary act, and, finally, the effect of the utterance on the listener as the perlocutionary act. Thus if a person says "It's warm in here," the locutionary act is a simple declarative, but it may be interpreted by the listener as a request to open a window or to turn on an air conditioner. And the listener may then get up and do one of those two things, either of which would appear to be the result of the utterance.

The illocutionary act (the interpretation made by the listener) is also called the **speech act** (Bach & Harnish, 1979; Katz, 1977). Speech acts can be organized functionally; that is, they may be organized according to the intentions that are being conveyed. Table 9.7 shows several speech acts and examples. One conclusion that can be drawn from Table 9.7 concerns the relationship between linguistic structure and linguistic function. For example, if we seek to give a congratulatory message, only a few linguistic structures are appropriate ("Let me congratulate you!" or "Congratulations!"). If a person were to use an inappropriate linguistic structure, such as an interrogative ("I guess I should congratulate you, shouldn't I?"), the listener might well conclude that this person did not really want to acknowledge the event.

However, linguistic structure does not constrain linguistic function completely. That is, there are situations in which we can legitimately use a particular linguistic structure to convey a speech act that is not normally associated with it.

············ **TABLE 9.7** Major types of speech acts

Speech Act	Definition	Examples
Constative	The speaker expresses a belief, with the intention of creating a similar belief in the hearer (*assert, predict, suggest, describe, conclude*)	*I assert the window is open.* *I conclude the case is closed.*
Directive	The speaker expresses an interest in the hearer's future action, with the intention that the utterance provide a reason for such action (*request, question, prohibit, authorize, recommend*)	*I recommend this class to you.* *I prohibit you from taking that action.*
Commissive	Obligates the speaker, by virtue of its occurrence, to do something (*promise, offer*)	*I promise you it will not happen again.* *I offer you the house for $300 a month.*
Acknowledgment	The speaker expresses feelings for the hearer, either true or socially expected feelings (*apologize, congratulate, thank, refuse*)	*I congratulate you on your appointment.* *I apologize for causing you inconvenience.*

Source: Bach and Harnish. (Copyright 1979 by the MIT Press. Adapted by permission of the publisher and author.)

For example, "It looks like you're having trouble performing up to your full potential in here" is superficially constative but may actually be a directive ("It's time for you to drop the class"). When a particular linguistic structure is used nonnormatively as a speech act, it is referred to as an **indirect speech act.**

Such usage may suggest that there is no rhyme or reason governing the intentionality underlying indirect speech. But most researchers (Clark & Lucy, 1975; Searle, 1975) argue that the interpretation of indirect speech is governed by certain principles that are shared by speaker and listener. In the next section, we'll deal with one such rule.

Role of Pragmatics in Language Comprehension   One rule that both speakers and listeners share is what we might call the "one-meaning convention." What this means is that, in most situations, we expect that a speaker has only a single intention. Further, the one-meaning convention also tells us that, if the speaker has more than a single intention, he or she is expected to give us some other clue to start looking for other meanings.

Let's consider a specific example to see how this rule would be used to identify the speech act. One time a colleague of mine began giving his students extra-credit points simply for coming to class in a somewhat ill-conceived attempt to boost attendance. When I asked him later how the plan was working, he said that attendance was up, but there were problems nevertheless. Why? "Well," he responded, "they're not coming because they want to be there." I'm sure you can tell what he meant, but if you simply look at what he said, the thought doesn't seem to be expressed very clearly. On the face of it, what my colleague's last comment seemed to assert was that the students weren't coming to class, but, parodoxically, the reason why they weren't coming to class was because they wanted to be in class. Taken that way, the comment doesn't seem to make much sense, especially in light of the fact that, immediately before making this comment, my colleague asserted that attendance was up. How do we go about figuring out the meaning of such an utterance? Well, first of all, we assume that the speaker does have a meaning—that he or she has not simply and suddenly gone completely insane. Then, applying the one-meaning convention, we can figure that the colleague's second comment was designed to continue and amplify the meaning of this previous comment, unless some other sign was given signalling us that some multiple meanings were intended. What might such signals be? We might consider facial expressions, including smiling or laughter, hand gestures, or obvious changes in tone, as cues that additional meanings are intended. Because none of these cues were present in my colleague's utterance, I concluded that its meaning must be an extension of the previous comment. Thus it seemed clear that the only thing he could have intended was that the students were indeed coming to class but that their attendance was not motivated by desire for learning, but by a desire for something else, probably a good grade. What the speaker might have said was, "Well, they're coming to class, but not for the reasons I had hoped."

Our analysis of this comment suggests that speakers and listeners know specific rules underlying speech acts. In the next section, we'll take a look at a related issue—rules that speakers follow to help listeners with the speech act.

Maxims of Conversational Coherence   Grice (1975) has postulated several principles (he refers to them as maxims) of conversational coherence. These maxims (shown in Table 9.8) are offered as guidelines that speakers might, and do, use to help their listeners interpret their utterances. Of course, all of us violate these maxims from time to time, but, usually, our violations are unintentional.

 ## READING

In some respects, understanding how people read is easier than the problem of speech perception. First, in order to perceive speech, people have to solve the "segmentation problem." That doesn't have to be done in reading. The words are almost always set off from one another, and even when they aren't, reading is still not too terribly difficult. And, at first glance, there doesn't seem to be any parallel transmission of information such as we saw in the speech perception literature. That is, the characters we use in reading don't seem to be influenced by those that have preceded them, nor do they seem to be influenced by those that follow. But these factors shouldn't mislead us: Understanding reading is still problematic. First, the alphabetic characters are far from a complete specification of their phonetic equivalents. Although the written symbol in an alphabetic system such as ours represents a phoneme (Foss & Hakes, 1978), the correspondence between

· · · · · · · · · · · · · ·   **TABLE 9.8**   **Four conventions for conversations**

1. Quantity: Make your contribution as informative as is required, but not more informative than is required.
2. Quality: Try to make your contribution one that is truthful. That is, do not say anything you believe to be false.
3. Relation: Make your contribution relevant to the aims of the ongoing conversation.
4. Manner: Be clear. Try to avoid obscurity, ambiguity, wordiness, and disorderliness in your use of language.

Source: Grice. (Copyright 1975 by Academic Press. Adapted by permission of the publisher and author.)

phonetics and alphabetic symbols is not one-to-one. This lack of correspondence has created some difficulties. For example, we cannot analyze the phonological rules acquired by children as they learn to read and spell because, strictly speaking, our alphabet and its spelling rules are not always phonetic.

Another way of expressing this problem is to note that English does not have a one-to-one mapping between graphemes and phonemes (Wood, 1983). A **grapheme** is an alphabetic letter, or combination of such letters, that stands for a single phoneme. The s in *stop* and the *ss* in *kisser* are both graphemes. Coltheart (1978) illustrated several of the problems that are created by this lack of correspondence. First, when we hear a word, there are no general rules that enable us to make a graphemic representation with certainty. For example, the vowel combinations *oa* and *oe* are both derivable from the same phoneme as in *boat* and *hoe*. However, these graphemes do not always indicate the same phoneme. This is illustrated in the words *boa* and *poem*. The graphemes that previously indicated the same phoneme now point to different phonemes.

Second, even when a series of graphemic units is clearly known, there is no clearly understood, universal way to map them onto a phonetic code. For example, in the word *bread*, which can be broken down into the graphemes *b-r-ea-d*, there is no rule-based way to assign *ea* to a phoneme without considering the other graphemes. You can see why this might create problems for the youthful reader. Let's assume for a moment that reading is similar to speech comprehension in that the graphemes must be converted into a phonetic code before they can be processed like speech sounds. If this view of reading is accurate, children with reading difficulties who are asked to sound out the letters have their work cut out for them. Nobody has written a complete specification of grapheme-to-phoneme mappings because the task is impossible. Given these problems, an interesting question is produced: How does the typical person go about dealing with these and other issues in order to read effectively?

Generally, cognitivists conceive of the reading process as involving a series of operations on a written message, called simply "the text." These operations in turn involve creating and successively altering a cognitive code. You might assume that the creation of this cognitive code begins with the perception of individual letters or words and progresses from there to successively larger units of meaning. Such an analysis implies that the process of reading is largely "bottom-up" or data driven. Yet, as we'll see, readers seldom initiate the reading process in so neutral a fashion. Rather, all reading is done in some context, a context shaped by the reader's skill, purpose, expectations, and by the complexity of the written material. At this point in your reading of this book, words like "purpose" and "expectations" probably are signals telling you to be on the lookout for the phrase "top-down processing"—and so there it is. Top-down processing in reading means that moderately skilled readers are not simply passive spectators but are actively engaged in extracting the desired information from the text.

In the next section, we'll consider a particular perspective on reading, and we'll use this perspective as a model of some of the cognitive operations that seem to be used by skilled readers. In the later sections, we'll go into more depth regarding the specific processes outlined in the general model. As you read, remember to keep in mind the distinction between top-down and bottom-up processing.

Routes of Information Processing in Reading

There are numerous theories of reading, and they differ in terms of the number of stages or events required to read, the cognitive processes underlying each stage, and the names given to each stage. What's presented here is something that might approach a "cognitive consensus" theory (Perfetti & Curtis, 1986) of reading.

Figure 9.2 shows the architecture of Marshall's (1987) model of the routes of information processing in normal reading. As shown, the model postulates three quasi-independent, parallel routes in which the form, meaning, and pronunciation of a printed word are determined. We'll take some time to go through each of these three routes. Visual analysis (VA) determines the features and featural pattern of the text and may operate along the lines of the Pandemonium model that we looked at in Chapter 2. These featural patterns are next assigned to their ultimate graphemic categories by the visual to graphemic conversion (VGC) routine. In Marshall's theory, the graphemic code is visual, but nonphonological, and abstract. What this means is that the segments of the lines and contours have been acquired by the visual and cognitive system and have been assigned to a particular grapheme. But these conglomerates of segments have not yet been "named" by the cognitive system with their specific letter names. The literature in this area is not clear with regard to the use of so-called transgraphemic features (such as overall orthographic shape) as an aid in letter acquisition. At this point in the system, multiletter strings are represented explicitly by their component letters. So for example the word "cat" is coded as $C + A + T$ in the VGC routine.

Let's now consider what happens when the first of the major independent routes begins to process the code. The phonic route begins when the code is passed to the graphemic buffer (GB), and it is here that the letters are given their specific names. We'll have more to say later in the chapter concerning the role that the phonic route typically plays in normal adult reading. From the graphemic buffer, the code is passed to the graphemic reparser (GR), at which point the code is reanalyzed into its graphemic chunks. Graphemic chunks are letters or

FIGURE 9.2
. . . .
Architecture of normal reading. VA = visual analysis; VGC = visual to graphemic conversion; GB = graphemic buffer; GR = graphemic reparsing; GPC = graphemic to phonologic conversion; IOL = input orthographic lexicon; GM = graphemic morphology; SR = semantic representations; OPL = output phonological lexicon; PB = phonologic buffer. A = phonic route; B = direct route; C = lexico-semantic route.

(Copyright 1987 by Lawrence Erlbaum Assoc., Inc. Adapted by permission of the publisher and author.)

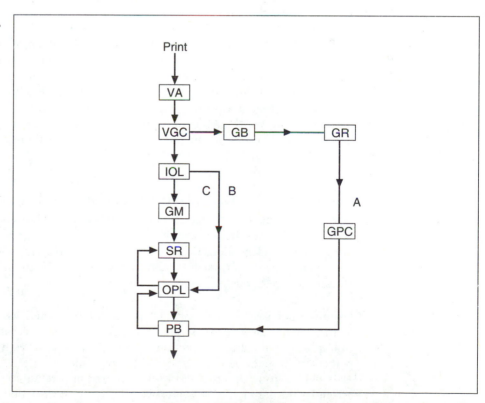

multiletter strings that map onto a single phoneme. For example, the reparser will leave D + O + G alone, because each chunk maps onto a single phoneme. But T + O + E will be reparsed as T + OE because the *oe* is a vowel digraph with a specific pronunciation. Notice that the oe is not a digraph in the word "poem," and this means that the phonic route will indeed misparse "poem" and other irregular uses of that vowel digraph. In the graphemic to phonological conversion (GPC) routine, the recoded grapheme will be assigned to its single most prevalent phonological representation. Thus grapheme *s* will be converted to phoneme /s/. However, let's consider what happens to a word like *shoe*. What happens in the GPC is that the *oe* is assigned its normal phonological representation (as in toe), and this means that *shoe* comes out of the GPC sounding just like the word *show* and is passed to the phonological buffer (PB) sounding just this way. This may seem like a theoretical mistake, but Marshall's model seeks to account for the reading of those individuals who rely upon the phonic route. Such individuals frequently read *shoe* aloud as *show*.

Turning to the direct route, from the VGC, the code also is passed to the input orthographic lexicon (IOL). This routine is the typical word-recognition device that underlies most explanations of "sight vocabulary." This code can be transferred intact to the output phonological lexicon (OPL) which is a repository of phonological information for all words that can be identified by the IOL. Here's how this works. First we have a printed word, let's say, *code*. This word's features are acquired by VA, and then these features are assigned to abstract, unnamed graphemes in VGC. From there the graphemes are passed to IOL which recognizes the string as an element in the system's lexicon, and finally they are passed to OPL which assigns a pronunciation to the entire word. The possession of such a route enables me to look at *code* and say *code*, but notice it doesn't entitle me to know the meaning of *code*.

To know the meaning of the word, I would have to use the third and final pathway, the lexico-semantic route. As we've seen, the IOL routine can recognize grapheme strings by sight. When this string, now recognized as a word, is passed to the graphemic morphology (GM) routine, operations are engaged that produce a morphological code suitable as an input for the semantic representation (SR) routine. This routine looks up the meaning of each morpheme in the string and passes this representation to OPL, which, as we've seen, assigns a phonological representation to the code. Understanding the function of the direct and lexico-semantic routes might be easier if you think of them as accessing different kinds of lexical knowledge.

Bottom-Up Cognitive Operations in Skilled Reading

We've looked at a typical model of the routes and stages involved in reading, and we've seen that researchers in this area conceptualize the reader as deploying a set of somewhat independent cognitive processes in order to read a word and say it out loud. In this section we'll consider what's involved in each of the stages required by the model.

Feature Processes   If you look back to Chapter 2, you'll see that I talked about feature extraction processes, and I happened to use features of letters as an example of such feature extraction processes. Now we'll see how such a theory of perception would operate in the context of reading.

As we know, a letter can be represented as a related group of features. For example, the letter *E* may be represented by a vertical line with three perpendicular horizontal lines, the letter *P* may be represented by a vertical line and a closed loop, and so on. This is the stage corresponding to the visual analysis in Marshall's model.

At the letter level, this stimulus is represented more abstractly, that is, independently of its particular configuration. Thus *f* and *F* are both examples of the letter *F*. Finally, the graphemes can be combined and reparsed to form words. A parallel processing model formulated by Johnston and McClelland (1980) is similar to the Marshall model in that it depicts these processes as operating hierarchically. Figure 9.3 shows their model. As the model shows, once the letters are positioned, their features are extracted, and these features activate the letters composed of those features. Thus, the detection of the curved line and the vertical line activates the recognition of the letter *R*, as shown by the solid lines from the feature detectors to the letter detectors. As you can see, the detection of the vertical line in the initial position of the word inhibits the system from detecting this as the letter G. A similar pattern of activation and inhibition takes place in the interaction of the letter and word detectors. Once the letter *R* has been identified, it activates those graphemic chunks that begin with *R*. Thus, *road*, *read*, *rend*, and *real* are activated but *head* is inhibited. As shown in Figure 9.3, these processes work for each word in the subject's lexicon: *Read* is the only word that has been activated by all the letter detectors, without having been inhibited by any of them.

The Johnston and McClelland model implies that the features of each letter are processed more or less independently, and, thus, letter recognition is determined by the pattern of activation and inhibition among the features that have been detected. Massaro and Hary (1986) explored these contentions in a study of ambiguous letter recognition. Subjects looked at ambiguous letters that varied between Q and G. The ambiguity was created by varying the openness of

FIGURE 9.3
. . . .
Hierarchical model of word and letter identification.

(From Johnston & Mc-Clelland. Copyright 1980 by Academic Press, Inc. Adapted by permission of the publisher and author.)

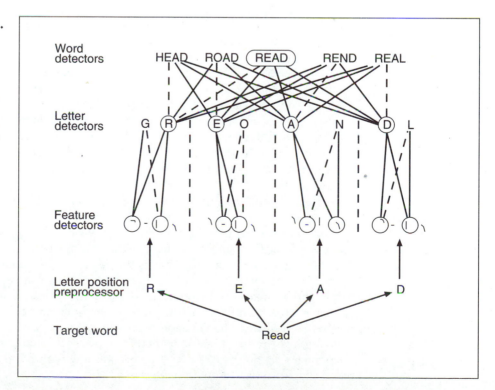

the oval and the obliqueness of the straight line in both characters. The results indicated that both sources of featural information were perceived and used by the subjects simultaneously, as predicted by the Johnston and McClelland (1980) model. Moreover, the evaluation of each source of featural information was carried out independently. The process of feature extraction supplied continuous information to another cognitive process, called "integration," that weighed the features adding up to "Q-ness" against the features adding up to "G-ness" and enabled the subjects to label the ambiguous letter either a Q or a G in a forced choice paradigm. In the integration process, the least ambiguous letter feature contributes the most to the letter judgment.

Letter-Recognition Processes   Of course, we use feature extraction processes to recognize letters. There are indications that such feature extraction processes are used in at least two different ways, depending upon whether we are trying to detect letters in isolation or in their normal context in reading. We'll consider each case in turn.

In Chapter 2, we saw that Neisser (1964) demonstrated that subjects typically found a straight-line letter (a Z) much more quickly when it appeared in a block of curved-line letters than they did when the target letter appeared in a block of other straight-line letters. (By the way, Chapter 2 will be helpful to us once again in a little while.) The Johnston and McClelland model (1980) offers a good explanation of what produces this effect. According to the model, the straight-line letter was detected quickly among the curved lines because the letter detectors for curved-line letters were all being inhibited by the features of the straight-line letter; in a sense the competing candidates were being suppressed by the features of the straight-line letter.

Of course, we don't usually process letters in isolation; we're much more likely to process letters in groups. And this leads to a bit of a problem: According to the purely hierarchical information-processing view, processing of words should not begin until all the letters have been processed and identified. But, if you looked back at Chapter 2 a little while ago, you may have seen some evidence that the hierarchical view is not completely accurate here. Recall the word superiority effect? Subjects are more likely to correctly identify a letter when it occurs in the final position of a word than when the letter is presented by itself, or in the context of a nonword letter string. However, the word superiority effect is observed only when the readers are at least nominally familiar with the words. Moreover, as also suggested in Chapter 2, the word superiority effect suggests that we may read in units that are "higher" than individual letters or individual strings. It's not crystal clear yet what some of these higher-order units might be, but some arguments suggest that some whole words might serve as such higher-order units.

Healy (1976) had her subjects scan a prose passage with the objective of locating all instances of the letter *t*. She found that subjects were much more likely to miss the letter when it occurred in the word *the* than when it occurred in other words, even when it occurred in other words that begin with *t*, such as *thy*. This finding suggests that the subjects had read *the* as a whole unit and had done so more or less immediately, rather than by detecting features, then letters, then words. If the subjects had engaged in all of these processes for all the words, they wouldn't have been able to read over *the* without first contacting its initial *t*. Healy observed this phenomenon even when *the* was embedded in a scrambled word passage, rather than in coherent prose. This finding suggests that the phenomenon is not based on *the's* functional role within a passage, but rather is based simply on *the's* status as a word.

Word-Recognition Processes   Given that we can process strings of letters of variable length, what factors tell us that a particular string of letters is a word? How do we determine that the word is a word we know, or don't know? We looked at some of these factors in Chapter 6 when we considered lexical access. There we looked at this term in its broadest possible sense to include all of our semantic knowledge about particular words. In this case, we will use the term lexical access in its more limited sense. That is, on what basis does letter-string perception access word recognition?

One variable seems to be the string's orthographic structure, that is, the patterns of letter placement within words including certain constraints of adjacency, and vowel-consonant combinations. For example, the reader who encounters *train* knows that this is an English word. Moreover, the skilled reader knows that a slight change in letter placement could produce *trian*. This is not a word, but it is orthographically well formed and thus could be a word. An equally minor variation, *rtian*, is orthographically deviant and so could not be a word (Perfetti & Curtis, 1986). From experience in reading, a skilled reader may encounter thousands of permissible patterns that could be summarized by the rules of English orthography (Venezky, 1970), and such rules could play a major role in word recognition.

Mechanics of Reading   We've focused on some of the cognitive operations that underlie the ability of the skilled reader, but we haven't yet seen how such processes are actually used by the reader. It's time to address this issue, and here we have to contact the literature that describes how readers go about engaging the cognitive processes we've been talking about.

During reading, our eyes are not in continuous motion over the page. We're capable of such eye movements, but they can be done only when we are tracking a moving object, such as a tennis ball. But in reading, the eye moves forward in a series of movements called **saccades.** The saccade is a ballistic movement; once launched forward, the eye must come to rest at some point, however briefly, and the movement of the eye cannot be altered in midmovement. During these motions, no information from the page can be gathered. Following the saccade, the reader fixates her eyes at one point on the page. During the fixation, the eyes are relatively motionless, and the cognitive processes we have described go to work. Typically, readers fixate for approximately 200 to 250 msec, and the saccade can be accomplished in 10 to 20 msec. If you look at the eyes of a skilled reader during reading, you can easily pick up the regular jump-stop-jump-stop rhythm that characterizes reading skill.

However, Just and Carpenter (1980) have pointed out that this rhythm is complicated. First, one of their basic findings is that people will occasionally launch a reverse saccade, called a **regression.** Regressions seem to be launched when the reader detects some comprehension difficulties requiring a reaccess of previously presented material. The number of regressions launched is one of the features that distinguishes good from poor readers. Not surprisingly, poor readers are much more likely than good readers to make numerous regressions, and poor readers do so more or less indiscriminately. Second, readers sometimes slow saccadic rate and saccadic "distance" when they encounter difficult material. At the intuitive level, you may feel that reading consists of "sampling" a relatively small percentage of all the words on a page and building from this sample a general idea of the passage's meaning. Certainly our subjective impression that we "skip" some words in prose is basically an accurate one. However, we actually fixate approximately 80 percent of the meaningful, content words in a prose passage, and we sometimes fixate the contentless function words (*the, an,* etc.) too. Especially in difficult material, the skilled reader samples much more from the printed page than you may have thought (Perfetti & Curtis, 1986). Given that skilled readers are likely to slow down and resample certain words more than once in some reading situations, Just and Carpenter (1980) make a distinction between the fixation (the amount of time that the eyes are motionless over a particular point on the page) and **gaze duration,** the total amount of time, summed over fixations, that the subject spends looking at a particular point on the page.

Figure 9.4 shows the gaze durations for one of Just and Carpenter's subjects who was reading a scientific passage. As it shows, the subject spent more time fixating on somewhat obscure, but nevertheless important, words such as *flywheels*, than on function words such as *the*. Given this finding, we might expect that a subject's fixation times are influenced by at least a couple of variables including the status of the word (i.e., content vs. function words) and the frequency with which the word currently being sampled occurs in the subject's lexicon.

Some of these variables were included in a study by Rayner and Duffy (1986). They found that the appearance of infrequently occurring nouns in a sentence influenced fixation times, with subjects fixating longer on such nouns. In addition, the mean length of the first fixation following such nouns also was increased, suggesting that the subjects may have used the next word fixated after an infrequent target to help pin down the meaning of the infrequent noun. Curiously, these effects were not observed for infrequent verbs. Rayner and Duffy also analyzed the fixation time that subjects spent on ambiguous nouns, those that may have had two meanings. They found that, when an ambiguous noun had two equally likely meanings, subjects were likely to spend a longer time fixating on it than when an ambiguous noun had one meaning that was substantially more likely than the other.

One other issue in reading mechanics concerns the amount of information that can be picked up in a single fixation. McConkie and Rayner (1974; Rayner, 1975) provided the initial answer to this question by using a computer system that

FIGURE 9.4

Eye fixations of a college student reading a scientific passage. Gazes for each word are numbered consecutively, and the gaze time (in msec) is indicated below the sequence number.

(Copyright 1980 by the American Psychological Association. Adapted by permission of the publisher.)

1		2	3		4		5		6		7		8		9		1
1566		267	400		83		267		617		767		450		450		400

Flywheels are one of the oldest mechanical devices known to man. Every

2		3		5	4	6	7		8		9
616		517		684	250	317	617		1116		367

internal-combustion engine contains a small flywheel that converts the

10	11		12		13	14	15	16	17		18
467	483		450		383	284	383	317	283		533

jerky motion of the pistons into the smooth flow of energy that powers

19	20	21
50	366	566

the drive shaft.

adjusted the window of visible text. Subjects wore a contact lens from which a reflection was picked up that indicated the subject's current fixation point. This information was fed into a computer, which clearly displayed the characters at the fixation point and for a short distance (measured in letters) around the fixation point. But the computer was programmed to mutilate letters beyond a certain range, which was accomplished by subtracting some of each letter's features. Letters outside this window of legibility therefore couldn't be read. As the subject's eyes moved across the computer screen, the machine continually updated this window. For all practical purposes, as soon as the subject's eyes moved to a new fixation point, the text around that new point became legible and what had been legible became mutilated.

Suppose the size of the window was only one character wide. What would happen to your reading speed in that situation? Under these circumstances, we can confidently predict that your reading speed would drop. Now suppose that we increased the size of the window to three characters, meaning that the fixation point and one character on each side of it were legible. Your reading speed would pick up. Continuing with this reasoning, if increasing the size of the window continues to produce increases in reading rate, we can assume that the subjects are picking up the additional information in that fixation. At some point, increases in the size of the window would not be accompanied by increases in reading rate. At that point, we can safely assume that the subject is extracting as many characters as possible from the fixation. McConkie and Rayner found that the reading rate leveled off when the window of legibility reached about twenty characters—ten on each side of the fixation point. Now the next question becomes, do subjects take in all of the information they can from the farthest reaches of the window of legibility? Or, do subjects take in different kinds of information from various points in the window?

Rayner (1975) argued that, if the letters from the edges of the window were being extracted in the same way as the letters near the center of the fixation, changes that occurred when the letters were fixated should influence processing time and fixation duration. One of Rayner's sentences was "The captain granted the pass in the afternoon." When the subject fixated on the word *granted*, it was presented as shown here. However, Rayner had modified the computer program so that other elements were present in place of *granted*, before the subject's fixation. For example, for some subjects the word *guarded* was available in the periphery before fixation. However, as the subject's eyes saccaded their way to *guarded*, it was suddenly changed to *granted* at the moment of fixation. Now let's think about what this might do to the subjects. If a subject was not actually extracting letters from the periphery, changing a word at the moment of fixation should have no influence on fixation duration because, if the subject hasn't extracted any letter information, then she has no reason to suspect that *guarded* has been changed to *granted*. But if the subject has been picking up at least some of the letters in the periphery, we should expect that the manipulation would affect fixation duration. This is just what Rayner found. Moreover, Rayner found that fixation duration could be altered by the presentation of nonwords such as *gnarbed*.

Using a similar methodology, Pollatsek, Rayner, and Balota (1986) found that visual information is picked up to about nine letter spaces to the right of the fixation point. At such far distances, peripheral information affected only the gaze duration (not first fixation duration) of the target word, but at closer distances, Pallatsek et al. found that first fixation duration as well as gaze duration increased.

Similar effects were observed in a study by Imhoff and Rayner (1986). Their subjects read sentences that contained a high-frequency or low-frequency target word. In some conditions **parafoveal** (i.e., peripheral) information to the right of the target was distorted when the subjects fixated on the target; in other conditions, the parafoveal word was left intact. Finally, the status of the parafoveal word was varied: In the intact conditions, some subjects encountered high-frequency parafoveal words, whereas in other conditions a low-frequency parafoveal word was encountered. As expected, readers showed shorter fixations on high-frequency words than they did on low-frequency targets. Also, however, the frequency of the parafoveal word influenced the fixation duration on the target. In other words, when subjects parafoveally encountered a high-frequency word, they were likely to reduce their fixation rate on the target word somewhat, even in those situations in which the target was a low-frequency word. This finding suggests that subjects were getting at least some contextual, and perhaps semantic, information from beyond the immediate range of the fixation point. This finding is consistent with previous research that indicated that semantic information is perceived to about four letter spaces to the right of the fixation point (Rayner, 1978).

You may have been curious about what happens to parafoveal information to the left of the fixation point. Because the direction of reading in English is left to right, the reader has access to only about four characters to the left of the fixation point.

Basically then, the literature we have reviewed suggests that the eye obtains useful information, that is, information that is sufficient by itself to enable lexical access to take place, from only a fairly narrow window surrounding the fixation point.

Recoding in Reading   One of the many controversies in the cognitive psychology of reading has concerned what exactly happens after readers have engaged a particular element in the text with their eyes. We know that this information is used for lexical access, but there are many other questions. For example, looking back at Marshall's model of the routes of information processing in reading, we might wonder if all three routes are automatically engaged in by all readers. That is, do skilled readers necessarily rely upon the phonic route to the same extent that they do the direct and lexico-semantic routes? Some cognitive psychologists argue that reading is accomplished by transforming the graphemic code into another, speech-based code, presumably one with acoustic, phonetic, or articulatory properties. This of course corresponds to Marshall's phonic route. The idea that readers must necessarily do this is called the recoding position, named for obvious reasons. Arrayed against these psychologists are others who believe that reading is typically accomplished directly from the graphemic code, without any need to access phonological information. These psychologists hold the **direct access** position.

Settling this question has been troublesome. Whatever the phonetic code might look like, it clearly does not involve recasting the graphemic code into a subvocal response. This can be easily demonstrated. First, if we had to subvocalize to read, reading rate would be limited by vocalization rate. However, most of the time, our speech rate comes nowhere near the reading rate of 250 words per minute that most of us can attain (Kolers, 1970). Similarly, an analysis of reaction times indicates that subjects don't have to subvocalize a word to comprehend it. Sabol and DeRosa (1976) have found that people have some semantic knowledge accessed within 200 msec of a word's presentation. Yet, other findings (Cosky, 1975) have demonstrated that more than twice that amount of time (i.e., 525 msec) is required to initiate a vocal response for a three-letter word. Also, if subvocalization were required for reading, people who presumably have no phonological or phonetic knowledge—that is, the congenitally deaf—would be completely unable to read. However, such individuals can learn to read (the learning is laborious, however).

Taken together, these findings suggest that a strict interpretation of the recoding hypothesis is out (Coltheart, 1980). However, some phonological encoding may take place nevertheless. For example, Patterson (1982) makes a distinction between **assembled phonology** and **addressed phonology.** In reading aloud, once a printed word is recognized, its pronunciation can be looked up or addressed. This indicates the existence of a sort of phonological lexicon in which the lexical items are catalogued by pronunciation. Presumably, this same lexicon is used to pronounce words in normal speech. This is addressed, or postlexical, phonology, and this type of phonology apparently does not play much of a role in reading. However, some phonological information may be, if not necessary, at least helpful in achieving word recognition in the first place. This type is assembled, or prelexical, phonology. The existence of an assembled phonological code does not necessarily disprove the direct access hypothesis. But it might help clarify the process of reading by specifying the conditions under which people rely more heavily on the graphemic code and the conditions under which phonological knowledge aids word recognition.

Some findings indicate that assembled phonology sometimes influences reaction times in certain tasks. First, phonemic similarity seems to affect the time required to make a lexical decision (Coltheart, Davelaar, Jonasson, & Besner, 1977; Rubenstein, Lewis, & Rubenstein, 1971). In these studies, subjects were given a string of letters and were asked to determine as quickly as possible whether the string was a word or a nonword (e.g., *fraze*). When the nonword was homophonic with an actual English word, the subjects required more time to make the decision than they did when the word was not homophonic. Thus, subjects would require more time to decide the fate of a nonword such as *brane* than they would a nonword such as *melp*. The obvious conclusion seems to be that the subjects were slowed by the resemblance of *brane* to *brain*. Although this effect demonstrably involves assembled phonology, it is limited to nonwords. Coltheart (1978, 1980) analyzed the response patterns and concluded that the recognition of real words is carried out on the basis of visual or graphemic information and is accomplished before the assembled phonology can play a role. Nonwords take longer to recognize as such, which gives the assembled phonology time to influence the cognitive processes involved in the recognition.

Direct Access Hypothesis Although some phonological coding seems to take place, most researchers believe that phonological recoding plays only a small role in the mature reader's cognitive processes. The alternative is the **direct access hypothesis,** a position whose basic premise is that a semantic code is produced directly from a translation of the graphemic code. What makes this view so plausible?

First, some studies (Green & Shallice, 1976; Klapp, Anderson, & Berian, 1973) have found that semantic decisions about real words are not influenced by phonemic factors. In these studies, a subject was given pairs of words. The first word denoted a category, and the subject's task was to determine if the second word was a legitimate member of that category. For example, in a pair such as SPORT–BASKETBALL, the subject had to respond yes, but in SPORT–PEACH, no was the correct response. The number of syllables in the second word was the variable of interest. Previous research (Eriksen, Pollack, & Montague, 1970) had determined that subjects take longer to begin pronouncing a multisyllable word than they do to pronounce a single-syllable word. Given this finding, we would expect that the category verification task would require more time when the subject had to make a lexical decision about a multisyllable word, provided that the subject was recoding the graphemes into a phonological code. But the expected effect was not observed. Subjects responded yes to SPORT–BASKETBALL as quickly as they did to SPORT–GOLF. This finding indicates that the subject apparently did not have to consult the phonological lexicon to derive the word's meaning as required in the task.

Kleiman (1975) arrived at a similar conclusion using a different approach. In this study, a disruption technique was used. It's plausible to assume that speaking an irrelevant message aloud while trying to read something completely different should disrupt any speech recoding. If speech recoding is critical to lexical access and reading, then speaking one thing while reading another should disrupt the reading process as well. Kleiman assessed this reasoning by having his subjects make judgments about pairs of words, which were presented in a tachistoscope. Over the course of the experiment, the subjects were required to make three kinds of judgments, examples of which are shown in Table 9.9.

In one-third of the trials, the subject had to make a graphemic decision for each pair. If the words were spelled the same following the initial letter, the subject was to respond yes, but if they were spelled differently, no was the correct response. On another one-third of the trials, the subject was supposed to make a phonemic decision, saying yes if the words of the pair rhymed and no if they didn't. Finally, on one-third of the trials, the subject was asked to make a semantic decision. Here, the subject was to say yes if the words of the pair meant the same thing and no if they didn't. On half of the trials, the subject was also asked to shadow a series of digits, with the assumption that this might disrupt the speech recoding necessary for lexical access.

Recall from Chapter 2 that shadowing refers to the immediate recitation of aurally presented material. Of particular interest in the Kleiman study was which types of trials (graphemic, phonemic, or semantic) the shadowing task would disrupt the most. Theoretically, the graphemic trials don't require any lexical access. Consequently, any increase in processing time on the shadowing trials here would presumably be produced by some general processing strain. That is, increases would simply be the result of the increased difficulty of shadowing the digits. The phonemic trials present a different story. Here, speech recoding must clearly be going on, because the subject must access the phonological code to know how the words are pronounced and in order to respond to the trial. We

·············· **TABLE 9.9**   **Stimuli from Kleiman's (1975) experiment**

TYPE OF DECISION	TRUE		FALSE		WITHOUT SHADOWING	INCREASE WITH SHADOWING
Graphemic	HEARD	BEARD	GRACE	PRICE	970(4.5)	125(0.4)
	NASTY	HASTY	SHADOW	FALLOW		
Phonemic	TICKLE	PICKLE	LEMON	DEMON	1,137(8.3)	372(7.7)
	BLAME	FLAME	ROUGH	DOUGH		
Synonymy	MOURN	GRIEVE	BRAVERY	QUANTITY	1,118(4.2)	120(3.8)
	INSTANCE	EXAMPLE	DEPART	COUPLE		

Source: Kleiman. (Copyright 1975 by Academic Press, Inc. Adapted by permission of the publisher and author.)
Note: The right columns show mean reaction times (in msec) and percentage of errors (in parentheses).

would expect that shadowing digits on these trials would result in a much greater increment in processing time than would be expected on the graphemic trials. The semantic trials are of particular interest. If speech recoding is necessary for lexical access, the shadowing task should produce a large increment in processing time, as would be expected for the phonemic trials. However, if speech recoding were not required for lexical access, the subject should be able to shadow the digits on the semantic trials with only a small increment in processing time. The right-hand side of Table 9.9 shows the results of the study: Shadowing resulted in a 125-msec increase in processing time on the graphemic trials. Shadowing produced a much larger increase—372 msec—on the phonemic trials. On the critical semantic trials, the shadowing increment was 120 msec—almost identical to what it had been for the graphemic trials, which didn't require any lexical access. These results support the direct access position, because the semantic increment was much closer to that seen on the graphemic trials than it was to the increment seen on the phonemic trials. Although these findings have been criticized (Baddely & Lewis, 1981; Besner, Davies, & Daniels, 1981; Patterson, 1982), they remain one of the pillars upon which the direct access hypothesis rests.

Other evidence supporting the direct access position has been produced by Blaxall and Willows (1984), who studied the errors second graders committed during oral reading. This study involved a challenge paradigm in which the child was asked to read passages of continually increasing difficulty. The researchers found that the proportion of graphemic errors (intrusions resulting from similarity in the visual form of the word) increased steadily as the material got more difficult. The increase in this type of error was accompanied by a decrease in the number of syntactically and semantically appropriate errors. At no point in the procedure did the proportion of phonemically induced errors increase. These findings therefore suggest that the second graders were converting the graphemic code directly to a semantic representation. As the material got more challenging, the breakdown apparently occurred in the matchup of the graphemic and semantic codes. The children were apparently willing to forgo a complete lexical search when the material was tough, settling instead for a visually based guess at the tough words.

Finally, and perhaps most provocatively, some evidence for the direct access hypothesis comes from the neuropsychological literature. Marshall and Newcombe (1973) have described a phenomenon that has since come to be called **deep dyslexia.** Some individuals who have suffered left hemisphere strokes retain the ability to read silently, but they no longer have the ability to assemble phonology for an unfamiliar letter string (Patterson, 1982). That is, they no longer have the ability to sound out orthographically conventional nonwords (e.g., *tride*). Since these individuals can repeat such nonwords if they hear them first, their problem is not simply articulatory but seems to result from an inability to convert a graphemic code to a phonemic one. For this reason, people with deep dyslexia are said to be "reading without phonology" (Saffran & Marin, 1977).

A case described by Patterson (1982) is particularly interesting, because the individual in question did not seem to suffer from some of the many reading deficits seen in other deep dyslexic patients (indeed, Patterson believes that this patient represents a new category: phonological dyslexia). A. M. (the patient) was a left-handed elderly man who had suffered damage to both the right frontal and the right tempero-parietal lobes. (His left-handedness may limit the generalizability of his case.) Patterson noted that A. M.'s inability to assemble phonology operated on at least two levels. First, A. M. could not produce the sounds corresponding to individual letters without extreme difficulty. For example, if given the printed letter *m* and asked what sound this made, A. M. might respond with "mother." Second, A. M. was unable to read nonwords. Table 9.10 shows the results of several testing sessions in which A. M. was asked to read a variety of nonwords.

As in other studies of people with deep or phonological dyslexia (Derouesne & Beauvois, 1979), A. M.'s reading of nonwords improved substantially on those occasions when the nonwords were homophonic with actual words. What accounts for this improvement? Patterson has suggested that A. M. and other patients with deep dyslexia shrewdly use a compensating strategy to pronounce nonwords. In this strategy, the patient finds a real word that is graphemically similar to the nonword, and pronounces it. The implication is that deep dyslexic patients should be able to handle only one type of nonword: those that are homophonic and visually similar to real words. For example, since the nonword *toun* is phonemically and graphemically similar to the real word *town*, we would expect the deep dyslexic to be able to pronounce it. But this strategy would not work with a homophonic nonword that was not also graphemically similar to a real word. For example, consider the nonword *phude*. The nonword has a homophonic relationship with a real word but little graphemic relationship. We would expect that the true deep dyslexic should have some difficulty assembling phonology for such nonwords. Patterson addressed this issue by comparing A. M.'s performance on these two kinds of nonwords. The finding is shown at the bottom of Table 9.10. A. M. did much better on the homophonic nonwords that were graphemically related to real words (.58 read correctly) than he did on homophonic nonwords that had little or no graphemic relationship with real words (.32 read correctly). Once again, this finding is most easily interpreted by the direct access hypothesis.

Still other evidence of the predominance of the direct route comes from studies of individuals who suffer from **surface dyslexia** which is something like the opposite of deep dyslexia (Marshall & Newcombe, 1973). These individuals can read out loud words that have a regular spelling (e.g., *mat, wheel*), and unlike the deep dyslexic, they can read orthographically regular nonwords as well as actual words. They read words whose pronunciation does not follow regular rules (e.g., *pint, yacht*) poorly. If such individuals are asked about the semantic content of the words they've read, their responses are based on what they've said, or apparently what they think they *would* say, rather than on the stimulus word itself. For

·············   **TABLE 9.10**   A. M.'s performance in oral reading of nonwords

LIST	DATE	NUMBER OF NONWORDS	SPECIAL CHARACTERISTICS	PROPORTION READ CORRECTLY
1	April 1978	24	—	0.00
2	July 1978	24	—	0.08
3	October 1978	36	Homophonic	0.47
			Nonhomophonic	0.26
4	July 1979	40	Homophonic	0.35
			Nonhomophonic	0.10
5	July 1979	26	Intermixed with words	0.19
Homophonic Nonwords from lists 3 and 4		37	High visual similarity	0.58
			Low visual similarity	0.32

Source: Patterson, 1982. (Copyright 1982 by Academic Press, Inc. Adapted by permission of the publisher and author.)

example, if a patient suffering from surface dyslexia is given the somewhat irregularly spelled word *listen* to read, this person may sound the normally silent *t*, and, as one of Marshall's subjects apparently did, then confuse *listen* with the name of the famous boxer of a generation ago, Sonny Liston. Such semantic confusions also occur when the patient is asked to define a word before saying it (Coltheart, 1981) and when the presented word has a homophonic, but not visual, relationship with another word. Thus, for example, when given *billed*, the surface dyslexic might say, "To build up, building" (Marshall, 1987).

These observations suggest that the surface dyslexic's problems stem from the relative inaccessibility of the direct and lexical routes. Because the surface dyslexic is deprived of these routes, he must rely on the phonic route in order to read. Whereas the deep dyslexic reads without phonology, the surface dyslexic reads without a lexicon. Again, the relative impoverishment of the surface dyslexic's reading ability when compared to normal people and to deep dyslexics suggests that most skilled readers rely chiefly upon the direct and lexical routes when reading. It seems that only when these routes are denied to us by a stroke or injury do we turn to the relatively less useful phonic route.

CONCLUDING COMMENTS AND SUGGESTIONS FOR FURTHER READING

Using language involves several different cognitive processes. Understanding speech requires the decoding of ambiguous stimuli. This is a matter of feature detection and pattern recognition. After the ambiguous stimuli have been recognized, the task of comprehension begins. The lexicon must be addressed, and these processes resemble those involved in the activation of nodes in semantic memory. All speech has gaps. We are usually not aware of these gaps, because the speaker has taken some pains to provide the audience with the main points of the discourse. Our inferential processes do the rest of the work. When we looked at the memory literature, we saw that providing someone with a theme for a story can enhance recognition. Remember the soap opera effect? When subjects were told that the woman in the story was pregnant, they recalled more of the story's details and interpreted the story in terms that were consistent with the script. Shared knowledge of such scripts enables the communication process to work. The only reason any narrative, written or told, has main points is because the participants share some mental organization. This sharing of mental organization seems to require more time or experience to develop than does phonological or lexical knowledge. If you doubt this, ask a five-year-old to tell you the plot of a movie sometime. The breakdown in communication won't occur at the phonetic or lexical levels. What the child sees as important in the story, however, will probably not overlap much with your viewpoint. When we use language to produce speech, the order of these processes is reversed. We start with a broad outline of what we're trying to say, which involves a judgment that our listeners have knowledge of the script we are about to use.

In summary, the use of language involves both top-down and bottom-up processes. In addition, the use of language requires perception and memory and, to a certain extent, reasoning. Although the organization of the book suggests that language is a separable phenomenon that can be unhitched from the other cognitive processes in the team, this organization is misleading. Language affects and is affected by the other cognitive processes we have studied; work is done because all cognitive processes pull together.

FOCUS ON RESEARCH
....
Disfluent Speech and the Brain

Even though we commit errors of syntax and pronunciation more often than we realize, our errors are unusual. Typically, we seem to be able to say just what we want to without any slip-ups. Unfortunately, for some people such fluency is seldom, if ever, achieved. Stutterers are plagued by a variety of handicaps including excessive hesitations, perseveration, and inability to articulate while maintaining normal speech rhythm. For some stutterers, producing speech is such an embarrassing agony they would rather remain silent.

Curiously, however, the stutterer doesn't seem to have as many problems when speaking under certain conditions. For example, stutterers can sometimes whisper fluently, and their singing ability is usually unimpaired. Also, the stutterer is often able to speak fluently in unison with other people. Some stutterers can improve their fluency by tapping their foot rhythmically and speaking at the rate of one word per tap (Kalat, 1984). These observances suggest that the stutterer's problem is not simply a loss of motor control over the tongue or breathing apparatus. The problem seems to be truly linguistic rather than muscular.

Recall that in Chapter 8 we examined the brain's role in normal language. In that chapter we saw that the left hemisphere of most people is the dominant one, and that this hemisphere contains Broca's and Wernicke's areas. Could these areas be involved in the stutterer's disfluency? The answer seems to be yes, although the involvement is indirect.

Jones (1966) performed surgery on the left hemispheres of four adults who had tumors near the speech centers. Such surgery would usually not be considered because of the risk it poses for speech. However, these patients were unusual: They had speech centers in both hemispheres of their brains (determined by anesthetizing only one hemisphere at a time). After the surgery, the patients were still capable of speech, apparently using the centers in their right hemispheres. Another striking finding was made: Before the surgery, all four patients routinely stuttered, but after the operation, none of them did. What's the interpretation?

For some people, the degree of lateral domination is not as great as it is for others. Essentially, such people have two speech centers that compete with each other. The failure to synchronize these centers is what contributes to the stuttering. When some rhythmic organization is imposed, the two centers have an easier time coordinating their efforts.

Several studies (Pinsky & McAdam, 1980; Rosenfield & Goodglass, 1980) have assessed this interpretation. Using a dichotic listening task similar to the ones we studied in Chapter 2, researchers have found more stutterers than nonstutterers with right hemisphere speech dominance, mixed dominance, or even fluctuating dominance. This last finding is interesting because it may account for why some stutterers experience lengthy periods of fluent speech followed by disfluencies.

The brain is not the sole cause of stuttering: Plenty of ambidextrous people don't stutter, but they would if hemispheric dominance were the only factor. Yet, competition between speech centers probably plays a role in some people's stuttering.

Readers who wish to find out more about speech perception will find no better starting place than Pisoni's article in the *Handbook of Learning and Cognitive Processes* (1978). Other material on speech perception can be found in *Psychology and Language* by Clark and Clark (1977). For a good discussion on feature detectors in speech (and the deficiencies of a theory based on them), see the articles by Remez (1979, 1980). Garret (1982) presents a complete account of speech production. Deese (1984) wrote a fascinating book in which he analyzed transcripts of naturally occurring speech.

There are several excellent general reviews of the research in reading. For example, the *Psychological Review* article by Just and Carpenter (1980) offers complete coverage of the stages of reading. Books by Crowder (1982), Kennedy (1984), and Beech and Colley (1987) also are good. Baker and Brown (1984) have written an account of the metacognitive influences on reading skill. The volume edited by Britton and Glynn (1987) describes variables that influence the top-down control of word recognition and sentence parsing. The edited volume by Tierney, Anders, and Mitchell (1987) deals with the cognitive processes readers use in comprehension.

KEY TERMS

Phoneme
Phonetics
Phonology
Place of articulation
Manner of articulation
Voicing
Distinctive features in speech
Phonemic restoration effect

Formants
Analysis by synthesis model
Pragmatics
Speech act
Indirect speech act
Grapheme
Saccade
Regression

Gaze duration
Parafoveal information
Direct access
Assembled phonology
Addressed phonology
Direct access hypothesis
Deep dyslexia
Surface dyslexia

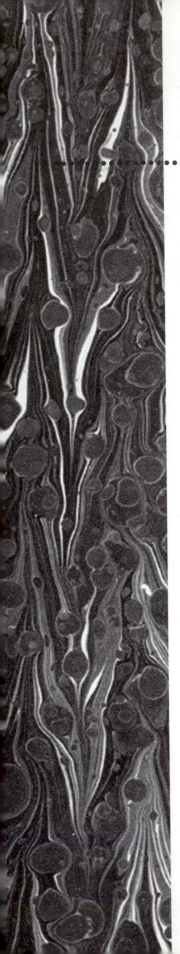

CHAPTER 10

LANGUAGE ACQUISITION AND COGNITIVE DEVELOPMENT

CHAPTER OUTLINE

OVERVIEW

When our younger son was about fifteen months old, he noticed a grass seed spreader in the garage at his grandparents' house. Looking at the spreader, he called it a "wagon," which of course is wrong, but interesting. I should point out that he did not say "wagon" when he saw an old bicycle wheel hanging on the garage wall. The fact that he called the spreader a wagon but didn't call a bicycle tire a wagon suggested to me that my son knew the difference between a wagon and a wheel. Now you might think that knowing the difference between a wagon and a wheel isn't really that much of an accomplishment. But let's consider what must be involved for a cognitive system to recognize and label an unfamiliar object in the world a "wagon."

Calling a spreader a wagon means (possibly) knowing that a wagon is a name that can be applied to things that have certain component structures, such as wheels, an open boxlike entity to which the wheels are attached, and a certain kind of handle attached to the boxlike entity. In other words, a very sophisticated feature analysis is required to take the object as it is in the world (the spreader) and decompose it mentally into its parts. However, in order to attach the label *wagon* onto the spreader, more than just the parts are required. The parts must stand in certain relationships to each other. For example, the wheels cannot be attached to the handle; they must be attached to the open box. This implies the presence of a conceptual structure in the mind of the toddler that specifies a number of things: the objects in the world to which names can be attached, the pieces of such objects, and the relationship of these pieces to one another within that concept. Not saying "wagon" when one of the concept's component

pieces is presented (the old bicycle wheel) implies that the toddler may also have the concept of "conjunction." That is, the toddler's cognitive system may have some rule that says, "Before you say 'wagon' you must have wheels *plus* box *plus* handle."

This description of the toddler's putative cognitive machinery is interesting for another reason, too. As you may have realized during my description of the conceptual processes underlying the naming of the spreader, there is a more-than-superficial similarity between the cognitive events that seem to enable concept formation in toddlers, and the rules by which more sophisticated humans produce grammatical sentences. In Chapter 8 we talked about the fact that sentences have component structures called noun phrases and so on; we described how sentences can be derived by an analysis of the rules that enable the parts of sentences to be assembled into larger components. Now, interestingly, we see that the rules that govern syntax may be generalizable to describe the way in which we build all of our concepts. For as long as humans have pondered their own mentality, they have wondered about the relationship of language to mind: Do you have to have a mind before you can speak? Or, are there are some concepts that we might call prelinguistic—a person doesn't have to be able to speak before these concepts can be used? What, then, is the relationship of linguistic development to cognitive development in its most general sense? Do these two types of development (if they really are two different types of development) almost always go hand in hand, or can one type of development outstrip the other? These are some of the questions that we will attempt to explore in this chapter.

STAGES OF LANGUAGE DEVELOPMENT

Table 10.1 shows the "stages" of language development. The word *stages* is in quotes to provide a clue about its meaning. Usually, children are not completely in one stage or another. Because children's behaviors show substantial overlap, the table indicates the dominant linguistic behavior at each age. Also, the ages given in Table 10.1 are only approximations. Some children begin producing their first words before their first birthdays; other children's first words don't occur until much later. The range of individual differences is fairly great. Also, a child who "misses" the average onset age for any given stage may not necessarily be behind at the next milestone. Children sometimes speed through several stages, only to spend a longer than usual time at a later point. Other children might go slowly at first and spend less time at the later stages. The order of events listed on Table 10.1 is probably invariant. For example, once children enter the stage of two-word utterances, they will not likely revert to babbling.

Crying and Cooing

For the first four weeks of an infant's life, his cries are undifferentiated. This means that the same cry is used regardless of the stimulus. During the second month, some differentiation occurs, which may be universal. For example, Ricks (1975) found that English parents could detect various messages in the cries of both English and foreign babies. Despite this finding, however, thinking of crying as truly linguistic is probably incorrect. Even babies of several months' age don't appear able to use their cries productively, and their behavior seems largely reflexive. However, crying does help lay the foundation for language by strengthening the vocal cords and the lungs (Aitchison, 1983). Also, the baby's cries usually elicit a response. This point is important. Early on, the baby has an opportunity to find out that vocalization can be functional, and speech almost always has that property.

Anywhere from six weeks to three months of age, children begin to coo. Cooing is hard to describe. The sounds are apparently vowel-like. Yet, the acoustic properties usually associated with adult vowels are not present in the infant's coos. Cooing seems to be universal. The child seems to be playing with her articulatory apparatus. Generally, this is a time during which the child explores the world, and cooing is probably best understood in that sense. Like

·············· **TABLE 10.1**   Milestones of Language Development

LANGUAGE STAGE	BEGINNING AGE
Crying	Birth
Cooing	6 weeks
Babbling	6 months
Intonation patterns	8 months
One-word utterances	1 year
Two-word utterances	18 months
Word inflections	2 years
Questions, negatives	2¼ years
Rare or complex constructions	5 years
Mature speech	10 years

Source: From *The Articulate Mammal: An Introduction to Psycholinguistics* (2d edition), by Jean Aitchison. © 1976, 1983 by Jean Aitchison. Reprinted by permission of Universe Books, New York.

crying, cooing is not truly linguistic but also bolsters the development of language. Adults seldom cry when babies cry, but they coo (or try to) when babies coo. Also, babies seem to be able to imitate some adult gestures (such as protruding the tongue) from a very early age (Meltzoff & Moore, 1977). The combination of adults' willingness to coo and babies' ability to detect and mimic various gestures suggests that babies begin to learn about reciprocity in vocalization before they begin to speak. By about six months of age, the child also uses consonantal sounds in her vocalizations. At this point, the child is said to have begun babbling.

Babbling and Single Words

Babbling has been described as a period of advanced motor play and vocal experimentation for the prelinguistic child. The consonantal and verblike sounds are strung together in lengthy chains that sound like words. Probably for eons, parents have incorrectly assumed that their progeny were addressing them with "dadada" or "mamama," and maybe it's just as well they don't know the truth. There is no available evidence to support the idea that babbling children attach any meaning to their utterances. It was once thought that, during the babbling period, children make almost every sound possible by the human vocal apparatus (Jespersen, 1922). This assumption is now known to be untrue; the variety of babbling sounds is not particularly great. Another past belief was that babbling is universal, that is, done by children everywhere, regardless of the cultural forces impinging on the child. However, there have been reports of children who never babbled yet nevertheless managed to acquire language. Babbling, however, is widespread and common.

One question that researchers pose concerns the role of the linguistic culture as a modifier of the child's utterances. If the babbling sounds are uninfluenced by the language that the child hears, this supports the idea that babbling is programmatic—a more or less innate and rigid stage of development. This idea has been supported by findings (Lenneberg, 1967) showing that congenitally deaf children babble. If, on the other hand, children are affected by the language they are exposed to, this suggests that, whatever the nature of the children's innate knowledge, it must be flexible.

Weir (1966) attempted to answer this question by examining the influence of tonality on children's babbling. Tonal languages are those in which variations in pitch can produce variations in meaning. For example, in Chinese, the same word may have different meanings when uttered at different pitches. Weir found that the longer babbling went on, the more likely Chinese babies were to produce monosyllabic utterances with a great deal of tonal variation. Nontonal babies (American, Arabian, and Russian) were more likely to show polysyllabic babbling. Interestingly, American mothers were often able to pick out American babies on the basis of their babbling sounds, as were Russian mothers able to pick out Russian babies, and Arabian mothers, Arabian babies. However, mothers of the three nontonal nationalities could not discriminate babies babbling in languages that were not the mothers' native tongues. This finding has been used to support the idea that, between the ages of nine to fourteen months, children undergo a **babbling drift** during which they gradually restrict their productions to only those sounds occurring in the language they will eventually master. At this point, children's utterances sound particularly like well-formed speech.

At approximately one year of age, the child begins to produce single words. During the interval from twelve to eighteen months, the child may acquire up to fifty words, although fifteen seems closer to the average. Some children may use as few as four or five words during this period. Babbling may continue for a short period after the production of true words, but it tends to disappear fairly rapidly.

This period is also referred to as the **holophrastic stage** of language development because the child seems to use a single word to stand for an entire sentence. These words are typically nouns or adjectives (McNeill, 1970) and usually refer to concrete objects that are present or to motivational or emotional states. Nelson (1973) found that animals, toys, and food were the three categories most frequently referred to by children who had learned their first ten words. These utterances have a variety of meanings. For example, the child who says "shoe" may be indicating that the shoe in question is his, that he wants to have his shoes put on, that someone has been observed who's not wearing shoes, and so on. Only by analyzing the context in which the utterance occurs can the child's intentions be understood.

Greenfield and Smith (1976) have stated that the content of the child's message may not be as important as the context. When the context is analyzed, the child's utterances are seen to express several sorts of functional roles. Greenfield and Smith followed two children around and recorded their utterances. They found that the children's initial utterances usually named things that were movers, or instigators of actions. Later, the children's utterances seemed to name movables, or things that were influenced by actions. Next, the children began referring to places and, finally, to possession, or recipients of actions. These functional roles and some examples of them are shown in Table 10.2.

When a child knows only five or so words, picking which one to say may not be too difficult a task, but by the time a child has learned 100 words, it may be very difficult to decide which word to use in a certain situation (Moskowitz, 1991). So how do children go about picking one word, of all the ones they know, to express a particular thought in a particular situation? Greenfield and Smith (1976) have suggested that children in the holophrastic period understand something of the informativeness of each of their holophrases in various situations. For example, a child who wants a banana and has the lexical items "want" and "banana" will pick the most informative of these two items to say. That is, the one-year-old will say "banana," not "want." Why is "banana" more informative than "want"? From the standpoint of the child, if you say banana, you may recognize that the adult caretaker will acknowledge that there are only a few relationships that could exist between you and a banana with "wanting one"

·············   **TABLE 10.2   Roles and Actions Talked About in One-word Utterances**

ROLE OR ACTION	UTTERANCE	CONTEXT
Agent	Dada	Hears *someone* come in
Action or state resulting from action	Down	When sits *down* or steps *down* from somewhere
Object affected by action	Ban	When wants *fan* turned off
State of object affected by action	Down	When *shuts* cabinet door
Object associated with another object or location	Poo	With hand on bottom while being changed, usually after bowel movement
Possessor	Lara	On seeing *Lauren's* empty bed
Location	Bap	Indicating location of feces on *diaper*

Source: Greenfield and Smith, 1976. (Copyright 1976 by Academic Press, Inc. Adapted by permission of the publisher and author.)

probably being the main relationship. Your caretakers will follow up on your comment by asking if you actually want a banana, to which you can respond "yes." But saying "want" doesn't accomplish the objective nearly as quickly. Once again, from the standpoint of the child, you may recognize that there are dozens or hundreds of things around the house, or around the kitchen, that you might want. And your caretakers really have no effective clue as to which one of these you might want, forcing them to go through a lengthy list ("What do you want? An orange, an apple, a cracker . . ."). This sort of analysis and the findings in Table 10.2 suggest that the child in the holophrastic period is not just learning about word meanings, but is also beginning to learn about syntax or word order too.

Overextensions and Underextensions The fact that children use a particular word in certain contexts is no guarantee that this word means the same thing to them that it does to older children or to adults. The deviations of a child's meaning from the standard meaning can be described in several ways. A child who says "doggie" in relation to dogs, and many other four-legged, hairy creatures, has **overextended** the word. A child who uses a general word to refer to only certain examples of its general meaning has **underextended** the word. A child who refers to only his or her cat, but not cats in general, as a "kitty" is underextending this term. Finally, a child may overextend a word in some cases, and underextend it in others; this is referred to as an overlap. Anglin (1986) observed an overlap in his daughter, who used the term "umbrella" to describe only open, not closed, umbrellas (underextension), but who also used the term umbrella to describe kites and a leaf that a character in a book used as a shield from the rain.

Most of us are probably familiar with the phenomenon of overextension because it tends to be a fairly noticeable error. Underextensions aren't so obvious. It's hard to tell if a child has restricted the range of a particular word, because he or she may nevertheless be labeling an object correctly. This may give the impression that overextensions are more common than underextensions, but that's not true. Kay and Anglin (1982) showed objects to one- and two-year-old children and then asked them questions ("What's this?" or "Is this a _____?"). The researchers found that underextensions were more common than overextensions. This finding fits in nicely with other findings of Greenfield and Smith (1976). They found that children are likely to be conservative with their recently acquired words in the sense that they are much more likely to use a recently acquired word as a label for a novel object in the environment than as a label for a familiar object or as a question.

Learning Word Meanings The fact that young children make errors of overextensions and underextensions shouldn't surprise us greatly, because, when you think about it, children in the holophrastic period are faced with a very difficult task in learning the meanings of many words. For example, in the literature on concept formation, which we'll look at more closely in a later chapter, we see that adults who are trying to learn a concept may frequently adopt a "win-stay, lose-shift" strategy. That is, if I'm asked to name elements of some arbitrary category, and I come up with some name that seems to work on a particular example, then I'll stick with this as a general name until I get some feedback indicating that my name has worked on some other example, at which point I'll modify my use of the name. Adults can use such a strategy fairly readily, but it's difficult for six-year-olds to generate new hypotheses in the face of negative information. Yet kids as young as two years of age learn new word meanings quite easily, seemingly doing something that older children can't do (Markman, 1990). Children have another, more abstract problem, too. As the philosopher Quine (1960) pointed out, for any finite set of data, there is an infinite number of logically possible hypotheses that are consistent with it. Because nobody has an infinite amount of time to test all possible hypotheses, technically, nobody, let alone small children, should be able to learn word meanings. But, obviously, we all seem to have the same meanings for thousands and thousands of words. So how do we accomplish this?

As Markman (1990) has indicated, the answer is that the child does not consider all possible hypotheses about what a particular lexical item might refer to. Rather, children seem to be constrained in what sorts of hypotheses about word meanings they will consider in the first place. This solves the strategy problem described above. Even though children are notoriously poor at being able to modify hypotheses in the face of negative information, they don't necessarily need such a skill to learn the meanings of words because they are biased in such a way as to not generate "wrong" hypotheses from the start.

There are several ways in which the hypotheses about word meanings may be constrained. First, children seem to follow the dictates of the **whole object assumption** (Carey, 1978), which means that children assume that a new word refers to an entire object, and not to a part of an object, or to a feature or property of the object. But even after children decide that a novel word refers to an entire object, they need some principle that tells them how far to extend that term. Here, Markman and Hutchinson (1984) have suggested that children are guided by the **taxonomic assumption.** The taxonomic assumption states that children will assume that a label can be extended to objects of the same kind, rather than to objects that are thematically related to the newly named object. Thematic relationships are those based on temporal, spatial, or causal properties rather than on categorical properties. Thus, according to the taxonomic assumption, if you say to a one-year-old, "Look, a train," the one-year-old will assume that the label refers to the whole object (the locomotive plus cars) but not to the tracks or the crossing gates (objects that are thematically related to trains). This assumption is particularly interesting because there is some evidence to suggest that young children (i.e., toddlers and preschoolers) are very sensitive to thematic relationships and use them in sorting tasks (Gelman & Baillargeon, 1983). This raises a question: Given that children have a propensity to use thematic relationships to sort, do they also know when to override them in order to learn new words?

Markman (1990) describes a study in which these elements were played out. Four- and five-year-olds were spoken to by a puppet (controlled by the experimenter) who said, "I'm going to show you something. Then I want you to think carefully and find another one." Following this, the puppet showed the children a picture of an object such as a cow. Then after inviting the children to look at this object, the puppet asked the children to find another object that was similar. Then the puppet put up two more pictures, one on each side of the target. Then the puppet said, "Can you find the other one?" One of the pictures was a pig, which has a taxonomic relationship with the target because they are both farm animals. The second picture was a pail of milk, which has an obvious thematic relationship with the target. In a second exercise, the condition was the same, except that the children were told that the puppet could talk in puppet language, and so they had to listen carefully to what the puppet had to say. In this condition the puppet said, "I'm going to show you a dax, then I want you to think carefully and find another one." Then the two pictures were displayed as before. If the taxonomic bias is operating here, children should be more likely to choose the taxonomic picture when the unfamiliar word is used than when no word is offered by the puppet. The findings confirmed this prediction. In the no-name condition, children chose the taxonomic category only 25 percent of the time. But in the name condition, 65 percent of the time subjects chose the picture that shared a taxonomic relationship with the target.

These findings suggest that the taxonomic bias guides children particularly when it comes to learning new words. Other evidence (Waxman, 1990) has suggested that children can use this information that they've learned to form conceptual hierarchies. However, it appears that there are some limitations on the taxonomic bias's ability to guide language acquisition.

Braine et al. (1990) studied the acquisition of a miniature, artificial language in children aged seven to ten years. Their subjects looked at a set of cards. Each card showed a monkey (Frippy) posed in one of three locations with regard to the object depicted on the card. Both the object depicted and Frippy's location relative to it were indicated in the artificial language. The object was represented by a word, and Frippy's location was represented by a suffix ending attached to the word. For example, the artificial language word for car was "garth." If Frippy was standing by the car, the suffix "–tev" was attached to the word. Consequently, the expression "Frippy garthtev" means Frippy is by the car. If Frippy was walking away from the car, the expression "Frippy garthgil" was used, and finally, if Frippy was walking over to the car, the expression "Frippy garthfoo" was used. The children attempted to learn a set of twenty-four nouns and suffixes. Of these, eighteen nouns took the "high-frequency" suffix; these nouns took the suffixes described above. The other six nouns took the "low-frequency" suffix. For these nouns, the children had to learn a different set of three suffixes to indicate the to, from, and at relationships. Of course the children were not told explicitly at the beginning of the study which nouns were in which category. One issue that concerned the researchers was the ability of the children to recognize that some of the nouns were secondary, and thus required the secondary suffix. This turned out to be extremely difficult for children to do. Approximately 80 percent of the time, children failed to put secondary suffixes on secondary nouns, and almost all of the mistakes were the result of the child using the high-frequency suffix inappropriately. Braine et al. (1990) report that this difficulty did not result simply because there were eighteen primary nouns and only six secondary nouns. Even in cases in which the number of nouns was balanced (twelve in each category), children had difficulty catching on to the distinction and generalizing to newly learned nouns.

There were many other findings that were of interest in this study, but I'll just mention a few that are particularly relevant to our purposes here. First, in learning the suffixes, the children almost always learned by rule instead of by rote. That is, there was very little evidence that the children learned simply by "brute forcing" particular noun-suffix combinations into their memories. Second, there was very little effect of immediate corrective feedback. Children who were given explicit information when they were right or wrong didn't do any better than children who were not given such information. Third, when adults were given the same task, in a similar format, they did statistically better than the children did. But the adults did not outperform the children in a practical sense; in some cases, the adults were getting only about 33 percent of suffixes correct on the secondary nouns.

There's also a sense in which these findings are quite counterintuitive. As you may know if you've studied some foreign languages, many feature something called "gender." That is, in some languages certain nouns are "masculine" and others are "feminine"; and adjectives sometimes have to take certain different suffix endings to modify a masculine or a feminine noun. Everybody who learns such a language as a native learns which nouns are which without any problem. Superficially, learning the gender of nouns seems comparable to the problems faced by the subjects in the Braine et al. study, and this resemblance leads to a question: How is it that native speakers learn the gender of the nouns (which often seems very arbitrary) without any apparent difficulty while Braine et al.'s subjects had such a hard time learning the arbitrary assignment of suffixes to certain categories of nouns? As Braine (1987) suggested, the arbitrariness of gender classes in other languages may be more apparent than real. In such languages, there is always a similarity of sound or meaning that clues the language learner how to subclass nouns. This tells us that the taxonomic bias that guides youthful language learners is not invincible: It can be defeated if we try to teach children languages that are truly arbitrary. In other words, there must be some shared similarity in meaning or in phonological shape if the child is to learn that certain nouns are members of the same category.

Two-Word Stage

Around age eighteen to twenty months, the child begins to produce utterances that are two words long—hence the unimaginative name, the **two-word stage.** All researchers agree that the increase in linguistic capabilities is dramatic during this period. First, vocabulary increases; the typical 2½-year-old knows several hundred words. Second, during this period, the average length of the child's utterances also increases dramatically. The length of an utterance is usually computed by counting all the basic units of meaning (the morphemes) that have appeared. Morphemes usually correspond to words, but this relationship is not perfect. For example, in English, *sad* is one word and one morpheme. However, *sadly*, although still one word, counts as two morphemes because the *ly* ending denotes meaning by itself. Therefore, the utterance "Daddy go" would be counted as three morphemes because the *y* carries meaning by itself. The **mean length of utterance (MLU)** is computed by determining the number of morphemes a child has produced, then dividing that number by the total number of utterances. When MLU is computed for children age two and beyond, a steady increase is seen across the entire period. Figure 10.1 shows the MLU graphed for two children studied by Roger Brown (1973). As mentioned earlier, different children may attain linguistic milestones at widely differing ages. This variation is evident for the two children referred to in Figure 10.1. Adam was three and one-half years old before his MLU reached four items; this placed him a full year behind Eve.

Another important change occurs during this period. Whereas during the holophrastic period, the child's caretakers are willing to analyze the context in which the utterance occurs to deduce the child's intention, caretakers are less likely to analyze context during the two-word stage. The child relies less on the context as a basis for meaning and begins to let the order of the words do some of the work. Using two utterances puts additional linguistic demands on the child, however. As we've seen, the child must now acquire the rules of syntax.

Bloom (1970) was among the first to realize that the child's two-word utterances show syntax. One of her subjects, Kathryn, used the expression "mommy sock" twice in one day. In the first instance, Kathryn produced the utterance while holding her mother's sock; the second time, Kathryn used that expression while her mother put one of Kathryn's socks on. A contextual analysis

FIGURE 10.1

·····················

Increases in mean length of utterance (MLU) as a function of age for two children.

(Adapted with permission of *The Free Press*, a division of Macmillan, Inc. from *Psycholinguistics*, by Roger Brown. Copyright © 1970 by The Free Press.)

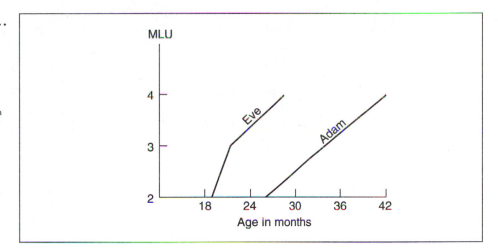

still must be done to understand the little girl's meaning, but the order of the words helps to express two meaningful relationships. In the first case, Kathryn was expressing the relationship of *possession*. In the second case, Kathryn was making use of the same sort of *agent* construction that also occurs during the holophrastic stage.

These kinds of utterances are called *telegraphic speech*. Just as in a telegram, where inessential words are omitted, the child seems to use only those words that are necessary to communicate a particular intention. Articles, pronouns, and auxiliary verbs have not yet appeared.

Brown (1970) analyzed the two-word utterances of small children and found that they typically express one of several meaningful relationships. These **structural relationships** are shown in Table 10.3. Notice that many of these relationships express the same things that children talk about during the holophrastic stage: namely, possession, the agent role, location, and so on.

Braine (1976) examined the two-word utterances of ten children (five were learning English, two Samoan, one Finnish, one Hebrew, and one Swedish). He found that all of these children spoke of movers or doers; that is, they all used the

·············· **TABLE 10.3** **Brown's Structural Description of Two-word Utterances**

STRUCTURAL MEANING	FORM	EXAMPLE
1. Nomination	that + N	that box
2. Notice	hi + N	hi belt
3. Recurrence	more + N	more cookie
4. Nonexistence	allgone + N	allgone kitty
5. Attributive	ADJ + N	big train
6. Possessive	N + N	mommy lunch
7. Locative	N + N	sweater chair
8. Locative	V + N	walk road
9. Agent-Action	N + V	mommy read
10. Agent-Object	N + N	mommy sock
11. Action-Object	V + N	put book
12. Conjunction	N + N	umbrella boot

Source: Adapted with permission of *The Free Press*, a division of Macmillan, Inc. From *Psycholinguistics*, by Roger Brown. Copyright © 1970 by The Free Press.

agent relationship. Moreover, all the children spoke of movable objects (the action-object relationship) and places (the locative relationships). Some of the other relationships were less commonly used. Braine noted that only some children used the possessive relationship, and the other relationships were used even less frequently.

The structural relationships described by Brown can be used as a basis for longer utterances. For example, three-word utterances can be made by combining certain two-word forms. The child who says "Bobbie take cookie" has combined the agent-action form ("Bobbie take") with the action-object form ("take cookie"). This linkage of primitive forms can take us only so far, however. Generally, after the creation of three-word utterances, the child seems to differentiate each of the noun classes contained in the basic utterance. *Differentiation* refers to the lengthening of a clause through elaboration and expansion. Bloom (1970) found that the initial elaboration of a sentence is right to left; that is, the object clause is elaborated first. This elaboration is accomplished by first adding articles or other modifiers to the object of the utterance, and later by the inclusion of possessive pronouns. In this way, an utterance such as "Mommy read story" might be elaborated into "Mommy, read my story." Although the differentiation of a sentence begins with the object clause and is therefore right to left, *within a clause* the differentiation is usually left to right. For example, articles begin to appear in front of the nouns that are the subjects of the sentence.

Such a view presupposes that all children in the two-word stage express the functional relationships in basically the same ways. However, Braine (1976) has pointed out that children in the two-word stage seem to adopt certain formulas to express certain relationships. For example, to talk about the location of an object, some children first mention the object (e.g., "baby") and then the location ("chair"). Other children take the opposite tack, stating the location first, then the object occupying it ("There doggie"). This approach inevitably colors the nature of later elaborations. The nature of the formula initially picked (which doesn't seem to have any rhyme or reason) may constrain the expansion process.

Bloom, Lightbown, and Hood (1975) and Nelson (1975) have also determined another variation that may affect the expansion process. They found that their subjects could be reliably grouped into one of two categories. Subjects in the first group used content words very early on in the two-word stage, just as the Brown model would predict. However, a second group of subjects used pronouns in the agent relationship. These children usually used the pronoun *I* in utterances such as "I do" and "I go." These children were also likely to use the demonstrative term *this* in the object relationship, in utterances such as "try this." This result is not what we would expect, given the differentiation process just outlined. In any case, within a few months, these early differences seemed to wash out. The "content" children started to include some pronouns in their utterances, and the "I" children began to use some content words. These findings suggest that substantial individual differences exist in the formulaic knowledge of children in the two-word stage. Whether such individual differences materially affect language development is not now known. These findings also suggest that the initial structural relationships proposed by Brown are used by some, but not by all, children. The early use of pronouns by some children seems to confound the notion that the structural relationships are the basis for longer utterances.

This discussion has emphasized the syntactic structure present in the two-word utterances of children, but we should not overlook a problem faced by children of this age, one that could overwhelm their syntactic structures.

Specifically, suppose that you are a child at the two-word stage and you have a thought that is just "longer" than any two words you can think of. What do you do then? Or, conversely, would this problem never come up because children of this age cannot have thoughts that are too complicated for a two-word utterance? The answer seems to be that two-year-old children do have complicated thoughts, and that they are also capable of solving the problem of expressing them in short sentences.

Consider the following dialogue between R. Scollon, a language researcher, and a two-year-old named Brenda:

> Brenda: Tape corder. Use it. Use it.
> Scollon: Use it for what?
> Brenda: Talk. Corder talk. Brenda talk. (Moskowitz, cited in Wang, 1991)

Here we see Brenda expressing a thought that we might translate as, "Turn on the tape recorder because I want to hear myself talking." But Brenda cannot encode this thought directly into a grammatical sentence because her knowledge of syntax is not extensive enough to permit that. So, what happens? Brenda takes her thought and breaks it down into a series of two-word utterances, which, when interpreted sequentially, contain enough information to permit a listener to infer Brenda's intention. The name for this process is **vertical construction** (Moskowitz, 1991), and it can be contrasted with the **horizontal construction** that most speakers use to translate their thoughts into a complete word-by-word specification of their intention. The process of vertical construction suggests that children have a sophistication about language structure that goes beyond their two-word utterances. In addition to the structural relationships that we looked at earlier, children also have the ability to take a fairly complicated thought and break it down into a series of utterances, each of which shows these structural properties.

Word Order and Inflections

As children begin to produce utterances of three and four words, they begin to rely more heavily on word order and **inflections** to signal their intents. For example, in English, inflections are used to show plurality of nouns and possession, among other things. Generally, a given language makes a trade-off between the stringency of its word order rules and the complexity of its inflections. For example, because English is not a highly inflected language, word order is quite important to meaning. If the word order is altered, the meaning of the utterance can be drastically revamped. As I recall, Latin is just the opposite: The actual order of the words can be shuffled around to a great extent without changing the sentence's meaning. It all works because each word is highly inflected, the ending reveals the noun's case, and adjectives have to agree in case with the nouns they modify.

The emergence of inflections has been studied by Bellugi (1964). Her findings are shown in Table 10.4. Once again, we see substantial timetable differences between Adam and Eve. For example, at twenty-six months, Eve began adding *s* to the verbs of third-person subjects. Adam was a full fifteen months behind in this ability. However, the order of emergence is identical for the two children. Moreover, the order of emergence is not strongly related to the frequency of use by the children's mothers. For example, the inflection mentioned previously was the last to appear in the children's speech although it was fairly common in their mothers' speech. Notice, too, that three of the inflections

·············· **TABLE 10.4**   The Emergence of English Inflections in the Speech of Two Children

Inflection	AGE OF APPEARANCE (IN MONTHS)		Combined Rank Order in Mother's Speech
	Adam	Eve	
Present progressive, -ing	28	19½	2
Plural on nouns, -s	33	24	1
Past on regular verbs, -ed	39	24½	4
Possessive on nouns, -s	39½	25½	5
Third person on verbs, -s	41	26	3

Source: Belugi. (Adapted by permission from Belugi, 1964.)

FIGURE 10.2
·····················
An example of one of Berko's stimulus cards.

(Adapted by permission from Berko, 1958.)

involve the production of an *s* sound. Yet, for Adam, the latency between the earliest /s/ inflection and the last to emerge was eight months. Even for Eve, whose progress appears to be much faster, this latency was two months. If the use of the inflection depended solely on the ability to produce the /s/ sound, no latency would occur between the emergence of the first of these inflections and the emergence of the last. The existence of the latency shows that the use of these inflections cannot be explained solely by phonemic development.

The development of inflectional markers has been researched in a classic study by Berko (1958). Preschool children were shown a card such as the one in Figure 10.2. While the children were looking at the card, Berko would say, "This is a wug." Berko next pointed to the two figures standing together and said, "Now there is another one. There are two of them." Then the child was asked to express this fact by providing the correct term in the statement "There are two _____ ." Most of the subjects correctly answered with *wugs* even though they were obviously unfamiliar with this term. Berko went on to demonstrate the power of the plurality rule in a follow-up study. The child was shown a picture of a goose and was told, "Here is a goose." Next, a card showing two geese was presented with the following statement: "Here are two *geese*. There are two _____ ." Even after hearing the correct form, most of the children responded with "gooses."

It's possible to identify six stages of development in the acquisition of plurals. In the first stage, the child uses the singular form in situations that require the plural form. At this point, the child does not appear to know that plurality can be designated linguistically, although he or she certainly appears to have the cognitive machinery necessary to represent the concept of "more than one." Thus, we find children at this stage saying "two cat." At the rather ambiguous second stage, the child seems to have learned that some nouns are irregular, and to express the concept of plurality, a different word altogether may be required. Thus for example, such a child may say "men" before he or she says "mans." At the third stage of development, the one in which many of Berko's subjects found themselves, the child adds an /s/ or a /z/ to a variety of words to express the concept of more than one. Consequently, the child may say "feets" or "gooses" and overgeneralizes this rule, now saying "mans." However, in the third stage, children do not routinely alter words that already end in an /s/ or /z/ sound to make them plurals. Thus for example, a child in stage three might not make a discrimination between one house and two house(s). For adults, there is a way of dealing with such words, and it consists of adding a /schwa-z/ to such words to get the "ehz" effect that adults pronounce in words like "houses," "roses," and "bushes." (Remember, the schwa is the unaccented vowel sound that we hear in "sofa.") When children catch on to this distinction, there may be a very short fourth stage in which they add the /schwa-z/ ending indiscriminately onto all words thus getting something like "boyzez" or "manzez." After perhaps only a few days of this, children begin to shift back to the simple "add /s/ or /z/" formula that was in use earlier. The rapid ditching of the /schwa-z/ formulation suggests that children probably had been working on such a rule during the third stage, mentally trying it out on all plural forms to see if it conformed to the linguistic rules that the community seemed to be playing by. When the child concludes that it's only the "end-in-/s/" singulars that take the /schwa-z/ plural ending, then he or she has learned just about everything there is to know about forming English plurals. The only remaining bit of business is to memorize the truly irregular forms such as "men" or "mice." As Moskowitz (1991) has pointed out, this task may seem like small potatoes to the five-year-old who may still have other more interesting linguistic problems to work on, so the child may remain at stage five ("housez," "ducks," "mans") for quite some time before entering stage six, at which point his or her knowledge and use conforms to that of the adult.

This sort of overregularization is interesting for several reasons. First, many of the forms thus created by children are not copies of adult speech, and so they cannot be explained as imitations. Second, the developmental pathway is similar for a variety of overregularization errors. For example, in the case of verbs, children of age three are fairly likely to use the correct past tense of some irregular verbs. The small child might say, "We went bye-bye." However, by the age of four or five, the child who had been producing the correct form now shifts to the incorrect form *goed*—a seeming regression. Usually by the age of six, the child once again consistently produces the correct form. Overregularization is sometimes called a "smart error" because it indicates that the child has mastered an inflection rule.

The fact that overregularization errors are often not imitative (what adult says "goed"?) has attracted the attention of researchers. Parents are not neutral with regard to these utterances, and parents sometimes try to get the child to imitate their correct usage. To produce such novel utterances, then, the child sometimes has to counteract the will of the caretakers. Children seem remarkably resistant to these pressures:

> Child: My teacher holded the baby rabbits and we patted them.
> Adult: Did you say your teacher held the baby rabbits?
> Child: Yes.
> Adult: What did you say she did?
> Child: She holded the baby rabbits and we patted them.
> Adult: Did you say she held them tightly?
> Child: No, she holded them loosely. (Cazden, 1972, p. 92)

More often, the attempts to influence the child take the form of **expansions** such as the following:

> Child: Daddy office?
> Adult: That's right, Daddy's gone to the office.

Such expansions are omnipresent in the linguistic environment of the child. Brown and Bellugi (1964) estimated that expansions make up over a third of all parental responses. Until Cazden (1972) completed her landmark study, it was commonly thought that such expansions helped the child acquire syntactic knowledge. Now the issue is not so clear.

The subjects in this study were children whose ages were less than three years, six months at the beginning of the project. In one group, an adult caretaker responded to the child's utterances with expansions. In a second group, the caretaker deliberately responded with well-formed utterances that were not expansions of the child's remarks. For example, the caretaker might respond, "Yes, but he'll be back soon" to the child's utterance noted previously. If expansions are useful for syntax learning, we would expect that the expansion group would outperform the nonexpansion group. But after three months, the children in these groups continued to perform at the same level. This somewhat puzzling finding has a variety of explanations that tend to have one theme in common. Language is a richly varied phenomenon, and language development seems to proceed faster when children are exposed to a good measure of this richness and variety. The Cazden finding also has a practical implication. Parents who overexpose their children to simple expansions or who subtly try to coerce their children into correct speech may be doing their children a disservice. Some errors, such as overregularization, seem to be an important part of the overall language development scheme. Well-meant interventions may be more disruptive than effective.

Later Developments

By the age of five or six, children appear to have mastered most of the rules of syntax and inflections, and so their knowledge of language seems complete. However, this apparent mastery is an illusion. Five-year-olds are readily able to make an interpretation of a sentence, but their interpretations are not always correct. Carol Chomsky (1969) demonstrated this by showing a blindfolded doll to a group of five- to eight-year-olds, who were then asked, "Is the doll hard to see or easy to see?" Chomsky found that all of the five- and six-year-olds thought that the doll was hard to see, and many of the seven- and eight-year-olds agreed. Although this particular study has been criticized, replications of it (e.g., Cromer, 1970) have confirmed the finding. Apparently, children of ages five and six don't realize that sentences such as "The rabbit is nice to eat" and "The rabbit is eager to eat" have completely different meanings (Aitchison, 1983). Language development apparently continues until the age of ten or eleven.

Summary of Language Development

In looking at language acquisition, we've seen evidence suggesting that infants and toddlers have an incredible cognitive sophistication that enables them to learn or know that there are such things as speech sounds and words, that words might mean something, that producing certain words in certain context is efficient in getting needs met, that words can be strung together to communicate even more complicated thoughts, and so on. Yet, paradoxically, we also see that it's very difficult to teach small children other things that are no more complicated than language. For example, from a strictly informational point of view, learning calculus is probably not as difficult as learning your native language at two years of age. (My sympathies are with you if you're actually in a calculus class at this point and thus find my assertion hard to swallow.) Despite the fact that learning a native language is harder than learning calculus, we recognize that children will learn their language pretty much on their own, but they probably could not be taught calculus at age two no matter how intensively we worked with them. How is it that the cognitive machinery that seems so sophisticated with regard to language doesn't seem nearly so smart when it comes to learning other things?

We can respond to this paradox in several ways. First, as Markman (1990) pointed out, children are guided in learning the meanings of words by a taxonomic bias that guides them to put the stimulus that we call a "word" in a special class, and to hunt for certain kinds of similarities among the members of this class. In other words, from the evidence supporting the taxonomic bias, it seems that children already know where to look in order to find the regularities inherent in word meanings. A second way of responding to the paradox of child language learning has been advanced by Newport (1990). Newport has formulated a position that has been labeled the **less is more (LIM) position**. Basically, Newport believes that, yes, children are relatively disadvantaged cognitively with regard to many kinds of learning, but their general cognitive shortcomings actually help them learn language. According to this position, a cognitively sophisticated learner faced with the problems of language would have quite a bit of work to do. In trying to learn the meaning of a word, such a learner might actually try to encode, in both short- and long-term memories, all of the features that had been present at the time a novel object had been named. But suppose the language learner had a relatively low-capacity short-term memory, as small children do. Such a learner would not bother trying to encode all the features that were presented, but rather might encode only the single most salient feature of the stimulus before him or her. But this single most salient feature is probably most likely to correspond to the actual meaning of the word. Consider this example: Suppose a caretaker is holding a small child, and they are both looking at a large tractor right next to them in a field. When the caretaker says, "That's a tractor," the child (technically) may not know for sure if "tractor" refers to the large thing sitting there, or the field itself, or the sky, or a bug crawling on the tractor. But the tractor is the most salient aspect of the scene, and the other elements will overcrowd the child's short-term memory and hence be eliminated. Thus, the child is left with the correct label for the most salient object presented.

This discussion has focused on the relationship between language and more general properties of cognition such as memory and attention. Moreover, in Newport's (1990) account, we've seen some evidence to suggest that children's language acquisition is paced by their general level of cognitive development. In the remainder of this chapter we'll explore several issues in cognitive development, and we'll try to see some of the parallels in cognition and language.

 **COGNITIVE DEVELOPMENT**

Conceptual Basis of Language

We might argue, as many have, that the function of language is to express some interior, or cognitive, event, and that the fundamental elements of such a cognitive event can be described as concepts. According to such a view, concepts are the atoms of thought, which can be arranged and rearranged in infinite ways to represent particular intentions. The rules of language enable this arrangement, and every particular arrangement, of conceptual atoms to be mapped onto a structured temporal code that preserves its underlying intentionality. According to such a view, it would be hard to imagine that much real language could take place early in a human's life, unless a theorist also wished to argue that young infants have a fairly strong conceptual basis for such language.

There is some evidence for such a point of view. Antell and Keating (1983) showed infants who were less than one week old arrangements of dot patterns. Antell and Keating used a habituation paradigm to measure the infants' interest in the dot patterns. That is, infants will suck harder on a pacifier if such sucking is followed by new and interesting sights, but their sucking rate declines if the same picture is on view too long. The phenomenon of habituation enables researchers to make some inferences about the conceptual apparatus of infants: If we show infants different stimuli, and their sucking rate continues to decline, we can infer that such young children do not detect the difference in the stimuli. Antell and Keating's subjects habituated to dot patterns showing three dots, even when the specific configuration of the dots was altered. But the subjects' interest perked right back up again when they were shown dot patterns consisting of either two dots or one dot. This finding suggests that even very young infants have a primitive number concept that can be used as the basis for later linguistic communication. In other words, when the child begins to develop the idea that language can reflect plurals, or "more-than-oneness," it is perhaps this primitive concept of numerosity that is the conceptual underpinning of the linguistic code.

A similar idea is seen in the research of Golinkoff and Kerr (1978). They presented fifteen- and eighteen-month-old children with short film clips showing a man A (an agent or actor) pushing a recipient B (either another man, or a chair). The subjects' heart rates were monitored as individual clips were shown, and the children eventually habituated. But when Golinkoff and Kerr showed the subjects a different clip, with B now pushing A, the children's heart rates accelerated, suggesting to the researchers that these young children had at least a primitive concept of "agency," or cause and effect. Once again, when we think back to the "agent-object" structural relationships that children express linguistically beginning around this time, we see a strong suggestion that such linguistic events are "anchored" on a conceptual framework that has been previously developed.

However, I should also say that there are a lot of questions left unanswered in this account. As Gross (1985) has pointed out, these studies don't explain what becomes a concept in the first place. For something to be a concept, it must have boundaries or borders specifying what's to be included and what's to be excluded. In other words, a "car" is defined just as much by what it's not as by what it is. Once these features are established, only then do we have a basis on which to categorize or conceptualize objects that we encounter in the natural world. But—and this is important—there's nothing about the natural world that tells us what concepts are the "natural" ones. Of the infinite ways in which we could use aspects of the world as a basis for grouping things, humans seem to show both consensus and diversity. That is, there are probably some universal concepts, but there are certainly many concepts that seem to be culturally generated and bound. The taxonomic bias that we discussed before doesn't help us solve this problem, either. It's true that the taxonomic bias helps children tremendously with the problem of mapping the child's interior, conceptual world onto language. But the taxonomic bias should not be understood as a way of enabling children to build their conceptual furniture in the first place. Another issue concerns the modification or development of concepts. However they do it, children build concepts. But the concepts they build may not always be the same as the adult version, a phenomenon we saw in my son's calling the seed spreader a wagon. Because we know that children almost invariably do eventually attain the adult forms of the concept, this means that they must have some reliable means of modifying their initial attempts in such a way as to get "closer" to the adult forms. We'll discuss some theories concerning this process in a later chapter, but for now we'll just say that this issue is far from settled.

However, one other cognitive process that's clearly implicated in both building and modifying the conceptual level is memory. In the next section we'll consider the development of memory capabilities and of children's knowledge of their own memorial processes.

Memory and Metamemory Development

Flavell (1971) used **metamemory** to refer to any aspect of the relationship between awareness and memory. Later, Flavell and Wellman (1977) refined the term and described metamemory as being any one of several different kinds of knowledge that people might have about their storage or retrieval processes. Specifically, metamemory can be broken down into three different categories of memory knowledge (Wingfield & Byrnes, 1981):

1. **Knowledge of One's Own Characteristics**   that are relevent to remembering. This kind of knowledge comprises our attitudes to our memories, as well as knowledge of our particular capacities and abilities. For example, you may know that you do better on essay tests than on multiple-choice tests because you find that retrieving information you've organized on your own is easier than making a judgment about the correctness of teacher-organized material. Similarly, you may know that remembering something that someone has explained to you is easier than remembering something you've read about. On the other hand, you may know that the mode of input is not particularly important to you. In these cases, we remember what has worked for us in the past, and we retrieve this knowledge to guide the encoding of new material.

2. **Knowledge About Differences Among Tasks**   that are important in storage and retrieval. This category contains the knowledge we have concerning the memory demands of a task and how well our memories will be able to meet those demands. For example, you know what happens when you are introduced to a large number of people at a party. As the introductions drone on, you probably become aware that you're not going to remember all the names you've just heard. The people being introduced sometimes challenge you to retrieve their names, which brings up a related point. If everyone knows that a long series of introductions imposes an almost impossible demand on someone's memory, then why do people

persist in doing it? Most adults have a fairly large fund of such task knowledge. For example, you probably know that you will remember the meaning and tone of a conversation but not the exact wording. You probably also know that memorizing a list of related words is easier than memorizing unrelated words, and so on.

3. Strategic Knowledge   refers to our ability to direct encoding and search processes. For example, you probably know many retrieval strategies. If asked what you had for lunch yesterday, you might try to retrieve this information by thinking about what day of the week it was, who your companions may have been, where you went for lunch, and so on. The point is, if one of these approaches doesn't work, you know that you can try an alternate retrieval strategy that may succeed.

Metamemory is implicit knowledge. Most people don't know where they learned about their memories or how they came by this knowledge, but they are nevertheless often fairly certain that their knowledge is accurate. This statement prompts two questions. First, can cognitivists outline the acquisition of metamemory? Second, is the assurance people have of their metamemorial knowledge well founded, or does people's knowledge of their memories contain some inaccuracies?

Development of Metamemory   Ample evidence indicates that small children don't have much knowledge in any of the three categories just mentioned. Flavell and Wellman (1977) found, for example, that their five-year-old subjects didn't rehearse a string of digits during a short-term retention task. This point is an interesting one. Children can easily be taught to rehearse strings of digits or lists of words, and when they do, their retention improves substantially. Even though children know the meaning of the phrase "Say these to yourself, over and over," and they have the ability to rehearse, they don't rehearse unless explicitly instructed. This type of failure is referred to as a **production deficiency**—a failure to use a strategy that one has the ability to execute. Production deficiencies can be contrasted with **process deficiencies** (Craik & Simon, 1980). The latter term is defined as an inability to execute some activity, because a memory process or capacity has not yet been fully developed.

Some findings suggest that, during the early school years, children's knowledge of the memory demands imposed by different tasks increases significantly. Yussen and Levy (1975) asked their five- and eight-year-old subjects to estimate how many things from a list they could recall without a mistake—in essence, an estimate of their memory span. Both groups overestimated the number of elements they could recall. The subjects then heard strings of nine or ten elements and attempted to recall them immediately after the presentation. Working memory was clearly overburdened by these demands. After several trials, the experimenters again asked the subjects to estimate their memory spans. The eight-year-olds revised their estimates appropriately—that is, downward. But the preschoolers didn't revise their estimates and were optimistic that they'd get all of them right during the next trial. The preschoolers were apparently unable to tell that their working memories were being overburdened.

This finding has some implications for other memory processes. In a series of studies, Brown and Smiley (1977, 1978; Brown, Smiley, & Lawton, 1978) found that children learn to pick out important factors in a story and use them as a basis for retrieval. First, the experimenters had a group of raters determine the structural importance of various idea units in a series of Japanese fairy tales that had been translated into English. The structural importance was a rating given to each of the passage's ideas and can be interpreted as an indicator of how necessary remembering that idea was to understanding the passage as a whole. Table 10.5 shows some of the idea units and their rated importance.

Next, Brown and Smiley gave the passage to third, fifth, and seventh graders, and to college students. After reading the story, the subjects were asked to recall as much as they could. When the proportion of recalled ideas was analyzed as a function of the idea's importance, the researchers found that all the subjects tended to recall the important ideas better than the less important ideas. Sixty-nine percent of all the subjects recalled the most important idea, but only 23 percent of all the subjects recalled the least important idea. Although this finding was true for all age levels, an age effect was nevertheless noted. Older subjects recalled more of the material regardless of its importance. That is, even of the less important material, the older subjects recalled more than the younger subjects did. Superficially, this finding suggests that the younger subjects had a process deficiency, meaning that they hadn't yet developed the ability to store large amounts of material.

Other findings have suggested a deeper interpretation. In an additional experiment, Brown and Smiley (1977) asked their subjects to make the structural importance ratings originally done by only the college students. The researchers discovered that the younger subjects were not very skilled at distinguishing the important ideas from the peripheral ones. Whereas the college students were able to distinguish four levels of importance in the passage, seventh-graders were able to distinguish only three levels, fifth-graders distinguished two levels, and third-graders distinguished only one level. Table 10.6 shows the numerical evaluation made of the least important and most important ideas in the passage by third-graders and college students. Note that there is no appreciable difference among the ratings made by the third-graders. If the younger subjects indeed have a process deficiency, it is an inability to detect the important aspects of a story. This apparent inability is bound to affect the subjects' encoding and comprehension of the story, because the meaning of such a passage is largely dependent upon the readers' ability to abstract important or thematic ideas.

Smiley, Oakley, Worthen, Campione, and Brown (1977) extended this idea in a study of retrieval among seventh-graders. They found that recall patterns of good readers corresponded closely with ratings of idea importance: Important ideas were consistently recalled by good readers. However, this correspondence

·············· **TABLE 10.5**   **Idea Units and Their Rated Importance**

UNIT	RATED IMPORTANCE
1. Once upon a time	162
2. there was a rich lord	356
3. who liked to collect carvings of animals	321
4. (those are like little wooden dolls)	106
5. He had many kinds	150
6. but he had no carved mouse	294
7. So he called two skilled carvers to him and said	341
8. "I want each of you to carve a mouse for me."	397

Source: Brown and Smiley, 1977. (Copyright 1977 by the Society for Research in Child Development, Inc.)

·············· **TABLE 10.6**   Ratings of Structural Importance by Subjects of
Different Ages in the Brown and Smiley Study

Subjects	IMPORTANCE RATING	
	Least Important Fact	*Most Important Fact*
Third-graders	2.41	2.56
College students	1.61	3.52

Source: Brown and Smiley, 1977. (Copyright 1977 by the Society for Research in Child Development, Inc.)

was not as good for poor readers. This finding suggests that the poor readers were not as sensitive to the structure of the story as were good readers. Perhaps more significant, it suggests that poor readers were not as sensitive to the importance of the story's structure as a vehicle, or medium, to aid memory.

Comparing the performance of college students with school-age children might give the impression that metamemory is fully developed among young adults and that their knowledge is invariably accurate. These impressions are false, however. Shaughnessy (1981) asked college students to predict which of two learning conditions would produce better performance on a memory test. In one case, a list of words was to be learned by simple rote repetition. In the second case, the list of words was to be learned using a procedure that prompted the subjects to elaborate the words' meanings. Subjects predicted that the two techniques would produce equivalent learning, but they actually performed much better in the elaboration condition. The subjects' memory knowledge was obviously incomplete and inaccurate. They persisted in their belief that rote repetition was an effective rehearsal strategy even though their own behavior provided evidence to the contrary. Subjects who were given permission to learn the list any way they wanted frequently reported that they learned by rote repetition. This knowledge also seems inaccurate, because these subjects outperformed the group that had been instructed to memorize the list using rote repetition.

Earlier I phrased two questions about metamemory, and I'll now summarize my answers. First, cognitive psychologists have provided a reasonably detailed outline of the course of metamemory improvement. Specifically, improvement during the grade-school years occurs in both the second and third categories of memory knowledge discussed earlier. That is, grade-school children begin to get a better idea of the demands that various memory tasks impose, and they begin to develop more effective encoding strategies as their sensitivity to story structures increases. In response to the second question, adults are apparently not infallible about their metamemory. Some evidence (Klatzky, 1984) suggests that people are strongly influenced by certain folk beliefs about memory, some of which are incorrect.

The Brown and Smiley studies suggest that as subjects become more knowledgeable about text, they will start to remember more about the material than they previously did. This implication in turn suggests that what happens during childhood could be interpreted as an improvement in learning about the nature of knowledge generally, and its organization. I suppose that we could term this a general kind of metaknowledge. But, in addition to these organizational improvements, there is also evidence that children simply become more skillful during their middle childhood years in using particular memory strategies.

Other findings suggest that there is also a developmental pathway in the acquisition of such strategies. That is, children develop different, and perhaps more complex, strategies at different points during their school years. A classic study by Moely, Olson, Halwes, and Flavell (1969) shows these effects. Children whose ages ranged from five to eleven were shown a group of pictures of objects drawn from different categories such as animals, articles of clothing, and so on. The pictures were arranged in a circle; no picture was placed next to another picture drawn from the same category. The children were asked to learn the names of the objects in the pictures, and, while the experimenter was gone for a few minutes, the children were invited to move the pictures around in any way that they thought might help them remember the names of the things shown. The variable of interest was the extent to which the children had learned that putting the pictures of category members together would help them remember the names of the objects. Surprisingly, only the ten- and eleven-year-old children used this grouping strategy spontaneously. This is interesting because, as we've seen, children who are much younger, perhaps as young as seven, know that subvocal rehearsal will help them remember a list. Here we see that even children who have learned something fundamental—namely, that there are things you can do to help you remember—don't seem to know that the picture situation offers the possibility of using such a strategy.

Development of Reasoning Ability

When we looked at the issue of memory development, we saw that the memory capabilities of children change in at least two ways during their school years. First, their conceptual knowledge of the world grows dramatically, enabling them to recognize connections and relationships among natural objects. Second, children's strategic knowledge also grows, and this enables them to encode and organize these new-found connections among objects with greater flexibility. When we look at the development of reasoning or problem solving, we see a similar phenomenon unfold. In part, older children reason better than younger ones because older children just know more about the world than younger children do. However, it also seems to be the case that older children know more than younger children do because older children are able to reason about their knowledge in ways that younger children cannot. In other words, it's as if the improvement in reasoning schemes seen in the school-age years enables children to widen their cognitive horizons and thus take in more information than they did when they were younger. And from all this knowledge that's been taken in, school-age children learn how to build schemes that are more effective in reasoning. If this discussion suggests to you that knowledge and reasoning have something like a "braided" relationship, that's probably right. In this section we'll explore some of the findings that bear on this relationship.

It's not too difficult to demonstrate that children frequently know less about the world than adults do. In one study, McCloskey and Kaiser's (1984) subjects watched a toy electric locomotive pull a flatcar carrying a ball. At one point, the ball fell through a hole in the moving flatcar and fell through the train tracks to the floor several feet below. The children were told that this would happen; their task was to predict the path the ball would take in its descent to the floor. Seventy percent of the children thought that the ball would fall straight down, rather than in a parabolic trajectory. When the children were asked to reconcile their predictions with what they had observed, many of the children claimed that the ball had indeed fallen straight down just as they had predicted! Some of the children claimed that the train had given the ball a small push just before it was released. Both of these explanations show that the children were trying to make their observations fit what they "knew" to be true about the world.

USING YOUR KNOWLEDGE OF COGNITION

If you want to remember to do something, but you fear you might forget, you may use a reminder. A reminder can be almost any sort of a stimulus, but usually it's (1) something visible that you're pretty sure you'll see, and (2) something that you'll see before you have to do whatever it is you're trying to remind yourself about. For most of us, it's not too hard to think of reminders and to use them. However the use of reminders requires more sophistication than we might think. Just as memory itself develops, the ability to recognize and use reminders also develops, and this implies that younger children may have to learn what to do in order to remind themselves of something. If you have some nieces or nephews or younger siblings available, you may be able to track the course of such development using some fairly simple apparatus.

Get four identical paper cups and show a four- or five-year-old that you are hiding a penny under one of the cups. Now tell the child that you are going to move two of the cups and slowly slide the cup with the penny under it into the position of another cup, while sliding that cup to the position that's now vacant. Ask the child where the penny is. He or she should know and be able to pick out the cup. If the child accomplishes this, then increase the number of switches by one on each

consecutive trial until the child's short-term memory is overloaded, and he or she can no longer tell where the penny is. At that point, produce a paper clip and tell the child that you will put the paper clip on top of the cup hiding the penny. Ask the child if this will help him or her remember, and the child's answer will almost certainly be yes. Does it help? Yes, now the child recognizes that the visible paper clip is an excellent reminder of the penny's whereabouts, and he or she can still find the penny after numerous switches. But it's also easy to demonstrate that many children of this age don't truly understand the reminding concept. Take the paper clip off the cup and ask the child if the paper clip would help them remember if it were placed inside the cup along with the penny. Surprisingly, Beal (1985) found that almost half of the four- and five-year-olds thought that this would be a good reminder, too. In contrast, none of the eight-year-old children tested by Beal thought that putting the paper clip in with the penny would help them remember. This demonstration points out that the kindergartners may have an incomplete notion of reminding: They recognize that a visible stimulus may help them remember, but they don't realize that in this case the stimulus *must* be visible if it is to be of any use.

But as children learn more about the world, their ability to reason about it also increases. For example, most adults use a concept of "cause and effect" to reason about some events in the world, and children also have this concept in some form or another. But, as the philosopher Hume originally observed over two centuries ago, "causes" are never observed in nature, they are inferred. Hume then went on to discuss three factors that seem to be involved in making a causal inference: The events must be close together in time and space (contiguity); the event labeled the cause must occur before the event labeled the result (precedence); and the presumed cause and effect must have occurred reliably together in the past (covariation). As you would probably hypothesize, the degree to which a person can infer "cause and effect" seems to depend in part on the degree to which he or she can observe and make inferences from contiguity, precedence, and covariation.

There is some good evidence to suggest that even very young children are sensitive to the effects of contiguity. Leslie (1982) demonstrated that four- and five-month-old children look longer at passive objects that begin moving without being first struck than they do at objects that begin moving after another object has collided with them. Presumably, the children's longer looking means that they sense that there is something "wrong" or "odd" about this violation of contiguity. By age three, when children observe three sequential events A, B, and C, and they're asked to tell "what made B happen," these preschoolers are almost as likely to say "C" as they are to say "A." However, by age five, kindergarteners seem to have the concept of precedence well established; at this point, on a variety of tasks, children always respond with the initial event. At this point in their lives, children will overlook the effects of covariation, especially when these effects conflict with contiguity. So, if one event always follows another event after a five-second interval, thus establishing covariation but not contiguity, five-year-olds will not necessarily see the causal connection. However, by age eight, children will see the temporally separate, but covariate events as causally connected (Mendelson & Schultz, 1976). Evidence from this developmental pathway suggests that children of various ages should be strategically different from each other in attempting to draw inferences about cause and effect, and that, by the age of eight or so, children should be relatively able to reason about cause and effect.

An interesting study by Schauble (1990) bears on this issue. The subjects were children ranging in age from nine to eleven; their task was to predict the speediness of race cars that had been generated by a computer. There were five variables that could be manipulated by the child-as-experimenter, who would then observe the performance of his or her design on a "track." The variables were engine size, wheel size, tail fins, the presence or absence of a muffler, and color. Prior to their experimentation, the children expected that cars with large engines, large wheels, and the presence of a muffler would be the fastest. In fact, large engines and medium-sized wheels were associated with faster cars; the muffler and the color had no causal influence. Tail fins helped a car go faster when the engine was large, but had no effect when the engine was small. Technically, this was not a difficult task: The children were given eight sessions to learn about the cars, and there was no variation in the cars' performance. Given the age range of the children involved, they should have been able to draw on their knowledge of the concepts on contiguity, precedence, and, especially, covariation to figure out what made some cars go faster than others. But it turned out to be a hard task for the children. Although the children had a good scheme for causal reasoning, this task necessitated that the children design "mini-experiments," holding all but one feature of a specific design intact while varying the one remaining feature. That is, the children had to design a situation in which they could bring their causal reasoning schemes to bear. But this is just what the children found difficult. Schauble (1990) found that most of the childrens' experiments were invalid: They typically manipulated two variables simultaneously, making a clear inference impossible. Even when they succeeded in designing a valid experiment, the children often seemed to ignore its conclusions if these disagreed with their prior expectations. Even after the children had developed a good scheme for interpreting events in a causal way, they still had to learn how to apply such schemes.

CONCLUDING COMMENTS AND SUGGESTIONS FOR FURTHER READING

We began this chapter with some questions about the relationship of language acquisition and general cognitive development. After reviewing some of this literature, we can see that, in some ways, at some points in the life span, there are certain aspects of language acquisition that seem to move "faster" than the child's overall cognitive development. For example, word acquisition during the period from eighteen months to age five or six grows at an explosive rate. Other rule-based aspects of language, such as plural learning, inflections, and syntax generally, are also acquired at a terrific pace from about age two to age six. But these findings show another picture too. We also saw that in many cases, language acquisition is supported by—that is, aided by—cognitive changes in concept formation, in memory, and in reasoning. That is, although two-year-olds may not be able to string lengthy sentences together—a linguistic problem—with the aid of vertical construction and a short-term memory whose capacity has gotten just large enough, the child is able to express some fairly complicated thoughts at a speed that is close to real time.

For those who are interested in language development, and in the interplay of language development and other forms of cognition, there are several excellent and very accessible books. First, Gross (1985) offers an overview of cognitive development in which the information-processing viewpoint is compared and contrasted with the Piagetian perspective. Siegler's (1991) book *Children's Thinking* is more comprehensive than the title might imply, and it's very readable too. Regarding language acquisition, Wang (1991) has edited a volume of articles from the magazine *Scientific American* that deals with a wide variety of issues, including the cultural origins of language. On a more narrow front, a special issue of the journal *Cognitive Science* (14(1), 1990) is concerned with the issue of constraints on learning, especially as these constraints of memory and attention may actually aid the child in the acquisition of language and concepts. Kail (1990) has written a comprehensive book on memory development in children. Finally, there are two books that deal with the issue of children's reasoning and their strategies for reasoning. Siegler and Jenkins (1989) present a coherent picture of children's arithmetic strategies. Bjorkland (1990) has edited a more general volume that includes chapters on children's strategies in reading, in paying attention, and in solving problems.

 **KEY TERMS**

Babbling
Babbling drift
Holophrastic stage
Overextensions
Underextensions
Whole-object assumption
Taxonomic assumption

Two-word stage
Mean length of utterance
  (MLU)
Structural relationships
Vertical construction
Horizontal construction
Inflections

Expansions
Less-is-more (LIM) position
Metamemory
Production deficiency
Process deficiency
Min strategy

FOCUS ON RESEARCH

Children's Addition

How do children go about adding two numbers, as in a problem such as "solve 2 + 9"? For many years, the standard answer to this question was the one provided by Groen and Parkman (1972) who discovered that children used what was termed the **"min" strategy.** To use the min strategy, a child looks at the two numbers to be added (these numbers are called the "addends"), determines which is smaller, and counts up that number of times beginning from the larger addend. To solve the problem shown above, the child's mental event would be something like "9, 10, 11—so the answer is 11." According to the min strategy, the only variable that should influence solution times is the size of the smaller addend, because the children count internally at a constant rate.

This hypothesis has been supported many times. Thus, children who are asked to add "9 + 6" require more time to get the answer than when they are given the problem "9 + 3," because it takes them longer to count up six places from the number nine than it does to count up three places from the number nine. However, educators have long reported that the children themselves maintain that they are capable of using a variety of strategies to solve such problems. Could it be that

the children were inaccurately reporting their use of strategies? Or, could it be that the chronometric analysis simply masked the fact that the children were arriving at the answer via a number of different routes.

Siegler (1987) asked his subjects, who were either kindergarteners, first-graders, or second-graders, to solve a number of addition problems and to describe what they were doing to get the answer. The data were remarkable. When the children reported that they were using the min strategy (which they actually used on only 36 percent of the problems), their solution times were beautifully correlated with the size of the smaller addend. But when the children said they were using a different strategy (such as simply counting from 1, which they might do if both addends were small), their solution times were rather poorly correlated with the size of the smaller addend. This suggests that when the children said they had used a non-min strategy, they indeed had used a non-min strategy to solve the problem. As this study shows, even these rather young children were capable of making a sophisticated decision from a menu of strategic choices that were available to them.

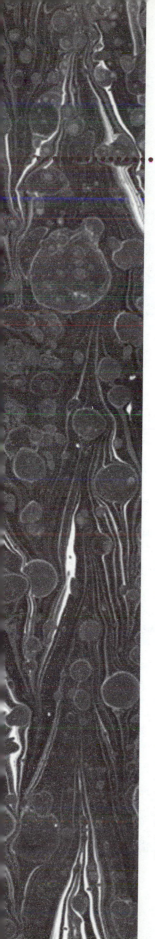

PART 6

THINKING

The book's final chapters discuss what have been called "higher" mental processes in humans. The word *higher* is in quotes for the following reasons. Generally, thinking, reasoning, and problem solving have been called higher processes because traditionally it's been thought that such events come at the end of the chain of information processing. This view of cognitive activity became particularly entrenched during the 1960s. Because perception and memory were strongly rooted in sensory and physiological psychology, they were thought to be closely related to neural processes. The cognitive activity related to thinking and reasoning, however, did not seem synonymous with any particular pattern of neural processing and in that sense seemed "higher" than other cognitive processes.

We now know the picture is much more complicated than that. First, as we've seen, information-processing theories of perception and memory have been formulated. These theories are abstract; that is, they do not deal with these phenomena in explicitly neural terms. Second, the idea that a chain of events occurs in cognition is also simplistic. Although the information-processing paradigm often treats mental events as though they occurred sequentially, we know that this is just a theoretical convenience. In reality, the so-

called higher processes don't necessarily occur after the so-called lower processes. What we perceive does form the basis of our thoughts, but our thoughts also influence what we perceive. The sequences of information processing are quite tangled, and they constantly loop and double back upon one another. Seen from this perspective, the term *higher mental processes* is really only a teaching or organizational device.

One important issue that this section deals with is the question of representation, or problem understanding. How a problem is represented or understood by the problem solver seems to have a powerful influence on the problem solver's effectiveness. In this regard, reasoning is much like problem solving. Although the principles of logic can be delineated clearly, humans often don't perceive these principles, which means that their representations of logic problems are sometimes different than those used by logicians. Earlier, we talked about the schema as an encompassing cognitive structure that organized incoming information and suggested which information should be forthcoming. In this context, the schema influences how problems are represented. This section examines schematic influences in both reasoning and problem solving.

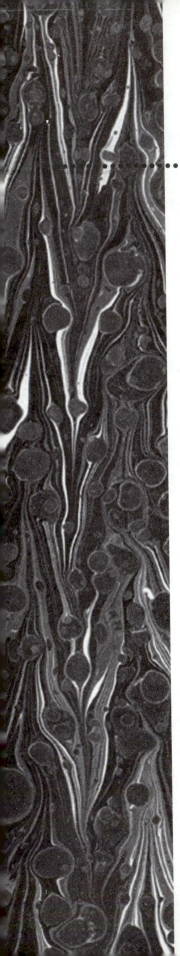

CHAPTER **11**

REASONING, CONCEPT FORMATION, AND CONCEPTUAL STRUCTURE

CHAPTER OUTLINE

OVERVIEW

LOGIC AND FORMAL REASONING
Human Thought and the Rules
of Logic
Validity, Truth, and Soundness
Cross-Cultural Studies
Conditional Reasoning
The Wason Selection Task
Mental Models
Summary of Formal Reasoning

NATURAL REASONING
Representativeness
Availability
Framing Decisions
How Biases Influence Decision
Making
Summary of Natural Reasoning

CONCEPT FORMATION
Artificial Concepts
Strategies in Concept Attainment Tasks
Summary of Artificial Concept
Formation Tasks

NATURAL CATEGORIES
Probabilistic Views of Conceptual
Structure
Exemplar-Based Views of Conceptual
Structure
Theory-Based Views of Conceptual
Structure
Theories of Conceptual Structure:
An Evaluation and Summary

USING YOUR KNOWLEDGE
OF COGNITION

CONCLUDING COMMENTS
AND SUGGESTIONS FOR
FURTHER READING

FOCUS ON RESEARCH

KEY TERMS

OVERVIEW

All the first-year students at my under-graduate college were required to take a course in logic. I remember looking forward to the course and thinking that I would become the possessor of some penetrating analysis that would enable me to immediately see the truth or falsity of things. Thus armed, I would be able to demolish my friends' arguments on any matter. My expectations were probably incorrect; the course turned out to be disappointing. First, I wasn't thrilled with the prospect of memorizing the form of all sixty-four categorical syllogisms—this didn't seem like any argument winner to me. Further, I found that logic didn't always seem logical. For example, logicians have developed truth tables that can be used to verify the truth of complex remarks. One of the truth tables concerns the truth of implications, such as "If P, then Q." I was surprised to find out that if P and Q were both false, the whole statement (If P, then Q) was nevertheless true! How could the whole statement be true when both of its parts were false? I had a realization: if this was logic, then my mind certainly wasn't logical all the time, because this didn't make much sense to me.

To what extent is this realization common to other people as well? This chapter considers the question of human reasoning. Success in **formal reasoning** seems somewhat dependent upon educational level. Individuals from cultures that don't emphasize Western education often perform poorly (by Western standards) on formal reasoning tasks. However, even highly educated Westerners sometimes perform poorly on such tasks. Does this mean that people have to be trained to be logical? We'll examine some of the findings from research on conditional syllogisms, and we'll see that people often seem to interpret logical information differently from the way that logicians do. We'll also consider natural reasoning—reasoning on problems that seem closely related to the kinds of judgments that are required of us every day. How do people accomplish such reasoning? Apparently, people typically make use of general rules of thumb that usually work quickly and efficiently. This chapter considers some situations in which these rules of thumb are pushed past their limits. Such situations occur more frequently than we think; reasoning that looks plausible and logical sometimes isn't.

The second part of the chapter investigates the nature of concept formation and how such concepts may be organized. The literature on so-called artificial concepts (i.e., concepts created by the experimenter) suggests that people formulate and, more or less systematically, test a hypothesis about which items or elements make up a particular category. However, when we look at natural categories, those that seem to be present in the everyday world—and which are represented internally—we see that there is much less evidence for the position that we form such concepts by explicitly evaluating hypotheses. This discussion of natural concepts will draw us into a discussion of similarity. Certainly, it seems that similar things are grouped into the same category. Such a position, then, would argue that concepts reflect our judgments of similarity: Things that are similar are similar because they share features. If they share enough features, then they'll be grouped together conceptually. As we'll see, it appears that the actual situation is more complicated than this.

LOGIC AND FORMAL REASONING

This section considers some of the findings that result when people try to solve formal problems by using **logic.** Several issues surface here: Do people without formal training in logic nevertheless use logic to solve such problems? From a failure to solve such problems, is it legitimate to conclude that people are illogical?

Human Thought and the Rules of Logic

If we think about all the people we know, we find that it is easy to categorize each individual as "logical" or "not logical." By "logical" we usually mean that individuals are capable of giving plausible reasons for events, or capable of making inferences implied by other facts. We seldom try to describe the behavior of the people we call illogical, but their actions need to be explained, too. Are such individuals following different rules of thought than logical people? If so, how did such individuals learn those illogical rules of thought? Perhaps the problem should be turned around. Maybe humans are inherently illogical, and they must be explicitly taught to use logic.

The idea that humans are inherently illogical would not have been accepted a century ago. Mill (1874) viewed the laws of logic as synonymous with the laws of thought. According to Mill, logical principles were not really discovered and developed. Mill understood logical principles as simply a formal account of the same principles used by people in their everyday thinking and reasoning. Mill was aware that people sometimes made logical errors, but he explained these as simply nonsystematic "slips." Similarly, James (1890) maintained that the two principal components of logical reasoning were analysis and abstraction. Analysis referred to our ability to break down an object into its component parts, letting one of the parts represent the entire object. For example, in the statement "Freud is a man," the thinker must represent Freud by using only one of Freud's components—specifically his maleness. Abstraction referred to our ability to designate a specific component as part of a broader classification. Thus from the statement "All men are mortal," it follows that Freud must be mortal. That is, Freud can be represented by his maleness, which can be grouped into the broader classification "mortal." Therefore, "Freud" can also be grouped into this broader classification. According to James, these two mental processes enabled logical reasoning to occur.

Validity, Truth, and Soundness

Logical analysis can take many forms, only some of which will be dealt with in this chapter. However, a few terms are common to all logical systems. One of these terms is **validity.** A logical argument is valid if according to the rules established by logicians, the conclusion of the argument necessarily follows from the earlier statements. Sometimes students think that the validity of an argument is synonymous with its **truth,** but that's a mistake. A logical argument can be valid but untrue. Consider the following statements:

All dinosaurs are animals.
All animals are in zoos.
Therefore, all dinosaurs are in zoos.

The conclusion is valid according to the rules used by logicians. However, not all dinosaurs are in zoos, so the conclusion is not true. On the other hand, if the argument's initial statements *are* true and the reasoning is valid, then the conclusion will also be true. All logical systems have this property, which is referred to as **soundness.** Soundness simply means that, given the truth of the argument's initial statements, valid reasoning will produce a truthful conclusion.

Soundness in reasoning doesn't necessarily imply that logical reasoning has taken place. For example, if given true initial statements, a person may be able to determine a valid, true conclusion with regularity. Under these circumstances, his reasoning would be sound. But if the person accomplishes this feat by applying an idiosyncratic reasoning system that he cannot explain, his reasoning is not logical. Logical reasoning implies that we have followed the rules of logical inference as established by logicians and described in textbooks. In other words, logical reasoning is defined as much by its methods as it is by its outcome. If we deviate from this method, our reasoning is not logical, no matter what other properties it might have.

Researchers face difficulty in trying to determine the logical abilities of humans. Even if a person succeeds in determining the validity or invalidity of an argument, this does not necessarily mean that she used logic to arrive at the conclusion. This assertion was clearly demonstrated in a well-known study by Henle (1962), who gave graduate students, with no formal training in logic, problems such as the one that follows:

> A group of women were discussing their household problems. Mrs. Shivers broke the ice by saying: "I'm so glad we're talking about these problems. It's so important to talk about things that are in our minds. We spend so much time in the kitchen that of course household problems are in our minds. So it is important to talk about them." (Does it follow that it is important to talk about them? Give your reasoning.)

Henle found that subjects often treated the logical problem as an empirical task. That is, they attempted to assess, for example, whether spending a great deal of time in the kitchen would necessarily imply that kitchen events would really be on the homemakers' minds. Frequently, subjects gave the correct answer (Mrs. Shivers is logically correct when she states that talking about such problems is important), but their reasoning was usually not logical. Although the ability to give the correct answer implies that the answer has been derived logically, this implication is deceptive. Henle's subjects did not perform in a logical fashion. As suggested by some commentators (Howard, 1983), the subjects may have performed illogically because everyday reasoning does not demand the knowledge and application of formal logical principles. When confronted with practical problems, we usually behave in a pragmatic or probabilistic way. We know, for example, that if a skunk is run over on the highway, a characteristic intense odor will be produced. If we're driving along some night and smell this scent, we're likely to conclude that a skunk has been hit, and we would probably feel that this conclusion is valid. But it isn't. The skunk may have been warding off an intruder, or perhaps a sensory psychologist had been conducting a field study on the effects of skunk scent on some aspect of driving performance. Henle's study implies that people do not typically distinguish between the everyday sort of probabilistic reasoning and logic.

Cross-Cultural Studies   If the laws of thought were truly synonymous with the rules of logic, then logic should be observable wherever human thought occurs.

Specifically, individuals who are reared and educated in non-Western ways should nevertheless be capable of reasoning logically. Debate on this issue was initiated by Levy-Bruhl (1910), who maintained that the "primitive mind" thinks in a "prelogical" way, governed by emotion, magic, and an inability to distinguish between mental and external events. Although Levy-Bruhl probably overstated the case, more recent anthropological studies (Cole & Scribner, 1977) have indicated that nonliterate, non-Western people employ reasoning strategies that are somewhat different from those observed among educated Westerners. Such individuals are capable of reasoning in an orderly fashion; consequently, their deductions are often sound. However, these nonschooled people seem to accomplish this reasoning without the aid of formal logic. For example, when Sylvia Scribner asked members of the Vai (a West African tribe) to respond to logical arguments as a part of a literacy program, she found that their answers, although reasonable, were not logical. What follows is a problem and response of one of the Vai:

> All women who live in Monrovia are married.
> Kemu is not married.
> Does she live in Monrovia?
> Answer and Explanation: Yes. Monrovia is not for any one kind of people, so Kemu came to live there. (Scribner, 1977)

Notice that the respondent answered the question by ignoring or discounting the first statement and insisted upon giving the correct answer, based upon what is known to be true: Anyone is permitted to live in Monrovia. This little protocol is a good illustration of what Scribner found to be a general finding in her work. As little as two years of schooling dramatically increased the likelihood of an individual's ability to reason logically. The protocol also shows a process that Henle observed in her Western subjects: The Vai tribesperson treated the task as an empirical problem—one that could be answered from one's observations of the world.

Are humans inherently logical? The answer appears to be a qualified no. Human reasoning may be inherently orderly and sound, but logical ability seems to be a by-product of education. But even people who are educated are not always logical. Their reasoning processes have offered cognitive psychologists a good "window" on what might be called the rules of thought.

Conditional Reasoning

One formal reasoning task that has been studied extensively by cognitive psychologists is known as **conditional reasoning**. Conditional reasoning takes place when an individual is given some statements called "conditions"—a rule for determining what outcomes can be expected if certain conditions are present, and a conclusion whose validity the reasoner tries to assess, using the previously given information. For example:

> If you have studied hard, you will do well in this course.
> You have studied hard.
> Therefore, you can expect to do well in this course.

Generally, the rule is expressed in an "if-then" format: If P (some sort of antecedent condition), then Q (some sort of consequent condition). One of the other statements establishes the truth or falsity of P or Q. The reasoner must establish the truth or falsity of the remaining term, or determine that its truth or falsity can't be established, given the existing information. Logicians have developed two inference rules that can be used to reason validly in these circumstances. The first of these is called **modus ponens.** In situations such as "If P, then Q" and "P is true," modus ponens allows us to validly infer that "Q is true." In other words, when we're given "if P, then Q," modus ponens enables us to infer that the presence of P implies the presence of Q. The studying example just used represents the valid use of modus ponens. The second rule is called **modus tollens.** Consider the following argument:

> If it snows on Thursday, I'll go skiing.
> I did not go skiing.
> Therefore, it did not snow on Thursday.

The conclusion is valid, and represents the correct use of modus tollens, which can be expressed in the following general format: Given, "if P, then Q" and "Q is false" or "not Q," then modus tollens allows to validly infer that "P is false" or "not P." Where P implies Q, the absence of Q implies the absence of P.

In addition to modus tollens and modus ponens, conditional reasoning can take place in two other forms, and both of these represent particular kinds of logical errors. Take a look at the following argument:

> If she likes me, she'll go out with me.
> She likes me not.
> Therefore, she won't go out with me.

If the conclusion looks valid to us, then we have made an error in reasoning known as "denying the antecedent." Notice that the error is named after the antecedent, the first part of the conditional rule. When we deny the antecedent, we assume that the consequent will be true *only if* the antecedent is true. That's an error because the consequent could be true even if the antecedent is false. That is, she may go out with you for some other reason even if she doesn't like you. Denying the antecedent is not the only error our love-stricken friends are likely to commit. Consider the following reasoning:

> If she likes me, she'll go out with me.
> She goes out with me.
> Therefore, she likes me.

Not necessarily. In this case, the reasoner has assumed that the truth of the consequent implies the truth of the antecedent, an error that is known as "affirming the consequent." These forms of conditional reasoning are summarized in Table 11.1.

We can be pretty sure that subjects who are untrained in logic are not familiar with these terms, but can educated people nevertheless reason successfully on formal conditional reasoning problems? Rips and Marcus (1977) presented their subjects, who were students untrained in the use of inference rules, with eight "concrete" (more about this term later) examples of conditional reasoning, such as the following:

> If a card has an A on the left, it has a 7 on the right.
> The card does not have a 7 on the right.
> The card does not have an A on the left.

They asked their subjects to judge whether the conclusion was always true, never true, or sometimes true. What's your answer? Perhaps the best way to proceed here is to convert the previous "concrete" phrases into a more general format

············ **TABLE 11.1**   Conditional Reasoning

FORM	NAME	EXAMPLE
If P, then Q P Therefore Q	Modus ponens (valid inference)	If the object is square, then it is blue. The object is square. The object is blue.
If P, then Q not Q Therefore not P	Modus tollens (valid inference)	If the object is square, then it is blue. The object is not blue. The object is not square.
If P, then Q not P Therefore not Q	Denying the antecedent (invalid inference)	If the object is square, then it is blue. The object is not square. The object is not blue.
If P, then Q Q Therefore P	Affirming the consequent (invalid inference)	If the object is square, then it is blue. The object is blue. The object is square.

Source: Adapted from Howard. (Copyright 1983 by Macmillan Publishing Co. Adapted by permission of the publisher and author.)

compatible with the information in Table 11.1. Thus, the "A on the left" phrase becomes "P," and the "7 on the right" phrase becomes "Q." Logicians have developed a symbol, $\supset$, sometimes called the horseshoe, to designate the idea of implication. The first line of the prior example then becomes "A on the left implies 7 on the right," or "$P \supset Q$." Logicians also make use of a symbol to designate "not" or "the absence of." This is the tilde, written like this: $\sim$. The phrase in the second line of the prior argument then becomes "not Q" or "$\sim Q$." Logicians sometimes use a three-dot pattern, $\therefore$, to indicate "therefore." Making the conversion for the prior argument, then, we have:

$$P \supset Q$$
$$\sim Q$$
$$\therefore \sim P.$$

Looking back to Table 11.1, we see that this is indeed a valid inference that represents the correct use of modus tollens. If we were one of Rips and Marcus's subjects, the correct answer in this case would be "always true." Table 11.2 shows the percentage of subjects responding "always true," "sometimes true," and "never true" for each of the eight types of problems used. The problems shown here are in the "abstract" format, but they were given to the subjects in the concrete form shown before. Problems 1 and 2 require the use of modus ponens, and as Table 11.2 indicates, subjects were quite adept in applying this inference rule. No errors at all were made on those two problems. Problems 7 and 8 also permit a valid inference through the use of modus tollens. That is, modus tollens enables us to say that problem 7 could never be true and problem 8 (the example used earlier) would always be true. The subjects were much less successful in applying modus tollens than they were in using modus ponens. More than a fifth of the subjects believed that the conclusion of problem 7 could sometimes be true. And over 40 percent made a reasoning error on problem 8.

No valid inferences can be drawn from the information in problems 3 through 6, and so the correct answer in each of those cases should be "sometimes

············ **TABLE 11.2** Percentage of Total Responses for Eight Types of Conditional Syllogisms

SYLLOGISM	ALWAYS	SOMETIMES	NEVER
1. P⊃Q P ∴ Q	100[a]	0	0
2. P⊃Q P ∴ ~ Q	0	0	100[a]
3. P⊃Q ~ P ∴ Q	5	79[a]	16
4. P⊃Q ~ P ∴ ~ Q	21	77[a]	2
5. P⊃Q Q ∴ P	23	77[a]	0
6. P⊃Q Q ∴ ~ P	4	82[a]	14
7. P⊃Q ~ Q ∴ P	0	23	77[a]
8. P⊃Q ~ Q ∴ ~ P	57[a]	39	4

Source: Adapted from Rips and Marcus. (Copyright 1977 by Lawrence Erlbaum Associates, Inc. Adapted by permission of the publisher and author.)

[a]The correct response.

true." However, we see that subjects sometimes insisted that valid inferences could be drawn. In problems 3 and 4, approximately 20 percent of the subjects believed that some valid inference could be drawn about Q from ~ P. This result represents denial of the antecedent. Similarly, about 20 percent of the subjects believed that valid inferences could be drawn in problems 6 and 7, which represents an affirmation of the consequent. From Q, we can't draw any valid inference concerning P or ~ P.

The errors on problems 3 through 6 can be explained by examining the subject's understanding of the logical term "if" when it is used in "if P, then Q" statements. People who have not been trained in logic apparently use this word differently than do logicians. Logicians make a distinction between the term "if," which is called the *conditional*, and the expression "if and only if," which is called the *biconditional*. The sentence

I will win if and only if I practice.

implies that practice is a necessary condition for my victory to take place. This wouldn't be so if I had used the connective "if."

To analyze the truth of implications containing the conditional or biconditional statement, logicians make use of truth tables. A truth table offers us a way of determining the truth of a complex remark based upon the truth of its

·············· **TABLE 11.3**   Truth Tables

IMPLICATION OR CONDITIONAL			BICONDITIONAL		
P	Q	P⊃Q	P	Q	P↔Q
T	T	T	T	T	T
T	F	F	T	F	F
F	T	T	F	T	F
F	F	T	F	F	T

component statements. Table 11.3 shows the truth tables for both the conditional "if," which is indicated by the horseshoe symbol, and the biconditional "if and only if," which is shown by the double-headed arrow.

To see how this table would be used in practice, let's consider an example:

If the switch is turned on, then the light will go on.
The switch is not turned on.
Therefore, the light does not go on.

Using the conditional truth table, we see that there are two conditions in which the complex remark is true while P, the antecedent, is false. In one of these two conditions, Q, the consequent, is false. In the other condition, it is true. All we can say about the conclusion is that sometimes it might not be true and sometimes it might be. Turning to the biconditional truth table, however, we see a different story. If P is false (i.e., ∼ P) and P ⊃ Q is true, then Q must be false. Also, if P is true and P ⊃ Q is true, then Q must also be true. If you go back to the previous example and change the word "if" to "if and only if," then you'll see that the conclusion is now valid. This means that neither the denial of the antecedent (as seen in Rips and Marcus's problems 3 and 4) nor the affirmation of the consequent (as took place in problems 5 and 6) is a fallacy in reasoning if one has interpreted the conditional as the biconditional.

Staudenmayer (1975) gave his subjects a series of conditional reasoning problems similar to the ones used by Rips and Marcus. He was able to demonstrate that subjects typically decide how the connective "if" is to be interpreted, and the subsequent reasoning processes are consistent with whatever interpretation the subjects make. For example, in cases in which an "if then" phrasing was used, 59 percent of the subjects treated the "if" connective as though it were the biconditional, "if and only if." This misuse increased to 77 percent when phrasings such as "P causes Q" were used in the problems. Once the interpretation of the "if" connective had been made, subjects' reasoning was fairly sound. Staudenmayer concluded that errors in these conditional reasoning problems were not errors of reasoning per se but rather failures to realize the distinction between the conditional and the biconditional phrasings.

The Wason Selection Task   Although such an analysis accounts for the errors made on problems 3 through 6 of Rips and Marcus's study, it does not explain the considerable number of errors made on problems 7 and 8. These errors seem to result from an inability to apply modus tollens. This inability is rather well documented, dating back to a study by Wason (1966). Wason presented his subjects with four cards showing the following symbols:

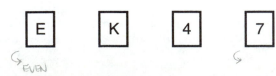

The subjects were told that each card had a number on one side and a letter on the other. Their task was to turn over the minimum number of cards necessary to verify (and this is an important term) the following rule: If a card has a vowel on one side, then it has an even number on the other side. You might try solving this problem. While you're thinking about it, I'd like to point out that this problem, now known to everyone as the Wason selection task, is one of the mainstays of the literature on reasoning, a fact that prompted Tweney and Doherty (1983) to comment that research on it and other logical tasks has become ". . . somewhat of a small industry, spawning a host of variations, dozens of studies, and more than its share of interpretational controversies."

In Wason's study, 46 percent of the subjects turned over both the *E* and the *4*. This response is incorrect and represents another example of affirming the consequent. We're really not interested in what's behind the *4* because, even if we found a consonant, that wouldn't invalidate the rule. Many subjects turned only the *E* over. This response is on the right track, but it's incomplete. Only 4 percent of the subjects got the problem right, by turning over the *E* and the *7*. Turning over the *7* represents an application of the important modus tollens step called **disconfirming the consequent.** If "vowel" implies "even number," the absence of an even number (in the case of the *7*) implies the absence of a vowel on the reverse side of the card.

Readers who are still in the dark on this problem are probably not alone. Wason and Johnson-Laird (1970) have pointed out that many people did not see why the *E* and *7* have to be turned over even after it had been explained to them. In some cases, subjects who picked the *E* and *4* initially seemed to have been "blinded" by their initial choices and seemed to be unable to consider the implications of the other cards. To see if the subjects were indeed blinded by their initial picks, Wason and Johnson-Laird (1970) presented their subjects with a specific form of the Wason selection task, one in which four cards were partially covered with cardboard masks, thus concealing some of the information on the cards. The subject's task was to determine which cards had to be unmasked in order to validate a conditional rule. When subjects got the problem wrong, the experimenters unmasked the correct cards and asked the subjects if they would like to change their minds, given what they could now observe. Seventy-four percent of the subjects who failed to get the answer initially also failed to correct themselves when the correct cards were unmasked! During an interview that followed with these subjects, 48 percent failed to correct themselves after the experimenter pointed out the nature of their logical error.

What makes the subjects do so poorly on this problem? One reason might be that the subjects simply don't have the logical competence required to do the task. That is, unless you've studied logic, you can't possibly do well. For example, Markovits (1985) found that, when subjects were given a particular conditional statement to interpret that was embedded in the context of other conditional statements, they performed better overall than when they were given only one conditional reasoning problem. However, subjects who profited the most from the additional information were those subjects who had already documented reasonable understanding of conditional rules on a pretest problem.

On the other hand, sheer logical competence, or the lack of it, may not be the only explanation for the poor performance of most subjects. The performance might result from the subjects' use of poor reasoning skills. According to this view, people actually have the reasoning competence necessary to solve the problem, but they deploy faulty reasoning strategies. In support of this position, Pollard (1985) found that subjects seem to use a matching strategy to solve the task.

Subjects who use the matching strategy turn over whatever cards are mentioned in the problem. So when the rule is "A card that has a vowel on one side doesn't have an even number on the other side," subjects still turn over the *E* and the 4—which happens to be the correct answer. However, when the rule is "A card that doesn't have a vowel on one side has an even number on the other side," subjects may still turn over the *E* and the *4*, although now the *K* and the *7* are the cards that should be flipped.

Further complications have been introduced by Johnson-Laird, Legrenzi, and Legrenzi (1972) who demonstrated that these sorts of errors don't have to occur. That is, the context in which the inference is demanded apparently influences the likelihood that a person will get the problem right. In their study, the subjects were given what have been called **thematic materials.** Subjects were shown the envelopes depicted in Figure 11.1, and they were asked to imagine that they were postal workers sorting letters. Specifically, they were asked to determine if the following postal regulation had been violated: "If a letter is sealed, then it has a 50-lire stamp on it." Subjects were asked to turn over the minimum number of envelopes necessary to verify the rule. In this case, 88 percent of the subjects were correct, turning over the sealed envelope and the envelope with the 40-lire stamp on it.

The so-called thematic materials effect is quite dramatic, altering for most people the likelihood of getting the correct answer from something under 10 percent to almost 90 percent. Given that people seem to be rather poor on the selection task, what accounts for the thematic effect? Needless to say, there has been some intense theorizing and experimentation concerning the necessary and sufficient causes of the effect. For the sake of clarity, I'll enumerate some of the possible explanations:

1. **The Concreteness of the Materials.** Some commentators (e.g., Mayer, 1983) have noted that the envelope task is more concrete than the original letter-numeral selection task.

2. **A Sense of Reality.** Johnson-Laird et al. (1972) thought that thematic materials established a natural, or down-to-earth, real-world context that enabled the subjects to reason about what they would do if they actually were in that situation.

FIGURE 11.1

Material used in the envelope experiment by Johnson-Laird, Legrenzi, and Legrenzi (1972). Subjects were asked which envelopes should be turned over to test the rule, "If a letter is sealed, then it has a 50-lire stamp on it."

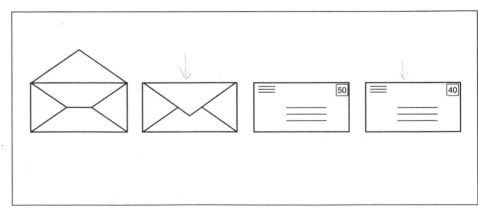

3. Instructional Set. Some researchers have pointed out that what we might be dealing with here is a linguistic phenomenon. In other words, the subjects simply interpret words like "verify" and "falsify" differently depending on their context.

4. Memory. Other researchers have maintained that the thematic materials effect extends as far as the subject's memory of the task. In other words, if the subjects can remember being in a situation that corresponds closely to the "cover story," they do well on the task. But if they've never been in such a situation, or if they can't retrieve their memory of it, they will fail.

5. Something Else in Addition to, or Instead of, the Above. Some researchers have argued that some altogether different variables may be involved.

Let's consider each of these. First, the "concreteness" of the materials probably isn't a relevant issue here. After all, looking at pictures of envelopes can hardly be considered more "concrete" than looking at pictures of cards.

Regarding the "sense of reality" established by the envelopes, some evidence suggests that simply giving people thematic materials won't produce improvements in reasoning unless the sense of reality established by the theme agrees with knowledge that people have stored in their memories. Thus, Griggs and Cox (1982) thought that it wasn't the thematic material per se in the envelope study that enabled the subjects to do so well; rather, the subjects were using remembered knowledge of the British postal system to help them make the deduction. Indeed, Griggs and Cox found that there was a defunct regulation that specified that a sealed envelope required more postage than did an envelope whose flap was simply tucked in. Griggs and Cox repeated the Johnson-Laird et al. study with University of Florida undergraduates as subjects, and they found that these subjects performed no better on the envelope problem than they did on the abstract letter-number problem. Next, Griggs and Cox constructed a problem representing facts and relationships that their subjects may have experienced directly. Subjects saw four cards labeled "beer," "Coke," "22 years," and "16 years." The subjects were told to turn over the minimum number of cards necessary to verify the following rule: "If a person is drinking beer, then the person must be over 19 years of age." In this situation, subjects performed much better than those people who had received the letter-number task. Griggs and Cox concluded that performance on card selection problems was enhanced when the thematic material cued retrieval of directly experienced knowledge stored in permanent memory.

Chrostowski and Griggs (1985) have supported this interpretation. Subjects who were given a memory cuing context outperformed subjects who were not given such a context; thus memory cuing was established as a necessary and sufficient condition to enhance performance on the selection task. However, the degree of improvement was influenced by the instructions that the subjects were given. Subjects who were given "true-false" instructions were not helped by the memory cuing conditions to the same extent that subjects given "falsification" instructions were helped.

This last finding does indeed suggest that the instructional set at least modifies in some way the cognitive processes that the reasoners bring to bear on this problem. Other studies provided some evidence for this contention. In a study by Yachanin (1986), subjects in some conditions were told to establish whether the rules were true or false (considered to be the most ambiguous instructional set), and in other conditions, the subjects were given a falsification instruction. For one of the rules, the subjects had direct experience; for the other rule, they did not. Performance was best when the subject had direct experience and falsification instructions; moreover, most of the effect seemed to be based on the instructions. That is, when subjects were given falsification instructions for a rule with which they were completely unfamiliar, their performance was nearly as good as the condition in which they were given falsification instructions for a familiar problem. This finding is in fundamental agreement with that of Chrostowski and Griggs (1985), although Yachanin's work seems to emphasize the linguistic component to a greater extent than does Chrostowski and Griggs' study. There is some reason to suspect the robustness of the instructional effect, however, if only for its volatility. In some studies, the instructional effect was very strong; in others, it was weak. In still other studies, the subjects' behavior was the opposite of what we would theoretically predict. Valentine (1985) argued that, if the subjects were to check those cards that were necessary to see if the rule was being violated, such an instructional set should induce a falsification strategy and thus produce a reasonable chance of success. But the subjects misbehaved: The instructions instead produced a verification bias. Given the falsification instructions, subjects were likely to turn over the cards that would be needed to *verify* the rule.

Margolis (1987) describes how these factors may produce poor performance. First, Margolis makes a distinction between **open** and **closed** scenarios in reasoning tasks. An open scenario is one in which the subjects are not given any information about how to search for an answer. A closed scenario is one in which the person is presented with simply a limited number of options. Margolis believes that in real life, we encounter closed reasoning tasks only after we have gone through an open phase. Consequently, Margolis believes that subjects in the selection task misinterpret it as an open task, when it really is a closed task. To illustrate, suppose you were told that each card in a collection of cards has either a "swan" or a "raven" on one side, while the other side is either "white" or "black." Then, suppose you are given a rule: "If a card says "swan" on one side, then it must say "white" on the other side of that card." Now, of the four categories of cards (swan, raven, white, black) you are asked to choose any category of cards (not just a specific card) that must be checked in order to see if the rule has been violated. When you pick a category, you are able to look at all the cards in that category, that is, all the cards that are black, or all the cards that have "swan" on them, or whatever. What would you do? The correct response is to look at either the cards that have "swan" on them, or the cards that are "black," but not both sets of cards! Looking at all the cards in either category would find any example of a black swan, and that's the only single case that would violate the rule. Now, let's add one other variable: Suppose that subjects make the logical error of reversing the rule (if swans are white, then ravens are black). Under these circumstances the two categories of cards that would be searched are "swans" as above and "white" cards, and, as we've seen, these are exactly the most common choices. When these sources of ambiguity are fixed (that is, when the subject understands that the scenario is closed, not open, and that the rule is not reversible), Griggs (1989) found that subjects averaged 74 percent correct answers in an abstract form of the selection task. Other research in support of Margolis's ideas (Griggs & Jackson, 1990) has shown that when the subjects are given the instruction set "Figure out which two cards violate the rule and circle them," the subject's attention is drawn to the not-P and not-Q cards, even though these are not the answer to the problem. As Margolis would predict, Griggs and Jackson (1990) found that 65 percent of the subjects getting these instructions looked at the not-P and not-Q cards. In the absence of these instructions, these alternatives are chosen only rarely by the subjects, typically by not more than 20 percent. Thus, as volatile as the instructional phenomenon seems to be, the weight of the evidence suggests that it indeed plays a role.

Returning to the memory cuing issue, Hoch and Tschirgi (1983) found that the effects of thematic materials were not limited to situations with which the subjects were personally familiar. They argued that people have general knowledge of circumstances that should make one wary or suspicious. One circumstance that might make a person suspicious is missing information. Hoch and Tschirgi reasoned that this *extralogical* information could be used as a basis to solve a card selection problem even in a situation outside the person's area of expertise. To test this assertion, they created the following scenario. Subjects were told to imagine themselves as quality-control inspectors for a firm that manufactured pocket calculators. Subjects in the "no-relation" condition were given information telling them how to decide if the calculators were acceptable. This information included a rule that could be verified by turning over some of the calculators. Next, the subjects looked at four drawings of calculators and circled the ones they thought should be turned over. Subjects in the "blank" condition were given a similar set of instructions, including a rule that could be verified by turning over some of the calculators. Next, these subjects looked at drawings of calculators, one of which was left blank. Again, the subjects' task was to circle those calculators that needed to be turned over to verify the rule. Figure 11.2 shows the instructional set and drawings for these two conditions. In the blank condition, you need to turn over the XT-10 calculator and the blank. In the no-relation condition, the XT-10 calculator and the technical instructions need to be turned over. Which problem did you find easier?

Hoch and Tschirgi's subjects found the blank problem substantially easier than the no-relation problem. Seventy-six percent of the subjects in the blank condition solved the problem, whereas 44 percent of the subjects in the no-relation condition were successful. What accounts for the discrepancy? Hoch and Tschirgi maintain that the subject notices the missing information in the blank condition, which may help to establish a "detective" orientation (van Duyne, 1974). That is, the subjects begin to suspect that something is wrong, and they turn over the calculator to investigate it. In so doing, Hoch and Tschirgi say that the subject is obviously not relying exclusively on personally experienced knowledge retrieved from memory to solve the problem.

Along the same lines, Hoch and Tschirgi (1985) suggested that "cue redundancy" might be used as an alternative to personally experienced knowledge in solving the selection task. According to their theoretical perspective, to solve the task, a subject could generate all of the possible antecedent-consequent pairs plus the four reverse orderings. Next, the subjects could identify the truth value of each pair [(p,q), $(-p,q)$, $(-p,-q)$ are true and $(p,-q)$ is false] and the reverse orderings. These two steps, according to Hoch and Tschirgi, represent the psychological equivalent of the mental construction of a truth table. Finally, the subjects select the two cards that represent the false pair. Hoch and Tschirgi argue that what typically stops the subject from doing this is the generative difficulty: The subjects don't stop to think about generating all four pairs, and they don't think about the reverse orderings. In their study, they provided some subjects with information that could be used to help generate the pairs; this information could

(A)

Imagine that you are a quality-control clerk for Microdigit. Inc. Your job is to inspect different models of pocket calculators moving along a conveyor belt. Your company markets two different calculator models: the XT-10 and XT-11. The two models are basically the same, but the XT-10 is sold in the United States and the XT-11 is exported to Canada.

Model numbers appear on the front side and a brief set of instructions can be glued to a panel on the back side. The instructions come in two versions, one technical (for the business market) and one quite simple (for the consumer market). The calculators move along a conveyer belt, some face up with the model number showing and some face down with the instruction panel showing. Clerks must make sure that the following rule is obeyed:

If a calculator is a model XT-10, then the simple instructions must be on the panel on the backside.

Clerks must work as quickly as possible, so you want to turn over the fewest number of calculators while making sure that the rule is followed in all cases. Below is a sample of 4 calculators on your conveyer belt. Circle the calculator or calculators that you would turn over to verify the rule.

Simple instructions

Technical instructions

(B)

Imagine that you are a quality-control clerk for Microdigit. Inc. Your job is to inspect different models of pocket calculators moving along a conveyor belt. Your company markets two different calculator models: the XT-10 and XT-11. The two models are basically the same, but the XT-10 is sold in the United States and the XT-11 is exported to other countries.

Model numbers appear on the front side and a brief set of instructions can be glued to a panel on the back side. The instructions are quite simple (directed toward the consumer market). In some cases, no instructions have been glued onto the panels. These are cases where different language instructions are supplied by the distributor at a later date. The calculators move along a conveyer belt, some face up with the model number showing and some face down with the instruction panel showing. Clerks must make sure that the following rule is obeyed:

If a calculator is model XT-10, then a set of instructions must be on the panel on the backside.

Clerks must work as quickly as possible, so you want to turn over the fewest number of calculators while making sure that the rule is followed in all cases. Below is a sample of 4 calculators on your conveyer belt. Circle the calculator or calculators that you would turn over to verify the rule.

Instructions

be understood as an elaborate prompt. As part of the instructions, some of their subjects read the following two sentences: "However, a card with a vowel showing may only have an even number on the back side. A card with a consonant showing may have either an odd or an even number on the back side" (Hoch & Tschirgi, 1985, p. 455).

When these redundant cues were used with subjects who had at least a master's degree (most of these degrees were in technical areas), 72 percent of the subjects got the problem right. When nonredundant instructions were used with master's degree subjects, only 48 percent of the subjects got the correct answer. For subjects who had a bachelor's degree, four percent of the subjects with the nonredundant instructions got the problem right, versus 36 percent who were correct when the redundant instructions were given. Finally, for subjects who had a high school education, eight percent of the subjects who received the nonredundant instructions got the problem right, versus 24 percent who were correct when the redundant instructions were given. Hoch and Tschirgi concluded that many of the master's degree subjects had adequate logical knowledge to solve the problems without the addition of redundant cues but that high school subjects had so little logical knowledge of the structure of conditional statements that they couldn't be helped much by the addition of the redundant cues.

Finally, another line of evidence suggests that these sorts of extralogical strategies and linguistic effects may be subsumed into an altogether different type of cognitive structure. Cheng and Holyoak (1985) agreed that individuals might solve the selection task through the use of internally generated and computed logical steps. They referred to this concept of internal logic as the "syntactic view." Alternatively, people may solve the problem because its cover story has cued a previously stored memory. They call this the "specific experience view." Although either of these might work in the selection task, Cheng and Holyoak proposed that people are more likely to use what they call **pragmatic reasoning schemas** to solve such reasoning problems. These are clusters of rules that are highly generalized and abstract, but nonetheless they are defined with respect to classes of goals and types of relationships. An example of a pragmatic reasoning schema is the set of abstracted rules for situations involving "permission," that is, situations in which some action A may be taken only if some precondition B is satisfied. If the semantic aspects of a problem suggest to people that they are dealing with a permission situation, all of the rules about permissions in general can be called on, including "If action A is to be taken, then precondition B must be satisfied," "Action A is to be taken only if precondition B is satisfied," and so on. In one of their studies, subjects were given a selection problem based on an abstract description of a permission situation: "If one is to take action A, then one must first satisfy precondition B." Subjects also were given an arbitrary card version that was syntactically (i.e., logically) identical to the permission problem. About 60 percent of the subjects solved the abstract permission problem correctly, whereas only 20 percent solved the abstract selection task problem.

It's important to realize that Cheng and Holyoak maintain that these effects will be observed only if the permission schema is "triggered" by the semantic content of the problem. For example in the problem above, in order to trigger the permission schema, the subjects were given instructions concerning the conversion of "if-then" conditional statements, which are normative in the Wason selection task, to permission-triggering statements of the form "only if." Thus, subjects were told in the instructions that statements like "If the tablecloth is brown, then the wall is white" could be converted to "The tablecloth is brown only if the wall is white."

Cheng, Holyoak, Nisbett, and Oliver (1986) reasoned that, if people are indeed using the pragmatic reasoning schemas, perhaps to the exclusion of logical principles, training in logical principles alone should have little influence on performance on the selection task because presumably the subjects would not know how to map the formal rules onto the selection task situation nor might they in fact even realize that such rules could be mapped onto the selection task. Their results confirmed this hypothesis: Training was effective only when abstract principles were coupled with examples of selection problems that enabled the subject to map abstract principles onto concrete instances. On the other hand, a brief training session on the use of a particular pragmatic reasoning schema dealing with obligation was sufficient to enable subjects who received "obligation" problems (such as "If one works for the Armed Forces, then one must vote in the elections") to lower their error rate to only eight percent, versus a 36 percent error rate for subjects who did not get the schema training.

Mental Models

We've looked at two ways that humans might accomplish formal reasoning tasks. First, it may be the case that humans have a kind of "psycho-logic" built right into them. Although such rules may not always be equivalent to the formal rules used by logicians, these psychological equivalents are nevertheless good enough to accomplish most of the reasoning tasks we are faced with. As an alternative account, some theorists argue that we reason by means of pragmatic reasoning schemes. Finally, there are theorists who argue that we reason deductively through the creation of mental models (Johnson-Laird & Byrne, 1991; Johnson-Laird, Byrne, & Schaeken, 1992).

Central to the idea of mental models is the idea that we reason by creating a representation of the world that is neither totally abstract (a truth table would be a totally abstract representation) nor completely specific (if our representation of the world were completely specific, we would not show any transfer of previous experience to new situations). Let's consider an example to show how a conditional statement could be represented at this level of abstraction. According to Johnson-Laird and Byrne (1991), the statement "If my son wakes up in time, then he watches 'Biker Mice from Mars' " would be represented as follows:

My son wakes up in time.	He watches "Biker Mice from Mars."
My son does not wake up in time.	He watches "Biker Mice from Mars."
My son does not wake up in time.	He does not watch "Biker Mice from Mars."

Each of the three lines represents a situation that could occur in the world, or we say that each line represents a possible model of the world. You may have noticed that one model seems to be missing, namely the situation in which my son wakes up in time, but for some reason does not watch the show. Why isn't this model included in the representation? This model is not included in the representation because the theory assumes that only models that are consistent with the meaning of the utterance are actually created. So in the original statement, "If my son wakes up in time, then he watches 'Biker Mice from Mars,' " the meaning of the utterance has to do with what he does if he wakes up or, by implication, what happens if he doesn't wake up. That's why only those situations are shown in the representation.

Now, let's move on to the next step, that of "reducing" the models. We'll use "a" to stand for "awaken" or "wakes up in time" and "w" to stand for "watches 'Biker Mice from Mars.' " So, then we have

```
    a      w
  ~a      w
  ~a     ~w
```

where the "~" or tilde means just what it meant earlier in the chapter, that is, either "not" or "the absence of."

There is a little more terminology to deal with before we can go on to discuss how the mental models approach explains the ease of modus ponens and the difficulty of modus tollens. According to mental models theory, the limitations on working memory that we all face impose a certain order to the way in which these models will be generated when we are given a proposition. In the following situation,

```
  [a]    w
       . . .
```

the top line represents the "exhaustive" representation of the statement "my son awakes in time." When a statement is "exhausted," it means that the statement cannot occur in any model without the statement "then he watches 'Biker Mice from Mars'" also occurring. In other words, when the "a" is exhausted, it means that the "a" cannot occur without the "w," and we show this by putting brackets around the "a." The three dots, or ellipsis, tell a different story. Because our working memory is almost inevitably filled up when we begin to reason with these models, we may try to represent some models implicitly rather than explicitly. That's the function of the model in the second line above, the ellipsis, which basically represents all of the other models about a conditional reasoning situation that I could create, but haven't yet created. In other words, the ellipsis is like a "mental place holder" that says, "I know there's more information to be represented, but I haven't gotten into the details of it yet."

Now we're ready to understand the model's explanation concerning the ease and difficulty of some conditional reasoning tasks. Consider the following syllogism:

If the Cubs win the division, then they'll go to the playoffs.
The Cubs win the division.

The first premise is modeled as follows:

```
  [w]    p
       . . .
```

and the second premise is modeled simply as

```
  w
```

Now to actually make an inference from these models, we must have a way of combining these two models, and in this case, that is not very difficult. The information is combined by adding the information from the second model into the first and then eliminating the ellipsis. So when the information is combined, we have

```
  w    p
```

which might be translated back into English as "The Cubs win the division and go to the playoffs." As you can see, making the modus ponens conclusion from this set of models is not very difficult because the set contains all the information that is needed.

Something different happens when we consider the situation for modus tollens. Consider the following syllogism:

If the Cubs win the division, then they'll go to the playoffs.
The Cubs didn't go to the playoffs.

Once again, the first premise may be represented by the model

[w]   p

and the second premise might be represented by the model

~p

Notice that there is no obvious way to combine the information from the second model with that of the first. According to the mental models position, this lack of an obvious linkage from the second model to the first is what stops most people from reasoning successfully in modus tollens situations. In order to combine the information from the two models, the first model must be fleshed out more extensively. Here's how that would look:

```
   w      p
  ~w      p
  ~w     ~p
```

Now, using the same procedure we used before to combine models, we can see that there is a linkage from the ~p model to the first set of models. Specifically, we can link the ~p model to the ~w model to arrive at

~w   ~p

Translating this model back into English, we might get a statement like, "If the Cubs don't go on to the playoffs, it means that they haven't won the division."

As this analysis shows, there are two reasons why modus tollens is difficult according to the mental models approach. First, modus tollens requires that the initial model be "fleshed out" or expanded from its first appearance. This requires cognitive effort to detect that the initial model must be expanded. As you'll recall, in the modus ponens case, the initial model does not have to be fleshed out in this way. Second, modus tollens is difficult because, for at least a short period of time, the reasoner must keep several distinct alternative representations in mind simultaneously. Doing so imposes a cognitive load on the memory of the reasoner. Once again, this cognitive load is not imposed in modus ponens reasoning.

Summary of Formal Reasoning

The study of conditional reasoning tasks tells us several interesting things about human reasoning. First, the untrained person's use of logical terms is sometimes far different from the logician's use. For example, we've seen that people typically take the term "if" to mean "if and only if." However, it's important to keep in mind that such transformations are usually orderly. Once subjects decide how they will interpret the "if" statement, they tend to stick with this interpretation, and their reasoning is appropriate, given their misinterpretation. It also seems that skill in formal reasoning is somewhat dependent upon Western education. Both logic and Western education may have been designed to meet the needs of a culture that emphasizes certain modes of thinking while de-emphasizing others. In cultures where other systems of thought are perhaps emphasized, then we might expect the culture to educate its people to reason accordingly. In other words, logic and education may simply be the by-products of a particular culture. If our culture were different, we would expect both logic and education to be different as well.

The modus tollens literature offers a fascinating picture of the ways in which people can circumvent, or somehow make up for, shortcomings in formal reasoning ability. When we looked at the work of Rips and Marcus (1977) and Wason (1966), we saw that people typically don't do well on tasks that require explicit knowledge of the modus tollens inference rule. However, in real life, people have developed several strategies that can be used to solve such problems. First, the subjects can check their memories for situations that seem similar to the one they encounter in the problem. Thus, the Johnson-Laird et al. subjects could use knowledge of the British postal system to help solve the problem. Although such knowledge was not available to the subjects of Griggs and Cox, these subjects could nevertheless imagine that they were checking identification at a bar. By mapping the conditions of the problem onto an easily visualizable action, these subjects also circumvented their apparent lack of explicit modus tollens knowledge. Finally, Hoch and Tschirgi demonstrated that some situations exist in which people's suspicion or curiosity is piqued. In such situations, people often choose to investigate further, and by doing so, they often solve a modus tollens problem. One condition that seems to produce these general **extralogical inferences** is the search for missing information.

This brings us to a related issue, an important one, although we've alluded to it only obliquely so far. This issue concerns the "rule-based" nature of reasoning (Rips, 1990). For example, is reasoning always accomplished by the application of some sort of rules? If it is, what kinds of rules are involved? Are these rules "hard and fast" or are these rules "fuzzy"? It's not very difficult to get some evidence for the hard and fast position. For example, if I tell you that Joe is taller than Bob, and Bob is taller than Alex, I'm sure you can tell me about Joe's height in relation to Alex's. It certainly seems in cases like this that you are consulting some internal calculus that has converted the specific statement into some more abstract rule of the form "If $A > B$, and $B > C$, then $A > C$," and moreover, built into the reasoning scheme is a tag that says "must be true." That is, in addition to knowing the rule and applying it, your cognitive system can also access that tag and know that whatever you substitute for A, B, and C, if the first two statements are true, the third must be also true. On the other hand, having access to hard and fast rules doesn't mean that we might not also use fuzzy rules. Here, the cognitive system's tag might read "could be true," or "not too confident that this is true," or "usually true," or whatever. Behaviorally, we would expect that reasoners who are using fuzzy rules should not be as confident of their reasoning as those who are using hard and fast rules, but the form and structure of the reasoning is identical in both cases. Of course, there is opposition to the basic premise here: There are plenty of theorists who argue that reasoning is always "just" the retrieval and comparison of the current situation with some previously experienced one. According to this view, errors in reasoning might result from poor analogies, from inexperience, from failures to encode or retrieve previous encounters, or whatnot. Can you see the difference between the two positions? The rule-based theorist seeks to find the underlying syntactical grammar of reasoning; the opposing camp maintains that there are only mere instances or examples of reasoning, and any behavioral similarities in reasoning outcomes are produced superficially by appearances of similarity in the reasoning tasks themselves. As you can see, this issue hinges somewhat on the notion of similarity across reasoning tasks. We'll examine the concept of similarity a little bit later in this chapter.

NATURAL REASONING

Most people don't know about logical inference rules, and so they can't possibly apply them explicitly when reasoning is required. The last section pointed out some of the tricks people use to overcome this lack of formal knowledge. One technique that can be used to study these strategies is to give people problems that are similar to the ones they are likely to encounter in real life. That is, although the reasoning process is still studied in the laboratory, the problems used involve making estimates of events that could take place in the real world. Thus, the objective here is not to see if people can reason their way to a valid conclusion. Instead, we are trying to find out whether people can reason their way to a true conclusion, given premises that could be true. In this sense, the emphasis in **natural reasoning** is on conditions that foster soundness in human reasoning. From the pattern of responses, the cognitive psychologist hopes to be able to say something about the underlying reasoning processes.

Representativeness

A series of studies by Kahneman and Tversky has been the basis for much of what is known about natural reasoning and decision making. In one study (Kahneman & Tversky, 1973), subjects were divided into two groups. Subjects in the "engineer-high" group were told that a person had been picked at random from a sample of one hundred people, seventy of whom were engineers, with the remaining thirty people being lawyers. Subjects in the "engineer-low" group were told that the sample had consisted of thirty engineers and seventy lawyers. Subjects in both groups faced the same task: they were required to estimate the odds that the person picked at random from the sample of one hundred was an engineer. Subjects in both groups were generally accurate. The engineer-high group correctly estimated that there was about a 70 percent chance that the person picked was an engineer, and those in the engineer-low group correctly estimated that the chances were about 30 percent. The subjects were then told that another person had been picked at random from the sample, and they were given the following thumbnail sketch of the person:

> Jack is a 45-year-old man. He is married and has four children. He is generally conservative, careful, and ambitious. He shows no interest in political and social issues and spends most of his free time on his many hobbies, which include home carpentry, sailing, and mathematical puzzles. (Kahneman & Tversky, 1973)

The subjects in both groups were asked to estimate the odds that this person was an engineer. Subjects in both groups now maintained that the odds that this person was an engineer were greater than the representational proportions in the sample. Both the engineer-high and engineer-low groups estimated that the odds that Jack was an engineer were greater than 90 percent. As you can see from the description, Jack has hobbies and interests that are somewhat stereotypical for an engineer, but his hobbies and interests are somewhat more unusual for a lawyer. In that sense, the profile of Jack is more representative of an engineer than it is of a lawyer. The subjects were apparently swayed by this fact. Because Jack was typical of engineers, subjects concluded that the odds were great that he *was* an engineer. The subjects in the engineer-low group did not take into account that the actual odds of selecting an engineer were only 30 percent.

A *heuristic* is a term used by psychologists to denote general problem-solving procedures that often work in solving everyday problems. A heuristic is a rule of thumb—a general, rather than precise, guideline for coming up with a solution. Subjects in the Kahneman and Tversky study were apparently using what has been named the **representativeness heuristic.** To make a quick judgment about odds, people compare the case in point with a concept that is at least similar to a prototype (see Chapter 3) and compute its deviation from that. If the deviation is small, people tend to assume that the odds are good that their judgment is true. In this case, the subjects in the engineer-low group overlooked some important information when they used the representativeness heuristic, namely that engineers were not very common in the original sample. Generally, people seem to have some difficulty evaluating the influence of the *base rate* in making such judgments. In situations in which the base rate is low, the representativeness heuristic can lead to serious misestimations. To see this, read the following problem and make the called-for judgment.

Pretend that a stranger told you about a person who is short, slim, and likes to read poetry, and then asked you to guess whether this person is more likely to be a professor of classics at an Ivy League University or a truck driver. Which would be your best guess (Myers, 1986)?

The previous problem has tipped you off, but those who are naive are likely to guess that the person is a classics professor rather than a truck driver. But this assumption is almost certainly wrong. To begin with, the Ivy League probably has about 40 to 50 classics professors. Perhaps half of these fit the prior description, which yields 25 people. In comparison with this result, the number of truck drivers is overwhelmingly large—perhaps 500,000 people. Truck drivers who fit the description may be relatively rare—let's say one in a thousand. This still gives us 500 cases in the truck driver pool against 25 in the Ivy League pool. The odds are rather good that the person is a truck driver rather than a professor, despite the typicality of the description for the latter.

Availability

The work of Kahneman and Tversky also found that people's reasoning is influenced by the availability of material in memory. In other words, when things come readily to mind, we assume that such things are more common than things that don't come to mind as easily. This heuristic is usually suitable for estimating likelihoods; that is, common things usually do come to mind more readily than do rare things. But like the representativeness heuristic, the **availability heuristic** can go astray, too.

Kahneman and Tversky (1973) asked their subjects to estimate the proportion of words in English that begin with k and the proportion of words in which k is the third letter. One way that the subjects might try to accomplish this task is by generating a list of words that begin with k and comparing this list with some hypothetical, uncomputed list of words that don't begin with k. Once this proportion has been estimated, the subject might generate a list of words that have k as their third letter and compare this list with another, not fully computed, list of words without this property. Spend a minute or two making these obviously speculative estimates. If you're like most people, producing the list of words beginning with *k* seems easier than producing the list of words with *k* in the third position, which may result in your saying that *k*-beginning words are more common. In reality, words with *k* in the third position outnumber *k*-beginning words by a ratio of about 3:1. This misestimation is thought to be related to the processes that we considered in Chapter 6 (Anderson, 1980). For example, a reasonable assumption is that words are more likely to be coded on the basis of initial letters rather than third letters. If this is so, then the spread of activation of *k*-beginning words to one another is likely to be stronger than the spread from words with *k* as their third letter. What happens is that more *k*-beginning words are likely to enter our awareness, and from this fact, we mistakenly figure that the contents of our minds are a good reflection of the proportions in reality.

This explanation has been supported in work done by Slovic, Fischoff, and Lichtenstein (1976), who asked their subjects to estimate the likelihoods of various occurrences. For example, which do you believe is more frequent: death as the result of all forms of accidents or as the result of strokes? From homicide or from diabetes? From all forms of cancer or from heart disease? Most people estimated that death was more likely from accidents, homicide, and cancer, but this assumption is incorrect. Although these events are often publicized, the less-recognized killers (strokes, diabetes, heart disease) actually take more lives. In this case, we see that the publicity surrounding homicide and cancer victims apparently makes these events more memorable and available.

The availability heuristic is also influenced by the ease with which certain computations can be made. Events that are easily computed are perceived as more common, and they are consequently more available than events whose likelihood is hard to compute. In another problem given by Kahneman and Tversky (1973) to their subjects, people were asked to form subcommittees from a group of ten people. In one group, the subjects were asked to estimate how many subcommittees of two people each could be formed from the original group of ten. In a second group, the subjects were asked to estimate how many subcommittees of eight people each could be formed from the original ten. The median estimate for subjects in the first group was seventy subcommittees, and the median estimate for subjects in the second group was twenty subcommittees. The number of subcommittees that can be formed is actually the same in each case: forty-five. Do you see why it's the same? Every group of two that is formed leaves a remainder of eight people who could make up a different subcommittee. Every subcommittee of eight that is made up also leaves a remainder of two from the original group. The subjects apparently didn't realize this point. Kahneman and Tversky maintain that the subjects probably began to compute the various groupings and succeeded in producing a fairly large number of two-people subcommittees in a short time. Subjects who started in the eight-person condition had a harder task. Computing the members of the subcommittee is difficult, as is storing the result. After a period of time, subjects in the eight-person condition probably hadn't generated as many subcommittees as the subjects in the other group, and so were inclined to estimate that there weren't that many of them.

Framing Decisions

As the previous section implied, the way in which a question is asked can influence an individual's reasoning process. Kahneman and Tversky (1982) refer to this process as **framing**. Essentially, framing refers to steering the reasoning processes by increasing the availability or representativeness of the desired outcome. Subjects read information such as the following:

> Imagine that the U.S. is preparing for the outbreak of an unusual Asian disease, which is expected to kill 600 people. Two alternative programs to combat the disease have been proposed. Assume that the exact scientific estimate of the consequences of the program are as follows:
> If Program A is adopted, 200 people will be saved.
> If Program B is adopted, there is a ⅓ probability that 600 people will be saved and a ⅔ probability that no people will be saved.

When asked which program they would pick, about 75 percent of the subjects chose Program A. The subjects were then given the following choice:

> If Program A is adopted, 400 people will die.
> If Program B is adopted, there is a ⅓ probability that nobody will die, and a ⅔ probability that 600 people will die.

In the latter case, about 75 percent of the subjects favored Program B. In the first case, the two-thirds probability that no people will be saved seems like a steep price to pay for the one-third probability (fairly low odds) of saving all the people. In contrast to this, two hundred people saved seems like a tangible, solid, and beneficial result. In the second case, the one-third probability that everybody can be saved looks like a long shot, but it seems better than ensuring the deaths of four hundred people if Program A were adopted.

How Biases Influence Decision Making

Suppose you were given a statement such as "Membership in a fraternity or sorority affects a student's likelihood of completing college in four years," and you were asked to indicate whether you thought the relationship between these variables was positive or negative. You might mentally note your own position on this matter. Now, suppose that you had access to various facts. What numerical data would you have to know in order to accurately evaluate your position? Basically there are four facts that we need to know, and we can easily imagine laying out these four bits of data in a table that we call a 2 × 2 contingency table. The numerical data should include the number of students who graduated in four years and who participated in the Greek system (let's call this cell "A" in the table), the number of students in the Greek system who did not graduate in four years (cell "B"), the number of independent students who did graduate in four years (cell "C"), and finally, the number of independent students who did not succeed in graduating in four years. Then, if you divide A by the sum of A + B, you get the percentage of all Greek students who graduated in four years. Similarly, if you divide C by the sum of C + D, you get the percentage of all independent students who got out in four years. If these two percentages are the same, then participation in a fraternity or sorority has no effect on the likelihood of on-time graduation. If the first percentage is greater than the second, we could argue that participation in a fraternity or sorority has a beneficial effect on graduation likelihood, whereas if the first percentage is less than the second, then we would say that participation in a fraternity or sorority might impair the chances of graduating in four years. Notice that in order to accurately evaluate your position, you need to have the data from all four cells before any argument becomes logically compelling: Just knowing one percentage or the other really doesn't allow any inferences to be made about the relationship between the two variables. Because you need all four cells in order to compute the two percentages, technically and logically, each of the four cells is mathematically equally important. However, Levin, Kao, and Wasserman (1991) found that people typically don't think that each cell is equally important. For the problem given above, university students who thought that the relationship was positive felt that cell A was a more important cell than cell B, which in turn was more important than cells C and D. The opposite was true for students who thought that relationship was negative: These students thought that cell D was more important than any of the other three cells. These findings are a good demonstration of the **confirmation bias** that is frequently seen in human reasoning. Humans have a tendency to seek information that may confirm what they expect to be true. In this light, even in the absence of any explicit framing information, people seem to "self-frame." That is, prior to reasoning, people may access whatever a priori biases they may have; if such biases are present, they will color decisions and reasoning processes.

Summary of Natural Reasoning

In one sense, people apparently don't perform much better on everyday reasoning tasks than they do on formal reasoning tasks. When we look at people's ability to estimate probabilities, we see that they seem to rely on several rules of thumb, and this reliance is more or less uncritical. People seem to think that, if a person or event is more representative of some category, then the likelihood is great that the person or event *is* a member of that category even though the base rate of such an event may be low. The representativeness heuristic produces errors when people fail to take base rates into account. People are also influenced by the ease with which certain events can be computed. What is easily computed and stored is thought to be more commonplace than rare or unusual things. Generally, the Kahneman and Tversky findings can be interpreted as showing that people seem to possess little sensitivity to these biases; they are unaware that they have them. As a general finding, therefore, we might say that people are far from optimal reasoners when asked to reason formally, or to estimate the likelihoods of outcomes (Wickens, 1984). This finding might seem discouraging, but we have to realize that the use of heuristics in reasoning doesn't guarantee anything. A heuristic is a tool, or reasoning device, that has the advantages of simplicity and speed. This ease of use requires a price to be paid. In some situations, the heuristic produces a biased estimate, and people are usually unaware of this bias.

CONCEPT FORMATION

Human reasoning has been studied in a variety of ways. Researchers have sometimes focused on the functional aspect of reasoning: its purpose. For most people, the purpose of reasoning seems to be the establishment of a workable truth. Here, by truth, I mean the establishment of a regularity between events that enables some degree of prediction and the reduction of uncertainty. People, and perhaps even some animals, often use a general method to establish these regularities. They begin by assuming or observing that some stated connection or relationship between objects or events exists. Next, they observe subsequent recurrences of the events to see whether the assumed relationship is verified or falsified. In a way, human reasoners act like scientists as they seek to support or disprove a hypothesis about the relationship between two events. When a hypothesis has been supported repeatedly, it may acquire the status of a rule. On the one hand, these rules can be used as statements of cause and effect, and thus as predictors of outcomes. In another way, such rules might enable linkages to be established between objects in the world, and such groupings of objects might then acquire the status of a category or a concept.

This approach was plainly obvious in the minds of researchers who first investigated concept formation. In an attempt to trace the course of concept formation from the ground up, such researchers used "artificial concepts"—geometric stimuli with which the subjects were obviously unfamiliar. As we'll see, from the standpoint of artificial concept research, the formation of a concept looks very much like a scientific reasoning task.

Artificial Concepts

Perhaps the granddaddy of the artificial concept literature is the work of Bruner, Goodnow, and Austin (1956). The stimuli used in this study consisted of eighty-one cards, which are shown in Figure 11.3. The set of cards had four dimensions, each of which had three *values*, or levels. *Shape* was one dimension; its three values were circle, cross, or square. *Color* was another dimension (values: red, black, green). *Border number* was the third dimension (values: 1, 2, or 3). *Object number* was the final dimension, with its values of 1, 2, or 3. Concepts were defined by rules that specified that certain cards were "in the concept"; that is, only certain cards of the set of eighty-one met the criteria implied by the rule. The subjects' task was to discover the rule that was currently in force. Several types of rules were used in the study; among them were *single value concepts*, which specified that all cards having one particular value of one particular dimension were in the concept. A rule specifying all green cards is an example of a single value concept. Somewhat more difficult for the subjects were *conjunctive concepts*. These rules specified the concept as having one value on one dimension *and* one value on some other dimension (e.g., green crosses). More difficult still were the *disjunctive concepts*—rules specifying that the concept had one value of one dimension *or* one value of some other dimension (e.g., green or cross).

The stimuli were presented to the subjects in one of two ways. In the **reception paradigm,** the subjects were shown a single card and were asked to state whether or not that card was in the concept. The experimenter then informed the subjects that the response was correct or incorrect. In the other procedure, the **selection paradigm,** the entire set of eighty-one cards was on view, and the subjects selected a particular card, stating whether or not it was in the concept. Following the selection and judgment, the experimenter informed the subjects about the correctness of the response.

The Bruner et al. study is perhaps most famous for its discovery of strategies used by subjects in both the reception and selection paradigms. In the reception paradigm, subjects used two strategies:

1. **Wholist Strategy.** With this strategy, subjects had to remember all the attributes common to those instances in which the response was correct and ignore everything else, thus eliminating attributes that were not part of a positive instance.

2. **Partist Strategy.** Subjects using the second strategy focused on one hypothesis at a time (for example, color green = yes), kept the hypothesis if it correctly predicted the membership of a stimulus card, and formed a new one based on all past experiences if it did not.

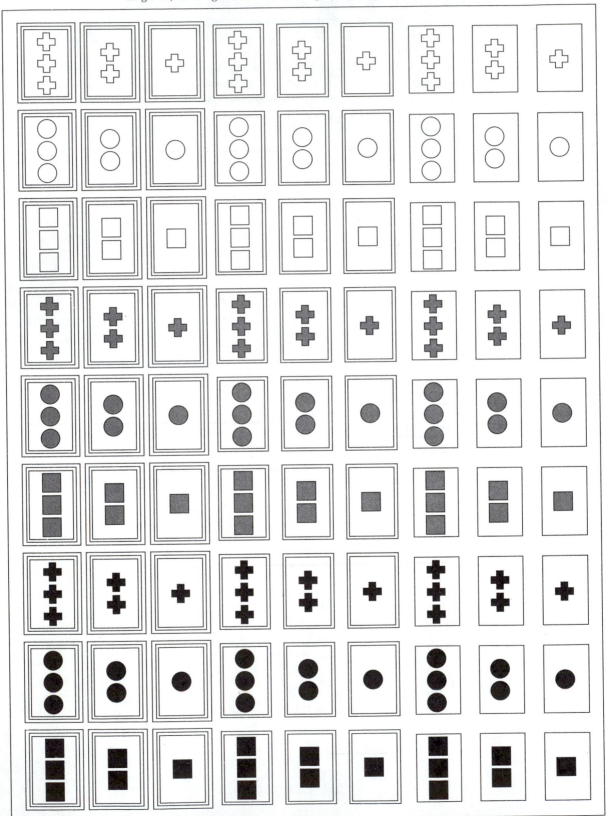

These strategies are shown in Table 11.4. Of these, the wholist strategy is the optimal one and was used by 65 percent of the subjects to a greater or lesser extent. The following example takes a look at the wholist strategy in practice. Suppose the first card the subject sees is

two borders, two red squares

and also assume that the subject is working on some conjunctive rule and correctly guesses that this card is in the concept. This card then becomes the *initial positive instance*, and all its features are encoded as the initial hypothesis about the concept. In this case, the features are two border lines, two objects, red colors, and square shapes. Suppose the subject is next given the card

one border, one red square

In this situation, the subject would judge this card as not being in the concept. If the subject is informed that the response is correct, then the current hypothesis is maintained. If the subject is told that the response is incorrect, that is, that the second card *is* in the concept, then the subject makes up a new hypothesis based on whatever the old hypothesis and the current card have in common, namely:

red squares

The wholist strategy is the optimal one for the reception paradigm because it puts a minimum load on memory. The subject has only the current hypothesis

·············· **TABLE 11.4** **Strategies in Concept Learning**

When subjects are presented with a series of instances selected from those shown and told whether each is a positive or negative instance, they may adopt one of the following strategies or a mixed combination.

Wholist Strategy
Take the first positive instance and retain all the positive attributes as the initial hypothesis. Then, as more instances are presented, eliminate any attribute in this set which does not occur with a positive instance.

	Positive Instance	Negative Instance
Confirming	Maintain the hypothesis now in force.	Maintain the hypothesis now in force.
Infirming	Take as the next hypothesis what the old hypothesis and the present instance have in common.	Impossible unless one has misreckoned. If one has misreckoned, correct from memory of past instances and present hypothesis.

Partist Strategy
Begin with part of the first positive instance as a hypothesis (for example, choose just one attribute). Then retain or change it in the following way.

	Positive Instance	Negative Instance
Confirming	Maintain hypothesis now in force.	Maintain hypothesis now in force.
Infirming	Change hypothesis to make it consistent with past instances, that is, choose a hypothesis not previously infirmed.	Change hypothesis to make it consistent with past instances, that is, choose a hypothesis not previously infirmed.

Source: Bruner, Goodnow, and Austin (1956). (Copyright 1957 by John Wiley and Sons. Adapted by permission of the publisher and author.)

to remember. Technically, the wholist strategy is easy to use, because the only time the subjects must take action is when they guess incorrectly.

Bruner et al. also discovered that the subjects would use strategies in the selection paradigm. They listed four possible strategies:

1. Simultaneous Scanning, in which the subject began with all possible hypotheses and eliminated the untenable ones after each instance.

2. Successive Scanning, in which the subject began with one hypothesis, kept it if it correctly predicted class membership, and changed it to another based on all past experience if it did not.

3. Conservative Focusing, in which the subject picked one positive instance and selected subsequent cards that changed one attribute at a time.

4. Focus Gambling, in which the subject picked one positive instance and selected subsequent cards that changed several attribute values at a time.

Let's consider the focusing strategies. Once again, let's assume that the subject is working on a conjunctive rule. Suppose the subject picks the following card:

three red circles and three borders

and correctly guesses that it is in the concept. This guess limits the number of possible correct solutions to fifteen. That is, the subject must continue to investigate only fifteen rules. The subject using the **conservative focusing** strategy might now attempt to find out which dimensions of the concepts are the relevant ones. Suppose the subject now selects

two red circles and three borders

If the subject is told this card is in the concept, then she can infer that number of shapes is not a relevant dimension and can limit future guessing to testing the three remaining dimensions. If the subject is told that the guess is *not* in the concept, then she can infer that number of shapes is a relevant dimension. If the guess is positive, only seven solutions remain possibilities, and if the guess is negative, only eight possibilities remain (Johnson, 1978). We might summarize the reasoning of the conservative focuser this way: If a positive instance and a negative instance differ in just one dimension, the dimension value of the positive instance is involved in the solution.

As stated before, the **focus gambler** changes more than one dimension following a positive trial. For example, suppose a subject made the same initial selection as did the previous subject. Using the focus gambling strategy, the subject now might select

two blue circles and three borders

If this trial is positive, the subject has eliminated two dimensions (number of figures and color figures) at once. A gamble is involved, however. If this guess is negative, then the subject must back up to figure out which of the two changed dimensions is relevant. (The possibility also exists that both of the changed dimensions are relevant.) Thus, the subject has to spend two trials finding this out, in addition to the one trial on which he made the gambling selection.

To summarize, the scanning strategies in the selection paradigm are similar to the partist strategy in the reception paradigm in that both impose a fairly heavy load on the memory of the subject. For that reason, focusing strategies are usually more efficient, and the majority of the subjects eventually settled on conservative focusing as their preferred approach for determining conjunctive concepts.

Strategies in Concept Attainment Tasks   For twenty years following Bruner et al.'s work, the interpretation of their findings was fairly straightforward. First, it was thought that human subjects treat the artificial concept as a hypothesis whose truth they seek to confirm. Second, human subjects are strategic on such tasks. That is, certain actions are preferred, while others are avoided. The preference for certain strategies appears to be based on the memory load required to use them; subjects prefer the strategy with the least "cognitive strain" (Johnson, 1978). In addition, it was thought that the subject who used a particular strategy was engaged in some distinct cognitive operations that wouldn't be taking place if the subject were using a different strategy. In other words, the mental operations of people using different strategies were really different from one another.

These basic interpretations were called into question by later findings. For example, Medin and Smith (1981) argued that the use of different strategies did not influence the nature of the cognitive operations taking place. Rather, the strategy being used affected only the amount of information that had to be retained. In other words, performance differences among the subjects simply reflected the cognitive strain associated with having to remember more or less information. Other studies (Eifermann, 1965a, 1965b; Wetherick, 1969) indicated some difficulty in isolating the various strategies behaviorally. As Johnson (1978) pointed out, some problems are involved in identifying focus gambling. Consider the following situation. Suppose the subject guesses correctly on her initial trial. If the subject alters only one dimension, then she will be classified as using conservative focusing. The subject would not bother altering all four dimensions, because they would surely not be in the concept, and no hypotheses would be eliminated from consideration. The subject has only two alternatives to conservative focusing: changing two or three dimensions. In either case, such a response would be classified as focus gambling. However, after the subject has gambled once successfully she cannot gamble again, because not enough untested dimensions remain to try. Johnson's (1978) point was that it seems unreasonable to classify a person's strategy as focus gambling on the basis of just one trial. For these and other reasons, some questions have arisen as to whether the subjects truly are strategic in artificial concept tasks. Several researchers have attempted to determine whether the selections made by subjects indicate some intention of testing a hypothesis that has been assumed to be true.

Johnson (1978) lists several characteristics of the subjects' behavior that should be present if their actions are to be considered truly strategic. One of these characteristics is referred to as *discontinuity*. Briefly put, if we were to give a problem to a group of subjects who were using two different strategies, and one of these strategies was more powerful or efficient than the other, then we would expect that on some performance measures, such as the number of trials to solution, the frequency distribution of the group would be bimodal. Can you see why? First, those subjects who were using the superior strategy should solve the problem faster on the average than those subjects who were using the less efficient strategy. Second, if the subjects are truly strategic on these tasks, then we would expect some sort of stability across time. In other words, referring to the subjects' behavior as strategic doesn't make sense if their behavior changes willy-nilly from problem to problem.

To establish whether these criteria are observed in actual human performance, Johnson (1978) developed a version of the Bruner et al. task, which is called the *zaps-duds* (ZD) *task*. In the ZD task, the subject is shown a string of six characters made up of X's and O's. The subject's task is to demonstrate knowledge of the rule that establishes some strings as zaps and others as duds. For example, if the rule were conjunctive, such as "3 and 5," this would mean any string that had an X in both the third and the fifth locations, such as

XXXOXO,

would be a zap, and any string without this property, such as

XXOXOX,

would be a dud. Subjects solved four such problems. On each trial, the subject had a choice of two actions. First, he could enter a string on a computer terminal, in which case the computer would inform the subject whether the string was a zap or a dud. Second, the subject could enter a hypothesis by typing "2 and 6," or whatever, in which case the subject would be told whether or not the hypothesis was correct.

When a frequency distribution of the trials to solution is made, based on over a thousand solutions, the figure has four modes, or peaks. Johnson argues that these peaks in the graph correspond to four commonly observed strategies. One peak occurs at around ten trials; apparently this is the mean number of trials for subjects who use some form of focusing strategy. Some subjects used a strategy called the *two X pattern*, in which only strings containing two X's were entered for thirteen trials. This enables the deduction of the correct pattern to be made on trial fifteen or sixteen and accounts for the second observed mode. A third group of subjects used a strategy in which they entered strings on the first few trials, then shifted to entering only hypotheses. These subjects produced the third peak in the distribution, which occurs at trial twenty-one. Finally, some subjects used what was called a *pure scanning strategy*, in which only hypotheses were entered. This produces the final peak, at trial thirty. Thus, the frequency distribution of the subjects' responses provides good evidence for discontinuity in selections on the ZD task. What about stability over time, another of Johnson's criteria?

Over the course of solving four problems, Johnson found that the subjects frequently used the same strategy on successive attempts. When the proportions of subjects using the same strategy two or three times were compared with the proportions of same strategy use expected by chance only, Johnson found that such regularity was unlikely to have occurred randomly. In other words, once the subjects settled on an approach to the ZD task, they didn't seem to do much shopping around for a different approach. This result was just as true for the subjects who were using the inefficient strategies as it was for those who were using the more powerful approaches. An analogy can be drawn between this finding and the work of Tversky and Kahneman. Just as their subjects did not seem to be aware of the biasing effects of representativeness and availability, neither did some of Johnson's subjects seem to be aware that other, unselected strategies may have been more powerful than the ones they were using.

The use of strategies in artificial concept tasks was also investigated by Laughlin, Lange, and Adamopulos (1982), who had their subjects play the popular logical deduction game **Mastermind.** This game is similar to the ZD task. The subject has to deduce a hidden code, which consists of a string of four colored buttons drawn from a pool of six different colors (repetitions of colors are allowed in the strings). Thus there are 6^4, or 1,296, plausible strings at the outset of the problem. The subject deduces the code by making a series of guesses, which also consist of strings of colored buttons. Following each guess, feedback is provided that tells the subject about the correspondence between the guess and the code. This feedback can be of two types. Each unit of white feedback tells the reasoner that one of the colors played in the string corresponds to one of the colors in the code.

Each unit of black feedback tells the reasoner that one of the colors in the just-played string corresponds in both the color and the location to one of the hidden code members. The object of the game, then, is to produce a guess that gets four black feedback units. In the following sequence of play:

Code: Red   Green   Blue   White
Guess: Blue   Black   Yellow   White

the reasoner would get one unit of black feedback (because the whites match) and one unit of white feedback (because of the color correspondence of the blues). With a little thought, you can see how a focusing strategy could be developed for this task. For example, you might hypothesize that your black feedback is being earned by the yellow button in the third position. On your next guess, you might put down the same three buttons in the other positions but put a different color in the third position. If you lose your black feedback, then you know yellow was right. If you keep your black feedback, then you know that it must be one of the other three buttons that's earning it.

In addition to the focusing strategy, Laughlin et al. also considered the use of a sophisticated tactical strategy. The tactician apparently anticipates the feedback that might be given following a guess and divides possible hypotheses about the code into two classes: those that will continue to be tenable if certain feedback is received and those that are no longer tenable. Such a strategy imposes a heavy demand on the reasoner's memory and requires a deep knowledge of the game's structure. For these reasons, Laughlin et al. consider the tactical strategy to be equivalent to the scanning strategy noted by Bruner et al. in their study.

Laughlin et al. found that many of the subjects adopted either a focusing or a tactical strategy. Thirty-six percent of their subjects used a focusing strategy, which enabled them to solve the deduction problem in 5.27 guesses, close to the theoretical limit of 4.5 guesses for an optimal focusing strategy. Thirty-one percent of the subjects used a tactical strategy. These subjects required 5.98 guesses to solve the deduction problem as against a 3.02 guess limit for optimal tactical performance. Although the tactical strategy is more powerful, subjects apparently have a difficult time applying it in the optimal way. Interestingly, subjects who used either of these strategies did better on the task than did subjects who used some other strategy. Moreover, when subjects were induced to use one of these strategies, their performance improved.

The Johnson and Laughlin et al. studies have cleared up some of the questions of strategy use in artificial concept tasks. They have pointed out that the variations in the human behavior are not random, and the choices made by the subjects apparently reflect distinct cognitive operations that have been carried out on an internal representation of the problem. The implication of this work is that humans form artificial concepts by strategically testing a hypothesis about observed events.

Summary of Artificial Concept Formation Tasks

In some respects the literature on artificial concept tasks is very much like that of the reasoning literature. In both cases, we see the reasoner applying strategies that have been generated by the reasoner; these strategies often work rather effectively, and they are not necessarily the strategies that would have been predicted by some independent, "objective" analysis of the task. In at least one other aspect however, we see a difference: From the reasoning literature, we saw that people are more or less unable to apply sophisticated reasoning analyses to problems.

Instead, it seems that people are afflicted with a host of biases and distortions in reasoning that hinder them. In contrast, we see that, at least for adults, behavior on artificial concept tasks seems remarkably rational.

But what about the underlying premise of all this work? That is, do people really go about forming real-life concepts in the way suggested by this literature? If you recall some of the information that we talked about in Chapter 3, you may have a hint that humans may treat their real-life experiences somewhat differently than they treat their experiences in a cognitive psychology laboratory. Let's examine in more depth some of the assumptions made by researchers of artificial concepts. Medin (1989) has argued that there are at least three arguments that can be raised against the classical position that we have outlined so far. We'll see all three of these arguments come into play, but let's lay out two of them at this point.

First, in the classical literature all concepts have defining features. A defining feature is an aspect of a concept that is necessary, or sufficient to admit specific instances into the concept. For example, you have the concept of a "car" don't you? But what makes a car a car? Four wheels? No, I've seen some three-wheeled cars. Internal combustion engine? No, because some cars are powered by electricity. We could go on, but I think you get the point. Lest you think the problem pertains to just some concepts, I invite you to think of some other concepts that you know about; I think you'll observe the same problem. For most concepts that you can think of, there are no features that must be present, and there are no features that are merely sufficient either: A school bus might have four wheels, an internal combustion engine, and a steering wheel, but it's still not a car.

The second problem in the classical literature stems from the first problem; this is the problem of unclear cases. In the classical view, and critical in the Bruner et al. research, is the idea that a given object is either clearly in or clearly not in the concept. As long as there are defining features, it's a simple matter to check for their presence to determine category membership. But without defining features, it's almost impossible to say what's clearly in or out of a concept. As Medin (1989) argues, should we think of a rug as "furniture"? If not, what is it? I should mention here that our political and legal system craves these defining features because they simplify things: For example, concepts like "property" and "ownership" enable the courts to determine who should pay whom for any damage that may be done to something. But this system will break down in a hurry when it begins to treat unclear cases as if they were clear: Just what exactly is a "human being"? Who or what exactly is "dead" or "alive"?

But if the classical view about concept formation and concept structure is wrong, what can we erect as an alternative? As Medin (1989) has pointed out, there are three alternative positions: probabilistic views of concept structure, exemplar views, and theory-based views. We'll examine each of these in turn.

NATURAL CATEGORIES

Probabilistic Views of Conceptual Structure

Once we reject the idea that we have defining features for our concepts, we might turn to the idea of "family resemblance" as a basis for membership in a concept, and indeed, we have seen this tactic used before in our study of cognition when we discussed prototypes and their formation. Here, the idea of category membership depends, not on some single feature, but rather on some group of features that seem to co-occur. Thus, it might be the case that there is a set of features that binds members of a category or concept together. No single feature is critical, but rather the more features that are possessed in common from among those in the set, the more likely it becomes that certain objects will be included in a particular category. Such a viewpoint gets around the problem of clear and unclear cases by treating the border around concepts as **fuzzy** (Rosch, 1973) rather than as crystal clear. In other words, because there is no single, defining feature, objects in the natural world might be "sort of" in a concept and "sort of" not. Things that are more clearly grouped together, and so become members of a concept, share more features from the set than do other objects.

These implications were tested in a study by Sokal (1977), who asked three experts (an entomologist and two paleontologists) to categorize the imaginary animals shown in Figure 11.4. Although these experts were in basic agreement

·············· **FIGURE 11.4   Caminalcules, imaginary animals created by J. H. Camin, illustrate individual differences in taxonomic judgment.**   Three taxonomists were asked to group the organisms by their similarities. Taxonomists A and C thought 13 was more similar to 8, but B placed it closer to 28. All three taxonomists thought 6 was most similar to 11. Whereas taxonomist C placed 5 and 18 together, taxonomist A grouped 5 with 22, and 18 with 23, and B did not form a close group with any of these Caminalcules. Taxonomist A thought 17 was most similar to 1, C held it most similar to 27, and B described the three organisms as equally similar. Taxonomists A and C recorded 19 most similar to 26, but B considered it closer to 20. By multiple regression of the similarities implied by the taxonomists on 112 objectively defined criteria differentiating the twenty-nine animals, the relative importance of various criteria in judging taxonomic similarity can be inferred. The judgments by persons A and C were more similar to each other than either was to B; most dissimilar were B and C. Table 11.5 shows which features of the organisms appeared important to each of the three taxonomists. No one feature was important to all three persons.

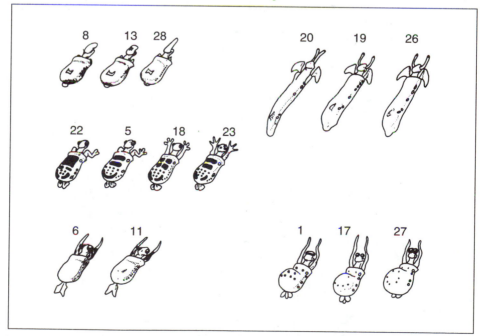

("Classification: Purposes, principles, progress, prospects," by R. R. Sokal. *Science, 185,* 27 Sept. 1974, pp. 1115–1123. Copyright 1974 by The American Association for the Advancement of Science.)

about each animal's classification, important differences arose concerning which features or aspects of the creature determined its classification. These effects are shown in Table 11.5. Consistent with the probabilistic viewpoint, we can see that no single feature of an animal determined its classification.

One other aspect of the probabilistic viewpoint concerns the **centrality** of some members of the category. Centrality in natural categories refers to the idea that some members of the category seem to be "better" examples than others, so that some birds are more birdlike than others, some games more gamelike, and so on. The feature of centrality is another way of stating that natural categories often have a prototype. Presumably, the most central member of a category is its prototype. Generally, natural category members are said to show centrality to some greater or lesser extent, whereas artificial concept members do not exhibit centrality. For example, thinking back to the Bruner et al. study for a minute, consider the concept *black squares*. Any card with a black square on it was in the concept, and all such cards were equally good members of the concept. However, not all members of a natural category are equally good examples. These effects are seen quite clearly in the work of Rosch and her colleagues (Rosch, 1973, 1975, 1977; Rosch & Mervis, 1975). Rosch (1975) presented her subjects with several lists of words referring to objects that shared category membership. The subjects were asked to rate each example on a 1 to 7 scale indicating how "good" a member of the category the example was. The subjects found this task quite reasonable. They were not perplexed by it, and they reached a reasonable consensus about the items. Table 11.6 shows the rankings and mean ratings for the category *fruit*. Here, it seems that the subjects are indirectly stating that apples and oranges are their idea of a prototypical fruit, basically round and about so big.

Subjects answered questions about central category members faster than they answered questions about peripheral members. Rosch (1973) asked children

·············· **TABLE 11.5**   Features of Caminalcules that Appeared Important to Three Taxonomists[a]

Feature of Caminalcules	TAXONOMISTS		
	A	B	C
Horns on head		+	
Stalked eyes	+		+
Groove in neck		+	
Anterior appendage			
Length	+		+
Flexion		+	
Subdivision	+		
Bulb		+	
Posterior appendage			
Disklike	+		+
Platelike	+		
Anterior abdomen spots			+
Posterior abdomen bars	+	+	
Abdomen			
Width	+		
Large pores	+		+
Small pores		+	

Source: Sokal, 1977. (Copyright 1977 by Cambridge University Press. Adapted by permission of the publisher and author.)

[a]A plus sign indicates a feature that the taxonomist considered important.

············· **TABLE 11.6**   Goodness-of-Example Ratings for Fruits

MEMBER	RANK	SPECIFIC SCORE[a]	MEMBER	RANK	SPECIFIC SCOREs[a]
Orange	1	1.07	Lemon	20	2.16
Apple	2	1.08	Watermelon	23	2.39
Banana	3	1.15	Cantaloupe	24	2.44
Peach	4	1.17	Lime	25	2.45
Apricot	6.5	1.36	Papaya	27	2.58
Tangerine	6.5	1.36	Fig	29	2.86
Plum	8	1.37	Mango	30	2.88
Grapes	9	1.38	Pomegranate	32	3.05
Strawberry	11	1.61	Date	37	3.35
Grapefruit	12	1.77	Raisin	39	3.42
Cherry	14	1.86	Persimmon	41	3.63
Pineapple	15	1.99	Coconut	43	4.50
Blackberry	16	2.05	Avocado	44	5.37
Raspberry	19	2.15	Tomato	46	5.58

Source: Rosch, 1975. (Copyright 1975 by the American Psychological Association. Adapted by permission of the publisher and author.)

[a]1 means highly typical; 7 means least typical.

and adults to respond to questions such as "Is an apple a fruit?" In some cases, the question concerned a highly typical category member such as a peach; in other cases, the question asked about a less typical, or peripheral, member such as a fig. Figure 11.5 shows the findings. Adults were faster than children in responding to these questions. However, for both children and adults, responses were faster for central rather than for peripheral category members. This effect was particularly striking in the children's responses.

Rosch has interpreted these and other findings as evidence that natural categories have *internal structure*. This term means that the center of each natural category is a prototype, and surrounding the prototype are the other category members. The category member that is judged to be the prototype is usually the member that has the most attributes in common with other category members and the fewest attributes in common with other categories.

Exemplar-Based Views of Conceptual Structure

According to the probabilistic view, concepts are organized around prototypes, and thus it is the prototype that gives the concept its mental coherence. Here's what I mean by mental coherence. If we were able to visualize the mental domain as a landscape, the concepts might look like a series of hills. At the top of each hill is the prototype. Lower down on each hill are other, less feature-laden members of the category. The farther down the hill you go, with greater and greater distance from the prototype, the less likely are people to judge that the object in question is a member of the category, until finally you get to the fuzzy border itself where things may or may not be judged as members of the category. Thus, according to the probabilistic view, the prototype becomes the "summary representation" of the concept (Medin, 1989).

It is this final statement that the exemplar viewpoint challenges. Rather than argue for the existence of prototypes, theorists of the exemplar view maintain that all we have is a collection of specific cases and situations (Smith & Medin, 1981). What happens to the prototypes in this situation? According to

FIGURE 11.5
....
Reaction times for
correctly answered
sentences about cen-
tral category and
peripheral category
members.

(Copyright 1975 by Aca-
demic Press, Inc. Adapted
by permission of the pub-
lisher and author.)

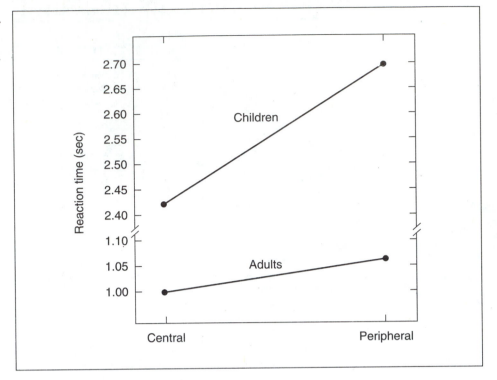

the exemplar view, they may be computed at retrieval or decision time, rather than being used as the basis for storing or encoding. In other words, I can use my cognitive system to figure out what example has more features than any other, if that's what the task requires, but that doesn't mean that I use my cognitive system that way all the time.

Although the exemplar view may seem somewhat far-fetched to you, there is some evidence to suggest that some people, particularly children, are likely to store examples rather than compute and store prototypes, and it makes sense that children might be likely to do so. As Carey (1978) has commented, for a child who hears the word "tall" used to describe a tall building, a tall woman, and a tall drink, there is nothing too similar about these cases in a metric sense. Given this, the child who is trying to learn the concept of "tall" must maintain fairly detailed information about specific examples at least long enough to infer the very nonconcrete relationship between tall and nontall objects. Consistent with this view, Kossan (1981) found that seven-year-olds learned new concepts better when the task encouraged them to pay close attention to specific examples than when the task encouraged them to try to abstract a general rule. In contrast to this finding, ten-year-olds did equally well under either condition. Kossan concluded that the difference in the younger children's performance reflected their learning style.

Theory-Based Views of Conceptual Structure

Both the probabilistic view and the exemplar-based view of conceptual structure are based on the idea that category members are similar to one another—this point doesn't seem at all controversial does it? After all, what could a concept be if it didn't include things that are similar to one another? However, according to theory-based views of conceptual structure, "similarity" is itself a very slippery word. In order for the term *similarity* to have any meaning at all, Medin (1989) argues that, first, the similarity between two things must increase as the number of shared features increases, and decrease as the number of shared features decreases. Second, the features must be independent of one another, and they must contribute to similarity in an additive way. Third, the features that contribute to similarity should be at the same level of abstractness. Fourth, these principles should be sufficient to describe the structure of a concept; thus, a concept should be more or less equal to a list of its features.

Stating that the features are independent of one another suggests that typicality judgments, and with such judgments, the emergence of prototypes, should be relatively invariant across different contexts. Thus, for example, if the features that contribute to my "bird" concept are independent and additive, then my judgment of "robin" as prototypical should occur whether I'm sitting in a cognitive science lab or sitting on a bench looking at a collection of stuffed birds in a natural history museum. However, it has been determined that context does influence typicality judgments. Roth and Shoben (1983) found that tea is the prototypical beverage in the context of secretaries taking a break, but milk is a more typical beverage than tea when the context is truck drivers taking a break.

Regarding additivity: There is some evidence that suggests that the features of prototypes are not additive either. Medin and Shoben (1988) found that small spoons are judged to be more typical of spoons than are large spoons. Similarly, metal spoons are thought to be more typical of spoons than are wooden spoons, leading one to think that large wooden spoons would not be likely to be judged as typifying spoons. But, no—people find large wooden spoons more typical than they do small wooden spoons or large metal spoons. Could it be, then, that similarity really isn't the engine of our conceptual structure, as we may have thought?

Let's consider some experimental work by Rips (1989). In one study Rips presented his subjects with a rather terse verbal description of an object; in fact, subjects were told about only one feature of the object—perhaps its diameter. This feature was previously determined to be in between the values of two categories. Then, Rips asked his subjects into which of the two categories the object in question should be placed. For example, if the subjects were told that the object was 3 inches in diameter, then they might be asked if this object was more likely to belong in the category "pizzas" or the category "US quarters." Now, even though an object that is 3 inches in diameter is closer to the size of a quarter (about 1 inch in diameter) and consequently is more similar to a quarter than it is to the size of a pizza (perhaps 12–16 inches in diameter), the subjects nevertheless judged the object to be a pizza rather than a quarter. You might be thinking, well, sure they did: Pizzas can come in different sizes, but official US quarters really can't. But do you see what this study is saying? The subjects applied their background knowledge and beliefs to consider the effects of variability and then to use this knowledge to override what they could perceive was a superficial similarity.

In a second study, Rips (1989) told the subjects that a particular animal had started out life having many birdlike features, but, in an accident, these properties had changed to insectlike features. This creature then mated with a normal member of its species, and the young that were produced were normal in appearance. Subjects were more likely to judge that the creature was a bird than an insect, but they were more likely to judge that it was more similar to an insect than it was to a bird. This study makes a point that is, well, similar, to that of the

USING YOUR KNOWLEDGE OF COGNITION

Here's an interesting demonstration involving concepts and reasoning in the real world. Take a look at Figure 11.6 and imagine that this is a metal tube lying flat on a table top. Then imagine a marble or ball bearing is inserted into the tube where the arrow indicates, and then finally imagine that the ball bearing is propelled rapidly through the tube, perhaps by a blast of compressed air. Now, what path will the ball take when it leaves the tube at the other end? Mentally note your response.

When McCloskey, Caramazza, and Green (1980) asked their subjects to do this, they found that fully 51 percent of the subjects believed that the ball would continue to go in a curved path for at least a little while, gradually straightening out as the distance between the ball and tube increased. That's the wrong answer. The right answer is that the ball will go in a straight line as soon as it leaves the tube. (Newton's laws tell us that an object in motion will continue in a straight line, unless some other force such as gravity is applied.) Forty-seven percent of the subjects got the right answer. Just for the record, the

"curved-line" position is, or was, called "impetus theory." Here the argument, first codified in the thirteenth century but doubtless believed before then, was that the tube imparted something called "impetus" or "movement force" to the ball-bearing. This impetus would dissipate, but not immediately; hence the ball would travel in a somewhat curved path when it left the tube. If your answer was based on impetus theory, at least you can console yourself with the knowledge that lots of smart people believed it 700 years ago.

Moving beyond the findings somewhat, we might ask what produced them. As McCloskey et al. were aware, we've had plenty of opportunities to observe objects in motion and to put objects in motion ourselves. Where in all that experience would "impetus theory" come from? How could our experience lead us so far astray? In an effort to make this demonstration a little more educational, you might ask yourself how a "prototype theory of motion," an "exemplar-based theory of motion," and a "theory-based theory of motion" would account for these findings.

first study: Subjects were not using similarity (in the sense of feature lists) to make an evaluation of conceptual structure, but rather were applying background, theoretical knowledge such as "creatures produce young of the same species as themselves." Seen in this light, we see that there may be a strong relationship between conceptual structure and our reasoning schemes. Taken together, these findings suggest that, although the probabilistic position and its resulting prototypes have been a tremendously popular account among cognitivists, there may nevertheless be some embarrassing shortcomings in this approach, because probabilistic and exemplar-based accounts are both based fundamentally on a concept of similarity that has not been empirically reliable. Now, if you were a cognitive scientist, you might engineer a way out of this problem by suggesting that there are subprototypes for each combination of attributes, but as you can see, such a maneuver would defeat the purpose of the prototype account in the first place.

According to the theory-based view, concepts have the structure they do not because people routinely build prototypes out of similar things, but because people's experiences have provided them with a kind of theory about motives, reasons, "real" changes and "surface" changes, and so on. When similar things are judged to be in the same category, it is only because some operative theoretical knowledge is being invoked. But this similarity can be overridden at any time by the invoking of a different theoretical perspective. Here's an example that appears

FIGURE 11.6

Stimulus used by McCloskey. Imagine that the curved tube is on a table top, and a ball or marble is tossed in (see arrow). Draw the path the ball takes when it exits the tube.

(Copyright 1980 by the American Association for the Advancement of Science. Adapted by permission of the publisher and author.)

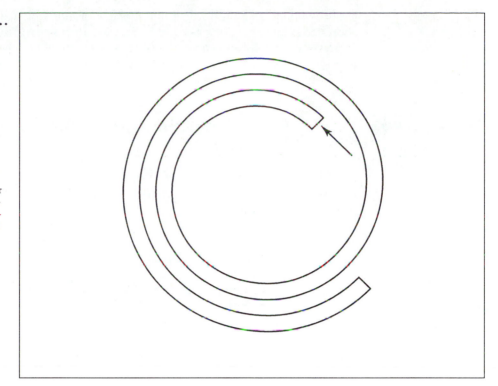

frequently in scientific papers in this area: What concept has as some of its members children, money, photo albums, and pets? Give up? The answer is "Things to carry out of the house in case of fire" (Barsalou, 1983).

Theories of Conceptual Structure:
An Evaluation and Summary

The earliest views of conceptual structure maintained that people formed concepts as they might approach a scientific reasoning task, developing a hypothesis and testing it, and modifying their concepts based on the evidence they acquired from the world. This approach did not make use of real-life concepts, but rather, artificial ones. It's true that such studies have given us a wealth of information about how people strategize in reasoning, but it's also true that real-life concepts have certain properties like centrality and fuzziness that proved to be the undoing of the classical view. Probabilistic views of conceptual structure argued that people construct prototypes by abstracting features from objects in the world and then grouping objects on the basis of their featural similarity. The exemplar position also endorsed the notion of feature abstraction based on similarity but argued that the prototype may be a retrieval phenomenon. Both positions have been supported empirically, but there are good reasons to doubt that either is the whole story. First, the prototypes don't always behave the way the theory predicts that they should. There are a lot of unanswered questions about the exemplar position, too: How many examples could you really keep in mind, especially when you did not know in advance how long you would have to keep them in mind? According to the theory-based view, both positions suffer from a misconception that similarity is the basis of conceptual structure. The theory-based viewpoint maintains that similarity is both hard to define and can be easily overridden if our knowledge, or context, or motives change. If, however, we accept that similarity does not seem to constrain concepts, then we have to ask ourselves what will constrain theories. How many theories does a person have and how could they be differentiated? Clearly, this is one of the tasks that the theory-based view must face.

CONCLUDING COMMENTS AND SUGGESTIONS FOR FURTHER READING

I think that three themes emerge from the literature on reasoning and concept formation. The first theme concerns the tremendous difficulty involved in specifying the contents of human knowledge. Thus, a very appropriate and seemingly answerable question like "Are humans logical or not?" becomes extremely difficult to answer in practice. On the one hand, humans can sometimes give responses that are congruent with those of logicians, suggesting that people can assemble some basic cognitive processes in a logical way. Of course, as we saw, humans are also subject to innumerable biases in reasoning. Sure, cognitive scientists have gotten very good at naming biases in reasoning, and we've gotten very good at predicting when people are likely to fall victim to a bias and when they might overcome one. But the bigger question still remains: If humans can assemble logical operations sometimes, and sometimes override their biases in doing so, why can't they override their biases all the time? Human knowledge must be very strange indeed if sometimes we have enough knowledge to chart a straight course in reasoning (assuming, that is, that the logical course is really "straight"), but sometimes we wander around pointlessly. Related to this first theme is a subtheme having to do with the question of strategies in reasoning. We saw that people sometimes develop what I called strategies that might compensate for their inability to use "logical" processes. But, are different strategies really different? That is, do such strategies really involve different cognitive processes? This is basically the issue that I was getting at when I described the Mastermind research: If we can establish that there are some basic cognitive operations in reasoning, and that the use of different strategies involves the assemblage of different components, then (I think) we will have met the requirement of "discontinuity" implied by the term *strategy*. We'll take this issue up again in the next chapter, too.

The second theme is related to the first; it concerns the specificity or generality of the rules used in reasoning. The basic issue is this: Do we have general-purpose, "contentless" reasoning schemes that we can use in a variety of situations? We did offer some evidence to that effect. But what happens to such schemes over time? One possibility is that, as such general reasoning schemes continue to "inhabit" a particular reasoning task, these schemes eventually conform themselves to the idiosyncrasies of that task. To see how this works, suppose you give me a reasoning task that's unfamiliar to me. I analyze the task and call up what I think is the most appropriate general reasoning scheme. The next time I see this task, I'll be likely to call up this scheme again, and with repeated use in that task, the generality of the scheme gradually fades, replaced with specific reasoning schemes for dealing with problems of that specific sort. Seen in this light, my reasoning schemes could be said to "evolve" so that, as I work with them in specific tasks, they no longer resemble the general reasoning scheme that was their progenitor.

The third theme has to do with the role of similarity in our conceptual structure. With the dawn of empirical work in this area, it was thought that concepts were the result of a kind of hypothesis testing. Then we moved to a position in which concepts became perceptual phenomena, involving feature abstraction, comparison of feature lists, and so on. Then many cognitivists began to theorize that similarity (which itself is a perceptual term) wouldn't do as the basis for our cognitive structure of concepts. At which point, many cognitivists moved back to a position in which they theorize that people treat concepts like a hypothesis testing situation. This looks like the same old theory we started with, except that in the current rendition the theory argues that people apply their background knowledge of the world in an effort to find meaningful linkages between the specific exemplars. Has there been progress? I think so. Cognitivists have come a long way in elucidating the difference between discovering concepts—using our perceptual processes to find out what similarities may exist in the natural world and impose concepts—and using the supreme flexibility of our cognitive systems to organize the stimuli in the world for whatever objective we may have established.

Many students find these topics the most fascinating of all the areas in cognition, and fortunately, there are many excellent papers and books that summarize this part of the field. Rips (1990) discusses the specificity/generality issue in depth. Kuhn (1989) treats the development of reasoning ability; her research deals with adults as well as with children. Along these lines, Voss, Perkins, and Segal (1991) discuss the issue of "reasoning skills," especially as such skills may be teachable in schools. Biases in reasoning are covered in detail in Evans (1989). Articles by Medin (1989) and Smith (1990) are excellent summaries of the concept formation literature.

 **KEY TERMS**

Formal reasoning	Thematic materials	Confirmation bias
Logic	Open scenario	Reception paradigm
Validity	Closed scenario	Selection paradigm
Truth	Pragmatic reasoning schemas	Conservative focusing
Soundness	Extralogical inferences	Focus gambling
Conditional reasoning	Natural reasoning	Mastermind
Modus ponens	Representativeness heuristic	Natural categories
Modus tollens	Availability heuristic	Fuzzy borders
Disconfirming the consequent	Framing	Centrality

FOCUS ON RESEARCH
....
Kids, Concepts, and Exemplars

In this chapter, we looked at the development of conceptual knowledge, and we saw that the exemplar model maintains that children especially are more likely than adults to organize their conceptual structure around specific examples. Although this may reflect the preferred style of children, it may nevertheless be true that children can use prototypical or even theory-based structures under some circumstances. Gelman and Markman (1986) developed the following procedure, which they first used with adult subjects. The subjects were shown three pictures that might show a flamingo (bird category), a bat (nonbird category), and a blackbird (bird category). The subjects were instructed to look at the flamingo picture and they were told that this bird's heart has a right aortic arch only. The subjects were next told that the bat's heart has a left aortic arch only. Then the subjects were asked about the blackbird's heart.

The subjects responded with right aortic arch 90 percent of the time. Here, the subjects were overriding similarity (a blackbird looks more like a bat than it does a flamingo) and making a decision based on what they knew about categories: flamingoes and blackbirds are birds and should therefore share the same heart structure, even though they don't look much alike. It's not too surprising that adults would respond this way, but what about children? Gelman and Markman repeated this procedure with four-year-olds (using simpler concepts) and found that even these preschoolers gave the "categorical" response 70 percent of the time! Clearly, although children of this age may prefer to organize their conceptual world around specific, similar examples, they have obviously developed a conceptual structure that is based on inferences made about abstract, invisible properties.

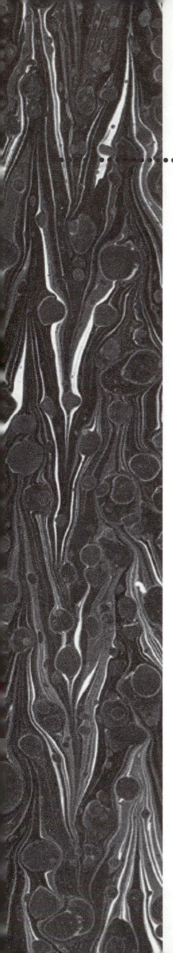

CHAPTER **12**

PROBLEM SOLVING

CHAPTER OUTLINE

OVERVIEW

What comes to mind when you think of the actions of the prototypical intelligent person? Phrased another way, what behaviors do you usually associate with being smart? This was essentially the question Sternberg (1982) asked his subjects, many of whom were not experts in the field of intelligence. To get people's everyday notions about intelligence, Sternberg went out into the real world and approached people in natural settings, such as commuter trains and supermarkets. Persons who agreed to participate in the study were given a blank sheet of paper and were asked to write down behaviors that were characteristic of **intelligence.** Sternberg found a substantial consensus about these behaviors. People's responses clustered around three categories of activities that were indicative of intelligence. Sternberg found that people think of social competence as one component of intelligence. He also found that people consider verbal ability to be indicative of intelligence. But according to many people, the most important indicator of intelligence is practical problem-solving ability. For example, a person who could "size up the situation accurately," "get to the heart of the problem," and then "reason logically" had the skills that were most often identified as indicating intelligence. When experts in the field of intelligence research were asked the same questions, Sternberg got similar findings. The experts listed "verbal intelligence" as the most important indicator of intellectual ability, but "problem-solving ability" was still mentioned as the second most important component of intelligence.

Given that both lay people and experts seem to agree that problem solving is one of the hallmarks of intelligence, it seems natural for cognitive psychologists to be interested in what mental events take place when a person tries to attain some goal in an unfamiliar situation. This chapter considers the phenomenon of problem solving from several perspectives. First, we'll examine a European psychological tradition, **Gestalt psychology.** The Gestaltists believed that thinking was much like perceiving. Finding a solution to a problem was like trying to see things from a different perspective. The information-processing approach to problem solving, which originated in this country approximately thirty years ago, really isn't an outgrowth of the Gestalt position. And as we'll see, the results of studies using the information-processing orientation have indicated that many of the Gestaltists' basic beliefs about thinking and problem solving have turned out to be inaccurate. Yet, some important studies have supported some of the Gestaltist's ideas, too.

In the first chapter, I mentioned that cognitive psychologists have become interested in exploring cognition in natural situations. Nowhere is this more true than in the area of problem solving. In the real world, an expert is a person who is skilled at solving problems in some particular domain. Cognitive psychologists have asked themselves several questions about the expert. How can expertise be described? What is the nature of the expert's knowledge, and how is it different from the novice's knowledge of the same material? All experts were novices once. How, then, does expertise develop? How does a person go from being a novice to being a pro? The last section of this chapter tries to answer these questions.

THE GESTALT HERITAGE

Before going on to examine the work of the Gestalt psychologists, we should have a definition of problem solving. A problem is a situation in which a person is trying to reach some goal and must find a means for arriving at it (Chi & Glaser, 1985). In Europe during the early part of this century, the Gestalt tradition flourished as several thinkers began to work on the issues of problem solving and other forms of creative thinking. According to members of the Berlin group, such as Max Wertheimer, Kurt Koffka, and Wolfgang Köhler, the goal of problem solving was the achievement of a Gestalt. *Gestalt* is a German word with no precise equivalent in English, but it's usually translated as "form" or "configuration." According to the Gestaltists, the end result of all perceptual processes was the formation of a Gestalt, and Gestalts were also the end result of all thinking processes. Thus, the Gestaltists believed that problem solving was much like perceiving. When we look at something, our task as perceivers is to arrange the separate elements of the visual field into a coherent whole. As problem solvers, our task is to mentally recombine the elements of a problem over and over again until a stable configuration, or Gestalt, is achieved.

The Gestaltists were intrigued by how frequently we use perceptual terms to describe our thinking processes. For example, if your friend doesn't understand a concept in physics, he says, "I don't see it." Similarly, we might encourage someone who is stumped by a problem to "try to look at it from a different perspective." We've probably all heard a confused person bemoan her problem with the words "I can't get a handle on it."

The Gestaltists were not particularly precise about how Gestalts were achieved. Yet, they were quite influential in their time, and they provided an outline of the issues that modern workers have sought to map more completely. This section examines the Gestalt approach to problem solving.

Stages of Thinking

All problem solving necessarily begins with the recognition that a problem exists. The solver must perceive a discrepancy between the current state of affairs and some desired state of affairs. The desired state of affairs becomes the goal, and the solver undertakes a series of mental operations with the intention of achieving the goal. Problem solving, then, consists of the recognition of a problem and the doing of some mental work to achieve a goal. The Gestaltists customarily thought that problem solving proceeded in a sequence of fixed stages. According to Wallas (1926), these stages were as follows:

1. **Preparation.** In the preparation stage of problem solving, the solver has recognized that a problem exists, and some preliminary attempts at understanding and solving the problem have been made.

2. **Incubation.** If the preliminary attempts fail, the solver may then put the problem aside for a while. At least on a conscious level, the thinker is no longer working on the task. However, at some unconscious level, work proceeds.

3. **Illumination.** Illumination refers to the famous flash of **insight** that ends the unconscious work and brings the answer to the surface of consciousness.

4. **Verification.** The verification stage refers to the confirmation of the insight. Generally, this stage is the least complicated and is usually nothing more than a simple checking to make sure that the insight worked.

In retrospect, this sequence of operations seems almost too rigid. We definitely have times when we put a problem aside, return to it, solve it, and never experience a flash of insight. Further, Wallas makes some assumptions that some modern psychologists might be unhappy about. One of these assumptions is the reference to unconscious thought. Another is the notion that problem solving is discontinuous. Like all stage theories, Wallas's model assumes that the activities at the different stages are qualitatively different from one another, meaning that the mental operations at the preparation stage are somehow fundamentally different from the operations at the other stages. However, modern theories of problem solving have tended to emphasize the continuous and accumulative nature of problem solving. Despite these concerns, Wallas's position has received support from artists and mathematicians who maintained that their own creative endeavors followed the course outlined by Wallas (Ghiselin, 1952; Harding, 1940). In particular, the concept that a period of unconscious work might follow the initially unsuccessful preparation phase has provoked a fair amount of research.

Incubation   Several demonstrations have been made of the so-called **incubation effect**. Fulgosi and Guilford (1968) asked subjects to first imagine some unusual event (e.g., all the power stations closing down) and then to list all possible consequences. Although subjects' performances were improved when a twenty-minute waiting interval occurred before the production of consequences began, these improvements were limited to the production of more obvious consequences, but not remote ones. Curiously, a ten-minute interval produced no effect.

Silveira (1971) demonstrated a similar effect when she presented her subjects with the cheap necklace problem, which is shown in Figure 12.1. Here are the instructions to this problem:

> You are given four separate pieces of chain that are each three links in length. It costs two cents to open a link and three cents to close a link. All links are closed at the beginning of the problem. Your goal is join all twelve links of a chain into a single circle at a cost of no more than fifteen cents.

You might try to solve this problem before reading further. Silveira's control group worked on the problem for half an hour; 55 percent of these subjects were

FIGURE 12.1
....
The cheap necklace problem.

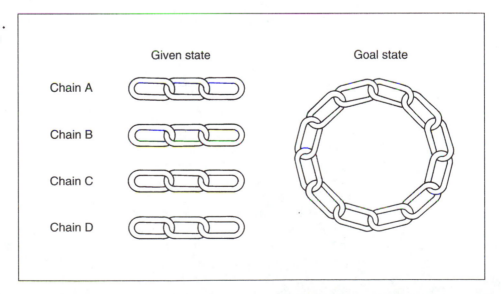

successful. Four experimental groups also worked on the task. Two groups worked briefly on the problem; one of these groups was then interrupted for four hours. Two other groups had a longer preparation period of uninterrupted work before one of them got a half-hour interruption and the other got a four-hour interruption.

Can you guess the findings? The two experimental groups that worked briefly on the problem showed no evidence of incubation; their performance was similar to that of the control group. However, the other two experimental groups showed the incubation effect. Of the long preparation-short interruption group, 64 percent of the subjects solved the problem, and 85 percent of the subjects in the long preparation-long interruption group were successful. (If you're still stumped, the answer to this and the other examples that appear in this chapter can be found in the appendix.) According to the Gestalt position, this pattern of results is the expected one. The long preparation groups had ample time to develop familiarity with the problem, and this familiarity in turn facilitated unconscious processing of the task. But not all cognitive psychologists would agree with this reasoning. Indeed, Silveira presented some evidence that argues against the hypothesis of unconscious thought. She had her subjects talk aloud as they solved the cheap necklace problem, and she tape-recorded what they said. She found that, when the subjects returned to the problem after the break, they had a tendency to pick up where they had left off. If the Gestalt position were completely correct, we should expect the subjects to show some progress during the interruptions; they should appear to be closer to the answer when they return from the break. But they weren't.

The Gestalt reasoning apparently requires some modification, but what alternative explanations can we offer? Simon (in Hunt, 1982) has suggested that incubation effects might best be explained by selective forgetting. He hypothesized that solving a problem is at least a two-stage task. Initially, we devise a plan for solving the problem that is held only in working memory. As our solution efforts proceed, we encode and store in permanent memory additional information that could easily be formulated into a successful plan, if only our attention could be shifted away from the initial plan in our working memory. During incubation, that's exactly what happens. We allocate our attention to permanent memory (thus letting the contents of working memory decay) and use the knowledge represented there to create a successful plan.

A second explanation of the incubation effect has been offered by Anderson (1981), who suggested that the effect is related to another Gestalt term known as *set*. Set refers to our tendency to perceive events and objects in a way that our prior experiences have led us to expect. That is, our perceptions are somewhat predetermined (set) by our experience. According to Anderson, when we begin to solve a problem, our prior knowledge is used as a resource that can be called up, or activated, to suggest at least an outline of effective procedures for solving the problem. If our set is appropriate, we'll call up effective procedures. However, if our set is inappropriate, we'll remain stuck with a list of ineffective procedures. During incubation, the solver is freed from these inappropriate procedures, thus giving him a chance to call up more effective ones. One important aspect of Anderson's argument is that it suggests that problem solving should not always be improved by interrupting it. To understand this, consider what might happen if we began to solve Silveira's problem and our set *was* appropriate. Following the interruption, we have no guarantee that we'll succeed in calling up the same appropriate set once again. And if we fail at this, we'll probably get stuck using an inappropriate set of operations, which may compromise our chance for solution. This helps explain why several studies (Dominowski & Jenrick, 1972; Murray & Denny, 1969) have shown decrements in problem solving following an interruption.

Insight and Creativity   The Gestaltists maintained that problem solving often resulted in a sudden awareness of the correct relationship among the problem's elements. This perception was often accompanied by the "aha!" experience—the solver is positive that she has discovered the problem's answer. In a famous passage, the mathematician Poincare (1913) describes one of his great insights:

> Just at this time, I left Caen, where I was then living, to go on a geological excursion under the auspices of the school of mines. The changes of travel made me forget my mathematical work. Having reached Coutances, we entered an omnibus to go some place or another. At the moment when I put my foot on the step the idea came to me, without anything in my former thoughts seeming to have paved the way for it, that the transformations I had used to define the Fuschisan functions were identical with those on non-Euclidean geometry. I did not verify the idea; I should not have had time, as, upon taking my seat in the omnibus, I went on with a conversation already commenced, but I felt a perfect certainty. On my return to Caen, for conscience' sake I verified the result at my leisure. (pp. 387–88)

Some of the comments in this passage are striking. Poincare says that "the idea came to me, without anything in my former thoughts seeming to have paved the way for it." Poincare is referring to the fact that his insight was not continuous with his previous thinking. In this, we see some anecdotal evidence of discontinuity in problem solving: When the insight would take place could not be predicted. Also, the passage refers to the effortlessness of the new thought; it was unforced and unbidden. This passage thus points out one of the Gestaltists' most cherished beliefs. Truly creative thought could never be predicted by previous behavior, because the creative work was essentially a break in the ongoing stream of problem solving. Such a break could be accomplished only by insight. We've all had experiences similar to Poincare's, but is there any empirical evidence to substantiate such discontinuities in human thought?

Katona (1940) compared the roles of memory and creativity (or as the Gestaltists called them, reproductive and productive thinking) in the solution of schematic matchstick problems. These problems are shown in Figure 12.2. The lines are drawn so that five squares are represented. The solver's task is to move three—and only three—matchsticks to create an array of four squares. The memory group was presented with the series of moves that would solve the problem. They were shown the sequence of moves seven times and were told to memorize it. The creative group was given some hints that might be helpful in fostering an understanding of what was involved in solving the problem. The presumption was that such hints might encourage the subjects to find some general principles that could be used to solve other problems of this class. In addition to the memory and creative groups, a control group solved the matchstick problem and was not given any help. All three groups were tested on the same and different matchstick problems after intervals of one and three weeks.

The results are also shown in Figure 12.2. The control group's performance was remarkably constant across the board, arguing that apparently not much learning is generalized from one problem to the next. Similarly, the memory group

·············· **FIGURE 12.2**   Katona's matchstick problem.

The Problem
Given matchsticks which form five squares, move three sticks to form four squares.

Group Mem
The complete solution steps are presented to the subject in order, moving one stick at a time, and repeating six times. For the above problem, the required moves shown are:

Group Help
The second method involves giving a series of hints to the subject accompanied by the comment "Try to understand what I am doing."

Results
Typical proportions correct on retention and transfer tests were as follows:

Group	Test after one week		Test after three weeks	
	Practice tasks	New tasks	Practice tasks	New tasks
Mem	.67	.25	.53	.14
Help	.58	.55	.52	.55
Con	.12	.12	.12	.12

(Original copyright 1940 by Columbia University Press. Adapted by permission of the publisher and author.)

had good retention of the original task after both one and three weeks, yet they hardly outperformed the control group after a three-week interval. The performance of the creative group is quite different from either of the other groups, however. Notice that they performed as well on new matchstick problems as they did on the original problem. The conclusion appears to be that Katona's hints were successful in prompting the subjects to develop a structural understanding of this type of problem. Thus, to the extent that the solution of these problems requires an insight, the nature of the creative group's experiences with matchstick problems did pave the way for future insights in solving this kind of problem.

Other researchers have used this procedure of giving their subjects hints in an effort to foster insight. For example, Duncker (1945) gave his subjects this problem: Why can you divide all numbers of the form abc,abc (e.g., 456,456) by 13? You might think about this for a while—it's a hard problem. Duncker found that general hints were not helpful (e.g., if a divisor of a number is divided by *p*, then the number itself is divisible by p), but only certain specific hints were helpful. An important hint was that the subject's attention be drawn to the number 1,001, for this is the key to the problem. If the subjects were given the hints "The numbers are divisible by 1,001" or "1,001 is divisible by 13," then they were likely to realize that each of the original numbers could be factored abc times into 1,001, and 1,001 is factored by 13.

What we need to realize about the findings of Katona and Duncker is their implication about the nature of insight and creativity. Rather than think of creative work as being accomplished by some discontinuous insight, which seems to arrive at unpredictable times and in unpredictable ways, a more reasonable approach is to emphasize the *continuity* of problem solving. The creative act is one of finding original arrangements of accumulated experiences.

Some research by Weisberg and Alba (1981) makes this point in a dramatic way. They gave their subjects the well-known "nine-dot" problem: The problem consists of nine dots arranged in three rows of three dots each. Each dot is placed so that it is equidistant from its row and column neighbors. The subject's task is to connect the nine dots using four and only four straight lines, without lifting the pencil from the paper. This task can be done, but most solutions involve drawing a line "outside" the boundary implied by the arrangement of the nine dots. According to the Gestaltists, most people assume that they must stay within the implied borders, and this set makes it impossible for them to solve the problem. In addition, according to the Gestaltists, success on this problem is achieved when the problem solver realizes that the boundary is an artificial one that must be crossed. Weisberg and Alba contested this theorizing by simply telling the subjects that they had to go outside the implied square (this advice came after the subjects had worked on the problem unsuccessfully for awhile). The Gestaltists would argue that the nine-dot problem should now become trivially easy; as soon as the subjects drew a line outside the imaginary square, they would restructure their representation of the problem and solve it. Weisberg and Alba found that the Gestaltists' predictions were wrong: Only 20 to 25 percent of the subjects who were given the "insight" succeeded in solving the problem. Analysis of the lines that were drawn indicated that the "insight" was of little or no help in figuring out the answer. In fact, several of Weisberg and Alba's subjects drew a line more or less randomly outside the dots and then said something like, "Okay, I'm outside the square. Now what do I do?" Such findings argue that insight is not the mechanism of creativity, nor is thinking in general, creative or otherwise, accomplished in discontinuous leaps.

Consider this final example. In 1797, Coleridge composed "Kubla Khan," one of the finest examples of English romantic poetry. Coleridge had fallen asleep while reading about Khan and (as he told it) composed the poem in his sleep without any conscious effort. Upon awakening, he immediately began to write down the whole 200-line poem he had composed in his sleep. Unfortunately, at line 54, he was interrupted by a bill collector, whom it took an hour to get rid of. When Coleridge returned to his work ... well, you guessed it, the rest of the poem had vanished. Not until many years after, when Lowes (1927) conducted a close analysis of Coleridge's notebooks, did the real origin of Kubla Khan come to light. Lowes was able to demonstrate that Coleridge had seen or read and, in many cases, had written down virtually every image or metaphor that occurred in "Kubla Khan." In other words, the raw material had already been encoded by Coleridge. Coleridge had taken some medication prior to his nap, and it was probably in his slightly disinhibited state that he was able to organize the material that made up the poem.

The Importance of the Correct Representation

According to the Gestaltists, perhaps no aspect of problem solving was more important than the activity involved in understanding or **representing the problem.** Consider the following problem (Wickelgren, 1974):

> You are given a checkerboard and thirty-two dominoes. Each domino covers exactly two adjacent squares on the board. Thus, the thirty-two dominoes can cover all sixty-four squares of the checkerboard. Now suppose two squares are cut off at diagonally opposite corners of the board [as shown in Figure 12.3]. Is it possible to place thirty-one dominoes on the board so that all of the sixty-two remaining squares are covered? If so, show how it can be done. If not, prove it impossible.

You might enjoy spending a few minutes solving this problem. If you became engrossed in this task, you are probably aware that you spent some time visualizing various configurations of dominoes being placed on the altered checkerboard, mentally noting whether any part of the domino would stick out over the edge of the checkerboard. Thus, your representation of the problem included information about area and edges. But until your representation of the problem includes at least one other important fact, your successfully solving this problem is unlikely.

The answer is that the checkerboard cannot be covered by the thirty-one dominoes. To see why this is so, you must realize that each domino must cover one white and one black square of the checkerboard. Covering two squares of the same color with one domino is impossible. But the checkerboard has been altered by taking away two white squares—leaving thirty-two black but only thirty white squares. We've solved this problem when we realize that the parity as well as the number of squares on the checkerboard has been altered. Notice that the problem's difficulty is not the result of logical or inferential complexity. The problem is difficult because one important element (what gets covered by every domino) is usually left out of most people's representations. As the Gestalt psychologists realized, the act of representation is done by the solver, and different solvers may arrive at equally valid representations.

Consider the game known as number scrabble (Newell & Simon, 1972). This game has the following rules:

FIGURE 12.3
....
The mutilated checkerboard.

A set of nine cardboard squares (pieces) like those used in the game of Scrabble is placed face up between the two players. Each piece bears a different integer, from 1 to 9, so that all nine digits are represented. The players draw pieces alternately from the set. The first player who holds any subset of exactly three pieces, from among those drawn, with digits summing to 15 wins the game. If all the pieces are drawn from the set without either player obtaining three whose digits sum to 15, the game is a draw.

I have played this game against students in my cognitive psychology classes, and I often win. When I watch the students to see how they may have represented this task, I usually find that they begin by listing all the combinations of three digits whose sum is 15. They then check off as "gone" any combination that involves a number that I have picked. Such a representation doesn't afford them many possibilities of victory. Are there any representations that might be somewhat more efficient?

When you were a child, you probably played tic-tac-toe, a game whose interest is generally limited to children. Although not apparent, tic-tac-toe and number scrabble are formally the same game. Figure 12.4 makes this relationship clear. The games are formally identical in the sense that a winning tic-tac-toe player would always have three digits from the "magic square" whose sum was 15. The converse is also true. Winning number scrabble players would also always have a winning tic-tac-toe configuration. My mastery of number scrabble now stands revealed: my superior representation of the game enables me to play a child's game against my students, who don't have the same representation.

The Gestaltists believed that improvements in thinking ability were accompanied by, or in fact were dependent upon, improvements in representation. What made the expert thinker superior was his ability to see things that the novice problem solver could not. We'll come back to this point again later, but apparently the Gestaltists were essentially correct on this point.

De Groot (1965, 1966) conducted a series of studies that have helped to clarify the role of perception in problem solving. He showed his subjects, most of whom were chess masters, a tactical position taken from an actual tournament game that had taken place between two grand masters. A tactical position is one in which many of the chess pieces are still on the board, and their arrangement is such that several moves are possible. In other words, in many tactical situations what the "correct" move should be is not obvious, and coming up with a good move involves a fairly lengthy analysis of the board.

·············   **FIGURE 12.4**   **Magic square for tic-tac-toe.**

The subjects were asked to analyze the board to determine what they thought would be white's best move. You might expect that chess masters should be much more able to do this than class A players, who make up the next lower rank. But when de Groot compared the responses of masters with class A players, he had a surprise. The masters were not overwhelmingly better than class A players in their ability to select the "correct" move. The class A player could analyze the board almost as well as the master. Yet, if a game were staged between players of these two ranks, the outcome would not be in doubt. The master would win an overwhelming proportion of such games. De Groot wanted to analyze the method used by the players to reach their decisions, and to do this, he had his subjects **think out loud** as they examined the chessboard. These comments were tape-recorded and analyzed. When de Groot compared the method of analysis used by the masters and class A players, he found similarities there as well. In both cases, the player looked at the board and selected a particular move as the basis for a continuation—a series of alternating white and black moves that the player would try to imagine. If you play chess, you're probably familiar with this type of "I'll do this, then they'll do this, then I'll do this" thinking. Generally, the continuation went on until the player felt that some clear evaluation point had been reached, such as the capture of an opponent's piece or the achievement of some identifiable strong position. After one continuation ended, the player selected another base move and explored a different continuation until another evaluation point was achieved. After several continuations had been explored, the player evaluated the outcomes and picked the base move that led to the best one.

Although the method of analysis and the move picked by the players were similar for players of different abilities, de Groot found that the differences between the two classes were in the number of moves that were selected for continuation. Surprisingly, masters explored fewer moves than did players of lesser ability. In other words, the masters seemingly had a good idea about which moves should be explored in the first place. According to de Groot, the masters were able to see certain moves better than class A players because their interpretation and organization of the chessboard were more likely to be deadly accurate, when accuracy was defined on the basis of independent postgame analysis by other masters.

De Groot and other researchers (Chase & Simon, 1973) also learned something about the nature of this organization when they asked chess masters to reproduce tournament positions (i.e., configurations of chess pieces that had occurred in a tournament) from memory. As you might expect, chess masters are quite good at this task. De Groot found that his masters could reproduce a position of greater than twenty pieces after only five seconds of study. De Groot noticed that, when the players reconstructed the position, they did not put down pieces on the board one at a time at a constant rate. Rather, in retrieving the position from memory, the master placed a group of four or five pieces on the board in their correct locations. A short latency then occurred, followed by another group of four or five pieces being placed.

What does this mean? The masters had apparently encoded the position in several chunks, where each chunk consisted of a group of pieces that were somehow related to one another. For example, one such chunk was the pawn chain, a group of mutually supporting pawns (Chase & Simon, 1973). It's also important to realize that the relationships between the pieces were expressible in chess terms. For example, fianchettoed bishops are those that operate on long diagonals on the chessboard and consequently have freedom of movement. The masters might retrieve the fianchettoed bishops simultaneously, even though the bishops themselves were not necessarily close to one another on the chessboard. The chess masters were not simply using a geographical code to organize the pieces on the basis of their place on the board. Rather, the masters were apparently using a much more abstract coding scheme, which was dependent upon their extensive knowledge of chess configurations.

This contention was supported in another study by Chase and Simon (1973). They showed chess masters and novices chess positions that were produced by random assignment of pieces. In that situation, chess masters were no better than novices in reconstructing the position. Simon and Gilmartin (1973) have speculated that the typical chess master, after countless hours of examining and analyzing chess positions, has encoded perhaps fifty thousand such chunks of related pieces.

Very similar findings have been obtained in a much different domain, that of computer programming. McKeithen, Reitman, Rueter, and Hirtle (1981) asked their subjects, who were computer programmers of differing skill levels, to recall programs that had been briefly presented on a computer screen. Both meaningful and meaningless programs were presented; the latter were created by scrambling the lines of code in a meaningful program. As you might expect, expert programmers were quite good at recalling the meaningful programs. However, experts did no better than novices in recalling the scrambled programs. McKeithen et al. hypothesized that the superiority of the experts was based on their organization of the elements of the computer program, and they tested this assertion by having experts and novices memorize and recall lists of programming "keywords" such as "string," "while," "do," "step," and so on. The dependent variable was the order in which the terms were recalled by various groups. Interestingly, they found that experts often retrieved words in an order that might correspond to the words' use in a computer program (e.g., "while—do," "for—step"). This organization was not observed in the retrieval patterns of novices, who tended to recall words in an order corresponding to natural language associations (e.g., "bits"—"of"—"string"). Such findings offer an intriguing foreshadowing of the literature on expertise that we'll take up later in the chapter.

Summary of the Gestalt Position

The Gestaltists emphasized **discontinuity in thinking.** That is, they believed that problem solving was accomplished in a series of stages that were qualitatively different from one another. Moreover, problem solving could sometimes be accomplished by unconscious work that would be terminated by insight. These matters have provided modern researchers with a host of interesting questions to explore, and as we've seen, these explorations have generally shown the Gestalt account to be lacking as an empirical prediction of what takes place when someone tries to solve a problem. That is, contemporary research has seemed to indicate that problem solving is not accomplished by insight, but rather is a continuous process. However, in emphasizing the importance of the correct representation, the Gestaltists were clearly onto something, and this establishes a theme for this chapter. Later, when we consider expertise in problem solving, we'll see that the expert seems to have a representation of the problem that includes some elements missing from the novice's representation. The next section examines some of the modern research in the area of problem solving.

DOMAIN-FREE PROBLEMS AND GENERAL STRATEGIES

Much of the contemporary research on problem solving has dealt with so-called **domain-free problems.** This term refers to problems that have a clearly specifiable answer but that require no explicitly specialized training to solve. For example, you may be familiar with any number of river-crossing problems in which a number of people or animals are to be transported across a river in a limited-capacity boat. Some constraints are usually imposed concerning who can be transported with whom. There are several reasons for the use of such problems. First, they are usually complicated enough to be challenging for most adults, but not so complicated as to be undoable. Second, the properties of such problems can often be specified in some formal way, such as in a mathematical representation or embodied in a computer program. This makes it possible to compare human performance on such problems with some idealized performance. The advantage of such an approach is that we might be able to discern some commonalities in various problems where human performance deviates significantly from ideal performance. If we find such deviations, they might tell us much about the characteristics of the human information-processing system in general. Finally, if we see some commonalities among people's attempts to solve such problems, we might be able to make some inferences about their strategies and, in turn, their representations of the problem.

Generally, cognitive psychologists have taken two complementary approaches to the study of domain-free problems. First, some psychologists have attempted to classify domain-free problems. This approach focuses on the problems themselves in the hope of finding out the cognitive skills that seem to be required to solve that class of problem. The ultimate—and perhaps unrealizable—objective of such a program would be a catalog of problem types, each type demanding a different set of cognitive skills.

An alternative approach is to look at problem solvers who are trying to solve a wide variety of domain-free problems. Here, the objective is to find some commonalities among people rather than among problems. The hope here is that some general strategies might be discovered that are used by people to solve a number of different domain-free problems. Part of the reason for searching for such general strategies is practical. If such strategies could be found, perhaps they could be taught to people, with the result that their problem-solving ability might be enhanced. This section explores the findings produced by both approaches.

Well-Defined and Ill-Defined Problems

One simple way of categorizing a problem is to determine whether it is well or ill defined. Most of the problems we have considered thus far in the chapter could be considered well defined (Reitman, 1964). A **well-defined problem** begins with a clearly defined start state and has clearly defined goals. If the problem is well defined, every proposed solution can be evaluated against the criteria implied by the goal. If the proposed solution matches the criteria implied by the goal, the problem is solved; if the criteria have not been achieved, the problem is still unsolved. For example, getting to the football game from your house in time for the kickoff is an example of a well-defined problem. The game of chess offers us another good example. The game starts from a clearly prescribed arrangement of pieces. Moreover, the goal can also be precisely stated: in chess we're trying to checkmate the opposing king. Checkmate has been achieved if one of our pieces is checking the opposing king and our opponent is unable to (1) move his king to a safe square, or (2) interpose a friendly piece between the king and the checking piece, or (3) kill the checking piece. Can you think of some other well-defined problems? For example, is the board game Monopoly well defined? The answer is yes. Monopoly and other board games such as Clue or Stratego are almost always well defined. Notice that a well-defined problem does not have to specify every path to the goal state; finding such a path is the solver's task.

Not all problems are well defined. The goal state or the start state or both are sometimes left only partially specified. A problem that has some component missing in this sense is said to be **ill-defined.** We are confronted with plenty of ill-defined problems in this world; indeed, most of the interesting problems we face, such as achieving success in life, are ill-defined. That is, how will you know when you're a success? Our intuitions tell us that our concept of success will vary throughout our lifetimes, and so there can be no precise criteria for determining its presence or absence. Generally, specifying the actions that should be taken to solve ill-defined problems is much more difficult than it is for well-defined problems (Chi & Glaser, 1985). Generally speaking, then, a problem is ill defined if the start state is vague or unspecifiable, if the goal state is unclear, or if the operations required to change the start state into the goal state are unclear.

Little research has been done on ill-defined problems, but what has been discovered is interesting. Voss and his colleagues (Voss, Greene, Post, & Penner, 1983; Voss, Tyler, & Yengo, 1983) asked their subjects to imagine that they were the minister of agriculture for the Soviet Union. The subjects were told to imagine that crop productivity had been too low for the last several years and that they were to come up with a plan to increase crop production. Notice that this problem is quite ill defined: All three components of a well-defined problem are missing from the description given the subjects. They are told crop production is low, but the problem goes far beyond this. To specify what has made the crop production low, subjects need to know something about the Soviet Union, agriculture, and so on. Similarly, the subjects were told to increase crop production, but they were not given any clue about how this might be achieved. Finally, the goal is also unclear. How much of an increase is reasonable and significant? Would a 5 percent increase represent a solution to the problem, or is a 50 percent increase required?

Three groups of subjects were used, who differed in their knowledge of the Soviet Union. One group of subjects consisted of political scientists specializing in Soviet affairs. A second group was comprised of students taking a course in Soviet domestic policy, and the third group consisted of chemistry professors. Voss et al. found that predictable effects resulted from prior knowledge. In 24 percent of their solutions, the Soviet experts mentioned that the problem's initial state needed to be elaborated more fully to achieve a solution. This need was mentioned in only 1 percent of the solutions offered by students and chemistry professors. However, some commonalities were noted in the approaches of the various subjects. They usually realized that the best way to solve a problem of this sort is to eliminate its causes. The subjects generally tried to determine what the causes of low productivity might be and then thought of ways of counteracting those effects. Typically, subjects realized that the problem wasn't produced by a single cause but rather by a series of possibly separate causes. Subjects who realized this usually proposed various ways that such separate causes could be dealt with. For example, one expert identified three separate causes of low productivity: the Soviet bureaucracy, the attitudes of Soviet farmers toward modernization, and the lack of infrastructure (e.g., pesticide production, farm equipment production, transportation deficiencies). Notice that these problems are somewhat more precise than the original problem.

This research therefore suggests that people solve ill-defined problems by performing some transformations that result in the problem's being broken down into a series of smaller, more manageable subproblems. The more knowledge a person has in a particular area, the more able she seems to be in creating such solvable subproblems. That is, the problem solver seems to rely on her knowledge to create more or less well-defined subproblems from the original ill-defined problem.

However, we should be aware of several other aspects of the well-defined–ill-defined distinction. First, the boundary between the two classes of problems is occasionally blurry (Simon, 1973). For example, the proof of a theorem in logic is usually considered a well-defined problem. However, as Simon notes, a person may not restrict his problem solving to the symbols of formal logic, but rather may make use of analogy to other logic problems. Viewed in this light, although the proof of a logic theorem might be well defined, the rules for going about such proofs are themselves ill defined. Second, some evidence has suggested that, unless people perceive a rigid procedure for converting start states into goal states, they are likely to treat well-defined problems as ill defined—just the opposite of what Voss et al. found.

Greeno (1976) presented high school students in geometry class with a series of problems that involve the proof of various theorems. He asked his subjects to think out loud as they solved the problems, and he tape-recorded their comments. Analysis of these utterances indicated that the subjects tended to break the problem down into smaller subproblems, as Voss and his colleagues had found. What was surprising about the findings, however, was the apparent vagueness of the subjects' subgoals. When asked if he had any specific theorems in mind, one student answered:

> I don't know. I was just sort of letting . . . I was just sort of letting the information . . . I shouldn't have said that I was running through all the theorems, I was just letting this stuff, the given information, sort of soak through my head, you know. (p. 483)

Typologies of Problems

As we've seen, the well-defined–ill-defined distinction offers us one way of categorizing problems, but its usefulness is somewhat limited. An alternative scheme for classifying problems has been developed by Greeno (1978). He analyzed several different problems that he maintains can be considered examples of the three basic forms of problem solving. Greeno also argues that each of these three basic forms can be associated with a particular cognitive operation or skill necessary to solve problems of that type.

Problems of Inducing Structure   The first of Greeno's three basic forms he calls **problems of inducing structure**. These consist of determining the relationship among several given elements of the problem. A common example is the analogy problem in which four elements are supplied, and the solver must determine whether they can be related in some way that fits the structure A:B::C:D (i.e., A is to B as C is to D). Greeno states that the principal cognitive ability required for problems of this type is some form of understanding. What processes are required to do analogy problems successfully?

Pellegrino (1985) theorized that three classes of cognitive skills are necessary to do analogy problems. The first class of cognitive operations consists of attribute discovery or encoding processes. If verbal items are presented, encoding consists of activating some aspects of semantic memory. If the analogy consists of figural or pictorial elements, the encoding processes are based on feature extraction. In either case, a representation of the elements is created and stored. This representation is critical because subsequent operations are carried out on it. After the elements of the analogy have been encoded, the problem solver begins the process of comparing the encoded attributes. This process is the second cognitive skill needed to solve analogies. The attributes might be compared in several ways. For example, the subject might use the process of inference making to determine what the first two elements of the analogy have in common with each other, as well as some of the things that are different between them.

Mapping the attributes is another way the encoded attributes might be compared. This refers to the solver's attempts to find a comparison between the first and third terms of the analogy. For example, if the analogy were Dog:Wolf::Cat: ? the solver must first activate the semantic nodes of *dog* and *wolf*, noting perhaps that they are both canine, and noting also that dogs are domestic whereas wolves are wild. In the mapping process, the solver would activate the *cat* node, noting that cats are feline and domestic.

Another way of comparing the encoded attributes is called application. Here, the solver attempts to relate the inference drawn from the A–B comparison to the differences noted in the C term, in an effort to generate what the "ideal" D candidate might be. The solver working on the prior analogy might convert its form into the following: Domestic Canine is to Wild Canine as Domestic Feline is to (perhaps) Wild Feline. Thus, the ideal candidate as produced by the application process might be lion, tiger, or panther.

After the solver has encoded the attributes of the analogy and compared them, it's time to engage in the final class of processes necessary to do analogies. This process consists of evaluation. In the example just given, determining the ideal candidate was fairly simple, and so making a response or picking out the most appropriate response from among several alternatives would be easy. However, in other situations, the complexity of the analogy might be increased if the elements differ in a wide variety of features. In those situations, evaluating the alternatives to pick the best one may be a complicated cognitive act in its own right.

According to Pellegrino's account, these processes should be enacted sequentially; that is, you cannot go to the evaluation process until you have completed all of the attribute comparison processes. Moreover, the attribute comparison processes should be affected by the complexity of the elements in the analogy and by the degree of the difference between features among the elements of the analogy. If the analogy has many features, or if the elements of the analogy share few features, this should make the analogy harder.

A study by Mulholland, Pellegrino, and Glaser (1980) tested these assertions. Subjects were shown the analogies depicted in Figure 12.5 and were asked to state whether the analogy was true or false (the analogy had to be exact in order to be true). Notice that the analogies had been varied in complexity by altering both the number of elements in the figures and the number of transformations between the elements. Figure 12.6 shows the findings of this study, which support the predictions of Pellegrino. The two factors affecting complexity combined in an orderly way to produce increases in latency for more complex analogies. Each element in the original analogy added about 300 msec to

·············· **FIGURE 12.5** Examples of true and false figural analogies varying in item complexity.

Item class	True analogies	False analogies
1 Element 1 Transformation		
1 Element 3 Transformations		
2 Elements 2 Transformations		
3 Elements 1 Transformation		
3 Elements 3 Transformations		

(From Mulholland, Pellegrino, & Glaser. Copyright 1980 by Academic Press, Inc. Adapted by permission of the publisher and author.)

FIGURE 12.6
·····················
Reaction times for figural analogy solution, showing the separate effect of elements and number of transformations (1).

(From Mulholland, Pellegrino, & Glaser. Copyright 1980 by Academic Press, Inc. Adapted by permission of the publisher and author.)

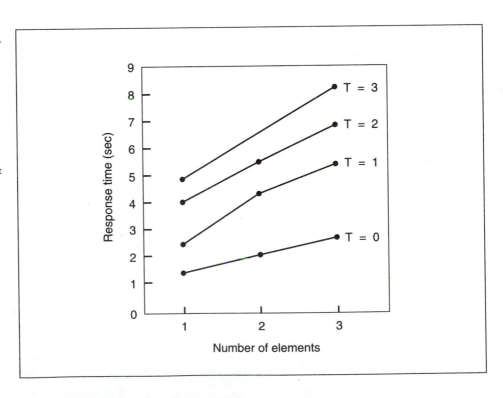

the average subject's solution time, and each transformation added about 400 msec.

In our everyday problem solving, we rely on analogies quite a bit; generally we use the analogy to take us from one domain of knowledge to another, or from one kind of problem to another within a domain. Novick and Holyoak (1991) have theorized that, in addition to the mapping process that we've already discussed, people must engage in a separate adapting process in order to complete an analogy. So, in other words, even after a particular problem reminds us of another problem that we might use as the basis for our solution efforts, we still must endeavor to see if the solution process that we used in the reminded problem can be tailored to work for the problem at hand. According to Novick and Holyoak (1991), it is this adaptation process that often spells the difference between success and failure in the use of analogies. To show these effects, Novick and Holyoak first gave their subjects a problem like this one to solve:

> Mr. and Mrs. Renshaw were planning how to arrange vegetable plants in their new garden. They agreed on the total number of plants to buy, but not on how many of each kind to get. Mr. Renshaw wanted to have a few kinds of vegetables and ten of each kind. Mrs. Renshaw wanted more different kinds of vegetables, so she suggested having only four of each kind. Mr. Renshaw didn't like that because if some of the plants died, there wouldn't be very many left of each kind. So they agreed to have five of each vegetable. But then their daughter pointed out that there was room in the garden for two more plants, although then there wouldn't be the same number of each kind of vegetable. To remedy this, she suggested buying six of each vegetable. Everyone was satisfied with this plan. Given this information, what is the fewest number of vegetable plants the Renshaws could have in their garden?

Would solving such a problem permit some "general" learning to take place that might enable a person to solve other problems? To find out, Novick and Holyoak gave their subjects additional problems, one of which, the Marching Band Target Problem follows:

> Members of the West High School Band were hard at work practicing for the annual Homecoming Parade. First they tried marching in rows of twelve, but Andrew was left by himself to bring up the rear. The band director was annoyed because it didn't look good to have one row with only a single person in it, and of course Andrew wasn't very pleased either. To get rid of this problem, the director told the band members to march in columns of eight. But Andrew was still left to march alone. Even when the band marched in rows of three, Andrew was left out. Finally, in exasperation, Andrew told the band director that they should march in rows of five in order to have all the rows filled. He was right. This time all the rows were filled and Andrew wasn't alone any more. Given that there were at least 45 musicians on the field but fewer than 200 musicians, how many students were there in the West High School Band?

Some subjects were given additional information as well. Some of the subjects were given a simple retrieval hint; others were given a number-mapping hint but were not given any conceptual information. These subjects got a statement similar to this one: The 12, 8, and 3 in the band problem are like the 10, 4, and 5 in the garden problem. Also, the 1 in this problem is like the 2 in the garden problem. Finally, the 5 in this problem is like the 6 in the garden problem. Other subjects got a conceptual hint but did not get specific numerical information. These subjects read the following passage:

> In particular, your goal in this problem is to arrange band members into rows or columns so that each row (or each column) has the same number of people in it, with no one left over. That's like the goal you had in the garden problem of grouping

plants into different types so that there were the same number of plants of each type, with none left over. In the garden problem the major difficulty encountered was that once the Renshaws finally figured out how many plants they had room for in their garden, all of the arrangements they had thought of failed to accommodate two plants. There is a similar difficulty in the marching band problem. There, each formation the band director thought of failed to accommodate one person. So to summarize, the band members are like plants, the rows and columns of band members are like kinds of plants, and the number of band members per row or column is like the number of plants of each kind.

Both problems can be solved by using a Least Common Multiple (LCM) approach. In each problem, the solver must generate the lowest common multiple of the first three divisors mentioned in the problem that leaves a constant remainder, generating multiples of this LCM, adding the constant remainder to each multiple, and then selecting from this set the generated multiple that can be evenly divided by a fourth number—the divisor that is mentioned last in the problem.

The subjects wrote down the approach that they used, and all their mathematical work was shown. A score of 2 was given to a subject who used the LCM procedure on the band problem; a 1 was given if the subject partially transferred the LCM procedure to the band problem, and a zero was given to subjects who showed no transfer. The number-mapping subjects showed the greatest degree of transfer (mean transfer score = 1.4); the concept-mapping subjects had a significantly lower transfer score (mean = 0.84). This finding suggests that understanding the numerical relationships in the two problems was crucial for success. But, importantly, understanding the numerical relationships was not sufficient for successful transfer. In other words, simply knowing that "12" in one problem is like "10" in another problem doesn't enable subjects to apply the LCM procedure in the second case. Indeed, Novick and Holyoak found that even in the "number-mapping" condition, which had the highest mean transfer score, still only 50 percent of the subjects successfully transferred the LCM procedure intact to the band problem. As the researchers suggested, this finding suggests that the major source of difficulty in transferring knowledge across to the target problem is the adaptation process rather than the mapping process per se.

Problems of Transformation   The second of Greeno's three types of problems is the transformation problem. **Problems of transformation** involve finding a sequence of operations that transform the initial situation into a goal state. A characteristic example of such a problem is the well-known **Tower of Hanoi** problem. Figure 12.7 illustrates a four-disk version of the Tower of Hanoi. The four disks have holes in them so that they can be placed on the three pegs. The disks may be moved one at a time to any other peg provided that no disk is ever stacked on top of a smaller disk. Only the top disk of a stack may be moved. The goal is to move the entire stack on peg 1 over to peg 3. You can duplicate the Tower of Hanoi using different size coins placed on pieces of paper labeled "peg 1" and so forth. If you try it, you'll see that the problem is far from trivial. According to Greeno, the major cognitive skill required to do this task is means-end analysis. Means-end analysis (Newell & Simon, 1972) refers to the perception of differences between the current and desired states. Moreover, means-end analysis suggests some sort of action that will reduce the discrepancy.

The Tower of Hanoi puzzle has been extensively studied for a variety of reasons. First, although usually not clear initially to the subjects, the puzzle has an

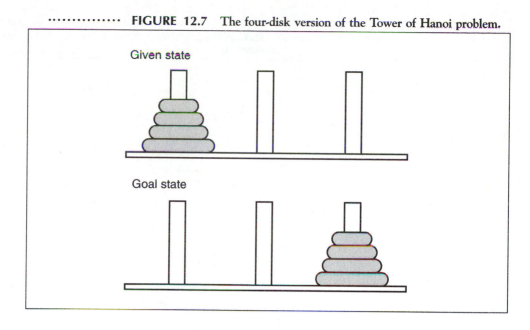

·············· **FIGURE 12.7** The four-disk version of the Tower of Hanoi problem.

orderly structure that significantly constrains the subjects' choices. Figure 12.8 shows this organization.

As the figure shows, each move in the Tower of Hanoi can be thought of as producing a different configuration of disks, or what we can call a different state. This version of the Tower of Hanoi problem has twenty-seven states. In general, a Tower of Hanoi has 3^n states, where n is the number of disks. The minimum number of moves necessary to solve a Tower of Hanoi problem is $2^n - 1$. You can therefore see that increasing the number of disks in a Tower of Hanoi by 1 essentially triples the number of states that could be entered, but it only doubles (more or less) the minimum number of moves necessary for solution. What produces this discrepancy? Again, it's not apparent, but the Tower of Hanoi problem has a feature known as recursion, which means that the larger versions of the problem contain the smaller versions. In other words, on the way to solving a four-disk version of the problem, the solver actually solves two three-disk versions. Solving the five-disk version consists of solving two four-disk problems and so on.

The nature of this organization is not initially clear to the problem solver, but Karat (1982) has determined that subjects do have some limited understanding of how to solve the problem. However, this understanding is not complete enough to permit the subject to generate the complete solution. For example, subjects quickly realize that moving the same disk on two consecutive moves is not useful, because such a movement could always be accomplished in a single move. This realization is often followed by the solver's understanding that the smallest disk in any Tower of Hanoi should be moved on the odd-numbered moves, while some other disk should be moved on the alternate, even-numbered moves. Together, these realizations suggest the following pattern of movement: (1) move the smallest disk, (2) move disk 2 (the second smallest disk) to the only available peg, (3) put disk 1 on disk 2, and (4) move the only other disk possible. Any deviation from this sequence of moves leads to the undoing of the most recently attained state (Polson & Jeffries, 1982). Although most solvers quickly

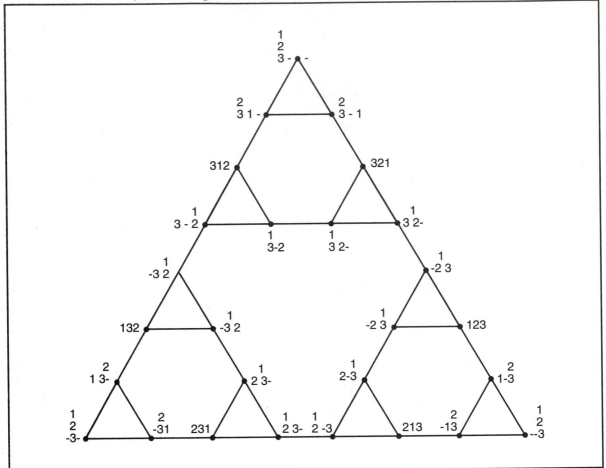

(From John Karat, *Cognitive Psychology,* Copyright 1982 by Academic Press, Inc. Adapted by permission of the publisher and author.)

latch on to these concepts, which Karat has called local knowledge, there's one thing that the four-step sequence doesn't indicate. That is, to what peg should the smallest disk be moved initially? This requires some additional knowledge—what we might call broader, or global, knowledge of Tower of Hanoi problems.

Karat has contended that both types of knowledge can be represented in three types of cognitive processes, which he has formalized as a three-stage model. These processes are called execute, propose, and evaluate. The executive system describes a group of cognitive processes that examine working memory to see if any from a list of approved moves (such as moving the smallest disk on an odd-numbered move) is available. If one such move is available, the person will make that move. If no such move is detected, this activates the propose system. The propose system considers the current condition of the array and tries to figure out if certain approved moves would become possible if the disks were rearranged somewhat. Here, Karat maintains that the solver has two kinds of knowledge. The first kind of knowledge we might call understanding; the solver knows what has to be done to rearrange the array so that the four-step sequence previously outlined can be executed. If understanding is not present, the solver will make certain available moves on a probabilistic basis, which constitutes the second kind of knowledge the solver might have. The final system, evaluation, simply checks the proposed move for legality. When Karat's model is compared with the performance of naive humans, its predictions about move choice and move latency agree closely with actual behavior. Although such findings don't prove that human subjects are endowed with and use the processes Karat has theorized, they suggest that humans have a few basic operations that are involved in these sorts of transformation problems.

Karat's research has suggested that human behavior on these types of tasks is fairly simple because the task constrains people's choices. This finding may give you the idea that, for most people, it is not hard to come up with a strategy or plan for dealing with the Tower of Hanoi. That is, because most people act in a very local sense, without seeming to take into account where they're ultimately going in the problem, you might get the idea that people are content simply to take "baby steps" in problems like the Tower of Hanoi. But actually, coming up with a strategy in these problems may be harder than it seems. For example, Anzai and Simon (1979) asked their subjects to make verbal statements of their thoughts while the subjects were solving the Tower of Hanoi. Anzai and Simon found that humans may actually use four different strategies in solving problems. Two of the strategies were particularly advanced. For example, many subjects' comments indicated the presence of a disk-moving strategy consisting of several moves that were designed to move a particular disk to a particular peg. In addition, many subjects possessed an even more advanced pyramid-moving strategy in which the subject produces a series of individual moves designed to move a stack of several disks to a particular peg.

VanLehn's (1991) work supports these notions. Using the same procedure as that of Anzai and Simon in a case study of a single subject, VanLehn found that the subject explicitly worked on developing particular strategies eleven times in the course of a problem-solving session on the Tower of Hanoi. One particularly interesting aspect of VanLehn's findings is that the strategies were usually discussed in terms of rules; moreover these rule acquisition events were not always driven by the subject's reaching an impasse. In some cases, the subject examined her strategies simply because she was seeking a more efficient (that is, fewer moves) solution.

Problems of Arrangement   Finally, in Greeno's third type of problem, that of arrangement, the solver is given some element that must be rearranged according to some criterion. A typical example of **problems of arrangement** is the anagram, and the principal cognitive skill needed to do such a problem is that of constructive search. That is, the solver must develop some way of systematically examining reasonable combinations of letters until the solution is found. This task is not easy. A five-letter anagram has 5! or 120 possible combinations. If you were to search through this number of combinations at the rate of one per second, coming up with the answer might take as long as two minutes. Since most people can solve such anagrams faster than that, however, the subjects don't seem to be searching the combinations randomly.

For most subjects not all 120 possibilities are examined. Consider the following anagram:

AIFMA

If you are even moderately aware of your own thought processes, you know you quickly became aware that the first two letters of the anagram almost certainly had to be separated. Few English words begin with the letters *AI*. Similarly, you know that the letters *MA* form a fairly common syllable in English that occurs at the beginning or ending of words (probably more often at the beginning). Perhaps you mentally shifted the *MA* combination around while visualizing various combinations of the remaining three letters. Greeno calls this type of thinking "generating partial solutions" (Greeno, 1978). That is, the problem solver produces what are believed to be the components of the entire solution, and these components are fabricated on the basis of the solver's knowledge.

This process is roughly analogous to the **local-global distinction** we made in regard to transformation problems. The person who is generating partial solutions has some local knowledge, but not complete global knowledge, of the task. This implies that an anagram would become more difficult if its letters could be combined systematically in a large number of ways. This hypothesis was supported in a study by Ronning (1965), who determined that anagrams are harder to solve if their letters can be organized in a variety of ways that are consistent with the rules of English phonology. In addition to this phonetic knowledge, other evidence indicates that knowledge of the anagram's semantic category (knowing, for example, that the anagram can be rearranged to make "a form of transportation") also facilitates the search process (Dominowski & Ekstrand, 1967; Richardson & Johnson, 1980), probably because it somewhat constrains the search process.

Greeno's work is an endeavor to identify various classes of problems that seem to require different classes of cognitive skills. We have seen that the problems that Greeno has identified as prototypical do require some different skills, but the skills required also seem to overlap. For example, constructive search is brought into play both for transformation problems and arrangement problems. This has led some cognitive psychologists to wonder if perhaps the problem should be turned around. Instead of trying to identify classes of problems that differ from one another, perhaps we should focus on what takes place in the solver's mind. This has resulted in a search for what we might call general problem strategies that can be used across a wide variety of problems. The next section reviews the outcome of this line of investigation.

Tactics for Solving Problems

Greeno's work has suggested that different types of problems can best be solved with relevant and particular skills. Are any sort of general strategies available that might be useful in solving a wide variety of problems?

Before we examine some of these all-purpose strategies, it's important to offer a definition of **strategy.** *Strategy* is derived from the Greek *strategos*, a root that originally meant "trick" or "deception." The Greeks later used this term to describe army generals; that is, a general was one who could trick the enemy. Notice that, although a trick or ruse is *indicated* by some behavior, a trick is more than *just* behavior. The trick implies that some mental action or planning has preceded it. Unintentional tricks are not possible.

A modern definition of strategy must take these things into account. Strategies are seen in behavior, but the behavior implies some sort of mental effort. A strategy can therefore be defined as a move, trial, or probe designed to effect some change in the problem and provide information by so doing. That is, the change is considered informative. Cognitive psychologists have described two broad classes of strategies: **heuristics** and **algorithms.**

An *algorithm* is a procedure that is guaranteed to produce an answer to the problem. Algorithms may not always be efficient, but they always work. We make use of algorithms whenever we multiply numbers together with paper and pencil or with a calculator. Similarly, we can solve any anagram problem if we follow the algorithm of arranging the letters in every possible combination until a word is found. If algorithms are so powerful, why don't we use them all the time? The answer to this question can be found by referring to the well-defined–ill-defined distinction made earlier. Successful solutions to ill-defined problems often can't be specified ahead of time; thus, no procedure can be developed that will necessarily produce solutions to them. We can't have algorithms for ill-defined problems. Even for well-defined problems, we are sometimes defeated in our attempts to find an algorithm because the problem is so vast. Chess is a good example of a problem that is too vast to permit the discovery of an algorithm. Starting from the conventional opening position, the estimate is that chess has 10^{40} different continuations or possible games. Assuming you had a computing machine capable of evaluating each entire game at the rate of three per micromillisecond (one-millionth of one-thousandth of a second), examining all the possibilities would still take the machine 10^{21} *centuries*. Don't hold your breath waiting for computers to discover the chess algorithm.

We've encountered heuristics in the last chapter. They are rules of thumb that have been developed from experience in solving certain problems. For example, if you've ever changed the tire on a car, you're probably aware of some useful heuristics such as loosening the bolts slightly *before* you jack up the car. Similarly, if you play chess, you probably know some of its heuristics, such as keeping the queen in the center of the action, keeping the knights away from the edge of the board, and so on. Unlike algorithms, heuristics don't guarantee the attainment of a solution. But they often make up this shortcoming by being easy and fast to use. Over the past several years, cognitive scientists have discovered that humans often use several all-purpose heuristics that don't appear to be closely tied to specific problems. The origin of much of this knowledge is the work of Newell and Simon.

Newell and Simon's Research   Perhaps the most imposing theory of problem solving to be erected by cognitive psychologists is that of Newell and Simon, which they developed over the past twenty-five years (Newell, 1962, 1965, 1966, 1967; Newell, Shaw, & Simon, 1958; Newell & Simon, 1961, 1972; Simon, 1969, 1978). This is an information-processing theory that begins with the concept of problem representation. Newell and Simon discuss two sorts of problem representations. The term **task environment** describes the representation of a problem in as complete and neutral a way as possible. The task environment therefore is an attempt to represent the problem in an objective way. In trying to understand human problem solving on a given task, Newell and Simon invariably begin by attempting to map out the problem's task environment. Why?

There are two major reasons. First, a complete understanding of a problem's task environment can be equated with an understanding of all the ways in which that problem could be represented. Clearly, for anything more than trivial problems, this ideal cannot be reached. But the solver, in the act of problem solving, chooses certain representations as being more desirable than others. Knowing which representations were chosen from an array of all possible representations affords a great deal of knowledge about the psychology of the solver.

A second reason for understanding the task environment stems from the fact that the task environment exerts a powerful influence on the apparent complexity of the solver's behavior. According to Newell and Simon, the human information-processing system is not very complicated. Consequently, if its behavior appears complex, it's probably because the task environment in which it is operating is complex.

The solver does not typically have complete knowledge of the task environment. When confronted with an unfamiliar problem, the solver must encode the relevant features of the problem to construct an internal representation of it. Newell and Simon label the solver's internal representation the **problem space**; and thinking of the problem space as a subset of the task environment is appropriate.

Newell and Simon conceptualize the problem space as a collection of nodes, similar in form to those specified by the theories of semantic memory examined in Chapter 6. In the problem space, each node stands for a particular state of knowledge. The nodes are linked by cognitive processes called **operators,** which convert one node into another. For Newell and Simon, problem solving consists of moving through the nodes of the problem space. This means that, as the solver works on the problem, she accesses, or enters, different states of knowledge. Newell and Simon describe this movement as being under the control of an executive system, and the movement itself is similar to the search processes that we observed when we studied activation models of semantic memory.

An example of Newell and Simon's research might help to clarify some of this terminology. They frequently use the case study as a method of investigation. Their procedure often involves making tape recordings of a subject who has been instructed to think out loud while solving a problem. Consider the following "cryptarithmetic" problem (Bartlett, 1958). (The answer to this problem is in the appendix. You might want to try it—but I'm warning you, it's not easy.)

$$
\begin{array}{r}
\text{DONALD} \\
+\text{GERALD} \\
\hline
\text{ROBERT}
\end{array}
$$

The subject is informed that each letter represents a single numeral and that the correspondence between the numerals and letters is one-to-one. The subject is asked to deduce the correspondence, such that when numerals are substituted for letters, the resulting addition problem is mathematically correct. The subject is given one correspondence (D = 5). The resulting output, called a protocol, is then broken down into a number of short behavior phrases labeled B1, B2, and so on. Finally, the behavior phrases are coded using fairly rigid criteria. Newell and Simon argue that such coded behavior phrases can be used as markers to indicate something about the state of knowledge or cognitive process that was taking place at the time the utterance was made. If, for example, the subject remarks:

B74: "But now I know that G has to be 1 or 2,"

we know that the solver is capable of considering disjunctive sets, that is, either-or assignments of numbers. When the protocol has been completely coded in this fashion, Newell and Simon use it to generate two different representations of the subject's problem space. The first representation is depicted in Figure 12.9.

These expressions probably won't be too meaningful to you at first. They are written in a formal notation known as Backus Normal Form (BNF). If you take a

············ **FIGURE 12.9**   Problem space for S3.

```
<digit> :: = 0|1|2|3|4|5|6|7|8|9
<digit-variable> :: = x|y
<general-digit> :: = <digit>|<digit-variable>
<digit-set> :: = <general-digit>∨<general-digit:>|<general-digit>∨<digit-set>
<letter> :: = A|B|D|E|G|L|N|O|R|T
<letter-set> :: = <letter>|<letter> <letter-set>
<carry> :: = c <column-number>
<variable> :: = <letter>|<carry>
<column> :: = column.<column-number>
<column-number> :: = 1|2|3|4|5|6|7
<column-set> :: = <column>|<column><column-set>
<assignment-expression> :: = <variable>←<general-digit>|
   <variable> = <general-digit>
<constraint-expression> :: = <variable><parity>|<variable> = ;<digit-set>|
   <variable><inequality><general-digit>|<variable><qualifier>
<parity> :: = even|odd
<inequality :: = >|<
<qualifier> :: = free|last
<expression> :: = <variable>|<assignment-expression>|<constraint-expression>
<state-expression> :: = <expression>|<expression><tag>
<tag> :: = new□|unclear|unknown|note
<knowledge-state> :: = <state-expression>|<state-expression><knowledge-state>
<operator> :: = PC[<column>]|GN|AV|TD
<goal> :: = get <expression>|get <letter-set>
   check <expression>|check <column-set>
Particular sets:
 all-letters, free-letters
 all-digits, free-digits
 all-columns
```

(From Allen Newell, Herbert A. Simon, *Human Problem Solving*, Copyright 1972, p. 168. Reprinted by permission of Prentice-Hall, Inc., Englewood Cliffs, N.J.)

close look at Figure 12.9, you'll see that the expressions formally define both the symbols that must be constructed in solving cryptarithmetic problems as well as the four operators that move the solver through the problem space. In other words, the BNF representation is a condensed, or collapsed, form of the subject's problem space. This means that, if Figure 12.9 is an accurate depiction of the solver's internal representation, we should be able to expand, or unpack, it. In other words, we should be able to use the rules implied by the BNF representation to develop a graph that charts the subject's movement through his problem space during the course of problem solving. This is the second of Newell and Simon's representations of the problem space, and they refer to it as a Problem Behavior Graph (PBG). We should understand the PBG as a trace of the subject's trajectory through a particular problem, that is, a record of his movement from state to state.

Table 12.1 lists the rules that Newell and Simon give for unpacking the PBG from the BNF notation, and Figure 12.10 shows the condensed version of a single subject's PBG for the Donald + Gerald problem.

As the PBG in Figure 12.10 implies, the subject's search is generally trial and error, particularly at the outset of his solution attempt. This is indicated by the fact that the subject, S3, has to back up fairly often, much like a novice chess

·············· **TABLE 12.1** **Rules for Problem Behavior Graph (PBG)**

A state of knowledge is represented by a node.

The application of an operator to a state of knowledge is represented by a horizontal arrow to the right: the result is the node at the head of the arrow.

A return to the same state of knowledge, say node X, is represented by another node below X, connected to it by a vertical line.

A repeated application of the same operator to the same state of knowledge is indicated by doubling the horizontal line.

Time runs to the right, then down: thus, the graph is linearly ordered by time of generation.

Source: From Allen Newell, Herbert A. Simon, *Human Problem Solving,* Copyright 1972, p. 173. Reprinted by permission of Prentice-Hall, Inc., Englewood Cliffs, N.J.

player who cannot carry the continuations very far forward and so must constantly return to the base move. In some cases, S3 has to back up to nodes occurring early in the problem-solving process. The bottom third of the PBG reveals the changing nature of S3's search in the late stages of problem solving. The graph shows much more horizontal than vertical movement, meaning that S3 has apparently latched onto the solution path. Newell and Simon have carried out extensive analyses of problem solving in chess (Newell & Simon, 1965; Simon & Simon, 1962) and logic problems (Newell & Simon, 1956) as well as in cryptarithmetic. Their work suggests that solvers' internal representations have certain invariant qualities, which are shown in Table 12.2.

A problem solver's effectiveness is determined by two major variables: the quality of the problem space and the mode of search. The solver is said to be searching for a solution path—a series of knowledge states—that leads through the problem space. Using the "thinking out loud" methodology, Newell and Simon were able to isolate a limited number of search modes, which they called heuristics, that seemed to have wide applicability across a number of domain-free problems. Generally, the solver operates by working forward from the initial knowledge state to the goal state. In such situations, Newell and Simon describe two general heuristics—means-end analysis and subgoal analysis—that seem to describe the mode of search. In some cases, the solver may elect to work backward from the goal state. The following sections consider some examples of these various search modes and their implications.

Subgoal Analysis   Consider the following problem (Wickelgren, 1974):

> Nine men and two boys want to cross a river, using a raft that will carry either one man or the two boys. How many times must the boat cross the river in order to accomplish this goal? (A round trip equals two crossings.)

This problem can be solved in a number of ways, but like many people, you probably intuitively adopted a subgoal approach. If you haven't solved this problem, try it again with the idea of determining how many crossings are necessary to get just one man across the river. Without too much difficulty, you've probably determined that getting one man across and returning the boat to the original bank takes four crossings. First, the two boys cross; then one boy brings the boat back. Next, the man crosses by himself, and finally, the boy on the far bank returns with the boat. To get all nine men across requires that this sequence be repeated eight more times for a total of thirty-six crossings. At that point, the boat will be on the original bank, and only the two boys will remain. They cross together, thus making a total of thirty-seven crossings. The key to this problem is

············· **FIGURE 12.10** Problem Behavior Graph of S3—overview.

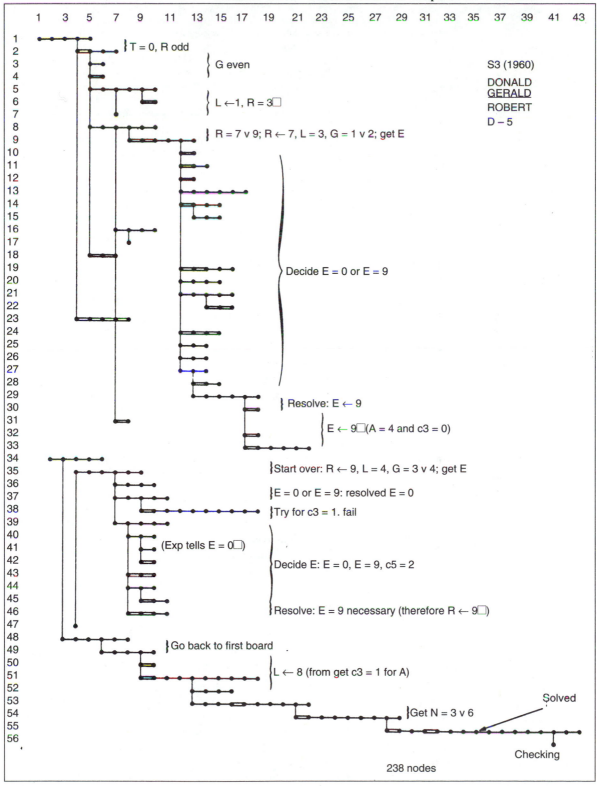

S3 (1960)

DONALD
GERALD
ROBERT
D − 5

T = 0, R odd

G even

L ←1, R = 3□

R = 7 v 9; R ← 7, L = 3, G = 1 v 2; get E

Decide E = 0 or E = 9

Resolve: E ← 9

E ← 9□(A = 4 and c3 = 0)

Start over: R ← 9, L = 4, G = 3 v 4; get E

E = 0 or E = 9: resolved E = 0

Try for c3 = 1. fail

(Exp tells E = 0□)

Decide E: E = 0, E = 9, c5 = 2

Resolve: E = 9 necessary (therefore R ← 9□)

Go back to first board

L ← 8 (from get c3 = 1 for A)

Get N = 3 v 6

Solved

Checking

238 nodes

(From Allen Newell, Herbert A. Simon, *Human Problem Solving,* Copyright 1972, p. 181. Reprinted by permission of Prentice-Hall, Inc., Englewood Cliffs, N.J.)

·············· **TABLE 12.2**   Invariant Features of Problem Spaces

1. The set of knowledge states is generated from a finite set of objects, relations, properties, and so on, and can be represented as a closed space of knowledge.
2. The set of operators is small and finite (or at least finitely generated).
3. The available set of alternative nodes in the space to which the problem solver might return is very small; in fact, it usually contains only one or two nodes.
4. The residence time in each particular knowledge state before generation of the next state is of the order of seconds.
5. The problem solver remains within a given problem space for times of the order of at least tens of minutes.
6. Problem solving takes place by search in the problem space—i.e., by considering one knowledge state after another until (if the search is successful) a desired knowledge state is reached. The moves from one state to the next are mostly incremental.
7. The search involves backup—that is, return from time to time to old knowledge states and hence the abandonment of knowledge-state information (although not necessarily of path information).
8. The knowledge state is typically only moderate in size—containing at most a few hundred symbols, more typically a few dozen.

Source: From Allen Newell, Herbert A. Simon, *Human Problem Solving,* Copyright 1972, p. 811. Reprinted by permission of Prentice-Hall, Inc. Englewood Cliffs, N.J.

realizing that the actions needed to get one man across can be duplicated to solve the entire problem; the nature of this problem is such that it can be broken into parts (Wickelgren, 1974, p. 91).

To understand the power of the subgoal heuristic more fully, another term must be introduced into our description. Imagine that the initial description of the problem were represented by a dot with some appropriate notation on a piece of graph paper. Also imagine that every action that could be taken from this initial point were represented by a line radiating from the original dot. Again, imagine that each line could be labeled with some notation to show what sort of action it represented (one boy crossing, one man crossing, or whatever). Each such line would terminate in another dot, which would represent the state of the problem as it had been transformed by the preceding action. Indeed, all the achievable states of the problem and all the actions possible from each state could be represented in a diagram of this sort. Such a representation is referred to as the state-action space, or **state-action tree.** You've probably recognized that the PBG and the diagram of the Tower of Hanoi are both versions of state-action trees. A hypothetical state-action tree is shown in Figure 12.11.

The power of the subgoal heuristic becomes more clear when we consider the nature of problem solving as movement through a state-action tree. Suppose we consider a hypothetical problem that has m alternative actions at each dot or state and requires a sequence of n actions for solution. If we mindlessly plow through the state-action tree of such a problem, we could well wind up pursuing some m^n alternative paths or action sequences needlessly. Assume, though, that you know just one state that could serve as a subgoal, and this state is on the correct path to the goal and is halfway through the sequence of n actions. This means that there are now $m^{n/2}$ paths to be investigated from the start state to the subgoal and a similar number from the subgoal to the final goal. The complexity of the entire problem has thus been reduced from m^n action sequences to $2m^{n/2}$ action sequences that are $n/2$ steps long.

The authenticity of this reduction becomes clear if you consider a problem in which $m = 10$ and $n = 10$. The number of possible action sequences to be investigated is awesome: 10^{10}. Knowing just a single subgoal with the conditions

················ **FIGURE 12.11   State-action tree for simple problem solving showing
how defining a subgoal on the correct path (action sequence) to the goal can reduce
the search.**   In this case, the search is limited to the region inside the two boxes,
which is eight action sequences each two steps long, instead of sixteen action sequences
each four steps long. Some simplifying assumptions are made, such as that one knows
that the subgoal is two steps from the beginning and two steps from the end. However,
the average problem is much longer, and the degree of reduction in search by defining
subgoals is far greater than in this simple example.

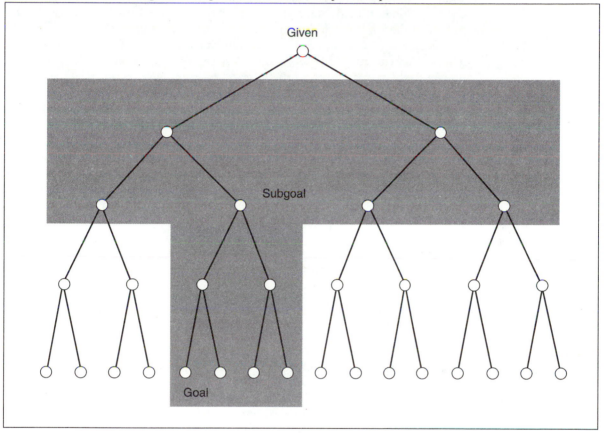

just described reduces the number of action states to $2(10^5)$, which is 1/50,000 of
the original number. This heuristic will not prove useful all the time. Oftentimes,
we're stumped in our search for subgoals, and being sure that the subgoal is on the
correct path to the goal is sometimes difficult. Nevertheless, the subgoal heuristic
can be a remarkable way to prune the state-action tree. For example, in the Tower
of Hanoi problem, it may have occurred to you that the movement of the bottom
disk to the appropriate peg is a subgoal that is halfway to the final goal state.
Accordingly, this makes the movement of the bottom disk a reasonable subgoal
for that problem.

Working Backward   Consider the following problem (Wickelgren, 1974):

> Three people play a game in which one person loses and two people win each game.
> The one who loses must double the amount of money that each of the other two
> players has at that time. The three players agree to play three games. At the end of
> the three games, each player has lost one game, and each player has eight dollars.
> What was the original stake of each player?

This problem can be devilishly difficult unless you work backward from the goal state, which in this problem is the only known state. That is, the goal state, or nth state of the action sequence is known, and our task could be represented as moving *backward* through the state-action tree from the nth state to the n − 1th state.

If you haven't solved this problem yet, stop here and try it again. We know what the state of affairs is after three games have been played; what happened in the third game? One person lost, and two won. The person who lost doubled the money of those who won. Because everyone has ended up with eight dollars, the two people who won the third game must have had only four dollars after two games. Consequently, the person who lost the third game had to pay out eight dollars to the two winners, so the loser of the third game must have had sixteen dollars after two games had been played. If you haven't solved the problem yet, I'll leave it up to you to use this same reasoning to determine what happened on the second and, finally, the first games. What conditions of the state-action tree must hold if the method of working backward is to be successful?

According to Wickelgren, these techniques will be useful if the problem satisfies two criteria. First, the problem should have a uniquely specified goal. The problem should have a single ending state that can be clearly described. The heuristic is particularly powerful in situations that involve a large number of plausible initial states. Here, the advantage of working backward accrues from the fact that the goal tells you where you must start to solve the problem, whereas the more conventional working forward techniques do not tell you which of the many initial statements will lead to the goal. Working forward in such a problem has been compared to finding a needle in a haystack (Newell, Shaw, & Simon, 1962), and working backward is analogous to letting the needle find its way out of the haystack.

General Problem Solver   These general heuristics that Newell and Simon discovered have been incorporated into a computer program known as the **General Problem Solver**, or **GPS.** The program is intended as a simulation of human problem solving, meaning that it is supposed to duplicate the outcome of human thought by duplicating the process of human thought. How does it work?

Basically, GPS has to be fed with a description of the problem to be solved. In this sense, the program does not really form its own problem space (although this shortcoming has been partially corrected in recent editions of GPS). Once the problem is presented, GPS proceeds by applying general heuristics, such as those we have been considering, to the state-action tree and evaluating its progress. The heuristic most typically used is means-end analysis, which we have examined before. For example, when confronted with the Tower of Hanoi problem, several sorts of activities are undertaken. First, the program represents the goal. Next, the difference between the current state of affairs and the goal is noted. After that, the program looks for a method that will reduce this discrepancy. The result of this processing is that a subgoal is set up, and generally the subgoal is accomplished by means-end analysis. GPS has been quite successful on the Tower of Hanoi and other more difficult problems.

Summary and Comments on the Newell and Simon Theory   Newell and Simon's theory emphasizes the relative invariance seen in people's strategies on domain-free problems. They argue that the similarity among people's strategies reflects that the human information-processing system is not very complex: people have a few basic, general heuristics for dealing with a wide variety of problems. The

Newell and Simon approach also emphasizes the importance of the correct representation. Building a problem space is probably the most important constructive act that occurs during problem solving, given that the mode of search is often fairly limited. This means that if your particular problem space doesn't include the "right" elements, this is like trying to solve the problem with a representation that may not include an adequate specification of the goal and may therefore be inadequate for the attainment of a solution. In essence, the problem solver may be searching through a problem space that is not a very good subset of the task environment. No matter how thorough the search is under those circumstances, the solver will not meet with success. The corollary of this assertion is that what differentiates an effective problem solver from a poor one is probably the quality of the internal representation used. We can examine de Groot's work as evidence of this.

Numerous questions have been raised about the Newell and Simon approach. One set of questions concerns the appropriateness of verbal reports as data. For example, Nisbett and Wilson (1977) maintain that humans have little or no introspective access to higher mental processes. This conclusion is based on several facts. First, humans are sometimes unaware of the existence of a stimulus that influenced their response. Second, they are sometimes unaware of all the responses they have made. Third, even if they are aware of the stimulus in question, they are unaware that they have been influenced by it. Nisbett and Wilson cite studies in which the subjects are given hints that are designed to facilitate their finding a solution. Typically, the subjects are not aware that hints have been given. Perhaps even more important, when false hints (which have previously been demonstrated to be ineffective) are given along with genuine hints, people are not very accurate in determining which hints are useful.

Several researchers (Ericsson & Simon, 1980; Kellogg, 1982) have commented on these findings. Ericsson and Simon (1980) have pointed out that the Nisbett and Wilson findings are not concerned with consciousness per se. Instead, the subjects in their studies could not be expected to have any awareness of their mental processes because of the nature of the judgments they were being asked to make. They argue that introspective evidence will be valid when the subjects are reporting about something that they are truly aware of, namely something that is currently being stored in working memory. In their view, subjects are capable of commenting on knowledge not currently stored in working memory, but this comment is an inference, not a report. Consequently, if people are probed in the correct fashion and at the correct time, then the introspections of subjects will be accurate on all except highly practiced tasks.

Perhaps a more serious concern is based on the nature of the problems used by Newell and Simon in their investigations. We should be aware that much of the research on problem solving has been based on fairly artificial games and puzzles that might have no genuine relationship with problem-solving ability in the real world. For example, if you take your bill stubs, receipts, W-2 forms, and so on to a tax person to prepare your income tax statement, we can imagine that the preparer uses knowledge of tax laws and other expertise to solve the problem of preparing your statement. My guess is that the preparer does not explicitly make use of general heuristics to do this task. Thus, even if we ask the person to think out loud à la Newell and Simon, the tax person would not likely make statements such as "Now I'm going to use a subgoal analysis to see what should be entered on Schedule A." This speculation implies that the sort of strategizing we have seen on problems like the Tower of Hanoi might not routinely occur in the knowledge-rich domains of everyday thinking. The next section takes up the question of problem solving in knowledge-rich domains.

 **PROBLEM SOLVING IN A DOMAIN OF KNOWLEDGE**

How Knowledge Guides Search

Chapter 3 examined the notion of schema as a coherent body of knowledge that can channel perception by producing expectations about the stimuli that will be displayed. The schema is therefore an active knowledge structure, and it plays a role in problem solving in knowledge-rich domains. That is, we can think of prior knowledge as activating certain slots, or nodes, in semantic memory. Naturally, these slots, or nodes, are organized. When enough nodes in a particular area of semantic memory are activated, this will trigger the activation of that area's organizing principle—its schema. Once the schema is activated, the subject is able to fill in some of the gaps observed in the existing display of stimuli. This sort of knowledge is exactly what enables the experienced pilot to bring in a plane for a landing when weather conditions are poor and enables a physician to make an accurate diagnosis on the basis of a few presenting symptoms. In both cases, schematic knowledge enables the problem solver to extrapolate, thus going beyond the information given. Once activated, the schematic knowledge suggests that the solver search the problem space in certain ways, looking for particular characteristics of the problem.

Hinsley, Hayes, and Simon (1978) have presented some findings that are consistent with this interpretation. They asked their subjects, who were high school and college students, to classify—not solve—algebra problems. The problems could be categorized in any way the subjects wished. Hinsley et al. found that the subjects' categorizations were similar and that the classification schemata were based on the solution procedures for the various kinds of problems. In other words, problems that were solved in similar ways were categorized together. Such a categorization schema is developed as a result of problem-solving experience with algebra problems.

The schematic nature of this knowledge became even more clear when Hinsley et al. asked the subjects to classify the problems as quickly as they could. They found that subjects were able to classify the problems after hearing only the initial sentence. For example, the subjects might hear a sentence such as "An airplane with a tail wind takes two hours to fly 230 miles." After hearing this sentence, subjects could quickly and reliably classify it as belonging to a "river current" problem in which some velocity has to be computed under aided and hindered conditions. The speed at which the problems are classified seems to rule out the possibility that the subjects are actually figuring the solution plan and categorizing accordingly. A more likely explanation is that they are able to guess accurately about the problem's forthcoming information, which enables them to guess what the solution procedure will be.

Unlike the general heuristics mentioned by Newell and Simon, however, the schemata learned in knowledge-rich domains are apparently highly specific to the types of problems encountered. That is, there is little generalization from one domain of knowledge to another. This inability to transfer schematic knowledge from problem to problem has been studied using problem isomorphs. Recall that problem isomorphs were discussed earlier in this chapter, when I described the number scrabble problem as being formally similar to tic-tac-toe. Generally, isomorphs are problems whose underlying structures and solutions are the same, but whose context may be quite different (Chi & Glaser, 1985).

Hayes and Simon (1974) studied the transfer of schematic knowledge using a problem called the tea ceremony. In this problem, three people are conducting an oriental tea ritual in which the responsibility for various aspects of the ceremony is shared among the participants according to an elaborate etiquette. The solver's task is to specify a sequence in which the various aspects of the ritual can be enacted in a way that does not violate the etiquette. The tea ceremony problem is isomorphic with the Tower of Hanoi, and anyone who realizes the **isomorphism** can easily solve the tea ceremony. However, Hayes and Simon found that almost none of their subjects, who were familiar with Tower of Hanoi problems, noticed the resemblance.

Simon and Hayes (1976) wondered what made this so. They investigated the variables that seem to play a role in the activation of the solver's schematic knowledge. They used the Tower of Hanoi once again as the basis for nine so-called Monster problems. The structure of all nine isomorphs is shown in Table 12.3.

As Table 12.3 depicts, sentence 3 of each problem refers to two classes of objects (for example, problem 5, sentence 3 refers to monsters and globes). In each problem, sentence 4 designates the objects of one class as fixed and the other as variable. Again, in problem 5, the globe held by each monster is fixed, and the monster's name is variable. Sentence 7 of each problem indicates that the legality of moves depends on the ordering of one of the attributes (e.g., in problem 5, the names are ordered by length). If the ordering referred to the variable objects, the problem was designated a transfer problem. If the ordering referred to the fixed objects, the problem was a change problem. Problems 1, 2, 5, 6, 8, and 9 are transfer problems, while 3, 4, and 7 are change problems.

Although some of the subjects in this problem were run through the typical thinking out loud procedure, other subjects were given paper and pencil and were allowed to record their moves. Of the 117 subjects who were presented with these isomorphs, more than half spontaneously used some form of state-matrix notation that offers strong evidence for the kind of representation in use. A state-matrix notation is a two-dimensional table showing the monsters on one dimension and the states of the problem on the other dimension. Here, the states of the problem refer to the successive changes or transformations made by the problem solver. In the body of the table are entries showing what size globe each monster is holding, what size the monster has become, and so on. A typical state-matrix notation used by the subjects in both transfer and change problems is shown in Table 12.4.

Of sixty-two subjects presented with a transfer problem, thirty-seven used a state matrix, as did thirty of the fifty-five subjects presented with a change problem. Of the sixty-seven subjects who used this notation to represent the problem, none used a notation form that was inconsistent with the isomorphs they were given. This can be seen by looking at the entries in Table 12.4. In the transfer problems, the variable attributes migrate from column to column. But in the change problems, the variable attributes change their values within the column. Clearly, although the form of the problems was structurally the same, the instructions seemed to exert a powerful influence on the nature of the schema guiding search. The use of the transfer terminology apparently resulted in the activation of a schema in which the variable attributes were thought of as being passed around from monster to monster, whereas the change instructions resulted in the calling up of a schema in which the subject apparently imagined the monster as changing the size of the globe she was holding. There was little or no evidence that the subjects attempted to alter the form of their internal representations once problem solving began. This observation was surprising because the change problems were quite difficult, requiring almost twice as much time as the transfer problems. Also, there were no formal indications that the subjects

·············· **TABLE 12.3**   **Monster Problem 1 and the Phrasing of the Nine Isomorphs**

S1.	Three five-handed extraterrestrial monsters were holding three crystal globes.
S2.	Because of the quantum-mechanical peculiarities of their neighborhood, both monsters and globes come in exactly three sizes with no others permitted: small, medium, and large.
S3.	The medium-sized monster was holding the small globe; the small monster was holding the large globe; and the large monster was holding the medium-sized globe.
S4.	Since this situation offended their keenly developed sense of symmetry, they proceeded to transfer globes from one monster to another so that each monster would have a globe proportionate to his own size.
S5.	Monster etiquette complicated the solution of the problem since it requires:
S6.	(1) that only one globe may be transferred at a time.
S7.	(2) that if a monster is holding two globes, only the larger of the two may be transferred, and
S8.	(3) that a globe may not be transferred to a monster who is holding a larger globe.
S9.	By what sequence of transfers could the monsters have solved this problem?

PROBLEM

Number	Type	Sentence 3	Sentence 4	Sentence 7
1	T	The small monster held the larger globe.	. . . to teleport globes . . . monster would have a globe proportionate to his own size.	If a monster is holding two globes . . . can transmit only the larger.
2	T	The small monster stood on the large globe.	. . . to teleport themselves . . . monster would have a globe proportionate to his own size.	If two monsters are standing on the same globe, only the larger . . . can leave.
3	C	The small monster was holding the large globe.	. . . to shrink and expand the globes . . . monster would have a globe proportionate to his own size.	If two globes are of the same size, only the globe held by the large monster . . . can be changed.
4	C	The small monster was holding the large globe.	. . . to shrink and expand themselves . . . monster would have a globe proportionate to his own size.	If two monsters are of the same size, only the monster holding the larger globe can change.
5	T	The monster with the small name was holding the large globe.	. . . to transfer names . . . monster would have a globe proportionate to the size of his name.	If a monster has two names . . . can transmit only the longer.
6	T	The monster with the small tail was holding the large globe.	. . . to transfer tails . . . monster would have a globe proportionate to the size of his tail.	If a monster has two tails . . . can transfer only the longer.
7	C	The small monster was originally large.	. . . to shrink and expand themselves . . . monster would have his original size back.	If two monsters are of the same size . . . only the monster who was originally larger can change.
8	T	The monster with the small name originally had the large name.	. . . to transfer names . . . monster would have his original name back.	If a monster has two names . . . can transmit only the longer.
9	T	The small monster was originally large.	. . . to transfer sizes . . . monster would have his original size back.	If a monster has two sizes . . . can transfer only the larger.

Source: Simon and Hayes. (Copyright 1976 by Academic Press, Inc. Adapted by permission of the publisher and author.)

·············· **TABLE 12.4**   State-matrix Notations used by Subjects[a]

	TRANSFER TYPE				CHANGE TYPE		
	M	**L**	**S**		**M**	**L**	**S**
0	L	S	M	0	L	S	M
1	—	L,S	M	1	L	L	M
2	M	L,S	—	2	L	L	S

[a]The columns correspond to the fixed attribute; the rows correspond to the successive problem situations after each move (0 is the starting situation). Within the cells are shown the current values of the variable attributes, which either (1) migrate from column to column (transfer type) or (2) change value within a column (change type).

Source: Simon and Hayes. (Copyright 1976 by Academic Press, Inc. Adapted by permission of the publisher and author.)

realized the equivalence of the Monster problem with the Tower of Hanoi problem, despite the fact that some of the subjects may have been familiar with the latter problem.

We've seen that schematic knowledge accrued from problem solving appears to be effective only when dealing with a particular class of problems—or maybe even a particular problem. This has led some researchers to wonder if an expert's organization of this highly specific knowledge is different from that of a novice.

Expertise

For the last several years, cognitive psychologists have come to appreciate that the knowledge of the expert is probably organized differently from knowledge in the mind of the novice. Reif (1979) analyzed this problem from the standpoint of hierarchical organization. According to Reif, the expert's knowledge is based on years of experience in which specific bits of information have been associated with other specific bits, which together have been placed in a more general category. This category is in turn placed under a more general category of knowledge. The expert's speedy and efficient problem solving is not necessarily the result of his better use of general heuristics. Rather, the expert's organization of material enables him to quickly get to the heart of the matter. Figure 12.12 will help to clarify this point.

Reif (1979) refers to the dotted lines as pointers. These are associations between specific elements of knowledge that connect the lower branches of this tree and provide what we might call mental shortcuts in the mind of the expert. If Figure 12.12 could be compared with a state-action tree, we can see that actions within this tree are not neutral for the expert, as they might be for the novice. Because the expert's knowledge suggests which branches of the state-action tree are the "right" ones, the reliance upon general problem-solving heuristics is lessened. One of the implications of Reif's position is that if specific facts were fed to the novices in a way that was similar to their representation in the mind of the expert, knowledge and problem solving in that domain might be improved.

Such a study was undertaken by Eylon (1979), who developed two different versions of a chapter on buoyancy and presented them to students in an introductory physics class. One account was organized conventionally, that is, like other physics texts on the market. The second chapter presented the information in a hierarchical fashion, based on an analysis of experts' knowledge of buoyancy. Students who used the hierarchical text showed a 40 percent improvement in

FIGURE 12.12

How knowledge is organized in the mind of an expert.

(From Reif. Copyright 1979 by Frank Reif. Adapted by permission of the author.)

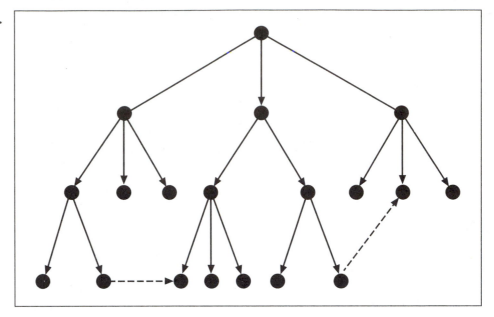

retention of the material and 25 percent better scores in problem solving than did students who used the conventional text.

Eylon and Reif (1984) and Heller and Reif (1984) have amplified these findings. Eylon and Reif found that subjects who were taught with hierarchical materials that mimicked an expert's organization of the material outperformed subjects who were taught with traditional "linear" models. Heller and Reif developed a model incorporating the procedures that experts use to organize and solve mechanics problems. Nonexpert subjects were induced to act in accordance with the model's prescriptions, and these subjects showed marked subsequent improvement in describing and solving mechanics problems.

The organization of experts' knowledge has been studied further by Chi, Glaser, and Rees (1982). They asked eight experts (Ph.D. students in physics) and eight novices (undergraduates who had had a semester of mechanics) to classify twenty-four physics problems that had been taken from a well-known physics text. Chi et al. found no major quantitative differences between the groups. The members of both groups used about eight different categories to classify the problems, and they each required about forty seconds to make the classification. However, there were major qualitative differences in the performance of the experts and novices. Essentially, the novices saw some problems as being quite similar to one another, but this resemblance was not used by the experts.

Figure 12.13 shows the diagrams for two pairs of problems that all eight novices grouped together. As this figure shows, the novices were heavily influenced by the diagram that accompanied the problem. For example, the bottom two problems were considered the same because they both showed an inclined plane. However, notice from Figure 12.14 that these diagrams did not play a strong role in the sorting processes of the experts.

The problems grouped together by the experts do not have any superficial similarity, but they can be solved using the same principle of physics, such as Newton's second law of motion. This means that the organizational principles used by the experts could be understood only by a physicist. In other words, since the problems that were grouped together by the novices looked alike, we might

Diagrams depicted from problems categorized by novices within the same groups

Novices' explanations for their similarity groupings

Problem 10 (11)

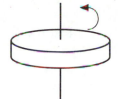

Novice 2: "Angular velocity, momentum, circular things"
Novice 3: "Rotational kinematics, angular speeds, angular velocities"
Novice 6: "Problems that have something rotating: angular speed"

Problem 11 (39)

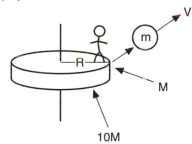

Problem 7 (23)

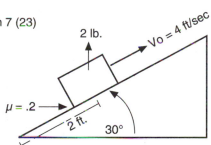

Novice 1: "These deal with blocks on an inclined plane"
Novice 5: "Inclined plane problems, coefficient of friction"
Novice 6: "Blocks on inclined planes with angles"

Problem 7 (35)

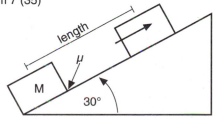

(From Halliday and Resnick, 1974. Copyright 1982 by Lawrence Erlbaum Associates, Inc. Publishers. Adapted by permission of the publisher and author.)

FIGURE 12.14 Examples from experts' problem categories. Problem numbers represent chapter and problem number.

Diagrams depicted from problems categorized by experts within the same groups

Experts' explanation for their similarity groupings

Problem 6 (21)

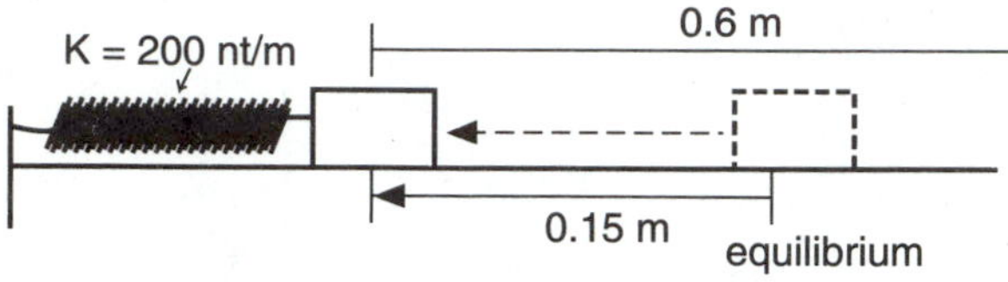

K = 200 nt/m

0.6 m

0.15 m

equilibrium

Expert 2: "Conservation of Energy"
Expert 3: "Work-Energy Theorem: They are all straightforward problems."
Expert 4: "These can be done from energy considerations. Either you should know the Principle of Conservation of Energy, or work is lost somewhere."

Problem 7 (35)

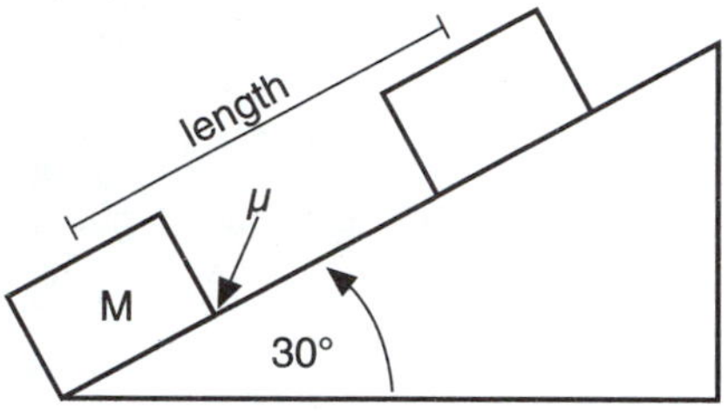

length

μ

M

30°

Expert 2: "These can be solved by Newton's Second Law."
Expert 3: "F = ma; Newton's Second Law"
Expert 4: "Largely use F = ma; Newton's Second Law"

Problem 5 (39)

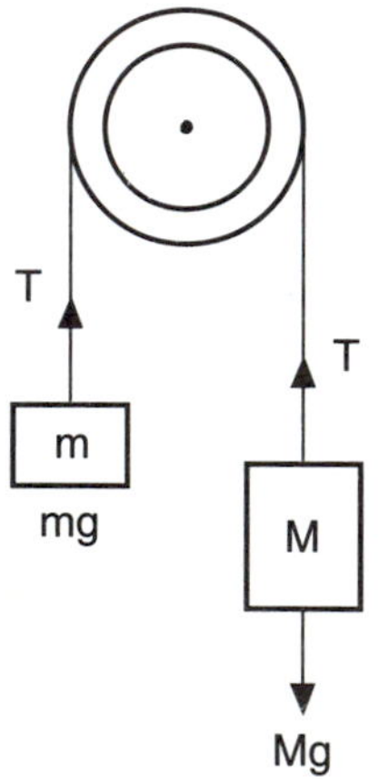

T

T

m

mg

M

Mg

Problem 12 (23)

Fp = Kv

mg

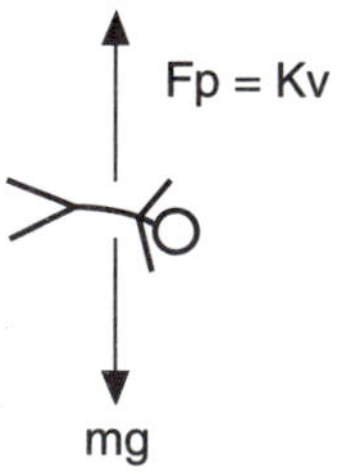

(From Halliday and Resnick, 1974. Copyright 1982 by Lawrence Erlbaum Associates, Inc., Publishers. Adapted by permission of the publisher and author.)

say that the basis of the grouping was perceptual appearance. But the basis of the experts' grouping was more abstract and resulted from their knowledge of physics. Chi et al. compare this to the deep-surface structure distinction examined in Chapter 8. The novices are influenced by the appearance of a problem—its surface structure; and the experts seem to be more able to extract the underlying meaning from the problem—its deep structure.

This finding suggests that the classification procedures of novices would be sensitive to variations in surface, but not deep, structure. Chi et al. corroborated this analysis in a follow-up study. They designed twenty problems in which they systematically varied the problems' appearance and objectives. When these specially designed problems were categorized by novices and experts, Chi et al. found once again that the novices were more influenced by the appearance of the problem than they were by the underlying physical principle involved. However, the experts were not affected by this manipulation. Regardless of the problem's text and diagram, the experts categorized it on the basis of abstract physical principles.

Other research (de Jong & Ferguson-Hessler, 1986) has corroborated these basic findings. In categorizing a problem, nonexperts are likely to be influenced by its appearance, while experts perceive its underlying structure.

The schematic and hierarchical nature of this knowledge was made apparent in another study by Chi et al. Here, the subjects had three levels of expertise. Experts were graduate students in physics. Intermediate subjects were fourth-year physics majors, and novices were students who had been in an introductory physics class and received grades of A, B, or C. The subjects were asked to sort forty physics problems, but in this study, several passes through the set were made. In the first step, the subjects simply sorted the problems. In the second step, the subjects were asked to look at their groups, and if they wished, they were permitted to further subdivide their original groups. In the third step, the subjects who had created subgroups were asked to examine them, and if they wished, they were permitted to further divide these subgroups they had just created. Finally, in the fourth step, the subjects reexamined their original groups and tried to combine them on whatever basis seemed appropriate.

Figure 12.15 shows the resulting hierarchical structure that was created for two novices and two experts. The circles represent the original sorting; the squares, the first subdivision; and the hexagons, the second subdivision. The final, combined stage is shown by the triangles. The numbers inside the geometric forms represent the number of problems sorted into that category. Figure 12.15 is a good way of showing the differences in the organization of knowledge in the minds of experts and novices. First, as we learned earlier, subjects typically needed eight categories to sort the problems. Here we can see that one of the novices required nine categories, which he could not divide any further. The other novice required fifteen categories. In contrast, both the experts required fewer than eight categories in their initial sorts.

Inspection of the figure also shows that the organization of knowledge is similar for both of these experts, but the organization of the novices' knowledge is quite different from each other. In one case, the novice was unable to divide the problems into subcategories, suggesting the categories were already at their lowest level (Chi, Glaser, & Rees, 1982). In the case of the other novice's groupings shown in Figure 12.15, the problems were so finely divided that each problem almost became its own category. This also suggests an inability to perceive any sort of abstract organizing principle. The experts' knowledge is not like this. Notice in Figure 12.15 that both of the experts were able to group all forty of the

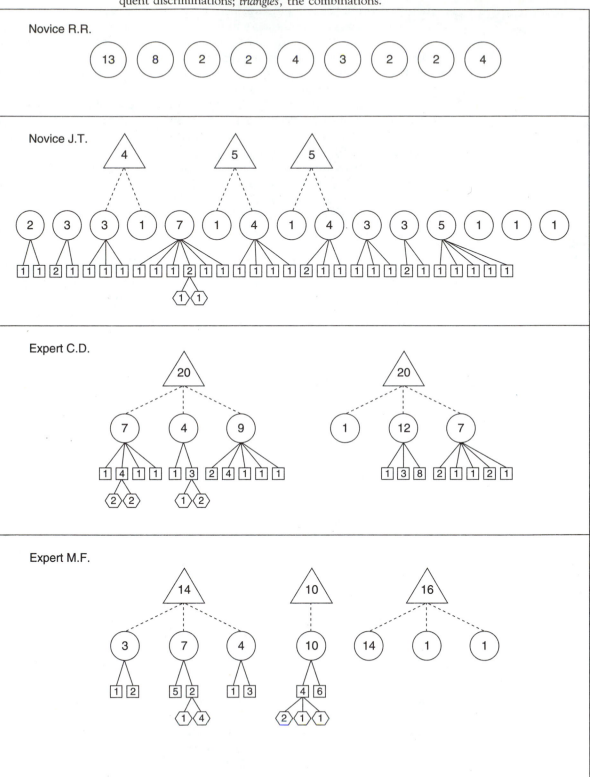

problems on the basis of some unifying principle. For example, in expert C.D.'s initial sort, the left group of circles represents problems dealing with conservation of energy, conservation of momentum, and conservation of angular momentum. The three groups of circles on the right represent problems dealing with force (i.e., $f = ma$), using $f = ma$ to find the resultant force, and simple harmonic motion. The left-most circles were in turn combined into the superordinate category *conservation laws*, whereas the right-most group of circles was collapsed into the category *equations of motion*. By contrast, only one of the novices was able to indicate any superordinate categories, and these accounted for only fourteen of the forty problems classified. This suggests that the hierarchical nature of knowledge seen in the experts is a developmental phenomenon. That is, the vertical organization seen in Figure 12.15 is produced by the expert's experience with physics problems.

Thus far, the text has focused on the acquisition of expertise in academic areas, such as physics, and this probably has given you the impression that expertise is usually acquired by formal training in some subject area. Actually, the importance of academic training, or even the usefulness of it for expertise, has been debated. Voss et al. (1986) compared the economics knowledge of college-educated subjects with that of people who hadn't gone to college. Perhaps not surprisingly, subjects who had been to college did better in answering questions requiring economics knowledge (regarding interest rates, the federal deficit, and so on) than did those who hadn't gone to college. Voss et al. determined, however, that classroom instruction in economics did not necessarily help the college-educated subjects in dealing with economics on a day-by-day basis, suggesting that academic training was of limited use in acquiring "hands-on" economic knowledge. This finding implies that our intuitions about everyday experience may be correct. That is, experience might be a good teacher.

Some support for this notion comes from the research of Ceci and Liker (1986), who studied the ability of fourteen expert horse-racing handicappers over a three-year period. In this case, expertise was defined as the ability to predict race-time odds on the basis of factual information about the horses (their lineage, the weight they were carrying, their ability to run under different track conditions, and so on). They asked these experts to handicap ten actual races and fifty fictitious ones that had been contrived to elucidate some of the variables the experts may have used in picking horses, as well as the importance of those variables in relation to each other. The researchers found that expertise in handicapping horses is dependent upon a very complex internal calculus in which several variables are related to one another in multiplicative, as opposed to additive, ways. Ceci and Liker administered a Wechsler Adult Intelligence Scale (WAIS) to the expert subjects and to several other nonexpert handicappers. They found that the experts were not necessarily more intelligent (as measured by the WAIS) than were the nonexperts, even though the experts consistently outperformed the nonexperts in handicapping ability. Cognitivists haven't determined yet what produces expertise, but it doesn't seem that classroom education, or vast amounts of intelligence, are crucial to the attainment of it.

CONCLUDING COMMENTS AND SUGGESTIONS FOR FURTHER READING

This chapter began with a discussion of the Gestaltists. They were a tremendously productive group of thinkers whose diversity of opinions nevertheless centered on

USING YOUR KNOWLEDGE OF COGNITION
••

One easy way to discover a problem's algorithm is to develop a notation that shows the problem's transformations. Sometimes, this notation also shows regularities in the problem's structure, and when these are revealed, an algorithm may also become apparent.

I've devised a notation for Tower of Hanoi problems. First, number the pegs 1, 2, and 3. Next, give each disk a name. In the convention I use, the disks have letter names; the biggest is always A, the next biggest B, and so on. Thus the (trivial) problem of transferring three disks from peg 2 to peg 3 could be written this way:

$$ABC_{(2)}—ABC_{(3)}$$

All disk moves can be shown as a letter with a numerical subscript that indicates the disk's destination. Thus, the solution to the prior problem could be written as follows:

$$C_3B_1C_1 \quad A_3 \quad C_2B_3C_3$$

There are seven moves. The first move (C_3) involves taking the smallest disk and transferring it to peg 3. If you make an arrangement of coins and duplicate each move, you'll see that this string of letters indeed represents a solution to the problem.

What about a four-disk problem? That is, how would we solve this one:

$$ABCD_{(2)}—ABCD_{(3)}$$

I'll show the solution to this problem and then we'll compare the two we've seen to see if they suggest an algorithm for all Tower of Hanoi problems. Here's the answer to the four-disk problem:

$$D_1C_3D_3 \ B_1 \ D_2C_1D_1 \ A_3 \ D_3C_2D_2 \ B_3 \ D_1C_3D_3$$

Do you see any similarities between the two solutions? You may have noticed that there is one A move in each problem, and it is the midpoint of both problems. The clusters of moves on both sides of A are symmetrical. Also, the smallest disk in each problem is in motion on exactly every other move. In both cases, the next to the smallest disk periodically moves between moves of the smallest disk. These regularities can be summarized as follows:

1. The A disk moves once in a Tower of Hanoi problem.
2. The B disk moves exactly twice as frequently as the A disk, and these moves are symmetrically distributed around the A disk move.

a few key ideas. One of these ideas was that perception and thinking were very similar. In both cases, the person mentally recombined and rearranged elements of a problem or visual array until a stable configuration, or Gestalt, was achieved. A second important idea was that thinking and problem solving took place in stages that were qualitatively different from one another. This means that problem solving was seen as a discontinuous process. When insights would come along was hard to tell in advance. Yet another idea was the notion that the solver's representation of the problem could be critical for success. Although we didn't explore the Gestalt literature on creativity, it generally discusses the ability of the creative person to overcome the effects of set by seeing the problem in a new way.

Time (and subsequent research) have put many of these ideas on the shelf. However, information-processing accounts of problem solving have seemed to converge on the notion that representation is perhaps the most critical act in problem solving. We've seen that cognitive psychologists have undertaken two different but complementary ways of understanding problem solving. One of these ways consists of isolating certain prototypical problems that seem to require particular cognitive skills. The second approach focuses on the solver in an effort to find those cognitive skills that seem general enough to be usable in a wide

USING YOUR KNOWLEDGE OF COGNITION

3. The C disk moves exactly twice as frequently as the B disk, and these moves are symmetrically distributed around the A and B disk moves.

4. The D disk moves exactly twice as frequently as the C disk, and these moves are symmetrically distributed around the A, B, and C disk moves. (Hence, the D disk move will always precede and follow C disk moves on a four-disk problem. By extension, the smallest disk will always precede and follow the moves of the next smallest disk.)

These rules enable us to expand any Tower of Hanoi problem—that is, write the string of letters that shows which disk is to be moved next. This is the first step in solving a Tower problem. These expansion rules don't indicate the subscript pattern, though. To determine this, the solution to the five-disk problem follows, which will show how the subscripts are derived:

$$ABCDE_{(2)}—ABCDE_3$$
$$E_3D_1E_1 \quad C_3 \quad E_2D_3E_3 \quad B_1 \quad E_1D_2E_2 \quad C_1 \quad E_3D_1E_3$$
$$A_3$$
$$E_2D_3E_3 \quad C_2 \quad E_1D_2E_2 \quad B_3 \quad E_3D_1E_1 \quad C_3 \quad E_2D_3E_3$$

Looking at the three- and five-disk problems, you'll see that the subscript pattern of the smallest disk (C in the three-disk and E in the five-disk problem) is the same. Specifically, the sequence repeats the sequence 3, 1, 2 over and over. Looking at the four-disk problem, we see a different pattern, but it also repeats. The D disk moves in the sequence 1, 3, 2 over and over. The first step in determining the subscript pattern is to count the number of disks in the tower. If odd, number all the smallest disk moves in the 3, 1, 2 sequence. If even, number all the smallest disk moves in the 1, 3, 2 sequence. In both cases, you'll end with a 3. You'll also notice that the moves of the next to the smallest disk always take the subscript of the following disk move. Number all these moves next. We also see that there are always only two B moves, and these go in the order 1, 3. Looking at the C disk moves, we see that they always move in the same sequence: 3, 1, 2. Similarly, the D disk moves are always the same, too: 1, 3, 2.

Do you see the subscript pattern? Besides the A and B disk moves, which are always locked in, and the two topmost disk moves, whose subscripts are derivable by counting the number of disks, all intervening disks have either a 3, 1, 2 pattern (if they're an odd-numbered disk up from the bottom) or a 1, 3, 2 pattern (if they are an even-numbered disk up from the bottom). Knowing these facts enables you to write a string of letters that represents the minimum solution to any Tower of Hanoi problem. You can demonstrate this to yourself by writing the solution to the six-disk problem.

variety of problems. Recently, psychologists have turned away somewhat from the study of games and puzzles and have begun to study expertise in solving real-world problems. As we've seen, such research seems to indicate that one important outcome of experience in a particular domain of knowledge is the restructuring of knowledge in the mind of the expert. Exploring the nature of this organization is sure to become one of the hot issues in problem solving in the foreseeable future.

Students who wish to find out more about the work of the Gestaltists should read Wertheimer's (1959) book *Productive Thinking,* which is the classic Gestalt account. Weisberg (1986) has written what might be called something of a rebuttal of the Gestalt position. The vast and challenging book by Newell and Simon (1972) has been the basis of much of the research in problem solving for the past twenty years. The information-processing approach to problem solving (among other things) is further expounded in two volumes edited by Sternberg (1982, 1985). Several of the chapters in the volume edited by Anderson (1981) deal with expertise.

FOCUS ON RESEARCH
. . . .
When One Problem Reminds Us of Another

If you've solved a certain type of problem, is it reasonable to expect that you'll recognize and do better on such types of problems in the future? That is, is it reasonable to expect that your cognitive system will retain and be able to apply something of your previous problem solving to a current situation? Ross (1989) has proposed a general framework for describing what might happen in such situations. Specifically, these are four processes that a cognitive system might engage in: (1) noticing a similarity to an earlier problem (i.e., being reminded of an earlier problem); (2) reconstructing that problem and its solution; (3) making an analogy from that problem and solution to the current problem; and (4) generalizing from the analogical process. In one study that dealt with the role of remindings, Ross's subjects learned six principles of probability theory by studying some abstract information and a word problem. Here's an example:

> To promote a hotel in Hawaii, the owners have imported thousands of oysters, 1/9 of them with pearls inside, and 8/9 with no pearl inside. When guests check in they are each given an oyster to open. What is the probability that the fifth guest finds the first pearl?

The principle here is derived from the formula for binary expansions, namely,

$$q^{k-1}p$$

where p is the probability of an event occurring, $q = 1 - p$ is the probability of an event not occurring, and k is the trial number of first occurrence, in this case, 5. As you can see, the Hawaiian story line is irrelevant to the probability principle. After subjects learned such problems, they were given test problems to solve and there were several conditions. Some subjects were given a test problem story line that was the same as the study problem story line for that problem. (This was called the appropriate condition because it was appropriate for the subjects to apply the same principle that they previously learned to the test problem.) Some subjects were given a test problem whose story line was similar to those that were studied in connection with different probability principles. (This was called the inappropriate condition because it was inappropriate for the subjects to use the principle in the previously seen story line in the current problem.) Finally, some subjects were given a test problem whose story line had not been seen before. These manipulations produced very large effects on the percentage of subjects solving the test problems: 77 percent of the subjects in the appropriate condition solved the test problem, but only 43 percent of the subjects in the no-relation condition did. In the inappropriate condition, a scant 22 percent of the subjects succeeded in solving the test problem. Clearly the subjects were influenced by the previous learning. What's also very interesting here is that the subjects were obviously reminded and in some cases negatively influenced by the irrelevant story line. Did the subjects really learn the underlying structure of the probability principles? Perhaps so, but there is also ample evidence here to suggest that the subjects also learned "what to do to solve an oyster problem," and they proceeded to do so whether the underlying probability principle matched up or not.

I suppose all of us would like to become better problem solvers, and I can recommend several books that might help you accomplish this objective. Neimark (1987) deals with a number of cognitive skills, as does Halpern (1984). Levine's (1988) book is very easy to read and shows the reader a general technique ("intimate engagement") that might help in both the cognitive and the affective domains. Kahney's (1986) book is somewhat more restricted in scope and is perhaps a bit more theoretical than the previously mentioned books.

We should be aware that many theorists have argued that a cognitive approach to thinking skills should be the underpinning of all, or much, classroom learning. Books by Whimbley and Lochhead (1986), Berger, Pezdek, and Banks (1986), and Phye and Andre (1986) each have some chapters devoted to this notion.

 **KEY TERMS**

Intelligence

Gestalt psychology

Incubation effect

Insight

Representing the problem

Thinking out loud

Discontinuity in thinking

Domain-free problems

Well-defined problems

Ill-defined problems

Problems of inducing structure

Problems of transformation

Tower of Hanoi

Problems of arrangement

Local-global distinction

Strategy

Heuristic

Algorithm

Task environment

Problem space

Operator

State-action tree

General Problem Solver (GPS)

Isomorphism

Expertise

APPENDIX

1. Answer to the "cheap necklace" problem. Realizing that a chain must be completely disassembled is the key to solving this problem. First, open a link of one of the three-link chains, let's say chain A. Take this open link and connect two different three-link chains, for example chains B and C. Then close this connecting link. Now we have one seven-link chain, one three-link chain, and one two-link chain. Next open a second link of chain A. Use this link to connect the seven-link chain with the remaining three-link chain (i.e., chain D). Then close the link. Now we have one eleven-link chain and just one closed link left from chain A. Open the last remaining link of chain A and link both ends of the eleven-link chain through it. Then close that link. We have opened and closed three links for a total cost of 15 cents.

2. Answer to DONALD + GERALD = ROBERT:

$$\begin{array}{r} 526485 \\ +197485 \\ \hline 723970 \end{array}$$

The real key to cracking this problem is deducing E = 9.

3. Answer to the "working backward" problem. Let's list the players using the notation P1, P2, and P3. Moreover, let's assume that P3 lost the final game. From the material in the text, we have already deduced that after playing two games P1 and P2 each had $4 and P3 had $16. Now, what happened in the second game? Since each player lost one game, we know that the second game was lost by either P1 or P2, and because they have the same amount of money, it doesn't matter which one we designate as the loser of game 2. Let P2 be the loser of the second game. We know that P2 had to double the current stakes of P1 and P3. Because P3 had $16 after two games had been played, and because P3's stake had been doubled in game 2,

P3 must have gotten $8 as a result of the second game, paid by P2. Similarly, we already know that P1 had $4 at the end of game 2 and this player's stake was also doubled by P2's losing in game 2. So P1 must have had $2 going into game 2 and earned $2 as a result of P2's loss. So in game 2, P2 paid $8 to P3, $2 to P1, and still had $4 remaining. Therefore, at the conclusion of game 1, P2 must have had $4 + $10, or $14. We've now established that at the end of the first game P1 had $2, P2 had $14, and P3 had $8. What took place in the first game? The only player whose loss is not accounted for is P1. Given that P2 had $14 at the end of game 1, this player must have been paid $7 by P1 in game 1 as a result of P1's loss. Similarly, we know that P3 had $8 at the end of game 1, so this player must have been given $4 as a result of P1's losing the first game. This establishes that the initial stake of P2 was $7 and P3 was $4. P1 paid out $7 + $4 = $11 dollars as a result of losing game 1 and still had $2 left, so P1's initial stake must have been $11 + $2 = $13.

REFERENCES

Abbott, V., Black, J. B., & Smith, E. E. (1985). The representation of scripts in memory. *Journal of Memory and Language, 24,* 179–199.

Adelson, E. H. (1978). Iconic storage: The role of rods. *Science, 201,* 544–546.

Adler, T. (1990, April). Different sources cited in major cognitive texts. *APA Monitor,* p. 8.

Aitchison, J. (1983). *The articulate mammal: An introduction to psycholinguistics* (2nd ed.). New York: Universe.

Aitchison, J. (1987). *Words in the mind.* New York: Blackwell.

Aitkenhead, A. M., & Slack, J. M. (Eds.). (1986). *Issues in cognitive modeling.* Hillsdale, NJ: Erlbaum.

Alba, J. W., & Hasher, L. (1983). Is memory semantic? *Psychological Bulletin, 93,* 203–231.

Anderson, J. A., & Rosenfeld, E. (1988). *Neurocomputing.* Cambridge, MA: MIT Press.

Anderson, J. R. (1976). *Language, memory, and thought.* Hillsdale, NJ: Erlbaum.

Anderson, J. R. (Ed.). (1981). *Cognitive skills and their acquisition.* Hillsdale, NJ: Erlbaum.

Anderson, J. R. (1983). *The architecture of cognition.* Cambridge, MA: Harvard University Press.

Anderson, J. R. (1990). *The adaptive character of thought.* Hillsdale, NJ: Erlbaum.

Anderson, J. R. (1993). *Rules of the mind.* Hillsdale, NJ: Erlbaum.

Anderson, J. R. (1993). Problem solving and learning. *American Psychologist, 48,* 35–44.

Anderson, J. R., & Paulson, R. (1977). Representation and retention of verbatim information. *Journal of Verbal Learning and Verbal Behavior, 16,* 439–452.

Anderson, J. R., & Ross, B. H. (1980). Evidence against a semantic-episodic distinction. *Journal of Experimental Psychology: Human Learning and Memory, 6,* 441–466.

Anderson, J. R., & Schooler, L. J. (1991). Reflections of the environment in memory. *Psychological Science, 2,* 396–408.

Anderson, R. C., & Pichert, J. W. (1978). Recall of previously unrecallable information following a shift in perspective. *Journal of Verbal Learning and Verbal Behavior, 17,* 1–12.

Anglin, J. M. (1986). Semantic and conceptual knowledge underlying the child's words. In S. A. Kuczaj and M. D. Barrett (Eds.), *The development of word meaning* (pp. 85–97). New York: Springer-Verlag.

Anisfeld, M., & Klenbart, I. (1973). On the functions of structural paraphrase: The view from the passive voice. *Psychological Bulletin, 79,* 117–126.

Antell, S. E., & Keating, D. P. (1983). Perception of numerical invariance in neonates. *Child Development, 54,* 695–701.

Anzai, Y., & Simon, H. A. (1979). The theory of learning by doing. *Psychological Review, 86,* 124–140.

Armstrong, S. L., Gleitman, L. R., & Gleitman, H. (1983). What some concepts might not be. *Cognition, 13,* 263–308.

Atkinson, R. C., & Shiffrin, R. M. (1968). Human memory: A proposed system and its control processes. In W. K. Spence & J. T. Spence (Eds.), *The psychology of learning and motivation: Advances in research and theory* (Vol. 1, pp. 89–195). New York: Academic Press.

Austin, J. L. (1962). *How to do things with words.* New York: Oxford University Press.

Babich, F. R., Jacobson, A. L., Bubash, S., & Jacobson, A. (1965). Transfer of a response to naive rats by injection of ribonucleic acid extracted from trained rats. *Science, 149,* 656–657.

Bach, K., & Harnish, R. M. (1979). *Linguistic communication and speech acts.* Cambridge, MA: MIT Press.

Baddeley, A. D. (1978). The trouble with "levels": A reexamination of Craik and Lockhart's framework for memory research. *Psychological Review, 85,* 139–152.

Baddeley, A. D. (1982). Reading and working memory. *Bulletin of the British Psychological Society, 35,* 414–417.

Baddeley, A. D. (1983). Working memory. *Philosophical Transactions of the Royal Society of London, 302B,* 311–324.

Baddeley, A. D. (1990). *Human memory: Theory and practice.* Boston: Allyn and Bacon.

Baddeley, A. D., & Dale, H. C. (1966). The effect of semantic similarity on retroactive interference in long- and short-term memory. *Journal of Verbal Learning and Verbal Behavior, 5,* 417–420.

Baddeley, A. D., & Lewis, V. J. (1981). Inner active process in reading: The inner voice, the inner ear, and the inner eye. In A. M. Lesgold & C. A. Perfetti (Eds.), *Interactive processes in reading* (pp. 107–129). Hillsdale, NJ: Erlbaum.

Baddeley, A. D., Logie, R., Bressi, S., Della Sala, S., & Spinnler, H. (1986). Dementia and working memory. *Quarterly Journal of Experimental Psychology, 38A,* 603–618.

Baker, L., and Brown, A. L. (1984). Metacognitive skills and reading. In D. Pearson (Ed.), *Handbook of Reading Research* (pp. 353–394). Newark, DE: International Reading Association.

Banaji, M. R., & Crowder, R. G. (1989). The bankruptcy of everyday memory. *American Psychologist, 44,* 1185–1193.

Banks, W. P., & Barber, G. (1977). Color information in iconic memory. *Psychological Review, 84,* 536–546.

Banks, W. P., & Barber, G. (1980). Normal iconic memory of stimuli invisible to the rods. *Perception and Psychophysics, 27,* 581–584.

Barclay, C. D., Cutting, J. E., & Kozlowski, L. T. (1978). Temporal and spatial factors in gait perception that influence gender recognition. *Perception and Psychophysics, 23,* 145–152.

Bargh, J. A. (1982). Attention and automacity in the processing of self-relevant information. *Journal of Personality and Social Psychology, 43,* 425–436.

Barrows, B. (quoting C. Stengel). (1977, April 5). Casey fields Kefauner's question with a bit of Stengelese. *Lewiston* (ID) *Morning Tribune.*

Barsalou, L. W. (1983). Ad hoc categories. *Memory & Cognition, 11,* 211–227.

Bartlett, F. C. (1932). *Remembering: A study in experimental and social psychology.* Oxford: Cambridge University Press.

Bartlett, F. C. (1958). *Thinking*. New York: Basic Books.

Bassili, J. N. (1978). Facial motion in the perception of faces and of emotional expressions. *Journal of Experimental Psychology: Human Perception and Performance, 4*, 373–379.

Beal, C. R. (1985). Development of knowledge about the use of cues to aid prospective retrieval. *Child Development, 56*, 631–642.

Beatty, W. W., & Butters, N. (1986). Further analysis of encoding in patients with Huntington's disease. *Brain & Cognition, 5*, 387–398.

Beaumont, J. G. (1987). *Understanding neuropsychology*. New York: Blackwell.

Beech, J. R., & Colley, A. M. (Eds.). (1987). *Cognitive approaches to reading*. New York: Wiley.

Begg, I. (1979). Trace loss and the recognition failure of unrecalled words. *Memory and Cognition, 7*, 113–123.

Bekerian, D. A., & Bowers, J. M. (1983). Eyewitness testimony: Were we misled? *Journal of Experimental Psychology: Learning, Memory, and Cognition, 9*, 139–145.

Bellugi, U. (1964). *The emergence of inflections and negation systems in the speech of two children*. Paper presented at New England Psychological Association Meetings.

Berger, D. E., Pezdek, K., & Banks, W. P. (Eds.). (1986). *Applications of cognitive psychology: Problem solving, education and computing*. Hillsdale, NJ: Erlbaum.

Berko, J. (1958). The child's learning of English morphology. *Word, 14*, 150–177.

Besner, D., Davies, J., & Daniels, S. (1981). Reading for meaning: The effects of concurrent articulation. *Quarterly Journal of Experimental Psychology, 33*, 415–437.

Besner, D., Twilley, L., McCann, R. S., & Seergobin, K. (1990). On the association between connectionism and data: Are a few words necessary? *Psychological Review, 97*, 432–446.

Bever, T. G., Lackner, J. R., & Kirk, R. (1969). The underlying structures of sentences are the primary units of immediate speech processing. *Perception and Psychophysics, 5*, 225–231.

Birnbaum, I. M., Taylor, T. H., Johnson, M. K., & Raye, C. L. (1987). Is event frequency encoded automatically? The case of alcohol intoxication. *Journal of Experimental Psychology: Learning, Memory, and Cognition, 13*, 251–258.

Bjorklund, D. F. (Ed.). (1990). *Children's strategies*. Hillsdale, NJ: Erlbaum.

Bjorklund, D. F., & Harnishfeger, K. K. (1987). Developmental differences in the mental effort requirements for the use of an organizational strategy in free recall. *Journal of Experimental Child Psychology, 44*, 109–125.

Blank, M. A., & Foss, D. J. (1978). Semantic facilitation and lexical access during sentence processing. *Memory and Cognition, 6*, 644–652.

Blaxall, J., & Willows, D. M. (1984). Reading ability and text difficulty as influences on second graders' oral reading errors. *Journal of Educational Psychology, 76*, 330–341.

Bloom, L. (1970). *Language development: Form and function in emerging grammars*. Cambridge, MA: MIT Press.

Bloom, L. M., Lightbown, P., & Hood, L. (1975). Structure and variation in child language. *Monographs of the Society for Research in Child Development, 40* (Serial No. 160).

Blumstein, S. E., Tartter, V. C., Nigro, G., & Statlender, S. (1984). Acoustic cues for the perception of place of articulation on aphasia. *Brain and Language, 22*, 128–149.

Bomba, P. C., & Siqueland, E. R. (1983). The nature and structure of infant form categories. *Journal of Experimental Child Psychology, 35*, 294–328.

Bovair, S., Kieras, D. E., & Polson, P. G. (1990). The acquisition and performance of text-editing skill: A cognitive complexity analysis. *Human Computer Interaction, 5*, 1–48.

Bower, G. H. (1981). Mood and memory. *American Psychologist, 36*, 129–148.

Bower, G. H., & Humphreys, M. S. (1979). Effect of a recognition test on a subsequent cued-recall test. *Journal of Experimental Psychology: Human Learning and Memory, 5*, 348–359.

Bower, G. H., Monteiro, K. P., & Gilligan, S. G. (1978). Emotional mood as a context for learning and recall. *Journal of Verbal Learning and Verbal Behavior, 17*, 573–587.

Braine, M. D. S. (1976). Children's first word combinations. *Monographs of the Society for Research in Child Development, 41* (Serial No. 164).

Braine, M. D. S. (1987). What is learned in acquiring word classes—A step towards an acquisition theory. In B. MacWhinney (Ed.), *Mechanisms of language acquisition* (pp. 65–87). Hillsdale, NJ: Erlbaum.

Braine, M. D. S., et al. (1990). Exploring language acquisition in children with a miniature artificial language: Effects of item and pattern frequency, arbitrary subclasses, and correction. *Journal of Memory and Language, 29*, 591–610.

Bransford, J. D., & Johnson, M. K. (1972). Contextual prerequisites for understanding: Some investigations of comprehension and recall. *Journal of Verbal Learning and Verbal Behavior, 11*, 717–726.

Brewer, W. F., & Nakamura, G. V. (1984). The nature and functions of schemas. In R. S. Wyer, Jr., & T. K. Srull (Eds.), *Handbook of Social Cognition* (Vol. 1, pp. 119–160). Hillsdale, NJ: Erlbaum.

Britton, B., & Glynn, S. M. (Eds.). (1987). *Executive control processes in reading*. Hillsdale, NJ: Erlbaum.

Broadbent, D. E. (1954). A mechanical model for human attention and immediate memory. *Psychological Review, 64*, 205.

Broadbent, D. E. (1958). *Perception and communication*. London: Pergamon Press.

Brooks, D. N., & Baddeley, A. D. (1976). What can amnesic patients learn? *Neuropsychologia, 14*, 111–122.

Brooks, L. R. (1967). The suppression of visualization by reading. *Quarterly Journal of Experimental Psychology, 19*, 289–299.

Brooks, L. R. (1978). Nonanalytic concept formation and memory for instances. In E. Rosch & B. B. Lloyd (Eds.), *Cognition and categorization*. Hillsdale, NJ: Erlbaum.

Brown, A. L., & Smiley, S. S. (1977). Rating the importance of structural units of prose passages: A problem of metacognitive development. *Child Development, 48*, 1–8.

Brown, A. L., & Smiley, S. S. (1978). The development of strategies for studying texts. *Child Development, 49*, 1076–1088.

Brown, A. L., Smiley, S. S., & Lawton, S. Q. C. (1978). The effect of experience on the selection of suitable retrieval cues for studying texts. *Child Development, 49*, 829–835.

Brown, J. (1968). Reciprocal facilitation and impairment of free recall. *Psychonomic Science, 10*, 41–42.

Brown, R. (1970). *Psycholinguistics*. New York: Free Press.

Brown, R. (1973). *A first language: The early stages*. Cambridge, MA: Harvard University Press.

Brown, R., & Bellugi, U. (1964). Three processes in the child's acquisition of syntax. In E. H. Lenneberg (Ed.), *New directions in the study of language*. Cambridge, MA: MIT Press.

Bruce, V., & Green, P. R. (1990). *Visual perception: Physiology, psychology, and ecology* (2nd ed.). Hillsdale, NJ: Erlbaum.

Bruner, J. S., Goodnow, J., & Austin, G. A. (1956). *A study of thinking*. New York: Wiley.

Burt, M. K. (1971). *From deep to surface structure: An introduction to transformational syntax*. New York: Harper & Row.

Cairns, H. S., & Kamerman, J. (1975). Lexical information processing during sentence comprehension. *Journal of Verbal Learning and Verbal Behavior, 14*, 170–179.

Cantwell, D., & Baker, L. (1987). Differential diagnosis of hyperactivity. *Journal of Developmental & Behavioral Pediatrics, 8*, 159–165.

Carey, S. (1978). The child as word learner. In M. Halle, J. Bresnan, & A. Miller (Eds.), *Linguistic theory and psychological reality* (pp. 264–293). Cambridge, MA: MIT Press.

Carroll, D. W. (1986). *Psychology of language*. Monterey, CA: Brooks/Cole.

Carroll, J. B. (Ed.). (1956). *Language, thought, and reality: Selected writings of Benjamin Lee Whorf*. New York: Wiley.

Caudill, M., & Butler, C. (1992). *Understanding neural networks* (Vol. 1). Cambridge, MA: MIT Press.

Cavanaugh, J. C., & Perlmutter, M. (1982). Metamemory: A critical examination. *Child Development, 53*, 11–28.

Cazden, C. (1972). *Child language and education*. New York: Holt, Rinehart & Winston.

Ceci, S. J., & Liker, J. K. (1986). A day at the races: A study of IQ, expertise, and cognitive complexity. *Journal of Experimental Psychology: General, 115*, 255–266.

Cermak, L. S., Butters, N., & Moreines, J. (1974). Some analyses of the verbal encoding deficit of alcoholic Korsakoff patients. *Brain and Language, 3*, 16–27.

Cermak, L. S., Naus, M. J., & Reale, L. (1976). Rehearsal strategies of alcoholic Korsakoff patients. *Brain and Language, 3*, 375–385.

Charniak, E. (1983). Passing markers: A theory of contextual influence in language comprehension. *Cognitive Science, 7*, 171–190.

Chase, W. G., & Simon, H. A. (1973). The mind's eye in chess. In W. G. Chase (Ed.), *Visual information processing*. New York: Academic Press.

Cheng, P. W., & Holyoak, K. J. (1985). Pragmatic reasoning schemas. *Cognitive Psychology, 17*, 391–416.

Cheng, P. W., Holyoak, K. J., Nisbett, R. E., & Oliver, L. M. (1986). Pragmatic versus syntactic approaches to training deductive reasoning. *Cognitive Psychology, 18*, 293–328.

Cherry, E. C. (1953). Some experiments on the recognition of speech with one and with two ears. *Journal of the Acoustical Society of America, 25*, 975–979.

Cherry, R. S., & Kruger, B. (1983). Selective auditory attention abilities of learning disabled and normal achieving children. *Journal of Learning Disabilities, 16*, 202–205.

Chi, M. T. H., & Glaser, R. (1985). Problem-solving ability. In R. J. Sternberg (Ed.), *Human abilities: An information processing approach* (pp. 227–248). New York: Freeman.

Chi, M. T. H., Glaser, R., & Rees, E. (1982). Expertise in problem solving. In R. J. Sternberg (Ed.), *Advances in the psychology of human intelligence* (Vol. 1, pp. 7–76). Hillsdale, NJ: Erlbaum.

Chomsky, C. (1969). *The acquisition of syntax in children from 5 to 10*. Cambridge, MA: MIT Press.

Chomsky, N. (1957). *Syntactic structures*. The Hague: Mouton.

Chomsky, N. (1959). Review of Skinner's verbal behavior. *Language, 35*, 26–58.

Chomsky, N. (1965). *Aspects of the theory of syntax*. Cambridge, MA: MIT Press.

Chomsky, N. (1972). *Language and mind* (enlarged ed.). New York: Harcourt Brace Jovanovich.

Chomsky, N. (1979). *Language and responsibility*. Hassocks, Sussex, England: Harvester.

Chomsky, N. (1983). On the representation of form and function. In J. Mehler, E. C. T. Walker, & M. Garrett (Eds.), *Perspectives on mental representation* (pp. 3–38). Hillsdale, NJ: Erlbaum.

Chomsky, N., & Halle, M. (1968). *The sound pattern of English*. New York: Harper & Row.

Chorover, S. L., & Schiller, P. H. (1965). Short-term retrograde amnesia in rats. *Journal of Comparative and Physiological Psychology, 59*, 73–78.

Chrostowski, J. J., & Griggs, R. A. (1985). The effects of problem, content, instructions and verbalization procedure on Wason's selection task. *Current Psychological Research and Reviews, 4*, 99–107.

Churchland, P. M. (1989). *A neurocomputational perspective: The nature of mind and the structure of science*. Cambridge, MA: MIT Press.

Churchland, P. M., & Sejnowski, T. J. (1989). Neural representation and neural computation. In L. Nadel, L. Cooper, P. Culicover, & R. M. Harnish (Eds.), *Neural connections, mental computation* (pp. 15–48). Cambridge, MA: MIT Press.

Clark, A. (1989). *Microcognition: Philosophy, cognitive science, and parallel distributed processing*. Cambridge, MA: MIT Press.

Clark, H. H., & Clark, E. V. (1977). *Psychology and language*. New York: Harcourt Brace Jovanovich.

Clark, H. H., & Lucy, P. (1975). Understanding what is meant from what is said: A study in conversationally conveyed requests. *Journal of Verbal Learning and Verbal Behavior, 14*, 56–72.

Cole, M., & Scribner, S. (1977). Cross-cultural studies of memory and cognition. In R. V. Vail, Jr., & J. W. Hagen (Eds.), *Perspectives on the development of memory and recognition*. Hillsdale, NJ: Erlbaum.

Collins, A. M., & Loftus, E. F. (1975). A spreading activation theory of semantic processing. *Psychological Review, 82*, 407–428.

Collins, A. M., & Quillian, M. R. (1969). Retrieval time from semantic memory. *Journal of Verbal Learning and Verbal Behavior, 8*, 240–247.

Coltheart, M. (1975). Iconic memory: A reply to professor Holding. *Memory and Cognition, 3*, 42–48.

Coltheart, M. (1978). Lexical access in simple reading tasks. In G. Underwood (Ed.), *Strategies of information processing*. New York: Academic Press.

Coltheart, M. (1980). Iconic memory and visual persistence. *Perception and Psychophysics, 27*, 183–228.

Coltheart, M. (1980). Reading, phonological recoding, and deep dyslexia. In M. Coltheart, K. Patterson, & J. C. Marshall (Eds.), *Deep dyslexia*. London: Routledge & Kegan Paul.

Coltheart, M. (1981). Disorders of reading and their implications for models of normal reading. *Visible Language, 15*, 245–286.

Coltheart, M., Davelaar, E., Jonasson, J. T., & Besner, D. (1977). Access to the internal lexicon. In S. Dornic (Ed.), *Attention and Performance* (Vol. 6). New York: Academic Press.

Conrad, C. (1972). Cognitive economy in semantic memory. *Journal of Experimental Psychology, 92,* 149–154.

Conrad, R. (1964). Acoustic confusions in immediate memory. *British Journal of Psychology, 55,* 75–84.

Conway, M. A. (1990). *Autobiographical memory: An introduction.* Philadelphia: Open University Press.

Cook, M. (1984). *Issues in person perception.* London: Methuen.

Cooper, L. A. (1976). Demonstration of a mental analog of an external rotation. *Perception and Psychophysics, 19,* 296–302.

Cooper, L. A., & Shepard, R. N. (1973). Chronometric studies of the rotation of mental images. In W. G. Chase (Ed.), *Visual information processing.* New York: Academic Press.

Cosky, M. J. (1975). *Word length effects in word recognition.* Unpublished doctoral dissertation, University of Texas, Austin.

Cowan, N. (1993). Activation, attention, and short-term memory. *Memory & Cognition, 21,* 162–167.

Cox, J. R., & Griggs, R. A. (1982). The effects of experience on performance in Wason's selection task. *Memory and Cognition, 10,* 496–502.

Craik, F. I. M. (1979). Human memory. *Annual Review of Psychology, 30,* 63–102.

Craik, F. I. M., & Lockhart, R. S. (1972). Levels of processing: A framework for memory research. *Journal of Verbal Learning and Verbal Behavior, 11,* 671–684.

Craik, F. I. M., & Simon, E. (1980). Age differences in memory: The roles of attention and depth of processing. In L. W. Poon, J. L. Fozard, L. S. Cermak, D. Arenberg, & L. W. Thompson (Eds.), *New directions in memory and aging: Proceedings of the George Talland memorial conference.* Hillsdale, NJ: Erlbaum.

Craik, F. I. M., & Tulving, E. (1975). Depth of processing and the retention of words in episodic memory. *Journal of Experimental Psychology: General, 104,* 268–294.

Craik, F. I. M., & Watkins, M. J. (1973). The role of rehearsal in short-term memory. *Journal of Verbal Learning and Verbal Behavior, 12,* 559–607.

Cromer, R. F. (1970). Children are nice to understand: Surface structure clues for the recovery of deep structure. *British Journal of Psychology, 61,* 397–408.

Crowder, R. G. (1976). *Principles of learning and memory.* Hillsdale, NJ: Erlbaum.

Crowder, R. G. (1982). *The psychology of reading.* New York: Oxford University Press.

Crowder, R. G. (1993). Short-term memory: Where do we stand? *Memory & Cognition, 21,* 142–145.

Crowder, R. G., & Morton, J. (1969). Precategorical acoustic storage (PAS). *Perception and Psychophysics, 5,* 365–373.

Curtiss, S. (1977). *Genie: A psycholinguistic study of a modern-day "wild child."* New York: Academic Press.

Curtiss, S., Fromkin, V., Krashen, S., Rigler, D., & Rigler, M. (1974). The linguistic development of Genie. *Language, 50,* 528–554.

Cutler, A. (1980). Errors of stress and intonation. In V. A. Fromkin (Ed.), *Errors in linguistic performance.* New York: Academic Press.

Cutting, J. E., & Kozlowski, L. T. (1977). Recognizing friends by their walk: Gait perception without familiarity cues. *Bulletin of the Psychonomic Society, 9* (5), 353–356.

Cutting, J. E., Proffitt, D. R., & Kozlowski, L. T. (1978). A biomechanical invariant for gait perception. *Journal of Experimental Psychology: Human Perception and Performance, 4,* 357–372.

Dale, R. H. I., & Cochran, B. (1989, November). *Do cognitive psychologists share a paradigm.* Paper presented at the annual meeting of the Psychonomic Society, Atlanta, GA.

Danks, J. H., & Glucksberg, S. (1980). Experimental psycholinguistics. *Annual Review of Psychology, 31,* 391–417.

Dannemiller, J. L., & Stephens, B. R. (1988). A critical test of infant pattern preference models. *Child Development, 59,* 210–216.

Dawes, R. M. (1988). *Rational choice in an uncertain world.* San Diego, CA: Harcourt Brace Jovanovich.

Dawson, M. E., & Schell, A. M. (1982). Electrodermal responses to attended and nonattended significant stimuli during dichotic listening. *Journal of Experimental Psychology: Human Perception and Performance, 8,* 315–324.

Dawson, M. E., & Schell, A. M. (1983). Lateral asymmetries in electro-dermal responses to nonattended stimuli: A reply to Walker and Ceci. *Journal of Experimental Psychology: Human Perception and Performance, 9,* 148–150.

Deese, J. (1984). *Thought into speech: The psychology of a language.* Englewood Cliffs, NJ: Prentice-Hall.

Deese, J., & Kaufman, R. A. (1957). Serial effects in recall of unorganized and sequentially organized verbal material. *Journal of Experimental Psychology, 54,* 180–187.

de Groot, A. (1965). *Thought and choice in chess.* The Hague: Mouton.

de Groot, A. (1966). Perception and memory versus thought: Some old ideas and recent findings. In B. Kleinmuntz (Ed.), *Problem solving.* New York: Wiley.

DeJong, G. (1982). On communications between AI and linguistics. In D. L. Farwell, S. C. Helmreich, & W. D. Wallace (Eds.), *Perspectives in cognitive science* (pp. 33–41). Urbana, IL: Linguistics Student Organization.

de Jong, T., & Ferguson-Hessler, M. G. (1986). Cognitive structures of good and poor novice problem solvers in physics. *Journal of Educational Psychology, 78,* 279–288.

Dennett, D. C. (1981). *Brainstorms.* Cambridge, MA: MIT Press/Bradford Books.

Denton, G. G. (1980). The influence of visual pattern of perceived speed. *Perception, 9,* 393–402.

Deregowski, J. B. (1972). Pictorial perception and culture. *Scientific American, 227*(5), 82–88.

Derouesne, J., & Beauvois, M. F. (1979). Phonological processing in reading: Data from alexia. *Journal of Neurology, Neurosurgery, and Psychiatry, 42,* 1125–1132.

Deutsch, F. A., & Deutsch, D. (1963). Attention: Some theoretical considerations. *Psychological Review, 70,* 80–90.

De Villiers, J. G., & De Villiers, P. A. (1978). *Language acquisition.* Cambridge, MA: Harvard University Press.

Dodd, D. H., & White, R. M., Jr. (1980). *Cognition: Mental structures and processes.* Boston: Allyn & Bacon.

Dodwell, P. D., & Caelli, T. M. (1984). *Figural synthesis.* Hillsdale, NJ: Erlbaum.

Dominowski, R. L., & Ekstrand, B. R. (1967). Direct and associative priming in anagram solving. *Journal of Experimental Psychology, 74,* 84–86.

Dominowski, R. L., & Jenrick, R. (1972). Effects of hints and interpolated activity on solution of an insight problem. *Psychonomic Science, 26,* 335–338.

Dooling, D. J., & Christiaansen, R. E. (1977). Episodic and semantic aspects of memory for prose. *Journal of Experimental Psychology: Human Learning and Memory, 3,* 428–436.

Dooling, D. J., & Lachman, R. (1971). Effects of comprehension on retention of prose. *Journal of Experimental Psychology, 88,* 216–222.

Dosher, B. A. (1984). Discriminating pre-experimental (semantic) from learned (episodic) associations: A speed-accuracy study. *Cognitive Psychology, 16,* 519–555.

Dretske, F. I. (1981). *Knowledge and the flow of information.* Cambridge, MA: MIT Press/Bradford Books.

Dretske, F. I. (1983). Précis of knowledge and the flow of information. *The Behavioral and Brain Sciences, 6,* 55–90.

Drewnoski, A. (1980). Attributes and priorities in short-term recall: A new model of memory span. *Journal of Experimental Psychology: General, 109,* 208–250.

Drewnoski, A., & Murdock, B. B., Jr. (1980). The role of auditory features in memory span for words. *Journal of Experimental Psychology: Human Learning and Memory, 6,* 319–332.

Dunker, K. (1945). On problem solving. *Psychological Monographs, 58* (5, Whole No. 270).

Eich, E. (1984). Memory for unattended events: Remembering with and without awareness. *Memory & Cognition, 12,* 105–111.

Eich, J., Weingartner, H., Stillman, R. C., & Gillin, J. C. (1975). State-dependent accessibility of retrieval cues in the retention of a categorized list. *Journal of Verbal Learning and Verbal Behavior, 14,* 408–417.

Eifermann, R. (1965a). Response patterns and strategies in the dynamics of concept attainment behavior. *Journal of Psychology, 56,* 217–222.

Eifermann, R. (1965b). Selection strategies in concept attainment: A reexamination. In R. Eifermann (Ed.), *Scripta hierosolymitana: Studies in psychology* (Vol. 14). Hebrew University of Jerusalem: Magnes Press.

Eimas, P. D., Siqueland, E. R., Jusczyk, P., & Vigorito, J. (1971). Speech perception by infants. *Science, 171,* 303–306.

Ellis, A., & Beattie, G. (1986). *The psychology of language and communication.* New York: Guilford.

Ellis, A. W., & Young, A. W. (1987). *Human cognitive neuropsychology.* Hillsdale, NJ: Erlbaum.

Erdelyi, M. H., & Kleinbard, J. (1978). Has Ebbinghaus decayed with time? The growth of recall (hypermnesia) over days. *Journal of Experimental Psychology: Human Learning and Memory, 4,* 275–289.

Ericksen, C. W., Pollack, M. D., & Montague, W. E. (1970). Implicit speech: Mechanism in perceptual recoding? *Journal of Experimental Psychology, 84,* 502–507.

Ericsson, K.A., Chase, W. G., & Faloon, S. (1980). Acquisition of memory skill. *Science, 208,* 1181–1182.

Ericsson, K. A., & Simon, H. A. (1980). Verbal reports as data. *Psychological Review, 87,* 215–251.

Evans, J. St. B. T. (1990). *Bias in human reasoning: Causes and consequences.* Hillsdale, NJ: Erlbaum.

Eylon, B. (1979). *Effects of knowledge organization on task performance.* Unpublished doctoral dissertation, University of California at Berkeley.

Eylon, B., & Reif, F. (1984). Effects of knowledge organization on task performance. *Cognition and Instruction, 1,* 5–44.

Falmagne, R. J. (Ed.). (1975). *Reasoning: Representation and process.* Hillsdale, NJ: Erlbaum.

Fantz, R. L. (1961). The origin of form perception. *Scientific American, 204*(5), 66–72.

Feldman, J. A. (1985). Connectionist models and their applications: Introduction. *Cognitive Science, 9,* 1–2.

Fiske, A. D., & Schneider, W. (1984). Memory as a function of attention, level of processing, and automatization. *Journal of Experimental Psychology: Learning, Memory, and Cognition, 10,* 181–197.

Fiske, S. T., & Taylor, S. E. (1984). *Social Cognition.* New York, NY: McGraw-Hill, Inc.

Flavell, J. H. (1971). First discussant's comments: What is memory development the development of? *Human Development, 14,* 272–278.

Flavell, J. H. (1978). Metacognitive development. In J. M. Scandura & C. Brainerd (Eds.), *Structural/process theory of complex human behavior.* Alpen an den Rijn, Netherlands: Sitjoff & Noordhoff.

Flavell, J. H., & Wellman, H. M. (1977). Metamemory. In R. V. Kail & J. H. Hagen (Eds.), *Perspectives on the development of memory and cognition.* Hillsdale, NJ: Erlbaum.

Flexser, A. J., & Tulving, E. (1978). Retrieval independence in recognition and recall. *Psychological Review, 85,* 153–171.

Flexser, A. J., & Tulving, E. (1982). Priming and recognition failure. *Journal of Verbal Learning and Verbal Behavior, 21,* 237–248.

Fodor, J. A., Bever, T., & Garrett, M. (1974). *The psychology of language.* New York: McGraw-Hill.

Fodor, J. A., & Garrett, M. F. (1967). Some syntactic determinants of sentential complexity. *Perception and Psychophysics, 2,* 289–296.

Fodor, J. A., & Pylyshyn, Z. W. (1988). Connectionism and cognitive architecture: A critical analysis. *Cognition, 28,* 3–71.

Fong, G. T., & Markus, H. (1982). Self-schemas and judgments about others. *Social Cognition, 1,* 191–205.

Foss, D. J. (1982). A discourse on semantic priming. *Cognitive Psychology, 14,* 590–607.

Foss, D. J., & Hakes, D. T. (1978). *Psycholinguistics: An introduction to the psychology of language.* Englewood Cliffs, NJ: Prentice-Hall.

Foti, R. J., & Lord, R. G. (1987). Prototypes and scripts: The effects of alternative methods of processing information on rating accuracy. *Organizational Behavior & Human Decision Processes, 39,* 318–340.

Franklin, M. B., & Barten, S. B. (Eds.). (1987). *Child language: A reader.* New York: Oxford University Press.

Franklin, N., & Tversky, B. (1990). Searching imagined environments. *Journal of Experimental Psychology: General, 119,* 63–76.

Fried, L. S., & Holyoak, K. J. (1978, November). *Learning fuzzy perceptual categories: Is feedback necessary?* Paper presented at the 19th meeting of the Psychonomic Society, San Antonio.

Fried, L. S., & Holyoak, K. J. (1984). Induction of category distributions: A framework for classification learning. *Journal of Experimental Psychology: Learning, Memory, and Cognition, 10,* 234–257.

Friedman, W. J. (1987). A follow-up to "Scale effects in memory for the time of events": The earthquake study. *Memory & Cognition, 15,* 518–520.

Fromkin, V. A. (1971). The non-anomalous nature of anomalous utterances. *Language, 47,* 27–52.

Fromkin, V., & Rodman, R. (1978). *An introduction to linguistics* (2nd ed.). New York: Holt, Rinehart, and Winston.

Frost, N. (1972). Encoding and retrieval in visual memory tasks. *Journal of Experimental Psychology, 95,* 317–326.

Fulgosi, A., & Guilford, J. P. (1968). Short-term incubation in divergent production. *American Journal of Psychology, 81,* 241–246.

Gallant, S. L. (1993). *Neural network learning and expert systems.* Cambridge, MA: MIT Press/Bradford.

Gardiner, J. M., & Tulving, E. (1980). Exceptions to recognition failure of recallable words. *Journal of Verbal Learning and Verbal Behavior, 19,* 194–209.

Garner, W. R. (1979). Letter discrimination and identification. In A. D. Pick (Ed.), *Perception and its development: A tribute to Eleanor J. Gibson.* Hillsdale, NJ: Erlbaum.

Garrett, M. F., Bever, T., & Fodor, J. A. (1966). The active use of grammar in speech perception. *Perception and Psychophysics, 1,* 30–32.

Garrett, M. F. (1982). Production of speech: Observations from normal and pathological language use. In A. W. Ellis (Ed.,), *Normality and pathology in cognitive functions* (pp. 19–76). New York: Academic Press.

Gelman, R., & Baillargeon, R. (1983). A review of some Piagetian concepts. In J. H. Flavell & E. M. Markman (Eds.), *Handbook of child psychology* (Vol. 3). New York: Wiley.

Gelman, S. A., & Markman, E. (1986). Categories and induction in young children. *Cognition, 23,* 183–209.

Geschwind, N. (1980). Specializations of the human brain. In R. C. Atkinson & R. L. Atkinson (Eds.), *Mind and Behavior* (pp. 206–215). San Francisco: Freeman.

Geyer, L. H., & DeWald, C. G. (1973). Feature lists and confusion matrices. *Perception and Psychophysics, 14,* 471–482.

Ghiselin, B. (1952). *The creative process: A symposium.* Berkeley: University of California Press.

Gibson, E. J. (1969). *Principles of perceptual learning and development.* New York: Prentice-Hall.

Gibson, J. J. (1960). The concept of stimulus in psychology. *American Psychologist, 16,* 694– 703.

Gibson, J. J. (1966). The problem of temporal order in stimulation and perception. *Journal of Psychology, 62, 141*–149.

Gibson, J. J. (1976). The myth of passive perception: A reply to Richards. *Philosophy and Phenomenological Research, 37,* 234–238.

Gibson, J. J. (1977). The theory of affordances. In R. Shaw & J. Bransford (Eds.), *Perceiving, acting, and knowing* (pp. 67–82). Hillsdale, NJ: Erlbaum.

Gibson, J. J. (1979). *The ecological approach to visual perception.* Boston: Houghton Mifflin.

Gillam, B. (1980). Geometrical illusions. *Scientific American, 242*(1), 102–111.

Glenberg, A. M., & Adams, F. (1978). Type I rehearsal and recognition. *Journal of Verbal Learning and Verbal Behavior, 17,* 455–463.

Glucksberg, S., Kreuz, R. J., & Rho, S. (1986). Context can constrain lexical access: Implications for models of language comprehension. *Journal of Experimental Psychology: Learning, Memory and Cognition, 12,* 323–335.

Godden, D. R., & Baddeley, A. D. (1975). Context-dependent memory in two natural environments: On land and under water. *British Journal of Psychology, 66,* 325–331.

Goldstein, E. B. (1984). *Sensation and perception.* Belmont, CA: Wadsworth.

Golinkoff, R. M., & Kerr, J. L. (1978). Infants' perception of semantically defined action role changes in filmed acts. *Merrill-Palmer Quarterly, 24,* 53–61.

Gorfein, D. S., & Hoffman, R. R. (Eds.). (1987). *Memory and learning: The Ebbinghaus centennial conference.* Hillsdale, NJ: Erlbaum.

Green, D. W., & Shallice, T. (1976). Direct visual access in reading for meaning. *Memory and Cognition, 4,* 753–758.

Greenfield, P. M., & Smith, J. H. (1976). *The structure of communication in early language development.* New York: Academic Press.

Greeno, J. G. (1976). Indefinite goals in well-structured problems. *Psychological Review, 83,* 479–491.

Greeno, J. G. (1978). Natures of problem-solving abilities. In W. K. Estes (Ed.), *Handbook of learning and cognitive processes* (Vol. 5, pp. 239–270). Hillsdale, NJ: Erlbaum.

Gregg, V. N. (1986). *Introduction to human memory.* London: Routledge & Kegan Paul.

Gregory, R. L. (1966). *Eye and brain.* New York: McGraw-Hill.

Grice, H. P. (1975). Logic and conversation. In P. Cole & J. L. Morgan (Eds.), *Syntax and semantics: Vol. 3, Speech Acts* (pp. 41–58). New York: Seminar Press.

Griggs, R. A., & Cox, J. R. (1982). The elusive thematic-materials effects in Wason's selection task. *British Journal of Psychology, 73,* 407–420.

Griggs, R. A. (1989). To "see" or not to "see": That is the selection task. Quarterly Journal of Experimental Psychology, 41 A, 517–529.

Griggs, R. A., & Jackson, S. L. (1990). Instructional effects on responses in Wason's selection task. *British Journal of Psychology, 81,* 197–204.

Groen, G. J., & Parkman, J. M. (1972). A chronometric analysis of simple addition. *Psychological Review, 79,* 329–343.

Gross, T. F. (1985). *Cognitive development.* Monterey, CA: Brooks/Cole.

Grossberg, S. (1988). *Neural networks and natural intelligence.* Cambridge, MA: MIT Press.

Gruenewald, P. J., & Lockhead, G. R. (1980). The free recall of category examples. *Journal of Experimental Psychology: Human Learning and Memory, 6,* 225–240.

Haber, R. N. (1983). The impending demise of the icon: A critique of the concept of iconic storage in visual inform0 ation processing. *The Behavioral and Brain Sciences, 6,* 1–54.

Hakes, D. T., & Foss, D. J. (1970). Decision processes during sentence comprehension: Effects of surface structure reconsidered. *Perception and Psychophysics, 8,* 413–416.

Halle, M., & Stevens, K. N. (1964). Speech recognition: A model and a program for research. In J. A. Fodor & J. J. Katz (Eds.), *The structure of language: Readings in the philosophy of language.* Englewood Cliffs, NJ: Prentice-Hall.

Halliday, D., & Resnick, R. (1974). *Fundamentals of physics* (2nd ed.). New York: Wiley.

Halpern, D. F. (1984). *Thought and knowledge: An introduction to critical thinking.* Hillsdale, NJ: Erlbaum.

Hampson, S. E. (1982). *The construction of personality.* London: Routledge & Kegan Paul.

Hannigan, J. L., Shelton, T. S., Franks, J. J., & Bransford, J. D. (1980). The effects of episodic and semantic memory on the identification of sentences masked by white noise. *Memory and Cognition, 8,* 278–284.

Hanson, S. J., & Burr, D. J. (1990). What connectionist models learn: Learning and representation in connectionist networks. *Behavioral and Brain Sciences, 13,* 471–518.

Hanson, S. J., Drastal, G. A., & Rivest, R. L. (Eds.). (1994). *Computational learning theory and natural learning systems* (Vol. 1). Cambridge, MA: MIT Press/Bradford.

Harding, R. (1940). *An anatomy of inspiration.* London: Cass.

Harris, J. E., & Morris, P. E. (Eds.). (1984). *Everyday memory, actions and absent-mindedness.* London: Academic Press.

Hasher, L., & Zacks, R. T. (1979). Automatic and effortful processes in memory. *Journal of Experimental Psychology: General, 108,* 356–388.

Hasher, L., & Zacks, R. T. (1984). Automatic processing of fundamental information: The case of frequency of occurrence. *American Psychologist, 39,* 1372–1388.

Hawkins, J. A. (Ed.). (1988). *Explaining language universals.* New York: Blackwell.

Hayes, J. R., & Simon, H. A. (1974). Understanding written problem instructions. In L. W. Gregg (Ed.), *Knowledge and cognition.* Hillsdale, NJ: Erlbaum.

Healy, A. F. (1976). Detection errors on the word *the:* Evidence for reading units larger than letters. *Journal of Experimental Psychology: Human Perception and Performance, 2,* 235–242.

Hebb, D. O. (1949). *The organization of behavior.* New York: Wiley.

Heft, H. (1982). Incommensurability and the "omission" in Gibson's theory: A second reply to Heil. *Journal for the Theory of Social Behavior, 12,* 345–347.

Heil, J. (1979). What Gibson's missing. *Journal for the Theory of Social Behavior, 9,* 265–269.

Heller, J. I., & Reif, F. (1984). Prescribing effective human problem-solving processes: Problem description in physics. *Cognition and Instruction, 1,* 177–216.

Henle, M. (1962). On the relation between logic and thinking. *Psychological Review, 69,* 366–378.

Herrmann, D. J., & Harwood, J. R. (1980). More evidence for the existence of separate semantic and episodic stores in long-term memory. *Journal of Experimental Psychology, Human Learning, and Memory, 6,* 467–478.

Hilgard, E. R. (1987). *Psychology in America: A historical survey.* San Diego, CA: Harcourt Brace Jovanovich.

Hinsley, D. A., Hayes, J. R., & Simon, H. A. (1978). From words to equations: Meaning and representation in algebra word problems. In P. A. Carpenter & M. A. Just (Eds.), *Cognitive processes in comprehension.* Hillsdale, NJ: Erlbaum.

Hintzman, D. L. (1965). Classification and aural coding in short-term memory. *Psychonomic Science, 3,* 161–162.

Hintzman, D. L. (1967). Articulatory coding in short-term memory. *Journal of Verbal Learning and Verbal Behavior, 6,* 312–316.

Hirst, W., Spelke, E. S., Reaves, C. C., Caharack, G., & Neisser, U. (1980). Dividing attention without alternation or automaticity. *Journal of Experimental Psychology: General, 109,* 98–117.

Hoch, S. J., & Tschirgi, J. E. (1983). Cue redundancy and extra logical inferences in a deductive reasoning task. *Memory & Cognition, 11,* 200–209.

Hoch, S. J., & Tschirgi, J. E. (1985). Logical knowledge and cue redundancy in deductive reasoning. *Memory & Cognition, 13,* 453–462.

Hockett, C. F. (1963). The problem of universals in language. In J. H. Greenberg (Ed.), *Universals of language.* Cambridge, MA: MIT Press.

Höffding, H. (1891). *Outlines of psychology.* New York: Macmillan.

Holding, D. (1975). Sensory storage reconsidered. *Memory & Cognition, 3,* 31–41.

Homa, D. (1978). Abstraction of ill-defined form. *Journal of Experimental Psychology: Human Learning and Memory, 4,* 407–416.

Homa, D., & Coltice, J. (1984). Role of feedback, category size, and stimulus distortion on the acquisition and utilization of ill-defined categories. *Journal of Experimental Psychology: Learning, Memory, and Cognition, 10,* 83–94.

Homa, D., & Vosburgh, R. (1976). Category breadth and the abstraction of prototypical information. *Journal of Experimental Psychology: Human Learning and Memory, 2,* 322–330.

Horn, B. K. P. (1986). *Robot vision.* Cambridge, MA: MIT Press.

Horrocks, G. (1987). *Generative grammar.* White Plains, NY: Longman.

Horton, D. L., & Mills, C. B. (1984). Human learning and memory. *Annual Review of Psychology, 35,* 361–394.

Houston, J. P. (1986). *Fundamentals of learning and memory* (3rd ed.). New York: Harcourt Brace Jovanovich.

Howard, D. V. (1983). *Cognitive psychology: Memory, language, and thought.* New York: Macmillan.

Hudson, R. (1984). *Invitation to linguistics.* New York: Blackwell.

Hull, C. L. (1920). Quantitative aspects of the evolution of concepts: An experimental study. *Psychological Monographs, 28*(1, Whole No. 123).

Hulse, S. H., Deese, J., & Egeth, H. (1975). *The psychology of learning* (4th ed.). New York: McGraw-Hill.

Humphrey, G. (1963). *Thinking: An introduction to its experimental psychology.* New York: Wiley.

Humphreys, G., & Bruce, V. (1989). *Visual cognition: Computational, experimental, and neuropsychological perspectives.* Hillsdale, NJ: Erlbaum.

Humphreys, M. S., & Bower, G. H. (1980). Sequential testing effects and the relationship between recognition and recognition failure. *Memory and Cognition, 8,* 271–277.

Hunt, M. (1982). *The universe within.* New York: Simon & Schuster.

Hunt, R. R., & Elliott, J. M. (1980). The role of nonsemantic information in memory: Orthographic distinctiveness effects on retention. *Journal of Experimental Psychology: General, 109,* 49–74.

Hyde, T. S., & Jenkins, J. J. (1973). Recall for words as a function of semantic, graphic, and syntactic orienting tasks. *Journal of Verbal Learning and Verbal Behavior, 12,* 471–480.

Imhoff, A. W., & Rayner, K. (1986). Parafoveal word processing during eye fixations in reading: Effects of word frequency. *Perception and Psychophysics, 40,* 431–439.

Ittelson, W. H., & Cantril, H. (1954). *Perception: A transactional approach.* New York: Doubleday.

Izard, C. (1971). *The face of emotion.* New York: Appleton-Century-Crofts.

Jacoby, L. L. (1983). Remembering the data: analyzing interactive processes in reading. *Journal of Verbal Learning and Verbal Behavior, 22,* 485–508.

Jacoby, L. L. (1988). Memory observed and memory unobserved. In U. Neisser & E. Winograd (Eds.), *Remembering reconsidered: Ecological and traditional approaches to the study of memory* (pp. 145–177). Cambridge: Cambridge University Press.

Jacoby, L. L., & Craik, F. I. M. (1979). Effects of elaboration of processing at encoding and retrieval: Trace distinctiveness and recovery of initial context. In L. S. Cermak & F. I. M. Craik (Eds.), *Levels of processing in human memory*. Hillsdale, NJ: Erlbaum.

Jacoby, L. L., Craik, F. I. M., & Begg, I. (1979). Effects of decision difficulty on recognition and recall. *Journal of Verbal Learning and Verbal Behavior, 18,* 585–600.

Jacoby, L. L., & Dallas, M. (1981). On the relationship between autobiographical memory and perceptual learning. *Journal of Experimental Psychology: General, 110,* 306–340.

James, W. (1890). *The principles of psychology*. New York: Holt, Rinehart & Winston.

Jenkins, J. G., & Dallenbach, K. M. (1924). Obliviscence during sleep and waking. *American Journal of Psychology, 35,* 605–612.

Jenkins, J. J. (1974). Remember that old theory of memory? Well forget it! *American Psychologist, 29,* 785–795.

Jespersen, O. (1922). *Language: Its nature, development and origin.* New York: Allen & Unwin.

Johnson, E. S. (1978). Validation of concept-learning strategies. *Journal of Experimental Psychology: General, 107,* 237–266.

Johnson, M. K., & Hasher, L. (1987). Human learning and memory. *Annual Review of Psychology, 38,* 631–668.

Johnson-Laird, P. N. (1987). Grammar and psychology. In S. Modgil & C. Modgil (Eds.), *Noam Chomsky: Consensus and controversy* (pp. 147–156). New York: Falmer Press.

Johnson-Laird, P. N., & Byrne, R. M. J. (1991). Deduction. Hillsdale, NJ: Erlbaum.

Johnson-Laird, P. N., Byrne, R. M. J., & Schaeken, W. (1992). Propositional reasoning by model. *Psychological Review, 99,* 418–439.

Johnson-Laird, P. N., Legrenzi, P., & Legrenzi, M. (1972). Reasoning and a sense of reality. *British Journal of Psychology, 63,* 395–400.

Johnson-Laird, P. N., & Steedman, M. (1978). The psychology of syllogisms. *Cognitive Psychology, 10,* 64–99.

Johnson-Laird, P. N., & Wason, P. C. (Eds.). (1977). *Thinking: Readings in cognitive science*. Cambridge: Cambridge University Press.

Johnston, J. C., & McClelland, J. L. (1980). Experimental tests of a hierarchical model of word identification. *Journal of Verbal Learning and Verbal Behavior, 19,* 503–524.

Johnston, W. A., Dark, V. J., & Jacoby, L. L. (1985). Perceptual fluency and recognition judgments. *Journal of Experimental Psychology: Learning, Memory, and Cognition, 11,* 3–11.

Johnston, W. A., & Heinz, S. P. (1978). Flexibility and capacity demands of attention. *Journal of Experimental psychology: General, 107,* 420–435.

Jones, R. K. (1966). Observations on stammering after localized cerebral injury. *Journal of Neurology, Neurosurgery, and Psychiatry, 29,* 192–195.

Just, M. A., & Carpenter, P. A. (1980). A theory of reading: From eye fixations to comprehension. *Psychological Review, 87,* 329–354.

Kahneman, D. (1973). *Attention and effort*. Englewood Cliffs, NJ: Prentice-Hall.

Kahneman, D., & Tversky, A. (1973). On the psychology of prediction. *Psychological Review, 80,* 237–251.

Kahneman, D., & Tversky, A. (1982). On the study of statistical intuitions. In D. Kahneman, P. Slovic, & A. Tversky (Eds.), *Judgements under uncertainty: Heuristics and biases* (pp. 493–508). Cambridge: Cambridge University Press.

Kahney, H. (1986). *Problem solving: A cognitive approach.* Philadelphia: Open University Press.

Kail, R. (1990). *The development of memory in children* (3rd. ed.). New York: Freeman.

Kalat, J. W. (1984). *Biological psychology* (2nd ed.). Belmont, CA: Wadsworth.

Karat, J. (1982). A model of problem solving with incomplete constraint knowledge. *Cognitive Psychology, 14,* 538–559.

Katona, G. (1940). Organizing and memorizing. New York: Columbia University Press.

Katz, J. J. (1977). *Propositional structure and illocutionary force.* New York: Thomas Y. Crowell.

Kausler, D. H., Lichty, W., & Hakami, M. K. (1984). Frequency judgments for distractor items in a short-term memory task: Instructional variation and adult age differences. *Journal of Verbal Learning and Verbal Behavior, 23,* 660–668.

Kay, D. A., & Anglin, J. M. (1982). Overextension and underextension in the child's expressive and receptive speech. *Journal of Child Language, 9,* 83–98.

Kellogg, R. T. (1982). When can we introspect accurately about mental processes? *Memory and Cognition, 10,* 141–144.

Kennedy, A. (1984). *The psychology of reading*. London: Methuen.

Keppel, G., & Underwood, B. J. (1962). Proactive inhibition in short-term retention of single items. *Journal of Verbal Learning and Verbal Behavior, 1,* 153–161.

Kessel, F. (Ed.). (1988). *The development of language and language researchers.* Hillsdale, NJ: Erlbaum.

Kihlstrom, J. F. (1980). Posthypnotic amnesia for recently learned material: Interactions with "episodic" and "semantic" memory. *Cognitive Psychology, 12,* 227–251.

Kinsbourne, M., & Wood, F. (1975). Short-term memory processes in the amnesic syndrome. In D. Deutsch & J. A. Deutsch (Eds.), *Short-term memory*. New York: Academic Press.

Kintsch, W., Miller, J. R., & Polson, P. G. (Eds.). (1984). *Methods and tactics in cognitive science*. Hillsdale, NJ: Erlbaum.

Klahr, D., Langley, P., & Neches, R. (1987). *Production system models of learning and development*. Cambridge, MA: MIT Press.

Klahr, D., & Kotovsky, K. (Eds.). (1989). *Complex information processing: The impact of Herbert A. Simon*. Hillsdale, NJ: Erlbaum.

Klapp, S., Anderson, W. G., & Berian, R. W. (1973). Implicit speech in reading reconsidered. *Journal of Experimental Psychology, 100,* 368–374.

Klatzky, R. L. (1980). *Human memory: Structures and processes* (2nd ed.). San Francisco: Freeman.

Klatzky, R. L. (1984). *Memory and awareness*. San Francisco: Freeman.

Kleiman, G. M. (1975). Speech recoding in reading. *Journal of Verbal Learning and Verbal Behavior, 14,* 323–339.

Kolers, P. A. (1970). Three stages of reading. In H. Levin & J. P. Williams (Eds.), *Basic studies on reading*. New York: Basic Books.

Kolers, P. A. (1983). Perception and representation. *Annual Review of Psychology, 34,* 129–166.

Kopell, S. (1979). Testing the attentional deficit notion. *Journal of Learning Disabilities, 12,* 52–57.

Kossan, N. (1981). Developmental differences in concept acquisition strategies. *Child development, 52,* 290–298.

Kosslyn, S. M. (1983). *Ghosts in the mind's machine*. New York: Norton.

Kroll, N. E., & Timourian, D. A. (1986). Misleading questions and the retrieval of the irretrievable. *Bulletin of the Psychonomic Society, 24,* 165–168.

Kuehne, C., Kehle, T. J., & McMahon, W. (1987). Differences between children with attentional deficit disorder, children with specific learning disabilities and normal children. *Journal of School Psychology, 25,* 161–166.

Kuhn, D. (1989). Children and adults as intuitive scientists. *Psychological Review, 96,* 674–689.

Kuhn, T. S. (1962). *The structure of scientific revolutions.* Chicago: University of Chicago Press.

Lachman, R., Lachman, J. L., & Butterfield, E. C. (1979). *Cognitive psychology and information processing.* Hillsdale, NJ: Erlbaum.

Larish, J. F., & Flach, J. M. (1990). Sources of optical information useful for perception of speed of rectilinear self-motion. *Journal of Experimental Psychology: Human Perception and Performance, 16,* 295–302.

Larkin, J. H. (1989). Display-based problem solving. In D. Klahr & K. Kotovsky (Eds.), *Complex information processing: The impact of Herbert A. Simon* (pp. 319–341). Hillsdale, NJ: Erlbaum.

Lashley, K. S. (1929). *Brain mechanisms and intelligence.* Chicago: University of Chicago Press.

Lashley, K. S. (1950). In search of the engram. *Symposia of the Study of Experimental Biology, 4,* 454–482.

Laughlin, P. R., Lange, R., & Adamopoulos, J. (1982). Selection strategies for "Mastermind" problems. *Journal of Experimental Psychology: Learning, Memory, and Cognition, 8,* 475–483.

Leahey, T. H. (1987). *A history of psychology: Main currents in psychological thought.* Englewood Cliffs, NJ: Prentice-Hall.

Lenneberg, E. H. (1964). *New directions in the study of language.* Cambridge, MA: MIT Press.

Lenneberg, E. H. (1967). *Biological foundations of language.* New York: Wiley.

Leonard, J. M., & Whitten, W. B. (1983). Information stored when expecting recall or recognition. *Journal of Experimental Psychology: Learning, Memory, and Cognition, 9,* 440–455.

Leslie, A. M. (1982). The perception of causality in infants. *Perception, 11,* 173–186.

Lettvin, J. Y., Maturana, H. R., McCulloch, W. S., & Pitts, W. H. (1959). What the frog's eye tells the frog's brain. *Proceedings of the IRE, 47,* 1940–1951.

Levin, I. P., Kao, S-F., & Wasserman, E. A. (1991, November). *Biased information usage in contingency judgments.* Paper presented at the meeting of the Midwestern Psychological Association, Chicago.

Levine, D. S. (1990). *Introduction to neural and cognitive modeling.* Hillsdale, NJ: Erlbaum.

Levine, M. (1988). *Effective problem solving.* Englewood Cliffs, NJ: Prentice-Hall.

Levy-Bruhl, L. (1966). *How natives think.* New York: Washington Square Press. (Original work published 1910.)

Lewis, J. L. (1970). Semantic processing of unattended messages using dichotic listening. *Journal of Experimental Psychology, 85,* 225–228.

Liberman, A. M., Cooper, F., Shankweiler, D. P., & Studdert-Kennedy, M. (1967). Perception of the speech code. *Psychological Review, 74,* 431–461.

Lieberman, P. (1967). *Intonation, perception, and language.* Cambridge, MA: MIT Press.

Light, L., & Carter-Sobell, L. (1970). Effects of changed semantic context on recognition memory. *Journal of Verbal Learning and Verbal Behavior, 9,* 1–11.

Lindsay, P. H., & Norman, D. A. (1977). *Human information processing* (2nd ed.). New York: Academic Press.

Lisker, L., & Abramson, A. S. (1970). The voicing dimension: Some experiments in comparative phonetics. *Proceedings of the Sixth International Congress of Phonetic Sciences.* Prague: Academia, 1970.

Loftus, E. F. (1975). Leading questions and the eyewitness report. *Cognitive Psychology, 7,* 560–572.

Loftus, E. F. (1977). Shifting human color vision. *Memory & Cognition, 5,* 696–699.

Loftus, E. F. (1979a). *Eyewitness testimony.* Cambridge, MA: Harvard University Press.

Loftus, E. F. (1979b). Reactions to blatantly contradictory information. *Memory & Cognition, 7,* 368–374.

Loftus, E. F. (1979c). The malleability of human memory. *American Scientist, 67,* 312–320.

Loftus, E. F., & Loftus, G. R. (1980). On the permanence of stored information in the human brain. *American Psychologist, 35,* 409–420.

Loftus, E. F., Miller, D. G., & Burns, H. J. (1978). Semantic integration of verbal information into a visual memory. *Journal of Experimental Psychology: Human Learning and Memory, 4,* 19–31.

Loftus, E. F., & Palmer, J. C. (1974). Reconstruction of automobile destruction: An example of the interaction between language and memory. *Journal of Verbal Learning and Verbal Behavior, 13,* 585–589.

Loftus, G. R., Johnson, C. A., & Shimamura, A. P. (1985). How much is an icon worth? *Journal of Experimental Psychology, 11,* 1–13.

Logan, G. D. (1990). Repetition priming and automaticity: Common underlying mechanisms? *Cognitive Psychology, 22,* 1–35.

Lombardo, T. J. (1987). *The reciprocity of perceiver and environment: The evolution of James J. Gibson's ecological psychology.* Hillsdale, NJ: Erlbaum.

Long, G. M. (1980). Iconic memory: A review and critique of the study of short-term visual storage. *Psychological Bulletin, 88,* 785–820.

Lorys, A. R., Hynd, G. W., & Lahey, B. B. (1990). Do neurocognitive measures differentiate Attention Deficit Disorder (ADD) with and without hyperactivity? *Archives of Clinical Neuropsychology, 5,* 119–135.

Lowe, D. G., & Mitterer, J. O. (1982). Selective and divided attention in a Stroop task. *Canadian Journal of Psychology, 36,* 684–700.

Lowes, J. L. (1927). *The road to Xanadu.* London: Constable.

Mace, W. M. (1974). Ecologically stimulating cognitive psychology: Gibsonian perspectives. In W. Weimer & D. Palermo (Eds.), *Cognitive and the symbolic processes* (Vol. 1, pp. 137–164). Hillsdale, NJ: Erlbaum.

Mace, W. M. (1977). James J. Gibson's strategy for perceiving: Ask not what's inside your head, but what your head's inside of. In R. Shaw & J. Bransford (Eds.), *Perceiving, acting, and knowing* (pp. 43–66). Hillsdale, NJ: Erlbaum.

MacKay, D. G. (1973). Aspects of the theory of comprehension, memory, and attention. *Quarterly Journal of Experimental Psychology, 25,* 22–40.

Mair, W. G., Warrington, E. K., & Weiskrantz, L. (1979). Memory disorders in Korsakoff's psychosis: A neuropathological and neuropsychological investigation of two cases. *Brain, 102,* 749–783.

Mandler, J. M. (1984). *Stories, scripts and schemes: Aspects of schema theory.* Hillsdale, NJ: Erlbaum.

Marcel, A. J., & Patterson, K. E. (1978). Word recognition and production: Reciprocity in clinical and normal research. In J. Requin (Ed.), *Attention and Performance* (Vol. 7). Hillsdale, NJ: Erlbaum.

Margolis, H. (1987). *Patterns, thinking and cognition: A theory of judgment*. Chicago: University of Chicago Press.

Markman, E. M., & Hutchinson, J. E. (1984). Childrens' sensitivity to constraints on word meaning: Taxonomic vs thematic relations. *Cognitive Psychology, 16*, 1–27.

Markman, E. M. (1990). Constraints children place on word meanings. *Cognitive Science, 14*, 57–77.

Markovits, H. (1985). Incorrect conditional reasoning among adults: Competence or performance? *British Journal of Psychology, 76*, 241–247.

Markus, H. (1977). Self-schemata and processing information about the self. *Journal of Personality and Social Psychology, 35*, 63–78.

Markus, H., & Sentis, K. P. (1982). The self in social information processing. In J. Suls (Ed.), *Psychological perspectives on the self* (Vol. 1). Hillsdale, NJ: Erlbaum.

Marr, D. (1982). *Vision*. San Francisco: Freeman.

Marr, D., & Hildreth, E. C. (1980). Theory of edge detection. *Proceedings of the Royal Society, London, B207*, 187–217.

Marr, D., & Nisihara, H. K. (1977). Representation and recognition of the spatial organization of three-dimensional shapes. *Proceedings of the Royal Society, London, B200*, 269–294.

Marshall, J. C. (1987). Routes and representations in the processing of written language. In E. Keller & M. Gopnik (Eds.), *Motor and sensory processes of language* (pp. 237–256). Hillsdale, NJ: Erlbaum.

Marshall, J. C., & Newcombe, F. (1973). Patterns of paralexia: A psycholinguistic approach. *Journal of Psycholinguistic Research, 2*, 175–199.

Massaro, D. W., & Cowan, N. (1993). Information processing models: Microscopes of the mind. *Annual Review of Psychology, 44*, 383–425.

Massaro, D. W., & Hary, J. M. (1986). Addressing issues in letter recognition. *Psychological Research, 48*, 123–132.

Mathieson, C. M., Sainsbury, R. S., & Fitzgerald, L. K. (1990). Attentional set in pure versus mixed lists in a dichotic listening paradigm. *Brain & Cognition, 13*, 30–45.

Matlin, M. (1983). *Cognition*. New York: CBS College Publishing.

Mayer, R. E. (1983). *Thinking, problem solving, cognition* (2nd ed.). San Francisco: Freeman.

Mayes, A. (1987). Human organic memory disorders. In H. Beloff & A. M. Colman (Eds.), *Psychology survey 6* (pp. 170–191). Cambridge, MA: MIT Press.

McCabe, V., & Balzano, G. J. (Eds.). (1986). *Event cognition: An ecological perspective*. Hillsdale, NJ: Erlbaum.

McClelland, J. L. (1981). Retrieving general and specific knowledge from stored knowledge of specifics. *Proceedings of the Third Annual Conference of the Cognitive Science Society*, 170–172.

McClelland, J. L., & Rumelhart, D. E. (1988). *Explorations in parallel distributed processing: A handbook of models, programs, and exercises*. Cambridge, MA: MIT Press.

McCloskey, M., Caramzza, A., & Green, B. (1980). Curvilinear motion in the absence of external forces: Naive beliefs about the motion of objects. *Science, 210*, 1139–1141.

McCloskey, M. E., & Glucksberg, S. (1978). Natural categories: Well-defined or fuzzy sets? *Memory & Cognition, 6*, 462–472.

McCloskey, M., & Kaiser, M. (1984). The impetus impulse: a medieval theory of motion lives on in the minds of children. *The Sciences*.

McCloskey, M., & Santee, J. (1981). Are semantic memory and episodic memory distinct systems? *Journal of Experimental Psychology: Human Learning and Memory, 7*, 66–71.

McCloskey, M., & Watkins, M. J. (1978). The seeing-more-than-is-there phenomenon: Implications for the locus of iconic storage. *Journal of Experimental Psychology: Human Perception and Performance, 4*, 553–564.

McConkie, G. W., & Rayner, K. (1974). Identifying the span of the effective stimulus in reading. *Final Report OEG 2-71-0531*. U.S. Office of Education.

McConnell, J. V. (1962). Memory transfer through cannibalism in planarians. *Journal of Neuropsychiatry, 3* (Supplement 1), 42–48.

McCoon, G., Ratcliff, R., & Dell, G. S. (1985). The role of semantic information in episodic retrieval. *Journal of Experimental Psychology: Learning, Memory and Cognition, 11*, 742–751.

McCulloch, W. S., & Pitts, W. (1943). A logical calculus of ideas immanent in nervous activity. *Bulletin of Mathematical Biophysiology, 5*, 115–133.

McKeithen, K. B., Reitman, J. S., Rueter, H. H., & Hirtle, S. C. (1981). Knowledge organization and skill differences in computer programmers. *Cognitive Psychology, 13*, 307–325.

McKoon, G. (1977). Organization of information in text memory. *Journal of Verbal Learning and Verbal Behavior, 16*, 247–260.

McKoon, G., & Ratcliff, R. (1979). Priming in episodic and semantic memory. *Journal of Verbal Learning and Verbal Behavior, 18*, 463–480.

McKoon, G., Ratcliff, R., & Dell, G. S. (1985). The role of semantic information episodic retrieval. *Journal of Experimental Psychology: Learning, Memory and Cognition, 11*, 742–751.

McNeill, D. (1970). *The acquisition of language: The study of developmental psycholinguistics*. New York: Harper & Row.

Medin, D. L. (1989). Concepts and conceptual structure. *American Psychologist, 44*, 1469–1481.

Medin, D. L., & Shoben, E. J. (1988). Context and structure in conceptual combination. *Cognitive Psychology, 20*, 158–190.

Medin, D. L., & Smith, E. E. (1981). Strategies and classification learning. *Journal of Experimental Psychology: Human Learning and Memory, 7*, 241–253.

Mehler, J., Segui, J., & Carey, P. (1978). Tails of words: Monitoring ambiguity. *Journal of Verbal Learning and Verbal Behavior, 17*, 29–37.

Meltzoff, A. N., & Moore, M. K. (1977). Imitation of facial and manual gestures by human neonates. *Science, 198*, 75–78.

Mendelson, R., & Schultz, T. R. (1976). Covariation and temporal contiguity as principles of causal inference in young children. *Journal of Experimental Child Psychology, 13*, 89–111.

Merikle, P. M. (1980). Selection from visual persistence by perceptual groups and category membership. *Journal of Experimental Psychology: General, 109*, 279–295.

Metzler, J. (1973). *Cognitive analogues of the rotation of three-dimensional objects*. Unpublished doctoral dissertation, Stanford University, Stanford, CA.

Meudell, P., Butters, N., & Montgomery, K. (1978). The role of rehearsal in the short-term memory performance of patients with Korsakoff's and Huntington's disease. *Neuropsychologia, 16*, 507–510.

Meudell, P., & Mayes, A. (1982). Normal and abnormal forgetting: Some comments on the human amnesic syndrome. In A. W. Ellis (Ed.), *Normality and pathology in cognitive functions* (pp. 203–237). New York: Academic Press.

Meyer, D. E., & Schvaneveldt, R. W. (1971). Facilitation in recognizing pairs of words: Evidence of a dependence between retrieval operations. *Journal of Experimental Psychology, 90,* 227–234.

Mill, J. S. (1874). *A system of logic* (8th ed.). New York: Harper.

Miller, G. A. (1956). The magical number seven, plus or minus two: Some limits on our capacity for processing information. *Psychological Review, 63,* 81–97.

Miller, G. A. (1958). Free recall of redundant strings of letters. *Journal of Experimental Psychology, 56,* 485–491.

Miller, G. A., Galanter, E., & Pribram, K. H. (1960). *Plans and the structure of behavior.* New York: Holt, Rinehart & Winston.

Miller, G. A., & Nicely, P. (1955). An analysis of perceptual confusions among some English consonants. *Journal of the Acoustical Society of America, 27,* 338–352.

Miller, G. A., & Selfridge, J. A. (1950). Verbal context and the recall of meaningful material. *American Journal of Psychology, 63,* 176–185.

Miller, R. R., & Springer, A. D. (1972). Recovery from amnesia following transcorneal electroconvulsive shock. *Psychonomic Science, 28,* 7–8.

Milner, B. (1959). The memory defect in bilateral hippocampus lesions. *Psychiatric Research Reports, 11,* 43–58.

Minsky, M., & Papert, S. (1969). *Perceptrons.* Cambridge, MA: MIT Press.

Mishkin, M. (1978). Memory in monkeys severely impaired by combined but not by separate removal of amygdala and hippocampus. *Nature, 273,* 297–298.

Moely, B. E., Olson, F. A., Halwes, T. G., & Flavell, J. H. (1969). Production deficiency in young children's clustered recall. *Developmental Psychology, 1,* 26–34.

Moray, N. (1959). Attention in dichotic listening: Affective cues and the influence of instructions. *Quarterly Journal of Experimental Psychology, 11,* 56–60.

Morris, C. D., Bransford, J. D., & Franks, J. J. (1977). Levels of processing versus transfer appropriate processing. *Journal of Verbal Learning and Verbal Behavior, 16,* 519–533.

Moscovitch, M. (1982). Multiple dissociations of functions in the amnesic syndrome. In L. Cermak (Ed.), *Human memory and amnesia.* Hillsdale, NJ: Erlbaum.

Moskowitz, B. A., (1991). The acquisition of language. In W. S-Y. Wang (Ed.), *The emergence of language: Development and evolution* (pp. 131–149). New York: Freeman.

Mowbray, G. H. (1953). Simultaneous vision and audition: The comprehension of prose passages with varying levels of difficulty. *Journal of Experimental Psychology, 46,* 365–372.

Mulholland, T. M., Pellegrino, J. W., & Glaser, R. (1980). Components of analogy solution. *Cognitive Psychology, 12,* 252–284.

Murdock, B. B., Jr. (1961). The retention of individual items. *Journal of Experimental Psychology, 62,* 618–625.

Murdock, B. B., Jr. (1962). The serial position effect of free recall. *Journal of Experimental Psychology, 64,* 482–488.

Murray, H. G., & Denny, J. P. (1969). Interaction of ability level and interpolated activity (opportunity for incubation) in human problem solving. *Psychological Reports, 24,* 271–276.

Myers, D. (1986). *Psychology.* New York: Worth.

Nadel, L., Cooper, L. A., Culicover, P., & Harnish, R. M. (1989). *Neural connections, mental computations.* Cambridge, MA: MIT Press.

Naveh-Benjamin, M., & Jonides, J. (1986). On the automaticity of frequency coding: Effects of competing task load, encoding strategy, and intention. *Journal of Experimental Psychology: Learning, Memory, and Cognition, 12,* 378–386.

Neches, R., Langley, P., & Klahr, D. (1987). Learning, development, and production systems. In D. Klahr, P. Langley, & R. Neches (Eds.). *Production system models of learning and development* (pp. 1–54). Cambridge, MA: MIT Press.

Neely, J. H. (1977). Semantic priming and retrieval from lexical memory: Roles of inhibitionless spreading activation and limited-capacity attention. *Journal of Experimental Psychology: General, 106,* 226–254.

Neely, J. H., & Durgunoglu, A. Y. (1985). Dissociative episodic and semantic priming effects in episodic recognition and lexical decision tasks. *Journal of Memory and Language, 24,* 466–489.

Neely, J. H., Crawley, E. J., & Velluntino, F. R. (1990, November). *Do words that are first syllables of other words access their semantic codes?* Paper presented at the 31st annual meeting of the Psychonomic Society, New Orleans, LA.

Neimark, E. D. (1987). *Adventures in thinking.* San Diego, CA: Harcourt Brace Jovanovich.

Neisser, U. (1964). Visual search. *Scientific American, 210,* 94–102.

Neisser, U. (1964). Visual search. *Scientific American. 210(6),* 94–102.

Neisser, U. (1967). *Cognitive psychology.* New York: Appleton-Century-Crofts.

Neisser, U. (1976). *Cognition and reality: Principles and implications of cognitive psychology.* San Francisco: Freeman.

Neisser, U. (1978). Memory: What are the important questions? In M. M. Gruneberg, P. E. Morris, & R. N. Sykes (Eds.), *Practical aspects of memory* (pp. 3–24). London: Academic Press.

Neisser, U. (1982). *Memory observed.* San Francisco: Freeman.

Neisser, U., & Harsch, N. (1992). Phantom flashbulbs: False recollections of hearing the news about Challenger. In E. Winograd, & U. Neisser (Eds.), *Affect and accuracy in recall: Studies of "flashbulb" memories* (pp. 9–31). New York: Cambridge University Press.

Neisser, U., & Winograd, E. (Eds.). (1988). *Remembering reconsidered: Ecological and traditional approaches to the study of memory.* New York: Cambridge University Press.

Nelson, D. L. (1979). Remembering pictures and words: Appearance, significance, and name. In L. S. Cermak & F. I. M. Craik (Eds.), *Levels of processing in human memory.* Hillsdale, NJ: Erlbaum.

Nelson, D. L., & McEvoy, C. L. (1979). Encoding context and set size. *Journal of Experimental Psychology: Human Learning and Memory, 5,* 292–314.

Nelson, K. (1973). Structure and strategy in learning to talk. *Monographs for the Society of Research in Child Development, 38* (Serial No. 149).

Nelson, K. (1975). The nominal shift in semantic-syntactic development. *Cognitive Psychology, 7,* 461–479.

Nelson, K. (1993). The psychological and social origins of autobiographical memory. *Psychological Science, 4,* 7–14.

Nelson, T. O. (1977). Repetition and depth of processing. *Journal of Verbal Learning and Verbal Behavior, 16,* 151–171.

Newell, A. (1962). Some problems of basic organization in problem-solving programs. In M. C. Yovits, G. T. Jacobi, & G. D. Goldstein (Eds.), *Self-organizing systems* (pp. 293–423). Washington, DC: Spartan Books.

Newell, A. (1965). Limitations of the current stock of ideas for problem solving. In A. Kent & O. Taulbee (Eds.), *Conference on electronic information handling* (pp. 195–208). Washington, DC: Spartan Books.

Newell, A. (1966). *On the representations of problems.* Computer Science Research Review, 18–33. Pittsburgh: Carnegie Institute of Technology.

Newell, A. (1967). *Studies in problem solving: Subject 3 on the cryptarithmetic task: DONALD + GERALD = ROBERT.* Pittsburgh: Carnegie-Mellon University.

Newell, A. (1990). *Unified theories of cognition.* Cambridge, MA: Harvard University Press.

Newell, A., & Rosenbloom, P. S. (1981). Mechanisms of skill acquisition and the law of practice. In J. R. Anderson (Ed.), *Cognitive skills and their acquisition* (pp. 1–56). Hillsdale, NJ: Erlbaum.

Newell, A., Shaw, J. C., & Simon, H. A. (1958). Elements of a theory of human problem solving. *Psychological Review, 65,* 151–166.

Newell, A., Shaw, J. C., & Simon, H. A. (1962). The processes of creative thinking. In H. E. Gruber, G. Terrell, & M. Wertheimer (Eds.), *Contemporary approaches to creative thinking* (pp. 63–119). New York: Atherton Press.

Newell, A., & Simon, H. A. (1956). The logic theory machine: A complex information processing system. *IRE Transactions on Information Theory, IT-2*(3), 61–79.

Newell, A., & Simon, H. A. (1961). GPS: A program that simulates human thought. In H. Billing (Ed.), *Lernende Automaten* (pp. 109–124). Munich: R. Oldenbourg.

Newell, A., & Simon, H. A. (1965). An example of human chess play in the light of chess playing programs. In N. Weiner & J. P. Schade (Eds.), *Progress in biocybernetics* (Vol. 2, pp. 19–75). Amsterdam: Elsevier.

Newell, A., & Simon, H. A. (1972). *Human problem solving.* Englewood Cliffs, NJ: Prentice-Hall.

Newport, E. L. (1990). Maturational constraints on language learning. *Cognitive Science, 14,* 11–28.

Nickerson, R. S. (1986). *Reflections on reasoning.* Hillsdale, NJ: Erlbaum.

Nisbett, R. E., & Wilson, T. D. (1977). Telling more than we can know: Verbal reports on mental processes. *Psychological Review, 84,* 231–259.

Norman, D. A. (1968). Toward a theory of memory and attention. *Psychological Review, 75,* 522–536.

Norman, D. A., & Bobrow, D. G. (1975). On data-limited and resource-limited processes. *Cognitive Psychology, 7,* 44–64.

Novick, L. R., & Holyoak, K. J. (1991). Mathematical problem solving by analogy. *Journal of Experimental Psychology: Learning, Memory, and Cognition, 17,* 398–415.

Obusek, C. J., & Warren, R. M. (1973). Relation of the verbal transformation and the phonemic restoration effects. *Cognitive Psychology, 5,* 97–107.

Oden, G. C. (1987). Concept, knowledge, and thought. *Annual Review of Psychology, 38,* 203–227.

Olson, J. N., & MacKay, D. G. (1974). Completion and verification of ambiguous sentences. *Journal of Verbal Learning and Verbal Behavior, 13,* 457–470.

Orne, M. T. (1962). On the social psychology of the psychological experiment: With particular reference to demand characteristics and their implications. *American Psychologist, 17,* 776–783.

Overton, D. A. (1972). State-dependent learning produced by alcohol and its relevance to alcoholism. In B. Kissin & H. Begleiter (Eds.), *Physiology and behavior* (Vol. 2). New York: Plenum.

Owens, J., Bower, G. H., & Black, J. B. (1979). The "soap opera" effect in story recall. *Memory and Cognition, 7,* 185–191.

Paivio, A. (1969). Mental imagery in associative learning and memory. *Psychological Review, 76,* 241–263.

Paivio, A. (1971). *Imagery and verbal processes.* New York: Holt, Rinehart, & Winston.

Paivio, A. (1978). Mental comparisons involving abstract attributes. *Memory & Cognition, 6,* 199–208.

Paivio, A., & te Linde, J. (1982). Imagery, memory, and the brain. *Canadian Journal of Psychology, 36,* 243–272.

Palmer, J. (1990). Attentional limits on the perception and memory of visual information. *Journal of Experimental Psychology: Human Perception and Performance, 16,* 332–350.

Palmer, S. E., & Kimchi, R. (1986). The information processing approach to cognition. In T. J. Knapp, & L. C. Robertson (Eds.), *Approaches to cognition: Contrasts and controversies* (pp. 37–77). Hillsdale, NJ: Erlbaum.

Palmere, M., Benton, S. L., Glover, J. A., & Ronning, R. (1983). Elaboration and recall of main ideas in prose. *Journal of Educational Psychology, 75,* 898–907.

Parker, E. S., Birnbaum, I. M., & Noble, E. P. (1976). Alcohol and memory: Storage and state dependency. *Journal of Verbal Learning and Verbal Behavior, 15,* 691–702.

Parkin, A. J. (1984). Levels of processing, context, and facilitation of pronunciation. *Acta Psychologia, 55,* 19–29.

Parkin, A. J. (1987). *Memory and amnesia: An introduction.* New York: Blackwell.

Patterson, K. E. (1982). The relation between reading and phonological encoding: Further neuropsychological observations. In A. W. Ellis (Ed.), *Normality and pathology in cognitive functions* (pp. 77–112). New York: Academic Press.

Pellegrino, J. W. (1985). Inductive reasoning ability. In R. J. Sternberg (Ed.), *Human abilities: An information processing approach* (pp. 195–226). San Francisco: Freeman.

Penfield, W., & Milner, B. (1958). Memory deficit produced by bilateral lesions in the hippocampal zone. *Archives of neurology and psychiatry, 79,* 475–497.

Perfetti, C. A., & Curtis, M. E. (1986). Reading in R. F. Dillon & R. J. Sternberg (Eds.), *Cognition and instruction* (pp. 13–57). Orlando, FL: Academic Press.

Petersik, J. T. (1982). Perception of eye scans with the Müller-Lyer stimuli: Evidence for filter theory. *Perceptual and Motor Skills, 54* (3, Pt. 1), 683–692.

Peterson, L. R., & Peterson, M. J. (1959). Short-term retention of individual verbal items. *Journal of Experimental Psychology, 58,* 193–198.

Phye, G. D., & Andre, T. (Eds.). (1986). *Cognitive classroom learning: Understanding, thinking, and problem solving.* Orlando, FL: Academic Press.

Piaget, J. (1968). *Le structuralisme.* Paris: Presses Universitaires de France.

Pinker, S., & Prince, A. (1988). On language and connectionism: Analysis of a parallel distributed processing model of language acquisition. *Cognition, 28,* 73–193.

Pinsky, S. D., & McAdam, D. W. (1980). Electroencephalographic and dichotic indices of cerebral laterality in stuttering. *Brain and Language, 11,* 374–397.

Pisoni, D. B. (1978). Speech perception. In W. K. Estes (Ed.), *Handbook of learning and cognitive processes* (Vol. 6, pp. 167–234). Hillsdale, NJ: Erlbaum.

Pisoni, D. B., & Sawusch, J. R. (1975). Some stages of processing in speech perception. In A. Cohen & S. G. Nooteboom

(Eds.), *Structure and process in speech perception* (pp. 16–34). Heidelberg, Germany: Springer-Verlag.

Poincare, H. (1913). The value of science. In *The foundations of science* (G. B. Halsted, Trans.). New York: Science Press.

Pollack, I., & Pickett, J. M. (1964). Intelligibility of excerpts from fluent speech: Auditory vs. structural context. *Journal of Verbal Learning and Verbal Behavior, 3,* 79–84.

Pollard, P. (1985). Nonindependence of selections in the Wason selection task. *Bulletin of the Psychonomic Society, 23,* 317–320.

Pollatsek, A., Rayner, K., & Balota, D. A. (1986). Inferences about eye movement control from the perceptual span in reading. *Perception and Psychophysics, 40,* 123–130.

Polson, P. G., & Jeffries, R. (1982). Problem solving as search and understanding. In R. J. Sternberg (Ed.), *Advances in the psychology of human intelligence* (Vol. 1, pp. 367–412). Hillsdale, NJ: Erlbaum.

Posner, M. I. (1969). Abstraction and the process of recognition. In G. H. Bower & J. T. Spence (Eds.), *The psychology of learning and motivation* (Vol. 3). New York: Academic Press.

Posner, M. I. (1973). *Cognition: An introduction.* Glenview, IL: Scott, Foresman and Co.

Posner, M. I., & Boies, S. J. (1971). Components of attention. *Psychological Review, 78,* 391–408.

Posner, M. I., & Keele, S. W. (1968). On the genesis of abstract ideas. *Journal of Experimental Psychology, 77,* 353–363.

Posner, M. I., & Keele, S. W. (1970). Retention of abstract ideas. *Journal of Experimental Psychology, 83,* 304–308.

Posner, M. I., & Snyder, C. R. R. (1975). Attention and cognitive control. In R. Solso (Ed.), *Information processing and cognition: The Loyola symposium.* Hillsdale, NJ: Erlbaum.

Postman, L., & Phillips, L. W. (1965). Short-term temporal changes in free recall. *Quarterly Journal of Experimental Psychology, 17,* 132–138.

Postman, L., Thompkins, B. A., & Gray, W. D. (1978). The interpretation of encoding effects in retention. *Journal of Verbal Learning and Verbal Behavior, 17,* 681–705.

Pritchard, R. M. (1961). Stablized images on the retina. *Scientific American, 204(6),* 72–78.

Purcell, D. G., Stanovich, K. E., & Spector, A. (1978). Visual angle and the word superiority effect. *Memory & Cognition, 6,* 3–8.

Quartermain, D., McEwen, B. S., & Azmitia, E. C., Jr. (1972). Recovery of memory following amnesia in the rat and mouse. *Journal of Comparative and Physiological Psychology, 79,* 360–370.

Quine, W. V. O. (1960). *Word and object.* Cambridge, MA: MIT Press.

Quillian, M. R. (1968). Semantic memory. In M. Minsky (Ed.), *Semantic information processing,* Cambridge, MA: MIT Press.

Raaijmakers, J. G. W., & Shiffrin, R. M. (1981). Search of associative memory. *Psychological Review, 88,* 93–134.

Rabinowitz, J. C., Mandler, G., & Patterson, K. E. (1977). Determinants of recognition and recall: Accessibility and generation. *Journal of Experimental Psychology: General, 106,* 302–329.

Rajaram, S. (1993). Remembering and knowing: Two means of acess to the personal past. *Memory & Cognition, 21,* 89–102.

Ratcliff, R., Hockley, W., & McKoon, G. (1985). Components of activation: Repetition and priming effects in lexical decision and recognition. *Journal of Experimental Psychology: General, 114,* 435–450.

Ratcliff, R. A., & McKoon, G. (1981). Does activation really spread? *Psychological Review, 88,* 454–462.

Rayner, K. (1975). The perceptual span and peripheral cues in reading. *Cognitive Psychology, 7,* 65–81.

Rayner, K. (1978). Eye movements in reading and information processing. *Psychological Bulletin, 85,* 618–660.

Rayner, K., & Duffy, S. A. (1986). Lexical complexity and fixation times in reading: Effects of word frequency, verb complexity, and lexical ambiguity. *Memory & Cognition, 14,* 191–201.

Reber, A. S. (1967). Implicit learning of artificial grammars. *Journal of Verbal Learning and Verbal Behavior, 6,* 855–863.

Reber, A. S. (1973). What clicks may tell us about speech perception. *Journal of Psycholinguistic Research, 2,* 287–288.

Reber, A. S., & Anderson, J. R. (1970). The perception of clicks in linguistic and nonlinguistic messages. *Perception and Psychophysics, 8,* 81–89.

Reed, E., & Jones, R. (Eds.). (1982). *Reasons for realism: Selected essays of James J. Gibson.* Hillsdale, NJ: Erlbaum.

Reicher, G. (1969). Perceptual recognition as a function of meaningfulness of stimulus material. *Journal of Experimental Psychology, 81,* 275–280.

Reif, F. (1979). *Cognitive mechanisms facilitating human problem solving in a realistic domain: The example of physics.* Unpublished manuscript.

Reiser, B. J., Black, J. B., & Abelson, R. P. (1985). Knowledge structures in the organization and retrieval of autobiographical memories. *Cognitive Psychology, 17,* 89–137.

Reitman, W. (1964). Heuristic decision procedures, open constraints, and the structure of ill-defined problems. In M. W. Shelley & G. L. Bryan (Eds.), *Human judgements and optimality.* New York: Wiley.

Remez, R. E. (1979). Adaptation of the category boundary between speech and non-speech: A case against feature detectors. *Cognitive Psychology, 11,* 38–57.

Remez, R. E. (1980). Susceptibility of a stop consonant to adaptation on a speech-nonspeech continuum: Further evidence against feature detectors in speech perception. *Perception and Psychophysics, 27,* 17–23.

Remez, R. E., Rubin, P. E., Pisoni, D. B., & Carrell, T. D. (1981). Speech perception without traditional speech cues. *Science, 212,* 947–950.

Richardson, J. T., & Johnson, P. B. (1980). Models of anagram solution. *Bulletin of the Psychonomic Society, 16,* 247–250.

Richardson, K., Bhavnani, K. K., & Browne, D. (1982). Abstraction of contingency in concept learning. *Current Psychological Research, 2,* 101–109.

Ricks, D. M. (1975). Vocal communication in pre-verbal, normal, and autistic children. In N. O'Connor (Ed.), *Language, cognitive deficits, and retardation.* London: Butterworth.

Riggs, L. A., Ratliff, F., Cornsweet, J. C., & Cornsweet, T. N. (1953). The disappearance of steadily fixated objects. *Journal of the Optical Society of America, 43,* 495–501.

Rips, L. J. (1989). Similarity, typicality, and categorization. In S. Vosniadou & A. Ortony (Eds.), *Similarity and analogical reasoning.* Cambridge: Cambridge University Press.

Rips, L. J. (1990). Reasoning. *Annual Review of Psychology, 41,* 321–353.

Rips, L. J., & Marcus, S. L. (1977). Supposition and the analysis of conditional sentences. In M. A. Just & P. A. Carpenter (Eds.), *Cognitive processes in comprehension.* Hillsdale, NJ: Erlbaum.

Rips, L. J., Shoben, E. J., & Smith, E. E. (1973). Semantic distance and the verification of semantic relations. *Journal of Verbal Learning and Verbal Behavior, 12,* 1–20.

Rock, I. (1983). *The logic of perception.* Cambridge, MA: MIT Press/Bradford Books.

Roediger, H. L. (1990). Implicit memory. *American Psychologist, 45,* 1043–1056.

Rogoff, B., & Lave, J. (1984). *Everyday cognition: Its development in social context.* Cambridge, MA: Harvard University Press.

Ronning, R. R. (1965). Anagram solution times: A function of the "ruleout" factor. *Journal of Experimental Psychology, 69,* 35–39.

Rosch, E. H. (1973). On the internal structure of perceptual and semantic categories. In T. E. Moore (Ed.), *Cognitive development and the acquisition of language.* New York: Academic Press.

Rosch, E. H. (1975). Cognitive representations of semantic categories. *Journal of Experimental Psychology: General, 104,* 192–233.

Rosch, E. H. (1977). Classification of real-world objects: Origins and representation in cognition. In P. N. Johnson-Laird & P. C. Wason (Eds.), *Thinking: Readings in cognitive science* (pp. 212–222) Cambridge: Cambridge University Press.

Rosch, E. H., & Lloyd, B. B. (Eds.). (1978). *Cognition and categorization.* Hillsdale, NJ: Erlbaum.

Rosch, E. H., & Mervis, C. B. (1975). Family resemblances: Studies in the internal structure of categories. *Cognitive Psychology, 7,* 573–605.

Rosenberg, C. R., & Sejnowski, T. J. (1987). Parallel networks that learn to pronounce English text. *Compex Systems, 1,* 145–168.

Rosenblatt, F. (1958). The perceptron: A probabilistic model for information storage and organization in the brain. *Psychological Review, 65,* 386–408.

Rosenfield, D. B., & Goodglass, H. (1980). Dichotic testing of cerebral dominance in stutterers. *Brain and Language, 11,* 170–180.

Ross, B. H. (1989). Reminders in learning and instruction. In S. Vosniadou & A. Ortony (Eds.), *Similarity and analogical reasoning* (pp. 438–469). Cambridge: Cambridge University Press.

Roth, E. M., & Shoben, E. J. (1983). The effect of context on the structure of categories. *Cognitive Psychology, 15,* 346–378.

Rubenstein, H., Lewis, S. S., & Rubenstein, M. A. (1971). Evidence for phonemic recoding in visual word recognition. *Journal of Verbal Learning and Verbal Behavior, 10,* 645–657.

Rubin, D. C., & Kontis, T. C. (1983). A schema for common cents. *Memory & Cognition, 11,* 335–341.

Rumelhart, D. E., & McClelland, J. L. (1986). *Parallel distributed processing: Explorations in the microstructure of cognition* (Vol. 1). Cambridge, MA: MIT Press.

Rumelhart, D. E., & Siple, P. (1974). Process of recognizing tachistoscopically presented words. *Psychological Review, 81,* 99–118.

Rundus, D. (1977). Maintenance rehearsal and single-level processing. *Journal of Verbal Learning and Verbal Behavior, 16,* 665–681.

Russell, W. R., & Nathan, P. W. (1946). Traumatic amnesia. *Brain, 69,* 280–300.

Sabol, M. A., & DeRosa, D. V. (1976). Semantic encoding of isolated words. *Journal of Experimental Psychology: Human Learning and Memory, 2,* 58–68.

Sachs, J. D. S. (1967). Recognition memory for syntactic and semantic aspects of connected discourse. *Perception and Psychophysics, 2,* 437–442.

Saffran, E. M., & Marin, O. S. M. (1977). Reading without phonology: Evidence from aphasia. *Quarterly Journal of Experimental Psychology, 29,* 515–525.

Salame, P., & Baddeley, A. D. (1982). Disruption of short-term memory by unattended speech: Implications for the structure of working memory. *Journal of Verbal Learning and Verbal Behavior, 21,* 150–164.

Salasoo, A., Shiffrin, R. M., & Feustel, T. C. (1985). Building permanent memory codes: Codification and repetition effects in word identification. *Journal of Experimental Psychology: General, 114,* 50–77.

Samuels, A. B. (1981). Phonemic restoration: Insights from a new methodology. *Journal of Experimental Psychology: General, 110,* 474–494.

Scardamalia, M., Bereiter, C., & Steinbach, R. (1984). Teachability of reflective processes in written composition. *Cognitive Science, 8,* 173–190.

Schacter, D. L. (1987). Implicit memory: History and current status. *Journal of Experimental Psychology: Learning, Memory and Cognition, 13,* 501–518.

Schacter, D. L. (1989). On the relation between memory and consciousness: Dissociable interactions and conscious experience. In H. L. Roediger & F. I. M. Craik (Eds.), *Varieties of memory and consciousness: Essays in honour of Endel Tulving* (pp. 355–389). Hillsdale, NJ: Erlbaum.

Schank, R. C., & Abelson, R. P. (1977). *Scripts, plans, goals, and understanding: An inquiry into human knowledge structures.* Hillsdale, NJ: Erlbaum.

Schank, R. C. (1982). *Dynamic memory: A theory of reminding and learning in computers and people.* New York: Cambridge University Press.

Schauble, L. (1990). Belief revision in children: The role of prior knowledge and strategies for generating evidence. *Journal of Experimental Child Psychology, 49,* 31–57.

Schneider, A. M., Tyler, J., & Jinich, D. (1974). Recovery from retrograde amnesia: A learning process. *Science, 184,* 87–88.

Schneider, W., Dumais, S. T., & Shiffrin, R. M. (1984). Automatic and control processing and attention. In R. Parasuraman & R. Davies (Eds.), *Varieties of attention* (pp. 1–27). New York: Academic Press.

Schneider, W., & Shiffrin, R. M. (1977). Controlled and automatic human information processing: I. Detection, search, and attention. *Psychological Review, 84,* 1–66.

Scoville, W. B., & Milner, B. (1957). Loss of recent memory after bilateral hippocampal lesions. *Journal of Neurology, Neurosurgery, and Psychiatry, 20,* 11–21.

Scribner, S. (1977). Modes of thinking and ways of speaking: Culture and logic reconsidered. In P. N. Johnson-Laird & P. C. Wason (Eds.), *Thinking: Readings in cognitive science* (pp. 483–500). Cambridge: Cambridge University Press.

Seamon, J. G., & Virostek, S. (1978). Memory performance and subject-defined depth of processing. *Memory and Cognition, 6,* 283–287.

Searle, J. R. (1975). Indirect speech acts. In P. Cole & J. L. Morgan (Eds.), *Syntax and semantics: Vol. 3. Speech Acts* (pp. 59–82). New York: Seminar Press.

Seidenberg, M. S., & McClelland, J. L. (1990). More words but still no lexicon: Reply to Besner et al. (1990). *Psychological Review, 97,* 447–452.

Selfridge, O. (1959). Pandemonium: A paradigm for learning. In *Symposium on the mechanization of thought processes.* London: HM Stationery Office.

Shaughnessy, J. J. (1981). Memory monitoring accuracy and modification of rehearsal strategies. *Journal of Verbal Learning and Verbal Behavior, 20,* 216–230.

Shepard, R. N. (1972). Psychological representation of speech sounds. In E. E. David & P. B. Denes (Eds.), *Human communication: A unified view* (pp. 67–113). New York: McGraw-Hill.

Shepard, R. N., & Metzler, J. (1971). Mental rotation of three-dimensional objects. *Science, 171,* 701–703.

Shepard, R., & Podgorny, P. (1978). Cognitive processes that resemble perceptual processes. In W. Estes (Ed.), *Handbook of learning and cognitive processes* (Vol. 5, pp. 189–237). Hillsdale, NJ: Erlbaum.

Shiffrin, R. M., Craig, J. C., & Cohen, E. (1973). On the degree of attention and capacity limitation in tactile processing. *Perception and Psychophysics, 13,* 328–336.

Shiffrin, R. M., & Dumais, S. T. (1981). The development of automatism. In J. R. Anderson (Ed.), *Cognitive skills and their acquisition* (pp. 111–140). Hillsdale, NJ: Erlbaum.

Shiffrin, R. M., Murname, K., Gronlund, S., & Roth, M. (1989). On units of storage and retrieval. In C. Izawa, (Ed.), *Current issues in cognitive processes: The Tulane Flowerree symposium on cognition* (pp. 25–68). Hillsdale, NJ: Erlbaum.

Shiffrin, R. M., & Schneider, W. (1977). Controlled and automatic human information processing: II. Perceptual learning, automatic attending, and a general theory. *Psychological Review, 84,* 127–190.

Shoben, E. J., Westcourt, K. T., & Smith, E. E. (1978). Sentence verification, sentence recognition, and the semantic-episodic distinction. *Journal of Experimental Psychology: Human Learning and Memory, 4,* 304–317.

Shulman, H. G. (1971). Similarity effects in short-term memory. *Psychological Bulletin, 75,* 399–415.

Shulman, H. G. (1972). Semantic confusion errors in short-term memory. *Journal of Verbal Learning and Verbal Behavior, 11,* 221–227.

Siegler, R. S. (1991). *Children's thinking.* Englewood Cliffs, NJ: Prentice-Hall.

Siegler, R. S., & Jenkins, E. (1989). *How children discover new strategies.* Hillsdale, NJ: Erlbaum.

Siegler, R. S. (1987). The perils of averaging data over strategies: An example from children's addition. *Journal of Experimental Psychology: General, 116,* 250–264.

Silveira, J. (1971). *The effect of interruption timing and length on problem solution and quality of problem processing.* Unpublished doctoral dissertation, University of Oregon, Eugene, OR.

Simon, H. A. (1969). *The sciences of the artificial* (1st ed.). Cambridge, MA: MIT Press.

Simon, H. A. (1973). The structure of illstructured problems. *Artificial Intelligence, 4,* 181–202.

Simon, H. A. (1978). Information processing theory of human problem solving. In W. K. Estes (Ed.), *Handbook of learning and cognitive processes* (Vol. 5, pp. 271–295). Hillsdale, NJ: Erlbaum.

Simon, H. A., & Gilmartin, K. A. (1973). A simulation of memory for chess positions. *Cognitive Psychology, 5,* 29–46.

Simon, H. A., & Hayes, J. R. (1976). The understanding process: Problem isomorphs. *Cognitive Psychology, 8,* 165–190.

Simon, H. A., & Simon, P. A. (1962). Trial and error search in solving difficult problems: Evidence from the game of chess. *Behavioral Science, 7,* 425–429.

Sitler, R. W., Schiavetti, N., & Metz, D. E. (1983). Contextual effects in the measurement of hearing-impaired speakers' intelligibility, *Journal of Speech and Hearing Research, 26,* 30–35.

Skinner, B. F. (1957). *Verbal behavior.* New York: Appleton-Century-Crofts.

Sleeman, D. (1982). Assessing aspects of competence in basic algebra. In D. Sleeman & J. S. Brown (Eds.), *Intelligent tutoring systems* (pp. 185–200). New York: Academic Press.

Slovic, P., Fischoff, B., & Lichtenstein, S. (1976). Cognitive process and social risk taking. In J. S. Carroll & J. W. Payne (Eds.), *Cognition and social behavior.* Hillsdale, NJ: Erlbaum.

Smiley, S. S., Oakley, D. D., Worthen, D., Campione, J. C., & Brown, A. L. (1977). Recall of thematically relevant material by adolescent good and poor readers as a function of written versus oral presentation. *Journal of Educational Psychology, 69,* 381–387.

Smith, E. E. (1978). Theories of semantic memory. In W. K. Estes (Ed.), *Handbook of learning and cognitive processes* (Vol. 6, pp. 1–56). Hillsdale, NJ: Erlbaum.

Smith, E. E. (1990). Categorization. In D. N. Osherson & E. E. Smith (Eds.), *Thinking: An invitation to cognitive science* (Vol. 3, pp. 33–53). Cambridge, MA: MIT Press.

Smith, E. E., & Medin, D. L. (1981). *Categories and concepts.* Cambridge, MA: Harvard University Press.

Smith, E. E., Shoben, E. J., & Rips, L. (1974). Structure and process in semantic memory: A featural model for semantic decisions. *Psychological Review, 81,* 214–241.

Smith, S. M., Glenberg, A., & Bjork, R. A. (1978). Environmental context and human memory. *Memory and Cognition, 6,* 342–353.

Smith, T. (1982). Chomsky's cognitivism at twenty-five from the perspective of Skinner's "behaviorism at fifty." *Papers in the Social Sciences, 2,* 23–32.

Smolensky, P. (1988). On the proper treatment of connectionism. *Behavioral and Brain Sciences, 11,* 1–74.

Snoddy, G. S. (1926). Learning and stability. *Journal of Applied Psychology, 10,* 1–36.

Sokal, R. R. (1977). Classification: Purposes, principles, progress, prospects. In P. N. Johnson-Laird & P. C. Wason (Eds.), *Thinking: Readings in cognitive science* (pp. 185–198). Cambridge: Cambridge University Press.

Solman, R. T., May, J. G., & Schwartz, B. D. (1981). The word superiority effect: A study using parts of letters. *Journal of Experimental Psychology: Human Perception and Performance, 7,* 552–559.

Sperling, G. (1960). The information available in brief visual presentations. *Psychological Monographs, 74* (Whole No. 498).

Spiro, R. J. (1977). Remembering information from text: The "state of schema" approach. In R. C. Anderson, R. J. Spiro, & W. E. Montague (Eds.), *Schooling and the acquisition of knowledge.* Hillsdale, NJ: Erlbaum.

Squire, L. R. (1987). *Memory and brain.* New York: Oxford University Press.

Srull, T. R., & Wyer, R. S. (Eds.). (1988). *Advances in social cognition, Vol. 1: A dual model of impression formation.* Hillsdale NJ: Erlbaum.

Staudenmayer, H. (1975). Understanding conditional reasoning with meaningful propositions. In R. J. Falmagne (Ed.), *Reasoning: Representation and process in children and adults.* Hillsdale, NJ: Erlbaum.

Stern, L. (1985). *The structures and strategies of human memory.* Homewood, IL: Dorsey.

Sternberg, R. J. (1982, April). Who's intelligent? *Psychology Today*, pp. 30–39.

Sternberg, R. J. (Ed.). (1982). *Advances in the psychology of human intelligence* (Vol. 1). Hillsdale, NJ: Erlbaum.

Sternberg, R. J. (Ed.). (1985). *Human abilities: An information-processing approach*. San Francisco: Freeman.

Sternberg, R. J. (1988). *The psychologist's companion: A guide to scientific writing for students and researchers*. Cambridge: Cambridge University Press.

Struhsaker, T. T. (1967). Auditory communication among vervet monkeys (Cercopithecus aethiops). In S. A. Altmann (Ed.), *Social communication among primates* (pp. 285–324). Chicago: University of Chicago Press.

Sulin, R. A., & Dooling, D. J. (1974). Intrusion of a thematic idea in retention of prose. *Journal of Experimental Psychology*, 103, 255–262.

Swinney, D. A., & Hakes, D. T. (1976). Effects of prior context upon lexical access during sentence comprehension. *Journal of Verbal Learning and Verbal Behavior*, 15, 681–689.

Tank, D. W., & Hopfield, J. J. (1987). Collective computation in neuronlike circuits. *Scientific American*, 257(6), 104–114.

Tarpy, R. M., & Mayer, R. E. (1978). *Foundations of learning and memory*. Glenview, IL: Scott, Foresmen.

Tate, D. F., Galvan, L., & Ungar, G. (1976). Isolation and identification of two learning-induced brain peptides. *Pharmacology, Biochemistry, and Behavior*, 5, 441–448.

Theeuwes, J. (1992). Perceptual selectivity for color and form. *Perception and Psychophysics*, 51, 599–606.

Thorndyke, P. W. (1977). Cognitive structures in comprehension and memory of narrative discourse. *Cognitive Psychology*, 9, 77–110.

Thorndyke, P. W. (1984). Applications of schema theory in cognitive research. In J. R. Anderson & S. Kosslyn (Eds.), *Tutorials in learning and memory: Essays in honor of Gordon Bower* (pp. 167–191). San Francisco: Freeman.

Thorpe, W. H. (1961). *Bird song: The biology of vocal communication and expression in birds*. Cambridge: Cambridge University Press.

Thorpe, W. H. (1963). *Learning and instinct in animals* (2nd ed.). London: Methuen.

Tierney, R. J., Anders, P. L., & Mitchell, J. N. (Eds.). (1987). *Understanding readers' understanding*. Hillsdale, NJ: Erlbaum.

Toye, R. C. (1986). The effect of viewing position on the perceived layout of space. *Perception & Psychophysics*, 40, 85–92.

Treisman, A. M. (1960). Contextual cues in selective listening. *Quarterly Journal of Experimental Psychology*, 12, 242–248.

Treisman, A. M. (1964a). Verbal cues, language, and meaning in selective attention. *American Journal of Psychology*, 77, 206–219.

Treisman, A. M. (1964b). The effect of irrelevant material on the efficiency of selective listening. *American Journal of Psychology*, 77, 533–546.

Treisman, A., & Gormican, S. (1988). Feature analysis in early vision: Evidence from search asymetries. *Psychological Review*, 95, 15–48.

Treisman, A. (1990). Variations on the theme of feature integration: Reply to Navon (1990).

Treisman, A., & Gelade, G. (1980). A feature integration theory of attention. *Cognitive Psychology*, 12, 97–136.

Tulving, E. (1972) Episodic and semantic memory. In E. Tulving & W. Donaldson (Eds.), *Organization of memory*. New York: Academic Press.

Tulving, E. (1979). Relation between encoding specificity and levels of processing. In L. S. Cermak & F. I. M. Craik (Eds.), *Levels of processing in human memory*. Hillsdale, NJ: Erlbaum.

Tulving, E. (1983). *Elements of episodic memory*. Oxford: Clarendon Press/Oxford University Press.

Tulving, E. (1985). How many memory systems are there? *American Psychologist*, 40, 385–398.

Tulving, E. (1986). What kind of a hypothesis is the distinction between episodic and semantic memory? *Journal of Experimental Psychology: Learning, Memory and Cognition*, 12, 307–311.

Tulving, E., & Thompson, D. M. (1973). Encoding specificity and retrieval processes in episodic memory. *Journal of Experimental Psychology: Learning, Memory, and Cognition*, 8, 336–342.

Turvey, M. T. (1977). Contrasting orientations to the theory of visual information-processing. *Psychological Review*, 84, 67–88.

Turvey, M. T., & Shaw, R. E. (1979). The primacy of perceiving: An ecological reformulation of perception for understanding memory. In L. G. Nilsson (Ed.), *Perspective on memory research* (pp. 167–222). Hillsdale, NJ: Erlbaum.

Tweney, R. D., & Doherty, M. E. (1983). Rationality and the psychology of inference. *Synthese*, 57, 139–161.

Ullman, S. (1980). Against direct perception. *Behavioral and Brain Sciences*, 3, 373–415.

Ungar, G., Desiderio, D. M., & Parr, W. (1972). Isolation, identification, and synthesis of a specific-behavior-inducing brain peptide. *Nature*, 238, 198–202.

Valentine, E. R. (1985). The effect of instructions on performance in the Wason selection task. *Current Psychological Research and Reviews*, 4, 214–223.

van Duyne, P. C. (1974). Realism and linguistic complexity in reasoning. *British Journal of Psychology*, 65, 59–67.

VanLehn, K. (1991). Rule acquisition events in the discovery of problem-solving strategies. *Cognitive Science*, 15, 1–47.

Venezky, R. L. (1970). *The structure of English orthography*. The Hague: Mouton.

von Frisch, K. (1954). *The dancing bees*. London: Methuen.

von Frisch, K. (1967). *The dance and orientation of bees* (L. E. Chadwick, Trans.). Cambridge, MA: Harvard University Press.

von Senden, M. (1960). *Space and sight: The perception of space and shape in the congenitally blind before and after operation*. New York: Free Press.

Voss, J. F., et al. (1986). Informal reasoning and subject matter knowledge in the solving of economics problems by naive and novice individuals. *Cognition and Instruction*, 3, 269–302.

Voss, J. F., Greene, T. R., Post, T. A., & Penner, B. C. (1983). Problem solving skill in social sciences. In G. Power (Ed.), *The psychology of learning and motivation: Advances in research and theory* (Vol. 17). New York: Academic Press.

Voss, J. F., Perkins, D., & Segal, J. (Eds.). (1991). *Informal reasoning and education*. Hillsdale, NJ: Erlbaum.

Voss, J. F., Tyler, S. W., & Yengo, L. A. (1983). Individual differences in the solving of social science problems. In R. F. Dillon & R. R. Schmeck (Eds.), *Individual differences in cognition*. (pp. 205–232). New York: Academic Press.

Wagenaar, W. A. (1986). My memory: A study of autobiographical memory over six years. *Cognitive Psychology*, 18, 225–252.

Walker, E., & Ceci, S. J. (1983). Lateral asymmetries in electrodermal responses to nonattended stimuli: A response to Dawson and Schell. *Journal of Experimental Psychology: Human Perception and Performance*, 9(1), 145–147.

Walker, N., Jones, J. P., & Mar, H. H. (1983). Encoding processes and the recall of text. *Memory and Cognition, 11*, 275–282.

Wallas, G. (1926). *The art of thought*. New York: Harcourt Brace Jovanovich.

Waltz, D. (1975). Understanding line drawings of scenes with shadows. In P. Winston (Ed.), *The psychology of computer vision* (pp. 19–92). New York: McGraw-Hill.

Wang, W. S-Y. (Ed.). (1991). *The emergence of language: Development and evolution*. New York: Freeman.

Warren, R. M. (1970). Perceptual restoration of missing speech sounds. *Science, 167*, 392–393.

Warren, R. M., & Obusek, C. J. (1971). Speech perception and phonemic restorations. *Perception and Psychophysics, 9*, 358–362.

Warren, R. M., Obusek, C. J., Farmer, R. M., & Warren, R. P. (1969). Auditory sequence: Confusions of patterns other than speech or music. *Science, 164*, 586–587.

Warren, R. M., & Warren, R. P. (1970). Auditory illusions and confusions. *Scientific American, 223*(6), 30–36.

Warrington, E. K., & Weiskrantz, L. (1970). Amnesic syndrome: Consolidation or retrieval? *Nature, 228*, 628–630.

Warrington, E. K., & Weiskrantz, L. (1973). An analysis of short-term and long-term memory deficits in man. In J. Deutsch (Ed.), *The physiological basis of memory*. New York: Academic Press.

Warrington, E. K., & Weiskrantz, L. (1978). Further analysis of the prior learning effect in amnesic patients. *Neuropsychologia, 12*, 419–428.

Wason, P. C. (1966). Reasoning. In B. M. Foss (Ed.), *New horizons in psychology* (Vol. 1), (pp. 135–151). Harmondsworth, Middlesex, England: Penguin.

Wason, P. C., & Johnson-Laird, P. N. (1970). A conflict between selecting and evaluating information in an inferential task. *British Journal of Psychology, 61*, 509–515.

Watanabe, I. (1980). Selective attention and memory. *Japanese Psychological Review, 23* (4), 335–354.

Watkins, M. J. (1974). When is recall spectacularly higher than recognition? *Journal of Experimental Psychology, 102*, 161–163.

Watkins, M. J. (1990). Mediationism and obfuscation of memory. *American Psychologist, 45*, 328–335.

Watkins, M. J., & Kerkar, S. P. (1985). Recall of a twice-presented item without recall of either presentation: Generic memory for events. *Journal of Memory and Language, 24*, 666–678.

Watkins, M. J., & Tulving, E. (1975). Episodic memory: When recognition fails. *Journal of Experimental Psychology: General, 104*, 5–29.

Waugh, N. C., & Norman, D. A. (1965) Primary memory. *Psychological Review, 72*, 89–104.

Waxman, S. R. (1990). Linguistic biases and the establishment of conceptual hierarchies: Evidence from preschool children. *Cognitive Development, 5*, 123–150.

Wegner, D. M., & Vallacher, R. R. (1977). *Implicit psychology: An introduction to social cognition*. New York: Oxford University Press.

Weimer, W. B. (1977). A conceptual framework for cognitive psychology: Motor theories of the mind. In R. Shaw & J. Bransford (Eds.), *Perceiving, acting, and knowing* (pp. 267–314). Hillsdale, NJ: Erlbaum.

Weimer, W. B., & Palermo, D. S. (Eds.). (1982). *Cognition and the symbolic processes* (Vol. 2). Hillsdale, NJ: Erlbaum.

Weir, R. H. (1966). Some questions on the child's learning of phonology. In F. Smith & G. A. Miller (Eds.), *The genesis of language*. Cambridge, MA: MIT Press.

Weisberg, R. W. (1986). *Creativity: Genius and other myths*. New York: Freeman.

Weisberg, R. W., & Alba, J. W. (1981). An examination of the alleged role of "fixation" in the solution of several "insight" problems. *Journal of Experimental Psychology: General, 110*, 169–192.

Weiskrantz, L., & Warrington, E. K. (1975). The problem of the amnesic syndrome in man and animals. In R. L. Isaacson & K. H. Pribram (Eds.), *The hippocampus* (Vol 2). New York: Plenum.

Wertheimer, M. (1959). *Productive thinking*. New York: Harper & Row.

Wessels, M. G. (1982). *Cognitive psychology*. New York: Harper & Row.

Wetherick, N. (1969). Bruner's concept of strategy: An experiment and a critique. *Journal of Experimental Psychology, 81*, 53–58.

Wheeler, D. D. (1970). Processes in word recognition. *Cognitive Psychology, 1*, 59–85.

Whimbley, A., & Lochhead, J. (Eds.). (1986). *Problem solving and comprehension* (4th ed.). Hillsdale, NJ: Erlbaum.

White, M. J. (1985). On the status of cognitive psychology. *American Psychologist, 40*, 117–119.

Whitney, P., & Kunen, S. (1983). Development of hierarchical conceptual relationships in children's semantic memories. *Journal of Experimental Child Psychology, 35*(2), 278–293.

Wickelgren, W. A. (1965). Size of rehearsal group and short-term memory. *Journal of Experimental Psychology, 68*, 413–419.

Wickelgren, W. A. (1973). The long and the short of memory. *Psychological Bulletin, 80*, 425–438.

Wickelgren, W. A. (1974). *How to solve problems*. San Francisco: Freeman.

Wickens, C. D. (1984). *Engineering psychology and human performance*. Columbus, OH: Merrill.

Wickens, D. D. (1970). Encoding categories of words: An empirical approach to meaning. *Psychological Review, 77*, 1–15.

Wickens, D. D. (1972). Characteristics of word encoding. In A. W. Melton & E. Martin (Eds.), *Coding processes in human memory* (pp. 191–215). Washington, DC: Winston.

Wiener, N. (1948). *Cybernetics*. Cambridge, MA: MIT Press.

Williams, K. W., & Durso, F. T. (1986). Judging category frequency: Automaticity or availability? *Journal of Experimental Psychology: Learning, Memory, and Cognition, 12*, 387–396.

Wingfield, A., & Byrnes, D. L. (1981). *The psychology of human memory*. New York: Academic Press.

Winograd, E., & Killinger, W. A. (1983). Relating age at encoding in early childhood to adult recall: Development of flashbulb memories. *Journal of Experimental Psychology, 112*, 413–422.

Wolff, P. H. (1966). The natural history of crying and other vocalizations in early infancy. In B. M. Foss (Ed.), *Determinants of infant behavior* (Vol. 4, pp. 81–109). London: Methuen.

Wood, G. (1983). *Cognitive psychology: A skills approach*. Monterey, CA: Brooks/Cole.

Wright, B., & Garrett, M. (1984). Lexical decision in sentences: Effects of syntactic structure. *Memory & Cognition, 12*, 31–45.

Wundt, W. (1900–1920). Volkerpsychologie (Vols. 1–10). Leipzig: Englemann.

Yachanin, S. A. (1986). Facilitation in Wason's selection task: Content and instructions. *Current Psychological Research and Reviews, 5*, 20–29.

Yarbus, A. L. (1967). *Eye movements and vision*. New York: Plenum.

Yantis, S. (1993). Stimulus-driven attentional capture. *Current Directions in Psychological Science, 2,* 156–161.

Yantis, S., & Jonides, J. (1990). Abrupt visual onsets and selective attention: Voluntary versus automatic allocation. *Journal of Experimental Psychology: Human Perception and Performace, 16,* 121–134.

Yekovich, F. R., & Walker, C. H. (1986). Retrieval of scripted concepts. *Journal of Memory and Language, 25,* 627–644.

Yussen, S. R., & Levy, V. M., Jr. (1975). Developmental changes in predicting one's own span of short-term memory. *Journal of Experimental Child Psychology, 19,* 502–508.

Zechmeister, E. B., & Nyberg, S. E. (1982). *Human memory: An introduction to research and theory.* Monterey, CA: Brooks/Cole.

GLOSSARY

Addressed phonology Postlexical phonology. Knowledge of pronunciation represented in a cognitive code produced after the specific word is recognized.

Affordance A combination of the properties of a substance and its surfaces taken with reference to an animal.

AI Artificial intelligence. A discipline that attempts to create software capable of executing actions thought to require intelligence when done by people.

Algorithm A procedure that specifies a correct solution to any particular example from a class of well-defined problems.

Allocation policy In capacity theories of attention, refers to the process of dividing cognitive resources among competing stimuli.

Analog representation A representation made by the nervous system that preserves many of the elements of a stimulus in a way that is closely related to the elements' appearance in the natural world.

Analysis by synthesis model A general model of speech perception and pattern recognition that maintains that bottom-up processes suggest to top-down processes the information that should be filled in or internally computed.

Angular disparity The difference, in degrees, in the orientation of stimuli.

Anterograde amnesia A general inability to encode durable memories following a trauma.

Aphasia A general term designating a wide variety of language disorders.

Articulatory loop A component of working memory having at least two parts: a phonological input store, and a rehearsal process capable of operating upon and extracting elements from the phonological store.

Assembled phonology Prelexical phonology. A cognitive code that may amplify graphemic information useful in reading.

Attenuation theory A theory of attention that maintains that unattended-to stimuli are damped down but not completely screened out.

Automaticity The establishment of automatic processing on some specific cognitive task.

Automatic processes Cognitive processes that can be initiated and run off without the allocation of attentional resources.

Availability heuristic A rule of thumb used to make estimates of likelihoods based on their commonness or ease of computation.

Babbling Prelinguistic motor play and vocal experimentation characterized by the production of both vowels and consonants.

Babbling drift In infants, the tendency to restrict the production of linguistic sounds of those of the language they will eventually learn.

Backward masking The presentation of a visual stimulus that prevents the recognition of a previously presented stimulus.

Bartlett tradition An orientation in memory research concerned with qualitative changes in the contents of retrieved material.

Binary code A representation of information using strings of symbols that can take on either of two values.

Brain writing Refers to the position that new memories produce some physical change in the brain's structure.

Canalization Refers to the idea that the contents of our minds are influenced and bounded by our affordances.

Capacity The volume of cognitive codes capable of being retained by a memory store.

Categorical perception The perception of phonemes as either-or. When ambiguous sounds are presented, subjects "hear" them as being a member of one category or another, not as having features of two categories.

Chunking Refers to associated elements being retained in short-term storage.

Closed scenario Type of reasoning that takes place when subjects are presented with a limited number of options for solving a particular problem.

Cognitive capacity Refers to the number of cognitive processes or resources that can be brought to bear on sensory stimulation.

Cognitive codes Representations of physical energy by the nervous system that are potentially capable of entering our awareness.

Cognitive maps Internal representations of spatial layouts.

Cognitive resources Cognitive programs, or routines, that process sensory stimulation or elaborate existing cognitive codes.

Comprehension The reception, analysis, and interpretation of an utterance.

Computer simulation The creation of software capable of executing actions in a way thought to mimic the cognitive processes of people.

Conceptual complexity Pauses in the stream of speech that seem to be associated with the translation of a thought into a linguistic code.

Conceptually driven processes (top-down processes) Cognitive processes involving feature abstraction and categorization that begin with expectations derived from context.

Conditional reasoning Logic problems involving the conditional, or "if-then," statement.

Confirmation bias Wason found that subjects in hypothesis evaluation tasks had a tendency to find evidence supporting particular hypotheses. This tendency to support hypotheses rather than refute them is called the confirmation bias.

Connectionist approach Essentially, connectionists approach the problem of cognition from an *analog* position in trying to show that cognitive events are the result of computations that could take place in neural-like systems that are organized in certain ways.

Conservative focusing A strategy useful in solving artificial concept attainment problems. It involves changing only a single element of an array and observing the outcome of the change.

Constituents Components of a sentence that can be arranged in a hierarchical structure. They loosely correspond to linguistic parts of speech.

Constructivist theory of perception A position that emphasizes the formation of prototypes and schemata used in recognition and categorization.

Content addressability The ability of our memory system to access or reinstantiate particular memories given specific probes. In other words, we don't have to search through an entire set of material to discover whether or not we know a particular fact.

Context Information surrounding stimuli being recognized, categorized, or searched for.

Continuity theory A theory of language that maintains that speech developed from the apparently intentional cries of animals.

Control processes The information-processing theory of memory maintains that control processes transfer material from one storage to another.

Controlled processes Effortful cognitive processes that seem to require the allocation of attention to sustain them.

Convolution A matrix algebra process that can be used in parallel distributed processing models of memory. In such models, convolution can be used to show how a network of neuronlike entities may store and retrieve information.

Correlational world structure Refers to the notion that distinctive features are not randomly assigned to objects in the world. Rather, such features can be useful in predicting the appearance of other features.

Data-driven processes (bottom-up processes) Cognitive processes involving feature abstraction that begin with sensory stimulation.

Data-limited processes The processing of ambiguous stimuli is limited by the poverty of information that can be extracted from them. Performance decrements are produced by limitations in the stimuli.

Decay The loss of a cognitive code resulting from the passage of time.

Declarative knowledge Typically refers to factual, describable information whose organization is flexible and, to some extent, under our control.

Deep dyslexia The ability to read silently without being able to convert a graphemic code into a phonological one.

Deep-surface structure distinction The distinction between meaning and its expression in a wide variety of phrase structures.

Delta rule The delta rule governs weight changes in neural networks. As a network is trained, the weights are changed more when the system makes a large error than when it makes a small one.

Demand characteristics Subtle aspects of the experimental situation that provide the alert subject with clues about the desired findings or outcome.

Depth of processing The nature of encoding is controlled by the subject. Semantic coding involves deeper processing than acoustic coding, because more knowledge is required to produce a semantic code.

Depth of search In chess-playing programs, refers to the number of moves and responses considered consecutively from some base move.

Design features Refers to attempts to define language in terms of presumed necessary characteristics.

Dichotic listening Listening to two unrelated messages played over stereo headphones.

Direct theory of perception A position that emphasizes the ability of the perceiver to pick up sensory information as it truly exists in the world.

Disconfirming the consequent Refers to the application of modus tollens in conditional reasoning. If P implies Q, then the absence of Q implies the absence of P.

Discontinuity in thinking Refers to the Gestalt notion that problem solving could be accomplished by insight, a phenomenon that the Gestaltists believed was unrelated to prior cognitive effort.

Displacement   All natural languages enable their possessor to refer to things that are distant in time or space.

Distributed network models   Theories that postulate that the phenomenon in question can be modeled by a system of interacting "neuronlike" entities that represent concepts and other knowledge as patterns of activity.

Domain-free problems   Problems whose solutions do not require extensive expertise.

Dual code position   The theoretical position that holds that our nervous system is capable of producing and sustaining two kinds of memories: verbal memories, and analog memories that have visuospatial properties.

Echo   Refers to the representation of acoustic events in the sensory register.

Ecological approach to visual perception   A position that emphasizes the information about the world that can be seen by moving through it.

Ecological validity   Refers to the trend in cognitive science to explain cognitive processes in everyday terms and to study mental processes in their "natural habitats."

Elaborative rehearsal   Rehearsal whose objective is to meaningfully associate incoming stimuli with previously learned material.

Electrodermal responses   Changes in the skin's electrical conductance, used as indicators of ongoing cognitive processing.

Encoding   Transforming a stimulus into a format that can be retained by the cognitive system.

Encoding specificity   At retrieval time, a cue will aid retrieval if the cue provides information that was also processed during the encoding of the to-be-remembered material.

Episodic memory   Memories that are autobiographical, personal, and sensitive to the effects of context.

Equipotentiality   As far as memory is concerned, all cortex areas seem to be equally important.

Expansions   A form of linguistic response to a child in which the intended meaning of the child's utterances is reformulated in the standard and complete form by the caretaker.

Expertise   Human knowledge or the representation of such knowledge in machines. In humans, such knowledge is acquired directly through experience.

Explicit memory   When a subject is asked to recognize or recall presented materials in a study, the subject must deliberately use his or her memory system. In these cases, the subjects are making use of their explicit memory.

Extralogical inferences   Inferences that are based on a person's general knowledge of the world. Although outside the realm of formal reasoning, such inferences can be useful as heuristics.

Fan effect   In ACT, the time required for activation to spread to associated nodes is inversely related to the number of associated nodes being activated.

Feature abstraction   Refers to the cognitive processes that take complex stimuli and abstract that is, draw out from them their simplest components.

Feature detection theory   A position that maintains that pattern recognition is accomplished by the abstraction and reassembly of specific aspects of sensory stimulation.

Filter theory   A theory of attention that maintains that unattended-to stimuli are completely screened out.

Finite state grammar   An attempt to formulate grammatical knowledge in left-to-right rules that specify the transitions between words.

Flashbulb memories   Vivid, seemingly accurate memories produced by unexpected, emotionally charged events.

Focus gambling   A strategy used on artificial concept attainment tasks. It involves simultaneously changing more than one element of the problem array and then observing the outcome.

Formal reasoning   Refers to the use of logical inference rules that have been developed by logicians.

Formant   Refers to the visual representation of a particular concentration of acoustic energy in the speech signal. Formants are typically distinguished by number. The fundamental frequency of speech (as produced by the vibrations of our vocal folds) is referred to as the first formant. The concentration of acoustic energy in the next higher frequency range, and the one produced by changes in the vocal cavity itself, is referred to as the second formant.

Framing   Refers to the influence of context on likelihood estimations.

Fuzzy borders   Refers to the fact that people treat many natural categories as though they were ill defined. The borders of the concept shift according to the context in which the category member appears.

Gaze duration   Refers to the total amount of time that the reader has spent fixating on a particular point of text; if there has been only fixation on that particular point, then gaze duration is equal to fixation.

Generate and recognize models   Models of this class maintain that retrieval is accomplished by two component activities. First, plausible candidates for the searched-for memory are internally generated. Then the list of candidates is examined and the most likely candidate is picked from among those generated.

Gestalt psychology   A European movement emphasizing the primacy of construction in perception and problem solving.

GPS   The General Problem Solver, a computer program designed by Newell and Simon whose purpose was to show how general heuristics could solve a wide variety of problems.

Graceful degradation Used to describe cognitive systems that remain relatively efficient at least up to a certain point under some adversity induced either by processing overloads or by impoverishment of incoming stimuli.

Grammar Our total linguistic knowledge, consisting of phonological, syntactical, and semantic components.

Grapheme A letter or combination of letters that stands for a single phoneme.

Habituation The tendency to cease responding to familiar, or extensively processed, stimuli.

Heuristic A rule of thumb for solving problems or reasoning in everyday situations.

Hidden units In a neural network, hidden units are those neurodes that intervene between input and output neurodes.

Higher-order invariances Regularities in patterns of stimuli that are available to be seen as we move through the world or as elements in the world move around us.

Hippocampus A large forebrain structure located between the thalamus and the cortex.

Höffding step The step between sensation and perception. The conversion of a cognitive code representing a stimulus into a code that enables the categorization of the stimulus.

Holophrastic stage At about one year of age, the child begins to produce single words that seem to symbolize entire sentences.

Human factors research A discipline that studies information processing by humans and machines in an attempt to find their optimal relationship.

Icon Neisser's name for the visual contents of sensory storage.

Ill-defined problems A problem is ill defined if the start or goal states are unclear, or if the operations required to change states are unspecified.

Implicit memory When a subject shows priming effects of materials that have been presented but not studied, and these priming effects occur in the absence of any deliberate attempt by the subject to use his or her memory system, we say that the subjects are making use of their implicit memory.

Incubation Refers to the unconscious work done by problem solvers who have left off conscious solving of the problem.

Indirect speech act When a speaker uses a linguistic structure nonnormatively, that is, to carry out a function for which the structure is not typically used, the speaker is relying upon the listener's ability to "go beyond" the typical use of the structure. This event is referred to as an indirect speech act.

Inferential intrusion errors Recall failures produced by general knowledge of the world. These errors occur when general knowledge is used to logically infer what must have taken place when a particular memory cannot be retrieved.

Inflection The process of adding linguistic markers to words to indicate plurality, possession, or case.

Information As defined by Shannon, the function of information is to reduce the uncertainty of future events.

Information-processing approach The metatheory of cognitive psychology that holds that mental events can be understood as complex cognitive codes that are often serially transformed.

Insight A conscious experience consisting of a sudden awareness of the correct organization of a problem's elements.

Intelligence Capabilities that seem to be reflected in the apparent purposiveness and goal orientation inferred from the behavior of humans and some animals. Intelligence can be represented as an organized amalgamation of cognitive structures and processes.

Intentionality Describes mental events that are the antecedents of certain actions and that perhaps play a causal role in producing those actions.

Interference In memory research, refers to the inability to retrieve material resulting from its confusion with other cognitive codes.

Intersection search In attempting to verify a relationship between two nodes in semantic memory, an intersection search fans out from both entry nodes until some path is found or until the search has verified that no common path exists.

Inter-stimulus interval In Sperling's study, the time interval between the offset of the stimulus and the onset of the cue to begin reporting.

Intrinsic characteristics The light reflected from an object carries with it information about the boundary characteristics and surface homogeneity of the object. These are the intrinsic characteristics.

Invariant features Information contained in the visual field that does not change regardless of our movement through it.

Isomorphism Formal equivalence. Usually used to describe the relationship between problems whose deep structure is the same, although their appearance, or surface structure, differs.

Late selection A theory of attention that maintains that almost all incoming stimuli are sent to working memory before any screening out is done.

Layout of perceivable space   Knowledge of the apparent alteration of the shapes of geometric objects in the visual field, acquired by motion.

Lexical access   Our ability to cognitively contact and retrieve the meanings of words and to be able to express the relationship of these elements to one another.

Lexical uncertainty   Refers to pauses in the stream of speech occurring just prior to the appearance of unusual words.

Linguistic universals   Used in two senses: the boundaries of language and characteristics of language that all languages share.

Local-global distinction   In problem solving, answering the question 'What to do next?' involves local knowledge. Understanding the big picture the problem's underlying structure is global knowledge.

Local network models   Theories of semantic memory that postulate that such knowledge is represented by a system of nodes, each one standing for a concept, and connections that show the associations among such concepts.

Logic   Any one of a variety of systems of reasoning used to determine the validity of certain premises.

Long-term storage   The information-processing theory of memory maintains that long-term storage is semantically organized and has an infinite capacity. Retrieval failures are produced by interference.

Maintenance rehearsal   Rehearsal whose objective is simply to retain information in working memory. This rehearsal seems to be accompanied by subvocalization.

Mand function   Skinner's term for the function of language referring to verbal operants reinforced through compliance.

Manner of articulation   In uttering consonants, refers to the way in which the constriction is produced.

Mass action   As far as memory is concerned, the brain seems to work en masse.

Mastermind   A logical deduction game in which the problem solver must deduce the color and location of a string of hidden buttons using only the ambiguous feedback provided.

Mentalism   A term used as a criticism by behaviorists for phenomena that seemed neither public nor reproducible.

Mental rotation   The creation and inspection of a rotating image.

Mental size   The amount of mental space that seems to be taken up by an image.

Metamemory   Personal knowledge about the operation of the memory system.

Metatheory   A set of basic presumptions thought to operate in a general domain. A metatheory is a schematic plan for building specific theories in particular domains.

MLU   The mean length of a child's utterance. Determined by counting the number of morphemes produced, then dividing the total by the number of separate utterances.

Modus ponens   An inference rule stating that, if P implies Q is true, then the presence of P implies the presence of Q.

Modus tollens   An inference rule stating that if P implies Q is true, then the absence of Q implies the absence of P.

Morpheme   The basic unit of meaning.

Müller-Lyer illusion   Refers to the famous "fins-out fins-in" illusion. The length of the middle bar seems to vary as the direction of the fins is changed.

Natural categories   Unlike the categories used in artificial concept tasks, everyday categories are ill defined, have fuzzy borders, and are sensitive to the effects of context.

Natural reasoning   The study of human reasoning in lifelike situations involving the estimation of likelihoods.

Neural code   A pattern of neural activity that represents a particular event.

Nonstrategic processing   The notion that some information such as the frequency of occurrence of some stimuli is encoded automatically, that is, without effort by the subject.

Open scenario   Type of reasoning that takes place when the subjects understand the task as one that involves searching for a particular method or form of reasoning.

Operator   A cognitive process that transforms one state of knowledge into another. Although a solver may access dozens of such states during the course of problem solving, the number of distinct operators is thought to be limited.

Optical flow pattern   The arrangement of changing and invariant aspects of the visual field.

Overregularization   A "smart error" in which a child treats an irregular noun or verb form as if it were regular. This indicates knowledge of general inflectional rules.

Overwriting   A position that maintains that inferences made at retrieval wipe out previous encodings.

Parafoveal information   Refers to information that can be picked up beyond the fixation point and used for word recognition, or lexical access.

Parallel processing   Refers to the simultaneous transformation of several different cognitive codes.

Partial-report technique   Used by Sperling, a technique that involves cuing the subject to report only certain elements of an array.

Pattern associator   In distributed network models, a pattern associator is a matrix of elements that, when premultiplied by specific vectors representing particular associated experiences, reproduce other vectors representing particular associated experiences, or memories.

Perceptual cycle Neisser's attempt to synthesize the direct and constructive viewpoints by conceiving of perception as on ongoing activity.

Perceptual fluency The ability to recognize a particular stimulus under impoverished presentation conditions.

Phoneme A separable, identifiable unit of sound. Phonemes are the basic acoustic building blocks of spoken language.

Phonemic restoration effect A speech illusion that occurs when a nonspeech sound is substituted for a deleted phoneme. The listener usually fails to detect the deletion.

Phonetics The discipline that attempts to categorize speech sounds. There are two approaches. Articulatory phonetics focuses on the movements of the tongue, and acoustic phonetics deals with linguistic sounds as physical energy.

Phonology The discipline that attempts to express the regularities in linguistic sounds as being rule based and principled.

Phrase structure A hierarchical, abstract formula, written in terms of constituents that can be used to generate and analyze utterances.

Place of articulation In speech, refers to the point of constriction in producing consonants.

Pragmatic reasoning schemas Clusters of highly generalized, and therefore abstract, rules that are organized on the basis of certain goals and conditions.

Pragmatics Describes the socially derived rules, principles, and conventions that speakers and listeners use to establish coherence across groups of sentences.

Preattentive analysis An analysis of stimuli that may extract acoustic, phonetic, and possibly prior semantic information prior to the material's entry into awareness.

Prestored knowledge Knowledge of "isnota" links in semantic memory that limit the extent of search.

Primal sketch A representation of the two-dimensional image that makes explicit the amount and disposition of the intensity changes or discontinuities present. The representation consists of place tokens and is hierarchical. The primitives at the lowest level represent raw intensity changes and their local geometry. Higher level primitives represent groupings and alignments among the lower level primitives.

Primary component Refers to the first part of the serial position effect seen in free-recall studies presumably the result of material retrieved from long-term storage.

Proactive interference Interference that results when some previously learned material hinders the formation of a memory for some recently learned material.

Problems of arrangement In Greeno's classification, refers to problems in which the elements of the problem must be rearranged according to a specific criterion.

Problems of inducing structure In Greeno's classification, refers to problems in which a relationship must be discovered among the problem's components.

Problems of transformation In Greeno's classification, refers to problems in which a sequence of moves or alterations must be determined to change the problem's initial state into the goal state.

Problem space A theoretical term that denotes the problem solver's internal representation of the problem.

Procedural knowledge Refers to knowledge that no longer enters awareness. Usually expressed as a skill.

Process deficiencies The inability to execute some cognitive process resulting from immaturity of the cognitive system.

Production Refers to the planning, lexical choice, and execution of speech.

Production deficiency A failure to use a memory strategy that one has the ability to execute.

Production rules Rules that can be used to guide intelligent actions. They have two parts. The state part lists conditions that might be observed in the world. The action part dictates the actions that should be taken if the conditions in the state part have been observed.

Productivity All natural languages permit their possessor to create novel utterances.

Propositional analysis Breaking down complex remarks into propositions, which are the smallest units of knowledge that can possess a truth value.

Prototype The psychological center of a category; the most typical instance of a category.

Psycholinguistics The study of language from a psychological rather than from a linguistic perspective.

Recency component Refers to the second part of the serial position effect seen in free-recall studies presumably the result of material retrieved from short-term storage.

Reception paradigm In artificial concept formation tasks, the reception paradigm describes situations in which the subject has no control over which exemplars will be examined.

Recursion Complete linguistic structures can be embedded within others. This process can theoretically be continued indefinitely.

Reductionist viewpoint A theoretical position that maintains that complex phenomena can be thought of as consisting of simpler, although qualitatively different, events.

Referential communication This occurs when a listener gathers additional information from a speaker in order to clarify a meaning previously produced by the speaker.

Regression   When a reader launches a **saccade** leftward during reading, this type of saccade is called a regression.

Rehearsal   The two types of rehearsal are maintenance rehearsal, which keeps a cognitive code intact for limited periods, and elaborative rehearsal, which establishes contact with semantic memory.

Representation problem   To solve unfamiliar problems, a person must construct an internal representation of the problem. The difficulty involved in constructing such a representation is known as the representation problem.

Representativeness heuristic   A rule of thumb used in estimating likelihoods. It is based on a subjective computation of the person or event's similarity to a prototype.

Resource-limited processes   Demanding, or unpracticed, tasks that require the heavy allocation of cognitive resources. Performance decrements are produced by unavailability of additional resources.

Response competition   This phenomenon occurs when an individual cannot determine which of several associations is correct.

Retinal image   The raw code produced by the retina and sent to the brain for perceptual processing.

Retrieving   Cognitive processing that recovers or elaborates stored cognitive codes.

Retrograde amnesia   Retrieval failure involving material encoded just prior to the occurrence of a traumatic shock.

Saccade   A rhythmic, ballistic eye motion used in reading.

Schema   A term that denotes what is essential in category membership and connotes a plan or expectation that can be used to receive or organize incoming stimulation.

Script   A general, context-free mental framework that can be used to organize particular sequences of common and familiar actions.

Secondary recall cues   Recalled material capable of cuing the recall of additional material.

Segment-and-label   An AI approach to computer vision that emphasizes bottom-up processes such as feature abstraction.

Selection paradigm   As used in artificial concept attainment tasks, refers to experimental procedures in which the subject picks the next exemplar in the series. The subject's choices indicate the nature of the strategy being used.

Selective attention   The capacity to focus cognitive processes on a narrow band of sensory stimulation.

Self-schema   A cognitive structure used to represent and assimilate information about the self.

Semantic memory   General, encyclopedic knowledge of the world and language.

Semantic priming   The activation of a word in semantic memory facilitates or primes the activation of subsequent, conceptually related words.

Semantics   Linguistic knowledge of meaning.

Sensory register   A storage location that retains an almost complete representation of sensory stimulation for a brief time.

Serial exhaustive search   Refers to a complete, one-at-a-time search of the elements in working memory.

Serial position effect   When a subject's memory is tested in a free-recall situation, initial and final items are more likely to be recalled than items presented in the middle of the list.

Serial processing   Refers to the sequential transformation of a cognitive code.

Serial self-terminating search   In a search of short-term memory, this refers to the ability of the subjects to conclude a search immediately upon encountering the target probe.

Shadowing   Reciting a message played over stereo headphones, as soon after hearing it as possible.

Short-term storage   The information-processing theory of memory maintains that this storage is acoustically organized, has a limited capacity, and loses material through decay.

Soundness   A system of reasoning is sound if, given true premises, it always produces true conclusions. All formal logical systems have this property.

Specializations for languages   Refers to certain features of the brain and larynx that may indicate innate predispositions for language ability.

Speech act   This refers to the interpretation by a listener of a speaker's intention. In other words, the speech act is the utterance as received and comprehended by a listener.

Spreading activation model   Retrieval from permanent memory can be thought of as activating elements in a semantic network.

State-action tree   A method of representing move problems in which the problem states are shown as nodes, and the actions transforming successive states are shown as connecting lines.

State-dependent learning   Retrieval is enhanced if the subjects are in roughly the same psychological state at both retrieval and encoding times.

Stimulus onset aynchrony   Refers to a difference in time between the appearance of two stimuli.

Storage   The capacity of the nervous system to retain cognitive codes.

Strategy   A move, or probe, designed to effect some change in the problem and provide information by so doing.

Structuralism   A theoretical position that regards the mind as an organized set of decomposable mental acts.

Structural relationships   Various sorts of underlying meanings, such as agent role, location, possession, and so on, that seem to be expressed by children in the holophrastic and two-word stages.

Sufficiency analysis   An analysis that focuses on how a particular cognitive process *may* be carried out.

Surface dyslexia   The ability to read out loud more or less normally without being able to recognize the words or their meanings.

Syntax   Linguistic knowledge of word order and inflections.

Tact function   Skinner's term for the function of language referring to verbal operants cued by discriminative stimuli.

Task environment   Theoretically, a neutral and complete representation of a problem that includes all possible problem spaces.

Template-matching theory   A position that maintains that pattern recognition is accomplished by comparing incoming stimuli with a fixed mental model of an ideal pattern.

Text model   The reader's internal representation, or understanding, of the text.

Texture gradient   The orderly and gradual loss of surface detail and clarity as we scan the visual field from nearby to distant objects.

Thinking out loud   Verbalizing the contents of working memory. A tape recording of the resulting utterances, known as a protocol, can be useful in analyzing a subject's problem solving.

TLC   Teachable Language Comprehender, one of the earliest models of semantic memory.

TOT phenomenon   William James referred to the "tip of the tongue" phenomenon as an "intensely active gap."

Tower of Hanoi   A transformation problem in which a stack of disks, situated on one of three pegs, must be transferred to another peg. Constraints limit the size of the disks that may rest on top of each other.

Transfer appropriate processing   The cognitive processes that are used to encode a stimulus interact with the processes that are used to retrieve it. When the retrieval processes match those that were used at encoding, retrieval may be enhanced.

Truth   In logic, refers to the reality of premises. An argument can be valid but untrue if the initial premises describe unreal situations.

Two-word stage   A period in which the child typically produces utterances of two words. This period indicates the beginning of syntactical knowledge.

Type-token distinction   The elements of semantic memory consist of nodes representing general categories (types) as well as specific examples of those categories (tokens).

Unattended speech effect   The processing of visually presented text is impaired by the presence of concurrent speech sounds. This impairment is observed even when the subject is told to ignore the speech sounds. This is not an acoustic effect per se because the presence of white noise does not produce the impairment in processing the visual materials.

Unlearning   This is similar to extinction of conditioned responses. The acquisition of new associations suppresses the associative strength of older associations.

Validity   An argument is valid if, according to the principles of reasoning developed by logicians, a conclusion necessarily follows from certain premises.

Visuospatial scratch pad   A component of working memory having at least two parts: an active storage for stimuli with visual properties or spatial extension, and a rehearsal process capable of extracting such material.

Voicing   The degree to which the vocal cords are involved in the production of a consonant. Voiced consonants are those in which the buzzing of the vocal cords is detected.

Well-defined problems   Those in which the start and goal states are clearly specified. A procedure that transforms the start state into the goal state must be at least potentially available.

Whole-report technique   Sperling's original methodology involved asking his subjects to report as much information as they could retrieve following the brief presentation of visual stimuli.

Widrow-Hoff rule   Describes the rate of change in the connective strength among elements in a distributed network model.

Width of search   In AI research, refers to algorithms that try to limit the number of different search pathways explored.

Word superiority effect   Subjects are better at identifying a letter when it appears in the context of a word rather than when it appears by itself.

XOR problem   The XOR ("exclusive or") problem refers to the fact that it is impossible for two layer neural networks like pattern associators to compute identical outputs from inputs that are completely uncorrelated.

Zero-crossing   The point where a function's value changes its sign from positive to negative or vice versa.

AUTHOR INDEX

SUBJECT INDEX